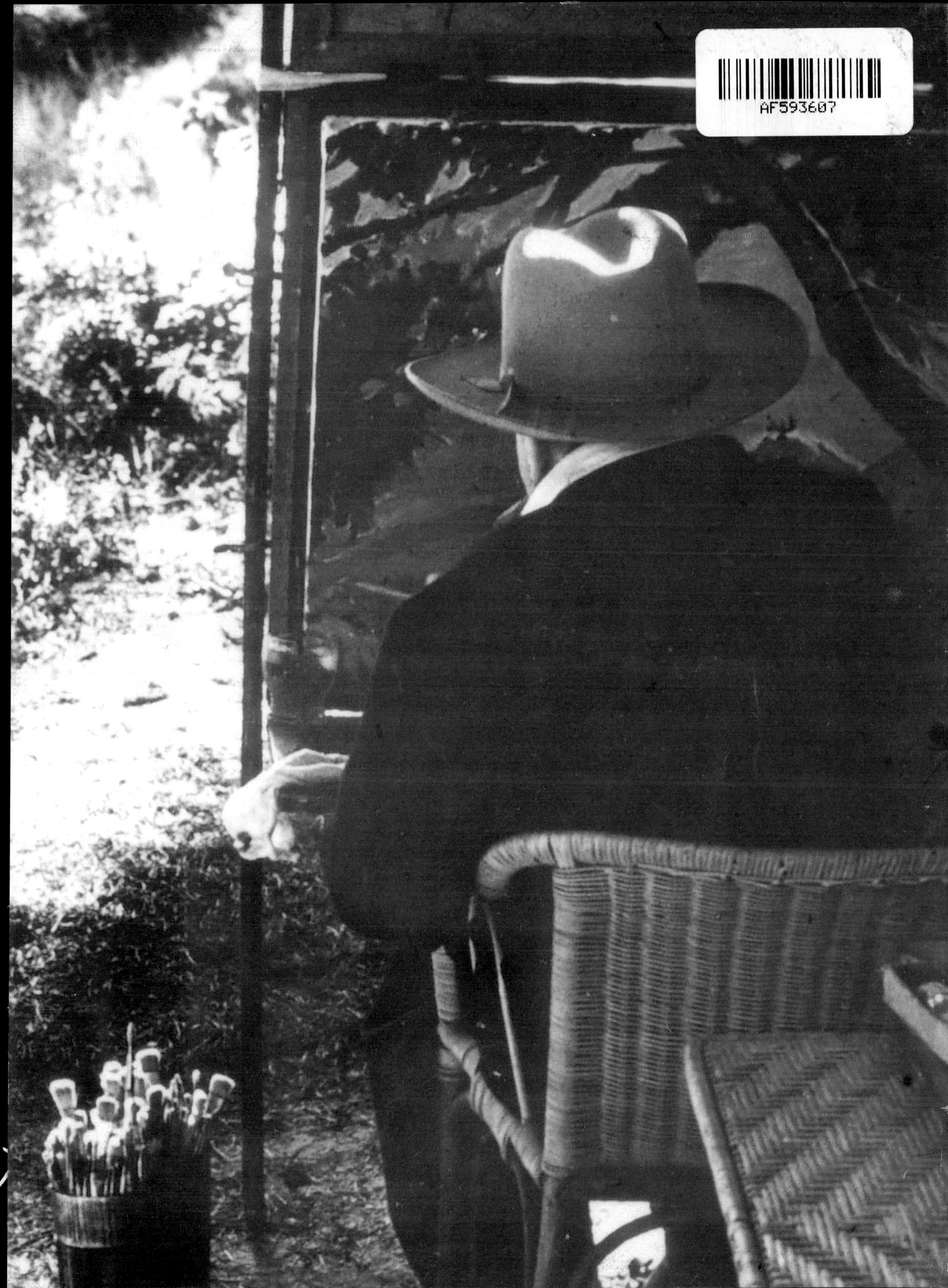

Sir Winston
CHURCHILL'S
Life Through his Paintings

This book is dedicated
to all who take pleasure
in painting as a pastime

Sir Winston CHURCHILL'S *Life Through his Paintings*

David Coombs
with Minnie Churchill
foreword by Mary Soames

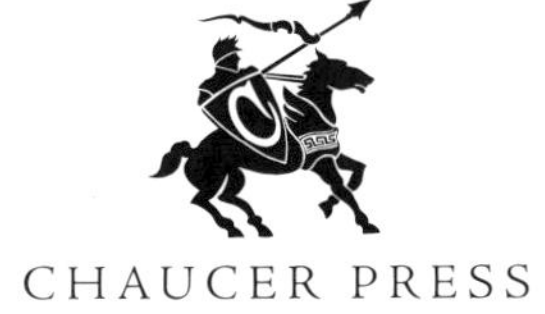

CHAUCER PRESS

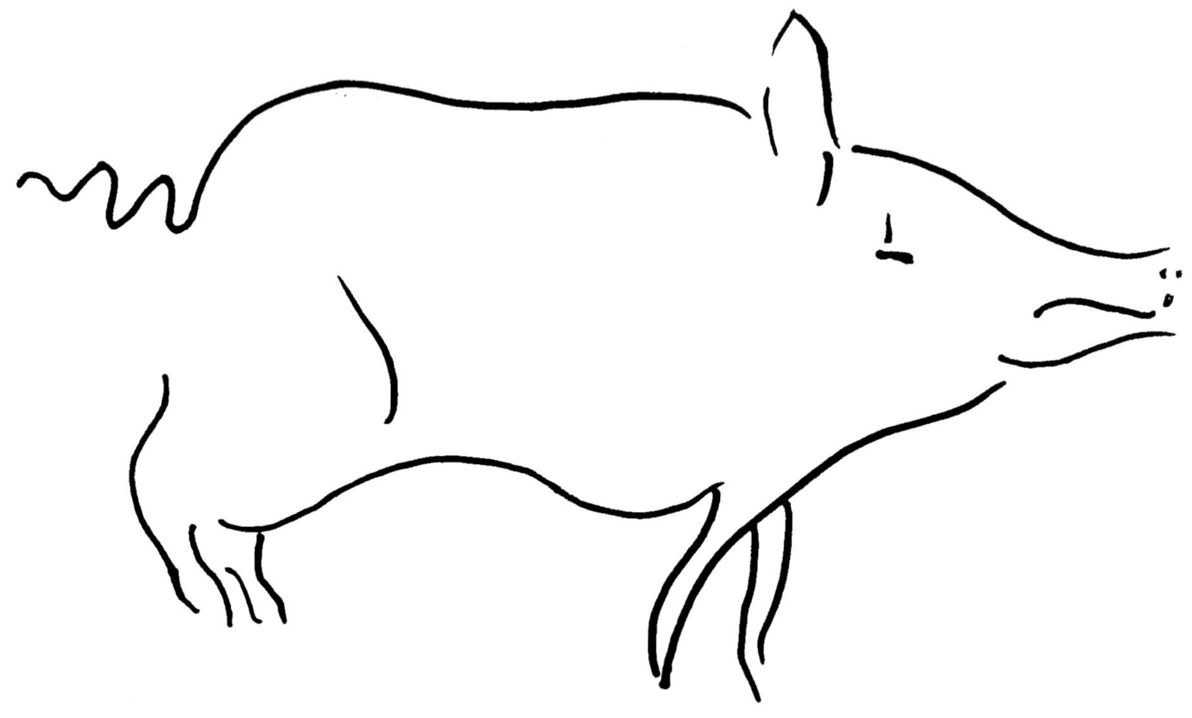

Published in 2003 by Chaucer Press
20 Bloomsbury Street
London WC1B 3JH

Book design by John Marsh Design Co
Cover design by Open Door Limited Langham, Rutland

Title: Sir Winston Churchill's Life Through his Paintings
ISBN: 1 904449 16 6

Printed in China

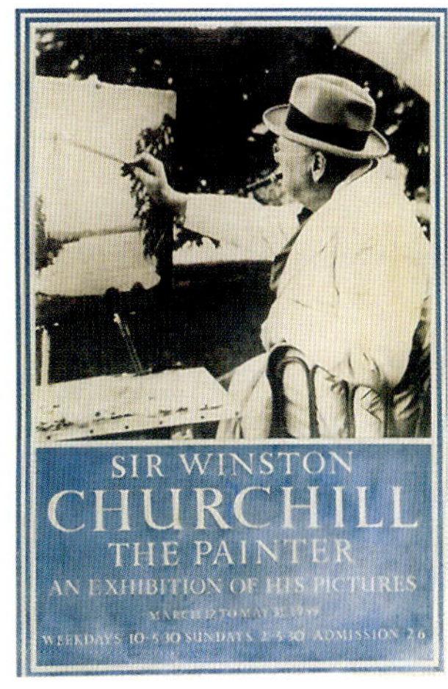

Following pages: Winston and Clementine Churchill at Mme Balsan's house, Miami, 1946.
Kindly reproduced from the original at Blenheim Palace.

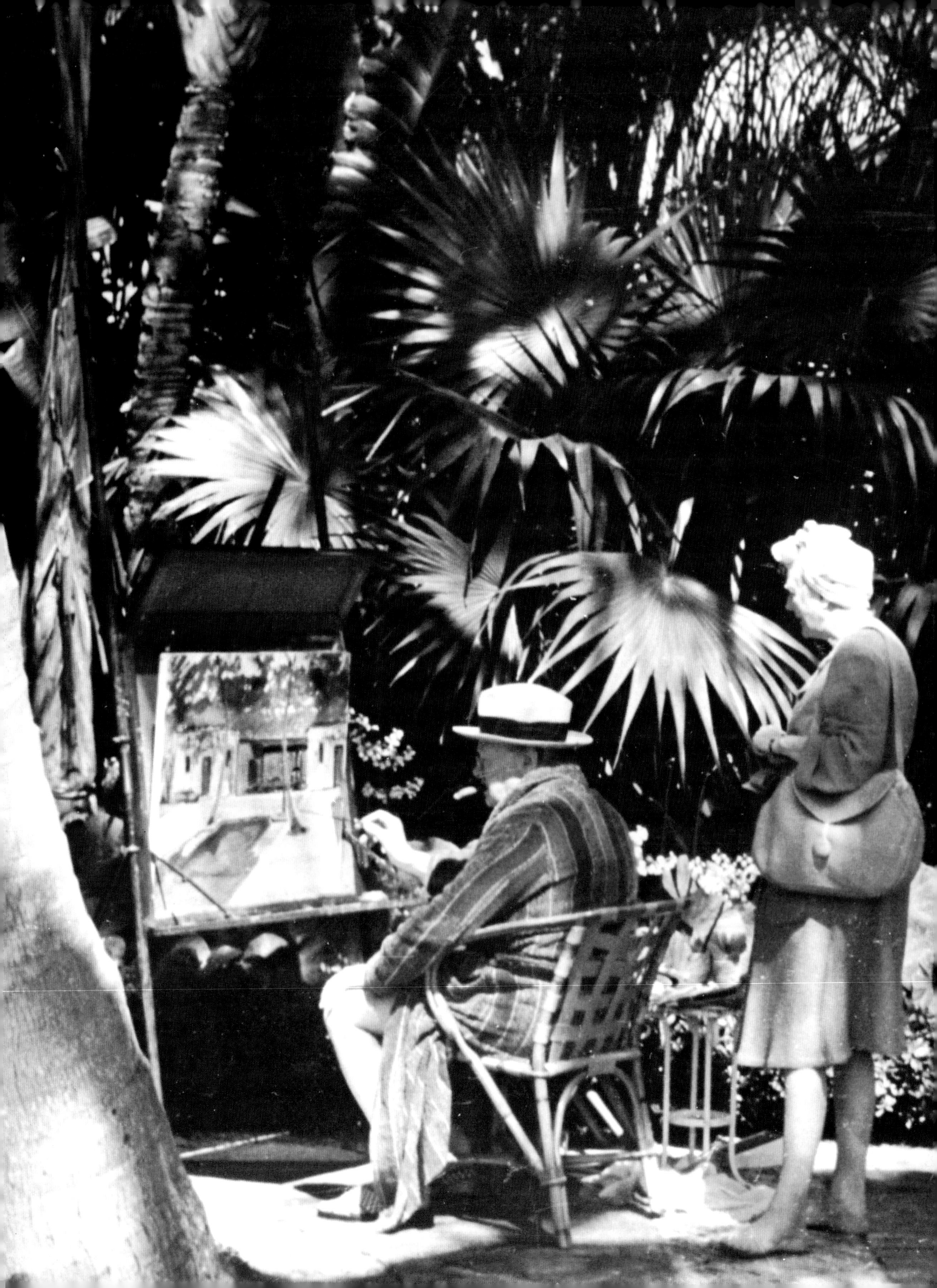

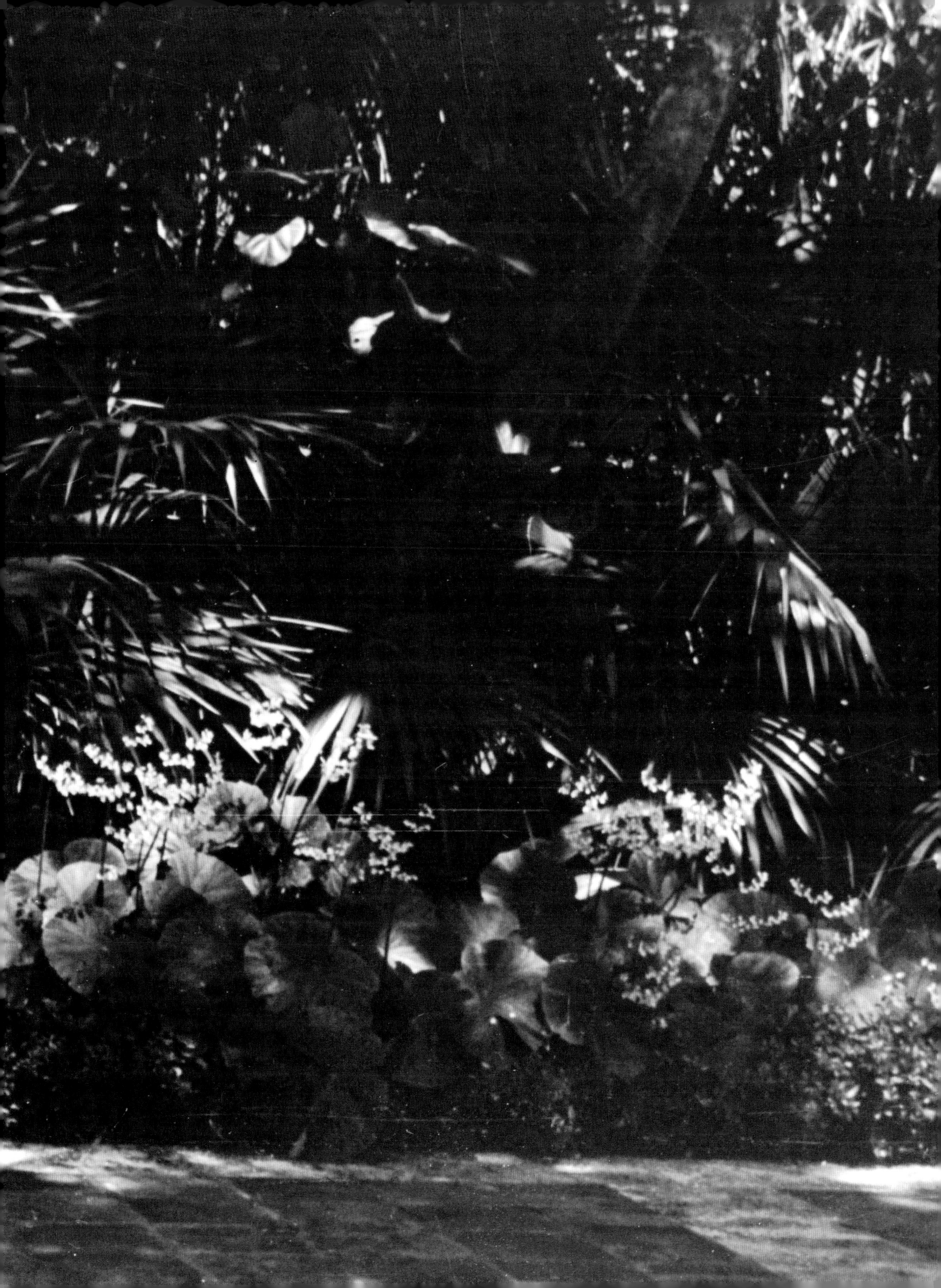

foreword by Mary Soames

It is most satisfactory and gratifying to members of our family that this uniquely comprehensive account of Winston Churchill's paintings is now accomplished - and I feel greatly privileged to have been asked to write a foreword to this beautiful and informative book.

We have been aware for many years now that an update of *Churchill: His Paintings* - David Coombs's first book on my father's paintings, published in 1967 - was long overdue, but the stimulus and opportunity to embark on a new and greatly enhanced version came from the wonderful exhibition of Churchill's paintings at Sotheby's in January 1998, in the preparation and mounting of which David Coombs, once more, after 30 years, became deeply involved in Winston Churchill's 'other' life - his painting.

This new book – *Sir Winston Churchill's Life Through His Paintings,* with its wealth of colour illustrations and copious information (much of it new) about the paintings and where each one fits into Churchill's life chronologically - is the fruit of intensive and dedicated work by David Coombs, helped by Minnie Churchill, over the last six years.

From childhood days I took for granted that painting was a grafted-in part of my father's life - at Chartwell painting had to fight it out with bricklaying - but both occupations had their share of the hours carved from full-time politics (in or out of office) and writing (mostly at night), the profession by which he kept us all. Before a holiday, the pile of painting impedimenta in the front hall was most impressive; and on his return home, it was a treasured treat for the stay-at-homes to have displayed the holiday pictures for them.

But it was not until I was in my late sixties, when I was writing *Winston Churchill: His Life as a Painter* (published in 1990), that I came to realize what painting had really meant to my father. Coming to him fortuitously and suddenly, at a moment of disaster in his political career after the Dardanelles catastrophe (when, as my mother would much later tell his biographer, Sir Martin Gilbert, 'I thought he would die of grief'), painting opened up to him a complete new world of colour, of light and shade, of proportion and perspective. But even more, this compelling occupation, I came to understand, nourished deep wells.

Winston Churchill in his earlier years was no stranger to depression - he labelled his depressive times 'Black Dog'. But in my opinion two events or circumstances in Winston's life increasingly and effectively kennelled 'Black Dog'. The first was his marriage and the build-up of the love, confidence and stability he found in his relationship with Clementine. The other was when, in his 41st year, painting literally 'grabbed' him, thereafter playing an increasing and abiding role in his life, renewing the source of his great inner strength and enabling him to face storms, ride out depressions and rise above the tough passages in his political life.

I hope many people will look at, read and enjoy this book - the vivid account of one man's 'joy-ride in a paint-box'!

Mary Soames

Below
Winston Churchill painting at Antibes. This photograph was included in his book 'Painting as a Pastime', 1948.

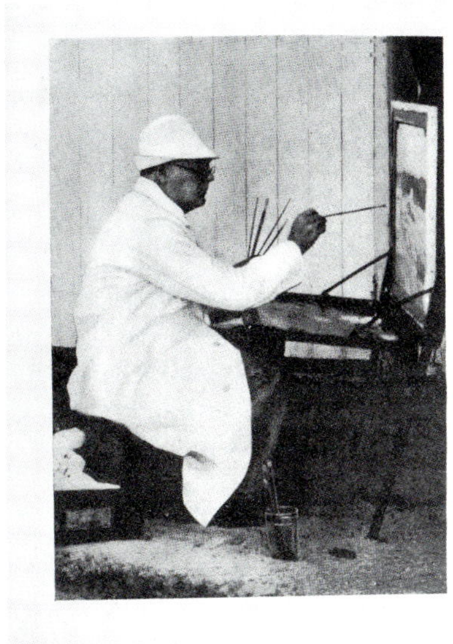

introduction by David Coombs

Although the principles and motives remain the same, much else has changed since the publication in 1967 of my first book of paintings by Sir Winston Churchill.

From the outset, Lady Soames has been closely involved in the making of this new and revised book of her father's pictures. Her interest and commitment have been unstinting and encouraging in equal proportions and she has happily engaged in often lengthy detective work when hunting for missing pictures. Neither I nor Minnie S. Churchill could have accomplished so much so quickly without Mary Soames's help, so the new book is, in every sense, the result of the joint work of the three of us.

The most obvious change is in the illustrations, which in this new edition are almost all in colour. This is entirely due to the efforts of Minnie S. Churchill, Director of Churchill Heritage, which owns the copyright in Sir Winston's paintings. With the devoted assistance of Simon Bird, Minnie Churchill has left no stone unturned in her efforts to find the present whereabouts of many of Sir Winston's paintings, which, as I foresaw after his death in 1965, have become scattered into collections round the world.

We all owe a considerable debt of gratitude to Anthea Morton-Saner, a director of Curtis Brown.

As well as pursuing known pictures so that they could be photographed in colour, Minnie Churchill has been eagerly seeking anecdotes from the owners and these have found their place in the new catalogue or in the text accompanying the illustrations, with much other material I have discovered for myself.

Not content with this often frustrating work, Minnie Churchill decided to look further for paintings that might have escaped my original net. Delving into the archives of the Witt Library at the Courtauld Institute of Art, she discovered a number of additional paintings sold at auction, including one or two that may not in fact be genuine.

On my own account I have taken a different route. By combing through journals published in Sir Winston's lifetime, I have found several paintings reproduced that have gone missing since. These, plus others, genuine or problematic, that have surfaced recently are illustrated also in the last chapter.

The archives in the care of the National Trust at Chartwell have proved to be a goldmine. With the ready agreement of Carole Kenwright, the Property Manager, I have delved into a large cache of several hundred original photographs that were originally kept in Sir Winston Churchill's Studio.

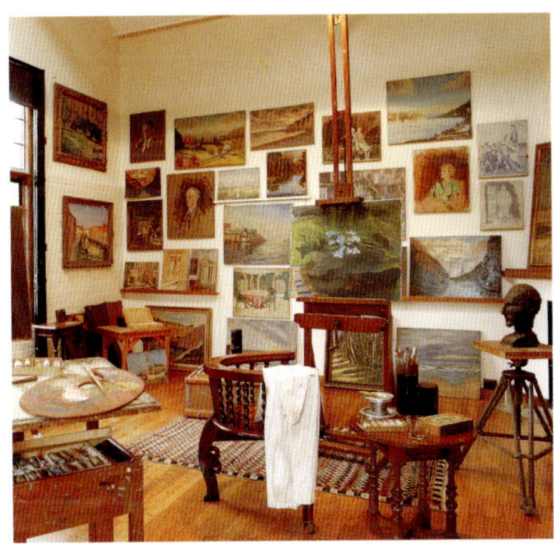

Sir Winston Churchill's Studio at Chartwell, his country home in Kent. In the care of the National Trust, the Studio displays a fine selection of Churchill's paintings from his first to the last.

It is known that Churchill, under Walter Sickert's tutelage, often used photographs to help him compose his paintings and it was exciting to find many that relate to specific examples, as well as others that do not. I have noted all the former in the new catalogue entries and some of the most interesting are illustrated here.

The Chartwell archives also included two hitherto unknown and unrecorded sketches by Churchill, both of which have been added to the catalogue. With these additions and paintings from a variety of other sources, the new catalogue now contains some 30 more pictures than the 500 or so listed previously.

At the time I made the first catalogue, some 36 years ago, relatively little was published about Sir Winston's life. Since then Sir Martin Gilbert's multi-volume biography has been completed, a task begun by Churchill's son, Randolph. In addition, Mary Soames has published her own unique memoir of her father's life as a painter.

All this information and much more that has been published or discovered since Sir Winston's death in 1965 has helped us achieve a greater accuracy than was originally possible in dating and identifying the subjects of many paintings.

Making use principally of Sir Martin Gilbert's biography and Mary Soames's memoir, plus other published sources, as well as the colossal archives held by Churchill College in Cambridge, I have been able to construct an outline chronology that relates Sir Winston's life as a painter to the broader historical events of his time. This weaves its way through the chapters that follow and is a revised and extended version of the text I first wrote for the catalogue of the 1998 Sotheby's exhibition in London. With more than 100 paintings on show, this was the largest exhibition to date of paintings by Sir Winston Churchill and was the idea of Hugo Swire, a Sotheby's director.

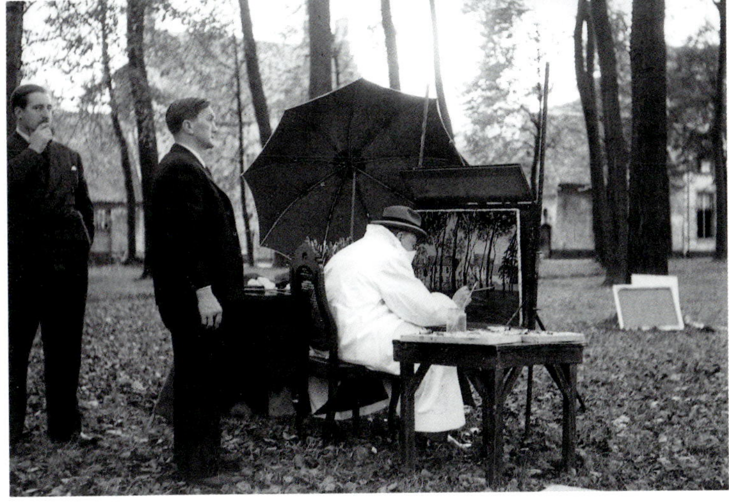

Sir Wintston Churchill painting at Le Beguinage, Bruges, in 1946. His picture is illustrated on page 195.

So much for the changes. As I have already stated, the principles and motives underlying this new book are the same as they were for my first. My prime purpose in making the catalogue was and is the protection of the reputation of the painter.

Why does anyone want to own or admire a painting by Sir Winston Churchill, however attractive or interesting it may be in itself? The answer is clear: because it is a genuine painting by the man himself.

In his lifetime, Sir Winston gave away or sold many more paintings than was generally realized at the time of his death. In all circumstances today, the key to authenticating a hitherto unknown yet possible Churchill painting is its provenance or, in other words, its history of ownership from the time of its painting. I have set out these points and others fully in my last chapter, 'Discoveries and Mysteries'.

In my original book and consequently in this revised version, many paintings are noted first as being in 'the Studio'. This refers to the paintings in Sir Winston's ownership that, on his death, passed into the hands of his executors. Many were given away by Lady Churchill to her family and friends, as well as to places and institutions that she knew would treasure such a memento. It was through her generosity that the major dispersal of Sir Winston's paintings began.

The reference in the catalogue to 'the Studio' was not in fact to Churchill's Studio in the grounds of Chartwell, so carefully restored since by the National Trust, but to the dining room in the house. This, now returned to its original form, served as a storeroom in post-war years for Sir Winston's paintings in his later years and no doubt, on occasion, as a warmer and more comfortable painting studio.

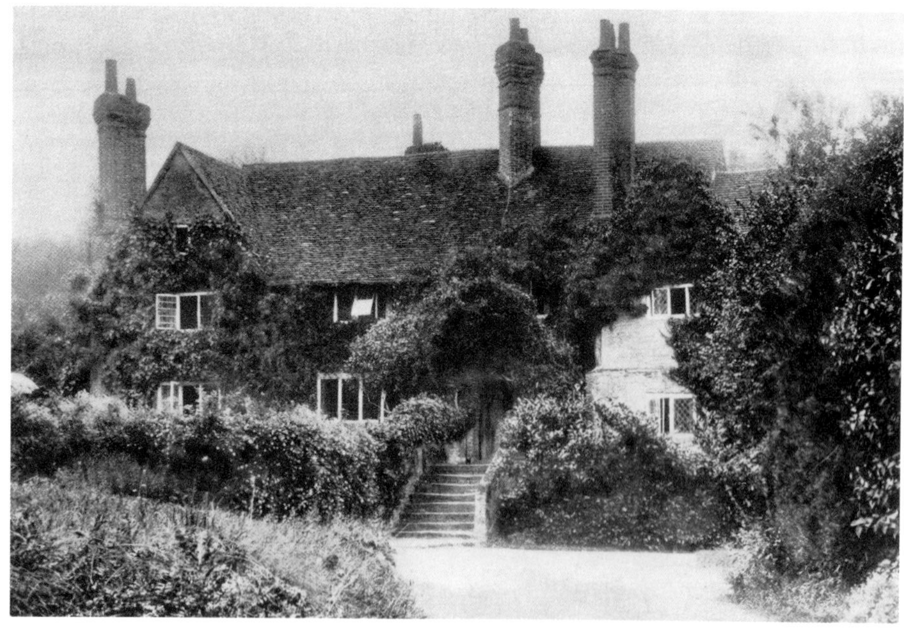

'Hoe Farm is the charming country residence, in the neighbourhood of Godalming, Surrey, where the late First Lord of the Admiralty [Mr Winston Churchill] passes his occasional leisure, occupied, it is announced, with landscape-painting, in which his work is said to show exceptionally high talent.'
From *The Illustrated War News*, September 1915.
Copyright reserved by the Trustees of Godalming Museum.

It was in this room in 1965 that I and the late Richard Pawsey, the probate valuer for Churchill's estate and a kind and generous mentor, found the paintings carefully stacked in two long rows. It was while we began to list them and to make our first attempts at dating the pictures and identifying their subjects that I first began to realize that Churchill's paintings in total must form a kind of visual diary of people and places that were important to him.

Furthermore, this opportunity to examine in detail and for the first time a large number of Churchill's pictures led me to my most startling personal discovery: that the paintings could have been done only by a sensitive man. Bearing in mind Churchill's reputation as a war leader and political fighter, this was not what I had expected. Although the charm and many insights of his book Painting as a Pastime had delighted me since boyhood, the beauty of Churchill's prose had hidden this aspect of his personality from me.

His book makes it absolutely clear that Churchill was more interested in the making of painting than he was in the meaning of painting. He had huge energy and so the act of painting was in itself a form of physical release. Also, the many technical problems associated with accurately depicting a landscape or any other subject in oil paint were sufficiently compelling to fill his mind, to the exclusion of almost everything else.

Confirmation of his remarkably thoughtful approach to painting can be found in a fundamental yet practical question posed by Churchill, which was to attract the admiration and attention of the great art historian Sir Ernst Gombrich in his influential book *Art and Illusion*. 'It would be interesting,' wrote Churchill in *Painting as a Pastime*, 'if some real authority investigated carefully the part which memory plays in painting.'

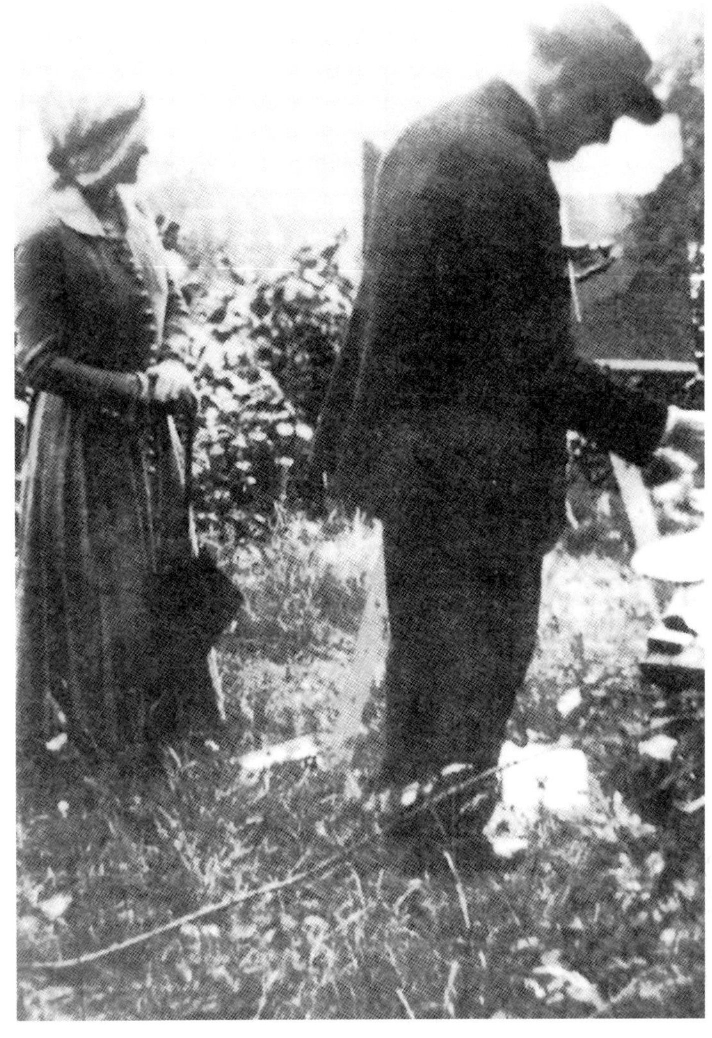

Clementine Churchill watches her husband Winston painting at Hoe Farm, one weekend in the summer of 1915. Reproduced by courtesy of Yvonne S. Churchill.

Thus apart from the paintings, which are the main focus of this book, at its heart are Churchill's essays 'Painting as a Pastime' and 'Hobbies' in the complete original texts that have been forgotten for more than 80 years. I am grateful to Winston S. Churchill, Sir Winston's grandson, for readily granting his permission for this. This chapter also contains an outline of the complicated history of both essays, which has thoroughly confused Churchill's dedicated bibliographers ever since.

The differences in the texts are significant and serve to confirm Churchill's essentially humble approach to painting. This can be inferred from the later, shortened versions but is substantial and specific in the original.

Any attempt to raise Churchill's paintings to a level of 'art' such as he never intended is, in my opinion, foolish and unnecessary. It is also unhelpful in that such an idea prevents us from seeing and enjoying his pictures for what they rightly are: an astonishing number of 'daubs' (Churchill's own modest description) ranging from the very good to the not so good, and in a surprising variety of styles by a technically audacious amateur painter.

Churchill's paintings represent the enduring pastime of one of the most remarkable world leaders of the 20th century. Herein lies their interest.

The chronology that follows, which is highly selective, has a single purpose: to set Sir Winston Churchill's painterly pastime in the context of the circumstances and experiences, concerns and interests that helped form and then encompassed the man. Where possible, his own words have been used to illuminate this.

To these have been added comments and reminiscences about Churchill's approach to painting by members of his family and his staff, as well as by friends, collectors and others, including several art critics, who admired his work in his lifetime. The text also reveals the extent of Churchill's friendship with a number of professional artists, as well as connoisseurs, which may come as a surprise to those unprepared for any such degree of sensibility in his temperament.

Overleaf: Sir Winston Churchill painting Mrs Cunliffe-Owen's house on the River Nivelle, 1945.

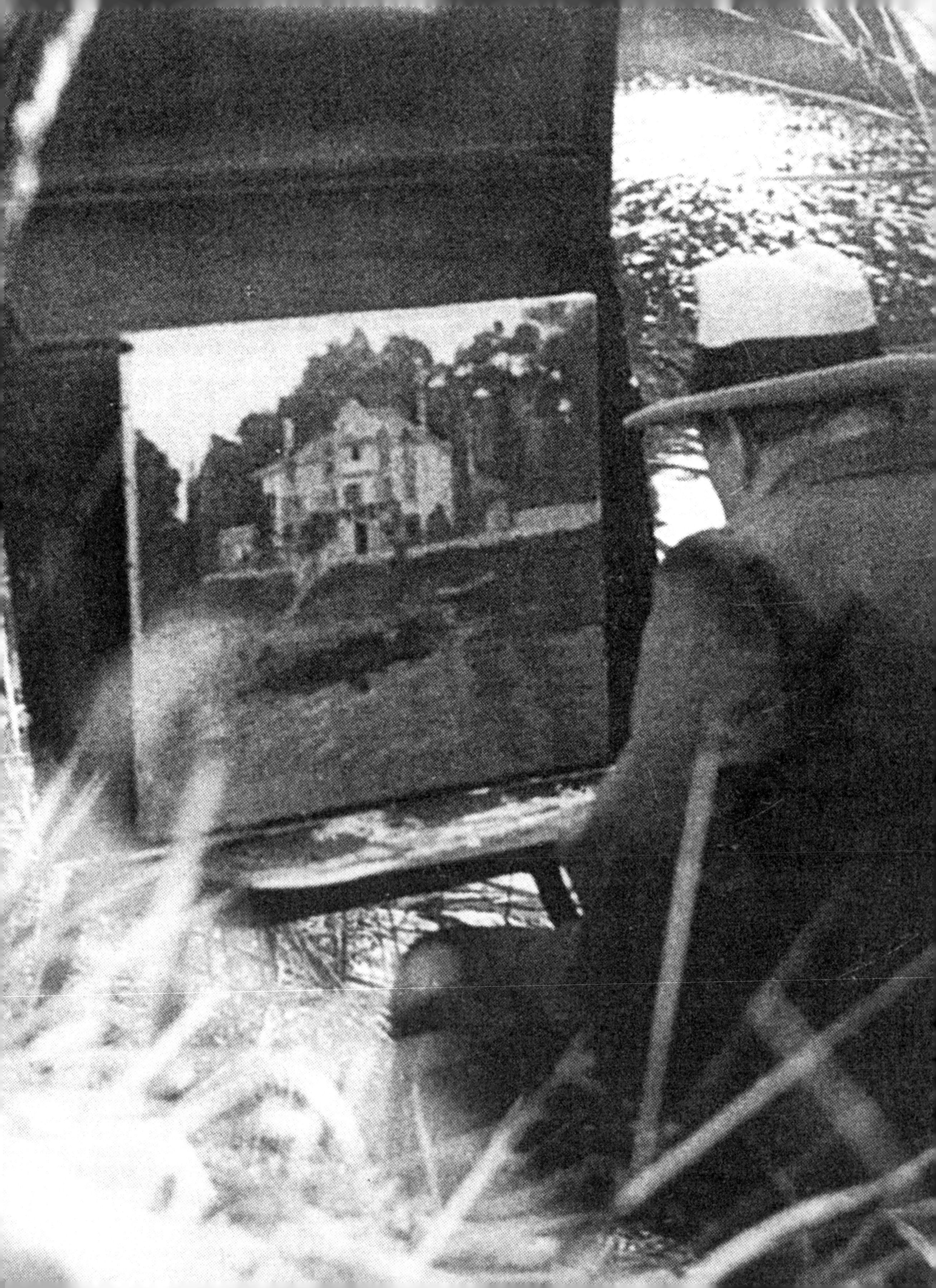

the beginning

1874 - 1921

1874 [Background] Winston Spencer Churchill was born November 30th at Blenheim Palace, home of his grandfather John, 7th Duke of Marlborough. Winston was the elder son of Lord Randolph Churchill and Jennie Jerome of New York. First Impressionist exhibition in Paris.

1886 [Background] Slavery abolished in Spanish Cuba. Lord Randolph Churchill became Chancellor of the Exchequer in the Conservative government but resigned when frustrated in his wish to create a more equitable taxation system.

1888 [Background] Suez Canal opened. Churchill went to Harrow School as a boarder, joined the school cadet force and later entered the Army Class.

1890 [Background] London-Paris telephone line opened. The German Emperor William II began personal rule as Kaiser. Churchill gave up the singing class at school to study drawing.

1892 [Background] Northern Rhodesia taken over by the British South Africa Company. Four Independent Labour Party Members of Parliament. Churchill won Public Schools fencing championship.

1893 [Background] United States Marines overthrew native government in Hawaii. Churchill passed entrance examination to Royal Military College, Sandhurst, at third attempt.

1895 [Background] Churchill's 21st year. Kiel Canal linked Germany with the North Sea. Lord Randolph Churchill died aged 45 and was buried in Bladon churchyard just beyond the walls of Blenheim. Winston gazetted a Second Lieutenant in the cavalry with the 4th Hussars. Steeplechasing and polo became interests. Travelled via New York, West Point and Florida to Cuba where the Spanish were fighting a rebellion; in his reports for *The Daily Graphic* Churchill expressed sympathy and understanding for the independence movement.

1896 [Background] Nobel Prizes established. Marconi demonstrated wireless telegraphy on Salisbury Plain. The Klondyke gold rush. Churchill sailed for India

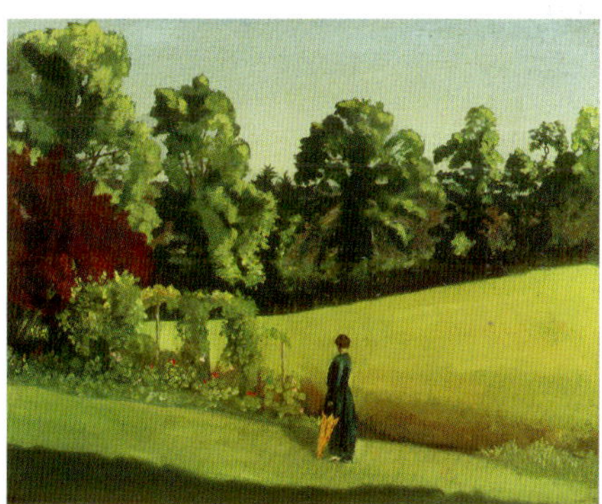

Fig 1 (C 146) above
It was at Hoe Farm in 1915 that Churchill first began to paint. His interest was prompted by his sister-in-law Goonie, Lady Gwendeline Churchill, shown in the garden there.

Fig 2 (C 148) below
The entrance to the drive at Hoe Farm, which is in the village of Hascombe near Godalming in Surrey. Winston's and his brother Jack's families shared the house as they did one in London at that time. Jack was away serving in the army during the war.

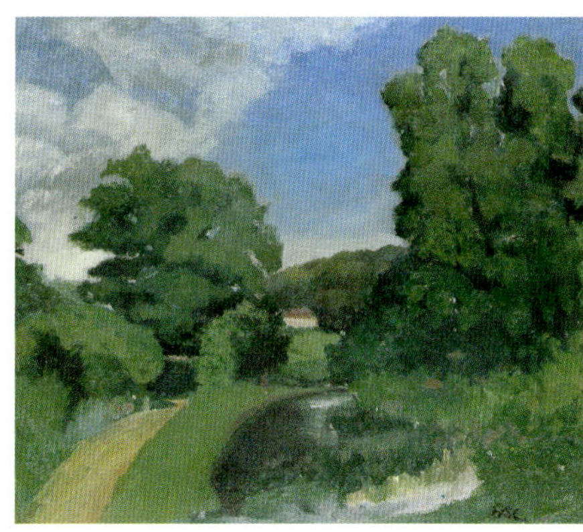

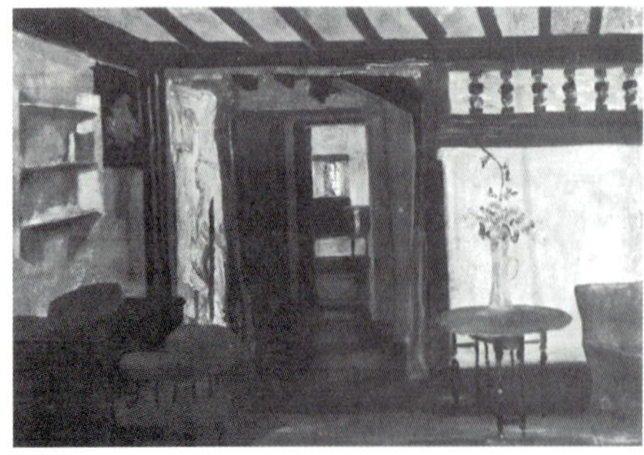

Fig 3 (C 23) above
The hall at Hoe Farm - part of the extension to the original medieval house, done for its owner Joseph Godman by the architect Edwin Lutyens in 1890

with the 4th Hussars. Continued an extensive course of self-education by reading, for example, Gibbon's *Decline and Fall of the Roman Empire*, Plato's *Republic*, Winwood Reade's *Martyrdom of Man*, Hallam's *Constitutional History* and Adam Smith's *Wealth of Nations*.

1897 [Background] Queen Victoria's Diamond Jubilee. Tate Gallery presented to the nation. After leave in England, during which he made his first political speech on behalf of the Conservative Party, Churchill returned to India and sent his mother the plot of a novel he intended to write. Travelled to the North-West Frontier, where the Afghan tribes were in revolt, as a correspondent for *The Daily Telegraph* and the *Allahabad Pioneer*. Attached to the Malakand Field Force, he joined the fighting and was mentioned in despatches for 'courage and resolution'. Decided to enter Parliament when an opportunity presented itself.

1898 [Background] Spanish-American war. United States acquired the Philippines. Churchill's book *The Story of the Malakand Field Force* published. This and the publication of his reports in *The Daily Telegraph* convinced Churchill that, henceforth, he could make his living by writing. Returned from India on leave and organized an attachment to Lord Kitchener's Expeditionary Force in the Sudan with the 21st Lancers. Commissioned to write for the *Morning Post*. Took part in a cavalry charge against the Dervish army at the Battle of Omdurman. Returned to London where he was offered serialization of his novel and continued to India where he decided to leave the army and go into politics.

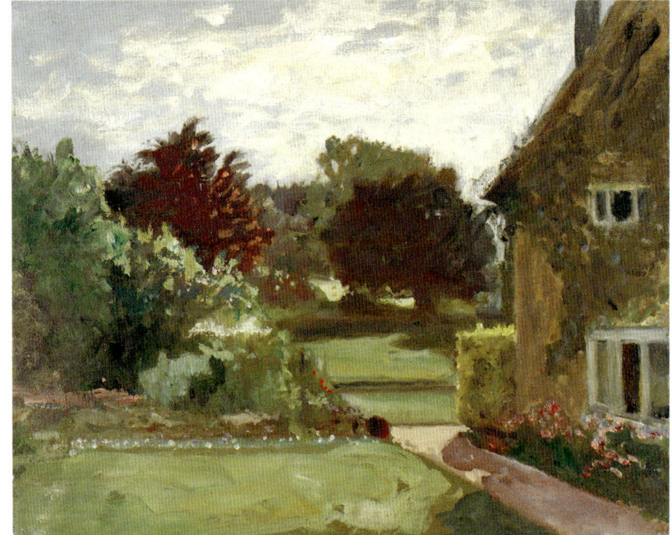

Fig 4 (C 149) above
The house and garden at Hoe Farm. Winston wrote to his brother Jack: "It really is a delightful valley, and the garden gleams with summer jewellery. We live very simply - but with all the essentials of life well understood & well provided for - hot baths, cold champagne, new peas & old brandy." Churchill was so entranced that he seriously considered buying a house in the locality.

1899 [Background] Anglo-Egyptian condominium over Sudan. War between British and Boers in South Africa. Churchill returned to England and was asked to stand for Parliament in Oldham but was unsuccessful. Travelled to South Africa as correspondent for the *Morning Post* in the war with the Boer Republic. His book *The River War* was published. Captured by Boers and held in a prison camp from which he made a daring escape and achieved national fame.

Winston's increasingly serious interest in painting, which required both mental and physical concentration, helped him deal with the grave depression which overtook him when he was forced to resign as First Lord of the Admiralty after the disastrous allied attack on the Dardanelles. Clementine was very worried about his state of mind: 'I thought he would die.' She told Churchill's biographer Sir Martin Gilbert many years later.

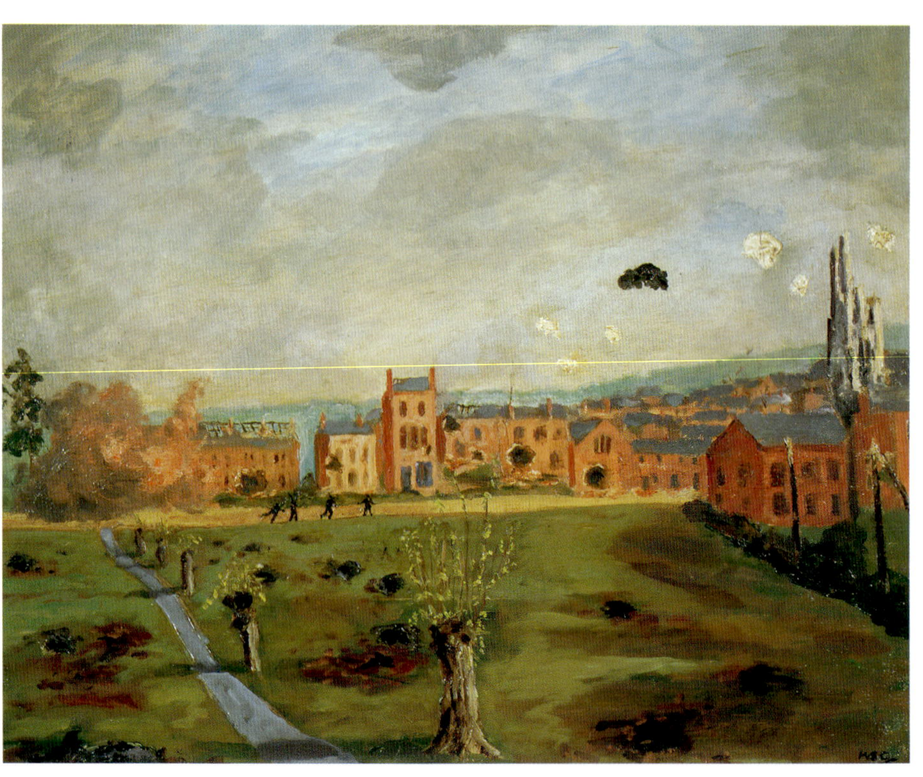

Fig 5 (C 4) right
Frustrated by political life, Churchill resigned from the government late in 1915 to rejoin the army while retaining his parliamentary seat. In 1916 Churchill took command of a battalion of the Royal Scots Fusiliers at Ploegsteert on the borders of France and Belgium. Here, enemy shells burst over his view of the village, which was known as 'Plugstreet' to the troops.

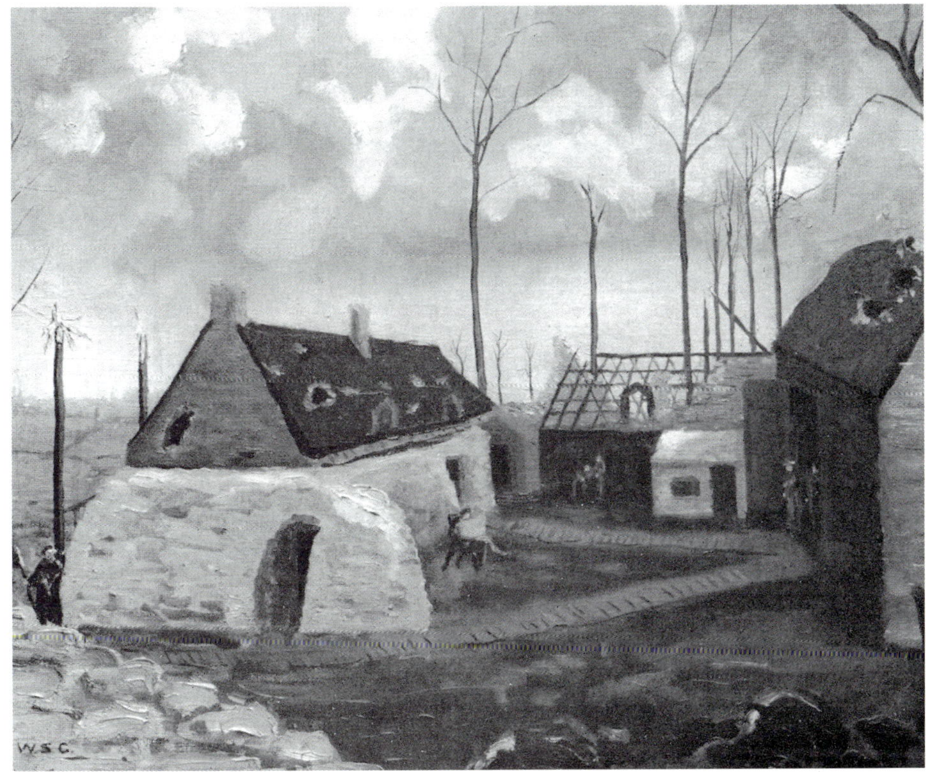

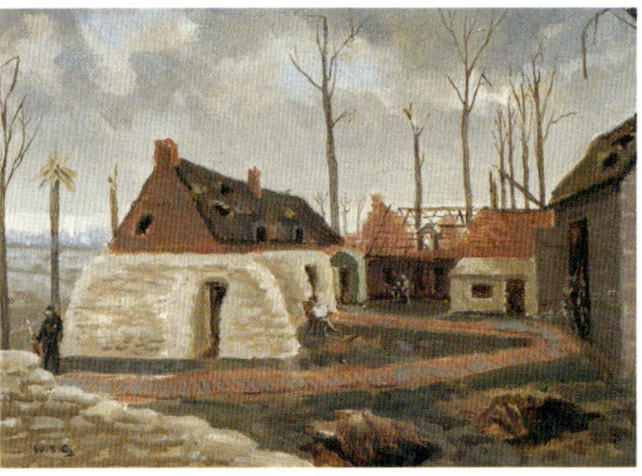

Fig 6 (C 2) above
Lawrence Farm at Plugstreet - Churchill's advance headquarters at the front line. Later he gave this little painting to his battalion, the 6th Royal Scots Fusiliers, which he had commanded from January 1916 until May when, faced with its amalgamation because of losses from shell-fire, he returned to London and to active political life.

Fig 7 (C 1) left
Lawrence Farm. The figure calmly reading the newspaper may be Churchill's second-in-command,ß Sir Archibald Sinclair, later Viscount Thurso, to whom he gave the painting.

1900 [Background] Socialist Revolutionary Party formed in Russia. Boxer Rebellion in China. First Zeppelin airship constructed in Germany. Churchill commissioned in the South African Light Horse and present at the relief of the siege of Ladysmith. His book *London to Ladysmith via Pretoria* was published, selling 11,000 copies in less than six weeks. Returned from South Africa and elected Conservative Member of Parliament for Oldham. His novel *Savrola* published. Began a career as a paid lecturer in England, also travelling to the United States and Canada.

1901 [Background] Marconi transmitted morse wireless signals across the Atlantic. First British submarine. Trans-Siberian railway opened. Queen Victoria died and Edward VII became King. Churchill took his seat in Parliament and made his maiden speech. Much affected by reading Seebohm Rowntree's book *Poverty: A Study of Town Life*. Learnt to drive a motor car.

1902 [Background] Boer War ended, Churchill calling for 'an honourable agreement between fighting races'. Churchill embarked upon a biography of his father. Frustrated by party politics, he proposed a centre party coalition. Travelled to Egypt to the opening of the new Nile dam at Aswan, visiting the temples and ruins of ancient Egypt.

1903 [Background] The Wright brothers made the first heavier-than-air flight in the United States. Hostile to the government's policies on military expenditure, Churchill now additionally opposed its proposals on trade tariffs.

1904 [Background] Churchill's 30th year. Construction of Panama Canal resumed. Churchill angered by the massacre of Tibetans by British forces. His support for Free Trade led to an invitation from the Liberals of Northwest Manchester to stand for Parliament and, having attacked the Government's Aliens Bill as undermining the practices of free entry and asylum, he joined the Opposition benches. Met 19-year-old Clementine Hozier.

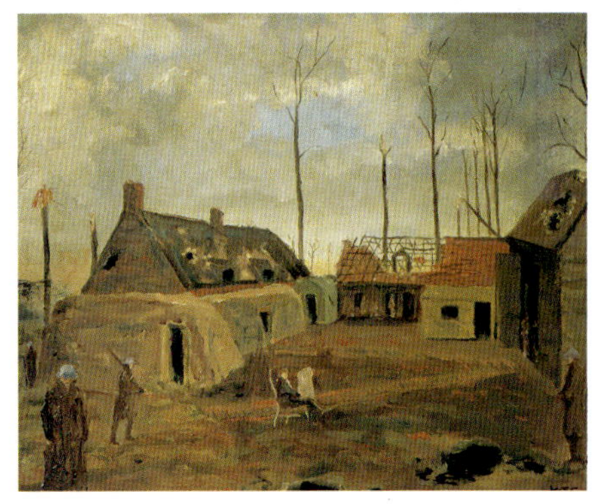

Fig 8 (C 3) above
Lawrence Farm - away from the professional influence of his friend Sir John Lavery, Churchill was painting in a more primitive style.

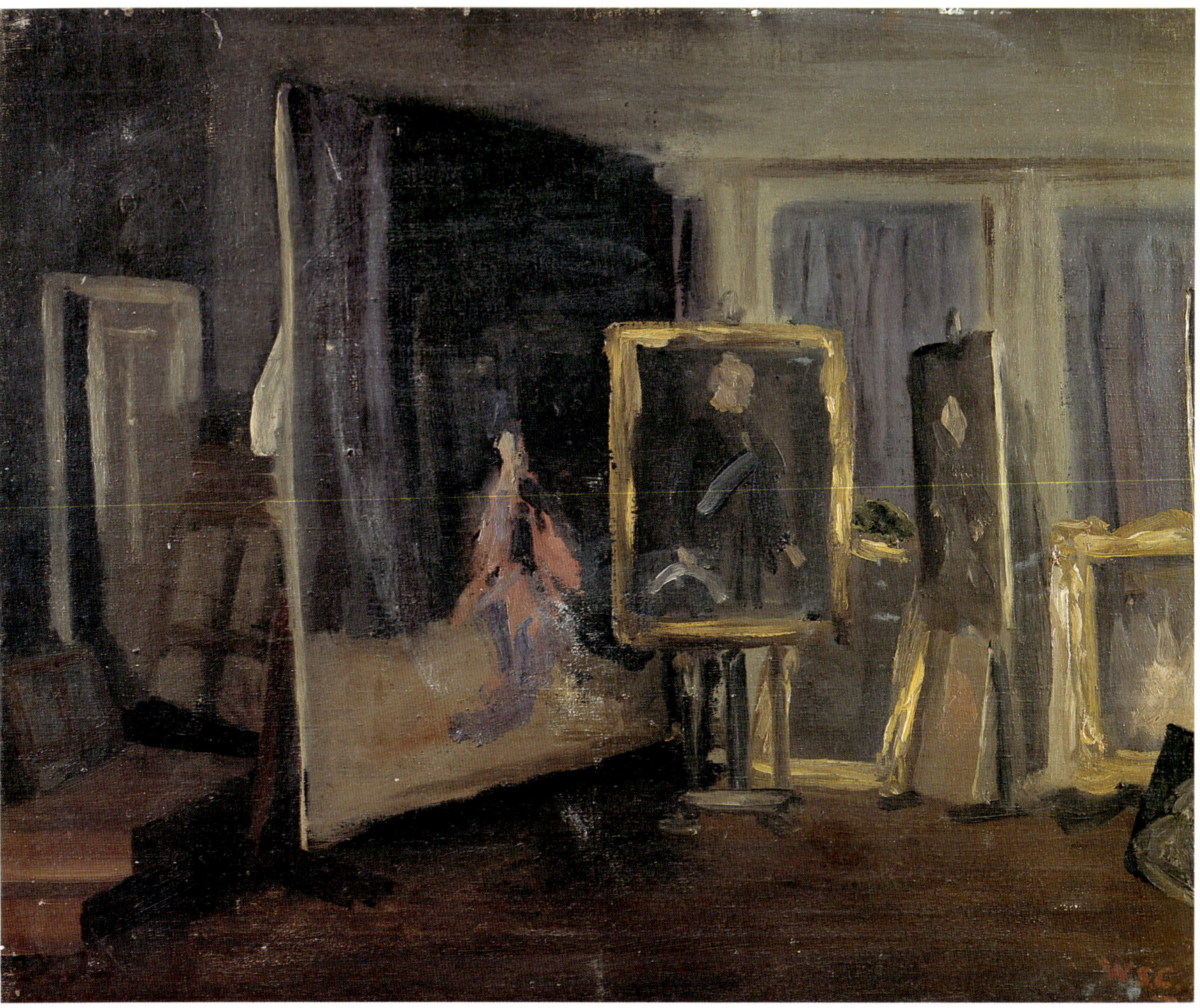

Fig 9 (C 27) above
Interior of Sir John Lavery's Studio in London where, from 1915, Churchill often worked and learnt from his first artist master. Lavery's studio was only a short walk from the London house which Winston, his brother Jack and their families were sharing for reasons of economy.

1905 [Background] Russian Baltic fleet destroyed by Japanese. First biography of Churchill by Alexander MacCallum Scott published. Conservative government resigned and was replaced by the Liberals. Churchill appointed Under-Secretary of State at the Colonial Office, where he met Edward Marsh who became his Private Secretary. Marsh was an important collector and patron of contemporary artists and remained a friend of Churchill until his own death in 1956.

1906 [Background] The first modern battleship, HMS *Dreadnought*, launched in Britain. Churchill's biography of his father Lord Randolph Churchill published. Churchill elected as Member of Parliament for Manchester in Liberal landslide. Promoted self-government for the former Boer Republic of the Transvaal. Travelled abroad for two months to Channel coast of France, then to Switzerland, to Silesia where he was the guest of the Kaiser, Venice and by car through Italy, back to Vienna and then into Moravia.

1907 [Background] Territorial Army introduced in Britain. Channel Tunnel scheme rejected by Parliament. Churchill returned to Italy, travelling down to Syracuse. Then embarked on a long official tour to Malta, Cyprus, Aden via the Suez Canal, Kenya, Uganda and down the Nile to Khartoum and Cairo. Wrote articles for *The Strand Magazine*, later published as *My African Journey*. Churchill proposed a system of social reform to the government.

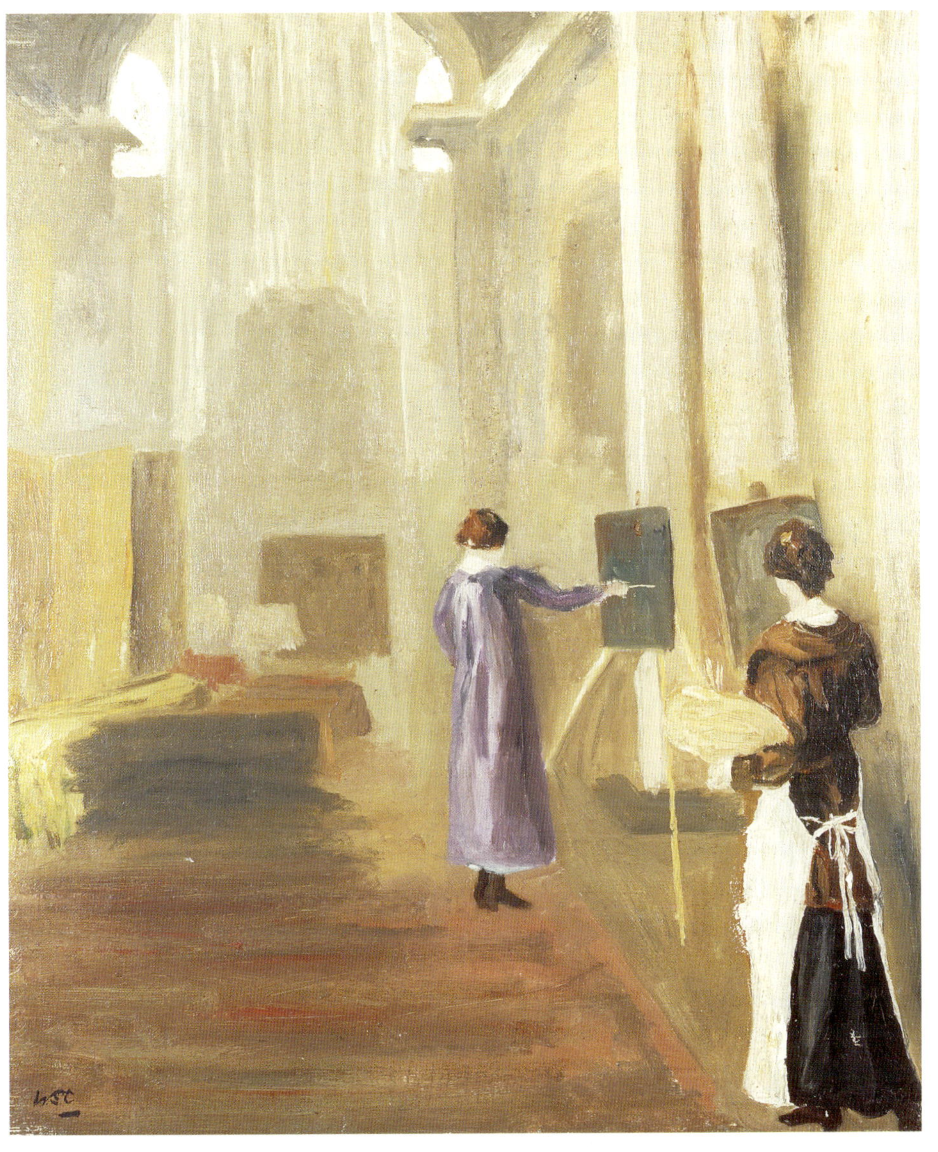

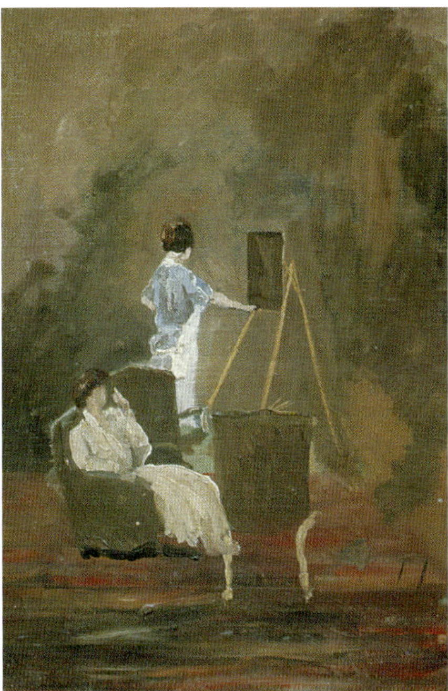

Fig 10 (C 26) above
A scene in Sir John Lavery's Studio with two unknown ladies.

Fig 11 (C 24) left
This is the Long Library at Blenheim in 1916 with Sir John Lavery's wife Hazel and Churchill's sister-in-law, Gwendeline.

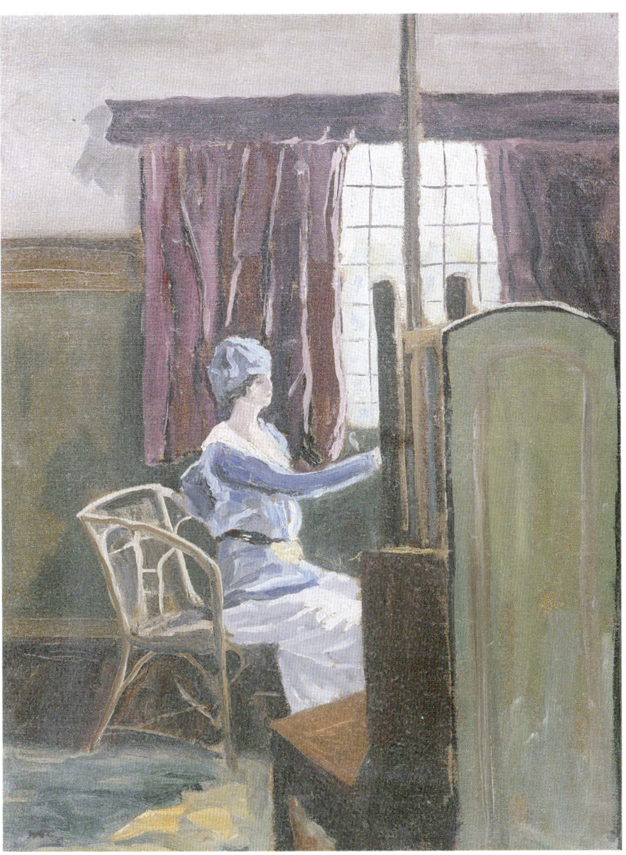

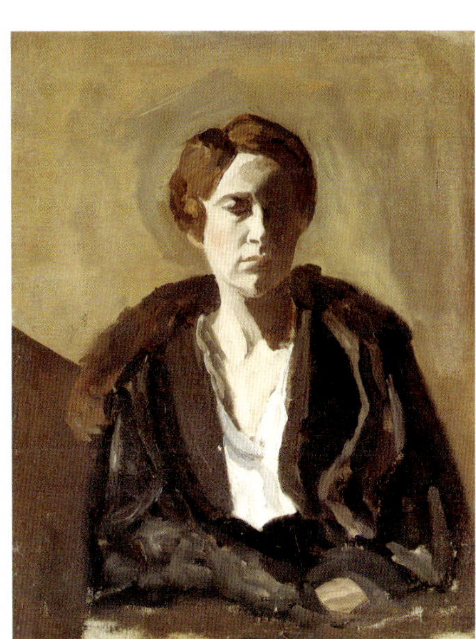

Fig 12 (C 29) above
Portrait of Churchill's sister-in-law Lady Gwendeline Churchill

Fig 13 (C 28) left
Lady Kitty Somerset painting at a studio easel.

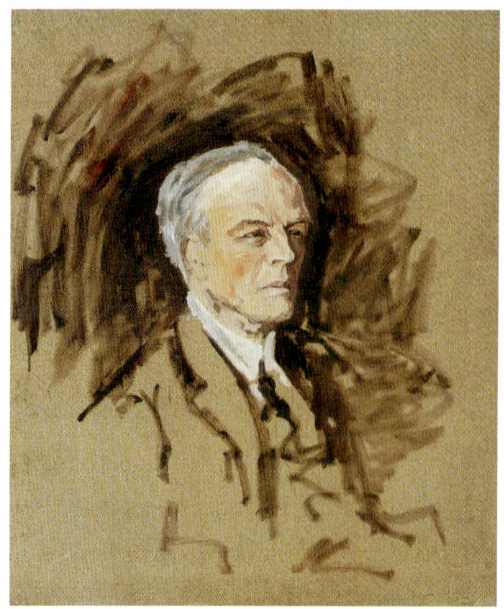

Fig 14 (C 40) above
Sketch portrait of Mr Justice Darling. Lord Darling was an original member of The Other Club, a dining society founded by Churchill and his friend F. E. Smith, Lord Birkenhead, in 1911.

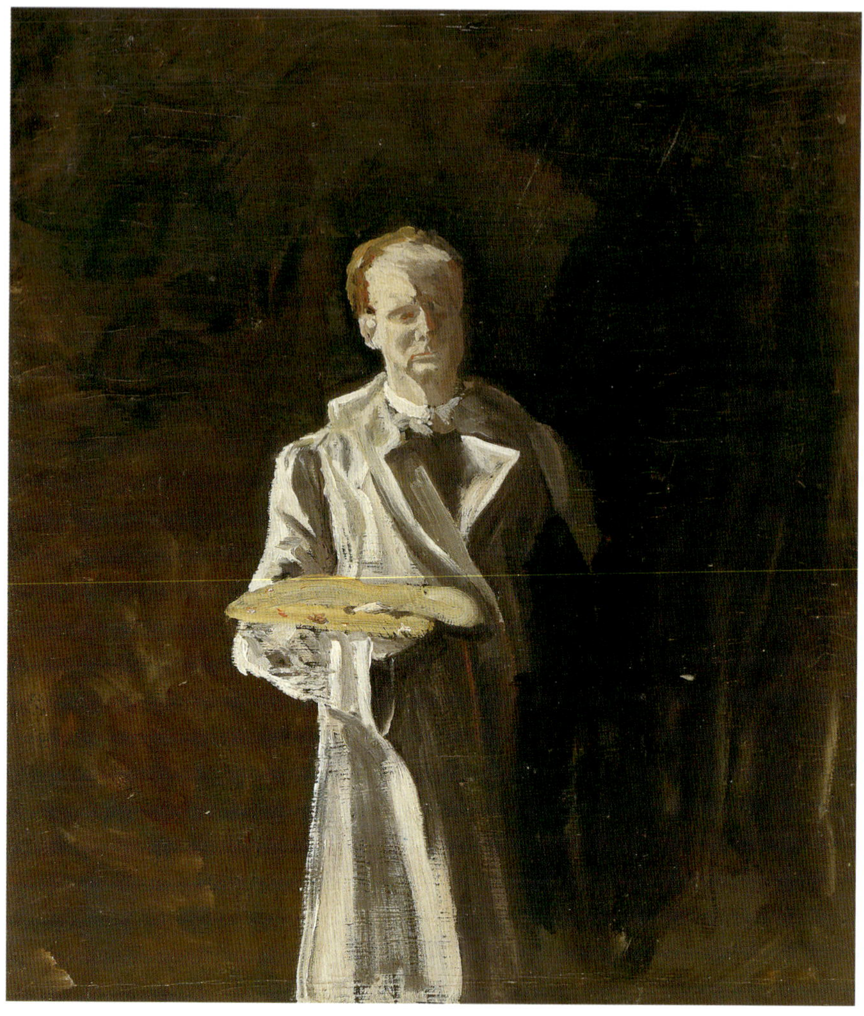

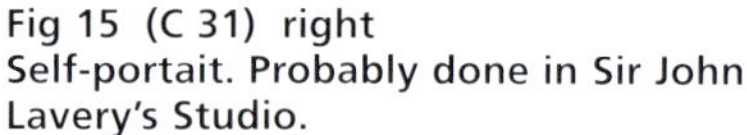

Fig 15 (C 31) right
Self-portait. Probably done in Sir John Lavery's Studio.

1908 [Background] Contributory old-age pension scheme in Britain. First production of Model T Ford motor car in United States. Churchill met Clementine Hozier again and invited her to Blenheim, where they became engaged. They were married in St Margaret's Westminster and honeymooned in Italy on Lake Maggiore and in Venice. Churchill appointed President of the Board of Trade; as a member of the cabinet had to stand for re-election, failed in Manchester but succeeded in Dundee. Conciliated in many industrial disputes.

1909 [Background] Blériot made first cross-Channel flight. Churchill began to take a close interest in developments in aviation; established principle of minimum wages; set up Labour Exchanges; proposed national unemployment and infirmity insurances. Alarmed by German naval expansion.
The Churchills' first child, Diana, was born.

1910 [Background] Braque and Picasso developed Cubism. House of Lords' opposition to budget forced a general election. Liberals returned and Churchill appointed Home Secretary. Embarked upon prison reforms, including the distinction between criminal and political prisoners. King Edward VII died. Churchill went on a summer cruise in the Mediterranean and the Aegean and travelled through Greece and Turkey. Violent coal strike in Wales put down by police; Churchill refused to use troops.

1911 [Background] Imperial Durbar at Delhi attended by King George V. Revolution in China. Churchill present at Siege of Sidney Street following the killing of three London policemen by burglars. Introduced bills to improve safety in coal mines and reduce the hours of shop-workers. Churchill attacked judges'

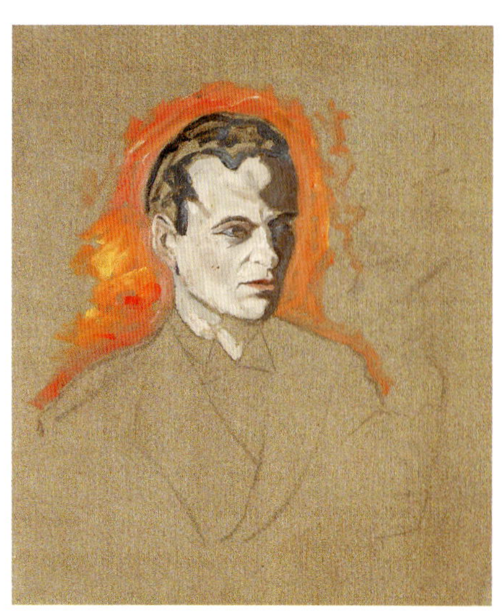

Fig 16 (C 37) above
Sketch portrait of Sir Archibald Sinclair, later Viscount Thurso; he was Churchill's second-in-command with the Royal Scots Fusiliers at Plugstreet.

unfairness in trade union cases. Dock and railway strikes, Churchill sympathetic to strikers. German/French crisis in North Africa threatened European war. Churchill appointed First Lord of the Admiralty and naval preparation became his priority.
The Churchills' second child, Randolph, was born.

1912 [Background] Italy bombarded the Dardanelles. Italo-Turkish war. Naval aeroplanes used in Britain to detect submarines and drop bombs. German naval plans for expansion matched by Britain. Churchill supported Irish Home Rule.

1913 [Background] War in the Balkans. Woodrow Wilson elected President of the United States. Churchill taught to fly by naval pilots. Attended the Royal Academy of Arts dinner and replied to the toast of the government. Travelled by train to Venice and then in the Admiralty yacht *Enchantress* to Malta, Sicily and Corsica.

1914 [Background] Churchill's 40th year. Ulster Unionists rejected Home Rule compromise in Ireland. Churchill stopped flying lessons at the request of his wife, following fatalities among his instructors and on verge of obtaining his licence. Churchill initiated government purchase of majority shareholding in Anglo-Persian Oil Company, so securing the fuel for Britain's warships. Archduke Ferdinand assassinated in Sarajevo. Germany declared war on Austria, which invoked treaty obligation of France, which was invaded by Germany through Belgium, whose neutrality Britain was pledged to defend. Britain at war. British Expeditionary Force sailed to France. Churchill set up Royal Naval Division. British and French armies fell back before German advances.

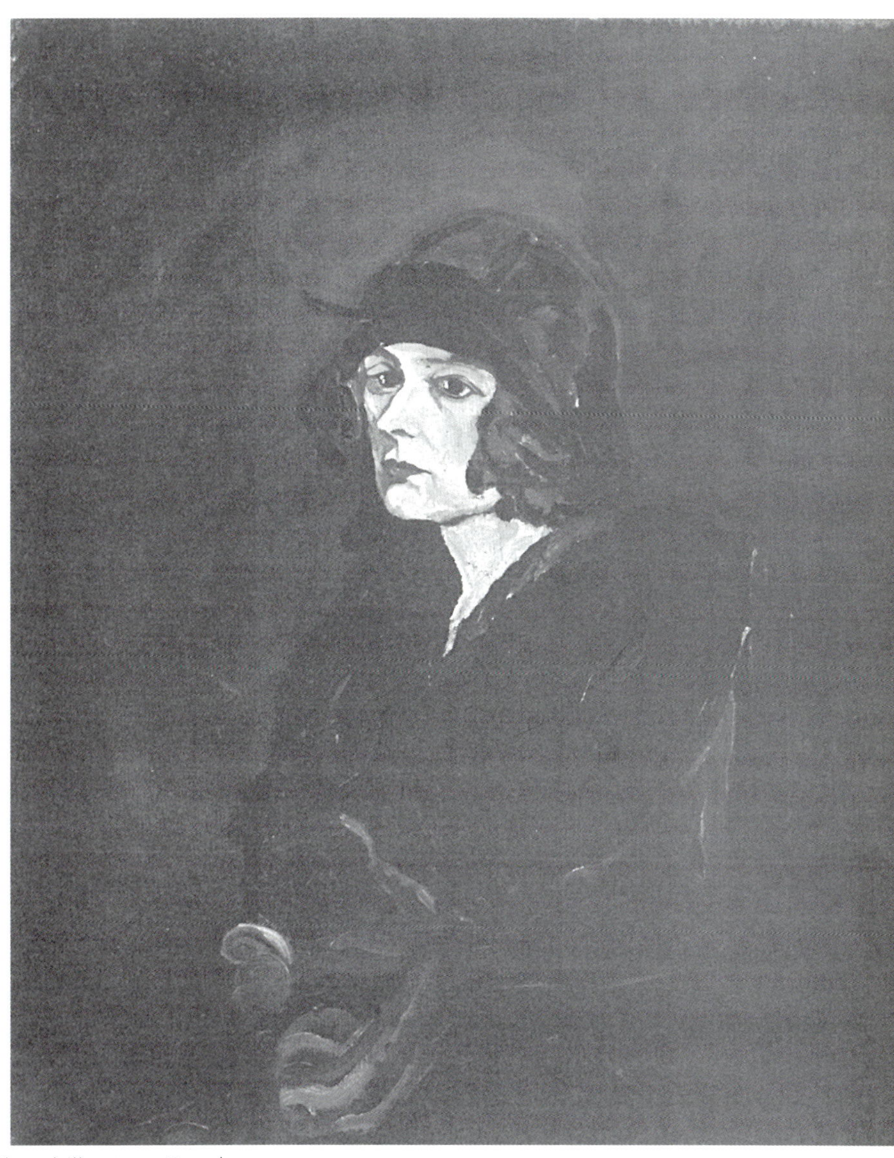
Fig 17 (C 30) above
Portrait of Hazel Lavery, Sir John's wife, and herself a professional artist whose portrait Lavery painted many times.

Churchill given responsibility for aerial defence of Britain. Naval aircraft sent to France. Allied forces began to drive Germans back. British cruisers sunk at the Dogger Bank. Churchill visited besieged Antwerp in attempt to persuade Belgian government not to abandon it to the Germans. Churchill expressed preference for military action rather than politics. German warships under Turkish control bombarded Russian Black Sea ports. Western Front established in Flanders to be held against the Germans. Churchill suggested a naval and military attack against Turkey on the Gallipoli peninsula. The Churchills' third child, Sarah, was born.

1915 [Background] Conditions worsened in the trench warfare on the Western Front; Churchill suggested armour-plated tractors containing machine guns using caterpillar tracks to cross trenches. *S.S. Lusitania* sunk by German submarine. Joint naval and military operation begun against enemy Turkish forces on the Gallipoli peninsula overlooking the Dardanelles straits; three battleships lost and naval attack suspended; army landings led to costly stalemate. National government formed and Churchill forced to resign as First Lord of the Admiralty for a nominal ministerial role. Subsequently, Churchill resigned from the government to serve in the army on the Western Front. Visited the French front line near Arras and was given a steel helmet.

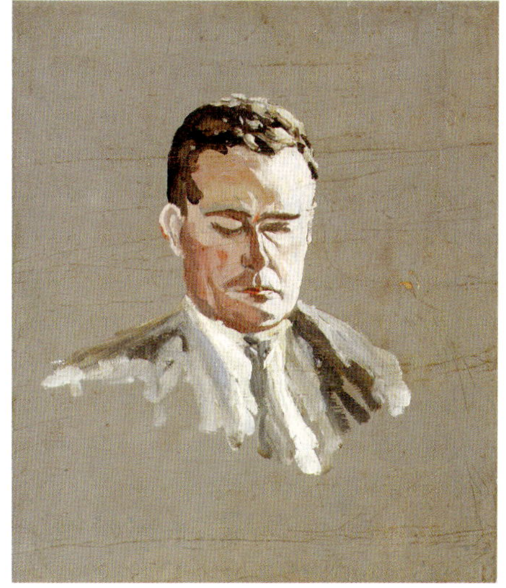
Fig 18 (C 38) above
Sketch portrait of Group Captain Jack Scott who, in 1919, when acting as co-pilot, saved Churchill's life when the plane he was
flying crashed at Croydon Aerodrome.

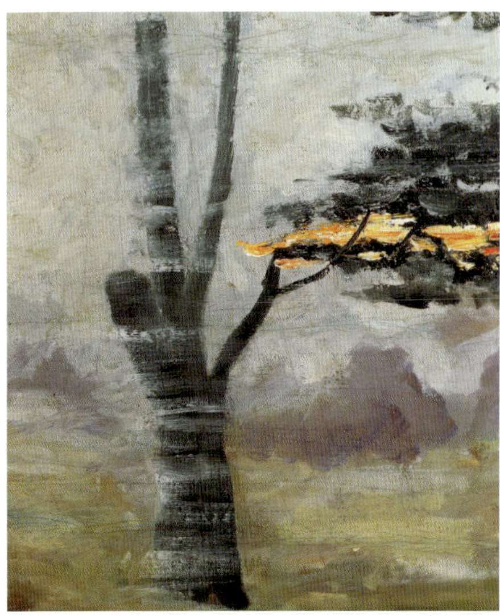

Fig 19 (C 50) above
Sunset through fog, painted at Roehampton in south-west London, where the Churchill family stayed with his cousin Freddie Guest after Lullenden had to be sold.

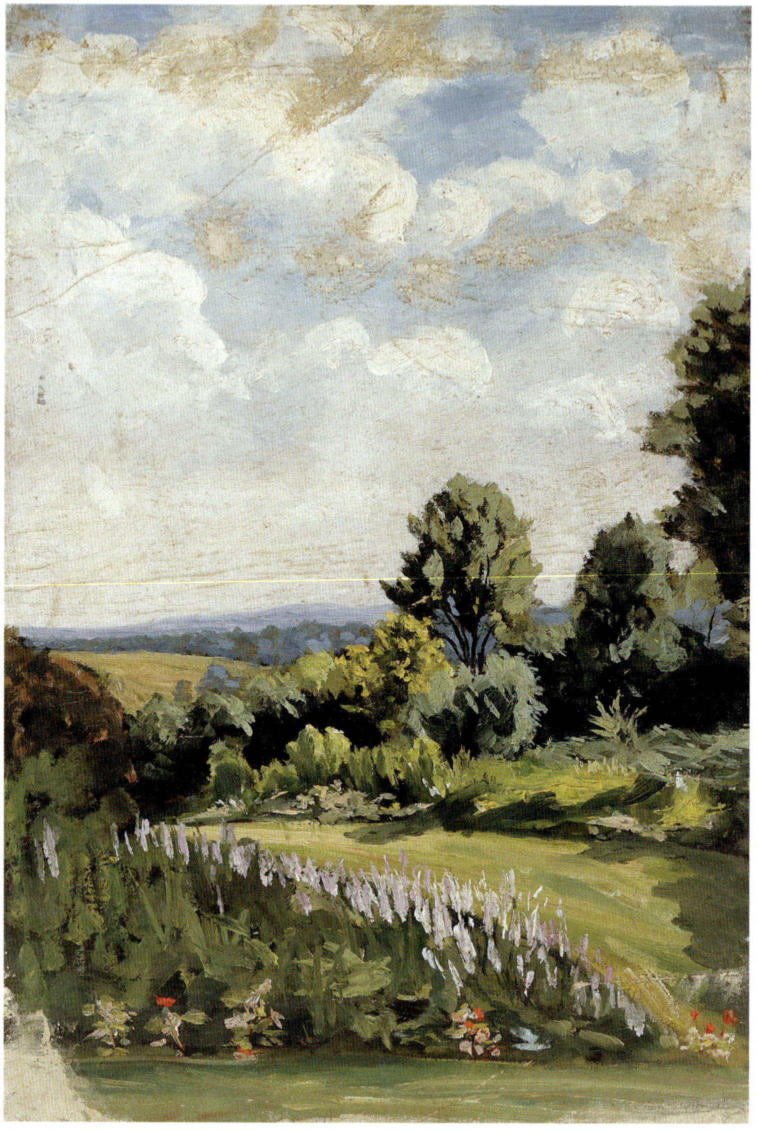

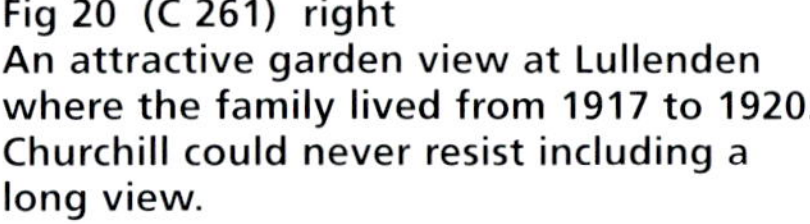

Fig 20 (C 261) right
An attractive garden view at Lullenden where the family lived from 1917 to 1920. Churchill could never resist including a long view.

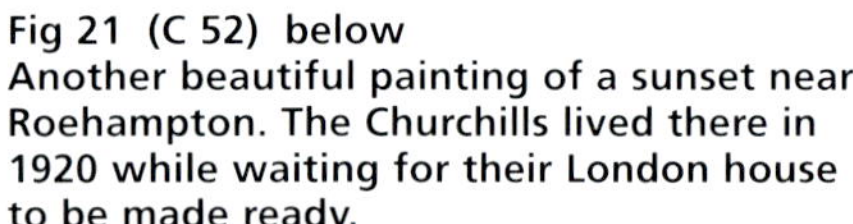

Fig 21 (C 52) below
Another beautiful painting of a sunset near Roehampton. The Churchills lived there in 1920 while waiting for their London house to be made ready.

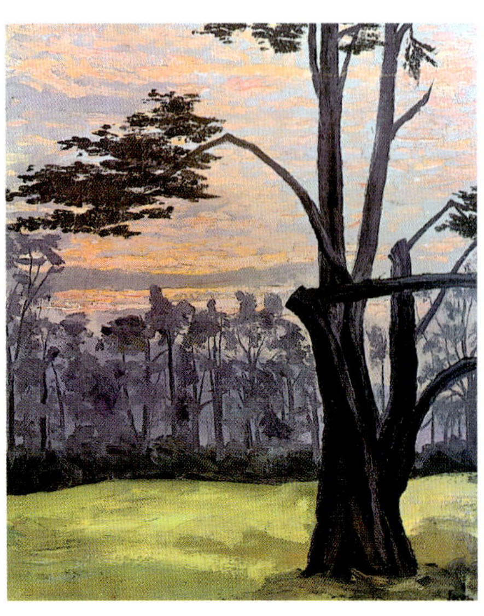

1915 [Painting] Churchill's enforced resignation as First Lord of the Admiralty was a devastating blow to him and he became profoundly depressed. Winston and Clementine rented Hoe Farm near Godalming in Surrey for the summer. They and their three children, Diana, Randolph and Sarah, spent weekends there, often with Lady Gwendeline Churchill, wife of Winston's younger brother, Jack, who was serving as a major in the army in Gallipoli, and their two children, John George and Peregrine. The two families were also sharing a London house in Cromwell Road, South Kensington; the painter Sir John Lavery and his artist wife Hazel lived near by.

One June day at Hoe Farm, Gwendeline sat in the garden sketching in watercolours. Winston, passing by deep in thought, noticed this and after watching for a few minutes borrowed her brush. Taking her son John George's painting box, Gwendeline encouraged Winston to paint a picture. He soon decided he wanted to experiment further by using oils and Clementine rushed into Godalming to buy whatever materials she could, without realizing the need for turpentine - hence Churchill found it virtually impossible initially to paint with the oils.

The Laverys learnt of his new interest and gave immediate practical help and advice. Churchill bought easel, palette, brushes, paints, turpentine and canvases in London and, directly encouraged by Hazel Lavery, he began to paint in oils. His first subjects were exterior and interior views of Hoe Farm.

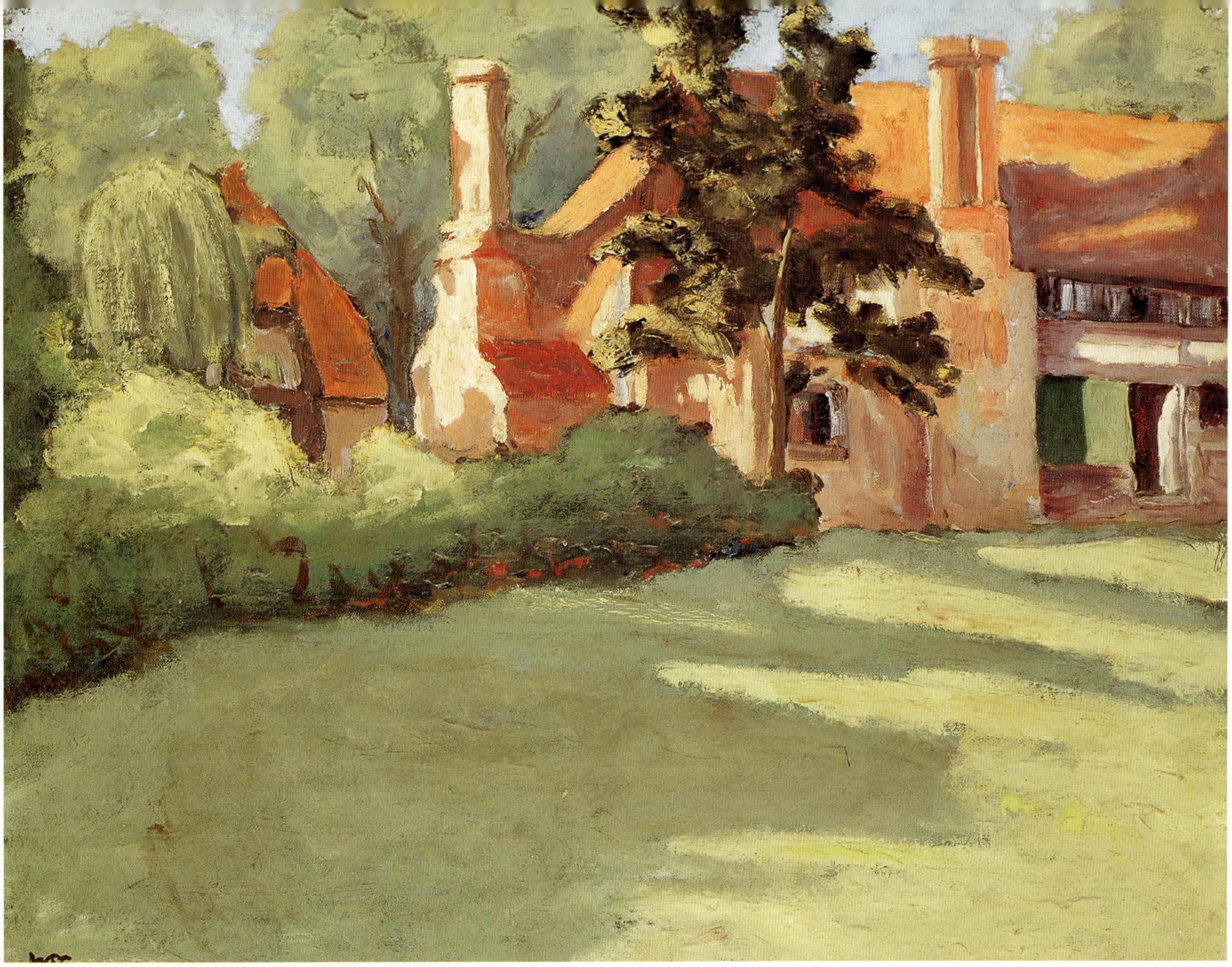

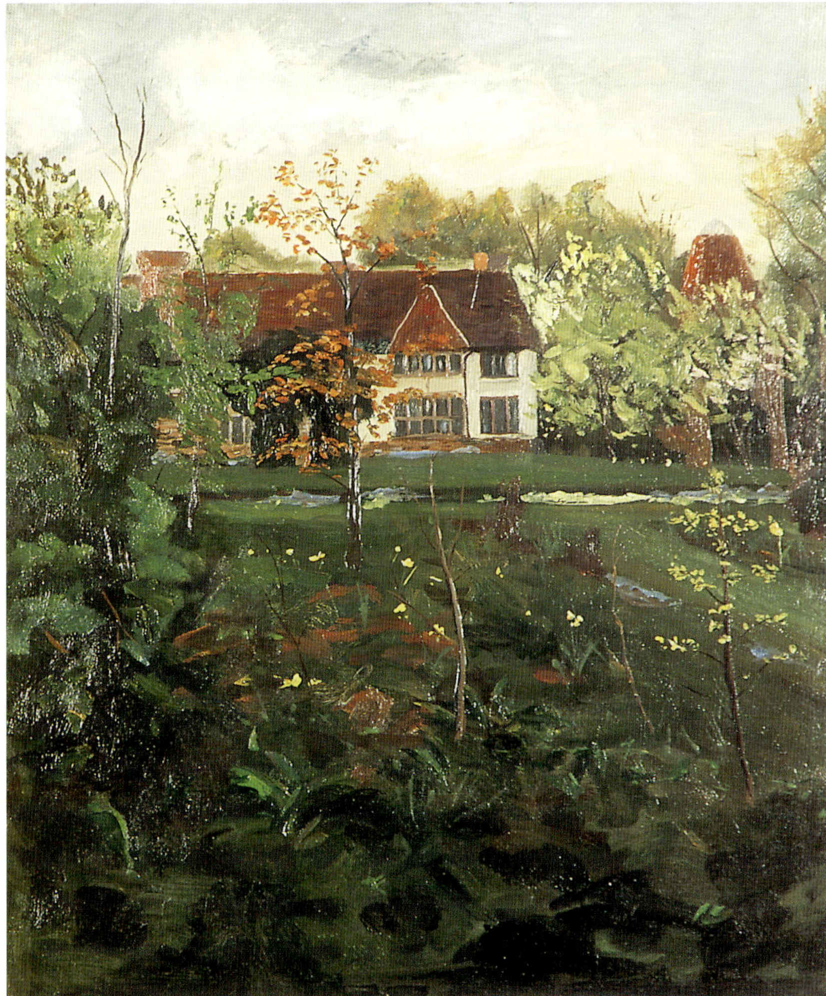

Fig 22 (C 143) above
In 1917, Churchill bought Lullenden Manor near East Grinstead in East Sussex so that his wife and children would be safe from Zeppelin raids on London.

Fig 23 (C 153) below
Green trees and poppies at Lullenden. It was in easy reach of London, so Churchill could visit his family at weekends and paint.

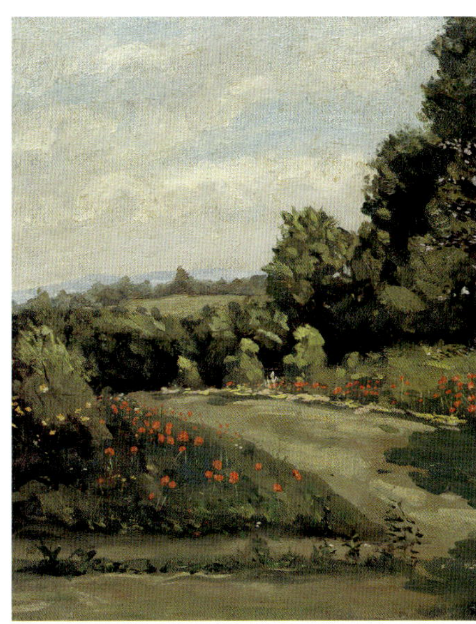

Fig 24 (C 151) left
The Churchills lived very happily at Lullenden until financial difficulties forced its sale in 1920. It was bought by his friend Sir Ian Hamilton.

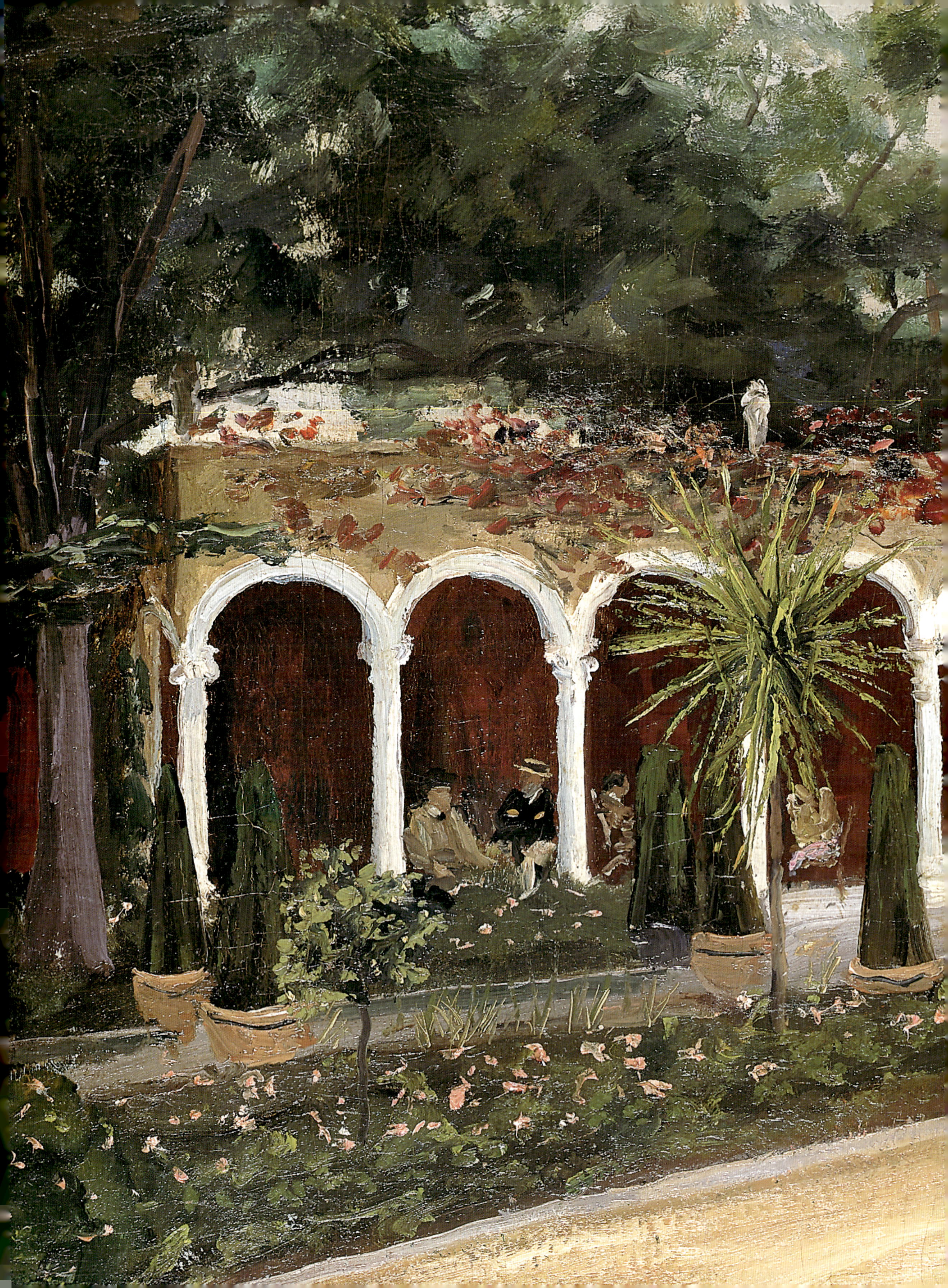

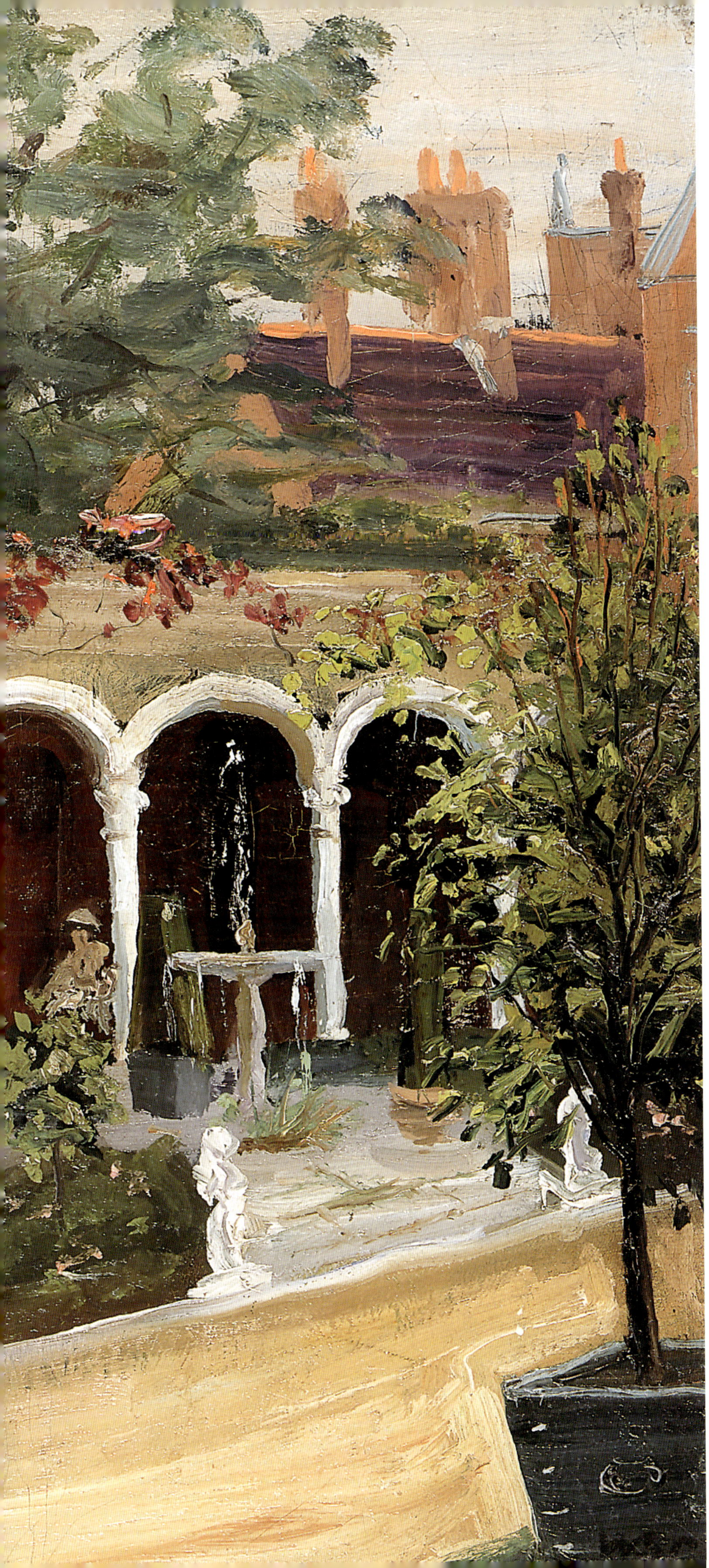

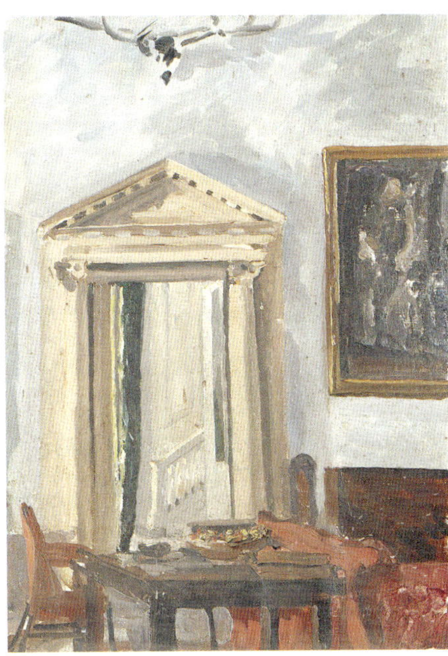

Fig 25 (C 15) above
A little painting of an unidentified interior; Churchill was obviously attracted by the strength of the architectural feature.

Fig 26 (C 137) left
Esher Place in Surrey was owned by Churchill's political colleague Viscount D'Abernon. It was built in the style of a French chateau; and this view of the Loggia shows Lord D'Abernon in the straw hat and Churchill himself in the beige raincoat.

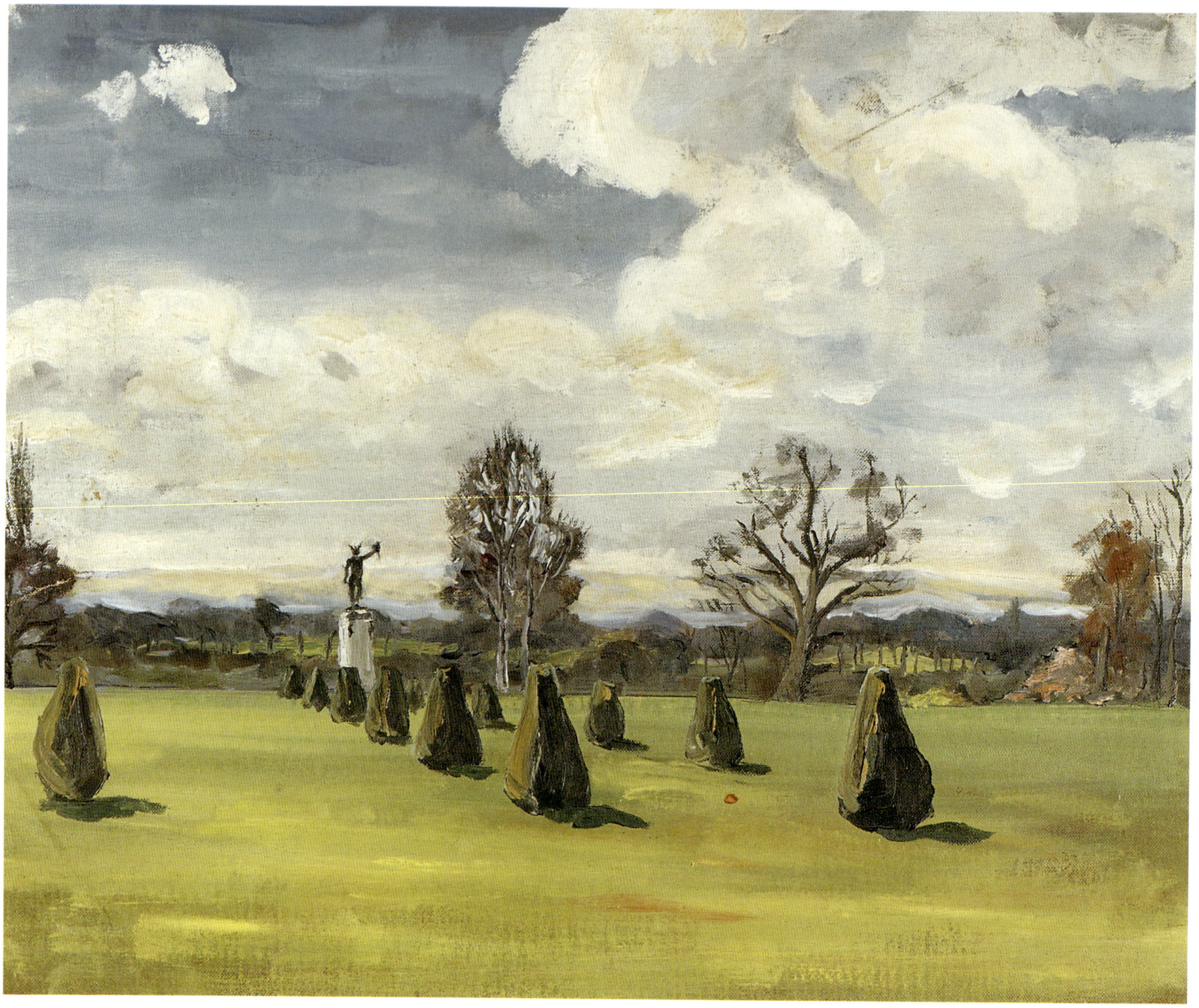

Fig 27 (C 255) above
The Italian Garden at Sutton Place, a great Tudor house near Guildford in Surrey owned by the Duke of Sutherland. (See also Fig 54)

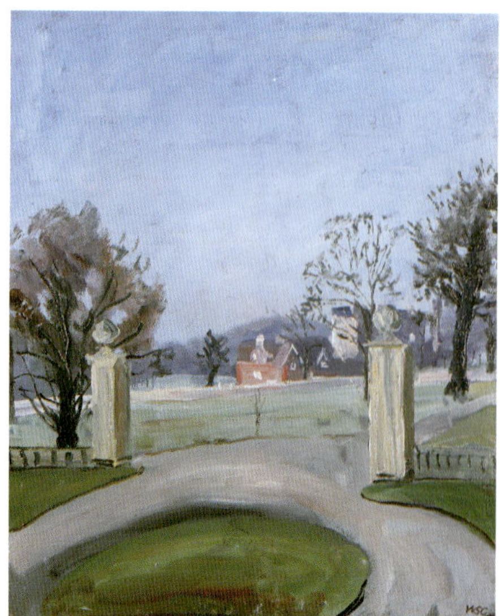

Fig 28 (C 141) above
The entrance to a drive of an unidentifed house.

Churchill worked often in John Lavery's studio in London where, among other pictures, he painted a self-portrait and another of Lavery at his easel - which Churchill gave to his friend. Lavery painted several formal portraits of Churchill and said of him: 'Mr Churchill has been called a pupil of mine, which is highly flattering, for I know few amateur wielders of the brush with a keener sense of light and colour, or a surer grasp of essentials.' Clementine Churchill took Winston on his first visits to the National Gallery in London.

At Blenheim, Churchill copied a painting by Daubigny, bought only a few years before by his cousin the Duke of Marlborough.

One day Churchill's friend Max Aitken, later Lord Beaverbrook, felt worried about him: 'I was disturbed because he was an obvious victim of depression and forebodings that distressed him. In consequence I asked him to spend a day with me at Cherkley, Leatherhead, in the hope that I could distract his mind ... I had noticed that he had placed on the car an easel and a box of colours ... The house was empty at the time. But Churchill's easel was soon out and planted on the terrace, where we looked out on the view that had fascinated so many politicians ... Churchill had turned to his painting. It was obvious that it absorbed his mind altogether. He could not talk while he painted and did not want to talk. I was glad to see him so engrossed in such a calm amusement.'

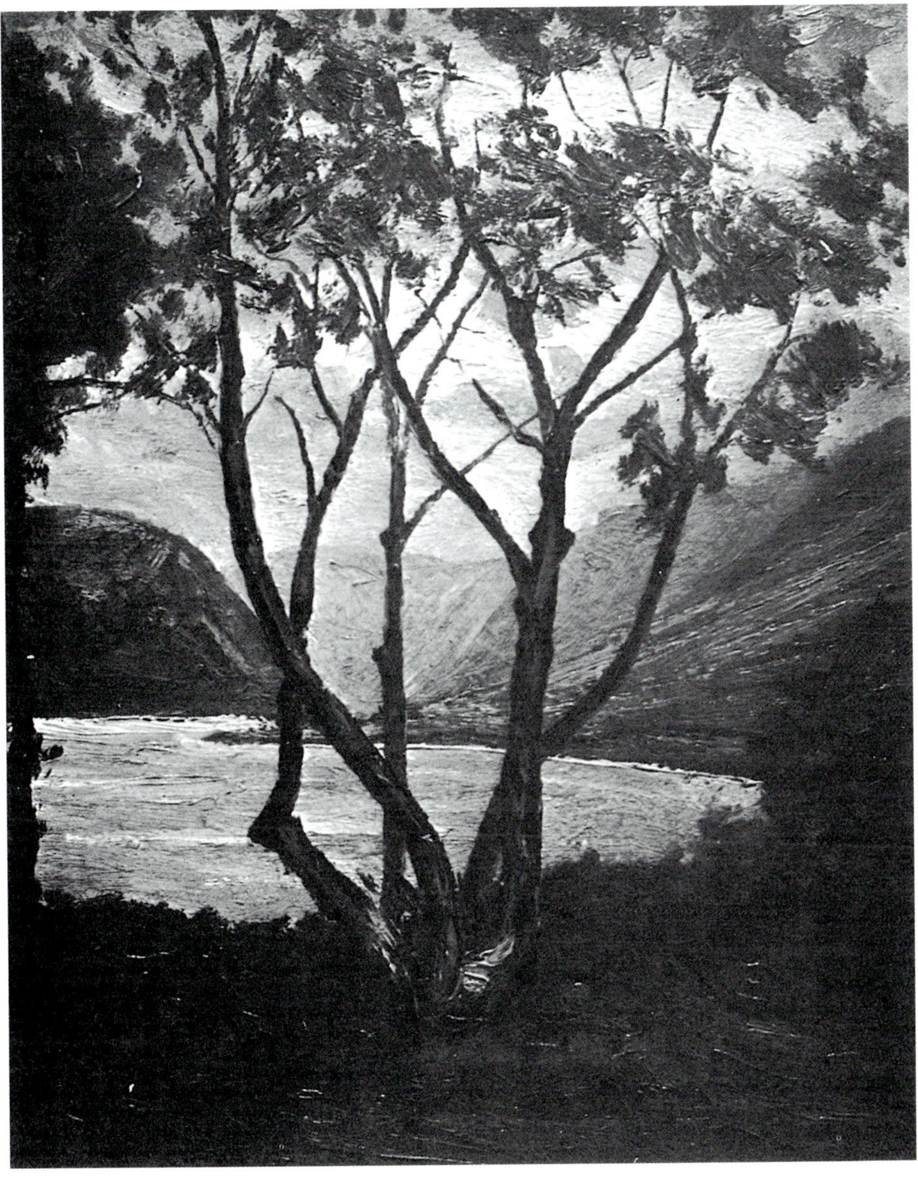

Fig 29 (C 51) left
Loch Choire in Scotland, painted in August 1919. Churchill gave this painting to the Duke of Sutherland who had an estate in the area.

In Paris, Churchill met Charles Montag, a landscape painter of Swiss origin, who took him round the galleries there and introduced him to the work of the Impressionists. Churchill and Montag became friends and, until the latter's death in 1956, enjoyed many painting expeditions together.

1916 [Background] Churchill was appointed Lieutenant-Colonel in command of the 6th Royal Scots Fusiliers. After several months at the front line and with many infantry battalions, including his own, facing amalgamation because of casualties, Churchill sought no further command and returned to London to resume his parliamentary duties. Tanks used for the first time at the Battle of the Somme. Allies evacuated Gallipoli. Easter Rebellion in Dublin. Lloyd George became Prime Minister.

1916 [Painting] Lavery painted a portrait of Churchill in service uniform, wearing his French military helmet, commissioned and presented to him by the officers of the Armoured Car Squadrons. This hangs at Chartwell.

From February, Churchill spent four months in the front line with the Royal Scots Fusiliers; his regiment was based just over the French/Belgian border in the village of Ploegsteert - called 'Plugstreet' by his troops - with his advanced headquarters at Lawrence Farm. 'The front was comparatively calm,' wrote Churchill, 'and the

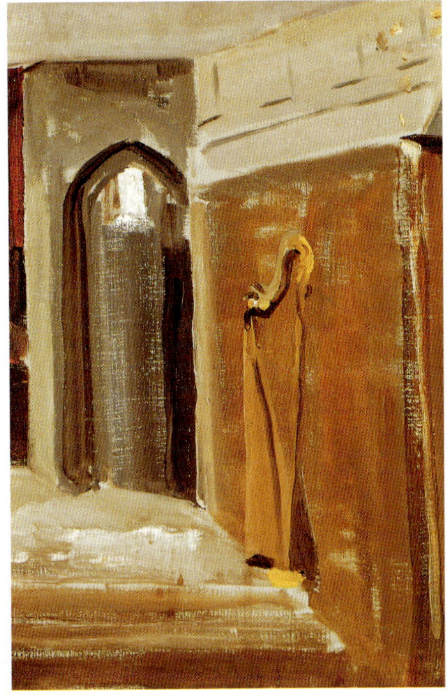

Fig 30 (C 17) above
Not a very successful painting of an unidentified music room.

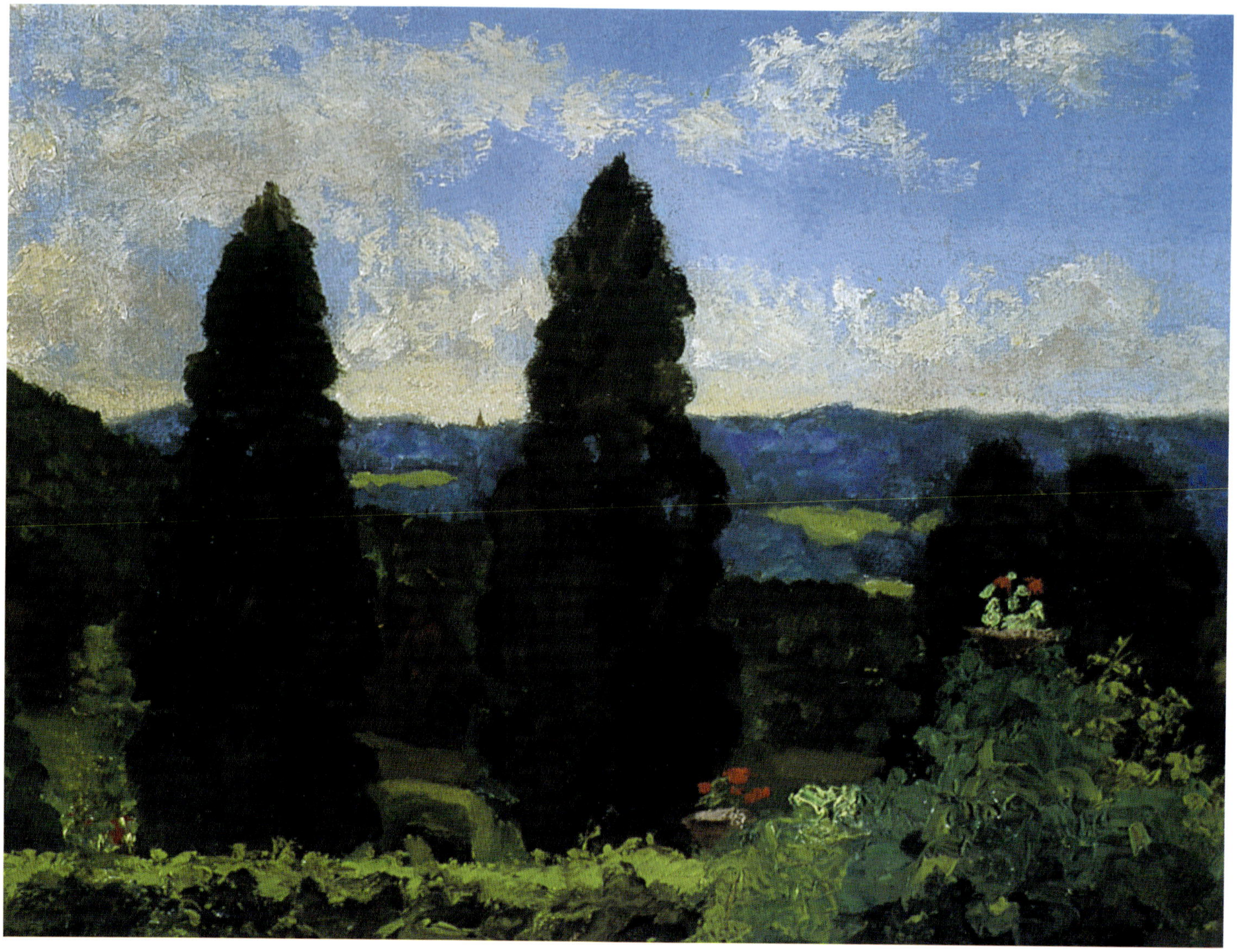

Fig 31 (C 73) above
In 1915, Max Aitken, later Lord Beaverbrook, felt very worried about Churchill and persuaded him to come down to his country home Cherkley, near Dorking in Surrey. Churchill painted this view from the terrace, which he gave Beaverbrook later as a 75th birthday present.

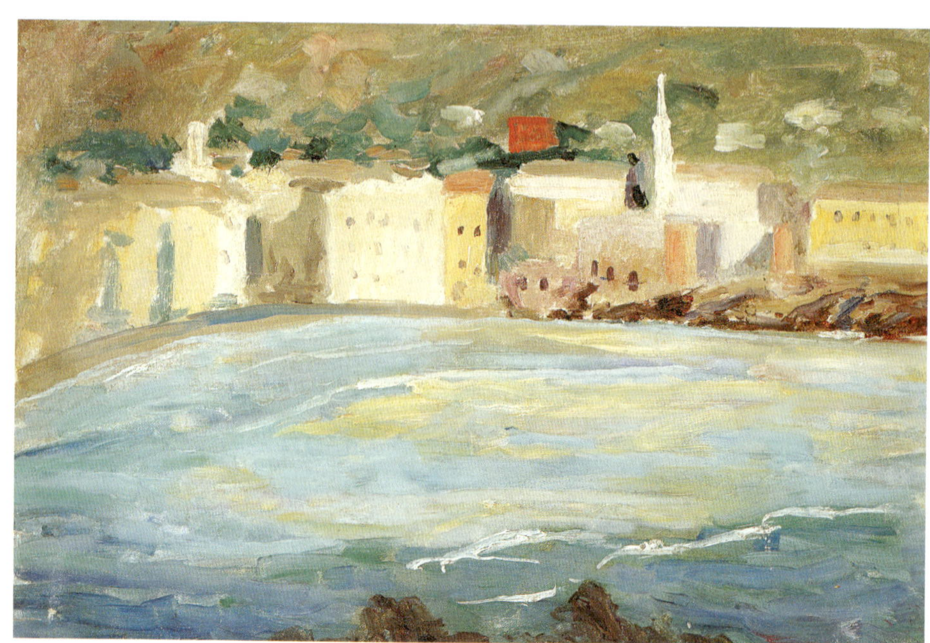

Fig 32 (C 111) right
A little sketch in oils of a town on the French Riviera. From his early manhood Churchill had travelled extensively throughout Europe. After being discovered by the 'Muse of Painting' he took his paints, brushes and easel wherever he went.

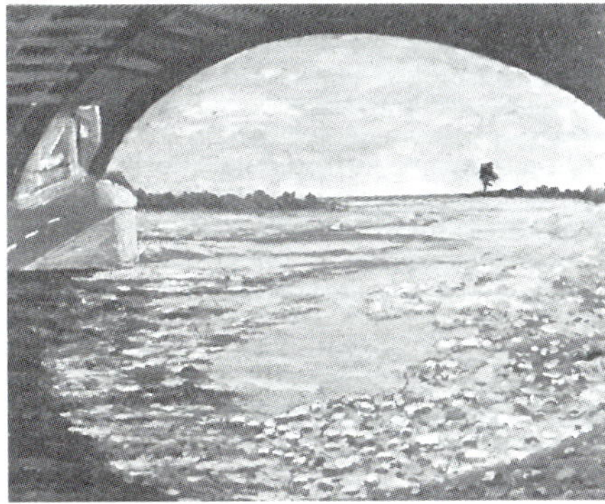

Fig 33 (C 342) above
A scene on the river Var near Nice in the South of France.

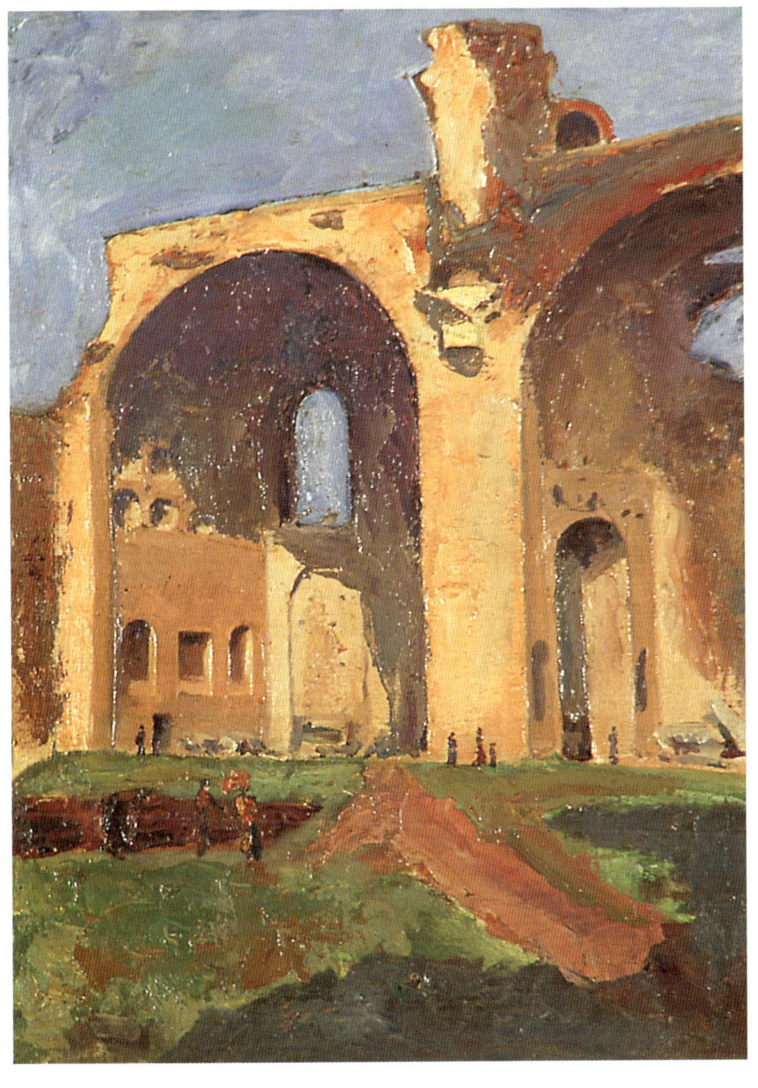

Fig 34 (C 239) left
A painting on canvas board of an unknown and ruined basilica.

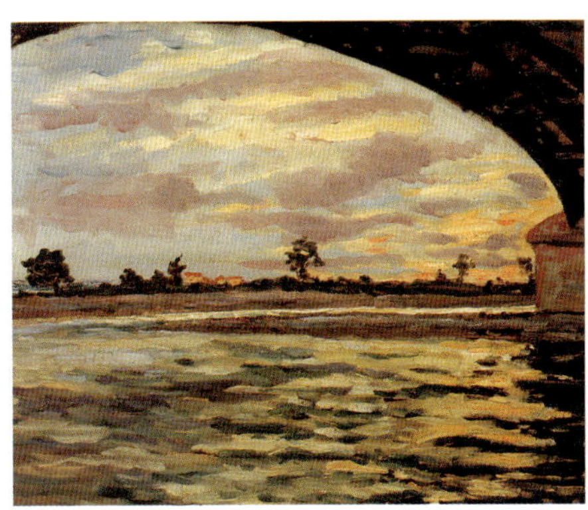

Fig 35 (C 343) above
Sunset over the river Var. Churchill was obviously very attracted by this view through the bridge.

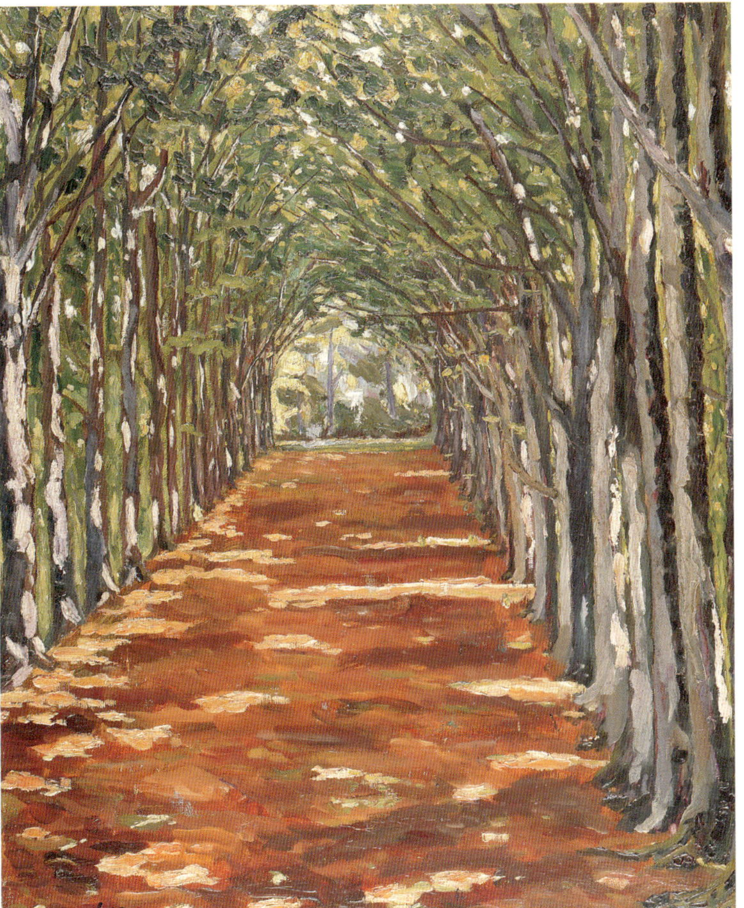

Fig 36 (C 75) left
This is a view of an avenue, known as 'The Cathedral', at Hackwood Park in Hampshire. Bought and restored by Lord Curzon, the house was subsequently owned by Lord Camose, to whom Churchill gave this painting.

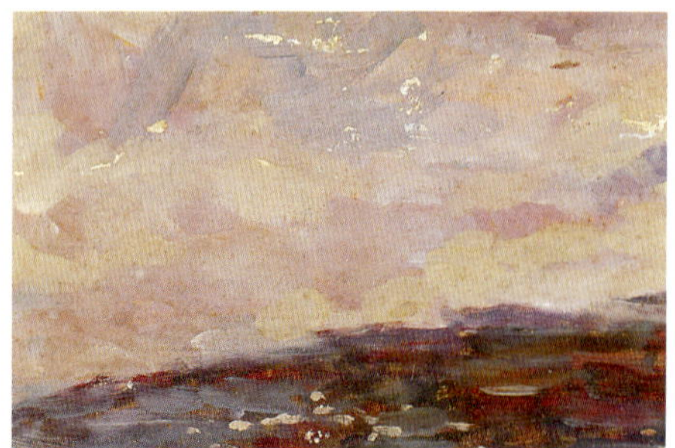

Fig 37 (C 109) above
An impression, painted on panel, of a cloud-swept landscape in the South of France.

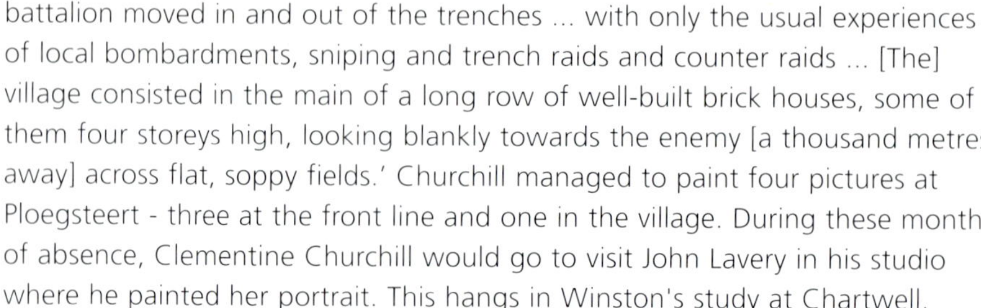

battalion moved in and out of the trenches ... with only the usual experiences of local bombardments, sniping and trench raids and counter raids ... [The] village consisted in the main of a long row of well-built brick houses, some of them four storeys high, looking blankly towards the enemy [a thousand metres away] across flat, soppy fields.' Churchill managed to paint four pictures at Ploegsteert - three at the front line and one in the village. During these months of absence, Clementine Churchill would go to visit John Lavery in his studio where he painted her portrait. This hangs in Winston's study at Chartwell.

On his return from France, Sir William Orpen painted Churchill's portrait. Thirty-three years later Churchill spoke of this picture to Sir John Rothenstein, Director of the Tate Gallery: 'Yes, it's good ... in fact when he painted it I'd lost pretty well everything.'

Churchill's first weekend at home with Clementine was spent at Blenheim, to which he took his paints, brushes, canvases and easel. He went to visit his friends Sir Ian and Lady Jean Hamilton at Postlip Hall in Gloucestershire. Jean noted in her diary: 'Winston is rather wonderful, very sincere and direct in his work, and paints like lightning; he loves being watched and being told how it is going all the time. He painted two pictures - one of the house which I instantly copied in pastel, and one of the view from the front of the house.'

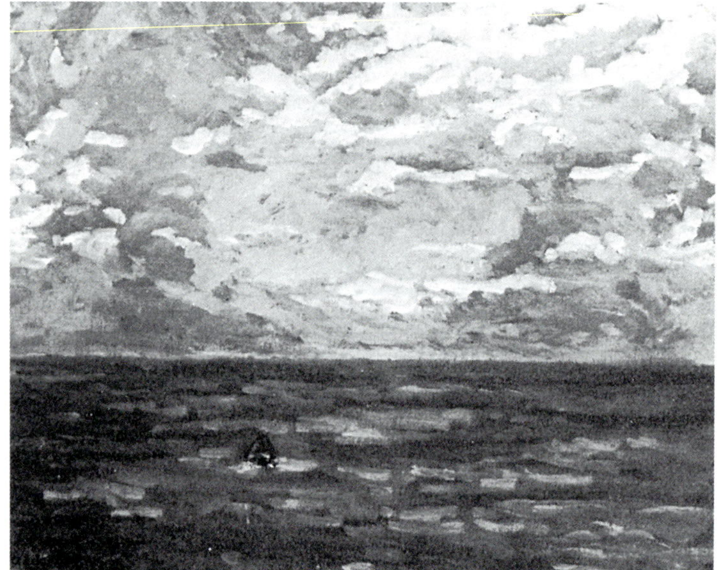

Fig 38 (C 107) above
A seascape with a conical buoy.

One summer weekend the Churchills and Violet Bonham Carter, daughter of Prime Minister Asquith, were guests of Claude Lowther at Herstmonceux Castle in Sussex. She went into the garden to watch Winston working at his easel. 'As he painted, his tensions relaxed, his frustration evaporated ... I was suddenly aware that this was the only occupation that I had ever seen him practise in silence ... rapt in intense appraisal, observation, assessment of the scene he meant to capture and to transfer to his canvas.'

On another occasion Violet Bonham Carter recalled them staying 'in a country-house set in a monochrome of dull, flat, uneventful country ... Looking over [Winston's] shoulder I saw depicted on his canvas range upon range of mountains rising dramatically behind the actual foregound. I searched the skies for a mirage and then inquired where they had come from, and he replied: "Well - I couldn't leave it quite as dull as all that."'

Churchill and Lavery worked together in the garden of General Sir Arthur and Lady Paget at Kingston Hill, near London, and Lavery painted a picture of Churchill at his easel.

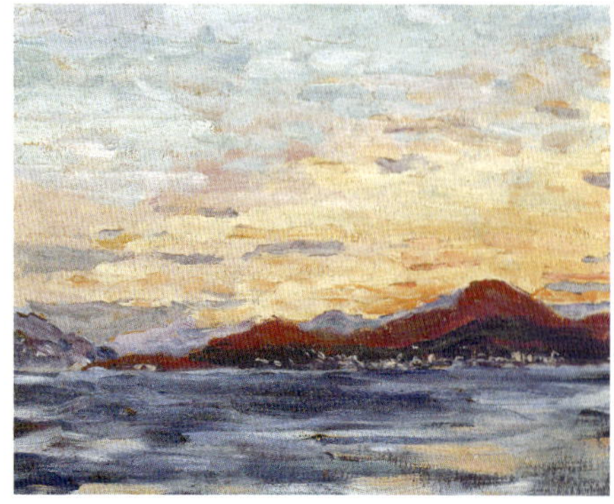

Fig 39 (C 108) above
Mountains and sea at sunset, a painting on panel.

1917 [Background] Churchill supported votes for women. Appointed Minister of Munitions by new Prime Minister Lloyd George. Resolved industrial dispute on the Clyde. His Munitions of War Bill ensured that no worker would be penalized for belonging to a trade union or for taking part in an industrial dispute. Churchill visited war zone in France. Battle of Passchendaele. British launched first tank offensive at Cambrai. United States declared war on Germany and, at request of Bernard Baruch, Churchill acquired war materials, including aeroplanes, for American expeditionary forces arriving in Europe. Established Anglo-American tank factory at Bordeaux. Jerusalem captured from the Turks and a Jewish National Home in Palestine promised. Revolution in Russia: the new Bolshevik government declared it would make peace with Germany.

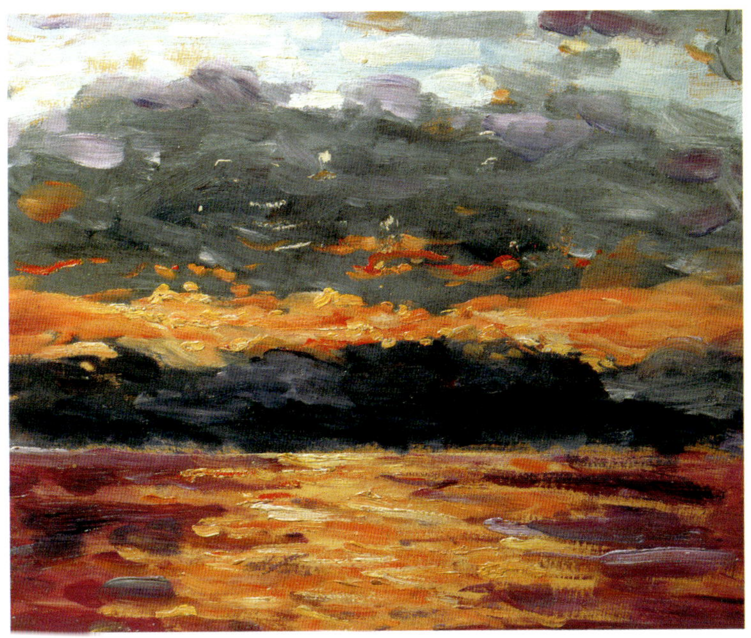

Fig 40 (C 104) left
Sunset over the sea, orange and purple, a painting on panel.

This series of very attractive paintings on panel may show the influence on Churchill of the sea painter Julius Olsson.
(See Chapter 5)

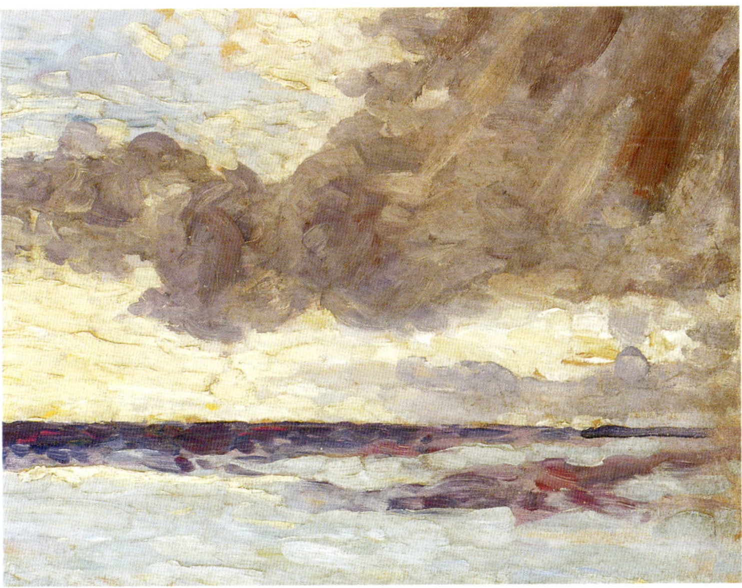

Fig 41 (C 105) left
Seascape with rain clouds, a painting on panel.

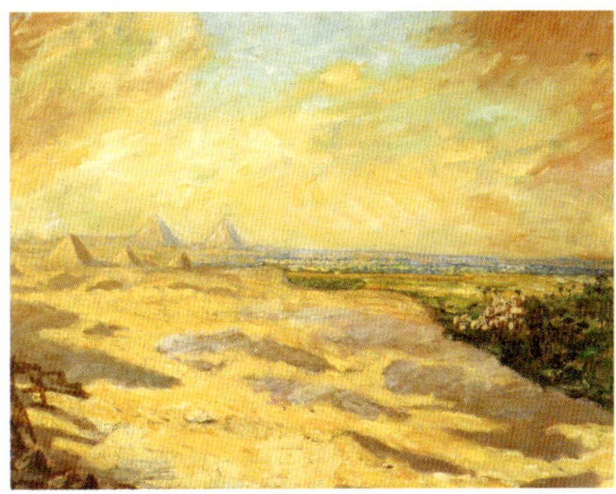

Fig 42 (C 85) above
A distant view of the Pyramids painted in 1921. Following the dissolution of the old Ottoman empire after the First World War, a conference was held in Cairo to discuss the political future of the Middle East. Churchill attended as the newly appointed Colonial Secretary and later went on to Jerusalem.

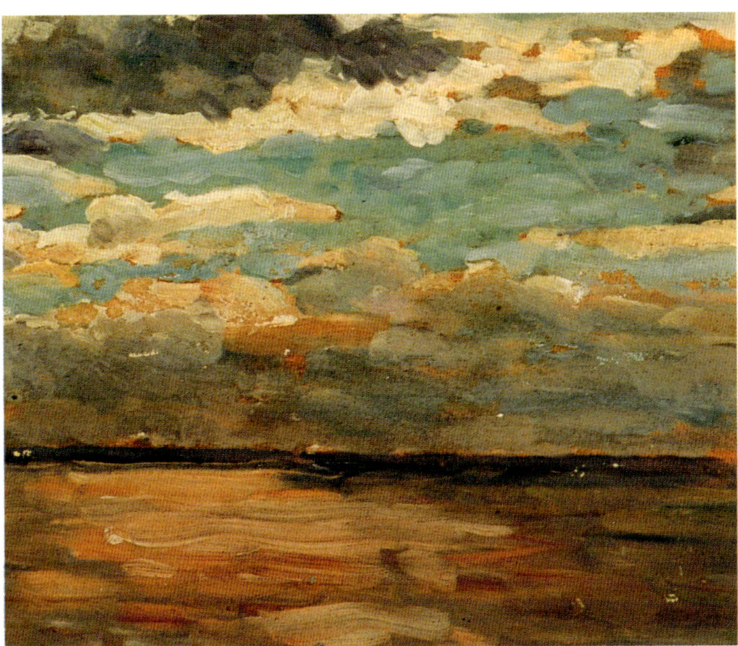

Fig 43 (C 106) left
Sunset over the sea, pink and mauve, a painting on panel.

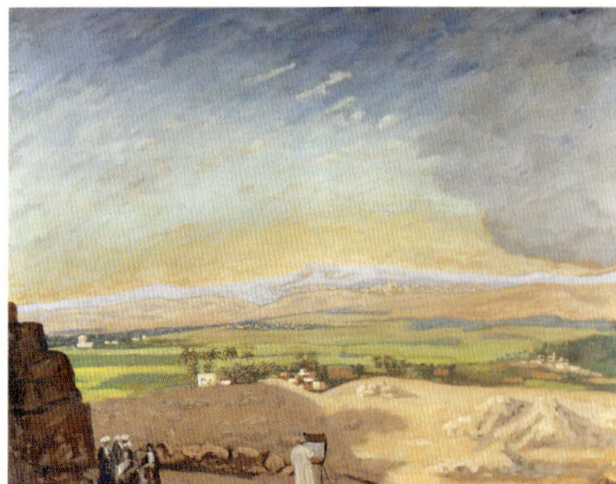

Fig 44 (C 84) above
This picture of Cairo from the Pyramids with the Artist working at his easel may well have been painted about 1946 when Churchill was experimenting with larger canvases.

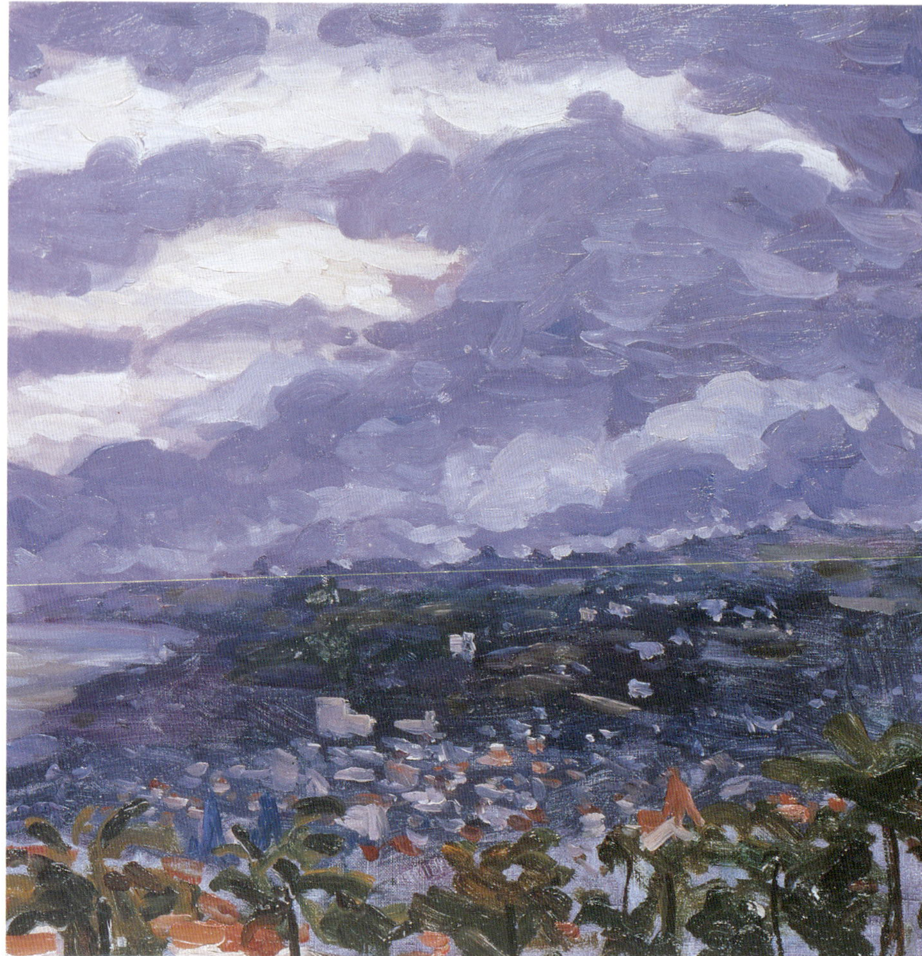

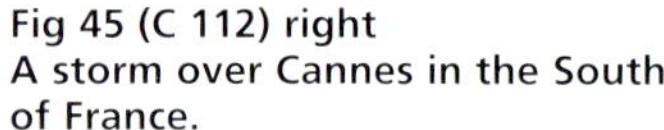

Fig 45 (C 112) right
A storm over Cannes in the South of France.

1917 [Painting] Churchill bought Lullenden, a house in the countryside near East Grinstead in Sussex where his wife and children would be safe from Zeppelin raids. Here he would paint at weekends.

1918 [Background] Churchill warned Lloyd George of the danger of German troops being transferred from the Eastern to the Western Front. Returned to visit the war zones. Proposed to the government a new offensive strategy for 1919 dominated by tanks and aircraft. Present at opening of the German offensive. Allied counter-attack forced German retreat. Turkey and Austria-Hungary surrendered. Allied-German Armistice November 11th. Civil war in Ireland. Lloyd George's government won general election. Women over 30 given vote in Britain. Churchill urged heavy tax on war profits and warned of danger of Bolshevism. The Churchills' fourth child, Marigold, was born.

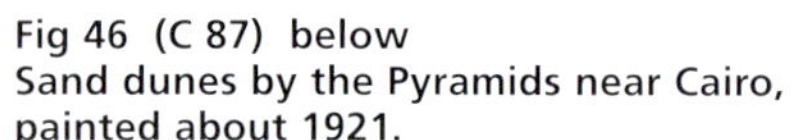

Fig 46 (C 87) below
Sand dunes by the Pyramids near Cairo, painted about 1921.

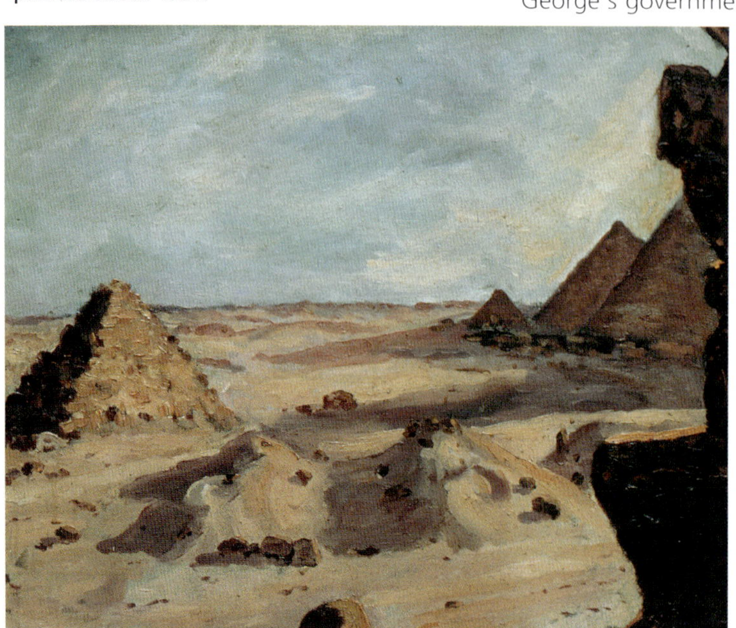

1919 [Background] Lloyd George appointed Churchill Secretary of State for War and Air with particular responsibility for demobilization. Versailles Treaty between Allies and Germany. League of Nations established. Civil war in Russia. Failure of Allied intervention against Bolsheviks: British troops withdrawn. Revolt in Egypt. Riots in the Punjab. First non-stop transatlantic flight by Alcock and Brown. Daily London-Paris air service begun. Winston took up flying again but after a near-fatal accident finally agreed to Clementine's pleas to stop. They both visited Cologne and the British army on the Rhine.

1919 [Painting] Sir John Lavery loaned the portrait of himself working in his studio, painted by Winston Churchill in 1915, to the Royal Society of Portrait Painters annual exhibition at the Grafton Galleries in London. The was the first-known public showing of a Churchill painting. Other exhibitors, besides Lavery himself, included Sir Oswald Birley and Frank Salisbury.

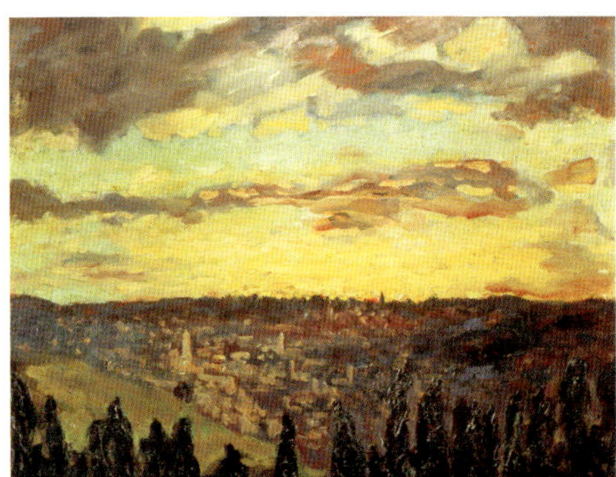

Fig 47 (C 110) above
A view of Jerusalem, painted in 1921.

1920 [Background] First meeting of the League of Nations. Britain to administer Palestine. Britain offered Ireland Home Rule with two parliaments, which was followed by terrorist campaign of murders; in response to threats of kidnap Churchill was provided with an armed bodyguard. Poland repelled Red Army attack. Rebellion in Iraq. Bolsheviks finally triumphed in Russia. Churchill began work on his war memoirs.

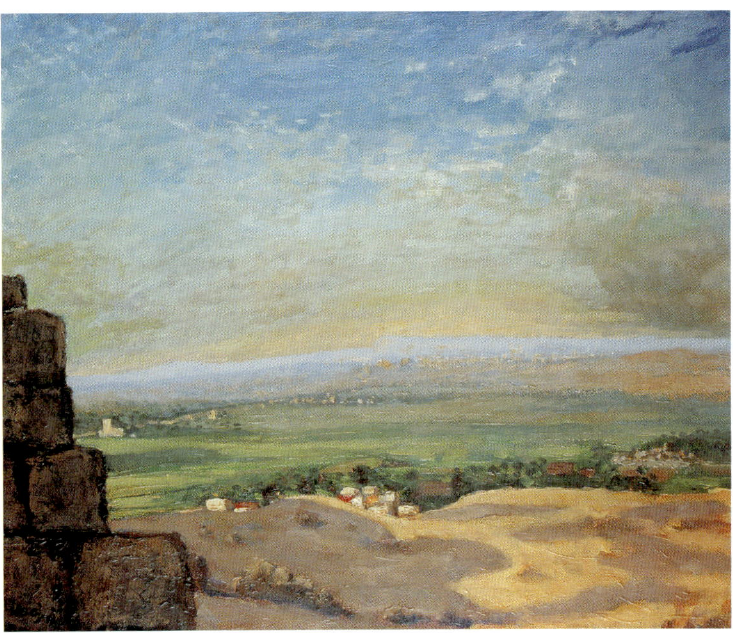

Fig 48 (C 79) above
A view of Cairo from the Pyramids, painted in 1921.

1920 [Painting] Lullenden was sold to Churchill's friend Sir Ian Hamilton because of financial difficulties and the Churchill family moved to Sussex Square in London where the mews building at the back was converted into a studio for Winston. In the interim the Churchills stayed with his cousin Freddie Guest at Templeton, Roehampton, near London, where several pictures were painted.

In her diaries, Jean Hamilton records a large weekend party at Panshanger as guests of Ettie and Willie Desborough. 'Winston painted dull pictures all day,' including one of the Orangery, 'and was quite happy,' she wrote.

Churchill went on holiday to Mimizan in the Landes, south of Bordeaux, where his friend the Duke of Westminster had a house near the Atlantic coast. Here he hunted wild boar and painted. Later that year, Winston took Clementine to Mimizan and then travelled to Italy to paint at Amalfi and to Cassis, in the South of France. Subsequently, John Lavery and Winston Churchill were fellow guests at Mimizan; they both painted pictures of the same subject, which were hung at Lochmore Lodge in Sutherland, the Duke of Westminster's Scottish home.

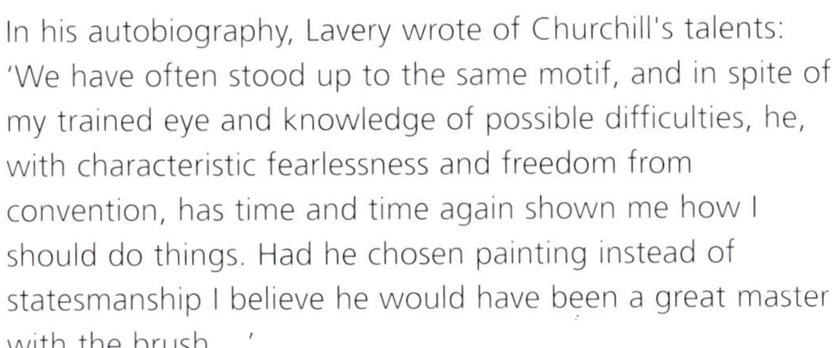

In his autobiography, Lavery wrote of Churchill's talents: 'We have often stood up to the same motif, and in spite of my trained eye and knowledge of possible difficulties, he, with characteristic fearlessness and freedom from convention, has time and time again shown me how I should do things. Had he chosen painting instead of statesmanship I believe he would have been a great master with the brush ...'

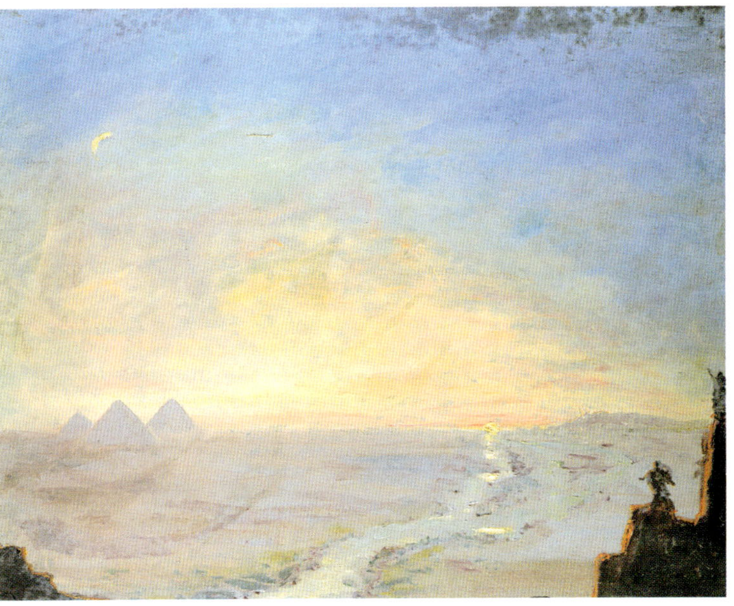

Following an approach by Francis Howard from the prestigious Grafton Galleries in London, Churchill wrote: 'I am much complimented by your kindness in suggesting that I should exhibit a couple of pictures ... But I am quite sure that none of them are worth showing, and I have made my mind up not to exhibit under my own name until I have succeeded in being selected on merits and under an assumed name. Perhaps you will give me the pleasure ... of coming and looking at some of my things. I should greatly appreciate your criticism and advice.'

Fig 49 (C 82) above
A distant view of the Pyramids near Cairo at sunset, painted in 1921.

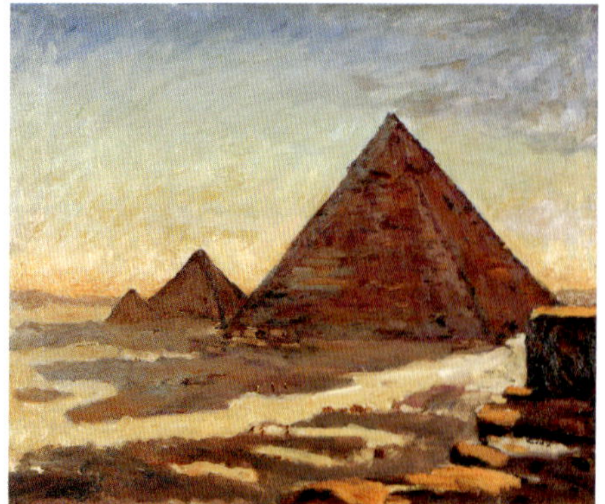

Fig 50 (C 86) above
'At the Pyramids.' Illustrated: 'Painting as a Pastime' The Strand Magazine, January 1922. Churchill went to Egypt for a conference on the Middle East in March 1921.

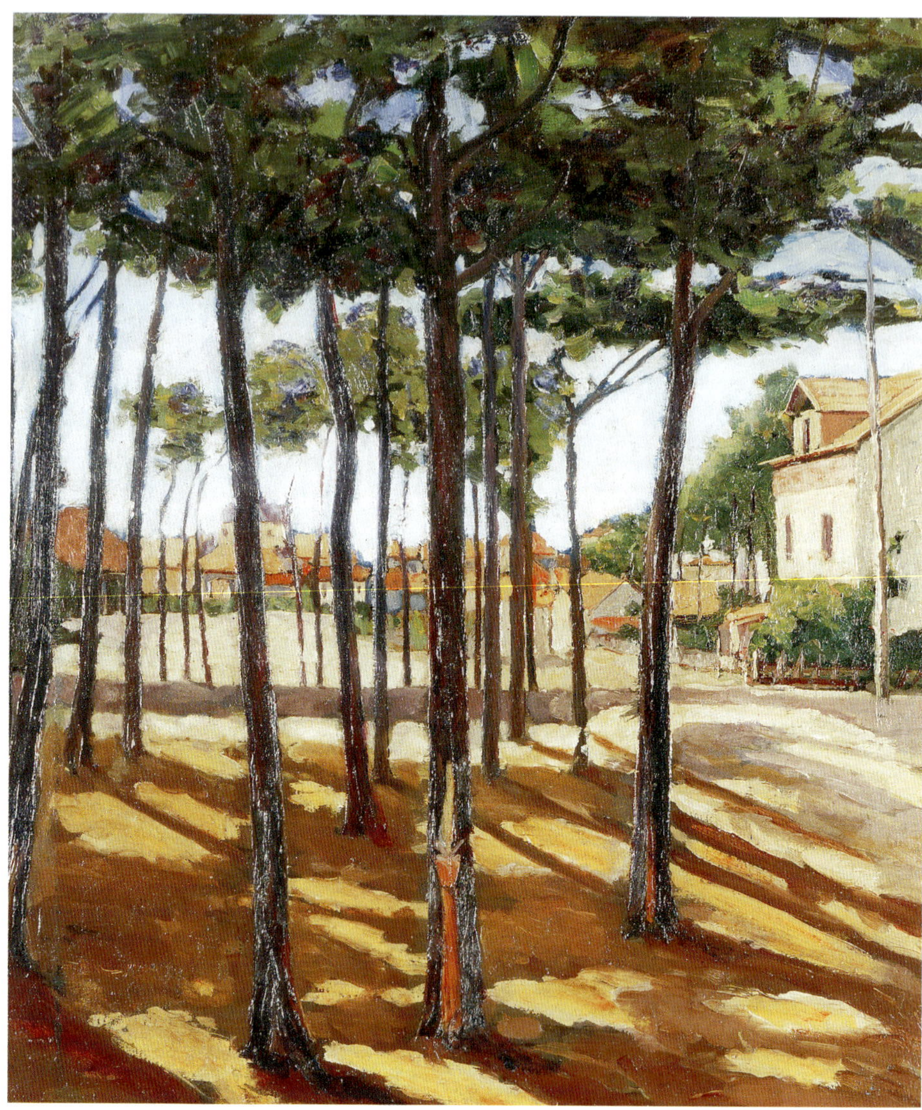

Fig 51 (C 69) right
'Mimizan Plage, Landes. This is the earliest of these sketches, and was painted during an afternoon in the Spring of 1920.' Illustrated: 'Painting as a Pastime' The Strand Magazine, December 1921. The Duke of Westminster had a home at Mimizan, near Bordeaux.

1921 [Background] Lloyd George appointed Churchill Colonial Secretary with responsibility for Iraq and Palestine; Churchill was already known as a supporter of Zionism. He appointed Colonel T. E. Lawrence (Lawrence of Arabia) as his adviser on Arabian affairs. Greeks defeated after attack on Turkey. Travelled with Clementine to Egypt for Middle East conference. Kingdom of Iraq established. United States refused to ratify Versailles Treaty and to join the League of Nations. Churchill proposed a treaty for Ireland with the south as an independent state; the rebellion there ended.

1921 [Painting] Churchill visited the Hamiltons at Lullenden. Ian's wife Jean noted in her diary that 'Winston approves of all we have done to the house - he has been painting a lovely picture of the Barn, with brilliant sunshine and shade effects all day ... ' In Paris, Churchill visited an exhibition, arranged by Charles Montag, at the prestigious Galerie Druet in the rue Royale, of works by a new artist named Charles Morin. Six paintings were said to have been sold; the artist was Winston Churchill showing under a pseudonym.

On his official travels with Clementine to the Middle East, Churchill landed at Alexandria, visited Aboukir Bay, then went on to Cairo where he painted the Pyramids. Later he rode on a camel round the Sphinx and made several sketches at Sakkara. Subsequently he travelled to Jerusalem, where he painted, and then to Tel Aviv.

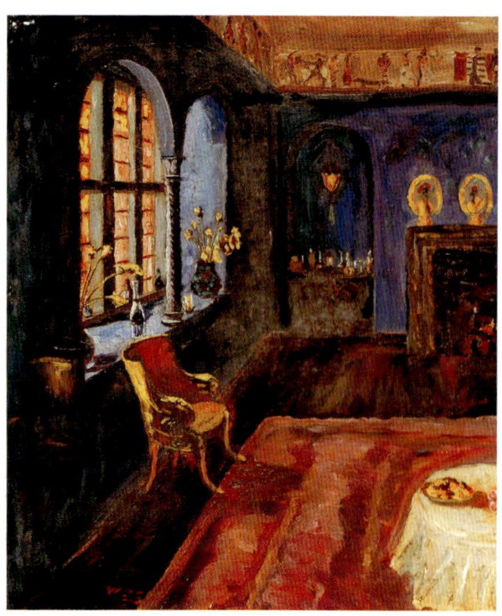

Fig 52 (C 189) above
'The Blue Room at Lympne.' Illustrated: 'Painting as a Pastime' The Strand Magazine, December 1921. Lympne was the country home in Kent of Sir Philip Sassoon who commissioned Rex Whistler to paint a series of murals there.

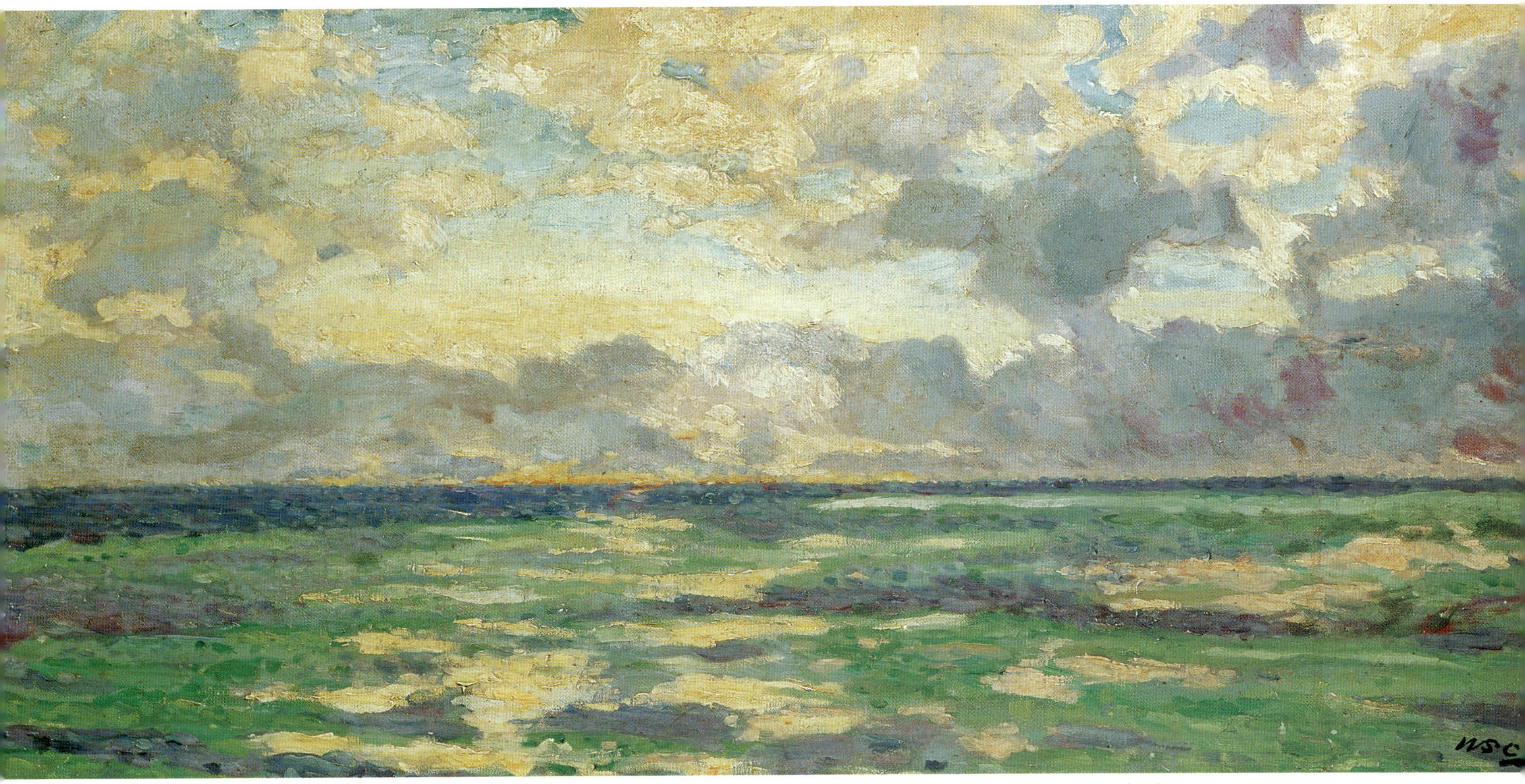

Fig 53 (C 103) above
'Daybreak at Cassis, near Marseilles. September 1920.' Illustrated: 'Painting as a Pastime' The Strand Magazine, December 1921. A beautiful painting of a difficult subject.

Fig 54 (C 25) left
'Long Gallery at Sutton Place, near Guildford.' Illustrated: 'Painting as a Pastime' The Strand Magazine, December 1921. Sutton Place belonged to the Duke of Sutherland. (See also Fig. 27)

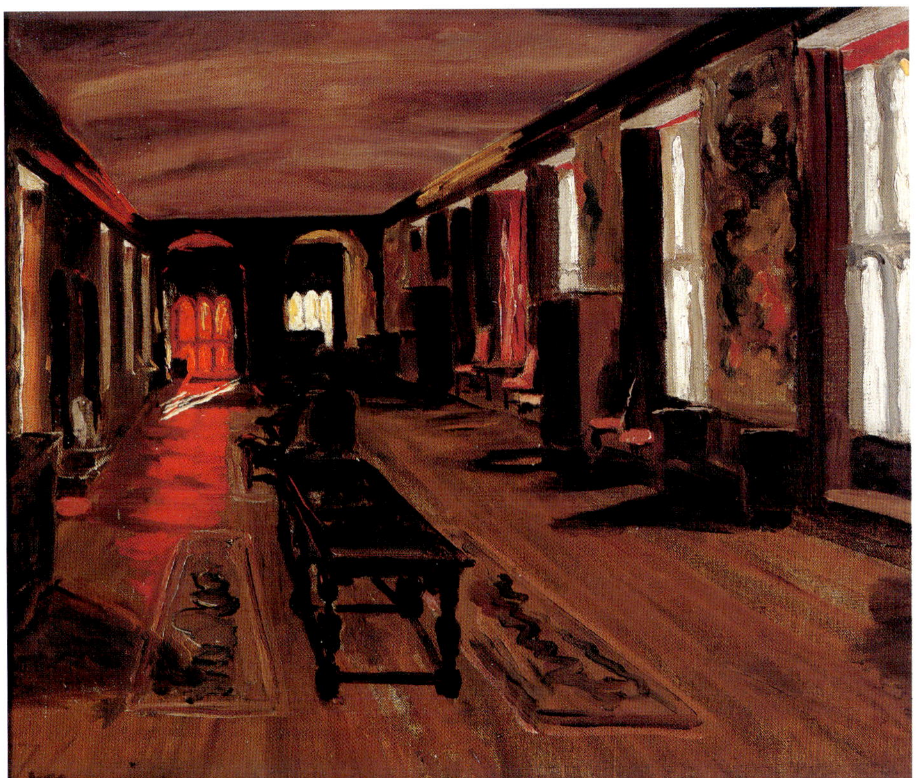

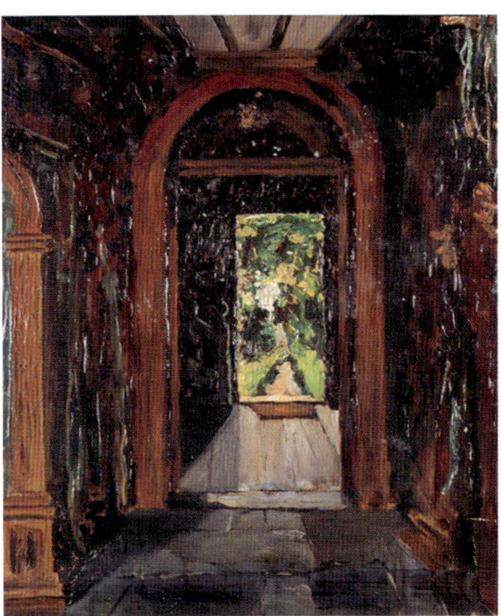

Fig 55 (C 16) above
'Newbuildings, Sussex. July, 1921.' Illustrated: 'Painting as a Pastime' The Strand Magazine, December 1921. This is the hallway of Wilfred Scawen Blunt's home.

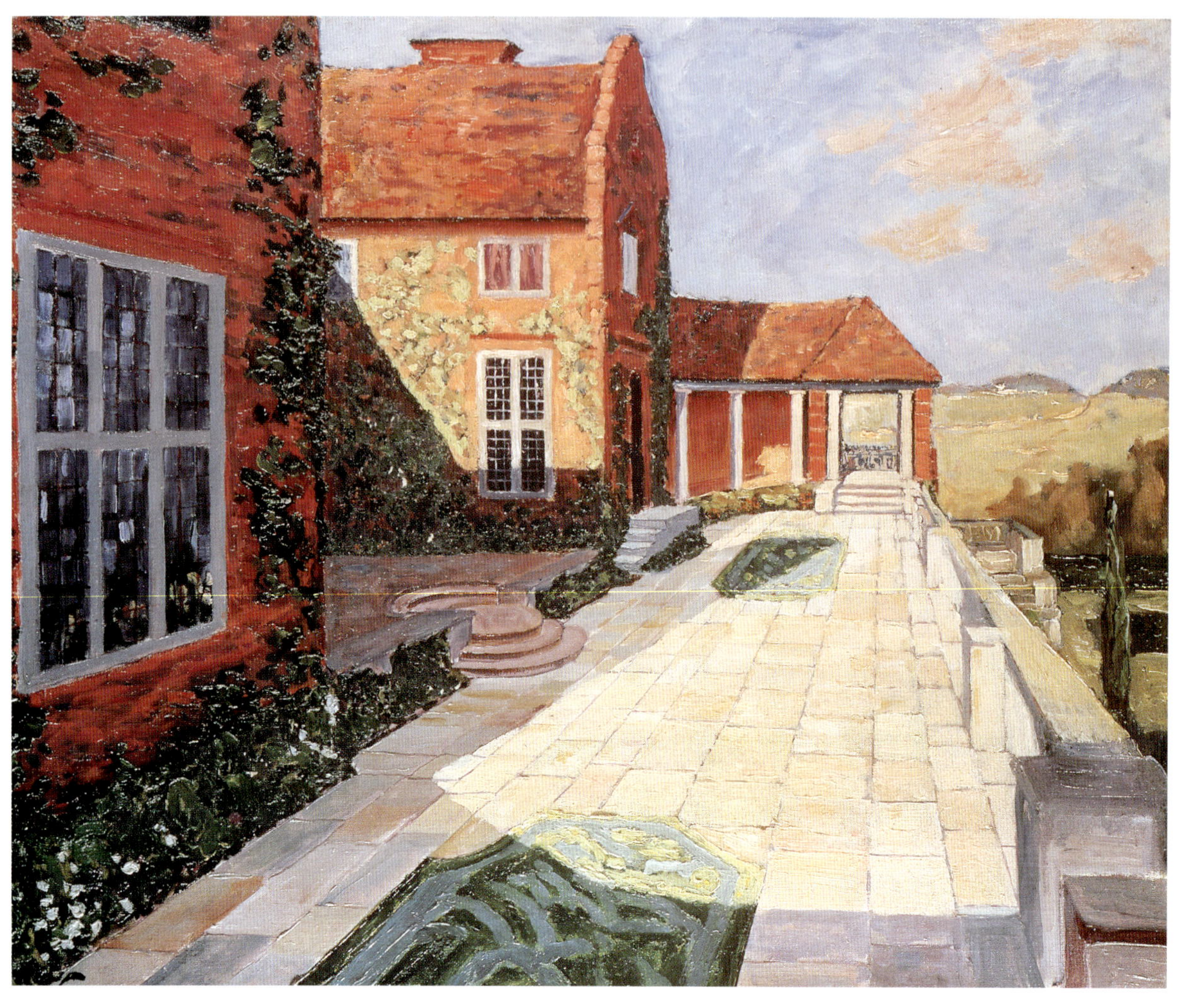

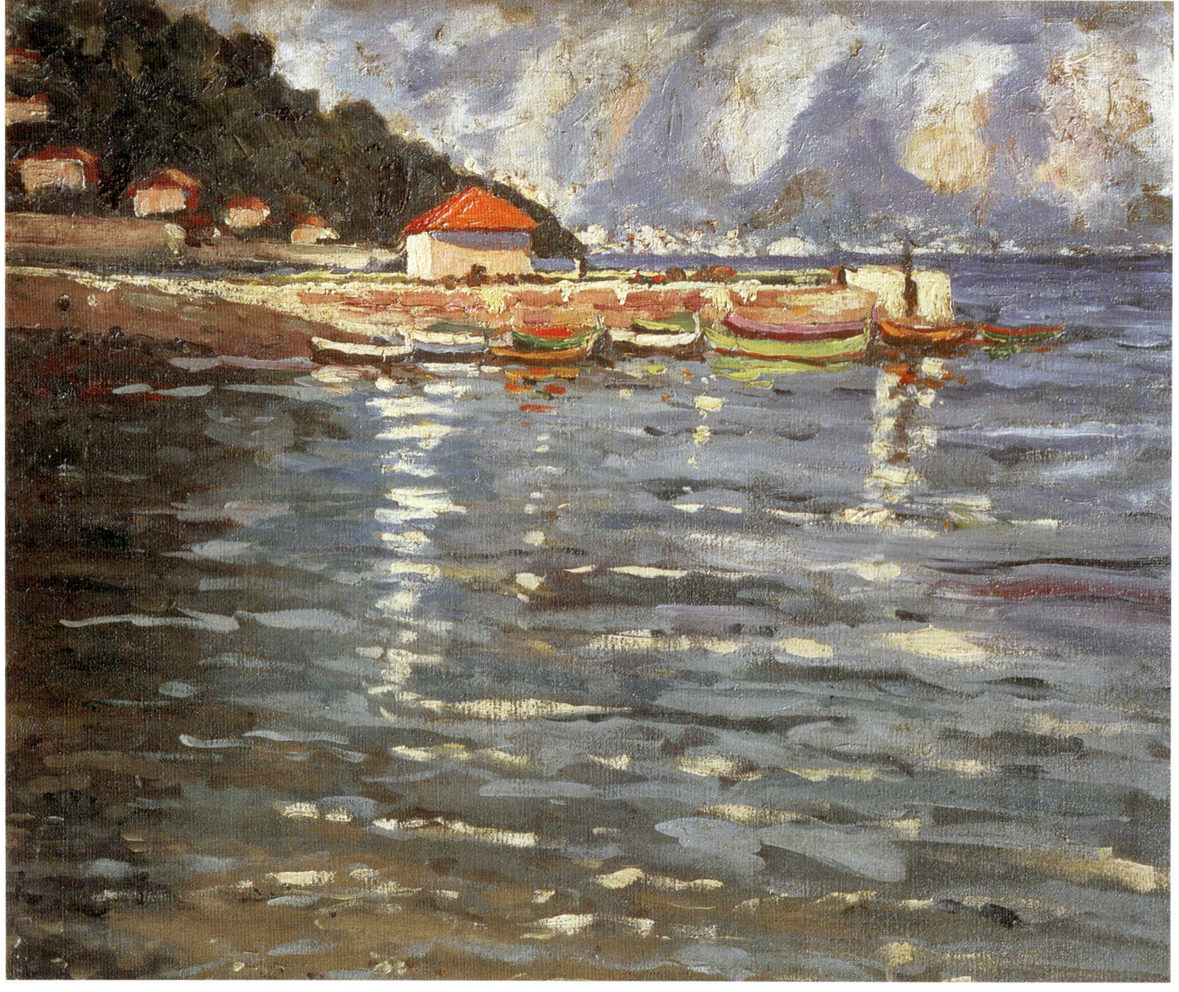

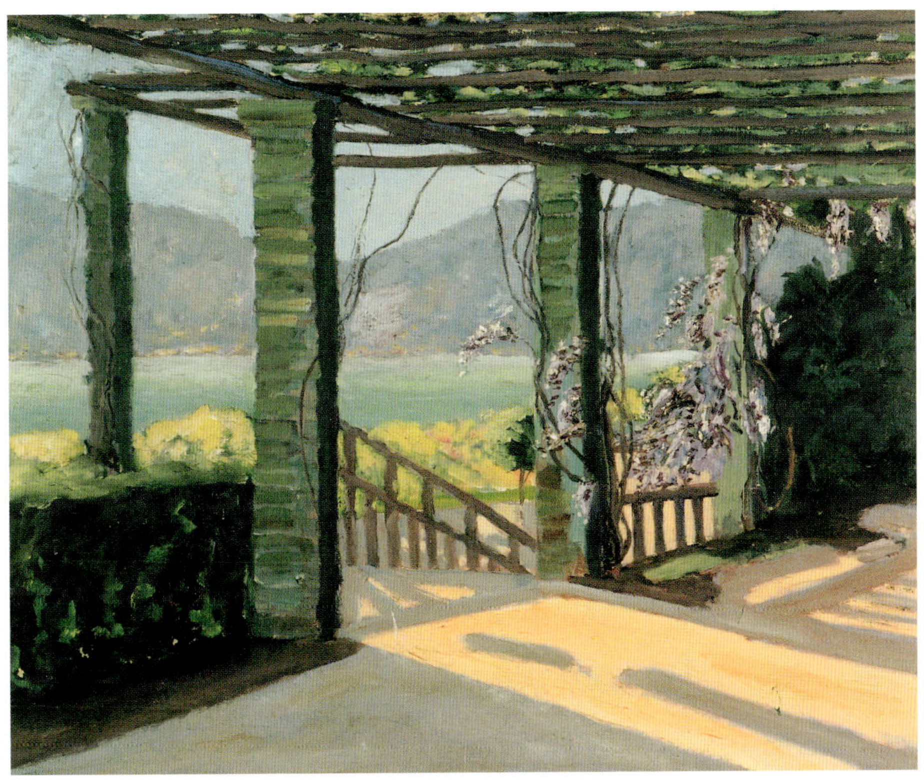

Fig 56 (C 278) left
'A Villa at the Riviera.' Illustrated: 'Painting as a Pastime' The Strand Magazine, December 1921. The exact location is unknown.

Fig 57 (C 222) opposite page above
'The Terrace, Lympne.' Illustrated: *'Painting as a Pastime'* The Strand Magazine, January 1922. Sir Philip Sassoon's spacious country house in Kent.

Fig 58 (C 309) opposite page below
'The harbour at St Jean Cap Ferrat. January 1921.' Illustrated: *'Painting as a Pastime'* The Strand Magazine, December 1921. This holiday resort on the French Riviera was a favourite of the Churchill family.

Fig 59 (C 235) below
'Ightham Moat.' Illustrated: 'Painting as a Pastime' *The Strand Magazine*, January 1922. Churchill sold this painting of the moat at Ightham Mote in Kent to Lady Jean Hamilton for £50.

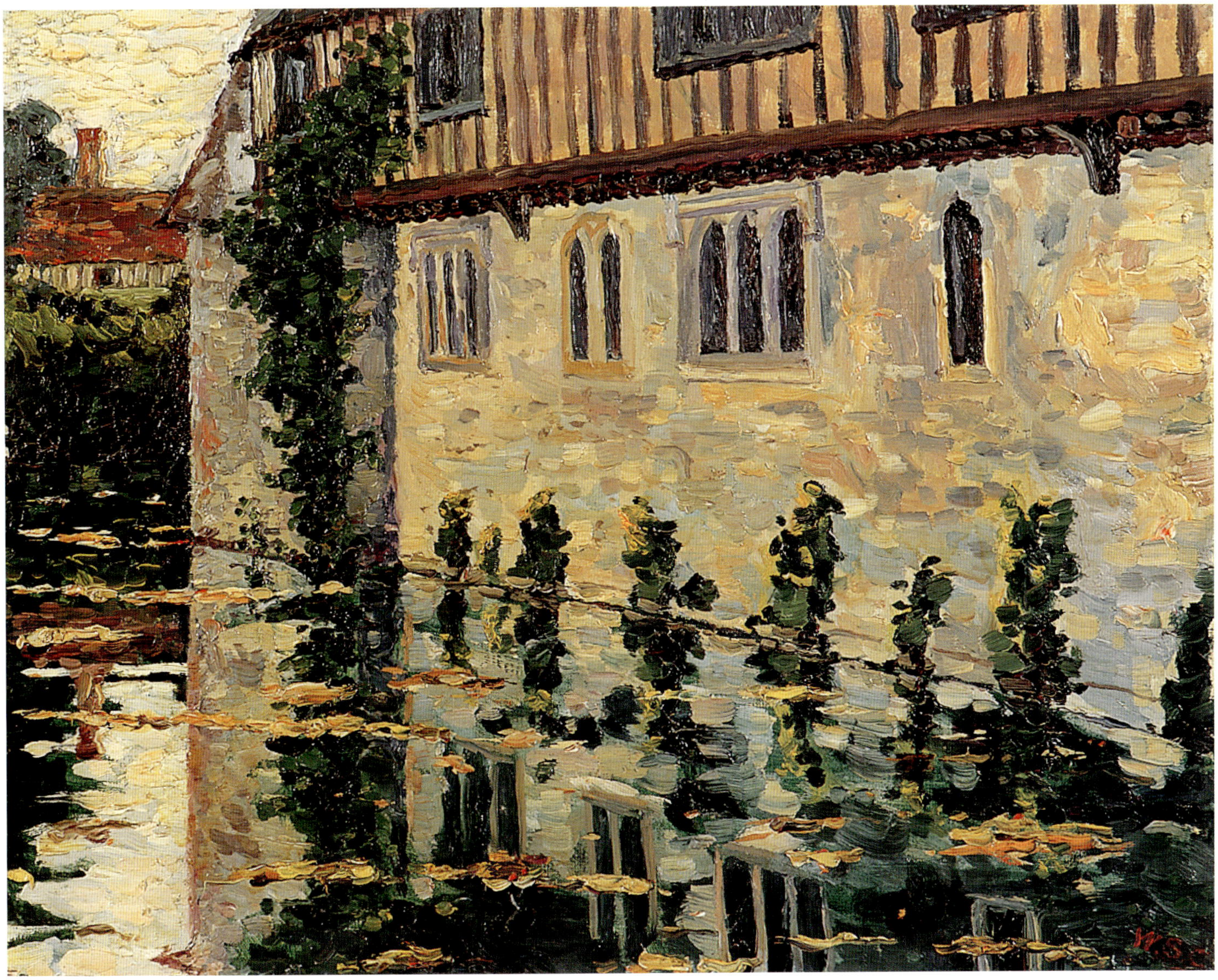

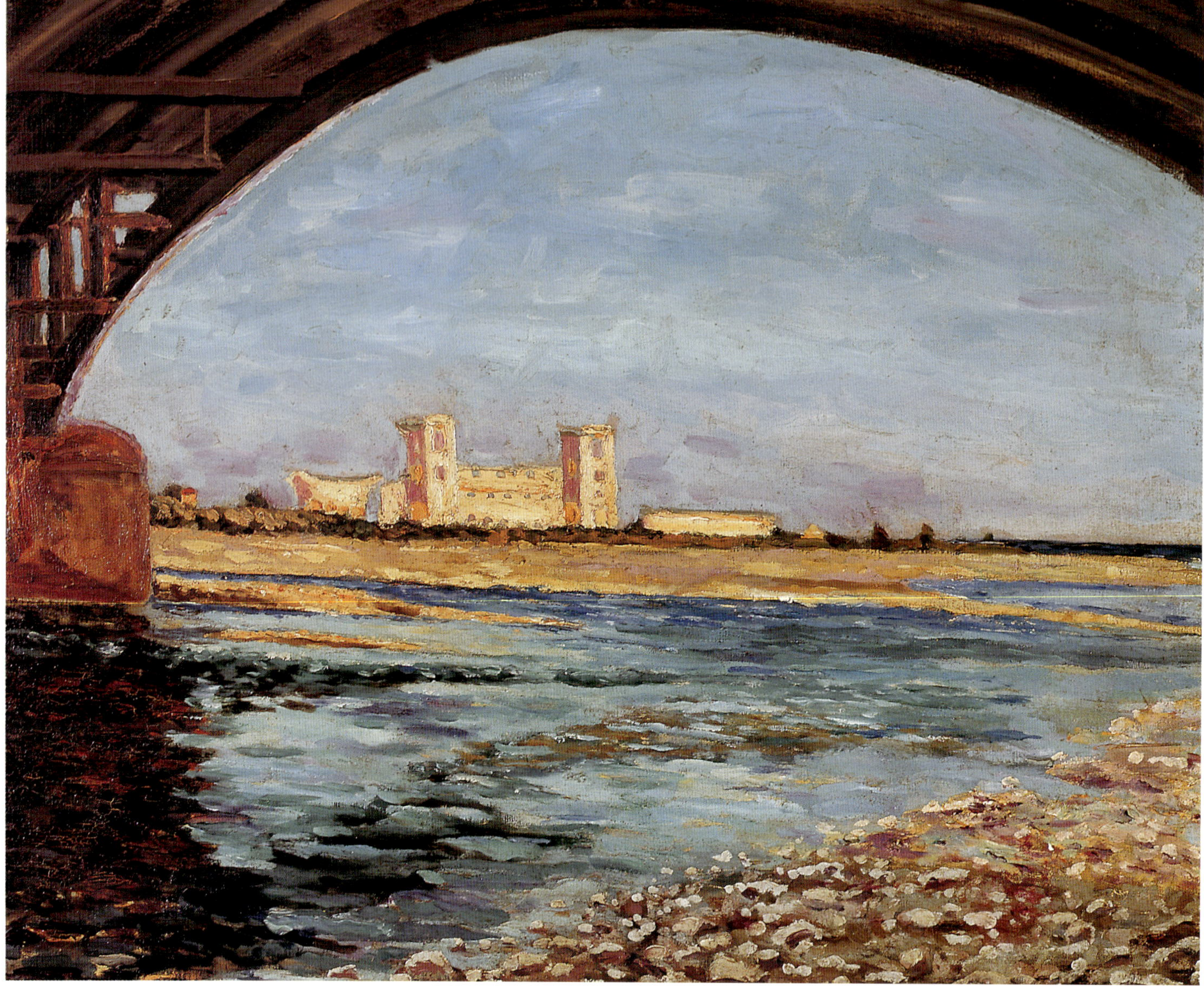

Fig 60 (C 341) above
'Racecourse, Nice, from under the railway bridge. January, 1921.' Illustrated: 'Painting as a Pastime' The Strand Magazine, December 1921. After the Second World War, in 1949, Churchill began horse racing himself with Colonist II.

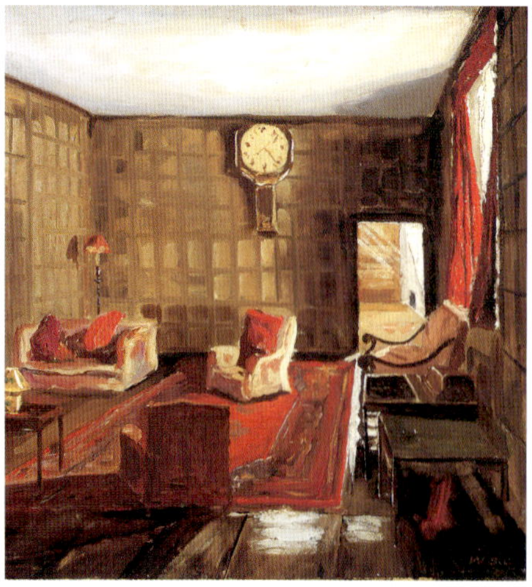

Fig 61 (C 186) above
'A room at Breccles, Norfolk. Whitsuntide, 1920.' Illustrated: 'Painting as a Pastime' The Strand Magazine, December 1921. Breccles was the home of Clementine Churchill's cousin Venetia Montagu. After it was first reproduced, Churchill decided for some reason to reduce the proportions of his painting.

Churchill's mother died, followed within two months by the death of Marigold, Winston's and Clementine's youngest daughter. They both went to Scotland to recover where, at Dunrobin Castle, home of the Duke and Duchess of Sutherland, Churchill painted.

Consuelo, former wife of Churchill's cousin Sunny, 9th Duke of Marlborough, married Jacques Balsan and moved with him to Lou Seuil on a clifftop above Eze-sur-Mer in France; both Clementine and Winston visited them there. Churchill and Lavery painted together in the South of France and Churchill contributed the foreword to the catalogue of Pictures of Morocco, the Riviera and Other Scenes, an exhibition of Lavery's paintings in London. Churchill wrote: 'Sir John Lavery is a plein-airiste if ever there was one, painting entirely out of doors, with his eye on the object, and never touching a landscape in his studio ... he is so quick that no coy transience of an effect can save it from his clutches...'

In two successive issues of *The Strand Magazine*, Churchill's essay 'Painting as a Pastime' was first published.

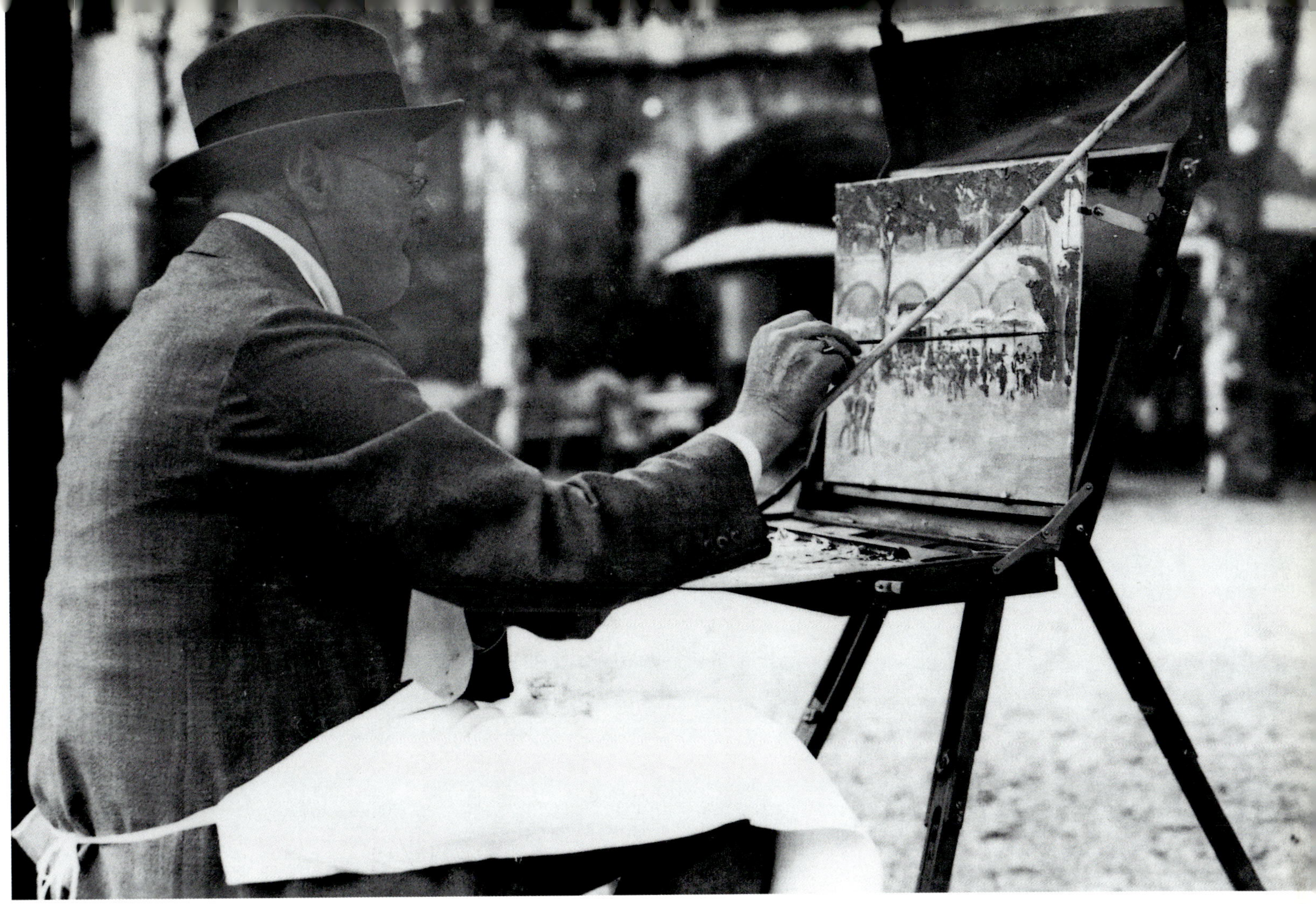

Winston Churchill painting in France. The picture is illustrated on page 244 (C 530).

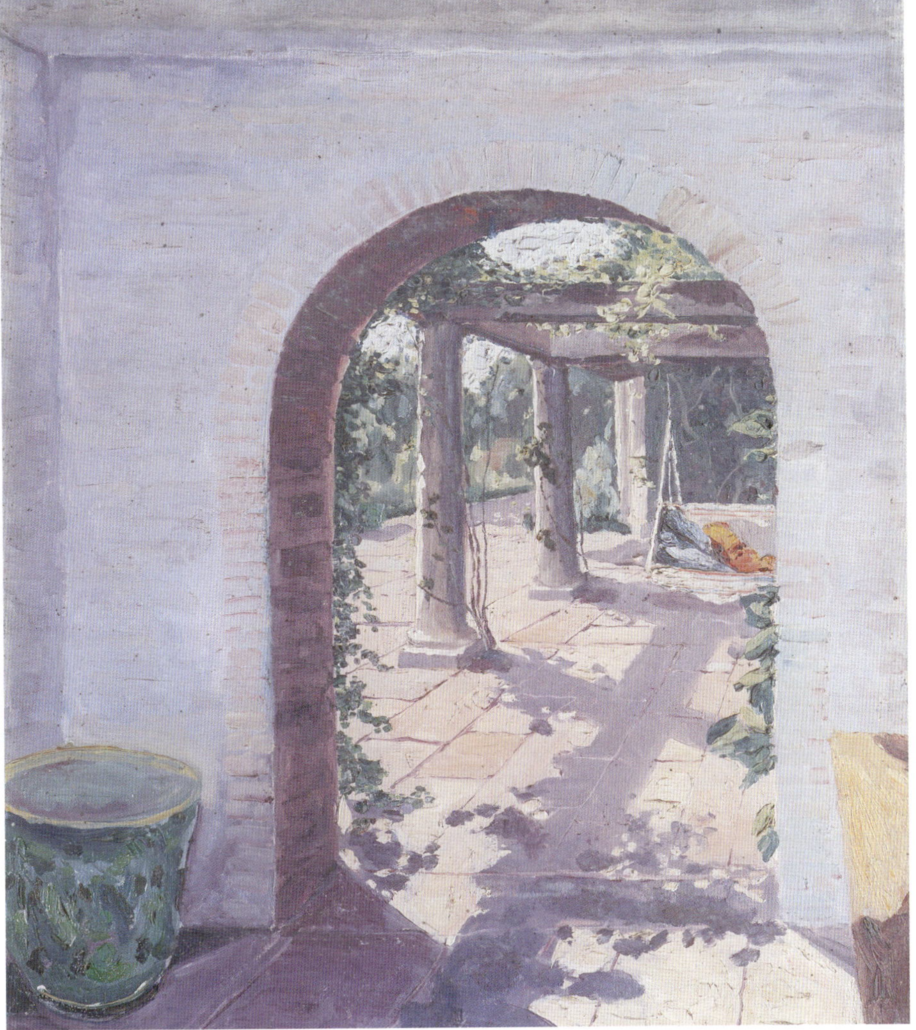

Fig 62 (C 144) left
'Mells, Somersetshire'. Illustrated: 'Painting as a Pastime' The Strand Magazine, January 1922. Mells, near Frome, was the home of Sir John and Lady Horner.

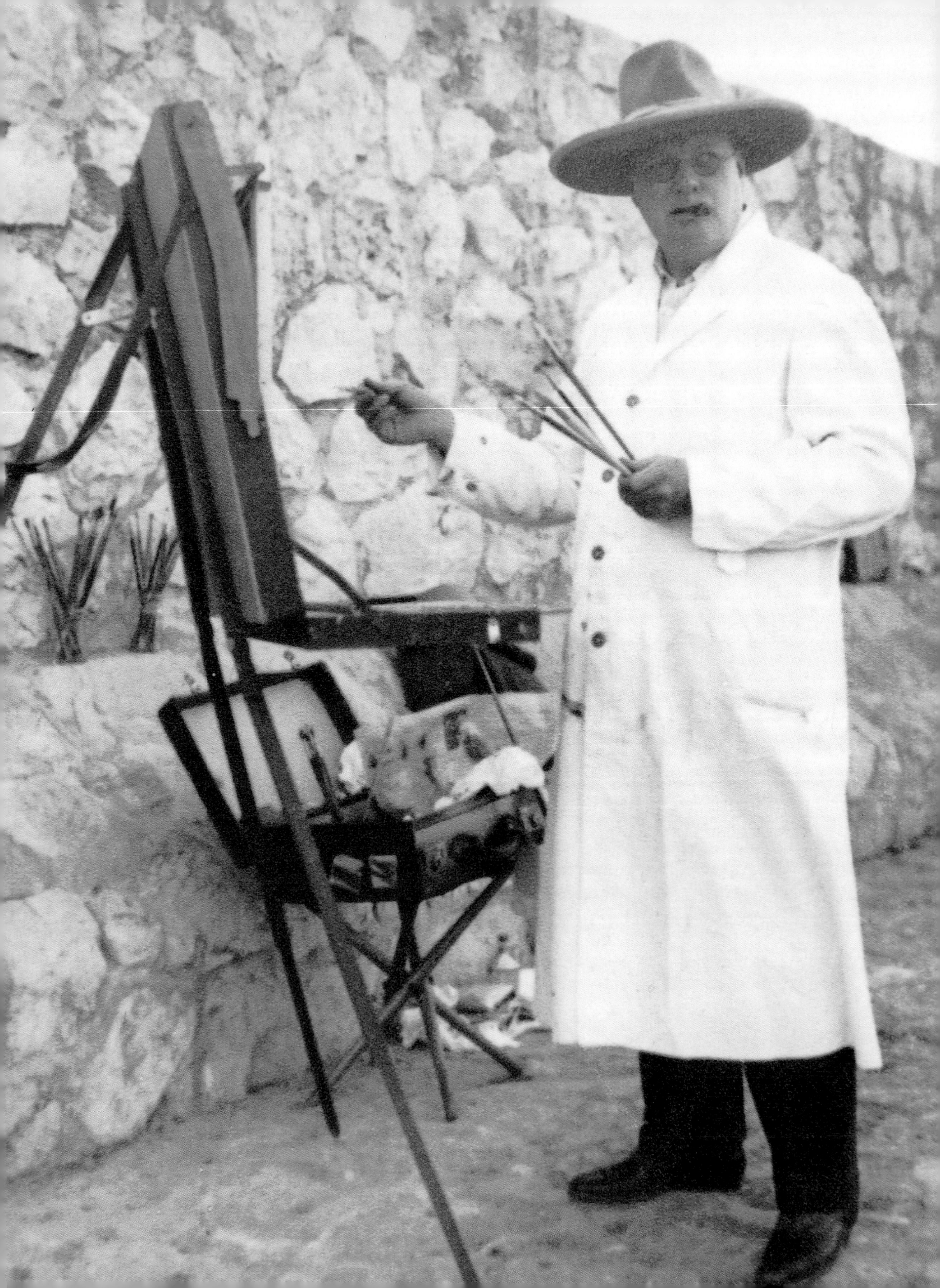

painting as a pastime

The Original Texts

The public was soon to learn of Churchill's summer weekend discovery of the 'muse of painting'. On September 1st, 1915, for example, *The Illustrated War News* published a photograph of an attractive old farmhouse fashionably covered with creepers. 'Hoe Farm is the charming country residence in the neighbourhood of Godalming, Surrey, where [Mr Winston Churchill] the late First Lord of the Admiralty passes his occasional leisure, occupied, it is announced, with landscape painting, in which his work is said to show exceptionally high talent.'

In 1915, Churchill had been a celebrity for nearly half his 40 years. His political humiliation and public shame consequent upon the disastrous allied invasion of Gallipoli was followed within two years by his entering the government once again. His renewed climb up the ministerial ladder reached a climax in 1921, when the Prime Minister, David Lloyd George, appointed him Colonial Secretary with responsibility also for Iraq and Palestine.

Early in the same year Churchill was approached by *The Strand Magazine* to write an article about his painting. (1) Winston wrote to his wife saying that the magazine had accepted his terms for a payment of '£1,000 for two articles with pictures reproduced in colour'. Clementine counselled caution: 'I expect the professionals would be vexed & say you do not yet know enough about Art.' As for reproducing his own pictures: 'The danger there seems to me that either it be thought naif or conceited.' However she expressed herself to be as 'anxious as you are to snooker that £1,000' and this jointly held need no doubt helped carry the day. More than 80 years ago this was a very significant sum of money.(2)

Churchill's article entitled 'Painting as a Pastime' was published in the December 1921 and January 1922 issues of *The Strand Magazine* with 19 of his paintings illustrated mostly in colour. In its day this monthly journal, published by George Newnes Limited, was unique both in terms of its prestige and in the writers it could attract. For example, the Christmas issue contained stories by P. G. Wodehouse, Edgar Wallace and Arthur Conan Doyle as well as an article on 'Singing as a Profession' by Enrico Caruso. The interval between commission and publication of Churchill's article allowed him to include an illustration of the Pyramids painted during a ministerial visit to Egypt.

Opposite
Churchill took his painting very seriously, buying the best quality paints, brushes, canvases, easels and palettes.
He also invariably used a painter's smock, and protected his head with a hat, often a sombrero.
Photograph probably from the early 1920s.

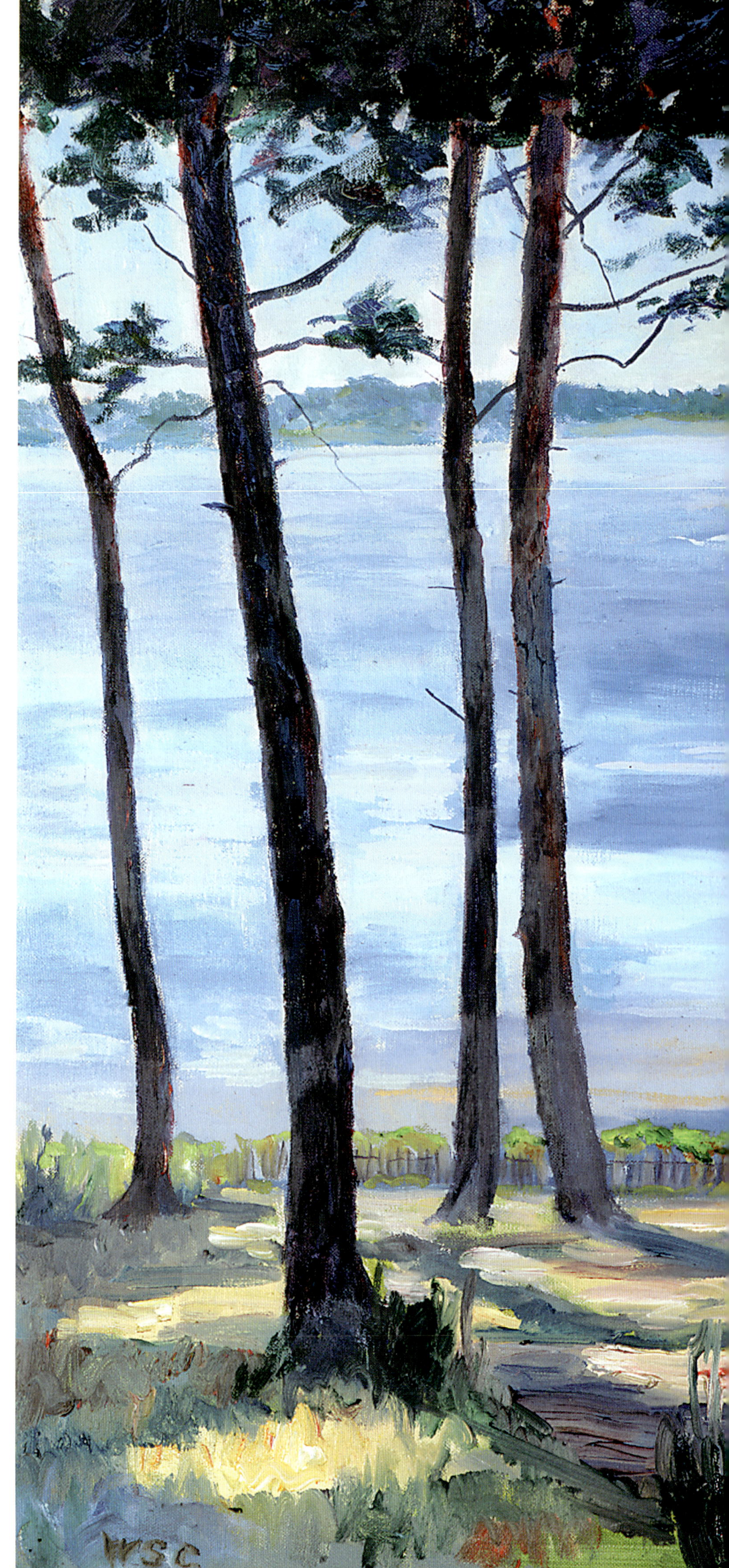

Fig 63 (C 70)
Mimizan, Landes, given by Churchill to the First World War Prime Minister, David Lloyd George, later Viscount Tenby.

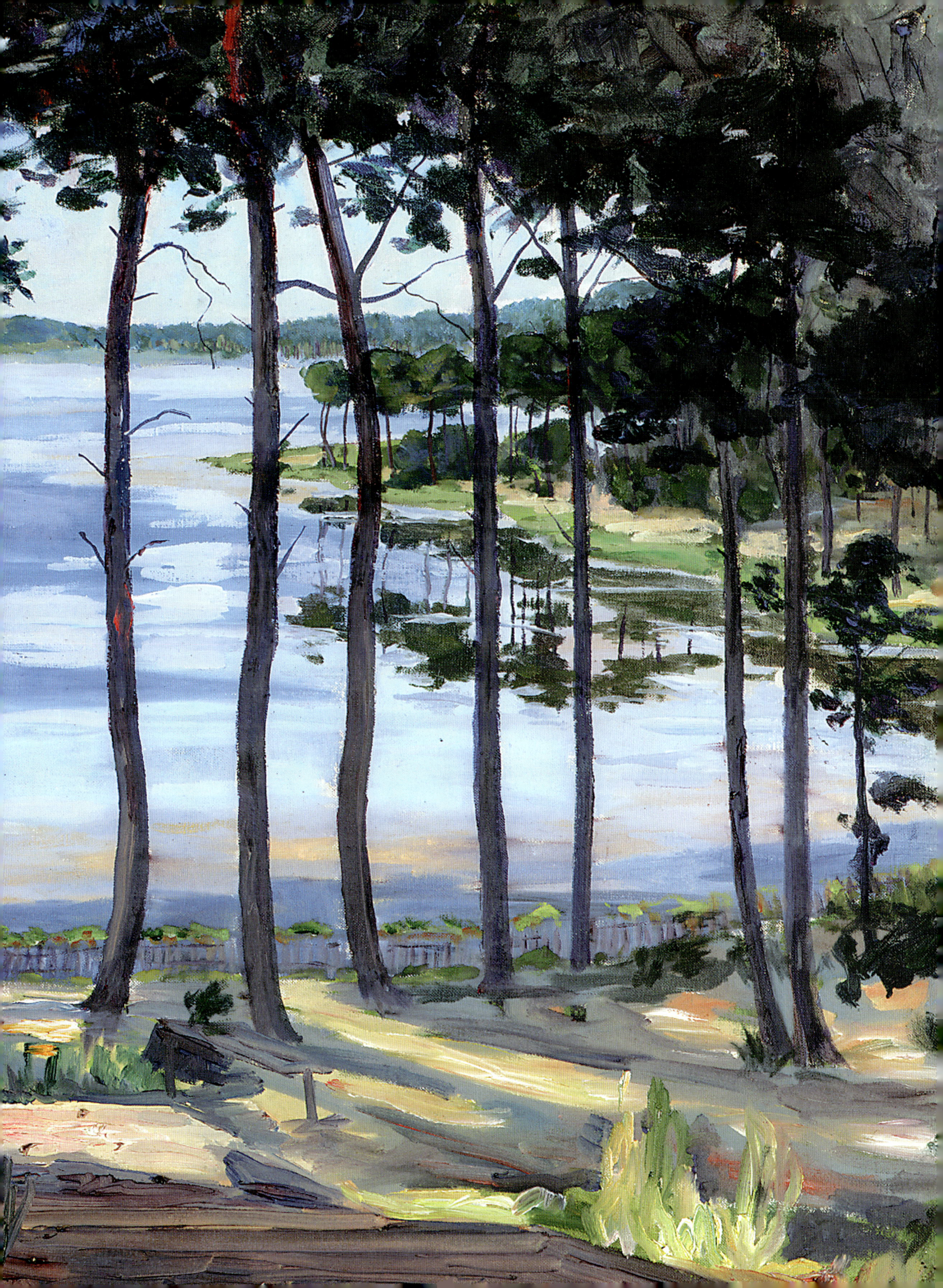

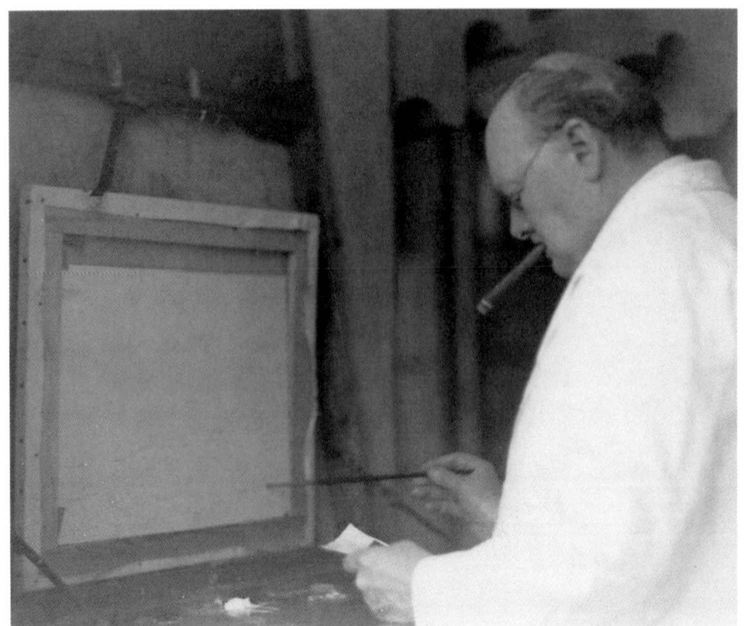

Winston Churchill sketching on the back of a canvas from a little snapshot held in his hand. This photograph is from the Studio archives at Chartwell.

The original text of 'Painting as a Pastime' clearly confirms what can be inferred anyhow from the later book, that Churchill was, perhaps surprisingly to some, essentially humble in his approach to painting.

In 1924 Churchill became Chancellor of the Exchequer, the second highest position in government, so achieving his ambition of emulating the success of his father, Lord Randolph. The following year brought Churchill an invitation to write another but more general article. He had acquired Chartwell three years before and had more or less immediately embarked upon what was to become another celebrated recreation as a builder of brick garden walls. The new article was commissioned by *Nash's Pall Mall Magazine*, which, since 1910, had been owned by the National Magazine Company, the British subsidiary of the American empire of the newspaper magnate William Randolph Hearst.

This second article was entitled 'Hobbies' and as its name suggested ranged rather more widely than 'Painting as a Pastime', although nearly half the space was devoted to that subject, touching on many of the same points but told in a fresh and different way.

In 1926, the US-based *Cosmopolitan*, another Hearst magazine, published a shortened version of 'Hobbies' under the title 'When Life Harasses me I Ride my Hobby'. The text was that part of the original article telling the story of Churchill's enthusiasm for painting.

Both articles were illustrated with a selection of Churchill's paintings with the addition of a photograph of the artist standing at his easel working on his picture of the Bridge over the Var in the South of France. In *Cosmopolitan*, this was captioned as 'Winston S. Churchill following his hobby in London's East End'. But the writer was meticulously described as 'Chancellor of the Exchequer in Great Britain, which corresponds to Secretary of the Treasury in the United States'.

In 1929, Churchill's complete original article 'Painting as a Pastime' was included in *The Hundred Best English Essays* selected by his friend the Earl of Birkenhead. The authors ranged from Sir Walter Raleigh to G. K. Chesterton by way of Samuel Pepys and John Stuart Mill. Lord Birkenhead was in no doubt about his choice, which 'in its revelation of character, in its gift of expression, and its fresh intellectual challenge is Mr Churchill at his best'.

Churchill was now out of office and at the beginning of his wilderness years, wholly dependent on writing and journalism for earning his living. In 1930, the complete version of 'Hobbies' was published once again but in newspaper form by *The Sunday Chronicle*, April 20th, with the title 'A Man's Hobbies'.

In 1932 a collection of Churchill's essays was published under the title *Thoughts and Adventures*. He was so busy that the introduction was written by his friend Edward Marsh in a fair pastiche of Winston's own style. The book included 'Hobbies' and 'Painting as a Pastime', both in considerably shortened versions. From this fact much later confusion has flowed.

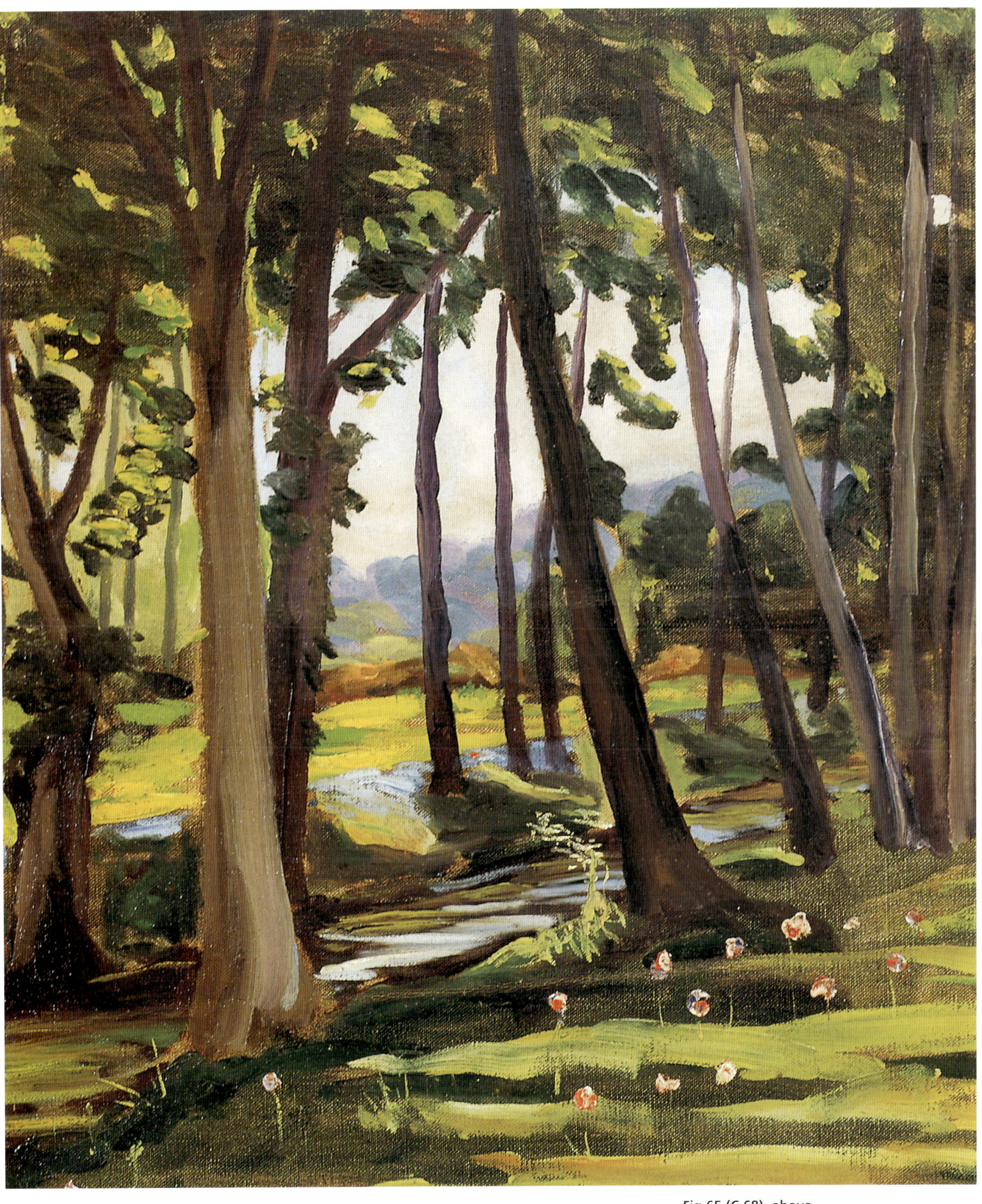

Fig 65 (C 68) above
Trees by a stream in Norfolk. This painting formerly belonged to Clementine Churchill.

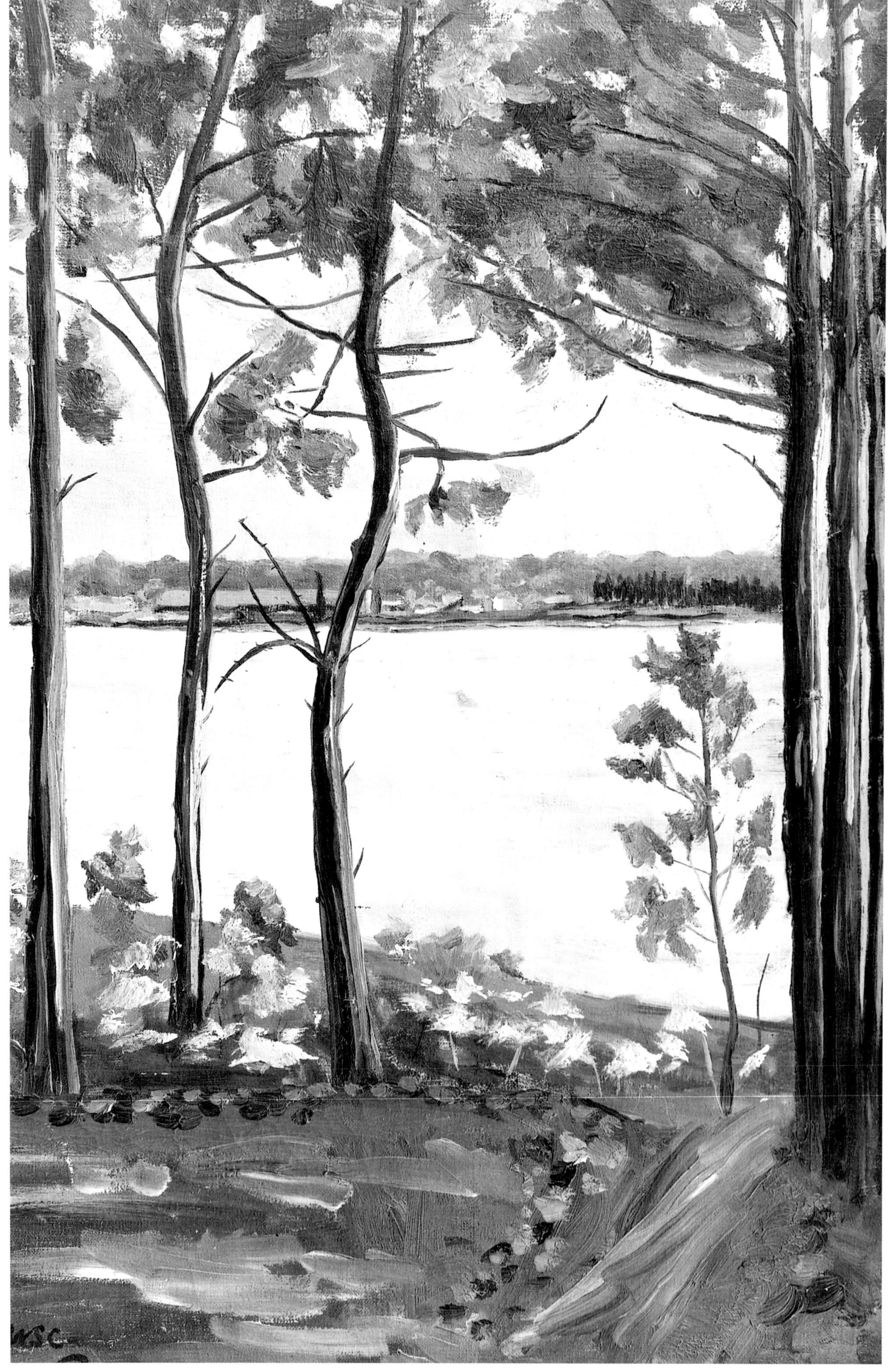

Fig 66 (C 62) above
A view at Mimizan, given by Churchill to Field Marshal Viscount Montgomery of Alamein.

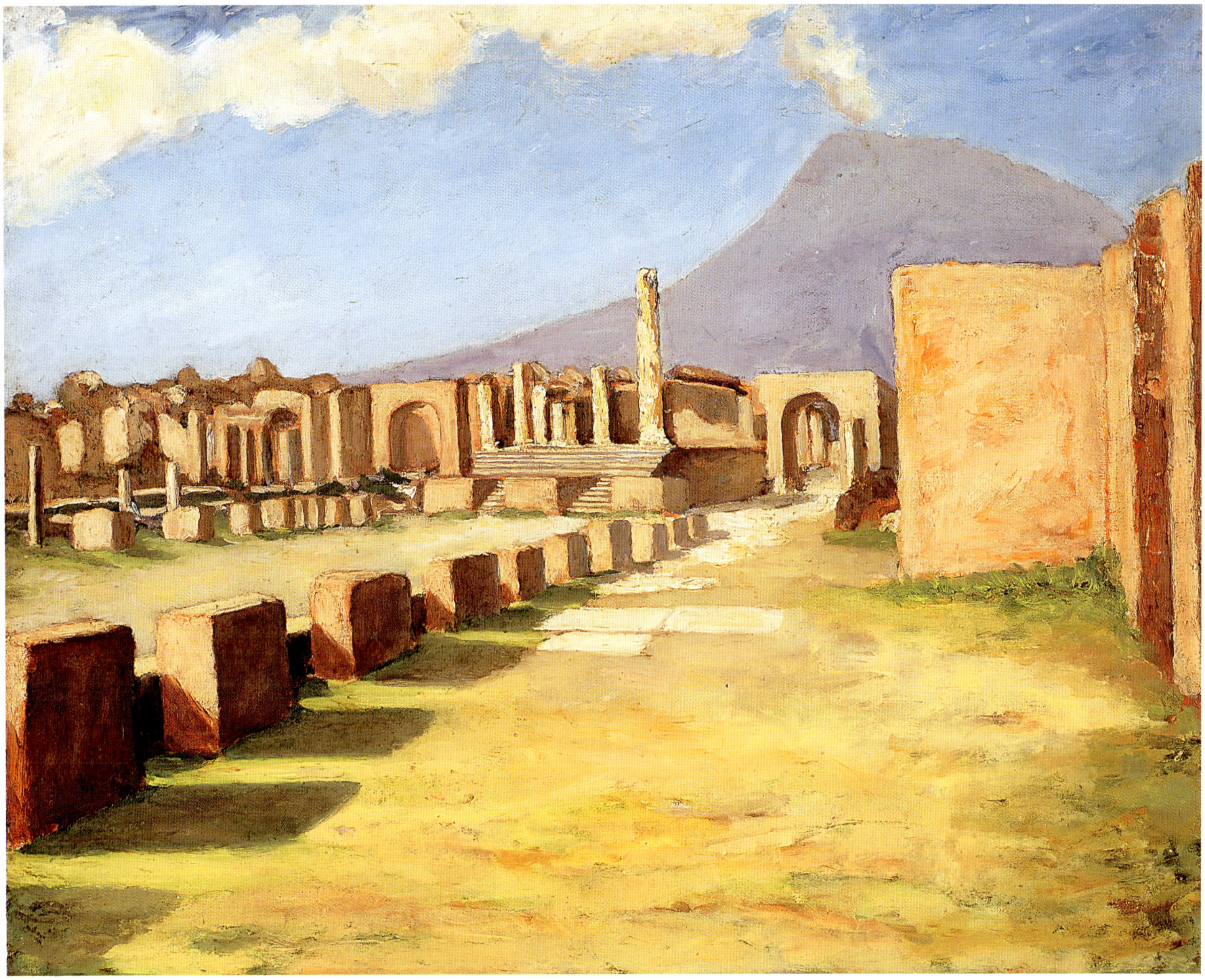

Fig 67 (C 237) above
'Vesuvius, from Pompeii.' Illustrated: 'Painting as a Pastime' The Strand Magazine, January 1922. The ancient Roman city near Naples buried by a volcanic eruption.

After the war, in 1946, *The Strand Magazine*, then a shadow of its former self, published in July and August two articles illustrated by Churchill's paintings. The first included an edited adaptation of the already shortened version of 'Painting as a Pastime' published in *Thoughts and Adventures*, but with a last paragraph so woodenly written it must have been added in the editorial office.

In 1947, John Benn from the publishers Ernest Benn approached Churchill with the idea that his two articles in *Thoughts and Adventures*, 'Hobbies' and 'Painting as a Pastime' should be combined to make a 'delightful gift book.' Odhams Press now had an interest in the copyright and they became joint publishers of what was to become, even by Churchill's standards, an outstanding literary success. The book was reprinted quickly and many times and was translated into Finnish, French, German and Japanese. In 1950, it was published in the United States. As a book, *Painting as a Pastime* has remained in print more or less constantly ever since. In 2002, for example, a handsome little leather-covered edition was published by Levenger Press in the United States.

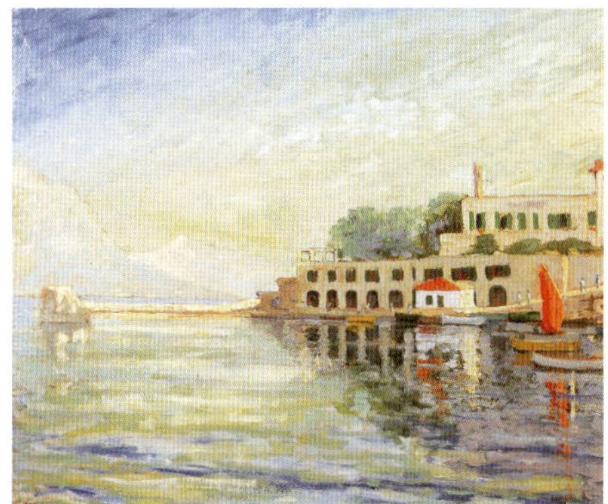

Fig 68 (C 315) above
'The harbour at St. Jean Cap Ferrat. January 1921.' Illustrated: 'Painting as a Pastime' The Strand Magazine, December 1921. This holiday resort on the French Riviera was a favourite of the Churchill family.

The texts that follow are Churchill's complete and unabridged original articles published here for the first time in nearly 80 years. The words and sentences in bold type have not been published since. Churchill's own later amendments to both texts are contained within square brackets.

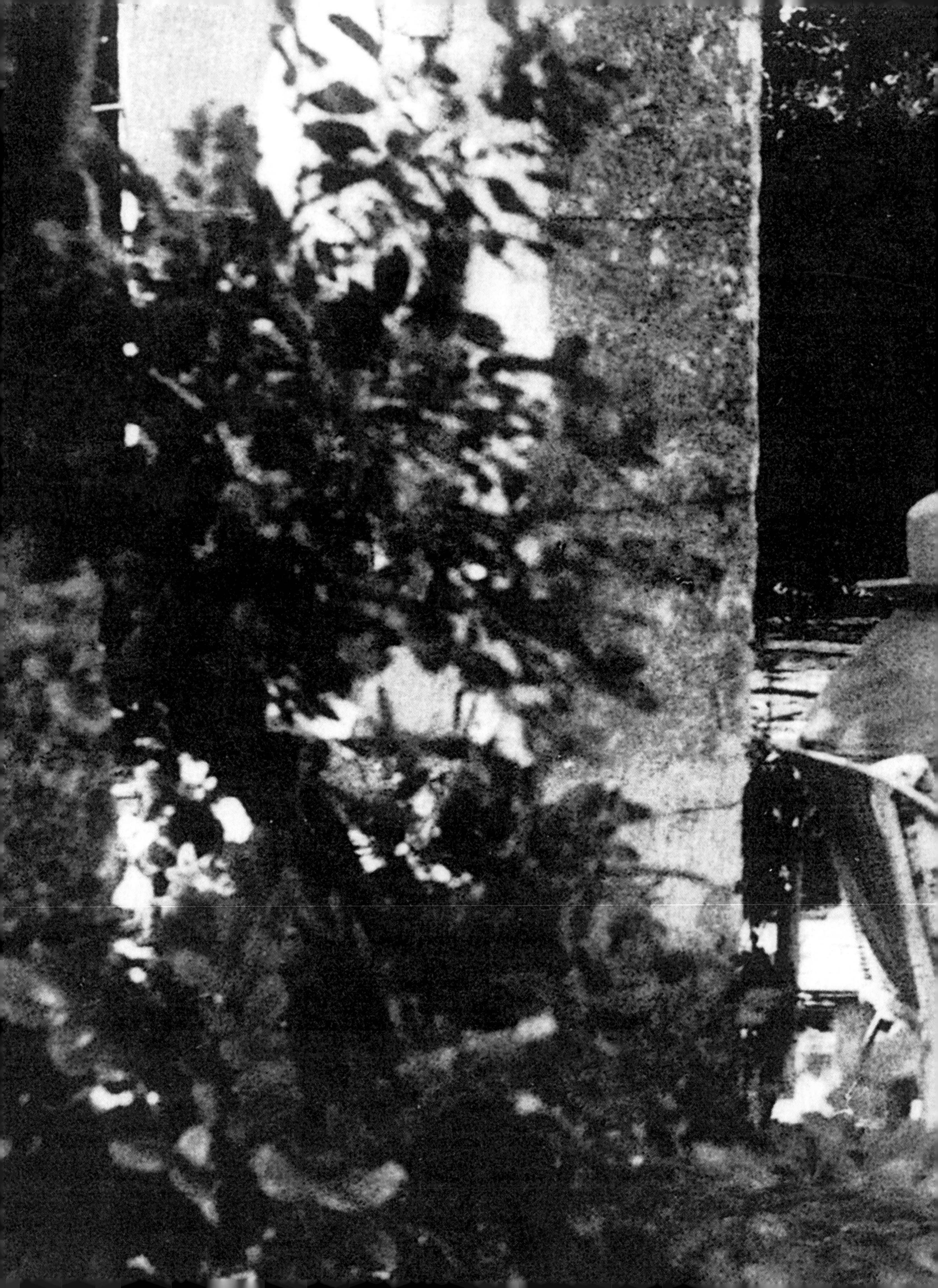

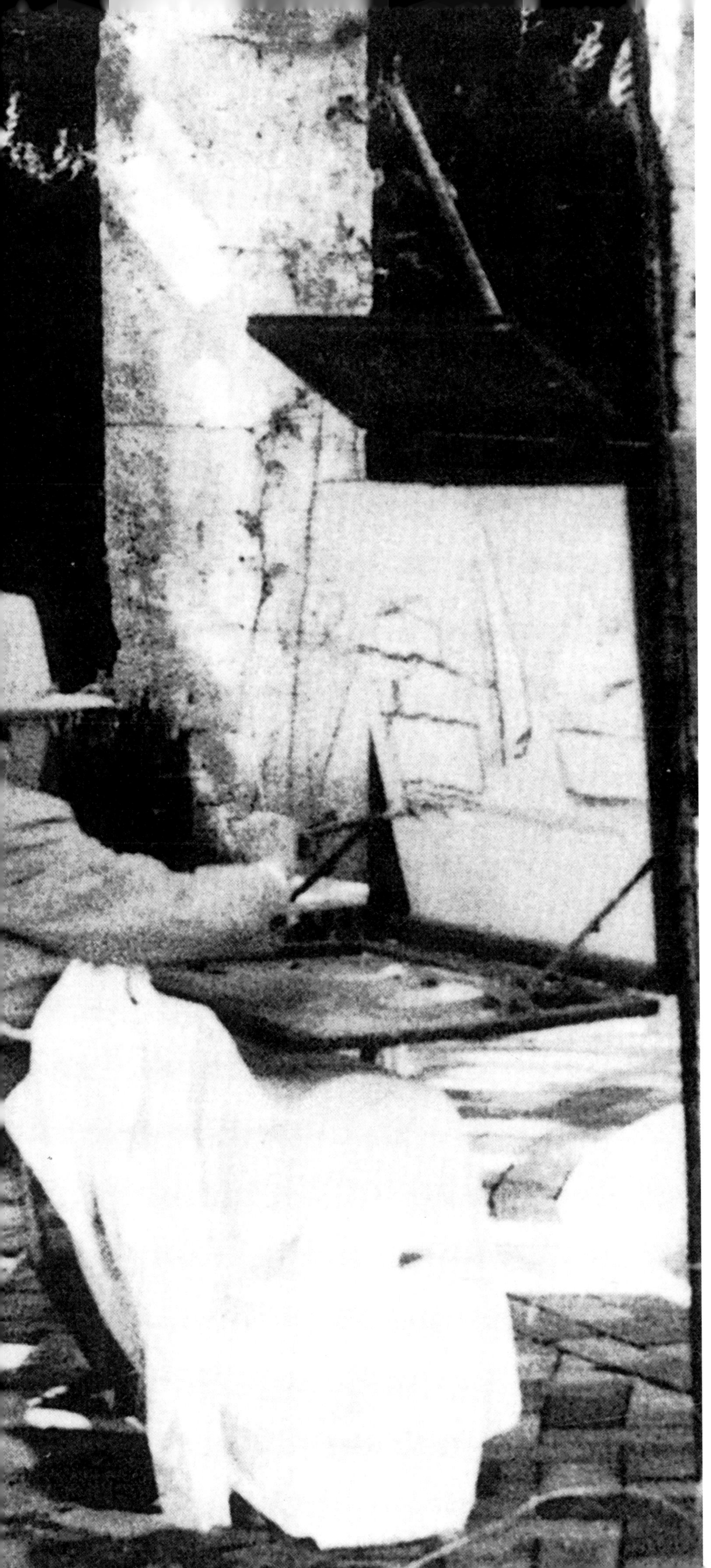

Sir Winston Churchill painting at La Capponcina, Cap d'Ail, 1960.

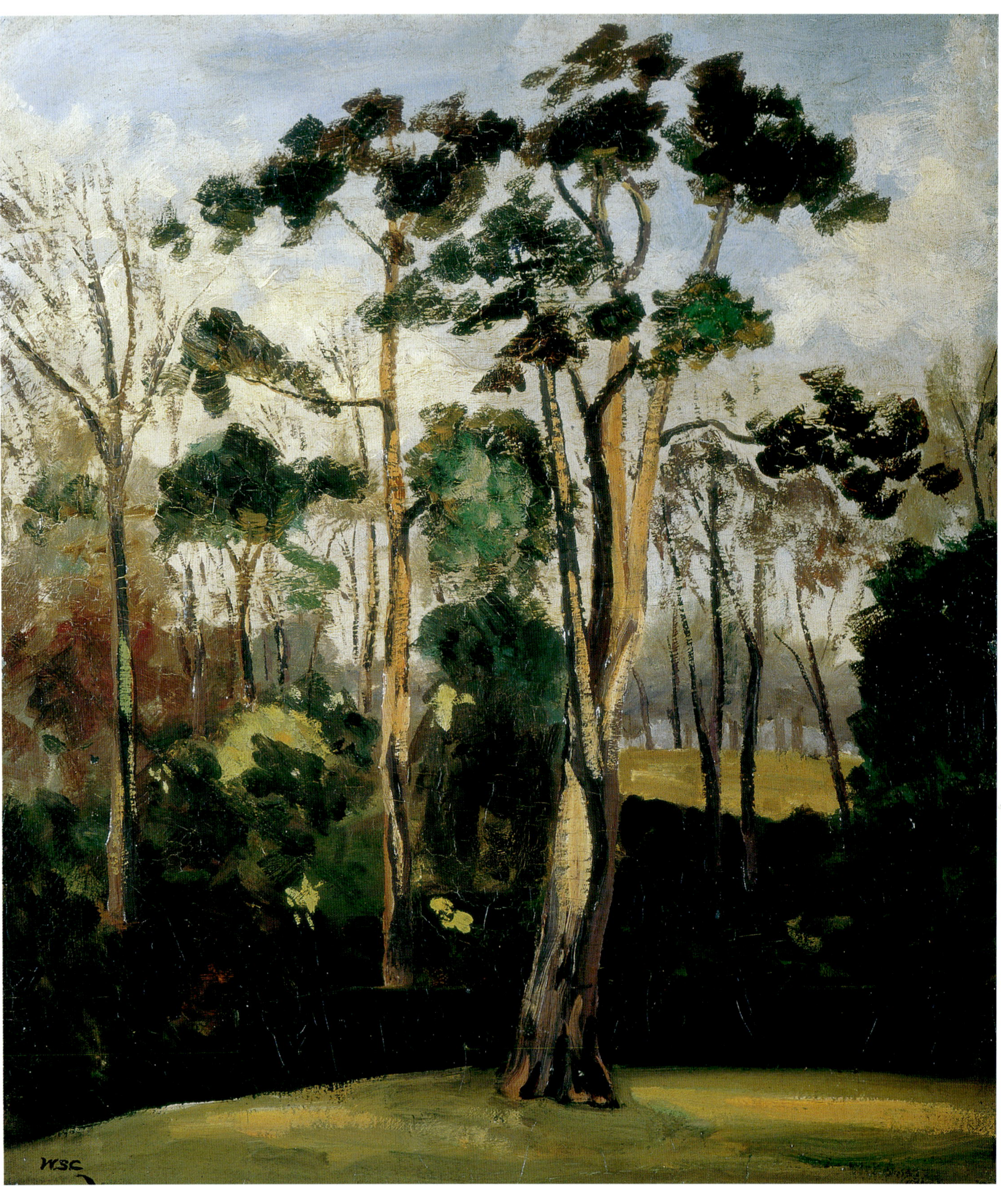
WSC

Painting as a Pastime

by The Rt. Hon. Winston Churchill

First published in *The Strand Magazine* 1921/2

[Part 1]

I do not submit these sketches to public gaze because I am under any illusion about their merit. They are the productions of a weekend and holiday amateur who during the last few years has found a new pleasure and who wishes to tell others of his luck. To have reached the age of forty without ever handling a brush or fiddling with a pencil, to have regarded with mature eye the painting of pictures of any kind as a mystery, to have stood agape before the chalk of a pavement artist, and then suddenly found oneself plunged in the middle of a new and intense form of interest and action with paints and palettes and canvases, and not to be discouraged by the results, is an astonishing and enriching experience. I hope it may be shared by others. I should be glad if these lines, I should be proud if these sketches, induced others to have tried the experiment which I have tried, and if some at least were to find themselves dowered with an absorbing new amusement delightful to themselves, and at any rate not violently harmful to man or beast.

I hope this is modest enough: because there is no subject on which I feel more humble or yet at the same time more natural. I do not presume to explain how to paint, but only how to get enjoyment. Do not turn the superior eye of critical passivity upon these efforts. Buy a paint-box and have a try. If you need something to occupy your leisure, to divert your mind from your daily round, to illuminate your holidays, do not be too ready to believe that you cannot find what you want here. Even at the advanced age of forty! It would be a sad pity to shuffle or scramble along through one's playtime with golf and bridge, pottering, loitering, shifting from one heel to the other, wondering what on earth to do - as perhaps is the fate of some unhappy beings - when all the while, if you only knew, there is a close at hand a wonderful new world of thought and craft, a sunlit garden gleaming with light and colour of which you have the key in your waistcoat-pocket. Inexpensive independence, a mobile and perennial pleasure apparatus, new mental food and exercise, the old harmonies and symmetries in an entirely different language, an added interest to every common scene, an occupation for every idle hour, an unceasing voyage of entrancing discovery - these are high prizes. Make quite sure they are not yours. After all, if you try, and fail, there is not much harm done. The nursery will grab what the studio has rejected. And then you can always go out and kill some animal, humiliate some rival on the links, or despoil some friend across the green table. You will not be worse off in any way. In fact you will be better off. You will know 'beyond a peradventure', to quote a phrase disagreeably reminiscent, that that is really what you were meant to do in your hours of relaxation.

But if, on the contrary, you are inclined - late in life though it be - to reconnoitre a foreign sphere of limitless extent, then be persuaded that the first quality that is needed is Audacity. There really is no time for the deliberate approach. Two years

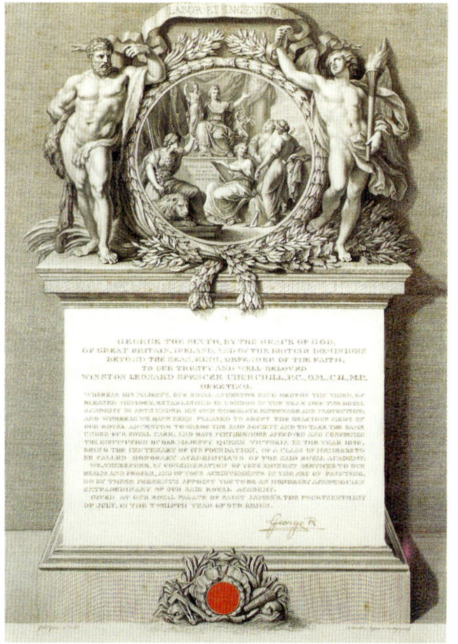

GEORGE THE SIXTH, BY THE GRACE OF GOD,
OF GREAT BRITAIN, IRELAND, AND OF THE BRITISH DOMINIONS
BEYOND THE SEAS, KING, DEFENDER OF THE FAITH,
TO OUR TRUSTY AND WELL BELOVED
WINSTON LEONARD SPENCER CHURCHILL, P.C., O.M., C.H., M.P.
GREETING.

WHEREAS HIS MAJESTY, OUR ROYAL ANCESTOR KING GEORGE THE THIRD, OF BLESSED MEMORY, ESTABLISHED IN LONDON IN THE YEAR [illegible] THE ROYAL ACADEMY OF ARTS UNDER HIS OWN IMMEDIATE PATRONAGE AND PROTECTION; AND WHEREAS WE HAVE BEEN PLEASED TO ADOPT THE GRACIOUS VIEWS OF OUR ROYAL ANCESTOR TOWARDS THE SAID SOCIETY AND TO TAKE THE SAME UNDER OUR ROYAL CARE; AND HAVE FURTHERMORE APPROVED AND CONFIRMED THE INSTITUTION BY HER MAJESTY QUEEN VICTORIA IN THE YEAR [illegible], BEING THE CENTENARY OF ITS FOUNDATION, OF A CLASS OF MEMBERS TO BE CALLED HONORARY ACADEMICIANS OF THE SAID ROYAL ACADEMY;

WE, THEREFORE, IN CONSIDERATION OF YOUR EMINENT SERVICES TO OUR REALM AND PEOPLE, AND OF YOUR ACHIEVEMENTS IN THE ART OF PAINTING, DO BY THESE PRESENTS APPOINT YOU TO BE AN HONORARY ACADEMICIAN EXTRAORDINARY OF OUR SAID ROYAL ACADEMY.

GIVEN AT OUR ROYAL PALACE OF SAINT JAMES'S, THE FOURTEENTH DAY OF JULY, IN THE TWELFTH YEAR OF OUR REIGN.

George R

In 1948, The Royal Academy of Arts unanimously appointed Winston Spencer Churchill an 'Honorary Academician Extraordinary'. This is Churchill's Diploma, signed by King George VI as the Academy's Patron and Protector, which proclaims that this unique appointment was made 'in consideration of your eminent services to our Realm and People, and of your achievements in the Art of Painting.'

**Fig 69 (C 53) opposite page
Woods at Mimizan.**

Churchill enjoyed many holidays on the Duke of Westminter's estate at Mimizan in France. It was set in Les Landes, a large area south of Bordeaux protected from the Atlantic ocean by colossal sand dunes; the original marshy wasteland was later planted with commercial pinewoods. Churchill was much attracted by the trees and their shadows as well as their lakeland setting. The artist Sir John Lavery was a fellow guest on at least one occasion and his general influence on Churchill's technique can be seen in this long series of paintings. Mimizan also gave Churchill the opportunity to enjoy a favourite sport - boar hunting.

Fig 70 (C 65) right
Woodland scene near Mimizan, given by Churchill to his wartime private secretary, Sir John Colville.

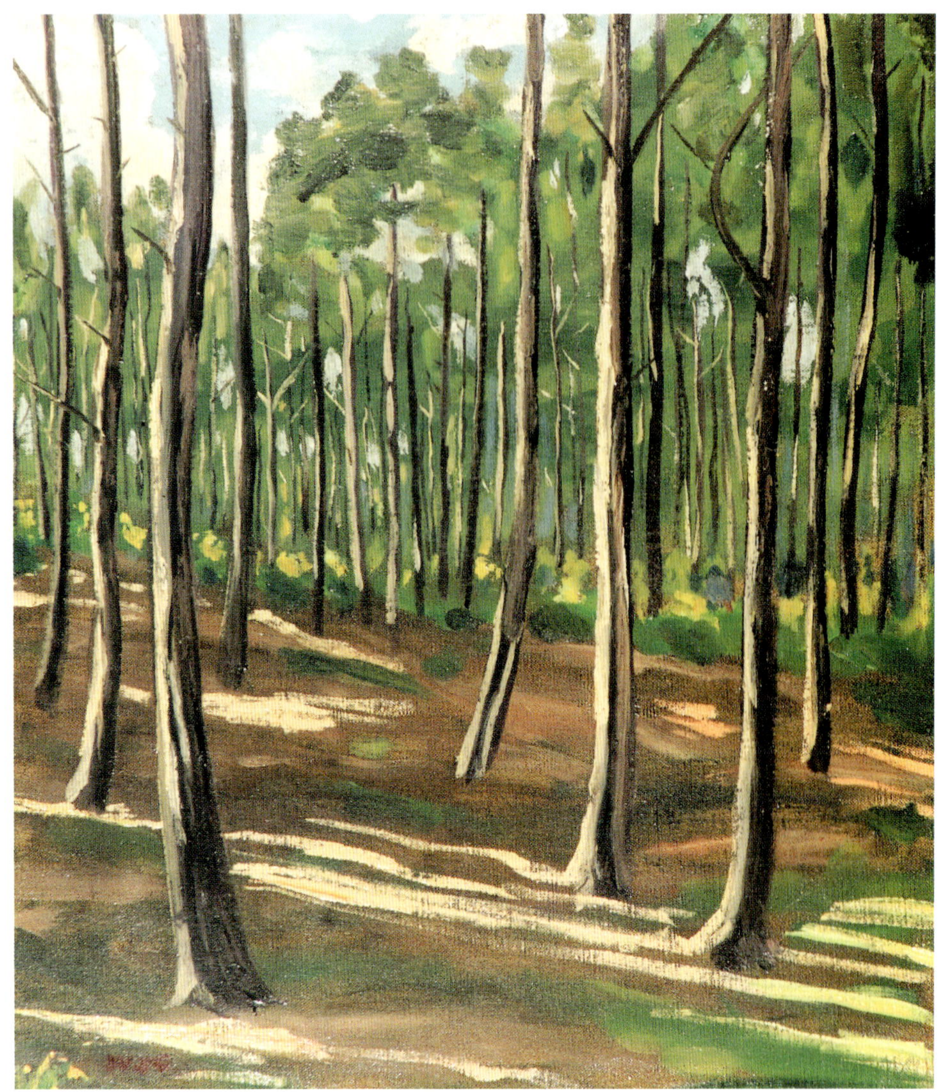

Fig 71 (C 66) below
Trees at Mimizan, given by Churchill to his wife, Clementine.

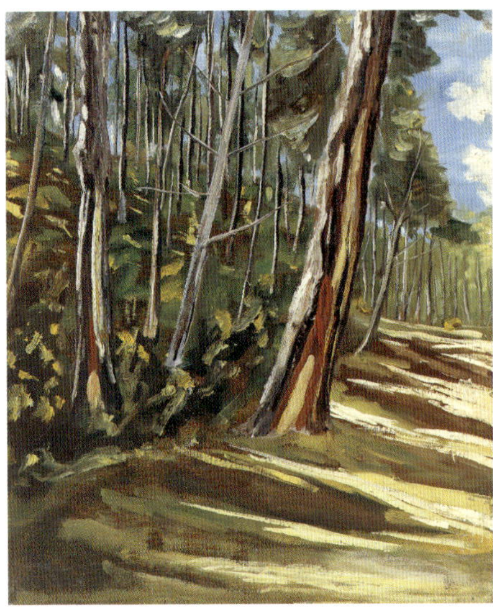

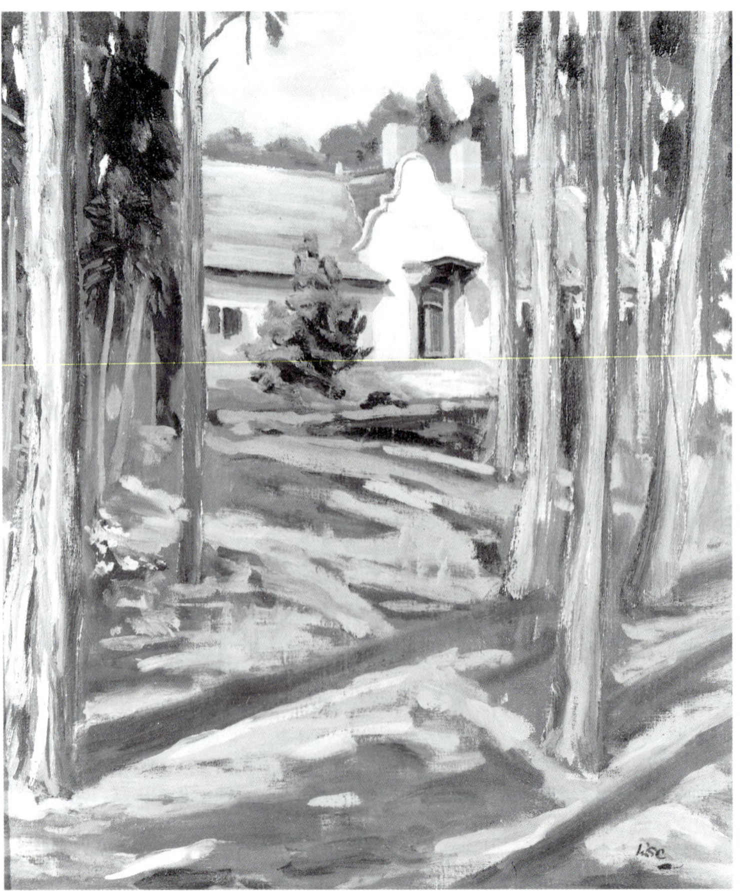

Fig 72 (C 67) right
Red-roofed house at Mimizan, given by Lady Churchill to Winston's last police bodyguard, Detective-Sergeant Edmund Murray.

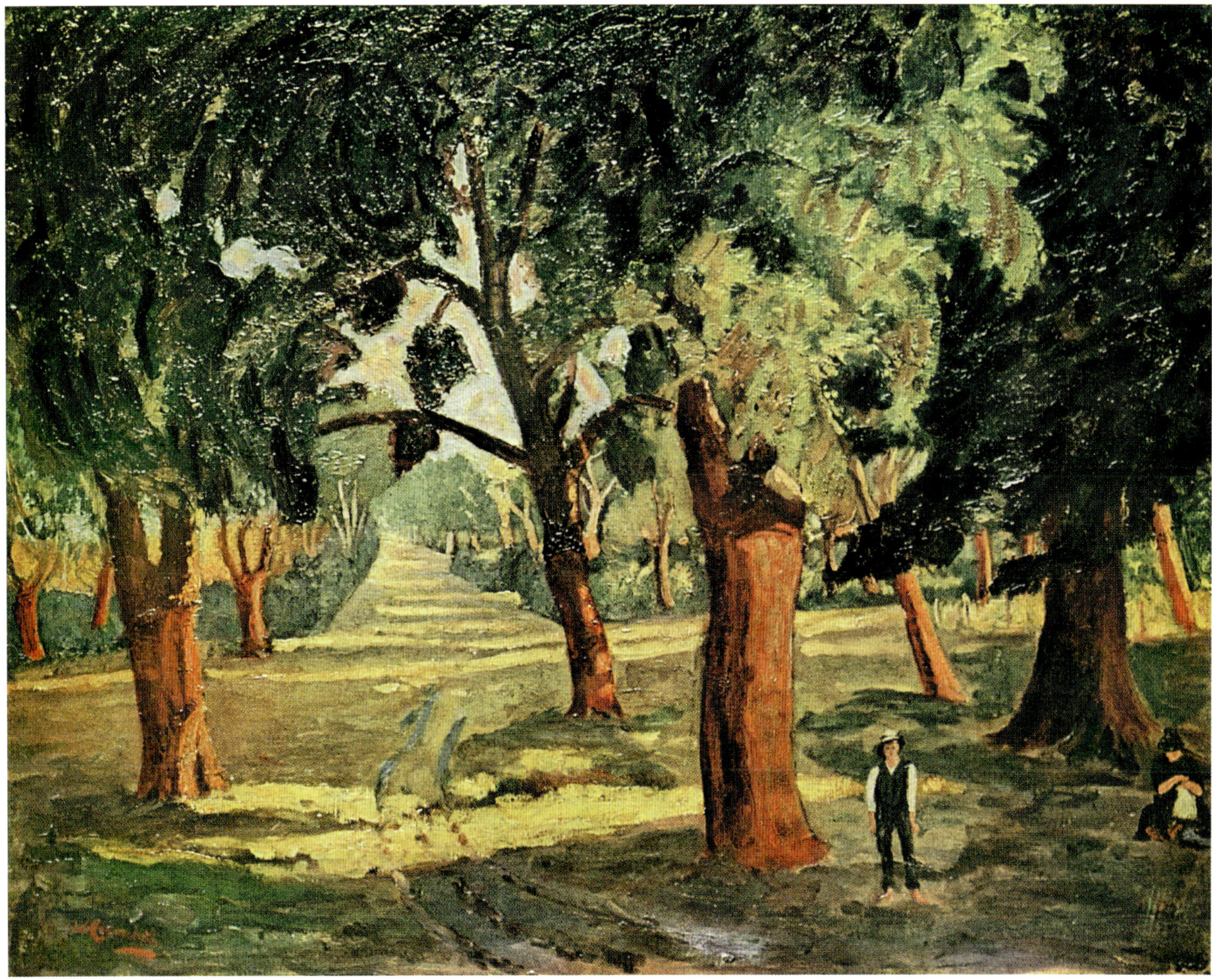

Fig 73 (C 74) above
Cork trees near Mimizan, sold at a London charity auction in 1961. Unusually this painting is signed in full.

of drawing-lessons, three years of copying woodcuts, five years of plaster casts - these are for the young. They have enough to bear. And this thorough grounding is for those who, hearing the call in the morning of their days, are able to make painting their paramount lifelong vocation. The truth and beauty of line and form which by the slightest touch or twist of the brush a real artist imparts to every feature of his design must be founded on long, hard, persevering apprenticeship and a practice so habitual that it has become instinctive. We must not be ambitious. We cannot aspire to masterpieces. We may content ourselves with a joy-ride in a paint-box. And for this Audacity is the only ticket.

I shall now relate my personal experience. When I left the Admiralty at the end of May, 1915, I still remained a member of the Cabinet and the War Council. In this position I knew everything and could do nothing. The change from the intense executive activities of each day's work at the Admiralty to the narrowly measured duties of counsellor left me gasping. Like a sea-beast fished up from the depths, or a diver too suddenly hoisted, my veins threatened to burst from the fall in pressure. I had great anxiety and no means of relieving it; I had vehement convictions and small power to give effect to them. I had to watch the unhappy casting-away of great opportunities, and the feeble execution of plans which I had launched and in which I heartily believed. I had long hours of utterly unwonted leisure in which to contemplate the frightful unfolding of the War. At a moment when every fibre of my being was inflamed to action, I was forced to

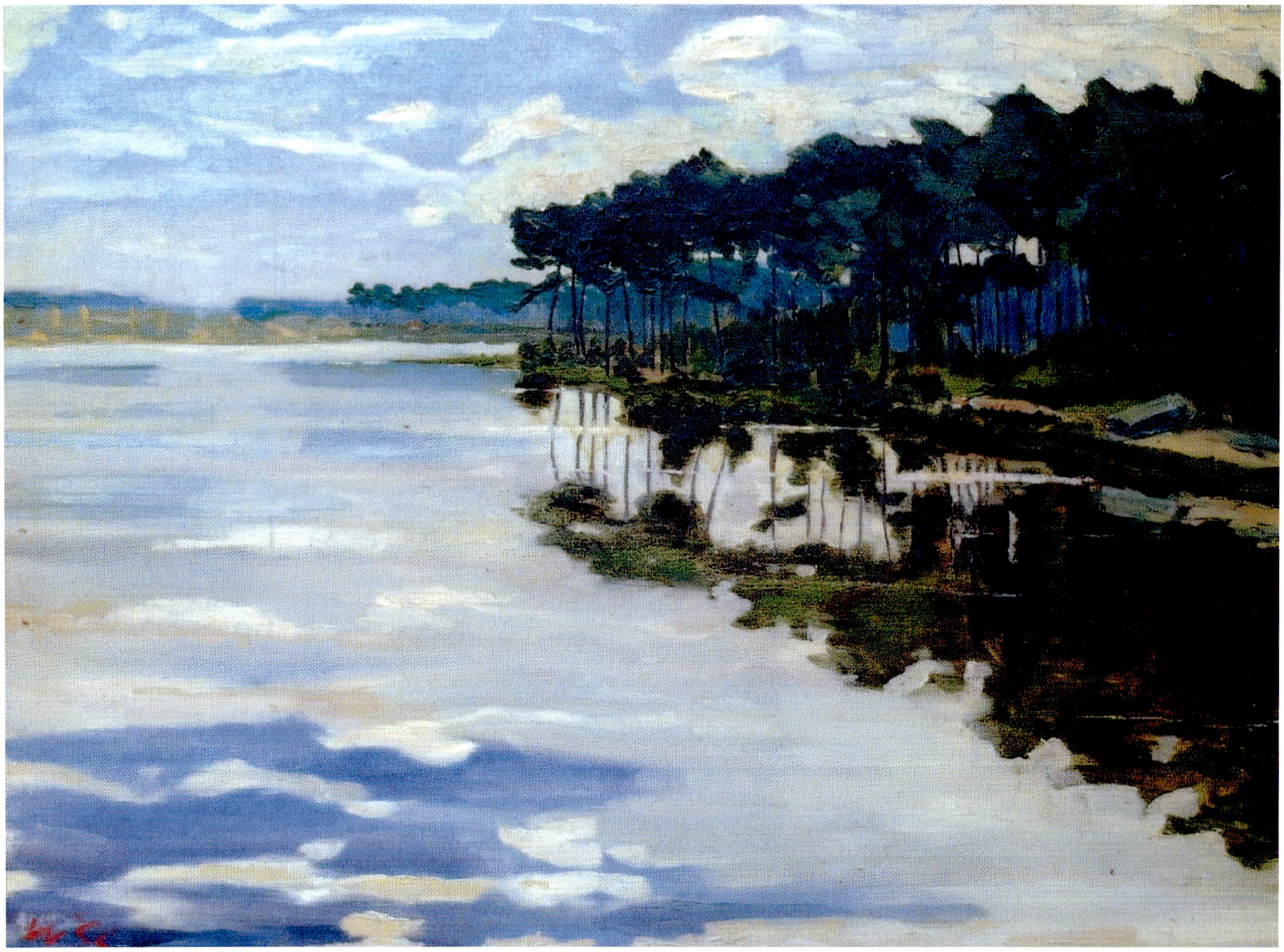

Fig 74 (C 498) above
A view at Mimizan, given by Churchill to Anne, wife of Bendor, 2nd Duke of Westminster, his host at Mimizan.

remain a spectator of the tragedy, placed cruelly in a front seat. And then it was that the Muse of Painting came to my rescue - out of charity and out of chivalry, because after all she had nothing to do with me - and said, 'Are these toys any good to you? They amuse some people.'

[Some experiments one Sunday in the country with the children's paint-box led me to procure the next morning a complete outfit for painting in oils.]

Having bought the colours, an easel, and a canvas, the next step was to begin. But what a step to take! The palette gleamed with beads of colour; fair and white rose the canvas; the empty brush hung poised, heavy with destiny, irresolute in the air. My hand seemed arrested by a silent veto. But after all the sky on this occasion was unquestionably blue, and a pale blue at that. There could be no doubt that blue paint mixed with white should be put on the top part of the canvas. One really does not need to have had an artist's training to see that. It is a starting-point open to all. So very gingerly I mixed a little blue paint on the palette with a very small brush, and then with infinite precaution made a mark about as big as a bean upon the affronted snow-white shield. It was a challenge, a deliberate challenge; but so subdued, so halting, indeed so cataleptic, that it deserved no response. At that moment the loud approaching sound of a motor-car was heard in the drive. From this chariot there stepped swiftly and lightly none other than the gifted wife of Sir John Lavery.(3) 'Painting! But what are you hesitating about? Let me have a brush - the big one.' Splash into the turpentine, wallop into the blue and the white, frantic flourish on the palette - clean no longer - and then several large, fierce strokes and slashes of

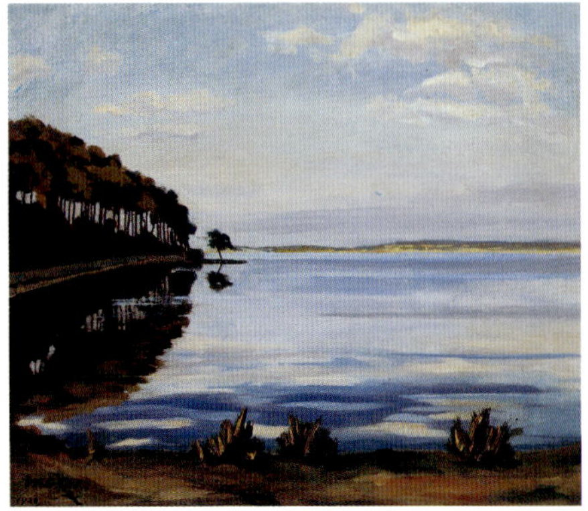

Fig 75 (C 502) above
A view at Mimizan, given by Churchill to the American financier Bernard Baruch. The painting is dated 1920.

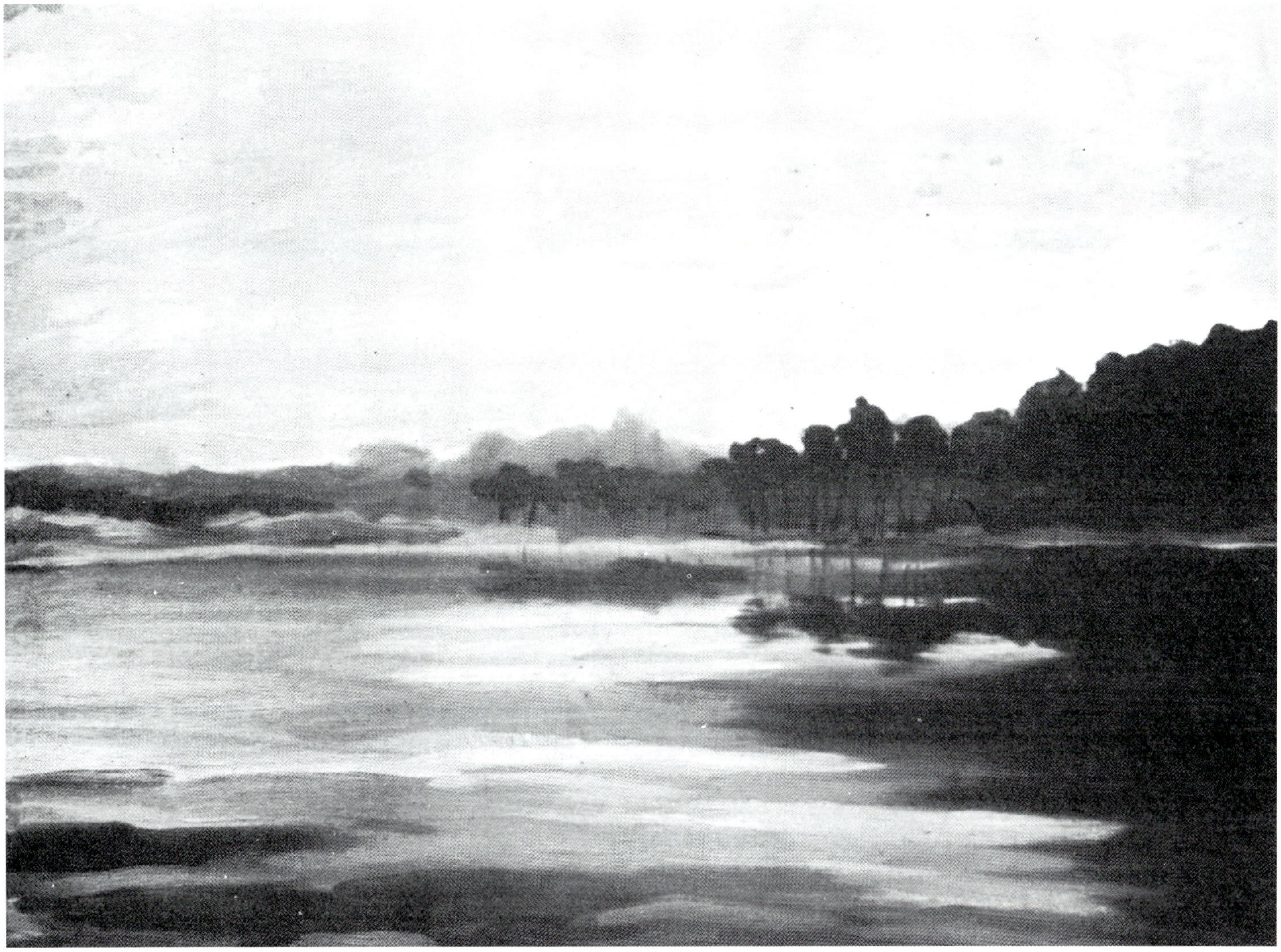

Fig 76 (C 63) above
Evening glow at Mimizan, given by Churchill to his eldest daughter, Diana.

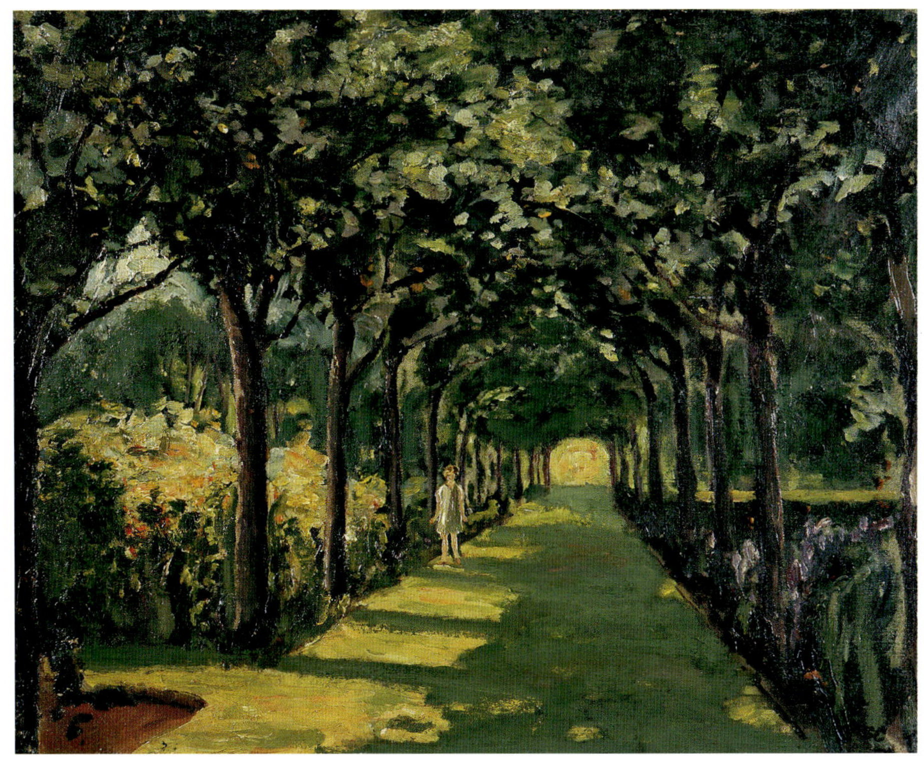

Fig 77 (C 276) left
In 1922 Clementine Churchill took her children on holiday to Frinton-on-Sea in Essex. In this painting, Winston portrays a shady avenue there with his eldest daughter, Diana.

Following pages
Detail of 'Daybreak at Cassis, near Marseilles' 1920. (See page 35, Fig. 53).

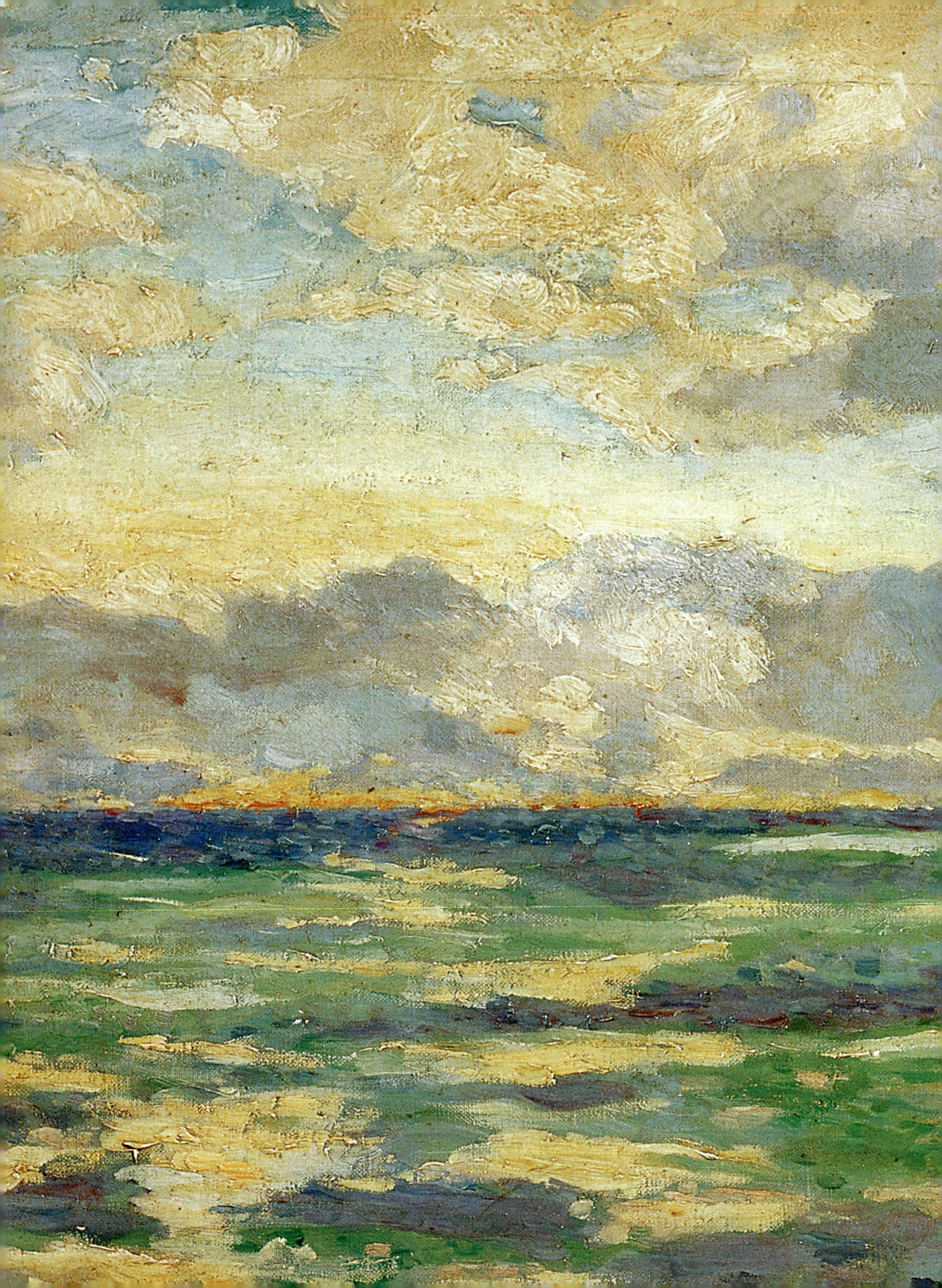

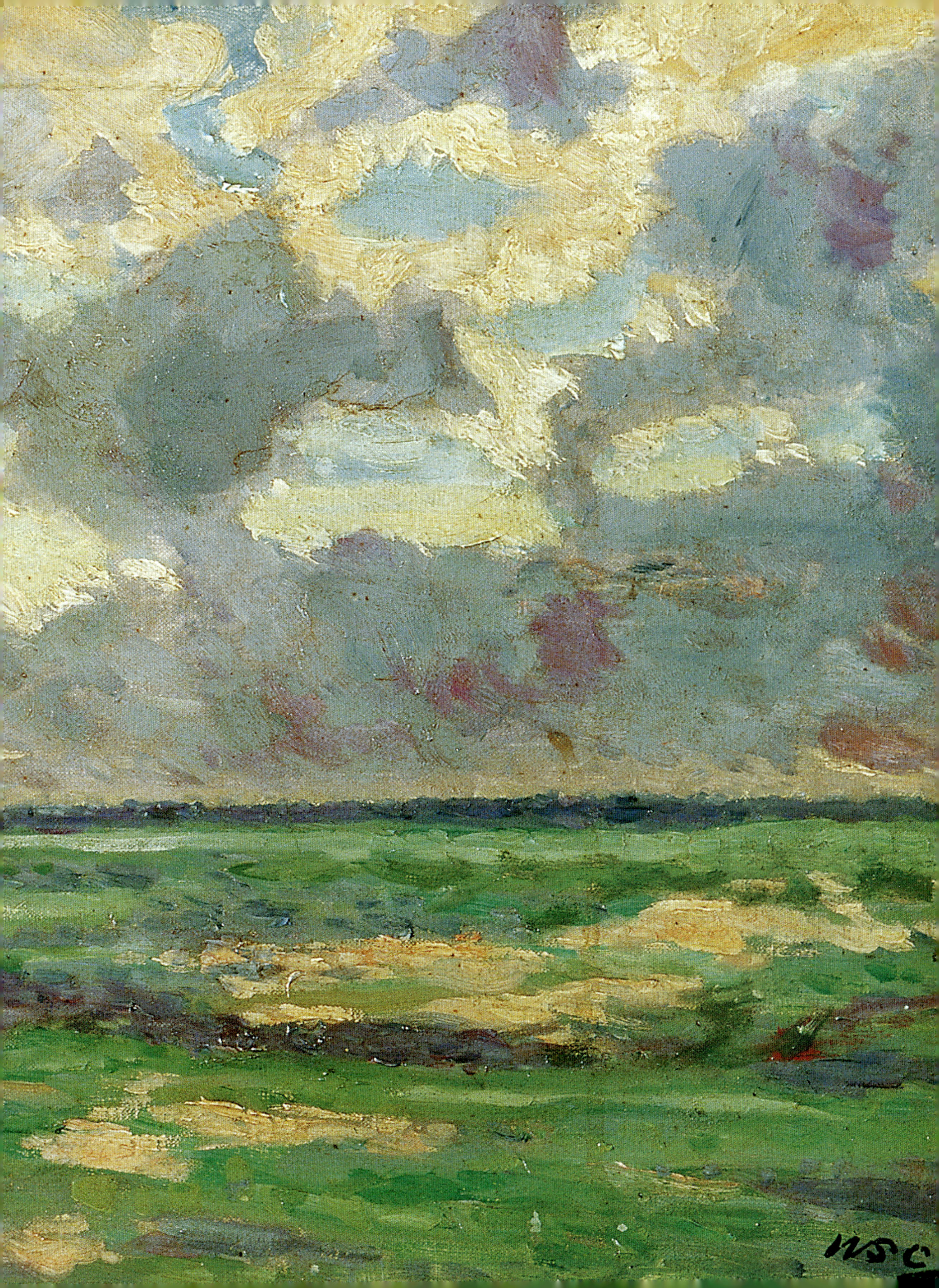

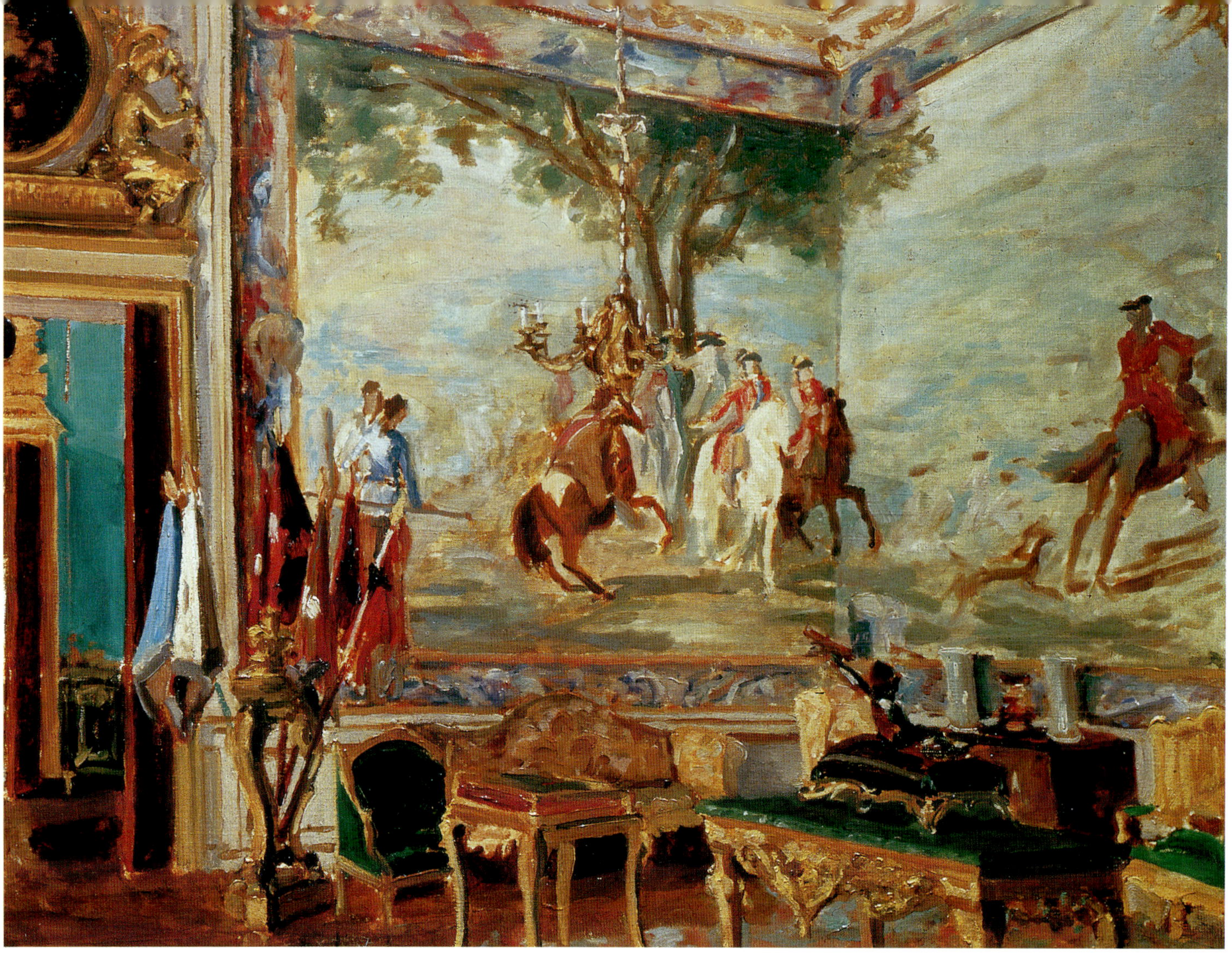

Fig 78 (C 11) above
Churchill gave this painting of the Marlborough tapestries at Blenheim to his youngest daughter, Mary. The tapestries commemorate the great military victory at Blenheim in 1704 of his ancestor the first Duke.

Winston was born at Blenheim Palace, the ancestral home of his family, built in the early 18th century. His grandfather was the 7th Duke of Marlborough; his father was Lord Randolph Spencer-Churchill, a successful politician and his mother, an American, Jennie Jerome. It was at Blenheim in 1908 that Winston proposed to Clementine who he had first met four years earlier.

Fig 79 (C 12) below
A State Room at Blenheim Palace.

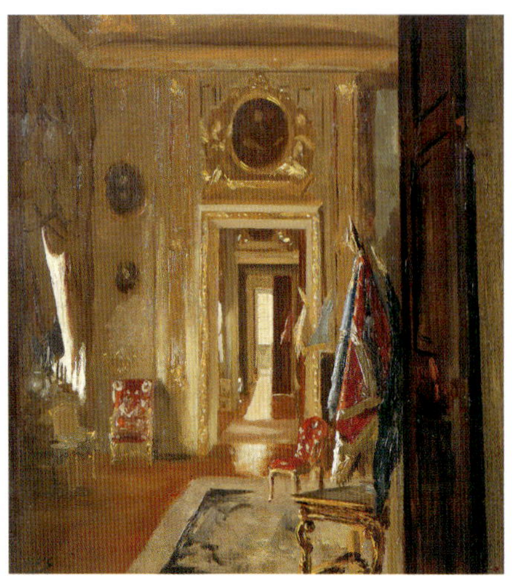

blue on an absolutely cowering canvas. Anyone could see that it could not hit back. No evil fate avenged the jaunty violence. The canvas grinned in helplessness before me. The spell was broken. The sickly inhibitions rolled away. I seized the largest brush and fell upon my victim with berserk fury.

I have never felt any awe of a canvas since.

Everyone knows the feeling with which one stands shivering on a spring-board, the shock when a friendly foe steals up behind and hurls you into the flood, and the ardent glow which thrills you as you emerge breathless from the plunge.

This beginning with Audacity, or being thrown into the middle of it, is already a very great part of the art of painting.

But there is more in it than that.

La peinture à l'huile
Est bien difficile,
Mais c'est beaucoup plus beau
Que la peinture à l'eau.

I write no word in disparagement of water-colours. But there really is nothing like oils. You have a medium at your disposal which offers real power, if you only can find out how to use it. Moreover, it is easier to get a certain distance along the road by its means than by water-colour. First of all, you can correct mistakes much more easily. One sweep of the palette-knife 'lifts' the blood and tears of a morning from the canvas and enables a fresh start to be made. [Indeed the canvas is all the better for past impressions.] Secondly, you can approach your

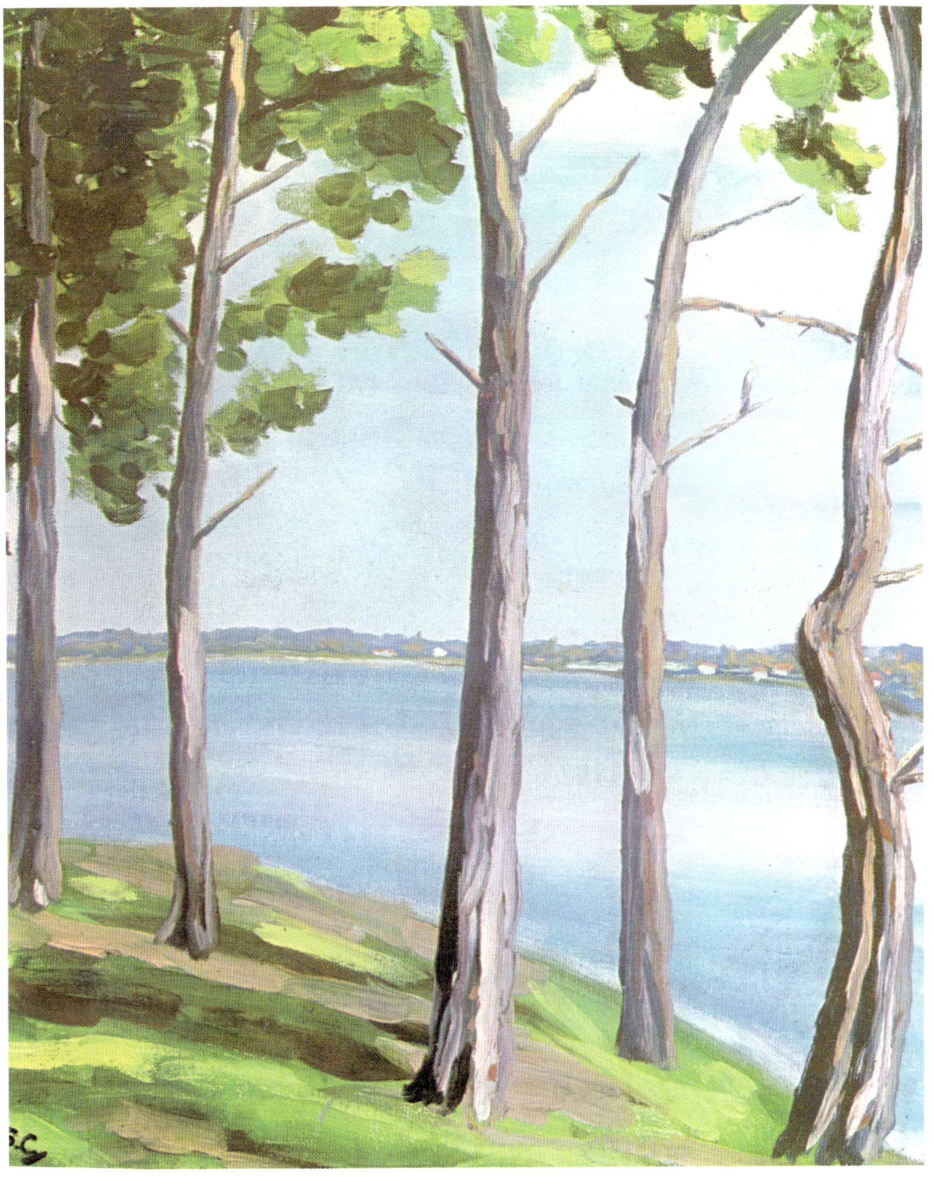

Fig 80 (C 71) left
This painting of Mimizan formerly belonged to Clementine Churchill.

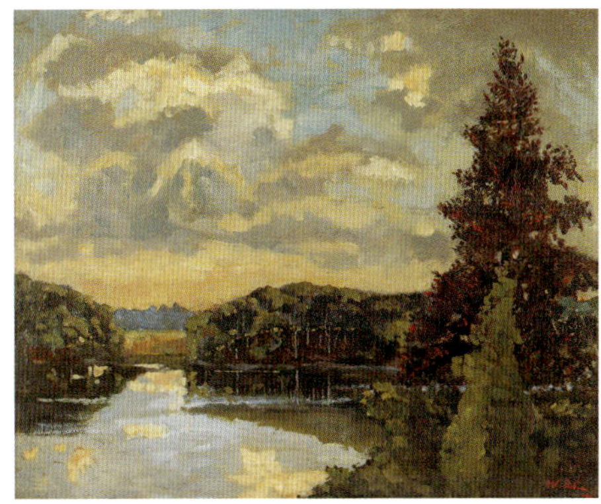

Fig 81 (C 59) above
Cannon Point, Blenheim Lake. Given by Churchill to the Duke of Marlborough.

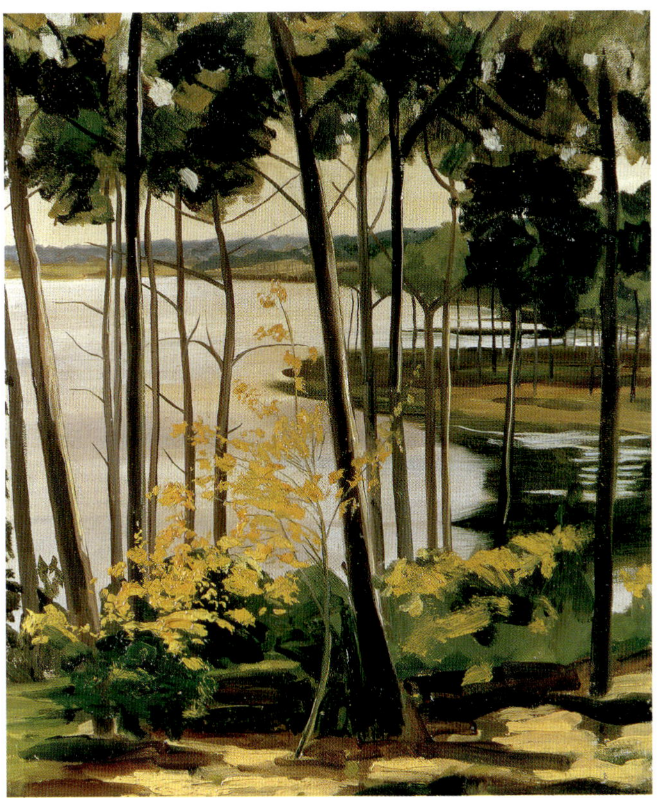

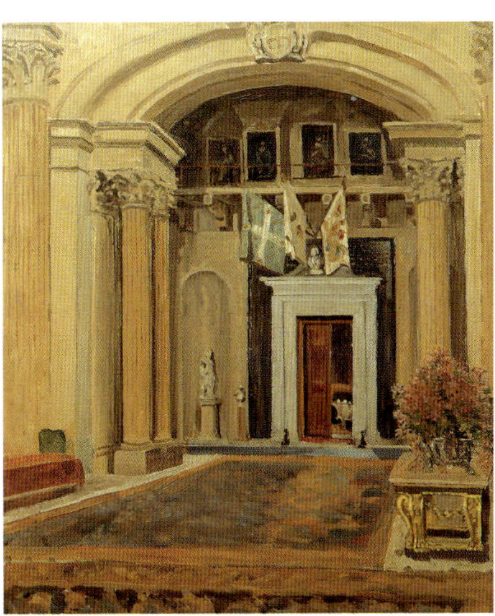

Fig 82 (C 13) above
The Great Hall at Blenheim Palace.

Fig 83 (C 72) left
Mimizan Lake. This painting was given by Lady Churchill to the Government Whips' Office after Sir Winston's death.

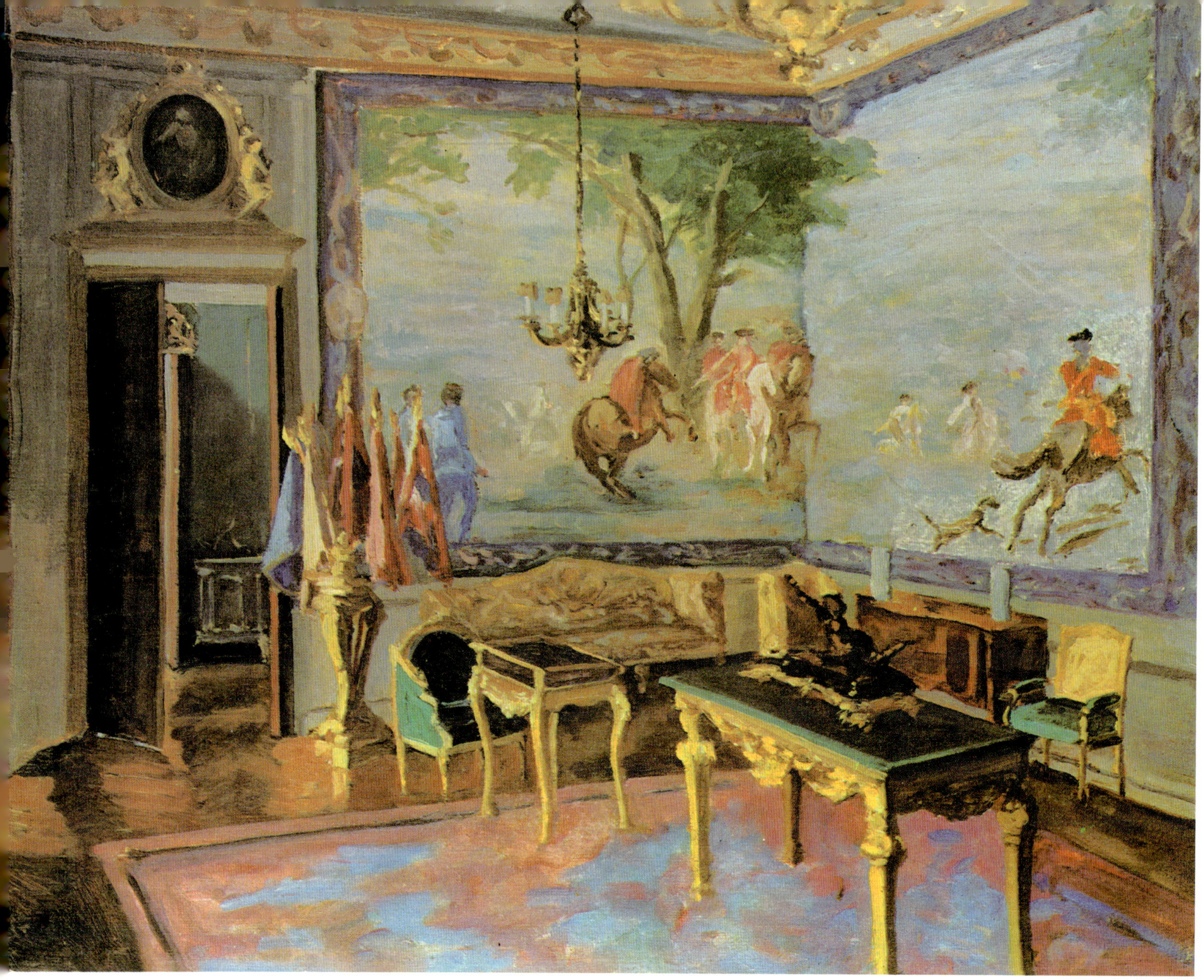

Fig 84 (C 14) above
The Marlborough Tapestries at Blenheim, given by Churchill to his son, Randolph.

problem from any direction. You need not build downwards awkwardly from white paper to your darkest dark. You may strike where you please, beginning if you will with a moderate central arrangement of middle tones, and then hurling in the extremes when the psychological moment comes. Lastly, the pigment itself is such nice stuff to handle (if it does not retaliate). You can build it on layer after layer if you like. You can keep on experimenting. You can change your plan to meet the exigencies of time or weather. And always remember you can scrape it all away.

Fig 85 (C 61) below
A view of the Boathouse on Blenheim Lake, given by Churchill to the Duke of Marlborough.

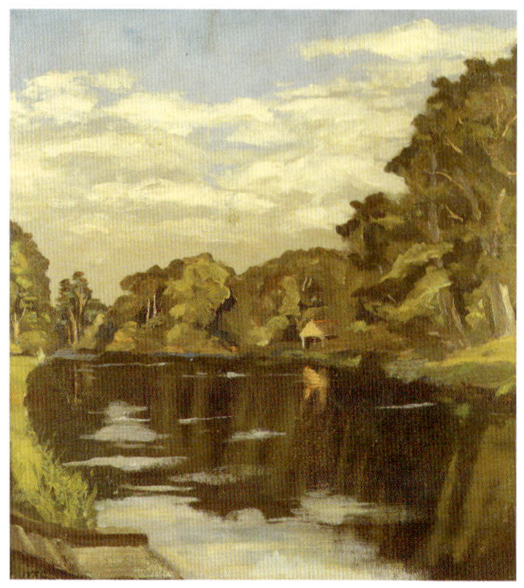

Just to paint is great fun. The colours are lovely to look at and delicious to squeeze out. Matching them, however crudely, with what you see is fascinating and absolutely absorbing. Try it if you have not done so - before you die. As one slowly begins to escape from the difficulties of choosing the right colours and laying them on in the right places and in the right way, wider considerations come into view. One begins to see, for instance, that painting a picture is like fighting a battle; and trying to paint a picture is, I suppose, like trying to fight a battle. It is, if anything, more exciting than fighting it successfully. But the principle is the same. It is the same kind of problem as unfolding a long, sustained, interlocked argument. It is a proposition which, whether of few or numberless parts, is commanded by a single unity of conception. And we think - though I cannot tell - that painting a great picture must require an intellect on the grand scale. There must be that all-embracing view which presents the

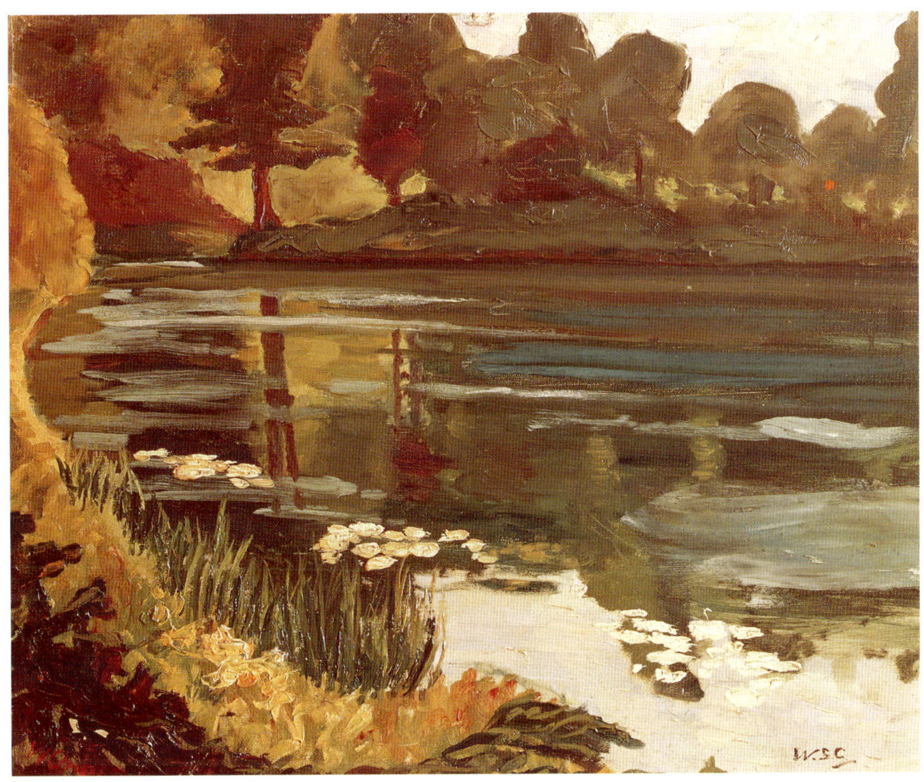

Fig 86 (C 64) left
The Lake at Blenheim, given by Churchill to Field Marshal Viscount Montgomery of Alamein. Uniquely, this painting is both signed in full and initialled.

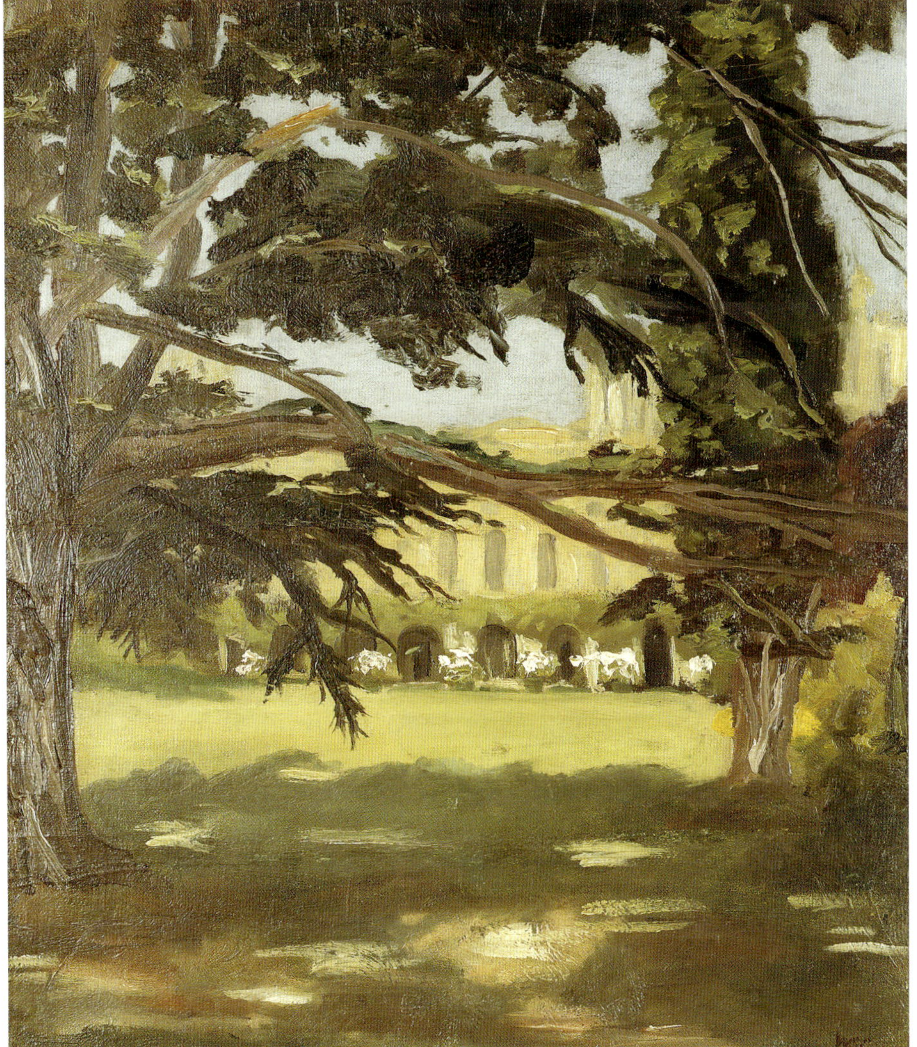

Fig 87 (C 269) left
The West Front of Blenheim Palace seen through the branches of a cedar tree. This was painted in the early 1920s before the building of the Water Terrace.

Fig 88 (C 60) below
Wooded water near Blenheim, given by Churchill to Sir Anthony Montague Browne, who was his Private Secretary during his last period as Prime Minister, and remained in that position until Churchill's death.

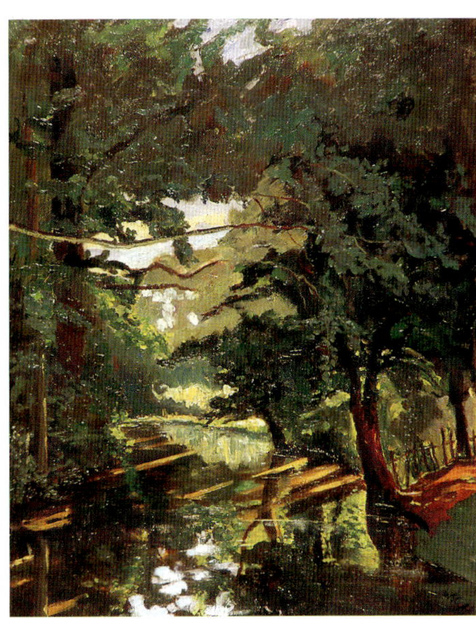

Fig 89 (C 246) right
The gardener's cottage at Mme Balsan's house, given by Churchill to Madeleine Whyte, a cousin of Clementine's and a bridesmaid at their wedding in 1908.

In 1895 Consuelo Vanderbilt, an American heiress, was forced into a loveless marriage with Churchill's cousin the 9th Duke of Marlborough. She left him a decade later and after her divorce in 1920, married a French air force officer, Jacques Balsan. They bought a property near the medieval fortified hilltop village of Eze, overlooking St-Jean-Cap-Ferrat to the west of Monaco, where they built a house, 'Lou Sueil'. Here Winston and Clementine Churchill were frequent guests.

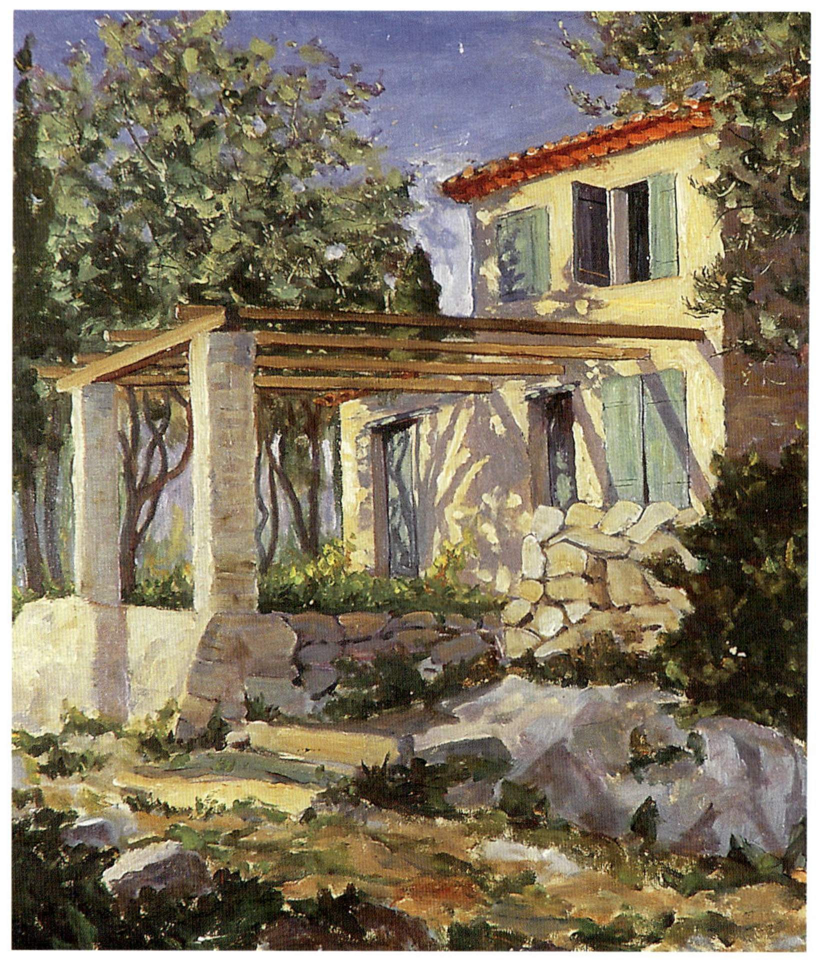

Fig 90 (C 203) below
A view of Eze in the Alpes-Maritimes.

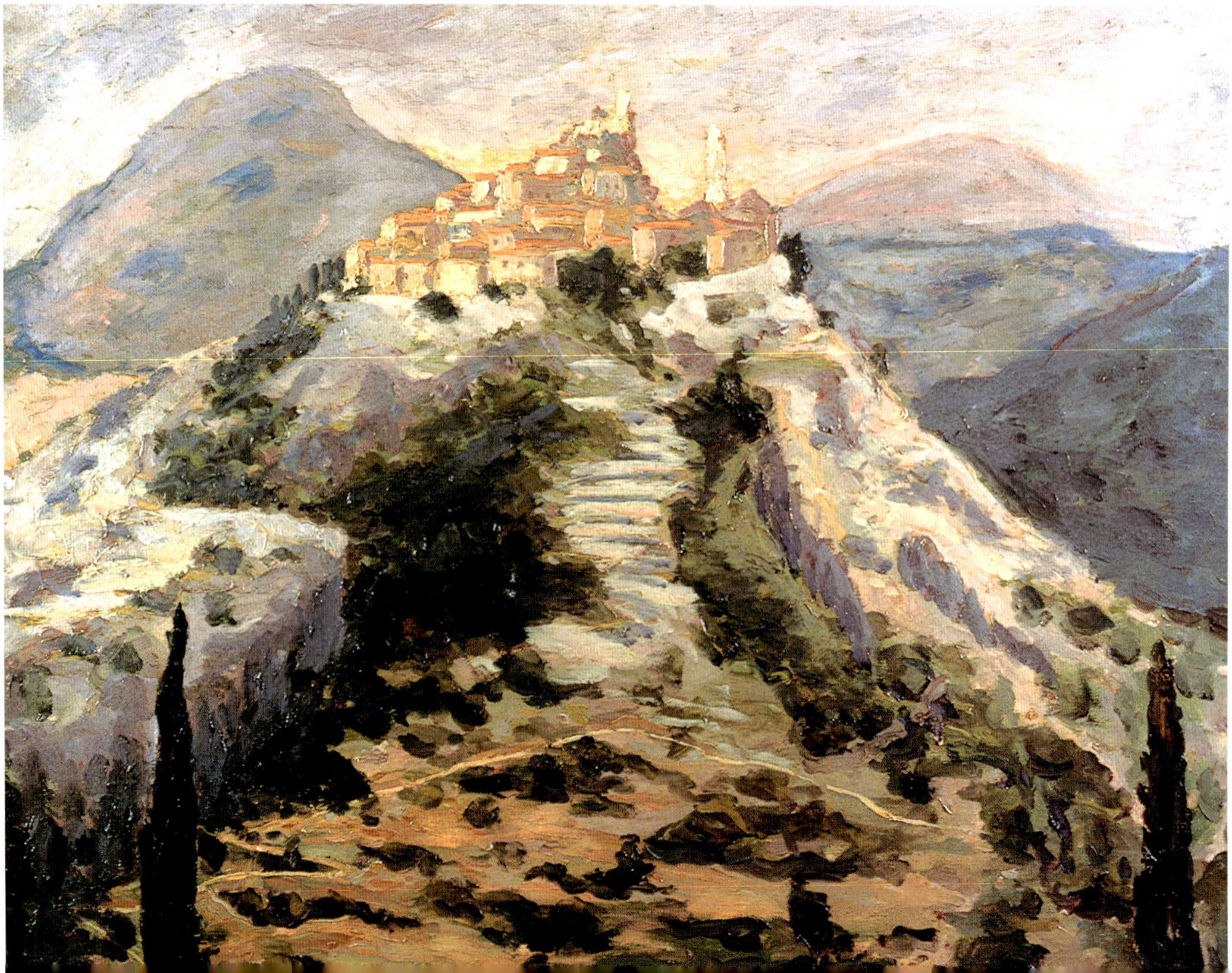

beginning and the end, the whole and each part, as one instantaneous impression retentively and untiringly held in mind. When we look at the larger Turners - canvases yards wide and tall - and observe that they are all done in one piece and represent one single second of time, and that every innumerable detail, however small, however distant, however subordinate, is set forth naturally and in its true proportion and relation, without effort, without failure, we must feel in the presence of an intellectual manifestation the equal in quality and intensity of the finest achievements of warlike action, of forensic argument, or of scientific or philosophical adjudication.(4)

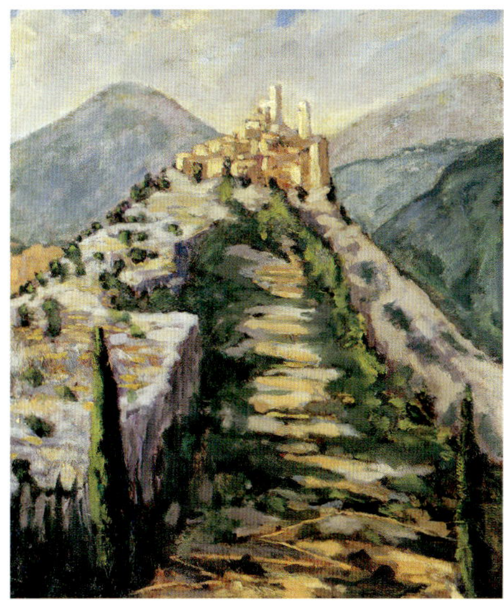

Fig 91 (C 204) above
A view of the fortified village of Eze.

In all battles two things are usually required of the Commander-in-Chief [firstly,] to make a good plan for his army and, secondly, to keep a strong reserve.(5) Both these are also obligatory upon the painter. To make a plan, thorough reconnaissance of the country where the battle is to be fought is needed. Its fields, its mountains, its rivers, its bridges, its trees, its flowers, its atmosphere - all require and repay attentive observation from a special point of view. One is quite astonished to find how many things there are in the landscape, and in every object in it, one never noticed before. And this is a tremendous new pleasure and interest which invests every walk or drive with an added object. So many colours on the hill-side, each different in shadow and in sunlight; such brilliant reflections in the pool, each a key lower than what they repeat; such lovely lights gilding or silvering surface or outline, all tinted exquisitely with pale colour, rose, orange, green or violet. [I found myself instinctively as I walked noting the tint and character of a leaf, the dreamy, purple shades of mountains, the exquisite lacery of winter branches, the dim, pale silhouettes of far horizons.] And I had lived for over forty years without ever noticing any of them except in general way, as one might look at a crowd and say, 'What a lot of people!'

Fig 92 (C 209) below
A distant view of Eze.

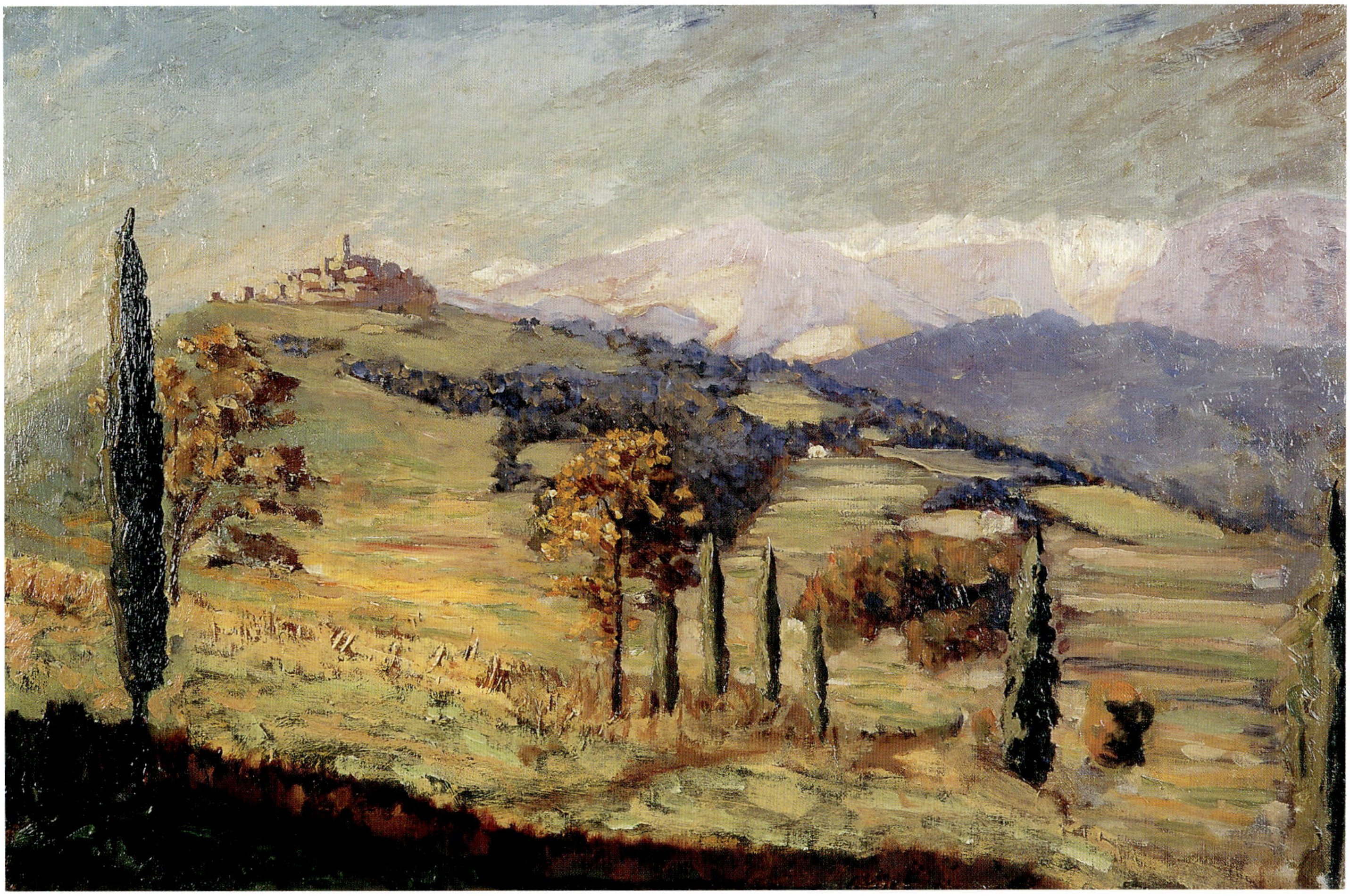

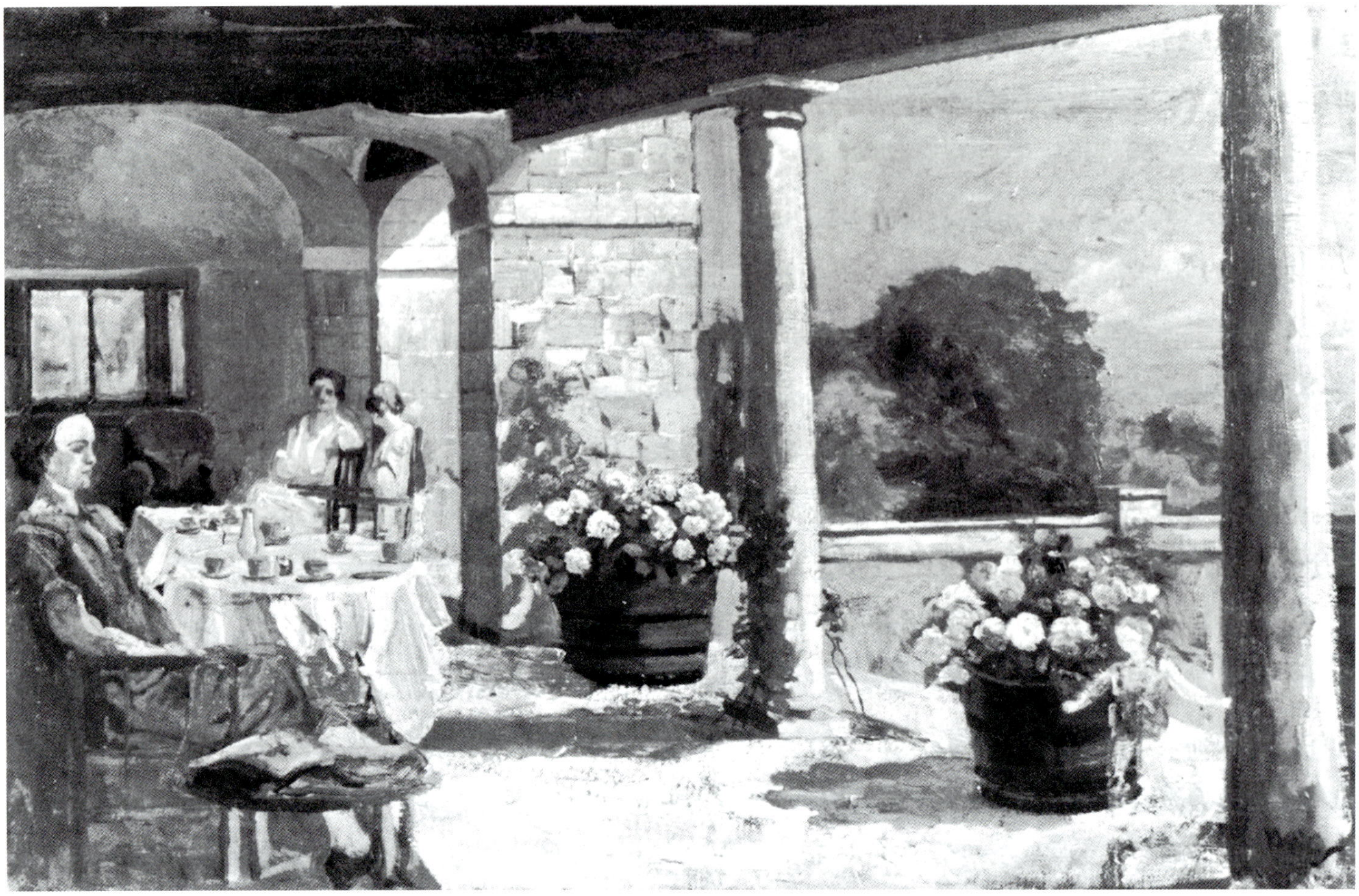

Fig 93 (C 42) above
Teatime in the Loggia at Chartwell. The principal figure on the left is Marryott Whyte, a cousin of Clementine Churchill who is shown in the background with her eldest daughter Diana. Nana Whyte was a trained children's nurse who in 1921 came to look after the family - especially the youngest daughter, Mary, shown beside the pillar on the right. Despite many efforts Churchill was never successful at painting figures.

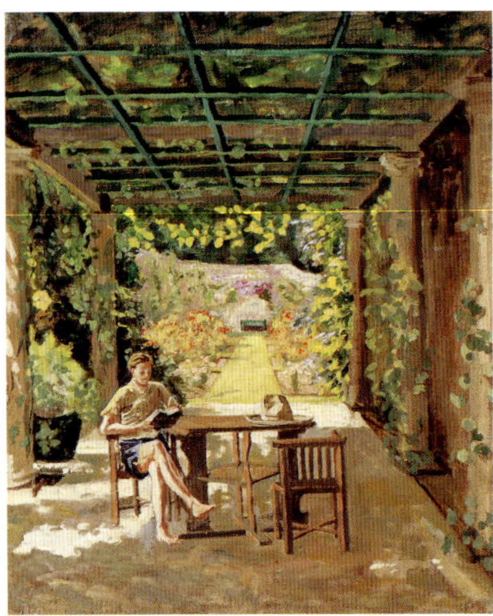

Fig 94 (C 46) above
Randolph Churchill, Winston's son, reading under the Pergola at Chartwell.

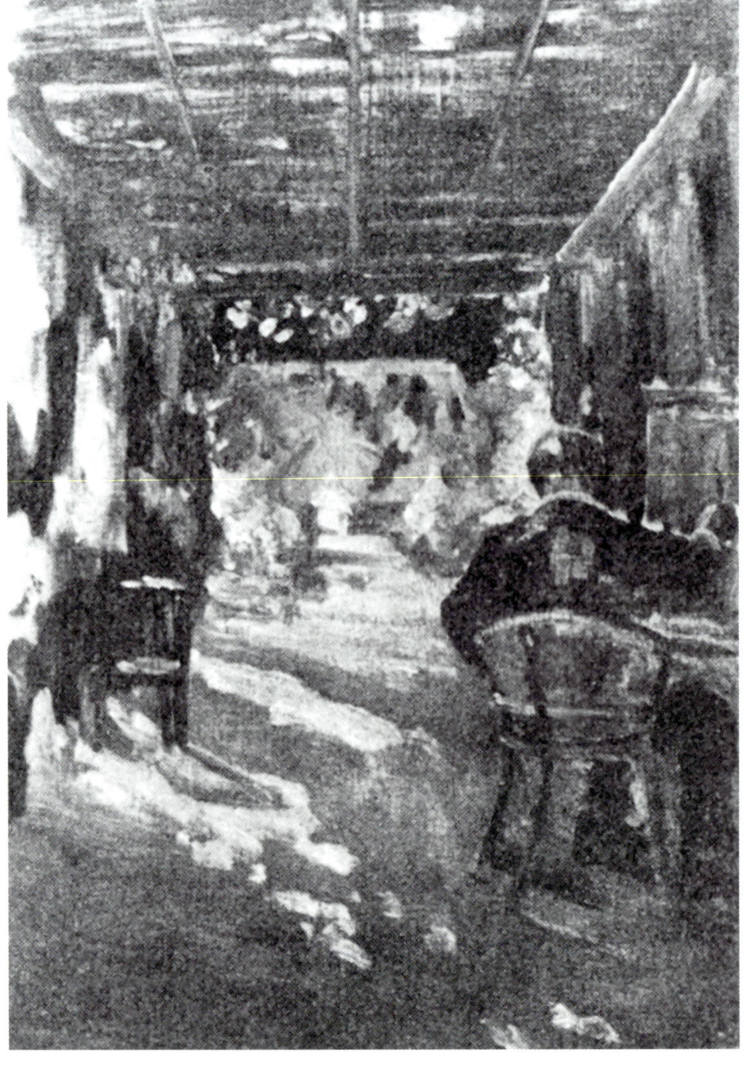

Fig 95 (C 43) right
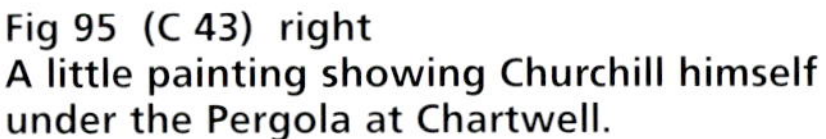
A little painting showing Churchill himself under the Pergola at Chartwell.

I think this heightened sense of observation of Nature is one of the chief delights that have come to me through trying to paint. No doubt many people who are lovers of art have acquired it in a high degree without actually practising. But I expect that nothing will make one observe more quickly or more thoroughly than having to face the difficulty of representing the thing observed. And mind you, if you do observe accurately and with refinement, and if you do record what you have seen with tolerable correspondence, the result follows on the canvas with startling obedience. Even if only four or five main features are seized and truly recorded, these by themselves will carry a lot of ill-success or half-success. Answer five big questions out of all the hundreds in the examination paper correctly and well, and though you may not win a prize, at any rate you will not be absolutely ploughed.

Fig 96 (C 150) above
View of the Loggia at Chartwell in the snow of 1924.

Later this became known as the Marlborough Pavilion after Winston's nephew John Spencer Churchill decorated it with murals.

But in order to make this plan, the General must not only reconnoitre the battle-ground, he must also study the achievements of the great Captains of the past. He must bring the observations he has collected in the field into comparison with the treatment of similar incidents by famous chiefs. Then the galleries of Europe take on a new - and to me at least a severely practical - interest. 'This, then, is how --- painted a cataract. Exactly, and there is that same light I noticed last week in the waterfall at --- .' And so on. You see the difficulty that baffled you yesterday; and you see how easily it has been overcome by a great or even by a skilful painter. Not only is your observation of Nature sensibly improved and developed, but you look at the masterpieces of art with an analysing and comprehending eye.

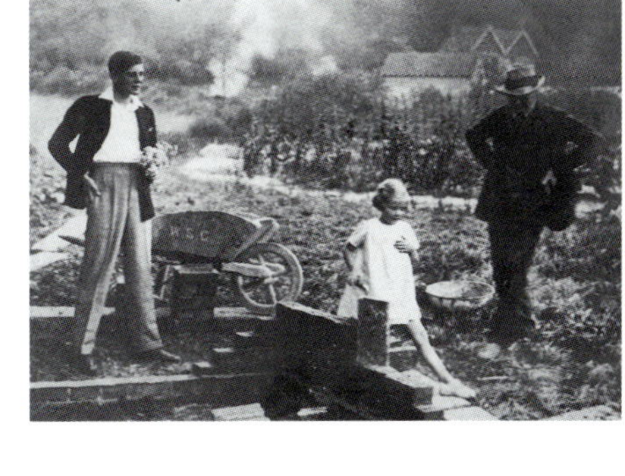

The whole world is open with all its treasures. The simplest objects have their beauty. Every garden presents innumerable fascinating problems. Every land, every parish, has its own tale to tell. And there are many lands differing from each other in countless ways, and each presenting delicious variants of colour, light, form and definition. Obviously, then, armed with a paint-box, one cannot be bored, one cannot be left at a loose end, one cannot 'have several days on one's hands'. Good gracious! what there is to admire and how little time there is to see it in! For the first time one begins to envy Methuselah. No doubt he made a very indifferent use of his opportunities.

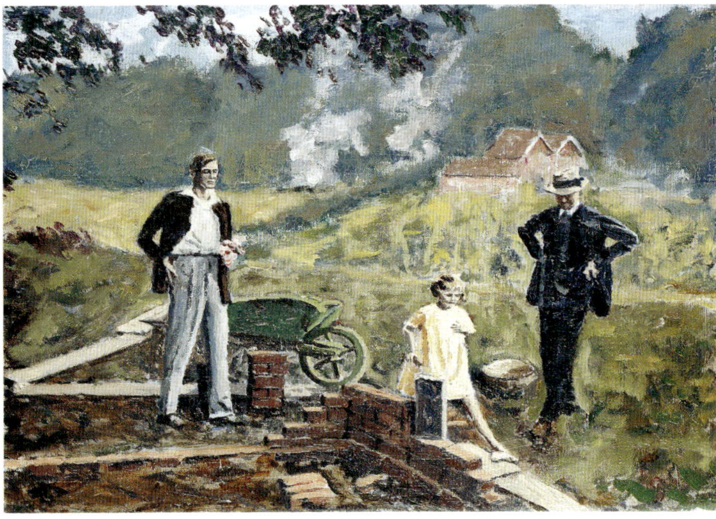

Fig 97 (C 47) above
Mary's First Speech. Attended by her brother Randolph carrying a little bouquet of flowers and Winston himself, his youngest daughter Mary lays the foundation stone for a little brick summer house Churchill built for her. This painting is based on a photograph (detail above) from the Studio archives at Chartwell.

But it is in the use and withholding of their reserves that the great commanders have generally excelled. After all, when once the last reserve has been thrown in, the commander's part is played. If that does not win the battle, he has nothing else to give. The event must be left to luck and to the fighting troops. But these last, in the absence of high direction, are apt to get into sad confusion, all mixed together in a nasty mess, without order or plan - and consequently without effect. Mere masses count no more. The largest brush, the brightest colours, cannot even make an impression. The pictorial battlefield becomes a sea of mud mercifully veiled by the fog of war. It is evident there has

Fig 98 (C 142) right
'Winter Sunshine, Chartwell.' A famous little picture by Churchill that in 1925 was entered anonymously in a London exhibition open to amateur painters and won first prize; and in 1947, when entered under a pseudonym, it gained Churchill his first entry at the Royal Academy's Summer Exhibition.

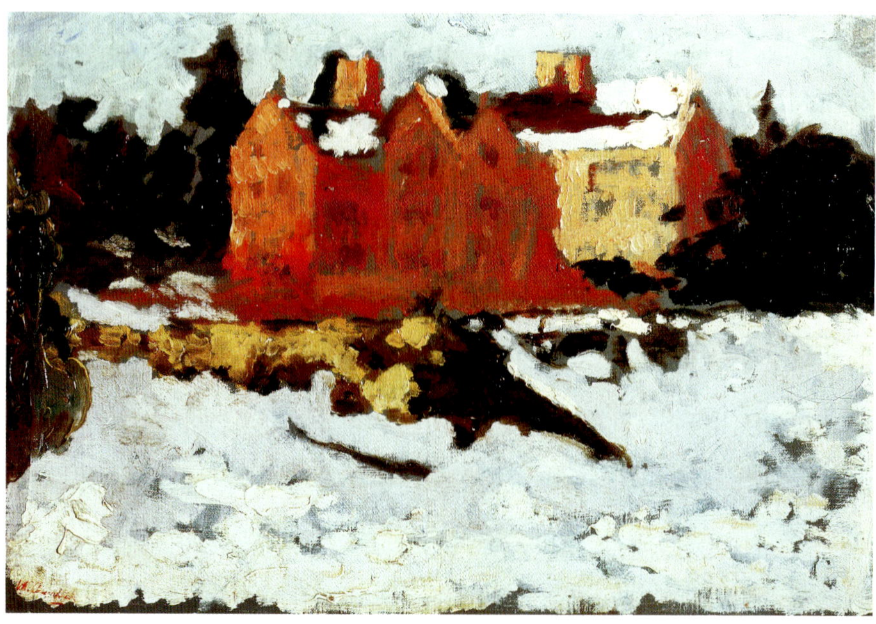

Fig 99 (C 123) below
A little painting of the Water Garden at Chartwell - one of Churchill's additions to the landscape.

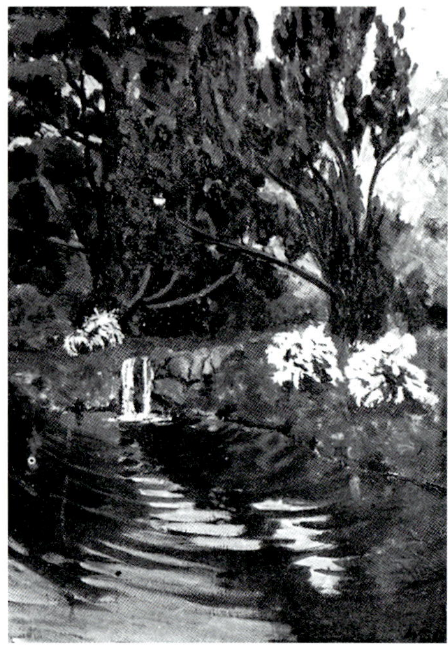

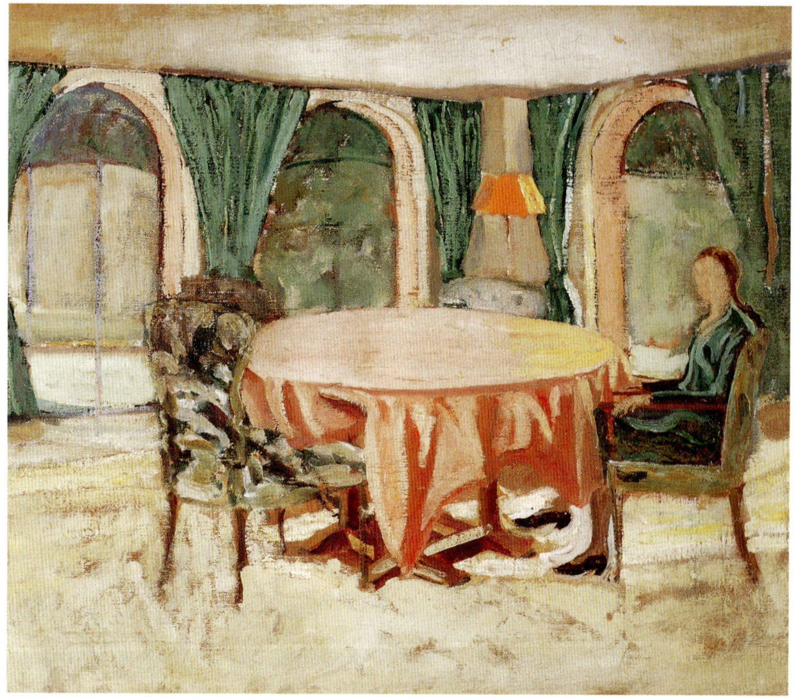

Fig 100 (C 157) centre right
The Churchill's eldest daughter, Diana, in the Dining Room at Chartwell.

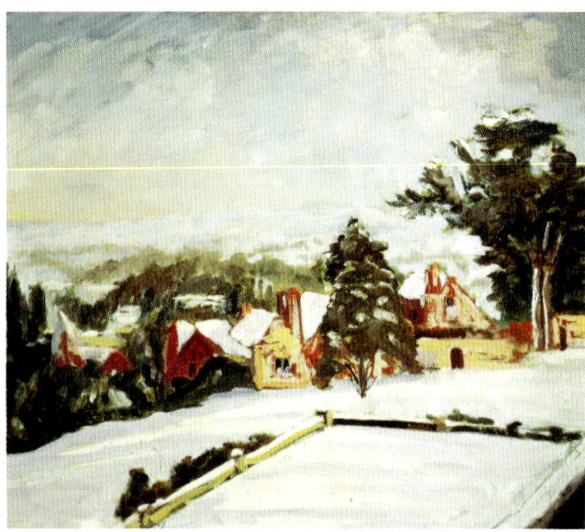

Fig 101 (C 287) above
A winter view of Chartwell showing Churchill's Studio in the centre foreground.

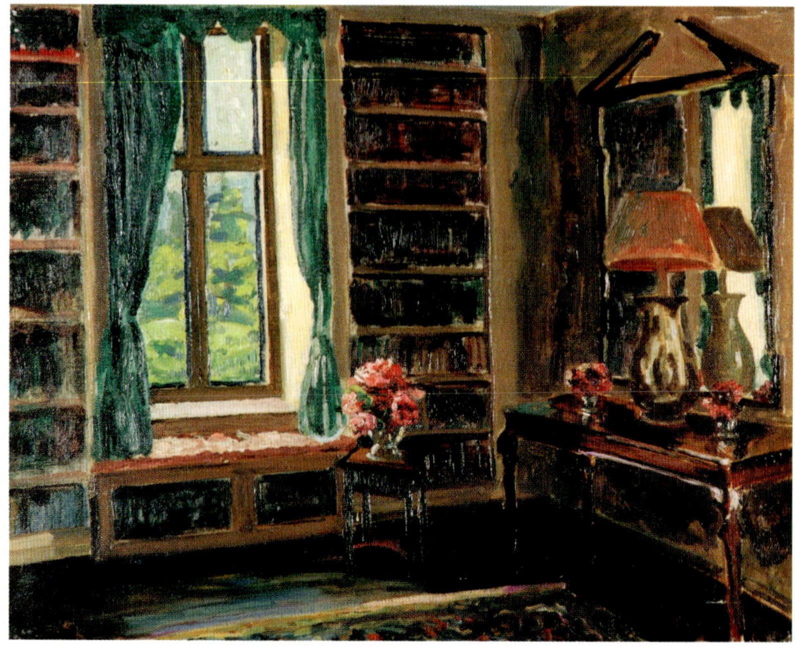

Fig 102 (C 184) right
A shady corner of the Drawing Room at Chartwell.

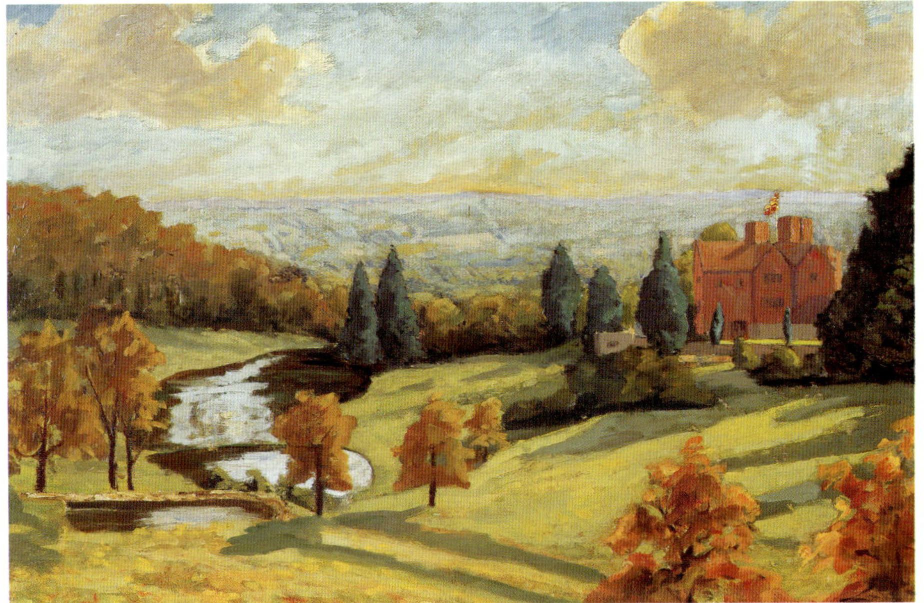

Fig 103 (C 286) left
View of Chartwell and its lakes showing the view in the background of the Kentish Weald that so attracted Churchill to purchase the house.

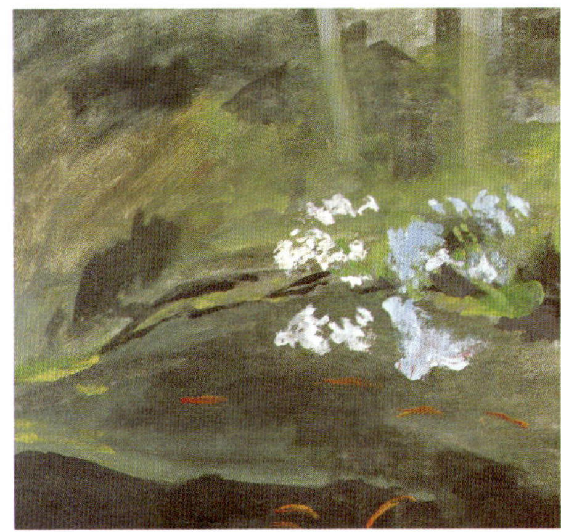

Fig 104 (C 348) above
Unfinished painting of the Goldfish Pool at Chartwell.

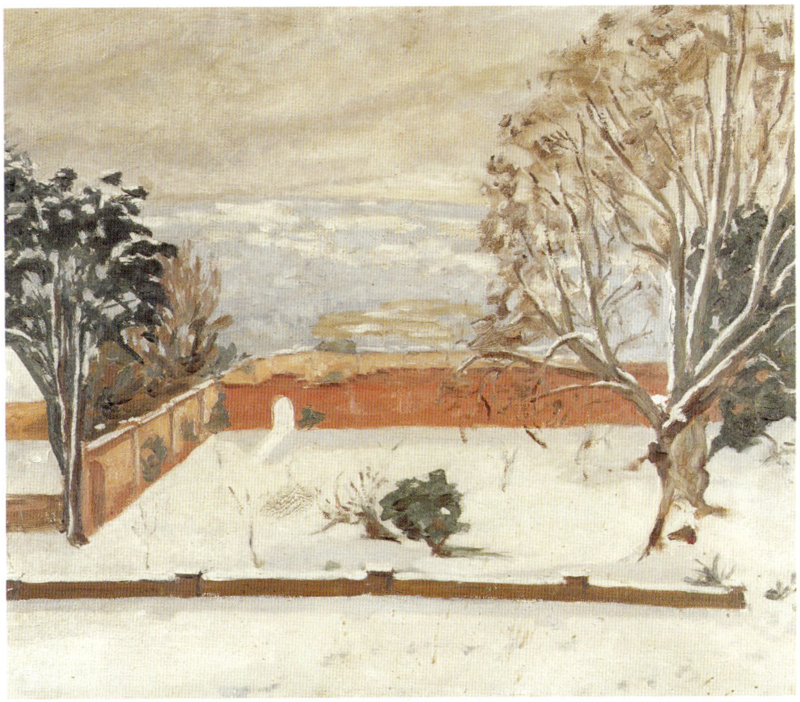

Fig 105 (C 284) left
A view of the Weald of Kent under snow, showing the garden walls at Chartwell built by Churchill himself. Winston gave this painting to his youngest daughter, Mary, in 1937.

Fig 106 (C 375) below
The Swimming Pool at Chartwell, one of Churchill's additions to the landscape. An almost identical view by the artist Sir William Nicholson was presumably painted at the same time; both hang in the Studio at Chartwell.

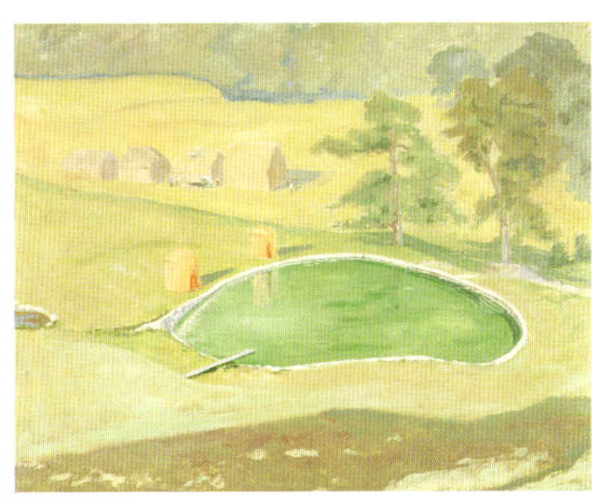

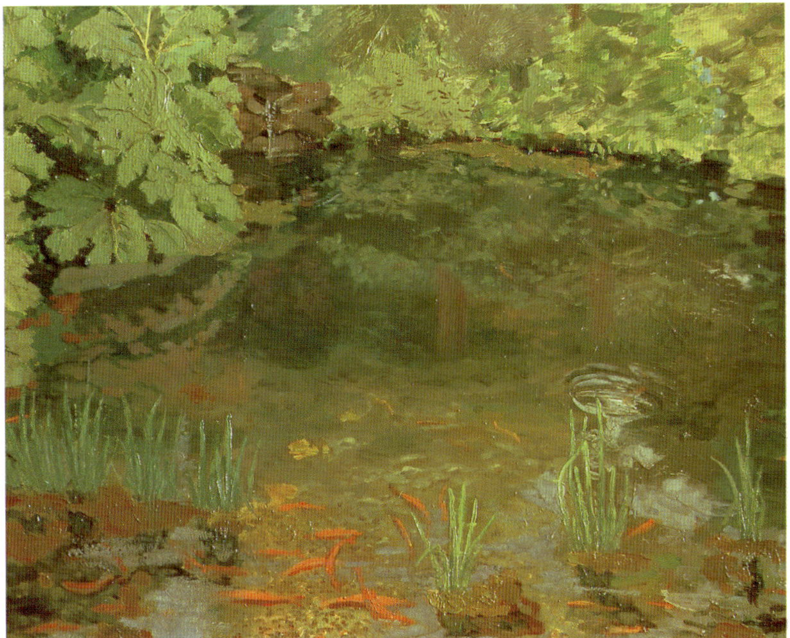

Fig 107 (C 344) left
The Goldfish Pool. This is one of the series of Water Gardens near the house at Chartwell that Churchill created, where he especially enjoyed feeding the Golden Orfe, whose descendants still swim there.

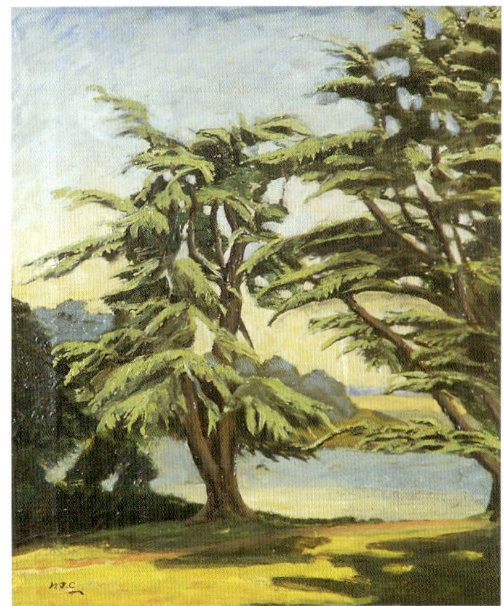

Fig 108 (C 266) above
Lakeland scene near Breccles.

Breccles was the home in Norfolk of Clementine's cousin, Venetia. The house was extended by the architect Edwin Lutyens for Venetia and her husband Edwin Montagu. Both Winston and Clementine were regular visitors.

been a serious defeat. Even though the General plunges in himself and emerges bespattered, as he sometimes does, he will not retrieve the day.

In painting, the reserves consist in Proportion or Relation. And it is here that the art of the painter marches along the road which is traversed by all the greatest harmonies in thought. At one side of the palette there is white, at the other black; and neither is ever used 'neat'. Between these two rigid limits all the action must lie, all the power required must be generated. Black and white themselves, placed in juxtaposition, make no great impression; and yet they are the most that you can do in pure contrast. It is wonderful - after one has tried and failed often - to see how easily and surely the true artist is able to produce every effect of light and shade, of sunshine and shadow, of distance or nearness, simply by expressing justly the relations between the different planes and surfaces with which he is dealing. We think that this is founded upon a sense of proportion, trained no doubt by practice, but which in its essence is a frigid manifestation of mental power and size. We think that the same mind's eye that can justly survey and appraise and prescribe beforehand the values of a truly great picture in one all-embracing regard, in one flash of simultaneous and homogeneous comprehension, would also with a certain acquaintance with the special technique be able to pronounce with sureness upon any other high activity of the human intellect. This was certainly true of the great Italians.

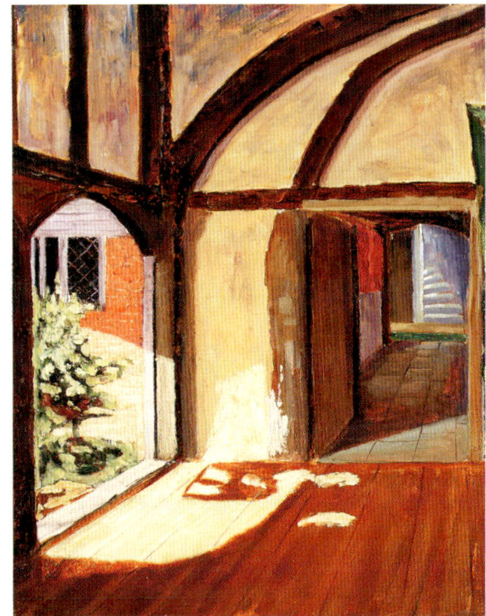

Fig 109 (C 187) above
Interior at Breccles.

Fig 110 (C 260) opposite page above
Trees near Breccles.

Fig 111 (C 57) right
Winter woodland at Breccles. Given by Churchill to Dame Pattie Menzies, wife of Sir Robert Menzies, Prime Minister of Australia.

Fig 112 (C 54) opposite page below left
Garden scene at Breccles.

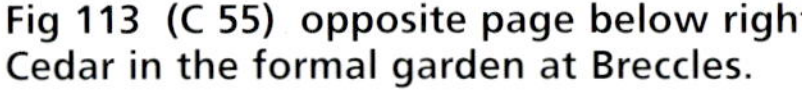

Fig 113 (C 55) opposite page below right
Cedar in the formal garden at Breccles.

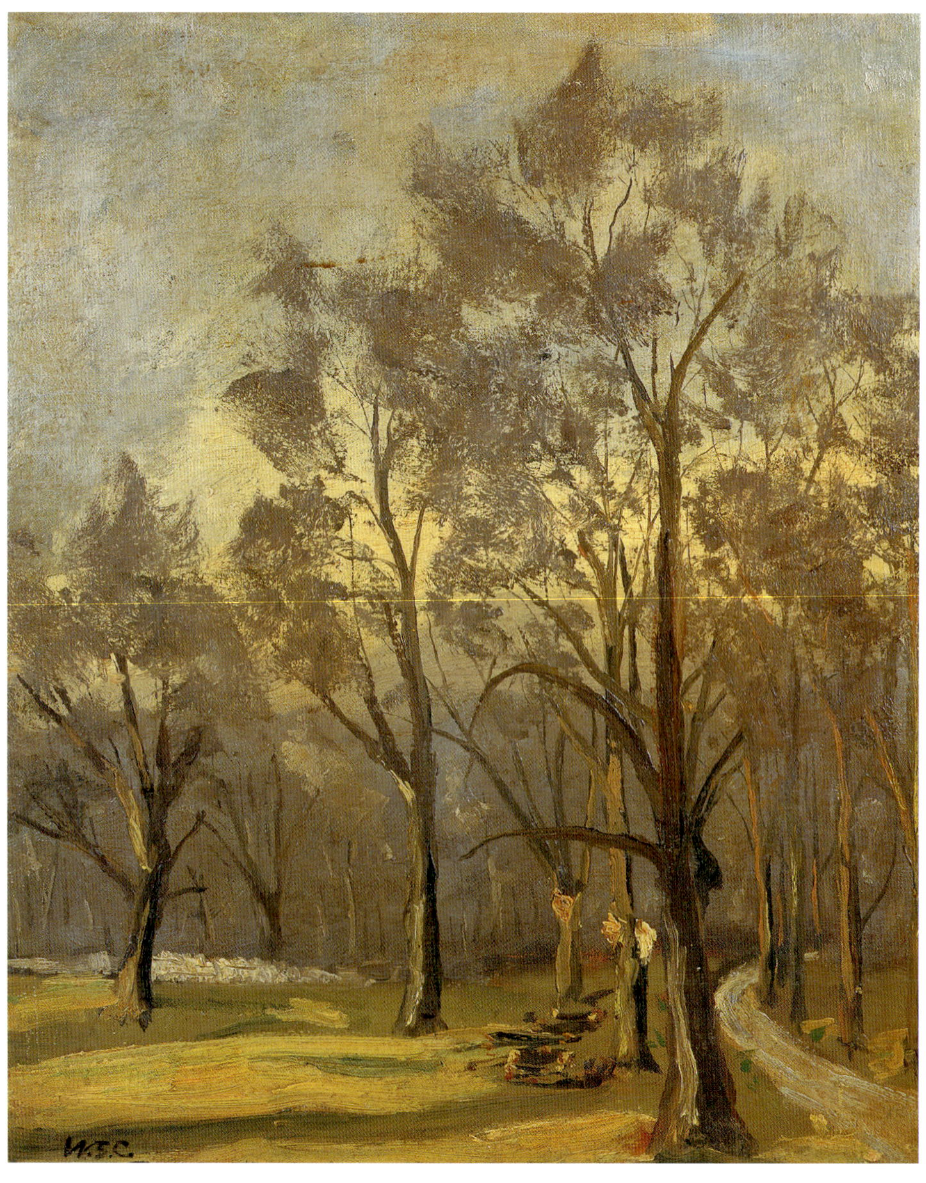

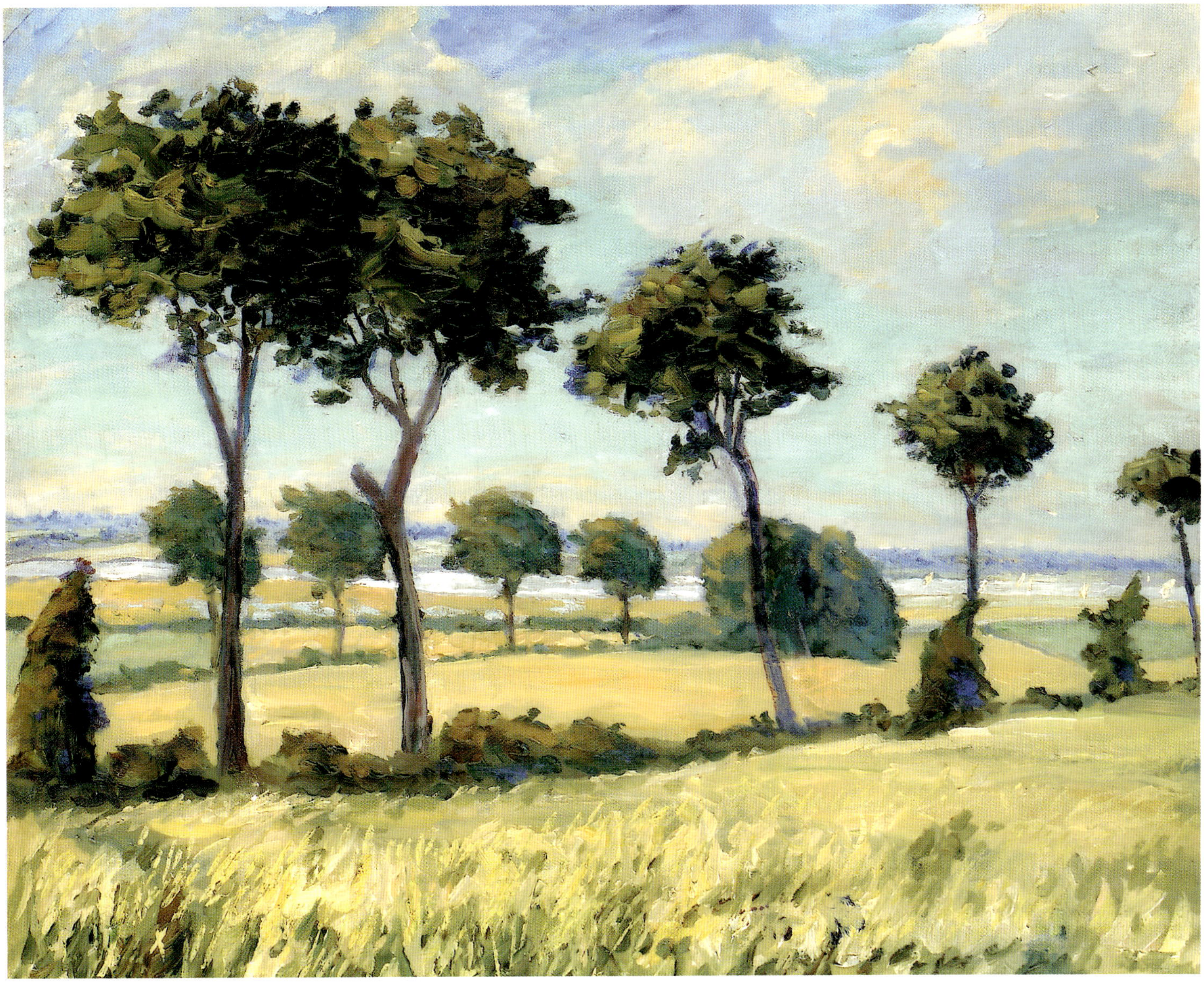

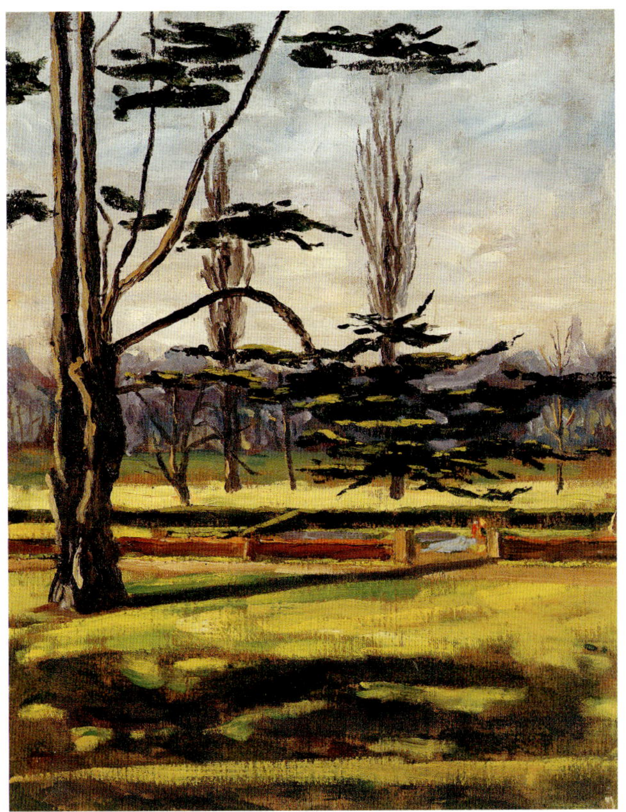

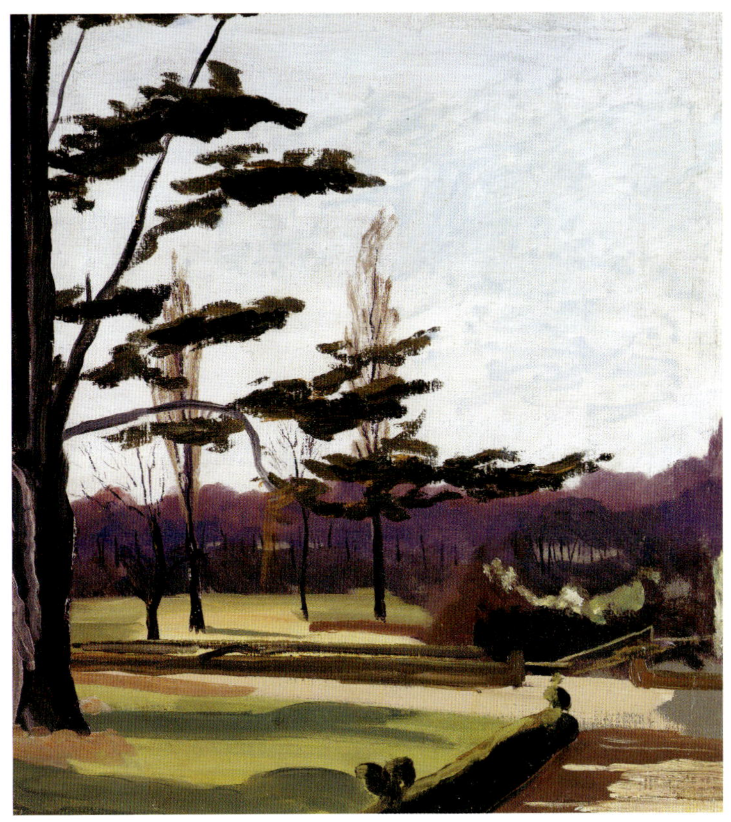

I have written in this way to show how varied are the delights which may be gained by those who enter hopefully and thoughtfully upon the pathway of painting; how enriched they will be in their daily vision, how fortified in their independence, how happy in their leisure. Whether you feel that your soul is pleased by the conception or contemplation of harmonies, or that your mind is stimulated by the aspect of magnificent problems, or whether you are content to find it fun to try to observe and depict the jolly things you see, the vistas of possibility are limited only by the shortness of life. Every day you may make progress. Every step may be fruitful. Yet there will stretch out before you an ever-lengthening, ever-ascending, ever-improving path. You know you will never get to the end of the journey. But this, so far from discouraging, only adds to the joy and glory of the climb.

Try it, then, before it is too late and before you mock at me. Try it while there is time to overcome the preliminary difficulties. Learn enough of the language in your prime to open this new literature to your age. Plant a garden in which you can sit when the digging days are done. It may be only a small garden, but you will see it grow. Year by year it will bloom and ripen. Year by year it will be better cultivated. The weeds will be cast out. The fruit-trees will be pruned and trained. The flowers will bloom in more beautiful combinations. There will be sunshine there even in the winter-time, and cool shade, and the play of shadow on the pathway in the shining days of June.

Fig 114 (C 372) below
Lake near Breccles in autumn.

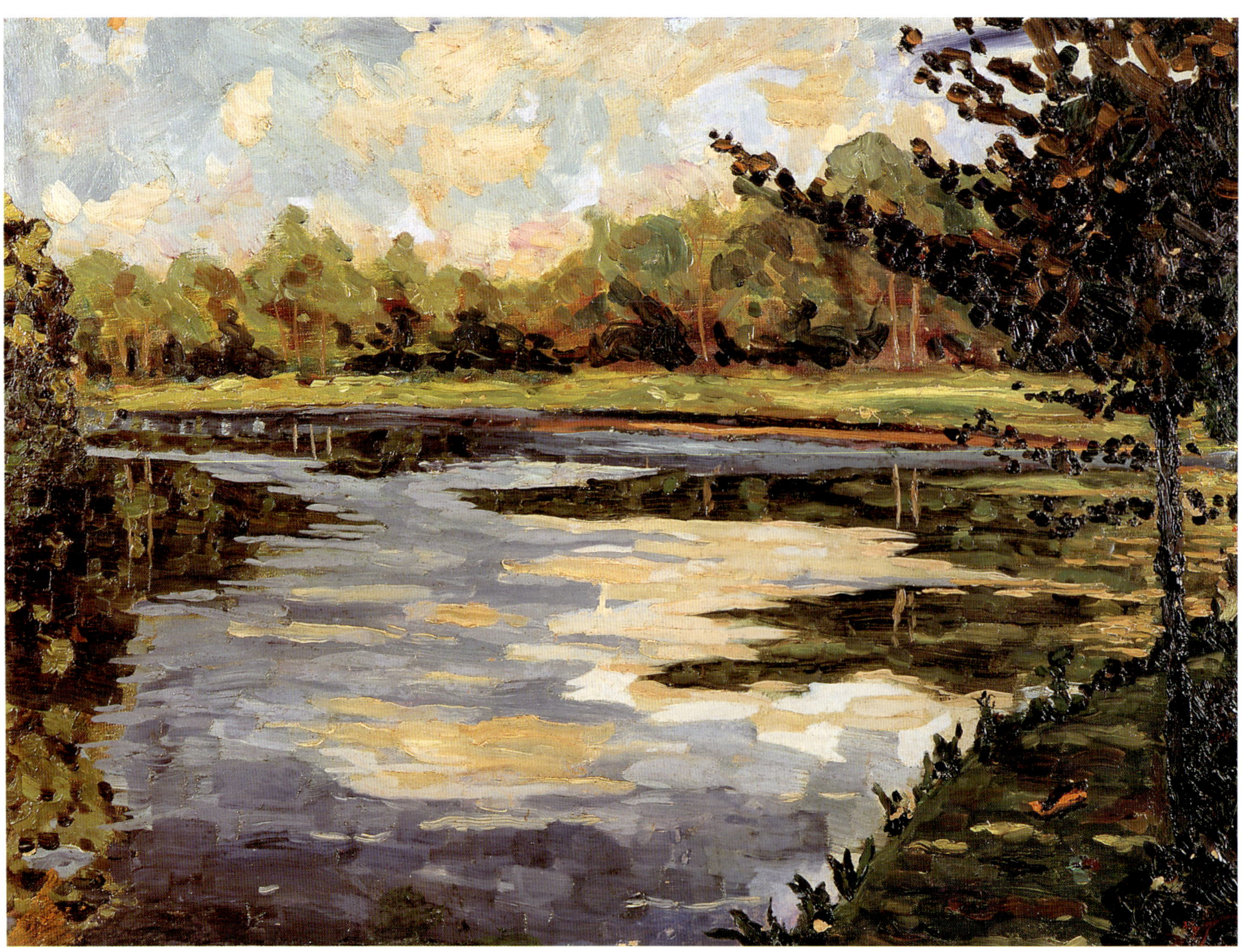

[Part 2]

I must say I like bright colours. I agree with Ruskin in his denunciation of that school of painting who 'eat slate-pencil and chalk, and assure everybody that they are nicer and purer than strawberries and plums'.(6) I cannot pretend to feel impartial about the colours. I rejoice with the brilliant ones, and am genuinely sorry for the poor browns. When I get to heaven I mean to spend a considerable portion of my first million years in painting, and so get to the bottom of the subject. But then I shall require a still gayer palette than I get here below. I expect orange and vermilion will be the darkest, dullest colours upon it, and beyond them there will be a whole range of wonderful new colours which will delight the celestial eye.

Chance led me one autumn to a secluded nook on the Côte d'Azur, between Marseilles and Toulon, and there I fell in with one or two painters who revelled in the methods of the modern French school.(7) These were disciples of Cézanne. They view Nature as a mass of shimmering light in which forms and surfaces are comparatively unimportant, indeed hardly visible, but which gleams and glows with beautiful harmonies and contrasts of colour. Certainly it was of great interest to me to come suddenly in contact with this entirely different way of looking at things. I had hitherto painted the sea flat, with long, smooth strokes of mixed pigment in which the tints varied only by gradations. Now I must try to represent it by innumerable small separate lozenge-shaped points and patches of colour -

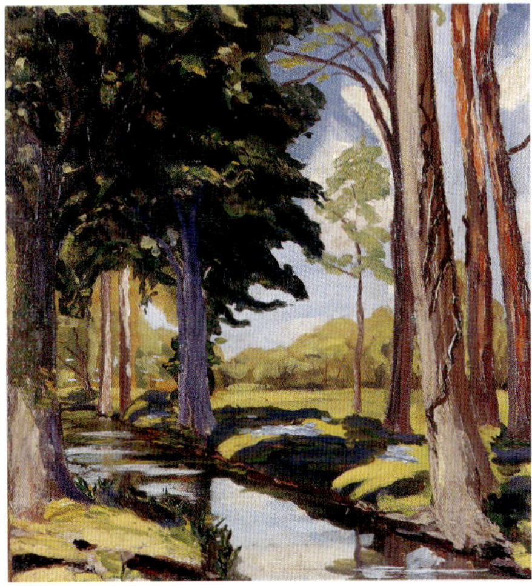

Fig 115 (C 359) above
The Moat at Breccles. This painting is almost identical to one, now missing, of the same subject published in The Strand Magazine, December 1921.

Fig 116 (C 373) below
Near Breccles.

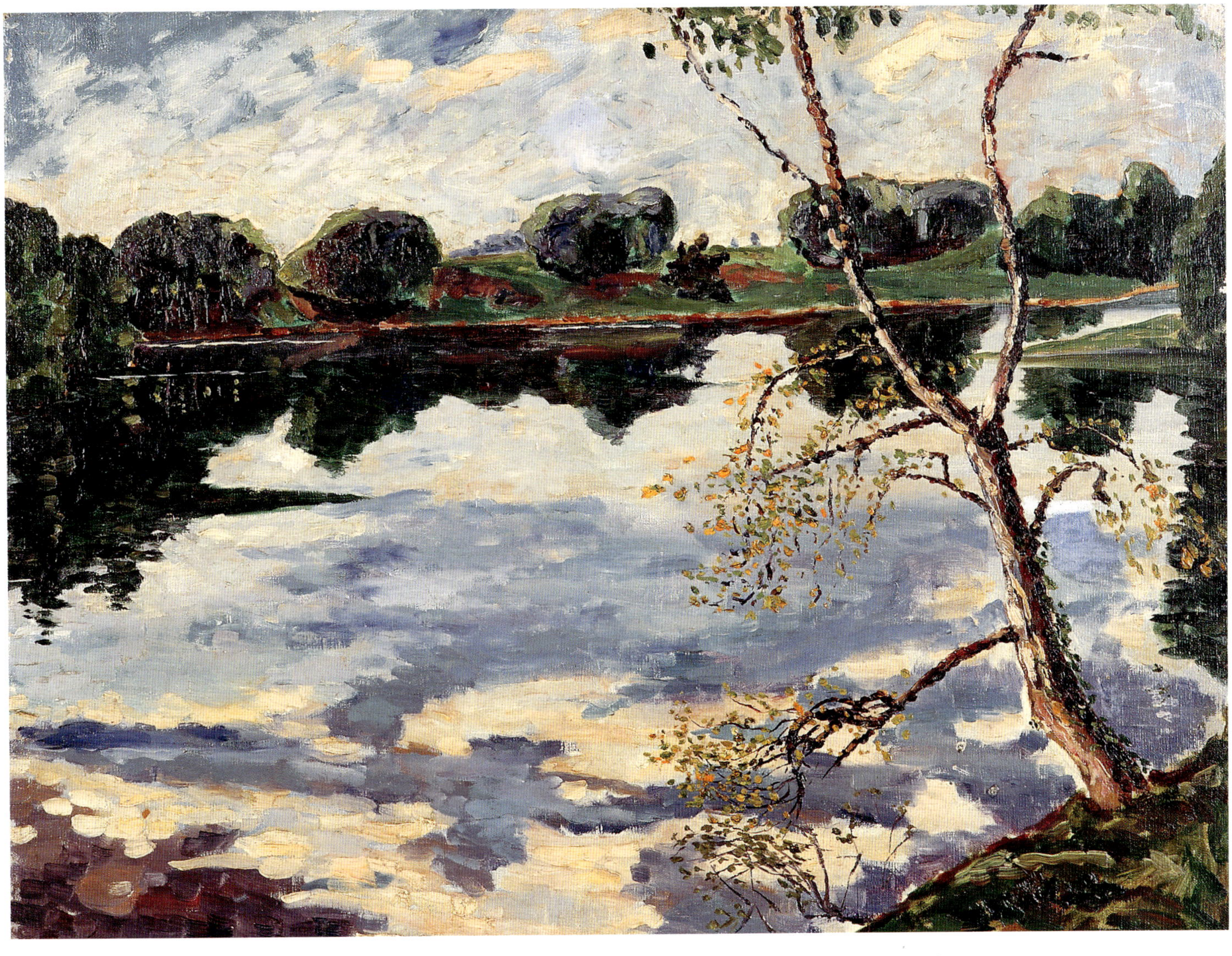

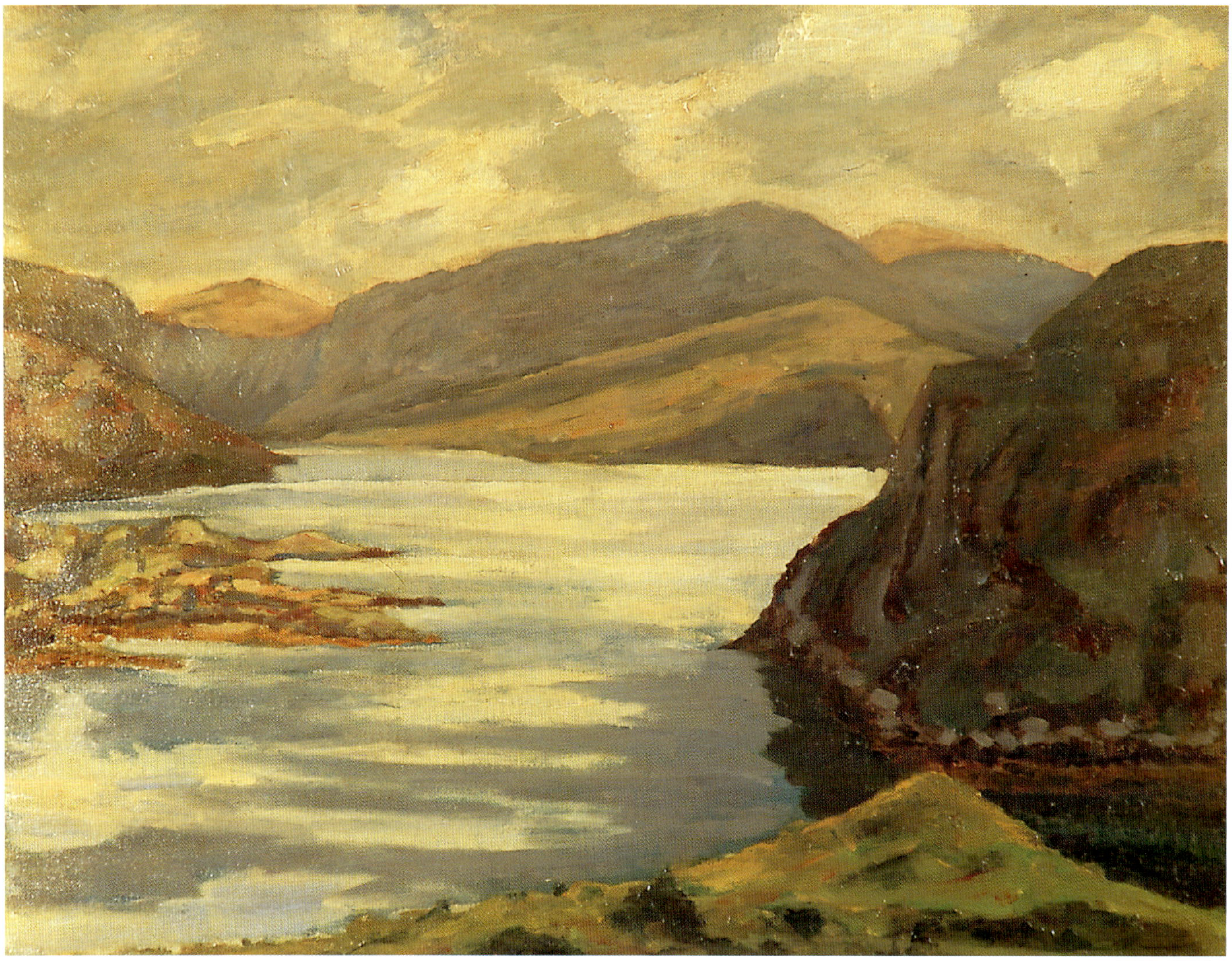

Fig 117 (C 192) above
Loch scene on the Duke of Sutherland's estate. The Duke lived at Dunrobin Castle near Golspie on the north east-coast of Scotland.

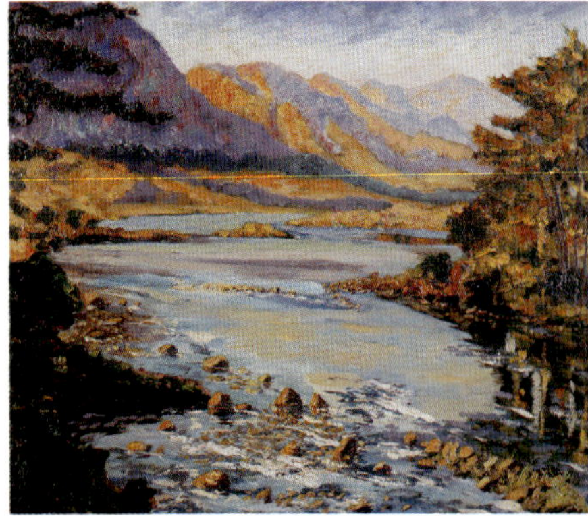

Fig 118 (C 99) above
Near Lochmore on the Duke of Wesminster's Scottish estate.

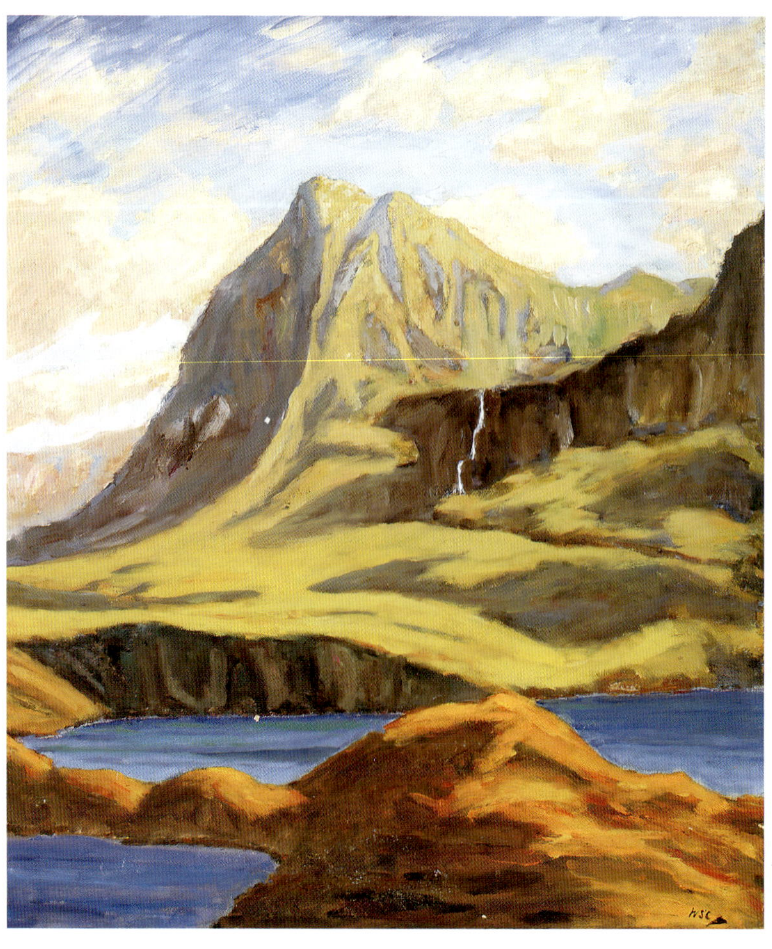

Fig 119 (C 195) right
Mountain near Lochmore.

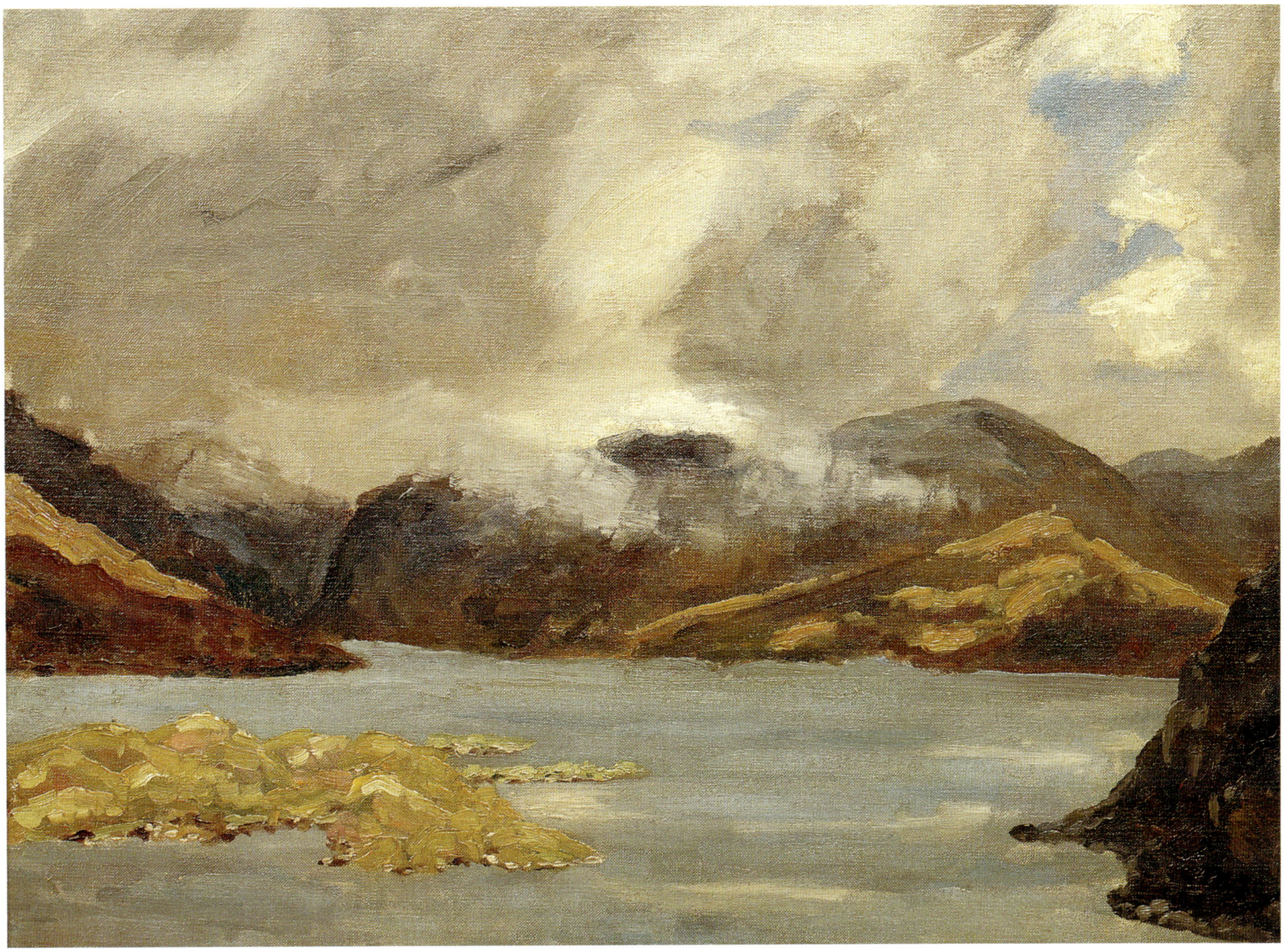

Fig 120 (C 194) above
Loch on the Duke of Sutherland's estate.

often pure colour - so that it looked more like a tessellated pavement than a marine picture. It sounds curious. All the same, do not be in a hurry to reject the method. Go back a few yards and survey the result. Each of these little points of colour is now playing his part in the general effect. Individually invisible, he sets up a strong radiation, of which the eye is conscious without detecting the cause. Look also at the blue of the Mediterranean. How can you depict and record it? Certainly not by any single colour that was ever manufactured. The only way in which the luminous intensity of blue can be simulated is by this multitude of tiny points of varied colour all in true relation to the rest of the scheme. Difficult? Fascinating!

Nature presents itself through the agency of these individual points of light, each of which sets up the vibrations peculiar to its colour. The brilliancy of a picture must therefore depend partly upon the frequency with which these points are found on any given area of the canvas, and partly on their just relation to one another. Ruskin says in his *Elements of Drawing*, from which I have already quoted, 'You will not, in Turner's largest oil pictures, perhaps six or seven feet long by four or five high, find one spot of colour as large as a grain of wheat ungradated.' But the gradations of Turner differ from those of the modern French school by being gently and almost imperceptibly evolved one from another instead of being boldly and even roughly separated; and the brush of Turner followed the form of the objects he depicted, while our French friends often seem to take pride in directly opposing it. For instance, they would prefer to paint a sea with up and down strokes rather than with horizontal; or a tree-trunk from right to left rather than up and down. This, I expect, is due to

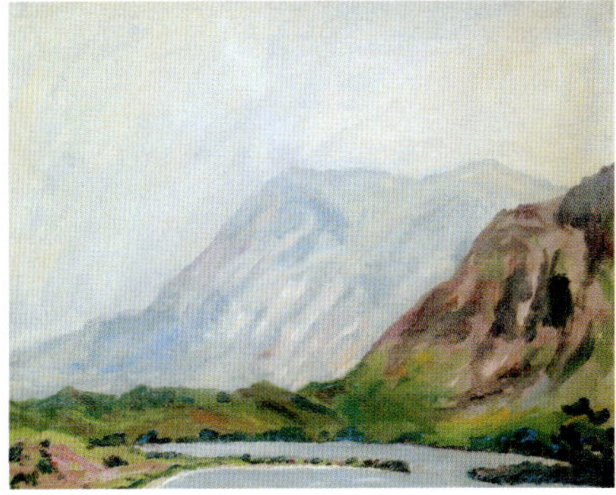

Fig 121 (C 193) above
View at Lochmore.

The Scottish Highlands had special meaning for the Churchills. In 1921, when their two year old daughter Marigold unexpectedly died, Winston and Clementine went after her funeral to stay at Lochmore where their three elder children were waiting for them. Churchill then went on his own to Dunrobin.

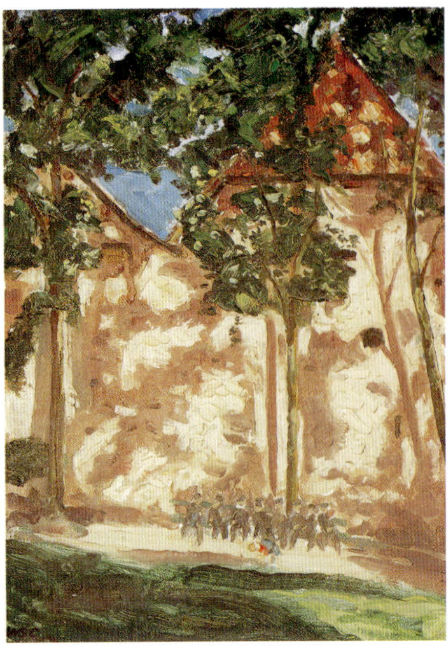

Fig 122 (C 147) above
This painting of trees and shadows is most likely to have been painted somewhere in southern France.

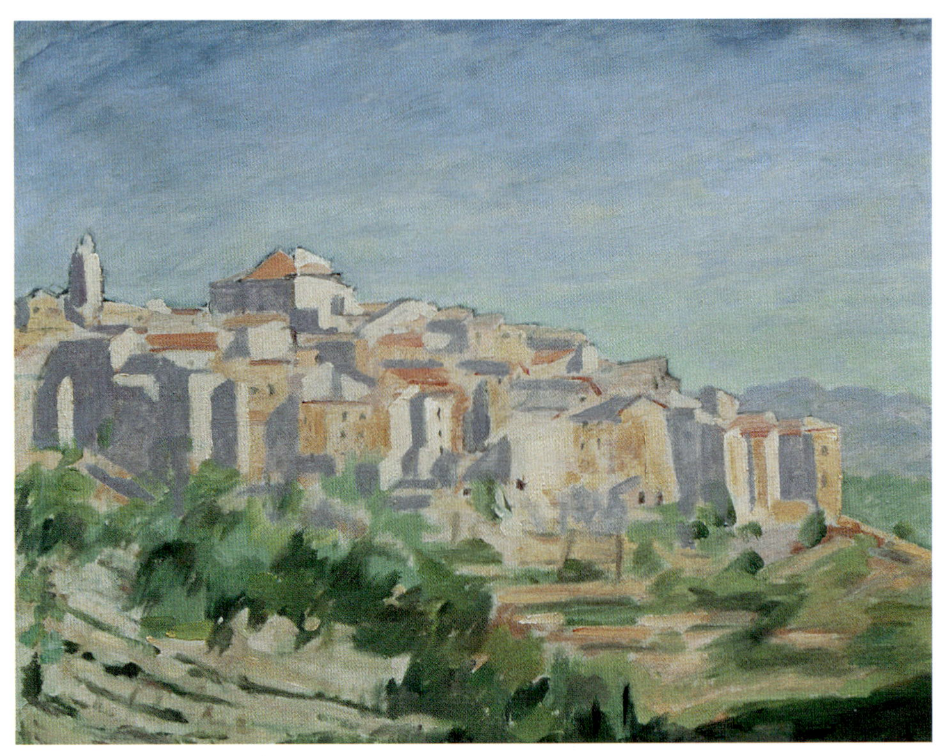

Fig 123 (C 207) above right
A view near Vence, west of Nice, in the Alpes-Maritimes.

Fig 124 (C 247) right
The Pont du Gard, the great Roman aqueduct built in the first century AD to serve the citizens of Nimes in Provence.

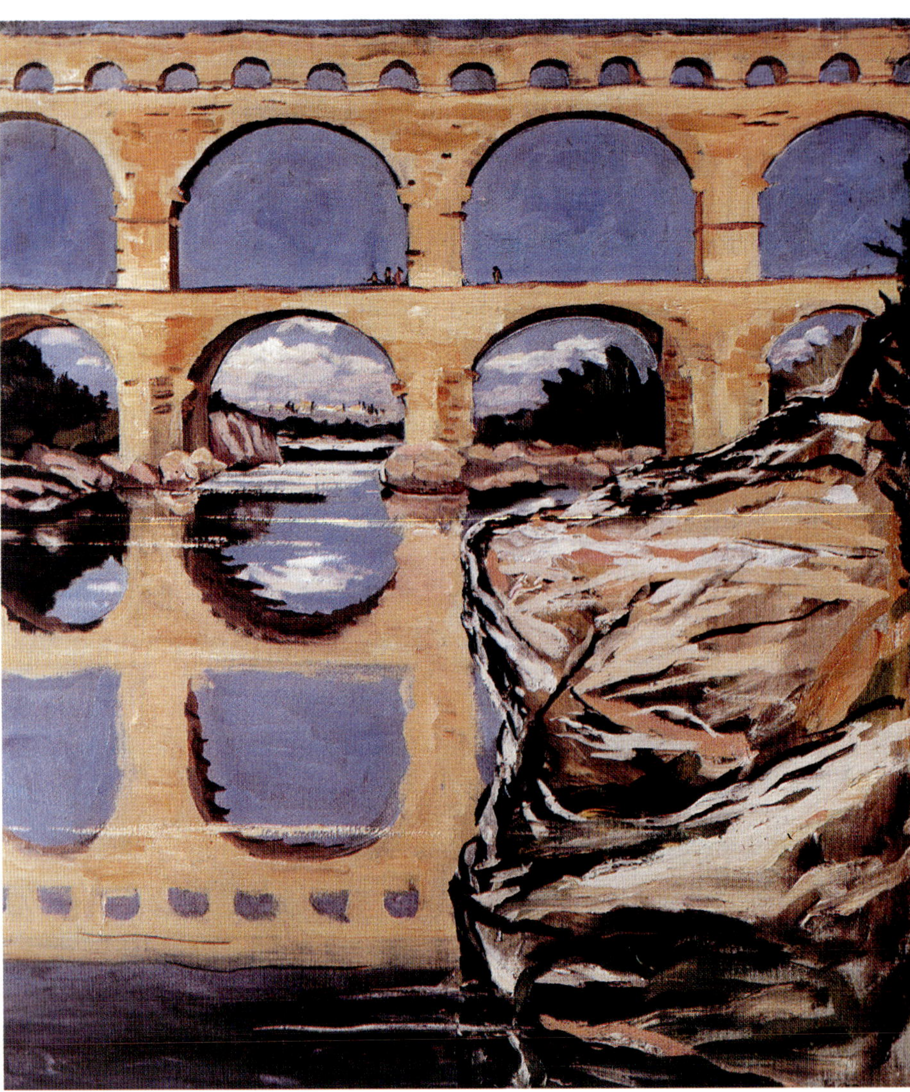

Fig 125 (C 283) below
A view of a valley somewhere in the South of France. Churchill loved the varied scenery of southern France and its coastline which he had visited first as a young man.

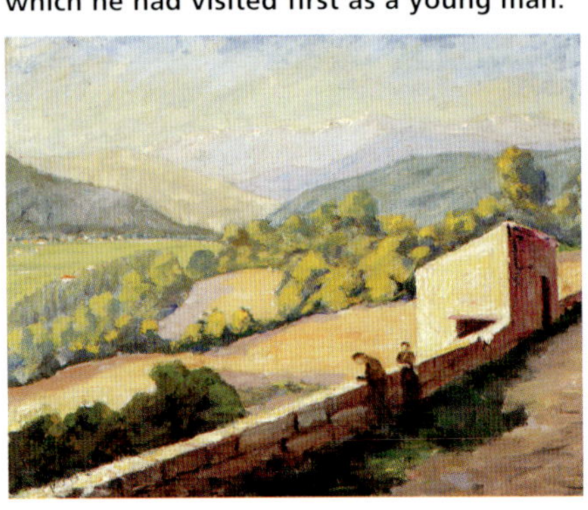

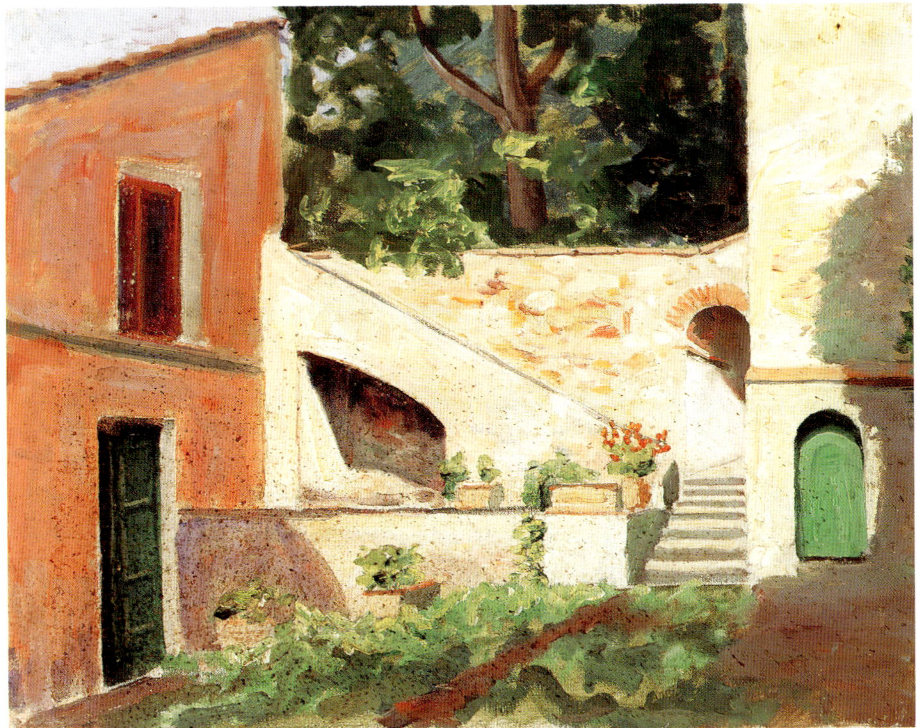

Fig 126 (C 236) left
Shadows on an open staircase somewhere in the South of France.

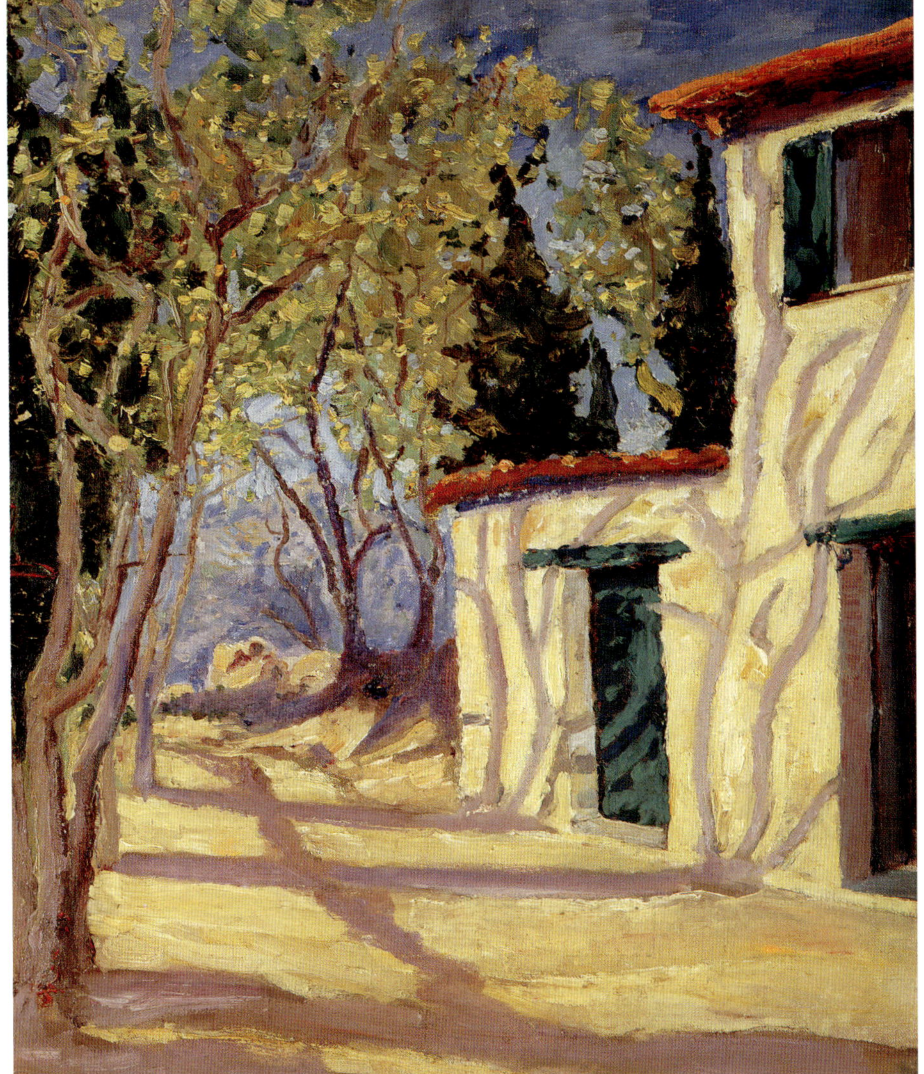

Fig 127 (C 228) left
Shadows on the wall of a village house somewhere in the South of France.

SFig 128 (C 499) below
A view in the south of France, possibly near Grasse, north of Cannes.

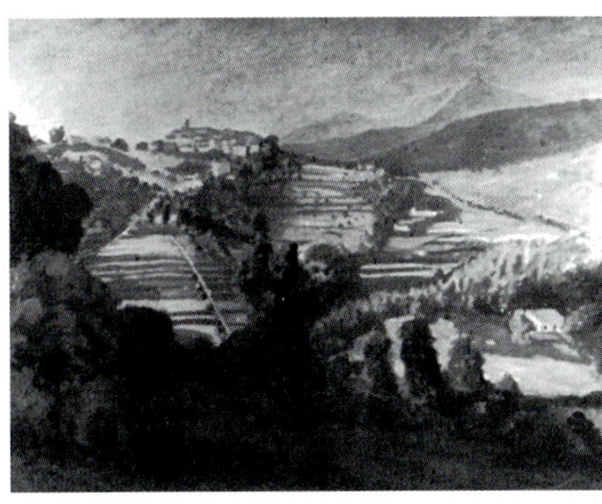

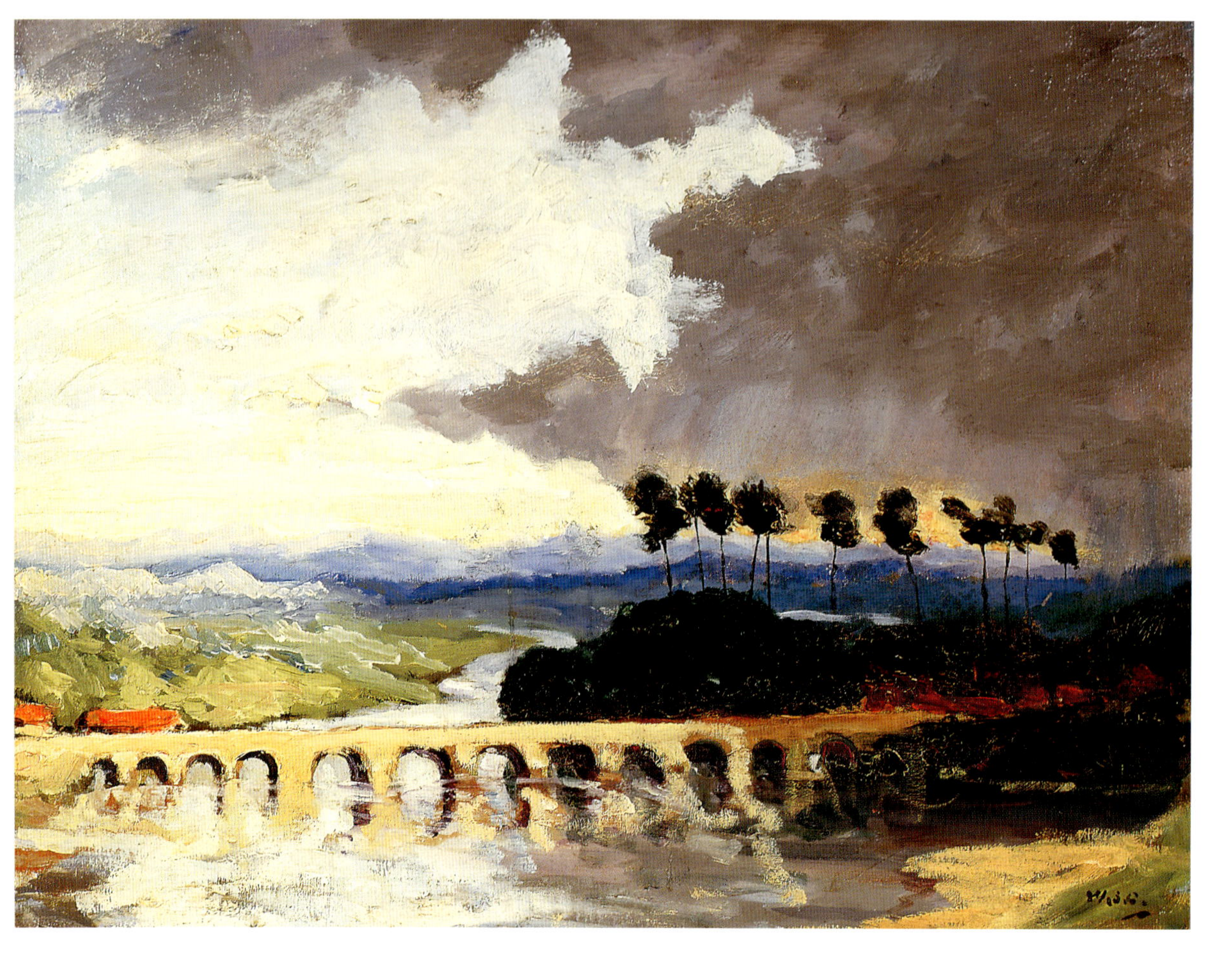

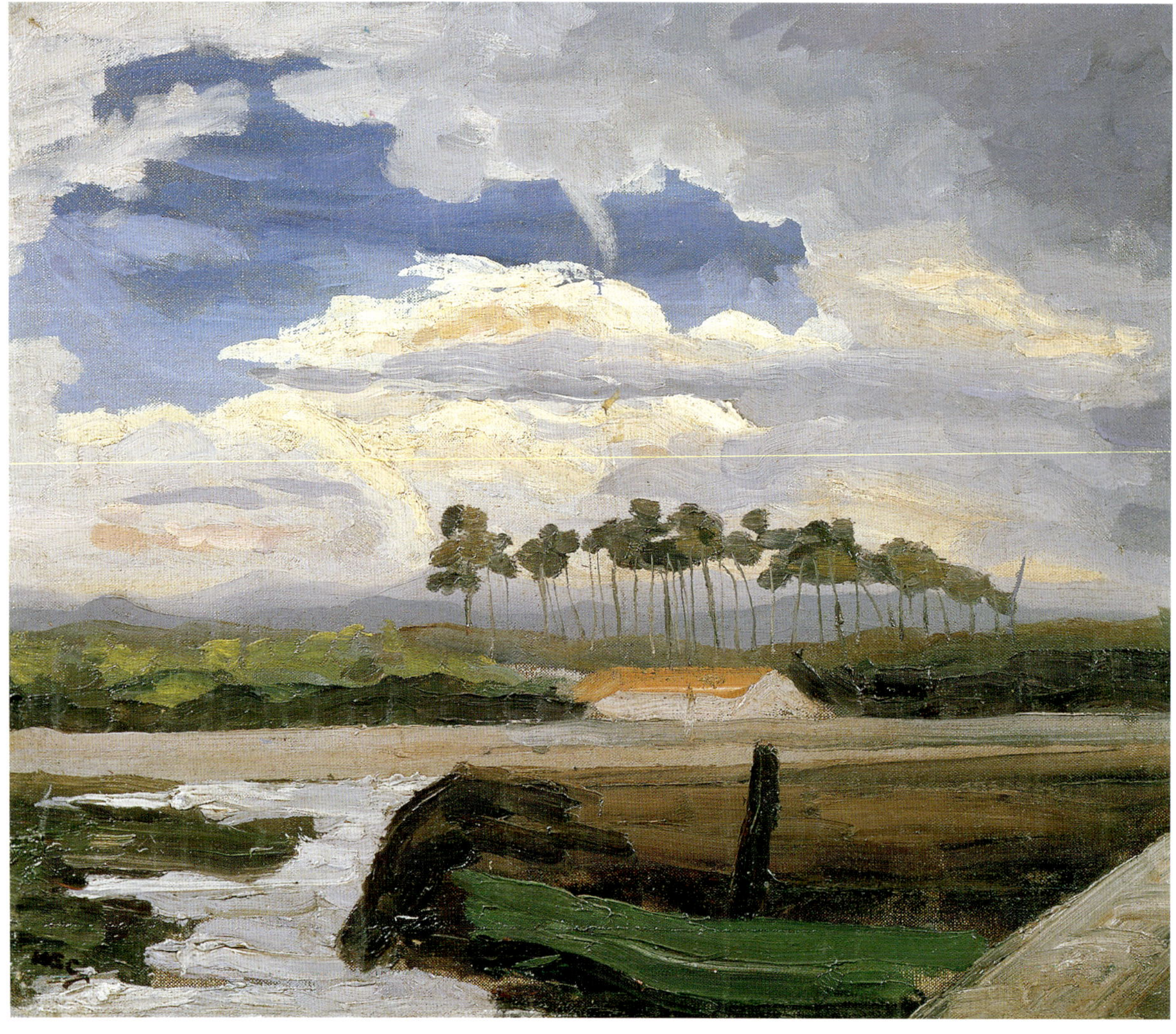

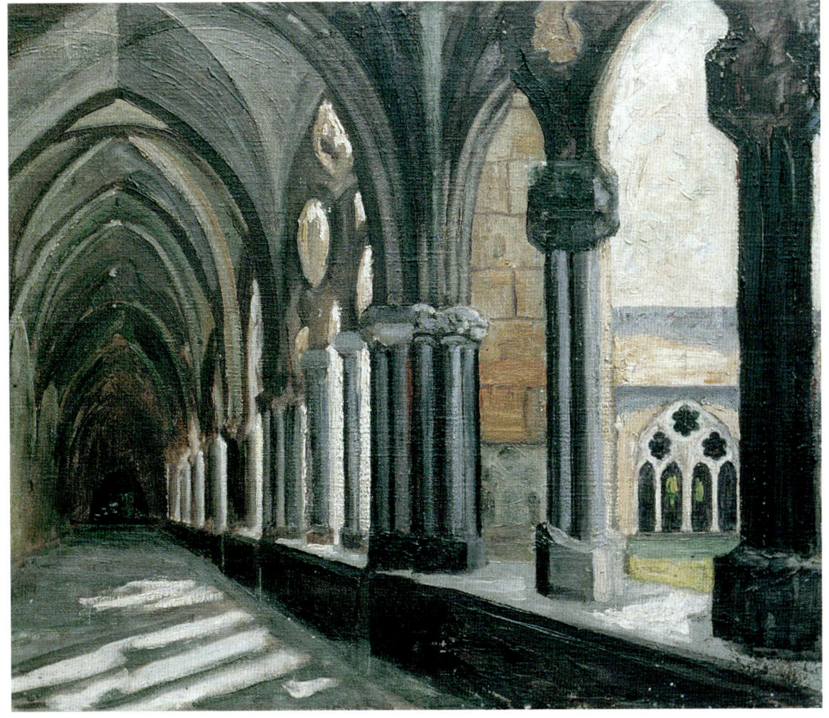

Fig 129 (C 371) opposite page above
A storm breaking above a bridge in the South of France. This painting formerly belonged to Clementine Churchill.

Fig 130 (C 188) left
A shady cloister, probably somewhere in southern France.

Fig 131 (C 370) opposite page below
This dramatic scene was painted somewhere in the South of France.

falling in love with one's theories, and making sacrifices of truth to them in order to demonstrate fidelity and admiration.

But surely we owe a debt to those who have so wonderfully vivified, brightened, and illuminated modern landscape painting. Have not Manet and Monet, Cézanne and Matisse, rendered to painting something of the same service which Keats and Shelley gave to poetry after the solemn and ceremonious literary perfections of the eighteenth century? They have brought back to the pictorial art a new draught of joie de vivre; and the beauty of their work is instinct with gaiety, and floats in sparkling air.

I do not expect these masters would particularly appreciate my defence, but I must avow an increasing attraction to their work. Lucid and exact expression is one of the first characteristics of the French mind. The French language has been made the instrument of the admirable gift. Frenchmen talk and write just as well about painting as they have done about love, about war, about diplomacy, or cooking. Their terminology is precise and complete. They are therefore admirably equipped to be teachers in the theory of any of these arts. Their critical faculty is so powerfully developed that it is perhaps some restraint upon achievement. But it is a wonderful corrective to others as well as to themselves.

My French friend, for instance, after looking at some of my daubs, took me around the galleries of Paris, pausing here and there.(8) Wherever he paused, I found myself before a picture which I particularly admired. He then explained that it is often quite easy to tell, from the kind of things I had been trying to do, what were the things I liked. Never having taken any interest in pictures till I tried to paint, I had no preconceived opinions.

I just felt, for reasons I could not fathom, that I liked some much more than others. I was astonished that anyone else should, on the most cursory observation of my work, be able so surely to divine a taste which I had never consciously formed. My friend

Fig 132 (C 357) below
A view on the river Var, above Nice in the South of France.

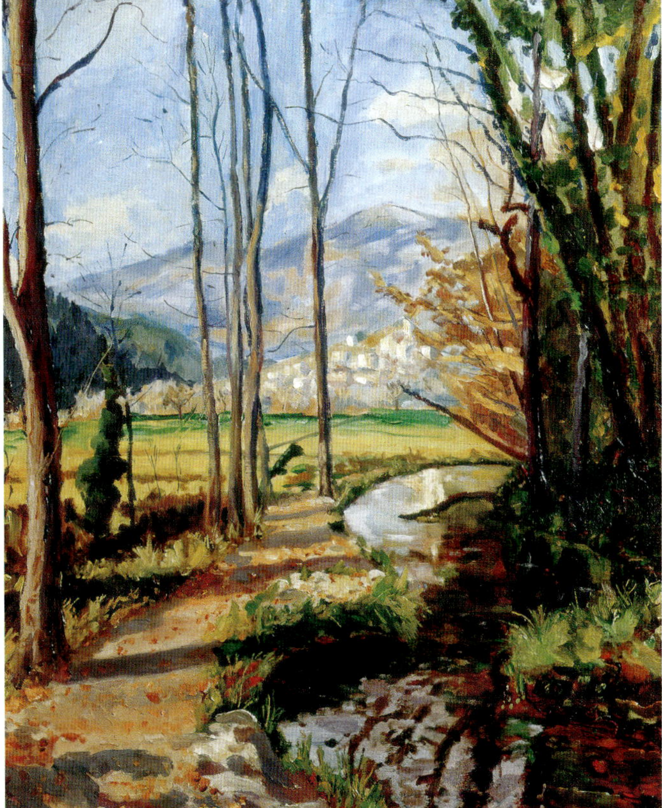

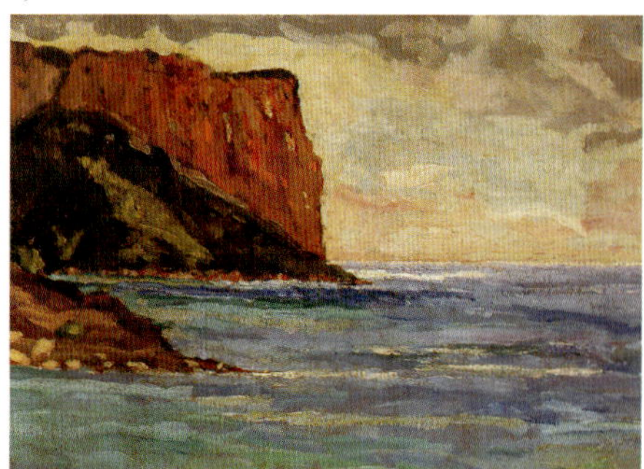

Fig 133 (C 332) above
The Mediterrenean coastline near Marseilles was often painted by Churchill.

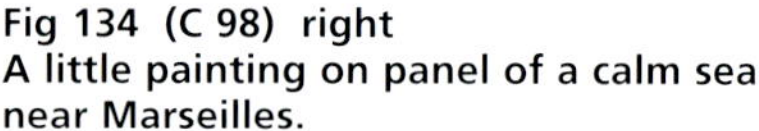

Fig 134 (C 98) right
A little painting on panel of a calm sea near Marseilles.

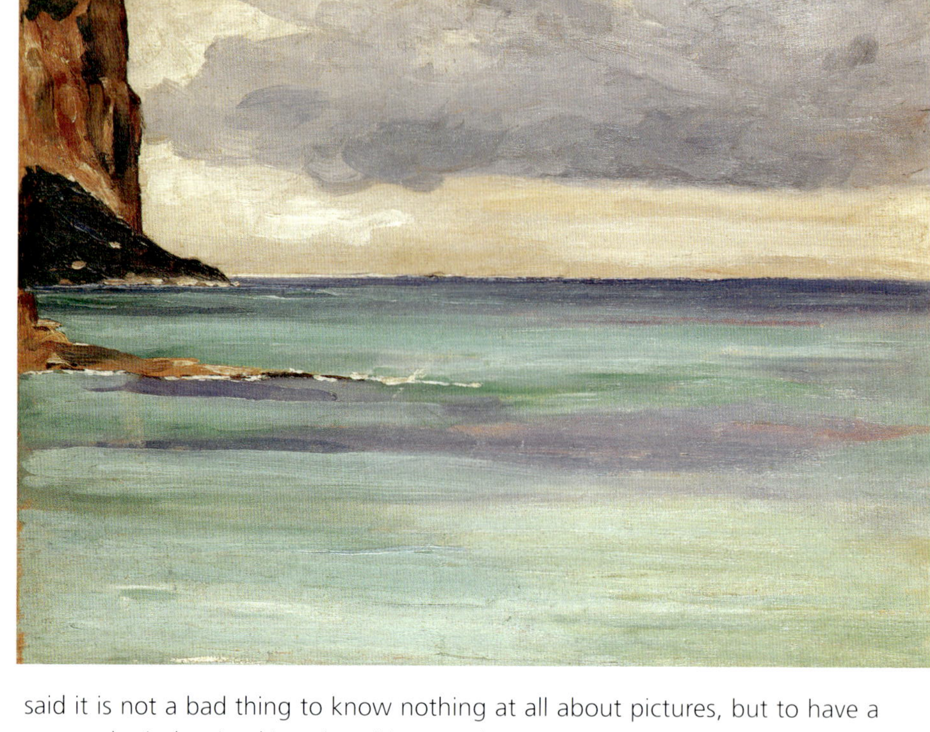

Fig 135 (C 330) below
This unusual painting, with uncharacteristic little figures at the edge of the sea, appears to be a copy by Churchill of a painting by Monet. When and where he saw the original or a reproduction of it is unknown.

said it is not a bad thing to know nothing at all about pictures, but to have a matured mind trained in other things and a new strong interest for painting. The elements are there from which a true taste in art can be formed with time and guidance, and there are no obstacles or imperfect conceptions in the way. I hope this is true. Certainly the last part is true.

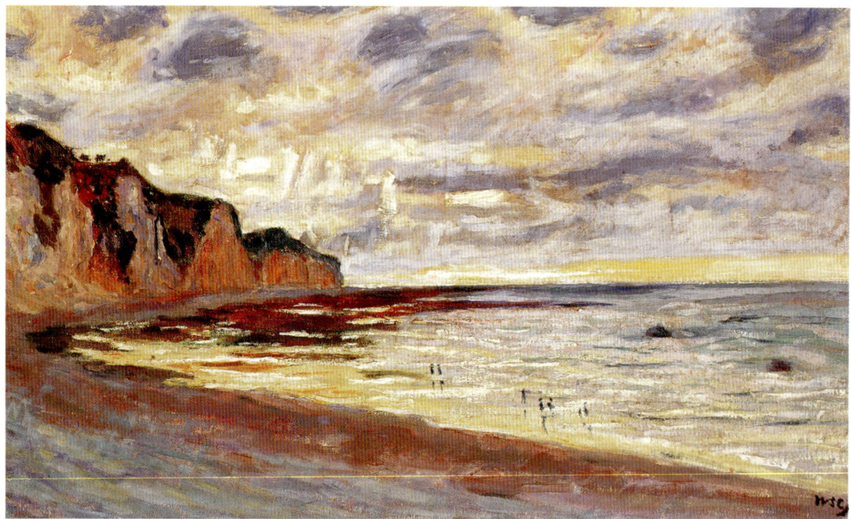

Once you begin to study it, all Nature is equally interesting and equally charged with beauty. I was shown a picture by Cézanne of a blank wall of a house, which he had made instinct with the most delicate lights and colours. Now I often amuse myself when I am looking at a wall or a flat surface of any kind by trying to distinguish all the different colours and tints which can be discerned upon it, and considering whether these arise from reflections or from natural hue. You would be astonished the first time you tried this to see how many and what beautiful colours there are even in the most commonplace objects, and the more carefully and frequently you look the more variations you do perceive.

But these are no reasons for limiting oneself to the plainest and most ordinary objects and scenes. Mere prettiness of scene, to be sure, is not needed for a beautiful picture. In fact, artificially made pretty places are very often a hindrance to a good picture. Nature will hardly stand a double process of beautification: one layer of idealism on top of another is too much of a good thing. But a vivid scene, a brilliant atmosphere, novel and charming lights, impressive contrasts, if they strike the eye all at once, arouse an interest and an ardour which will certainly be reflected in the work which you try to do, and will make it seem easier.

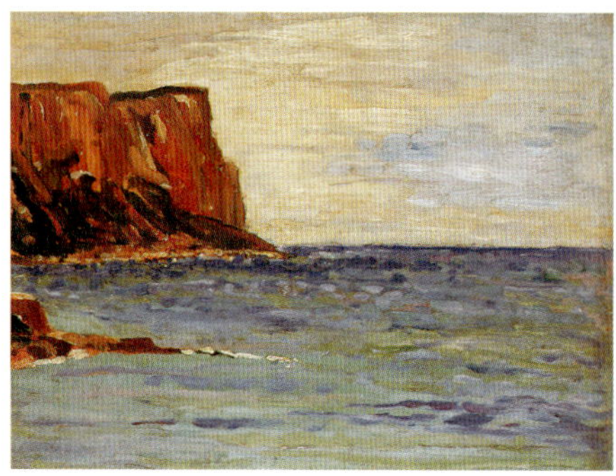

Fig 136 (C 331) above
A little painting on panel of the coast near Marseilles.

It would be interesting if some real authority investigated carefully the part which memory plays in painting.(9) We look at the object with an intent regard, then at the palette, and thirdly at the canvas. The canvas receives a message dispatched

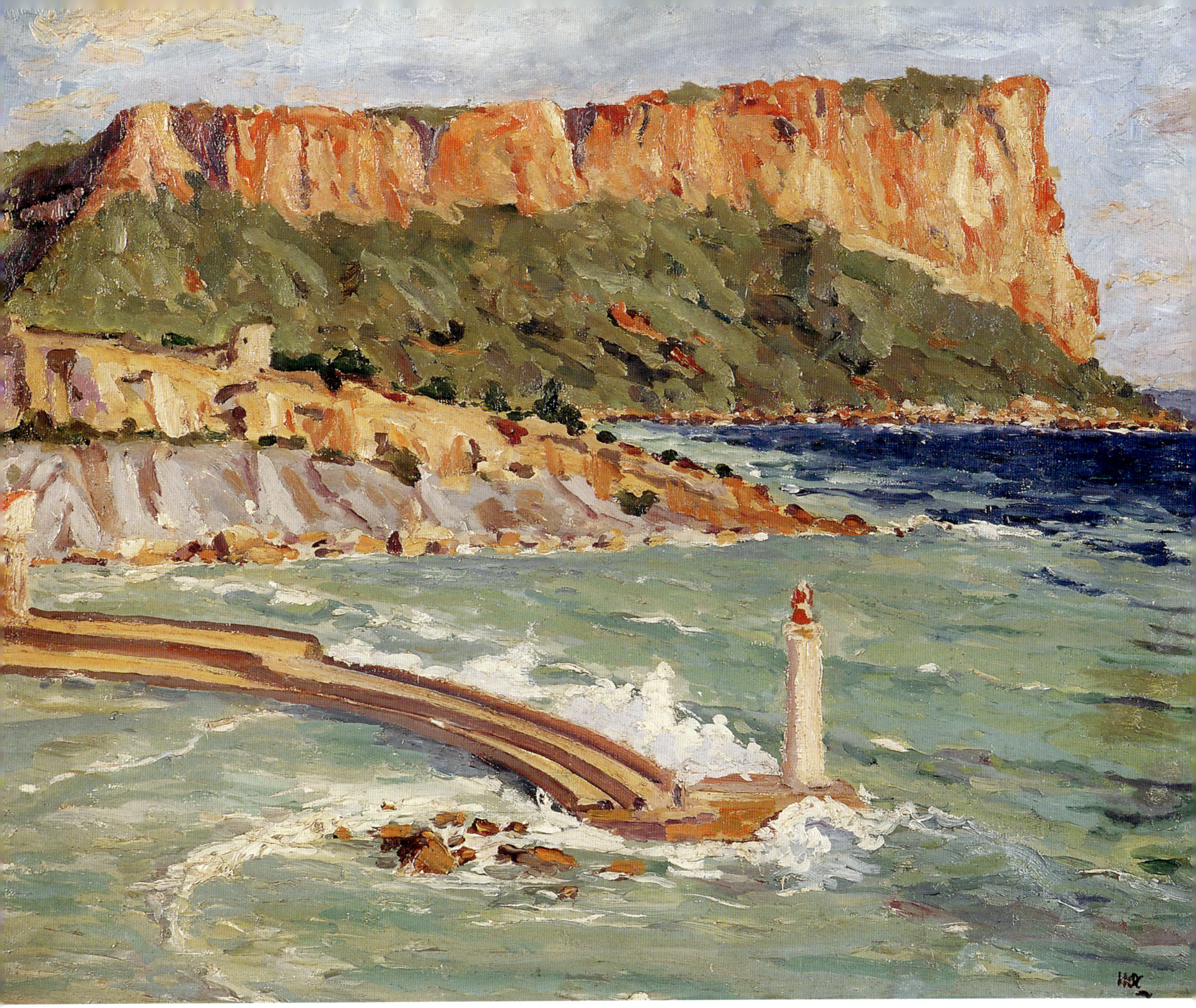

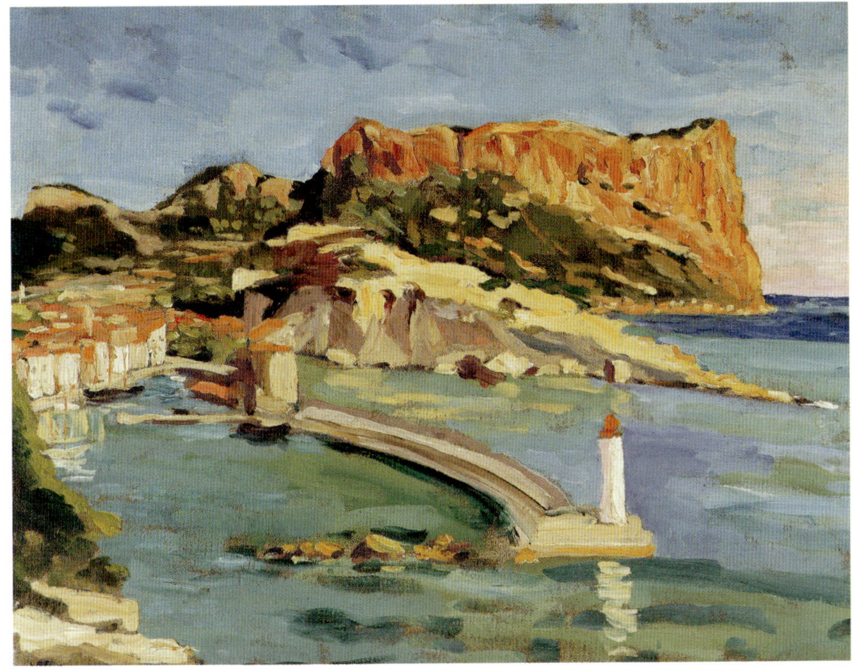

Fig 137 (C 334) above
A view somewhere near Marseilles.

Fig 138 (C 333) left
An unknown harbour near Marseilles.

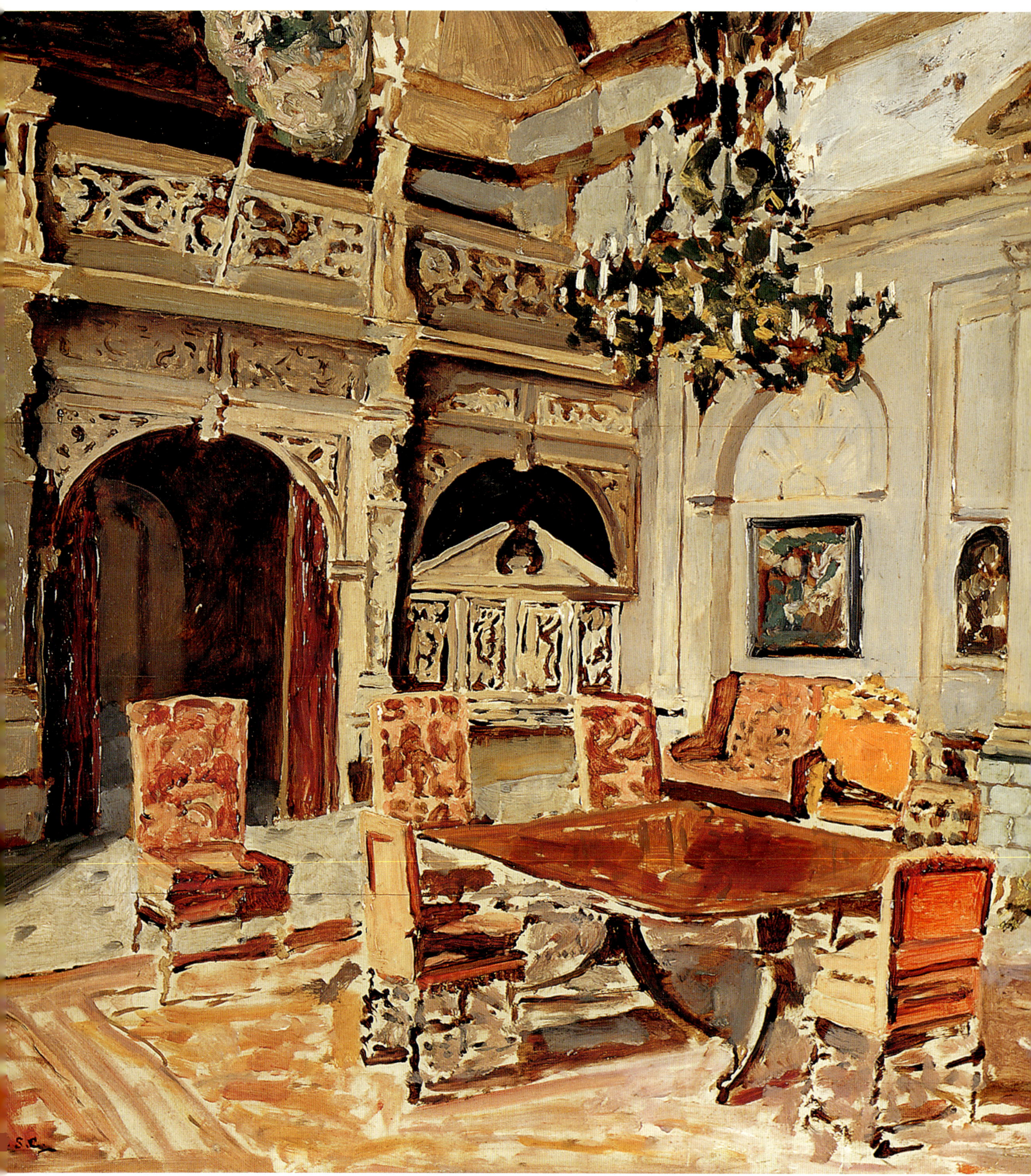

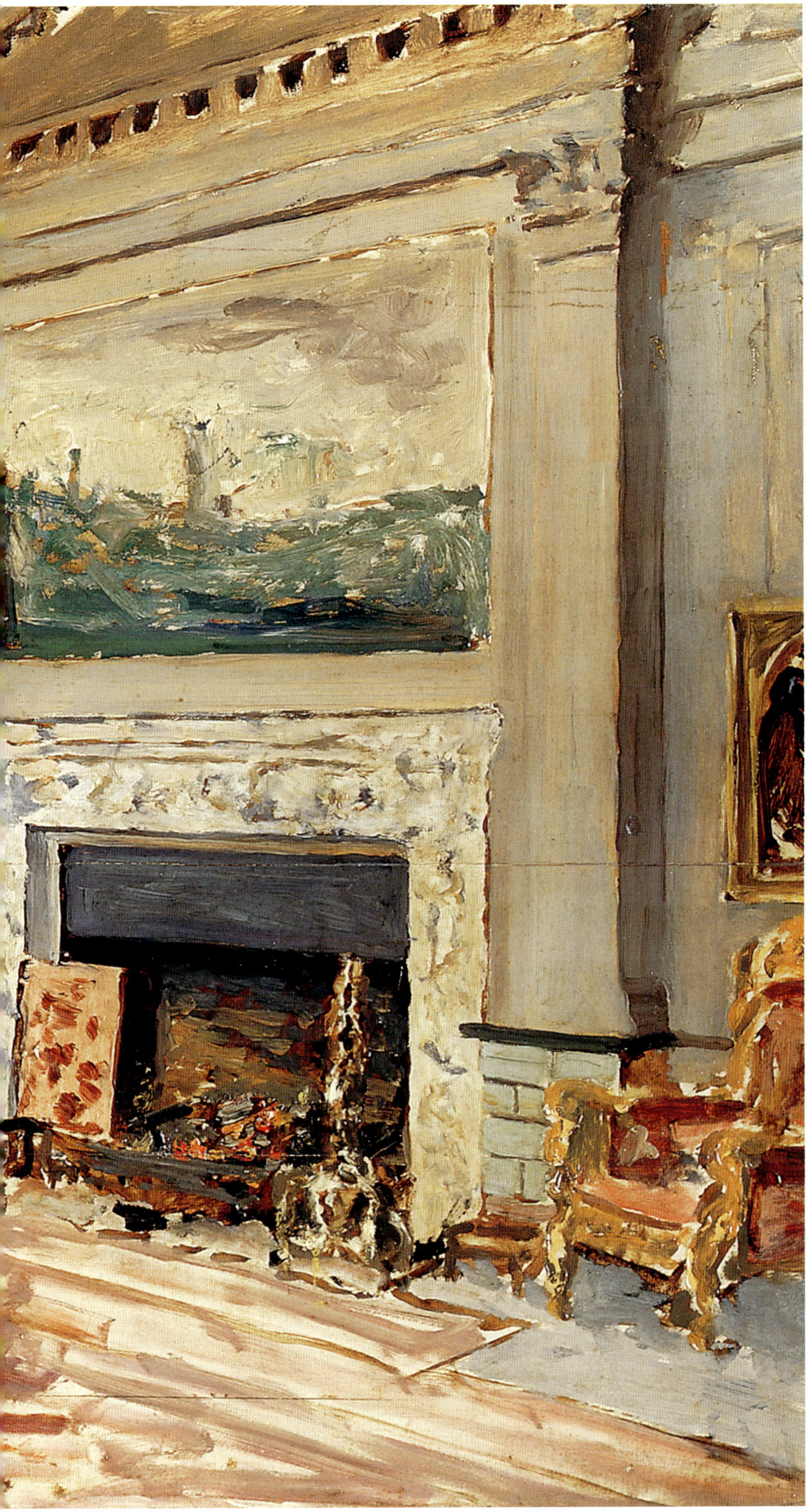

Fig 139 (C 10) left
Churchill gave this painting of the Jacobean Banqueting Hall at Knebworth House to Lady Lytton and it now hangs in this very room.

Knebworth, near Hatfield in Hertfordshire, was the home of the Earl and Countess of Lytton; the latter, born Pamela Plowden, was Winston's first great love. The house also contains rooms designed by the 20th century architect Sir Edwin Lutyens and a herb garden designed by his own first patron, Gertrude Jekyll.

Fig 140 (C 22) below
The dining room at Knebworth.

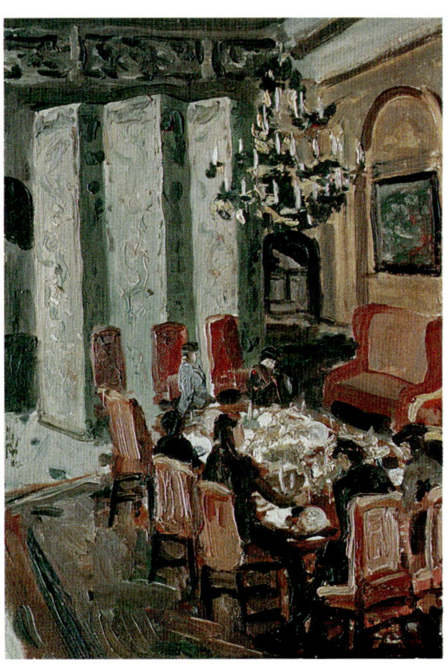

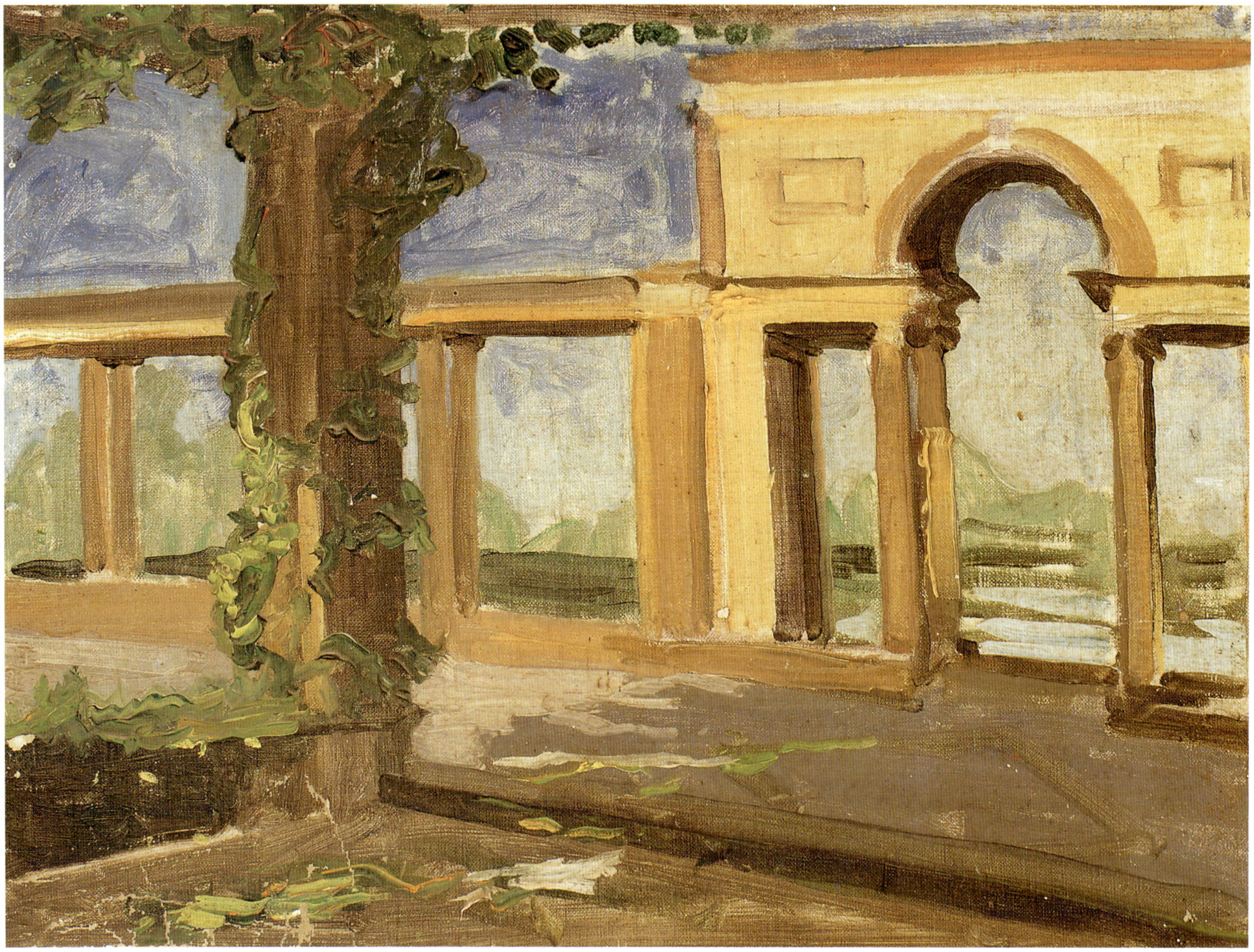

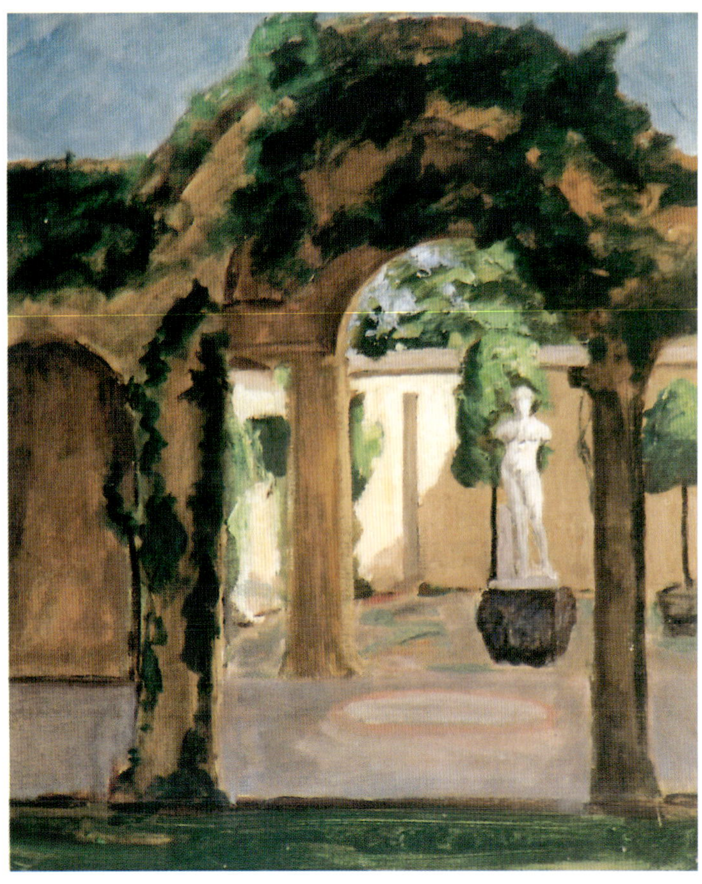

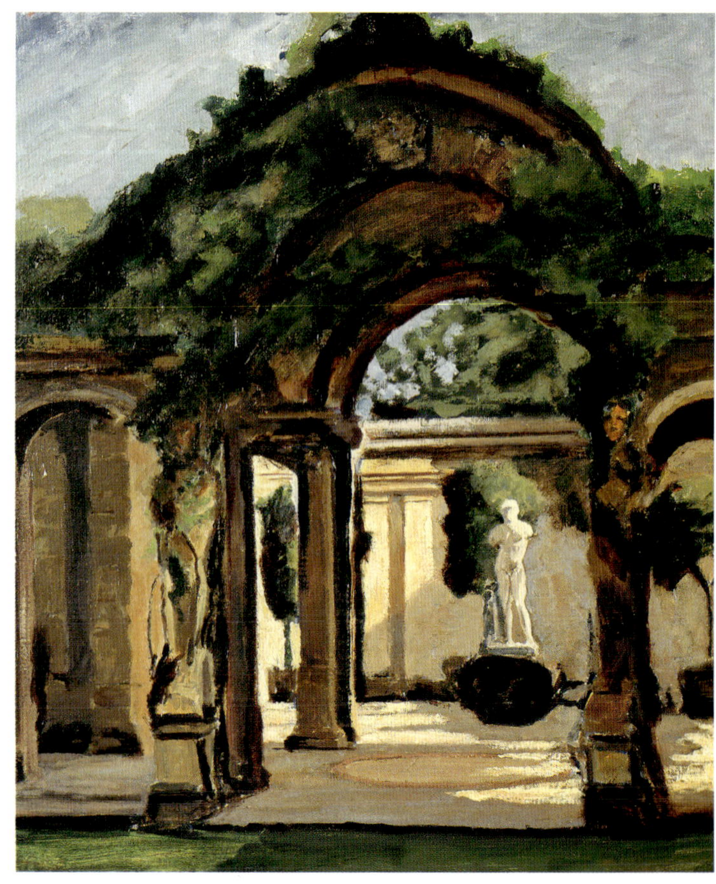

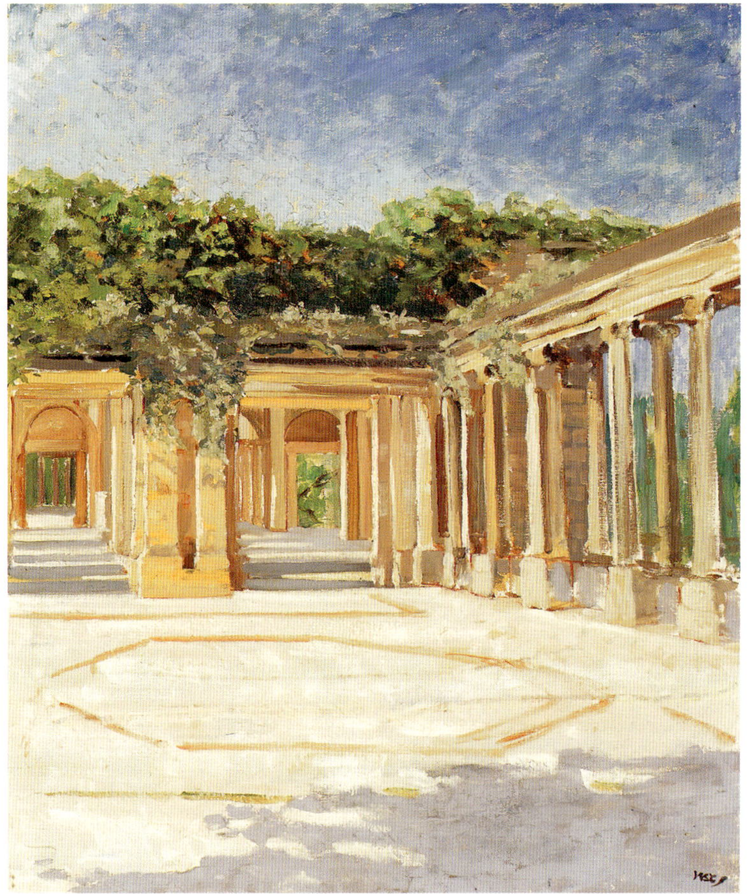

Fig 141 (C 125) opposite page above
A sketch of the Terrace at Hever.

Hever Castle, near Edenbridge in Kent, is only a few miles from Chartwell. It was the home of Lord Astor who restored the ancient castle and created an Italian garden, filling it with statuary. Churchill painted there in the 1920s and 1930s, and again after the Second World War, from when one or more of these paintings may date. Given the opportunity, Churchill might attempt the same view more than once.

Fig 142 (C 254) left
At Hever.

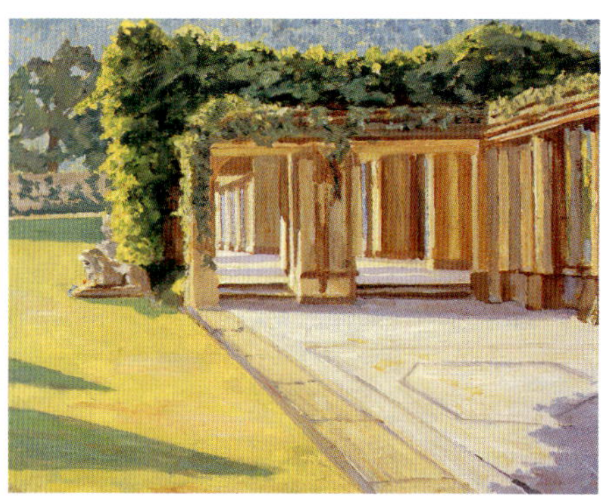

Fig 143 (C 258) above
The Terrace at Hever.

usually a few seconds before from the natural object. But it has come through a post office en route. It has been transmitted in code. It has been turned from light to paint. It reaches the canvas a cryptogram. Not until it has been placed in its correct relation to everything else that is on the canvas **or has yet to be put upon the canvas** can it be deciphered, is its meaning apparent, is it translated once again from mere pigment into light. And the light this time is not of Nature but of Art. The whole of this considerable process is carried through on the wings or the wheels of memory. In most cases we think it is the wings - airy and quick like a butterfly from flower to flower. But all heavy traffic and all that has to go on a long journey must travel on wheels.

In painting in the open air the sequence of actions is so rapid that the process of translation into and out of pigment may seem to be unconscious. But all great [the greatest] landscapes have been painted indoors, and often long after the first impressions were gathered. In a dim cellar the Dutch or Italian master recreated the gleaming ice of a Netherlands carnival or the lustrous sunshine of Venice or the Campagna. Here, then, is required a formidable memory of the visual kind. Not only do we develop our powers of observation, but also those of carrying the record - of carrying it through an extraneous medium and reproducing it, hours, days or even months after the scene has vanished or the sunlight died.

I was told by a friend that when Whistler guided a school in Paris, he made his pupils observe their model on the ground floor, and then run upstairs and paint their picture piece by piece on the floor above. As they became more proficient, he put their easels up a storey higher, till at last the elite were scampering with their decision up six flights into the attic - praying it would not evaporate on the way. This is, perhaps, only a tale. But it shows effectively of what enormous importance a trained, accurate, retentive memory must be to an artist; and conversely what a useful exercise painting may be for the development of an accurate and retentive memory.

Fig 144 (C 259) opposite page below left
Through an arch at Hever.

Fig 145 (C 256) opposite page below right
In the Italian Garden at Hever. This painting formerly belonged to Clementine Churchill.

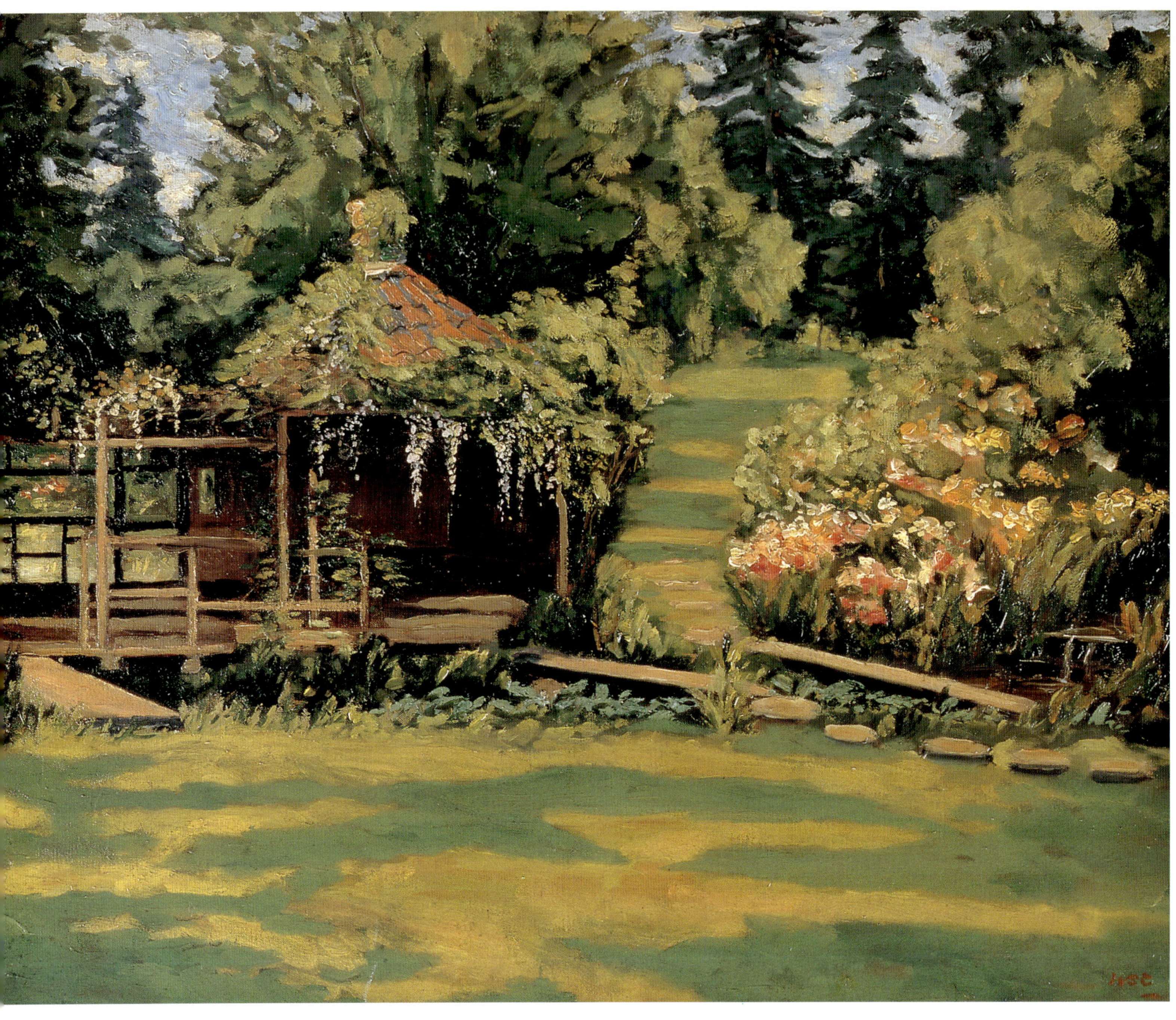

Fig 146 (C 257) above
The Summer House at Trent Park. This painting is owned by HRH the Prince of Wales.

Both Winston and Clementine were frequent guests at Trent Park and Port Lympne, both owned by Churchill's political colleague Sir Philip Sassoon. Trent Park was near London at New Barnet, and Port Lympne on the Kent coast overlooking the English Channel. Sir Philip was a collector and a connoisseur of art and a chairman of the Trustees of the National Gallery. He had his own private plane and had a considerable interest in the development of aircaft design. He was a patron of the artist John Singer Sargent and commissioned Rex Whistler to paint a series of murals - at Port Lympne, where the architect Philip Tilden (who worked for Churchill at Chartwell) designed a 'Moorish' courtyard: as a reminder perhaps of Sassoon's Levantine ancestry. Sir Philip greatly encouraged Winston's interest in art and loaned him several paintings to copy including two by Sargent.

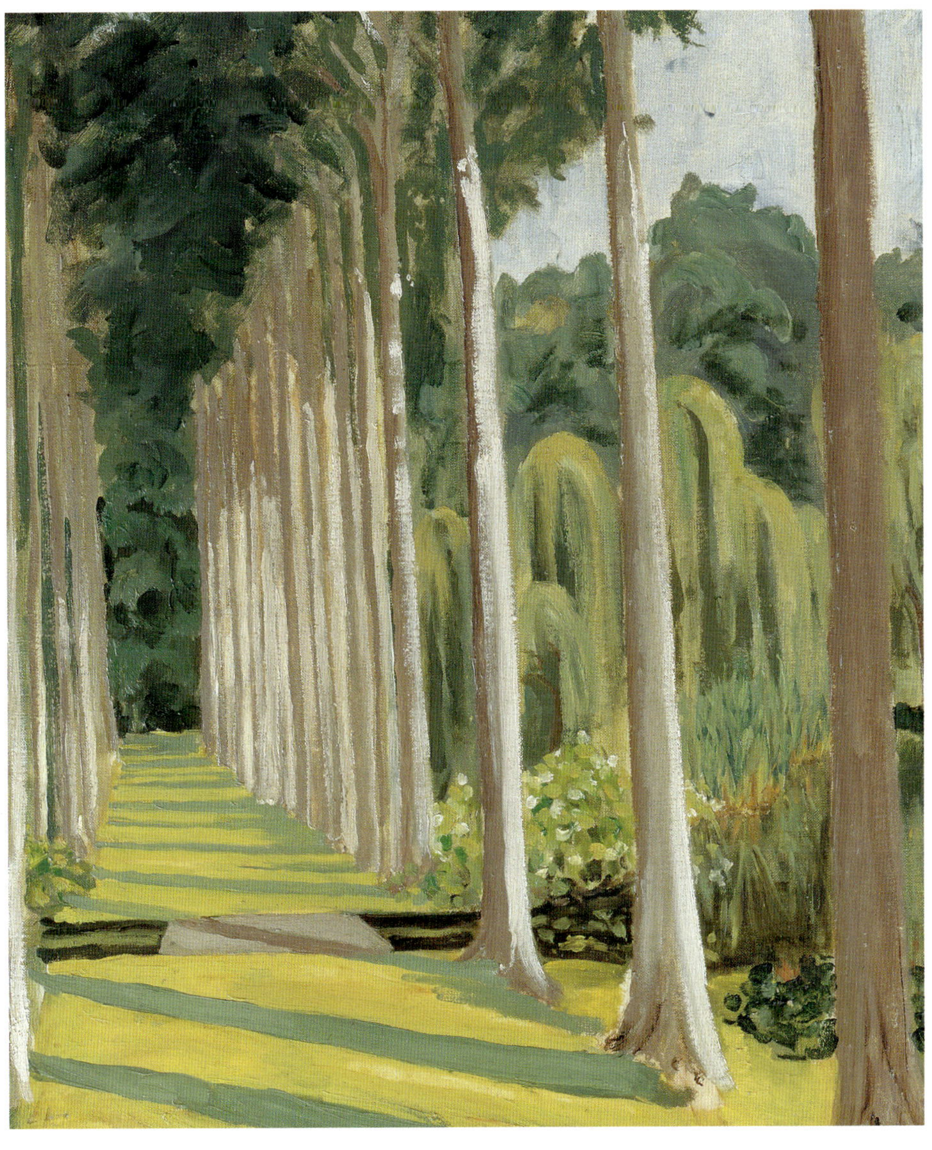

Fig 147 (C 274) left.
The Avenue at Trent Park. This painting formerly belonged to Clementine Churchill.

Fig 148 (C 20) below
The Blue Room at Trent Park.

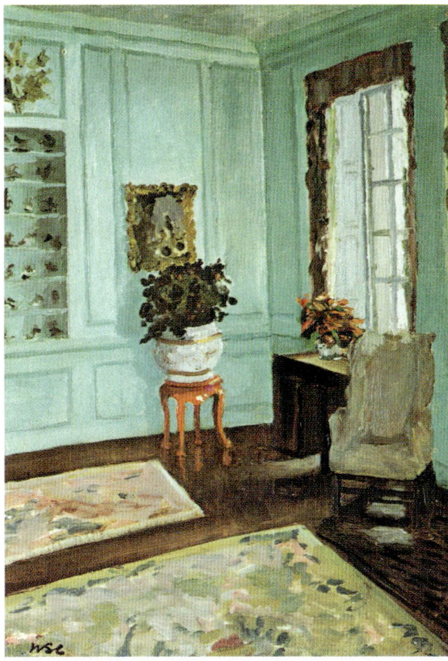

There is no better exercise for the would-be artist than to study and devour a picture, and then, without looking at it again, to attempt the next day to reproduce it. Nothing can more exactly measure the progress both of observation and memory. It is still harder to compose out of many separate, well-retained impressions, aided though they be by sketches and colour notes, a new, complete conception. But this is the only way in which great landscapes have been painted - or can be painted. The size of the canvas alone precludes its being handled out of doors. The fleeting light imposes a rigid time-limit. The same light never returns. One cannot go back day after day without the picture getting stale. The painter must choose between a rapid impression, fresh and warm and living, but probably deserving only of a short life, and the cold, profound, intense effort of memory, knowledge, and will-power, prolonged perhaps for weeks, from which a masterpiece can alone result. It is much better not to fret too much about the latter. Leave to the masters of art trained by a lifetime of devotion the wonderful process of picture-building and picture-creation. Go out into the sunlight and be happy with what you see.

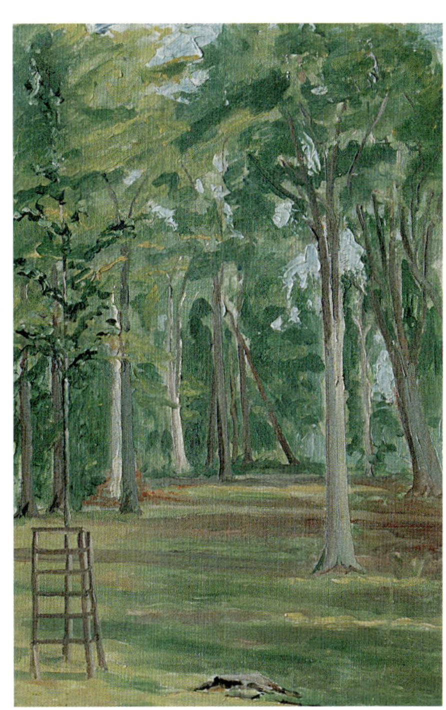

Fig 149 (C 78) above
At Trent Park.

Painting is complete as a distraction. I know of nothing which, without exhausting the body, more entirely absorbs the mind. Whatever the worries of the hour or the threats of the future, once the picture has begun to flow along, there is no room for them in the mental screen. They pass out into shadow and darkness. All one's mental light, such as it is, becomes concentrated on the task. Time stands respectfully aside, and it is only after many hesitations that luncheon

Fig 150 (C 275) right
The Pergola at Trent Park.

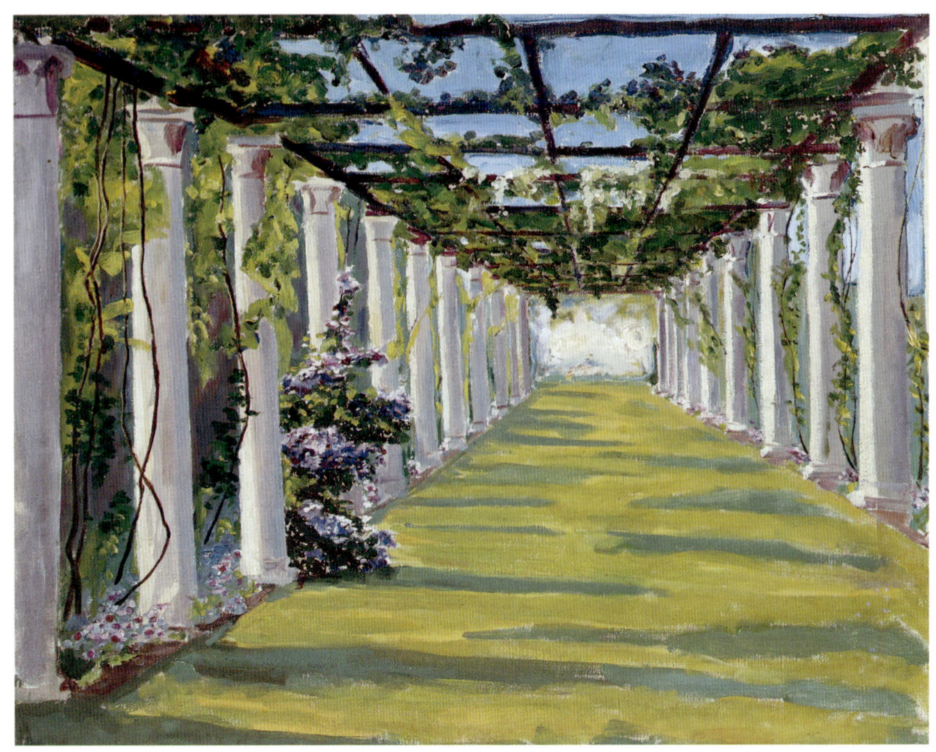

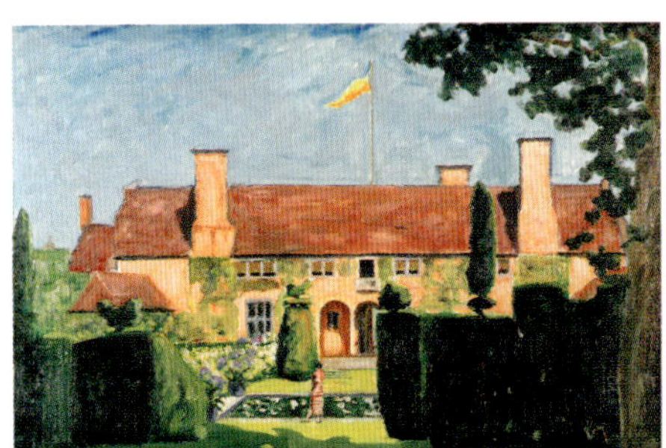

Fig 151 (C 225) above
The house at Lympne.

knocks gruffly at the door. When I have had to stand up on parade, or even, I regret to say, in church, for half an hour at a time, I have always felt the erect position is not natural to man, has only been painfully acquired, and is only with fatigue and difficulty maintained. But no one who is fond of painting finds the slightest inconvenience, [as long as the interest holds,] in standing to paint for three or four hours at a time [at a stretch.] **or for seven or eight hours in a day. Not, at least, as long as the interest holds.**

Lastly, let me say a word on painting as a spur to travel. There is really nothing like it. [Every day and all day is provided with its expedition and its occupation - cheap, attainable, innocent, absorbing, recuperative. The vain racket of the tourist gives place to the calm enjoyment of the philosopher, intensified by an enthralling sense of action and endeavour.] Every country where the sun shines and every district in it, has a theme of its own. The lights, the atmosphere, the aspect, the spirit, are all different; but each has its native charm. Even if you are only a poor painter you can feel the influence of the scene, guiding your brush, selecting the tubes you squeeze on to the palette. Even if you cannot portray it as you see it, you feel it, you know it, and you admire it for ever. When people rush about Europe in the train from one glittering centre of work or pleasure to another, passing - at enormous expense - through a series of mammoth hotels and blatant carnivals, they little know what they are missing, and how cheaply priceless things can be obtained. The painter wanders and loiters contentedly from place to place, always on the look out for some brilliant butterfly of a picture which can be caught and set up and carried safely home. **All he asks for is sunshine, and if it be really true that we are to have thirty-five years of drought, there ought to be no difficulty about supplying that. Côte d'Azur, Côte d'Argent, Côte Emeraude all present to him their world-famed beauties, which neither crowds nor casinos are needed to enhance.**

[Now I am learning to like painting even on dull days. But in my hot youth I demanded sunshine.] Sir William Orpen advised me to visit Avignon on account of its wonderful light, and certainly there is no more delightful centre for a would-be painter's activities: then Egypt, fierce and brilliant, presenting in infinite

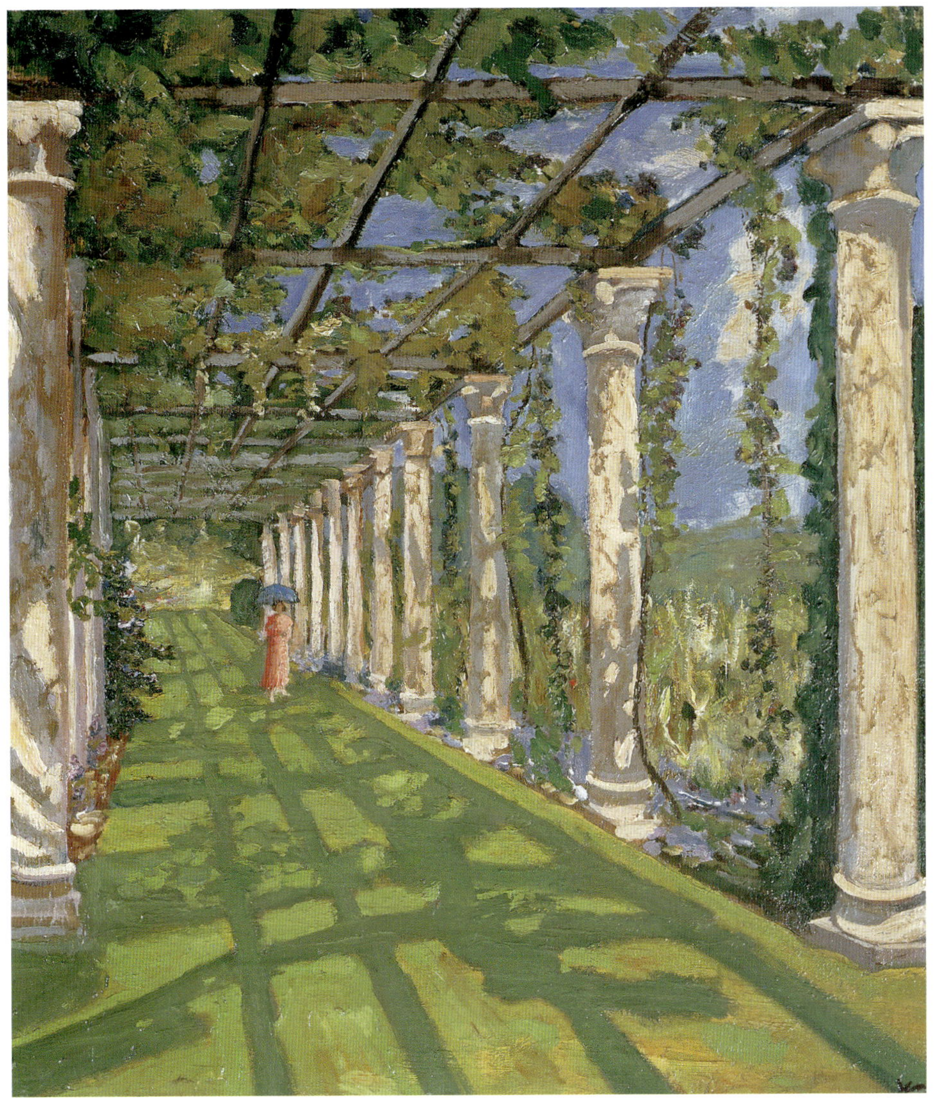

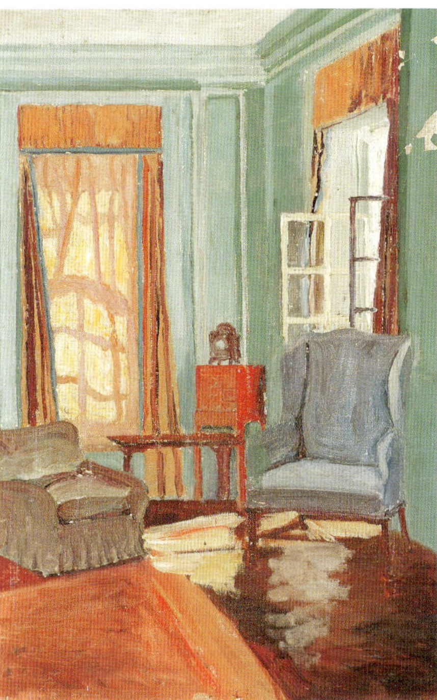

Fig 152 (C 21) above
The Blue Room at Trent Park.

Fig 153 (C 277) left
The Terrace at Trent Park.

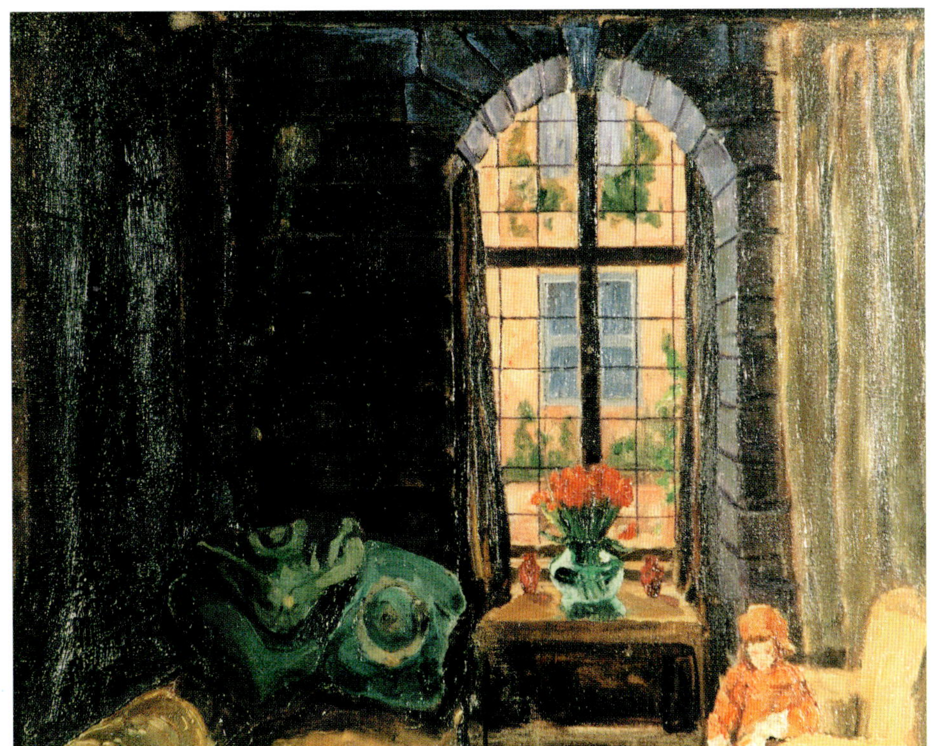

Fig 154 (C 18) left
The Living room at Lympne with Lady Pamela Smith, younger daughter of the Earl of Birkenhead.

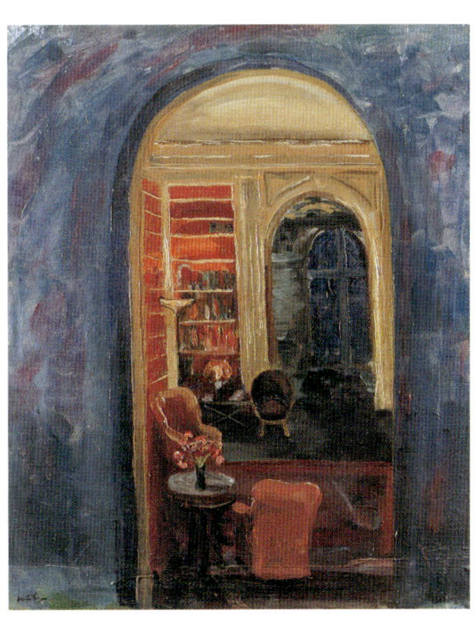

Fig 155 (C 19) above
The Library at Lympne.

Fig 156 (C 282) right
View from the Stone Terrace at Lympne.
The photograph below shows Winston Churchill working on this painting.

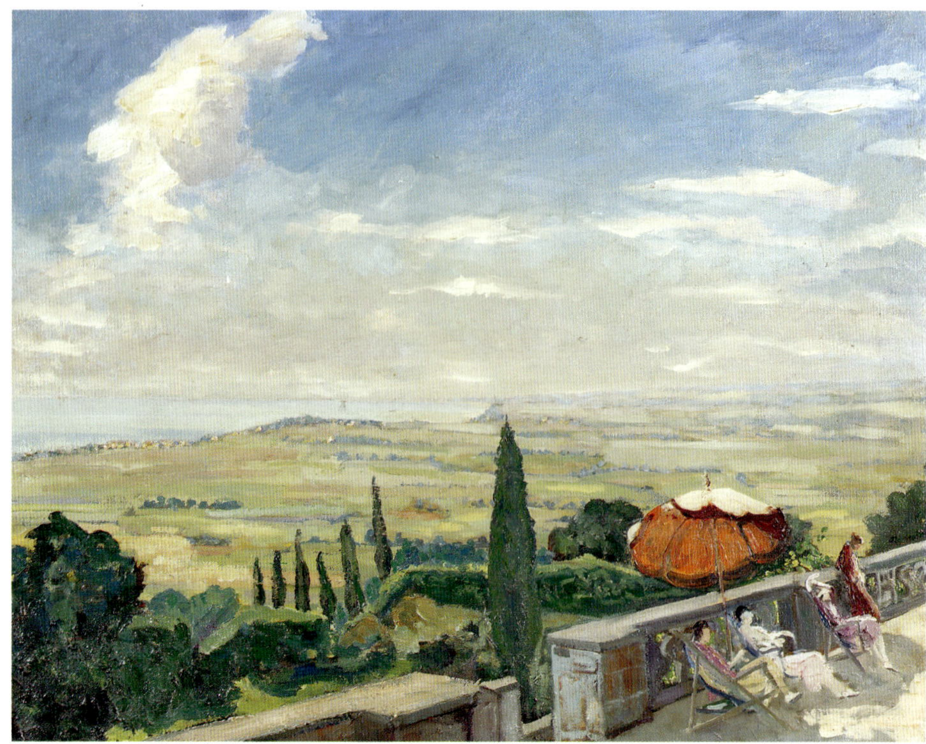

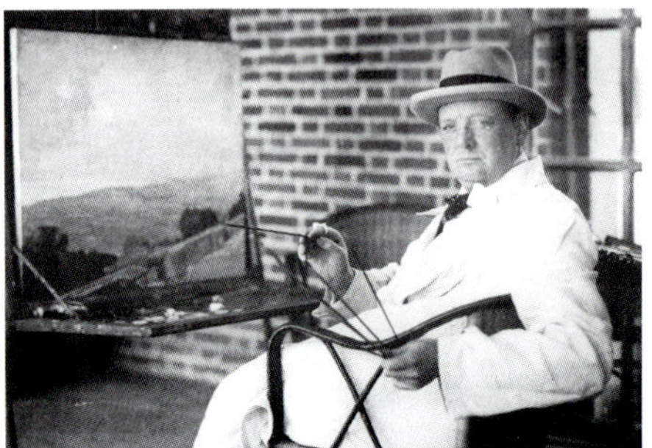

Fig 157 (C 292) opposite page above right
Coast scene near Lympne in summer.

Fig 158 (C 288) right
Landscape near Lympne.

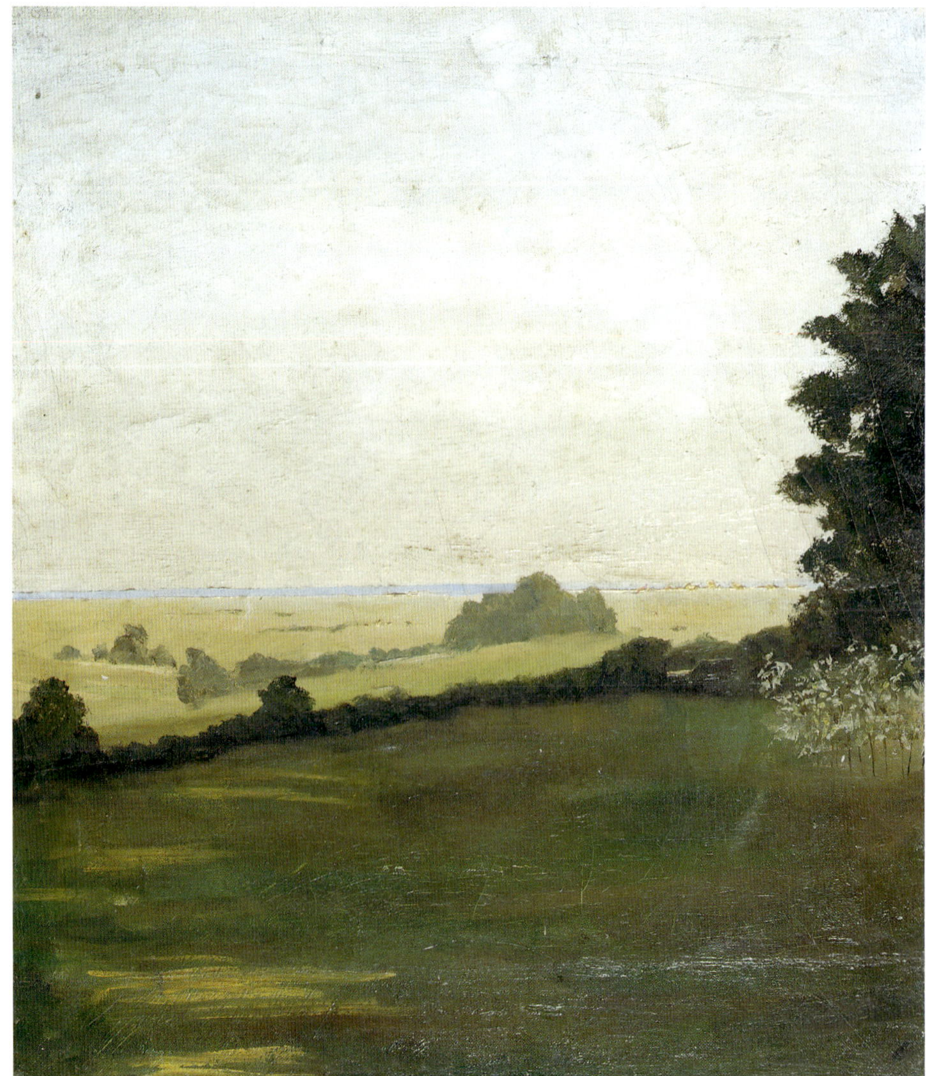

Fig 159 (C 221) opposite page below left
The Garden Entrance at Lympne,

Fig 160 (C 251) opposite page below right
Formal Garden and Pavilion at Lympne, painted in an unusual technique for Churchill.

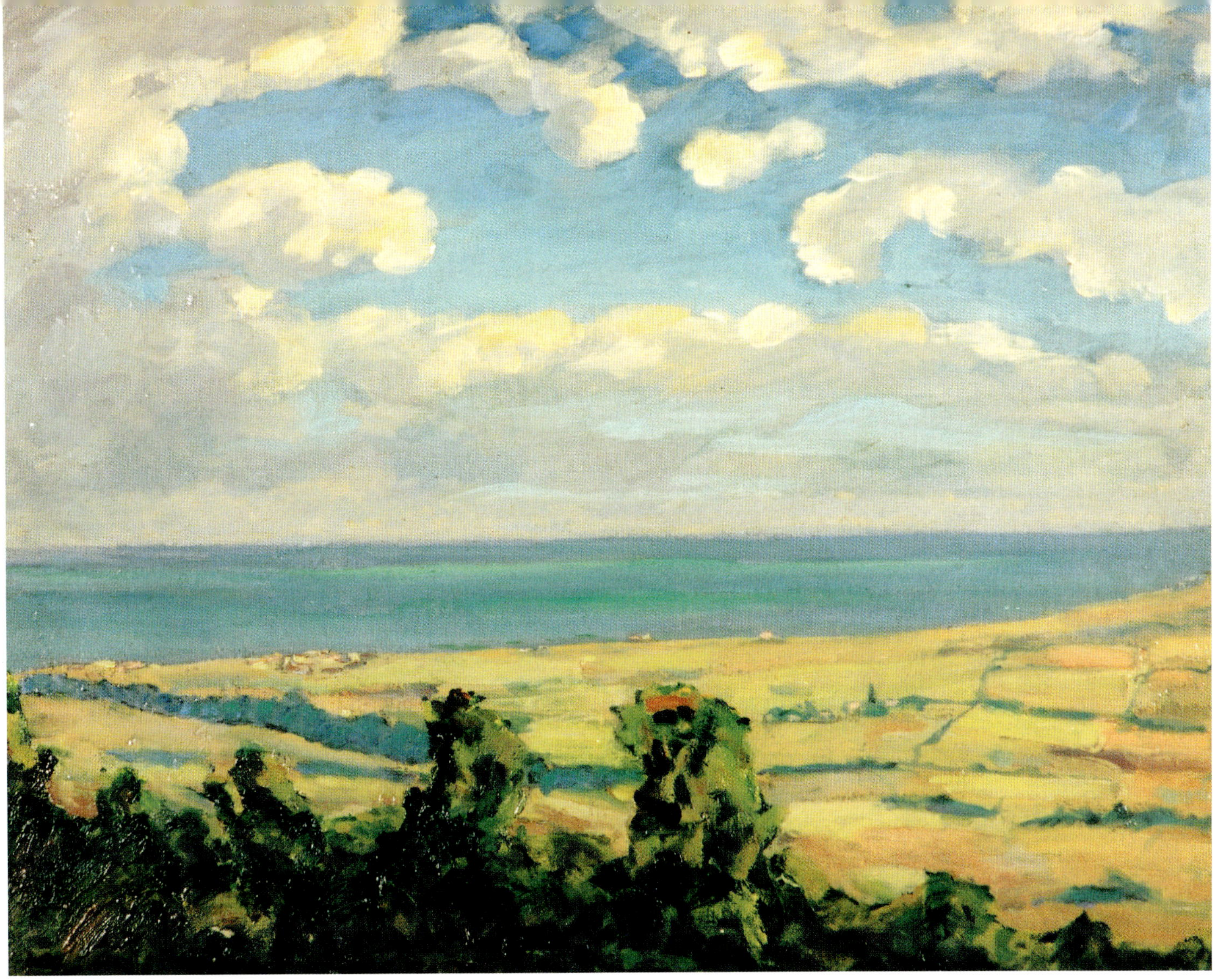

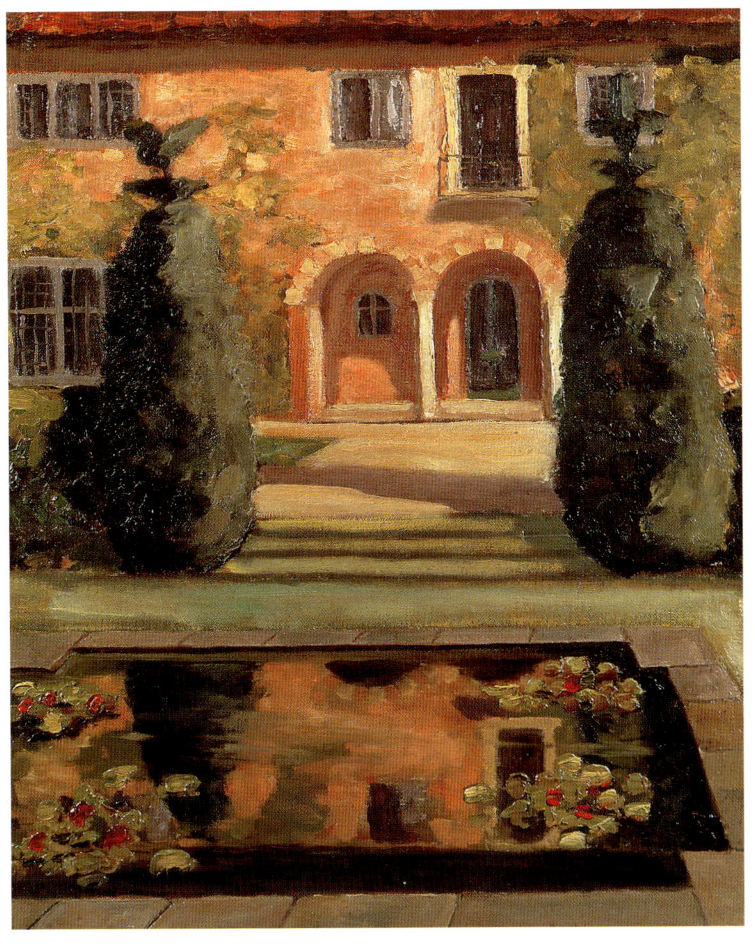

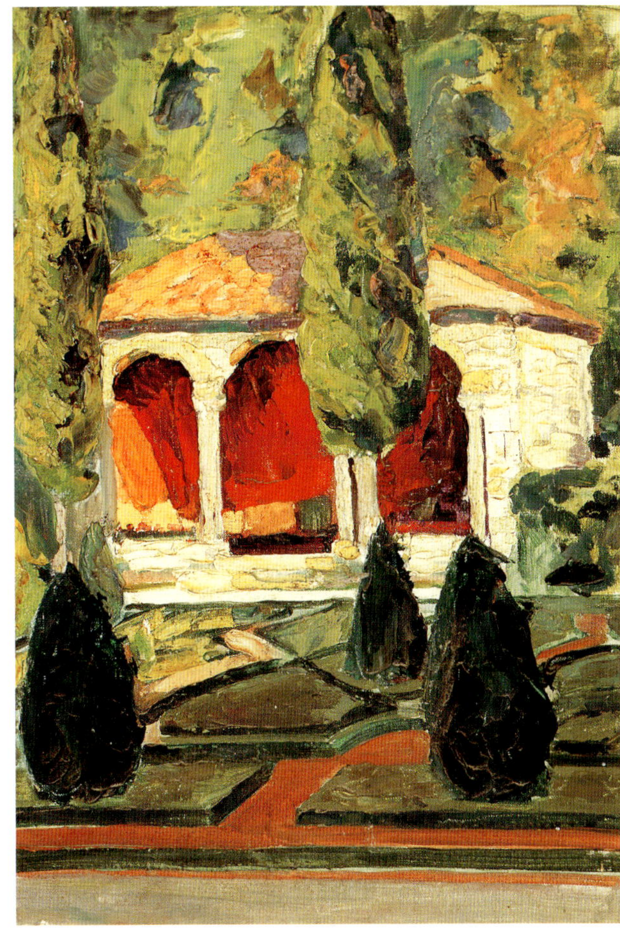

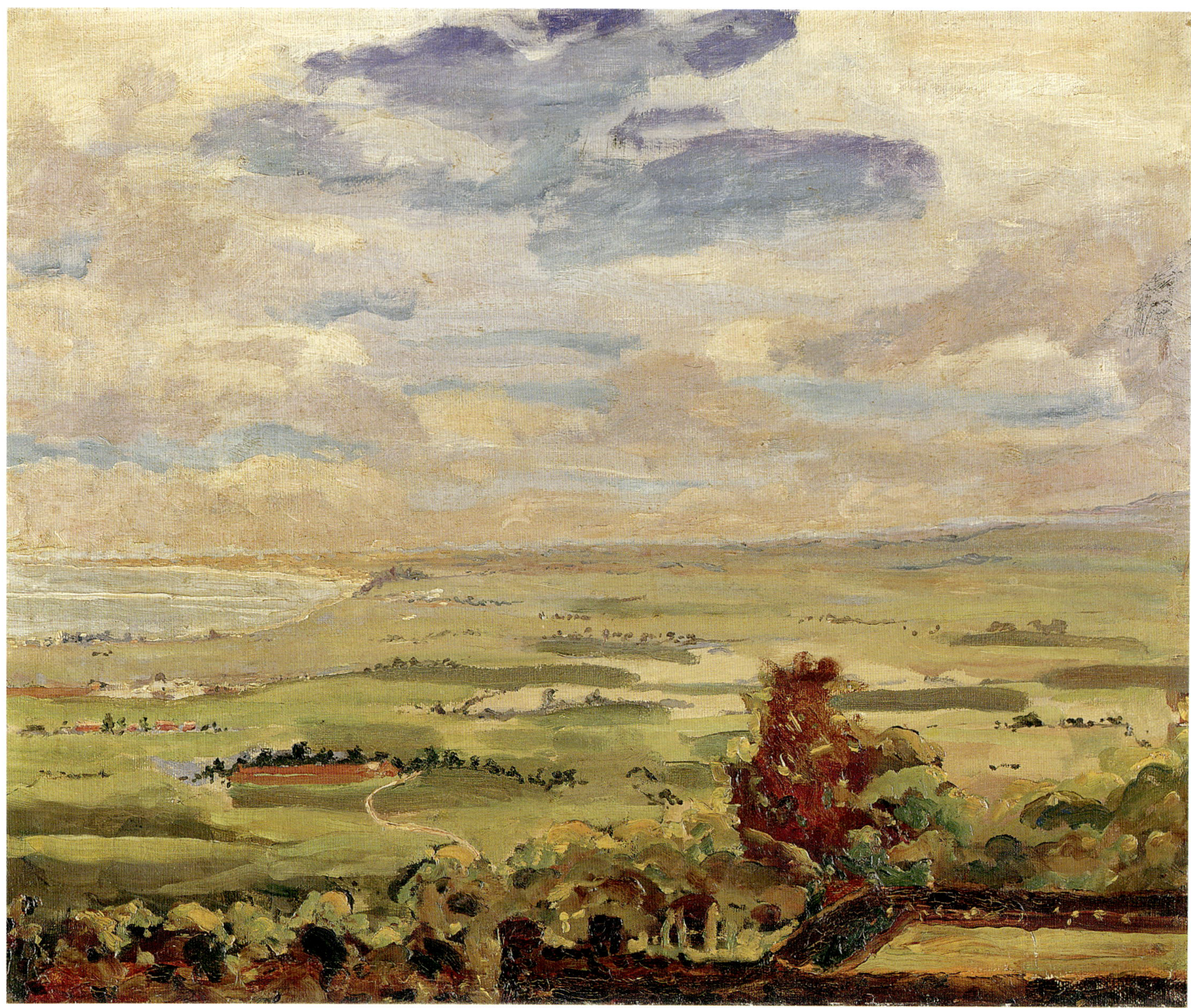

Fig 161 (C 80) above
View over the Lympne marshes. This painting was given by Winston to his son, Randolph.

variety the single triplex theme of the Nile, the desert, and the sun; or Palestine, a land of rare beauty - the beauty of the turquoise and opal - which well deserves the attention of some real artist, and has never been portrayed to the extent that it is due. And what of India? Who has ever interpreted its lurid splendours? But after all, if only the sun will shine, one does not need to go beyond one's own country. There is nothing more intense than the burnished steel and gold of a Highland stream; and at the beginning and close of almost every day the Thames displays to the citizens of London glories and delights which one must travel far to rival.

I end where I began; I hope sincerely that these notes and sketches may encourage others to find out whether they have not got within them that love of colour and faculty of observation which will enable them to enrich their leisure with the delightful amusement of painting. At any rate I shall dwell in the comfortable expectation of stirring some slumbering genius into action, or at least of investing a modest life with a new sense of fullness, security and independence.

Fig 162 (C 290) opposite page top
Coast scene near Lympne.

Fig 163 (C 289) opposite page below left
Coast scene near Lympne.

Fig 164 (C 293) opposite page below right
View of the sea from a clifftop at Lympne.

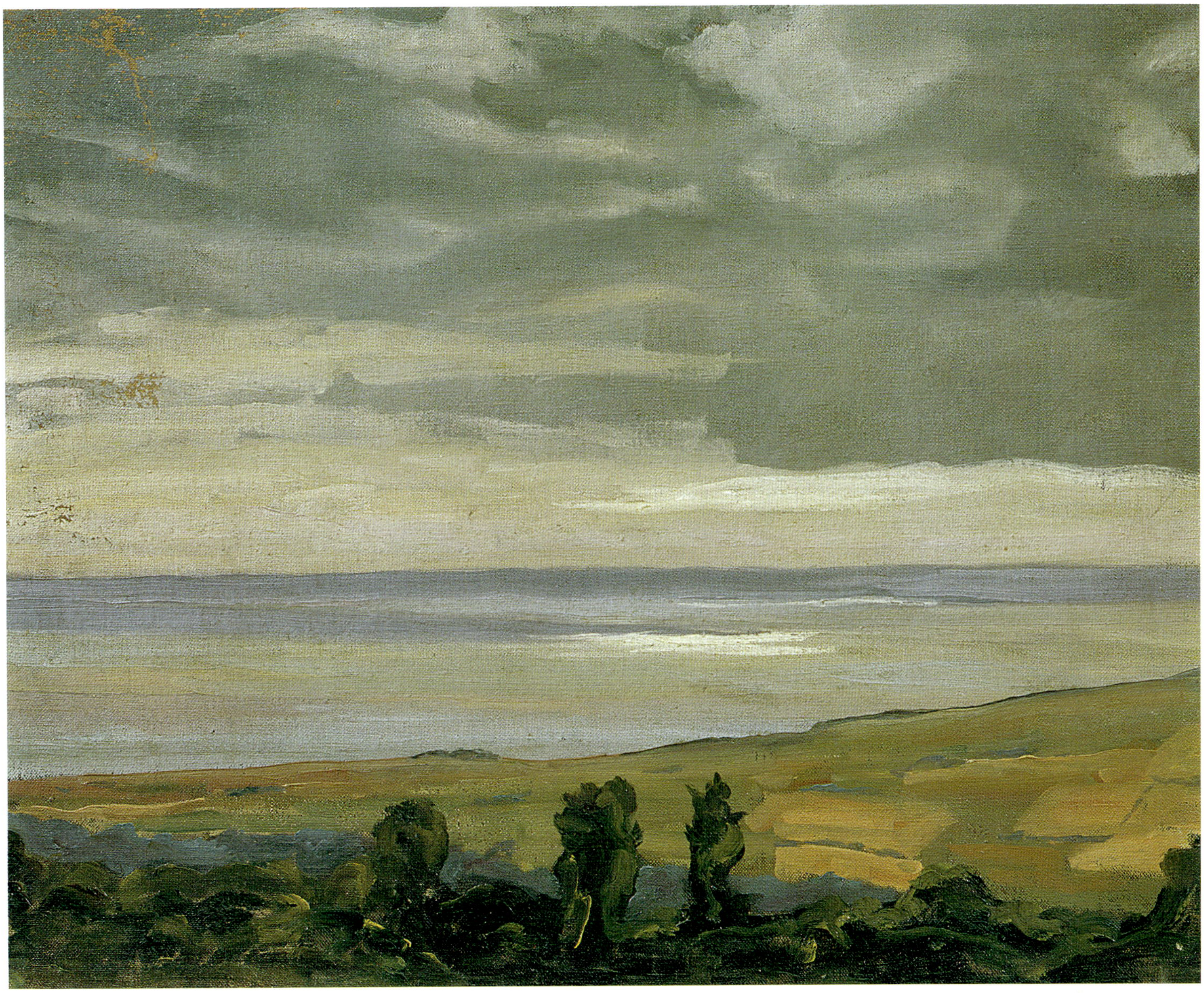

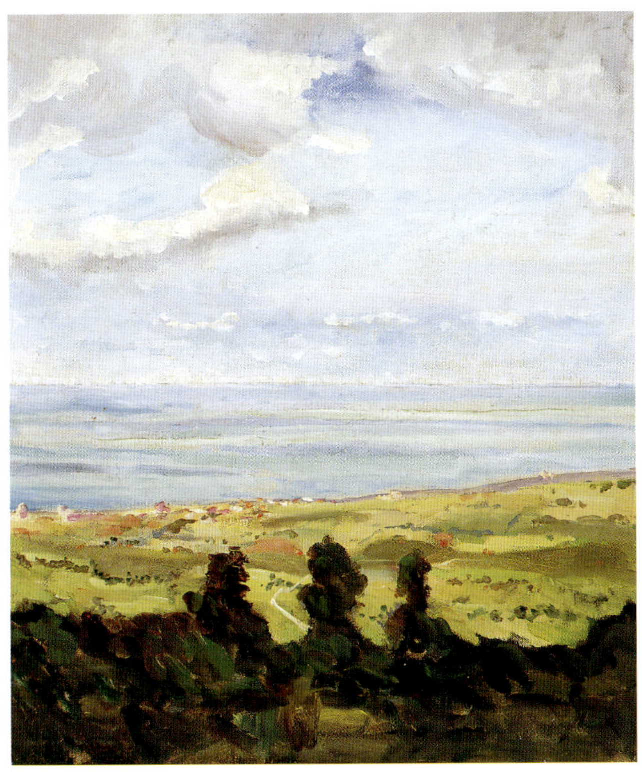

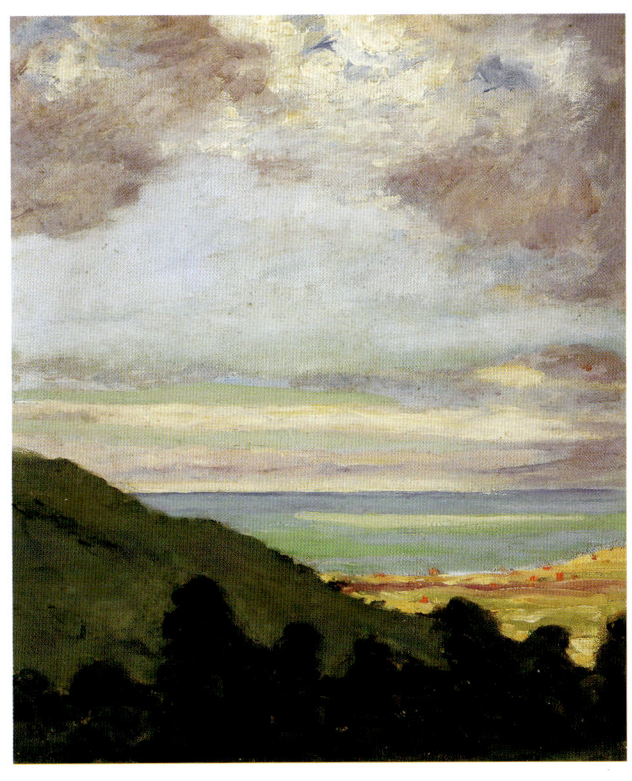

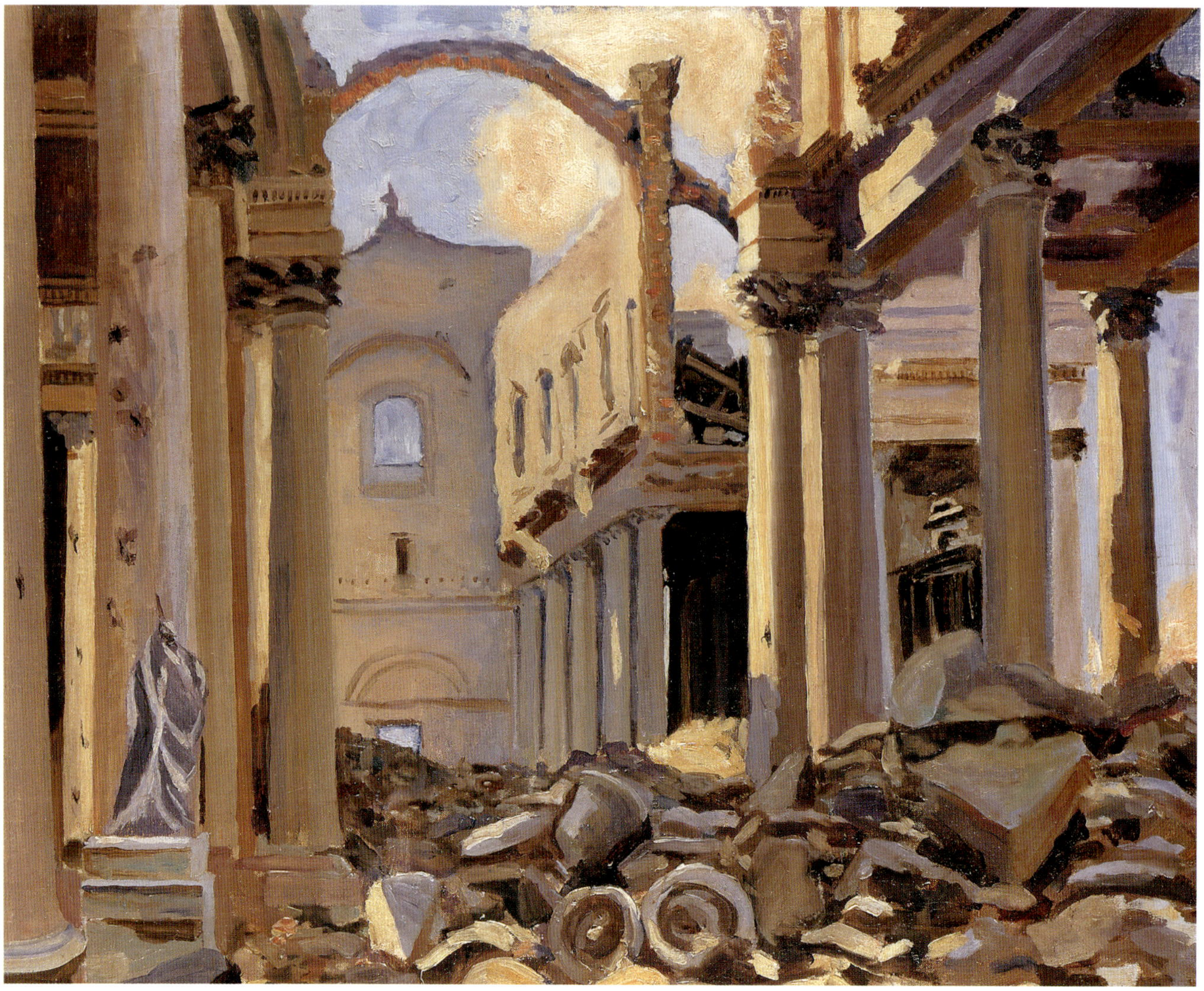

Fig 165 (C 440) above
Ruins of Arras Cathedral. Arras in north-west France was on the frontline during the First World War and suffered from considerable bombardment by both the German and Allied forces.

Both these pictures are excellent copies by Churchill of a painting by John Singer Sargent owned by Sir Philip Sassoon.

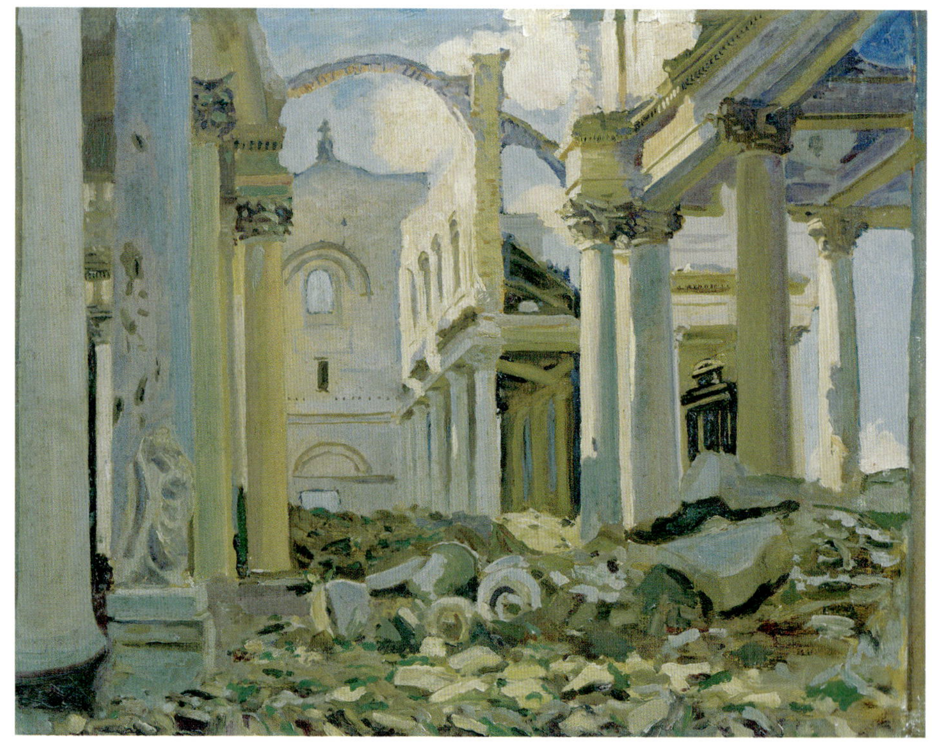

Fig 166 (C 116) right
Ruins of Arras Cathedral.

Hobbies

by The Rt. Hon. Winston Churchill P.C. M.P. etc

First published in *Nash's Pall Mall Magazine* 1925

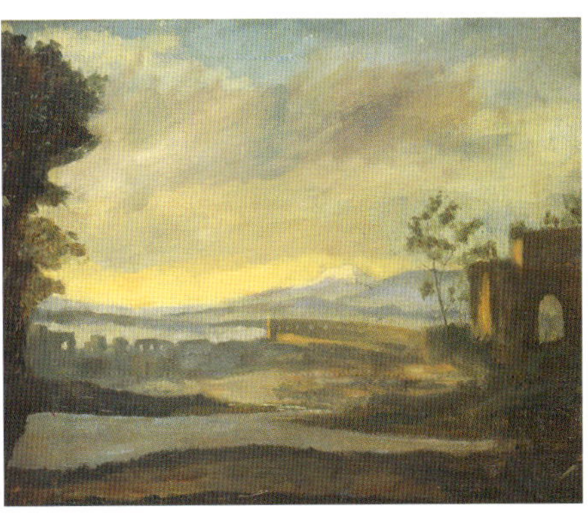

Fig 167 (C 100) above
A copy of a classical landscape: neither the artist nor its owner are known. From the outset in 1915, Churchill was fascinated by the techniques of the master painters and sought to learn from them by faithfully copying their works.

Many remedies are suggested for the avoidance of worry and mental overstrain by persons who, over prolonged periods, have to bear exceptional responsibilities and discharge duties upon a very large scale. Some advise exercise, and others, repose. Some counsel travel, and others, retreat. Some praise solitude, others, gaiety. No doubt all these may play their part according to the individual temperament. But the element which is constant and common in all of them is Change.

Change is the master key. A man can wear out a particular part of his mind by continually using it and tiring it, just in the same way as he can wear out the elbows of his coat. There is, however, this difference between the living cells of the brain and the inanimate articles: one cannot mend the frayed elbows of a coat by rubbing the sleeves or shoulders; but the tired part of the mind can be rested and strengthened, not merely by rest, but by using other parts. It is not enough to merely switch off the lights which play upon the main and ordinary field of interest; a new field of interest must be illuminated. It is no use saying to the tired 'mental muscles' - if one may coin such an expression – 'I will give you a good rest', 'I will go for a long walk' or 'I will lie down and think of nothing'. The mind keeps busy just the same. If it has been weighing and measuring, it goes on weighing and measuring. If it has been worrying, it goes on worrying. It is only when new cells are called into activity, when new stars become the lords of the ascendant, that relief, repose, refreshment are afforded.

A gifted American psychologist has said, 'Worry is a spasm of the emotion; the mind catches hold of something and will not let it go.'(10) It is useless to argue with the mind in this condition. The stronger the will, the more futile the task. One can only genuinely insinuate something else into its convulsive grasp. And if this something else is rightly chosen, if it is really attended by the illumination of another field of interest, gradually, and often quite swiftly, the old undue grip relaxes and the process of recuperation and repair begins.

The cultivation of a hobby and new forms of interest is therefore a policy of first importance to a public man. But this is not a business that can be undertaken in a day or swiftly improvised by a mere command of the will. The growth of alternative mental interest is a long process. The seeds must be carefully chosen; they must fall on good ground; they must be sedulously tended, if the vivifying fruits are to be at hand when needed.

To be really happy and really safe one ought to have at least two or three hobbies, and they must all be real. It is no use starting late in life to say: I will take an interest in this or that. Such an attempt only aggravates the strain of mental effort. A man may acquire great knowledge of topics unconnected with his daily work, and yet hardly get any benefit or relief. It is no use doing what you like; you have got to like what you do. Broadly speaking, human beings may

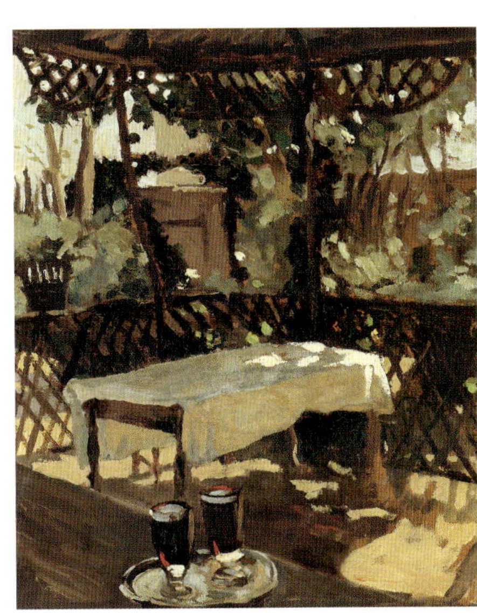

Fig 168 (C 179) above
Two glasses on a verandah, a copy by Churchill of a little painting by John Singer Sargent owned by Sir Philip Sassoon. Winston's copy formerly belonged to Clementine Churchill.

Fig 169 (C 129) right
An unfinished copy on panel by Churchill of a painting hanging in his Study at Chartwell.

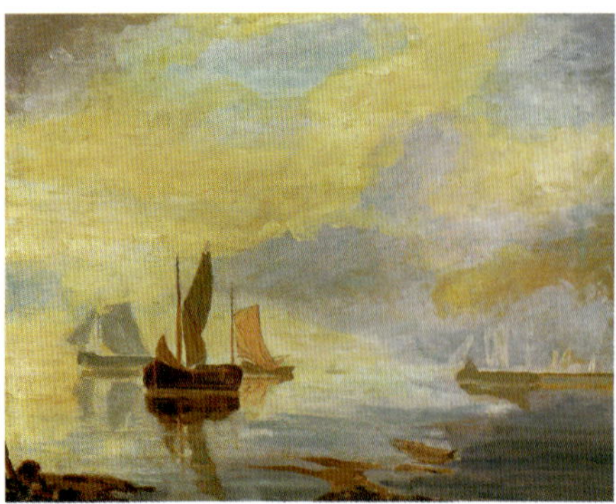

Fig 170 (C 133) above
Another copy by Churchill of the 19th century Dutch seascape that hangs in his Study at Chartwell.

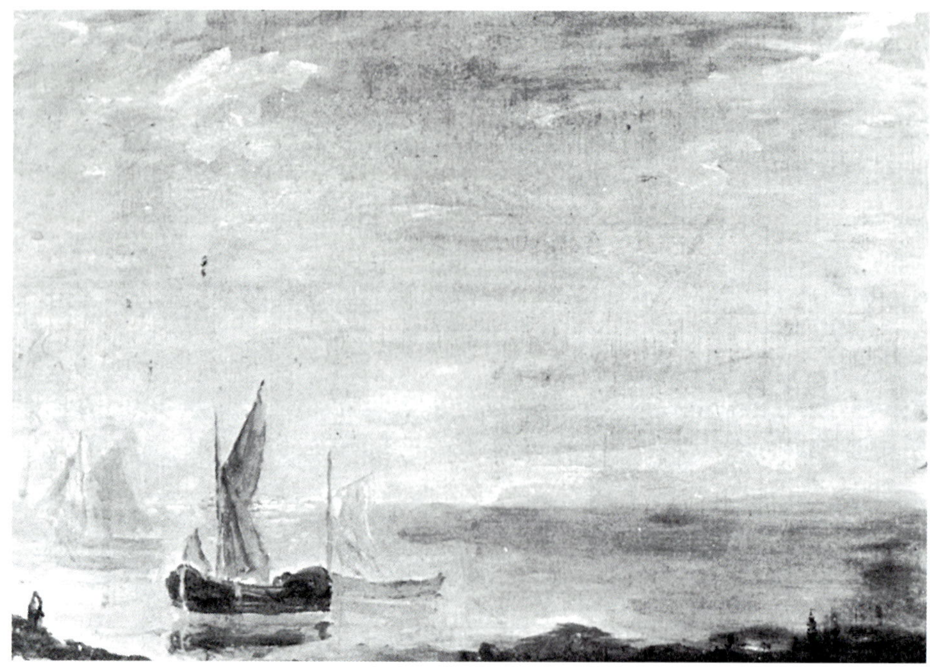

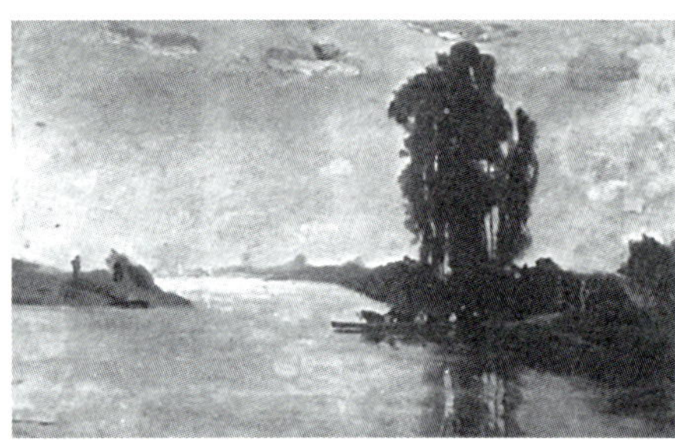

Fig 171 (C 165) above
Copy after Daubigny. All these copies seem to have been painted by Churchill as early as 1915.

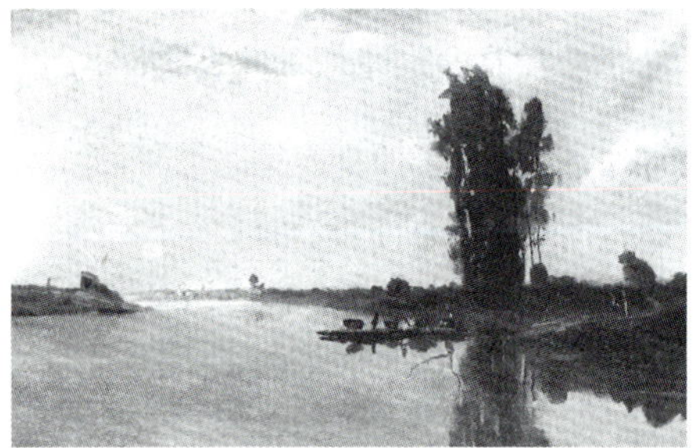

Fig 172 (C 162) above
Copy after Daubigny. All these copies by Churchill are of a painting by the 19th century French landscape painter Charles Daubigny owned by his cousin Sunny, the 9th Duke of Marlborough.

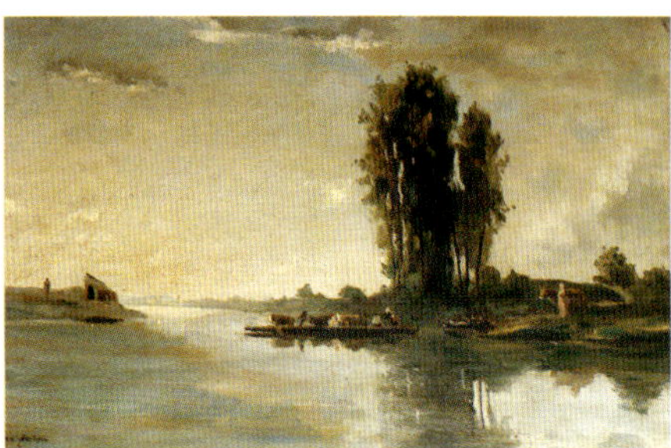

Fig 173 (C 164) above
Copy after Daubigny. Churchill gave this painting to the Earl of Birkenhead.

be divided into three classes: those who are toiled to death, those who are worried to death, and those who are bored to death. It is no use offering the manual labourer, tired out with a hard week's sweat and effort, the chance of playing a game of football or baseball on Saturday afternoon. It is no use inviting the politician or the professional or business man, who has been working or worrying about serious things for six days, to work or worry about trifling things at the week-end.

As for the unfortunate people who can command everything they want, who can gratify every caprice and lay their hand on almost every object of desire - for them a new pleasure, a new excitement is only additional satiation. In vain they rush frantically round from place to place, trying to escape from avenging boredom by mere clatter and motion. For them discipline in one form or another is the most hopeful path.

It may also be said that rational, industrious, useful human beings are divided into two classes: first, those whose work is work and whose pleasure is pleasure; and secondly, those whose work and pleasure are one. Of these the former is the common lot [are the majority]. They have their compensations. The long hours in the office or the factory bring with them as their reward, not only the means of sustenance, but a keen appetite for pleasure even in its simplest and most modest forms. But Fortune's favoured children belong to the second class. Their life is a natural harmony. For them the working hours are never long enough. Each day is a holiday, and ordinary holidays when they come are grudged as enforced interruptions in an absorbing vocation. Yet to both classes the need of an alternative outlook, of a change of atmosphere, diversion of effort, is essential. Indeed, it may well be that those whose work is their pleasure are those who most need the banishing of it at intervals from their minds.

The most common form of diversion is reading. In that vast and varied field millions find their mental comfort. Nothing makes man more reverent than a library. 'A few books', which was Lord Morley's definition of anything under five thousand, may give a sense of comfort and even of complacency.(11) But a day in a library even of modest dimensions, quickly dispels these illusory sensations. As you browse about, taking down book after book from the shelves and contemplating the vast, infinitely varied store of knowledge and wisdom which

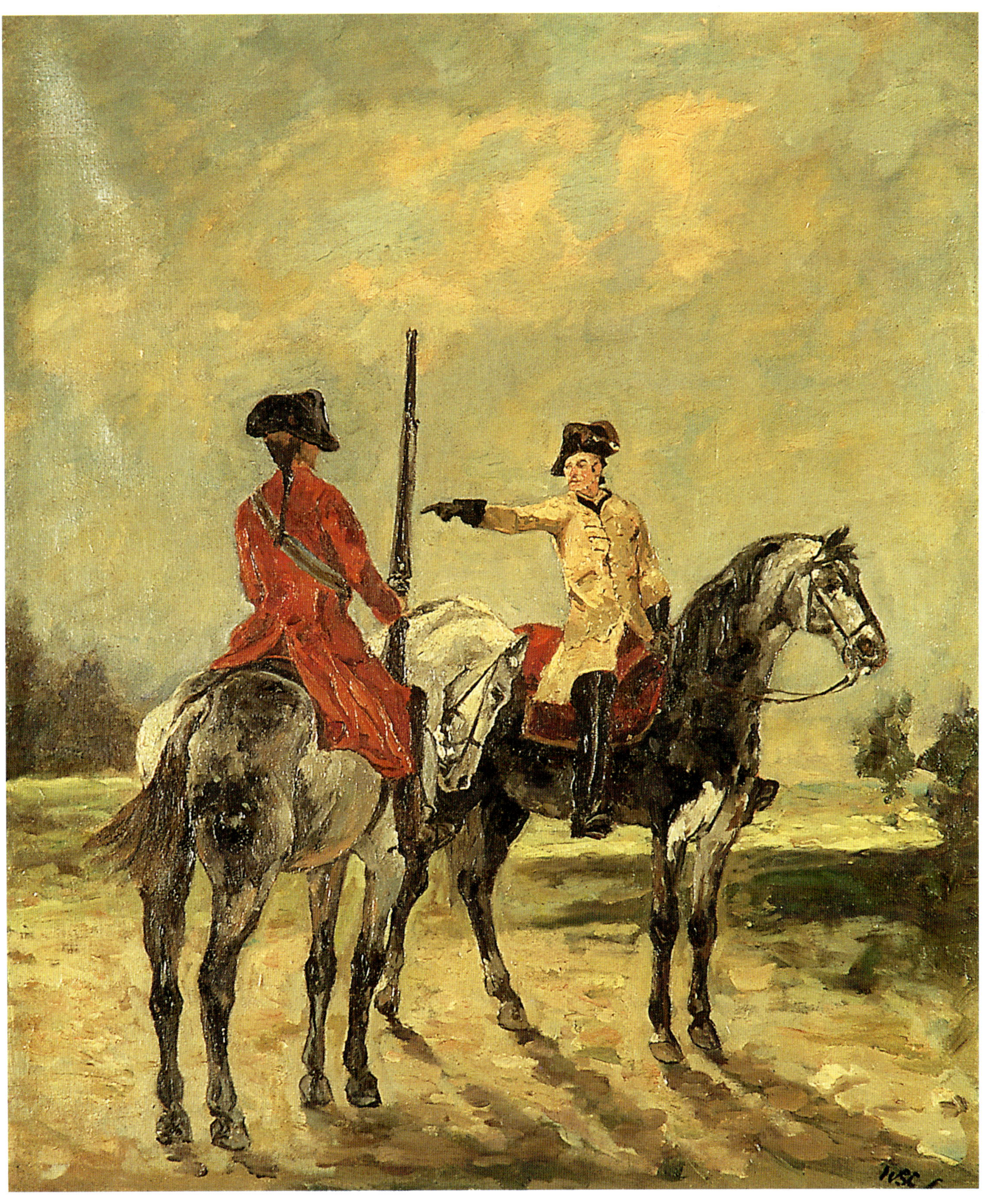

Fig 174 (C 163) above
Copy by Churchill of a painting by John Lewis Brown hanging in his Study at Chartwell. The original was a gift from Sir Philip Sassoon.

Fig 175 (C 130) right
A none-too successful painting of the church of San Giorgio in Venice.

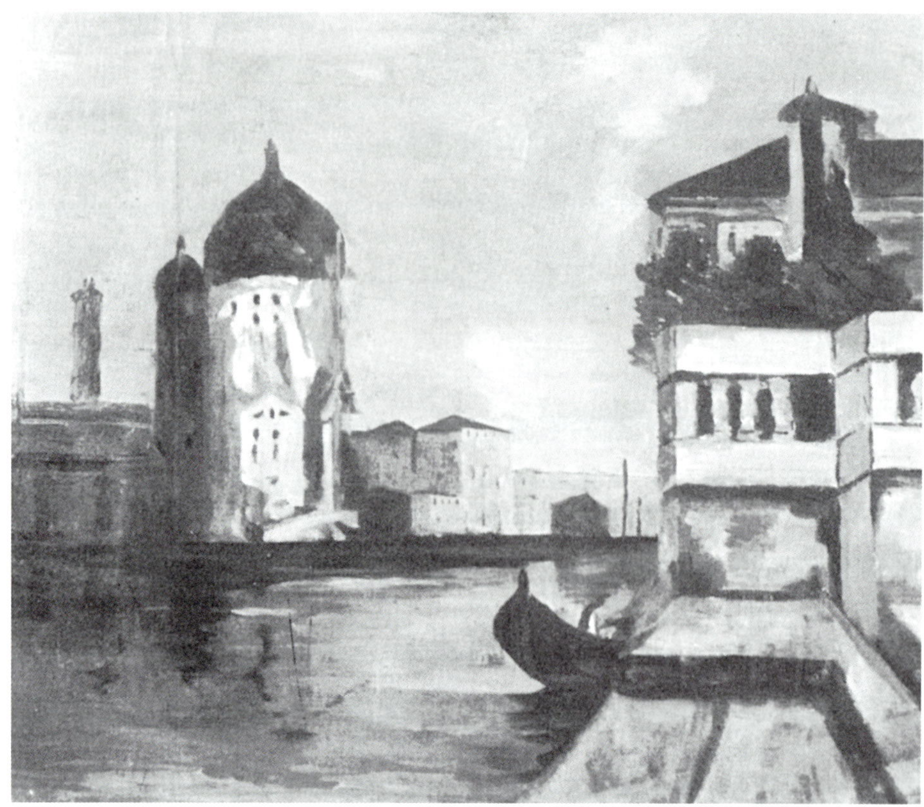

Fig 176 (C 119) right below
A painting of the Bridge of Sighs in Venice.

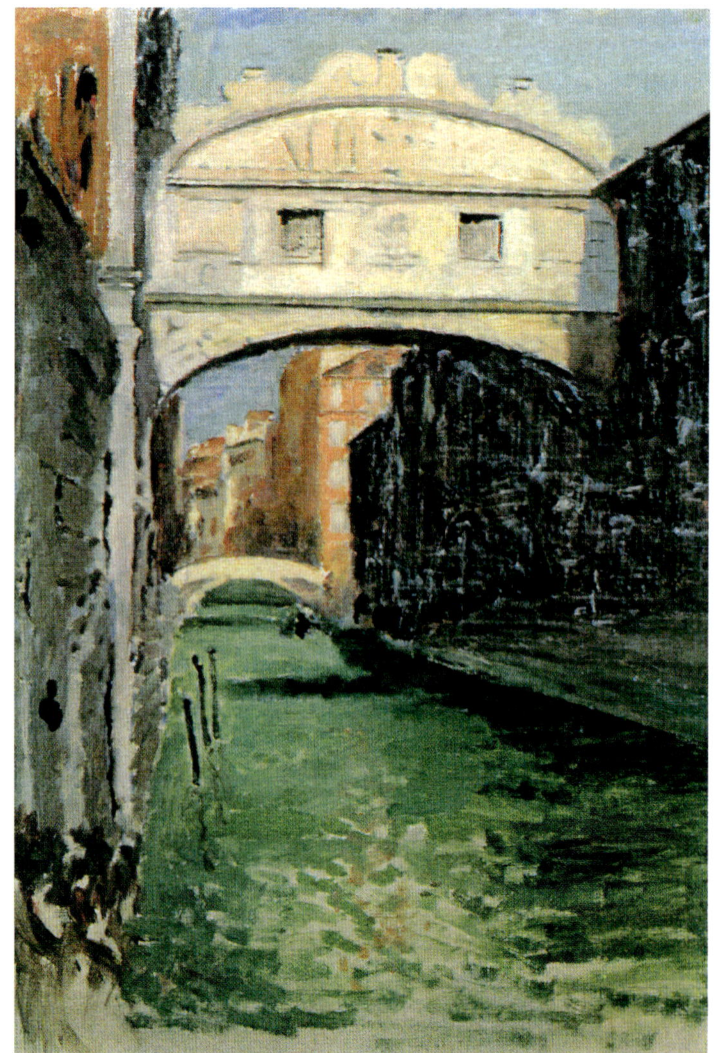

Fig 177 (C 44) below
The two ladies in a Gondola on the Venetian Lagoon are probably Clementine and Diana Churchill on holiday in 1927. This picture may have been painted from a photograph.

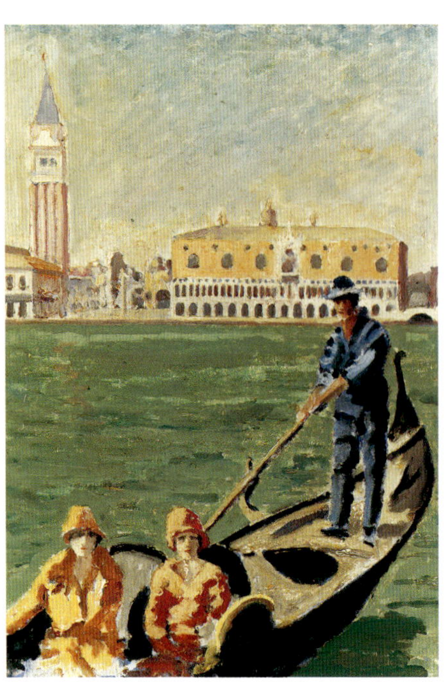

the human race has accumulated and preserved, pride, even in its most innocent forms, is chased from the heart by feelings of awe not untinged with sadness. As one surveys the mighty array of sages, saints, historians, scientists, poets and philosophers whose treasures one will never be able to admire - still less enjoy - the brief tenure of our existence here dominates mind and spirit.

Think of all the wonderful tales that have been told, and well told, which you will never know. Think of all these searching inquiries into matters of great consequence which you will never pursue. Think of all the delighting or disturbing ideas that you will never share. Think of the mighty labours which have been accomplished for your service, but out of which you will never reap the fruits [harvest]. But from this melancholy there also comes a calm. The bitter sweets of a pious despair melt into an agreeable sense of compulsory resignation from which we turn with renewed zest to the lighter vanities of life.

'What shall I do with all my books?' was the question; and the answer, 'Read them', sobered the questioner. But if you cannot read them, at any rate handle them and, as it were, fondle them. Peer into them. Let them fall open where they will. Read the first sentence that arrests the eye. Then turn to another. Make a voyage of discovery, taking soundings of uncharted sea. Set them back on their shelves with your own hands. Arrange them on your own plan, so that if you do not know what is in them, you at least know where they are. If they cannot be your friends, let them at any rate be your acquaintances. If they cannot enter the circle of your life, do not deny them at least a nod of recognition.

It is a mistake to read too many books when quite young. A man once told me that he had read all the books that mattered. Cross-questioned, he appeared to

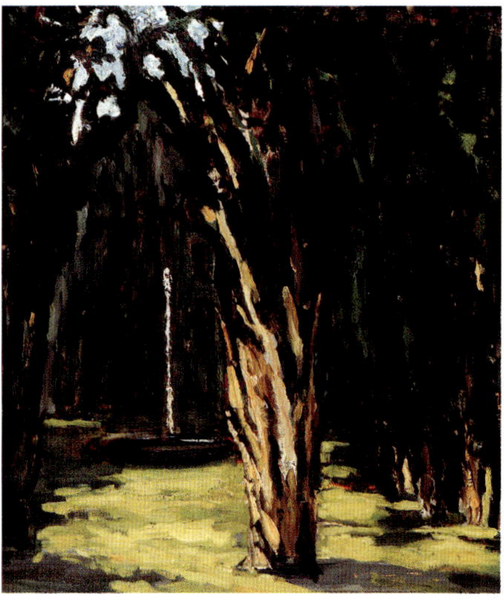

Fig 178 (C 77) above
Where this picture of a fountain in shade was painted is unknown; it is likely to be in Italy, perhaps near Florence.

Fig 179 (C 92) below
A lake scene in the Dolomites in north-east Italy. Churchill knew northern Italy well and it was a frequent source of inspiration for his brush.

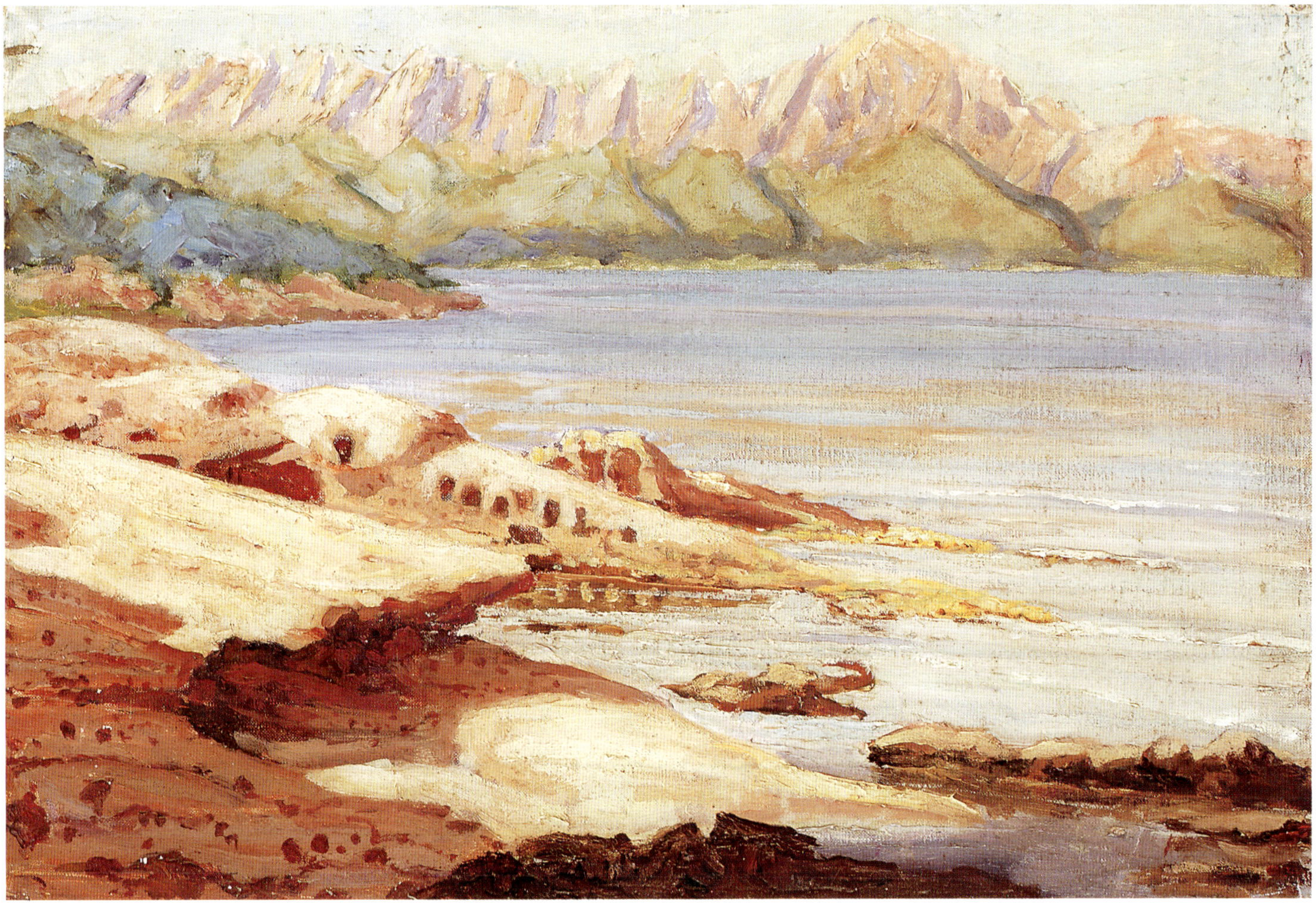

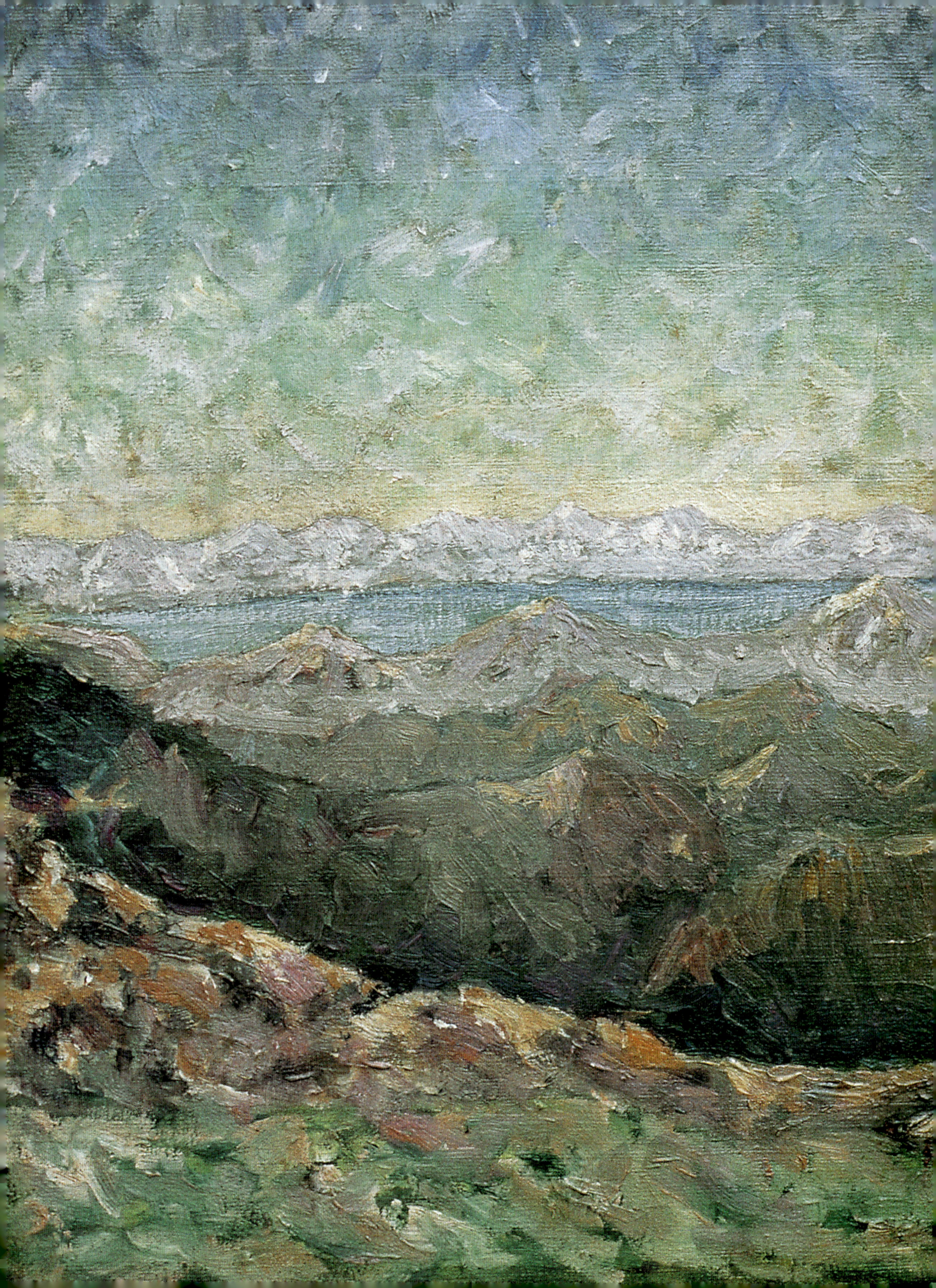

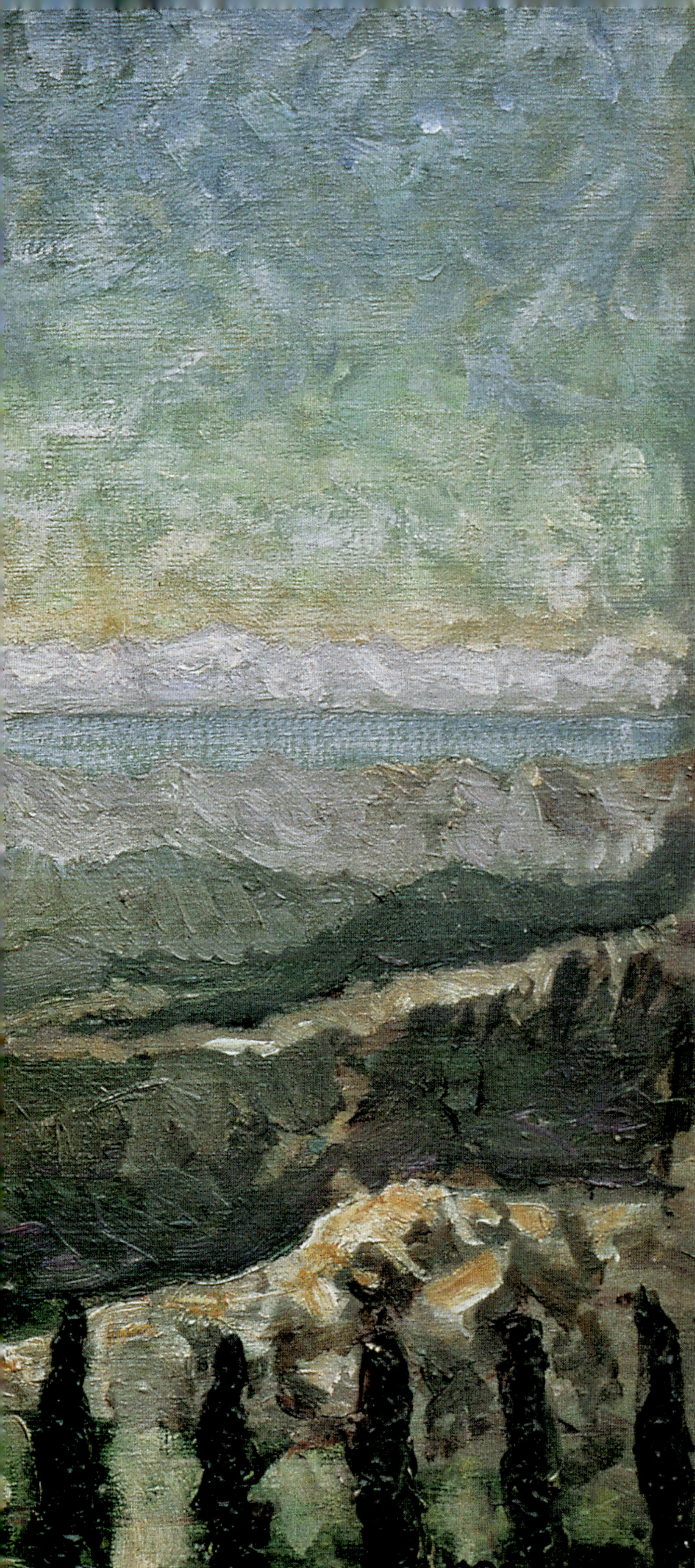

Fig 180 (C 200) left
This view in the Italian alps was formerly owned by Clementine Churchill.

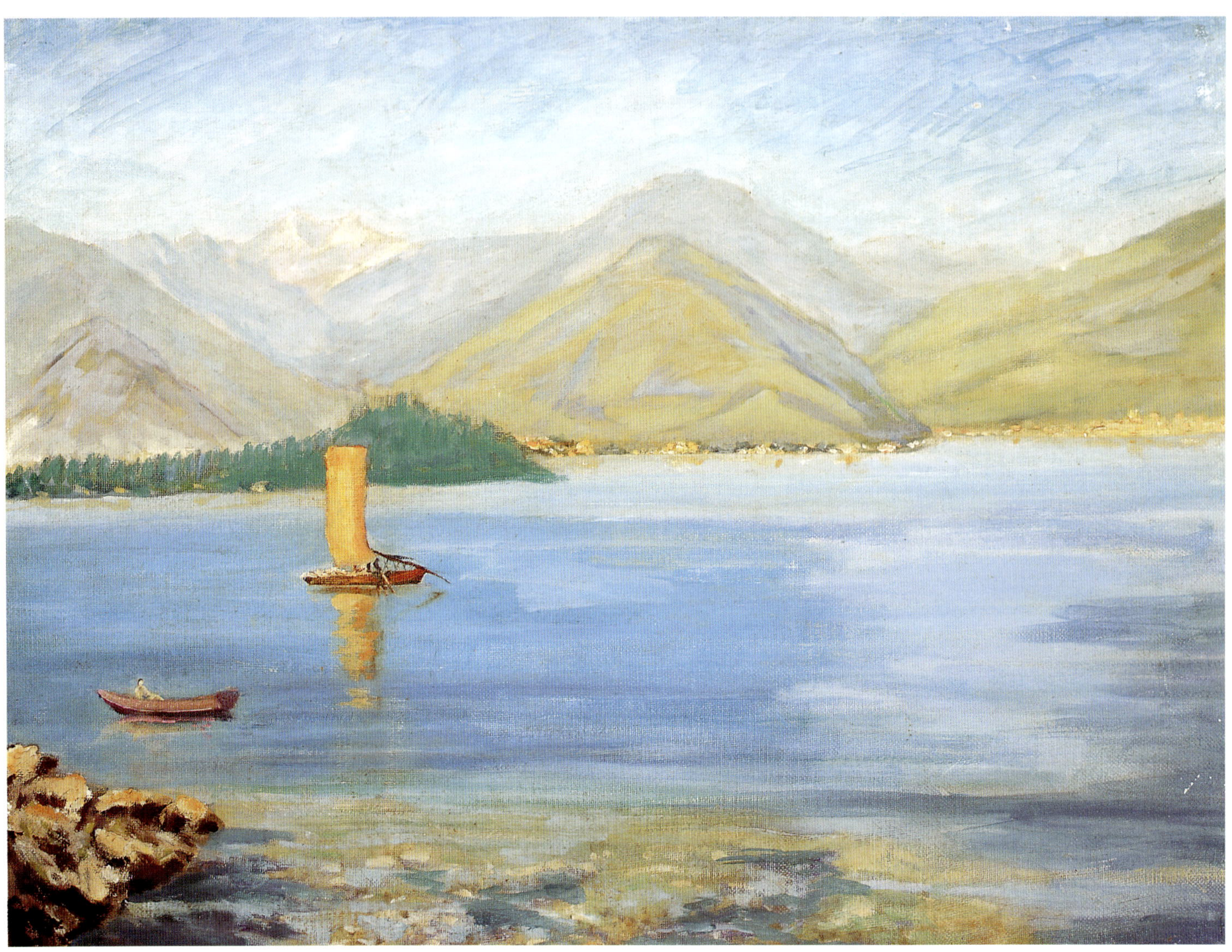

have read a great many, but they seemed to have made only a slight impression. How many had he understood? How many had entered into his mental composition? How many had been hammered on the anvils of his mind, and afterwards ranged in an armoury of bright weapons ready to hand?

It is a great pity to read a book too soon in life. The first impression is the one that counts; and if it is a slight one, it may be all that can be hoped for. A later and second perusal may recoil from a surface already hardened by premature contact. Young people should be careful in their reading, as old people in eating their food. They should not eat too much. They should chew it well.

Since change is an essential element in diversion of all kinds, it is naturally more restful and refreshing to read in a different language from that in which one's ordinary daily work is done. To have a second language at your disposal, even if you only know it enough to read it with pleasure, is a sensible advantage.

Our educationists are too often anxious to teach children so many different languages that they never get far enough in any one to derive any use or enjoyment from their study. The boy learns enough Latin to detest it; enough Greek to pass an examination; enough French to get from Calais to Paris; enough German to exhibit a diploma; enough Spanish or Italian to tell which is which; but not enough of any to secure the enormous boon of access to a second literature.

Fig 181 (C 190) above
A view of Lake Maggiore in northern Italy. In 1908 Clementine and Winston spent part of their honeymoon here.

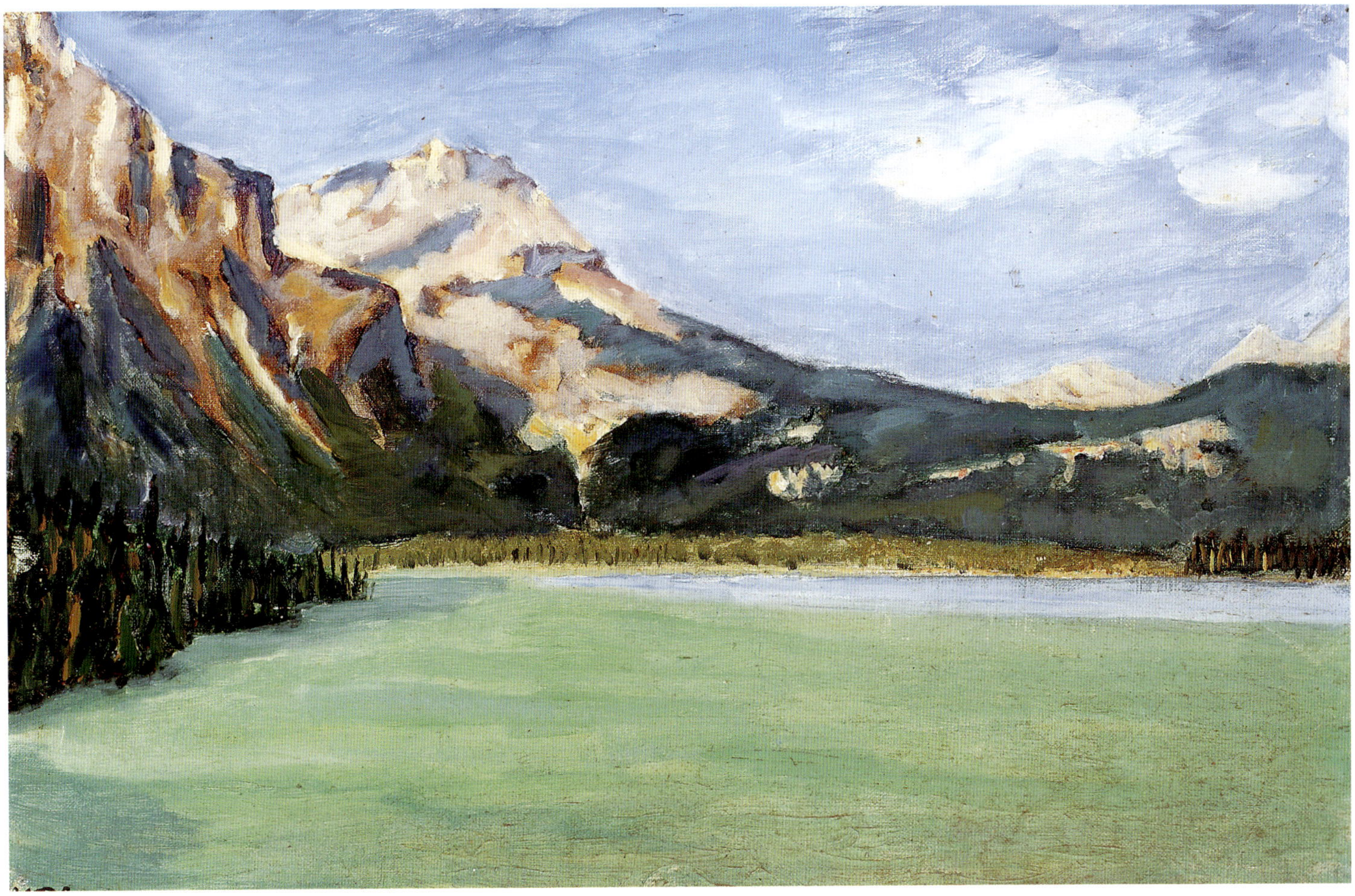

Fig 182 (C 191) above
A view in the Italian Dolomites.

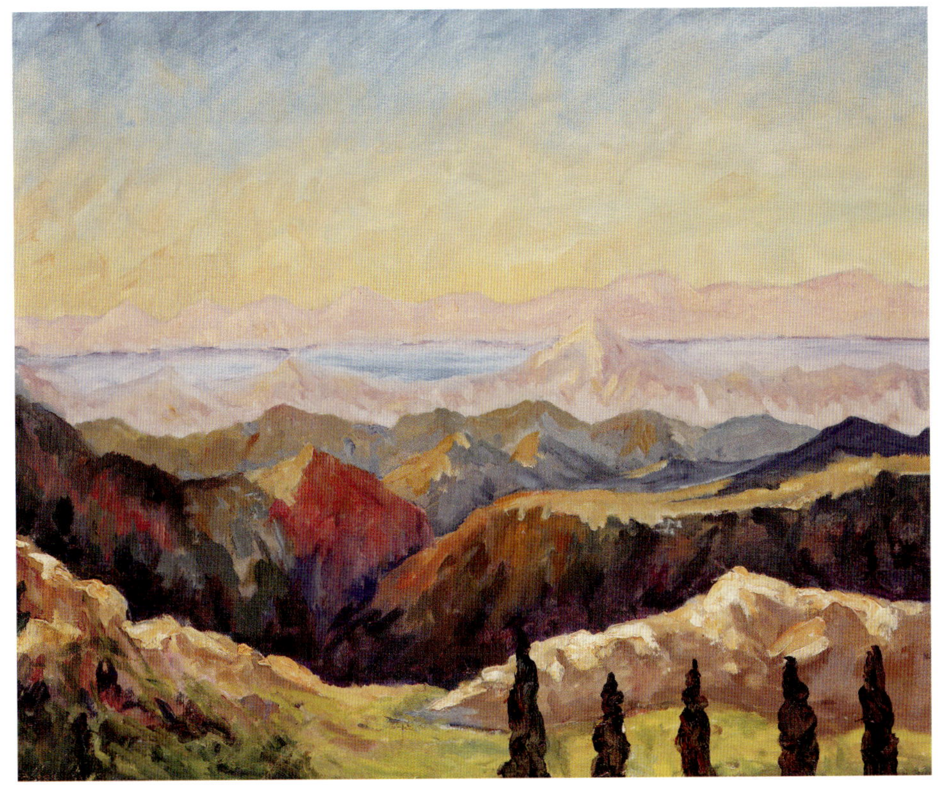

Fig 183 (C 198) left
A view in the Italian Alps.

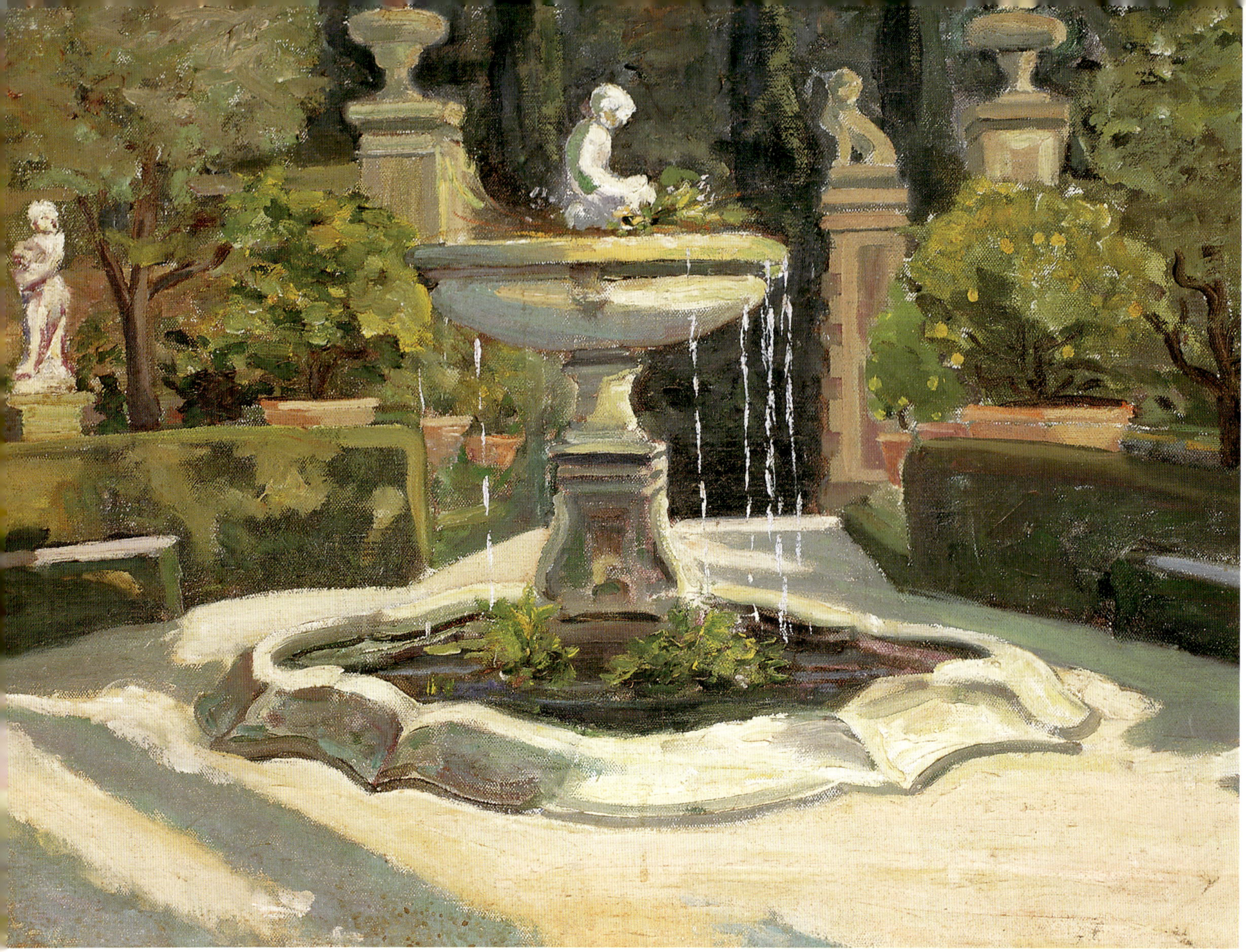

Fig 184 (C 262) above
Fountain in a garden near Florence. Perhaps at Mrs Keppel's villa.

Fig 185 (C 263) right
The Terrace at Mrs Alice Keppel's Villa d'Ombrellino near Florence.

Fig 186 (C 253) below
Probably an Italian garden scene.

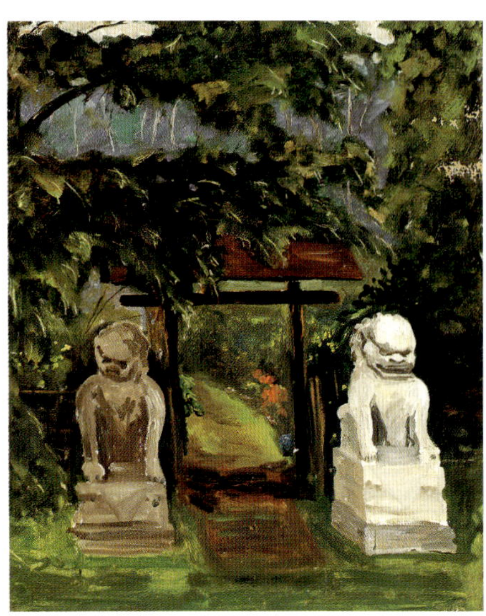

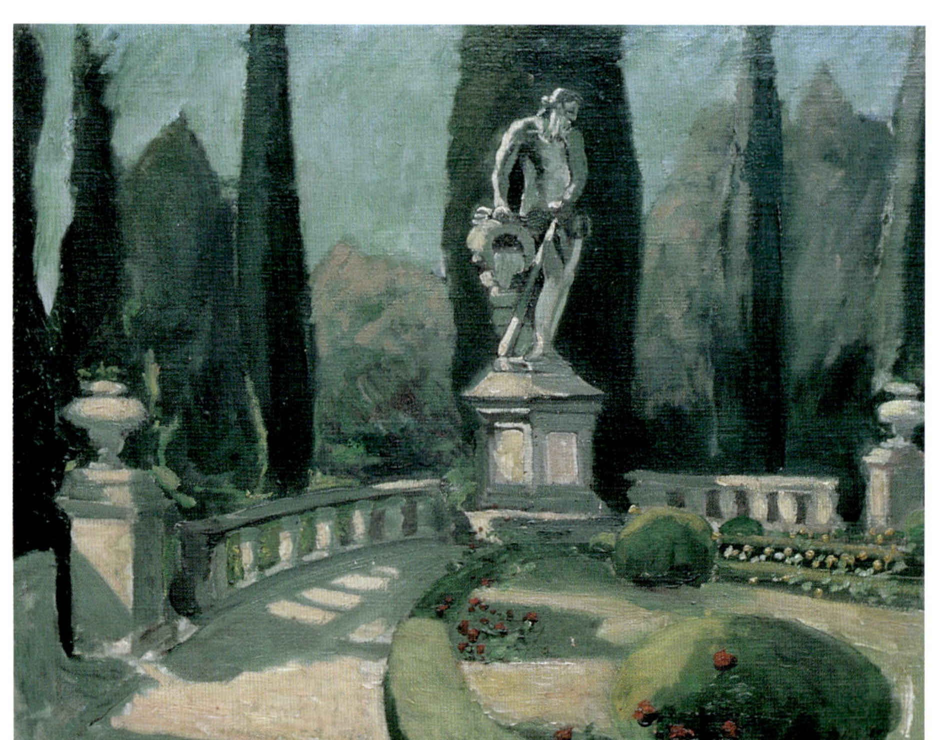

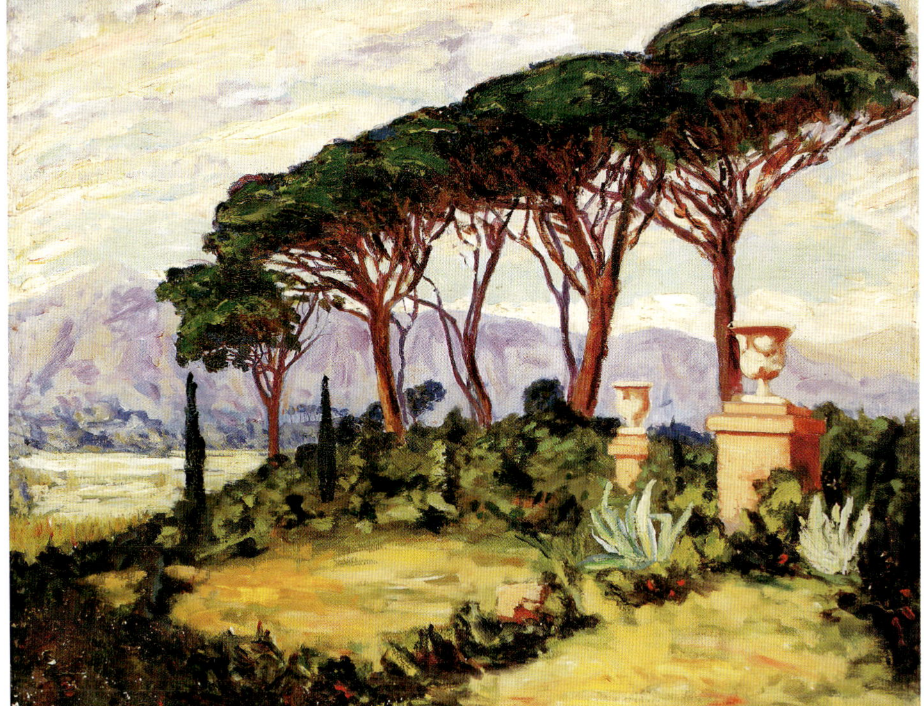

Fig 187 (C 265) left
A garden somewhere on the French Riviera.

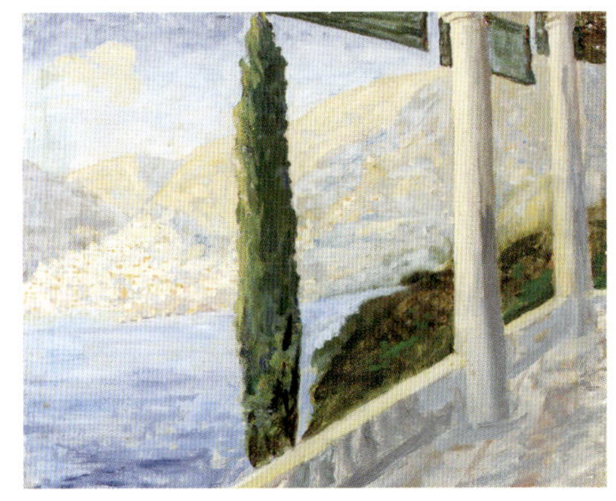

Fig 188 (C 280) above
A view of Monte Carlo and Monaco.

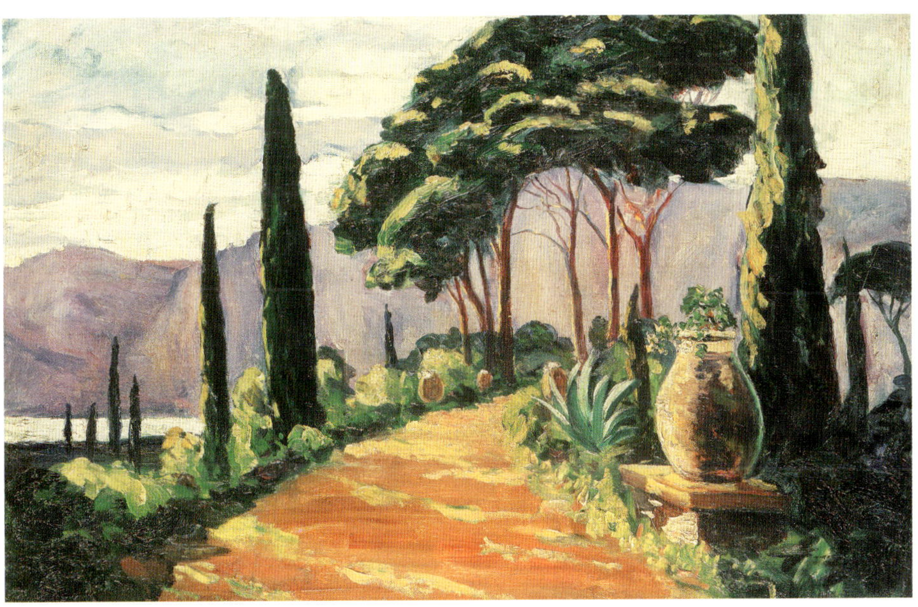

Fig 189 (C 264) left
This painting is initialled and titled 'Riviera Scene' on the back.

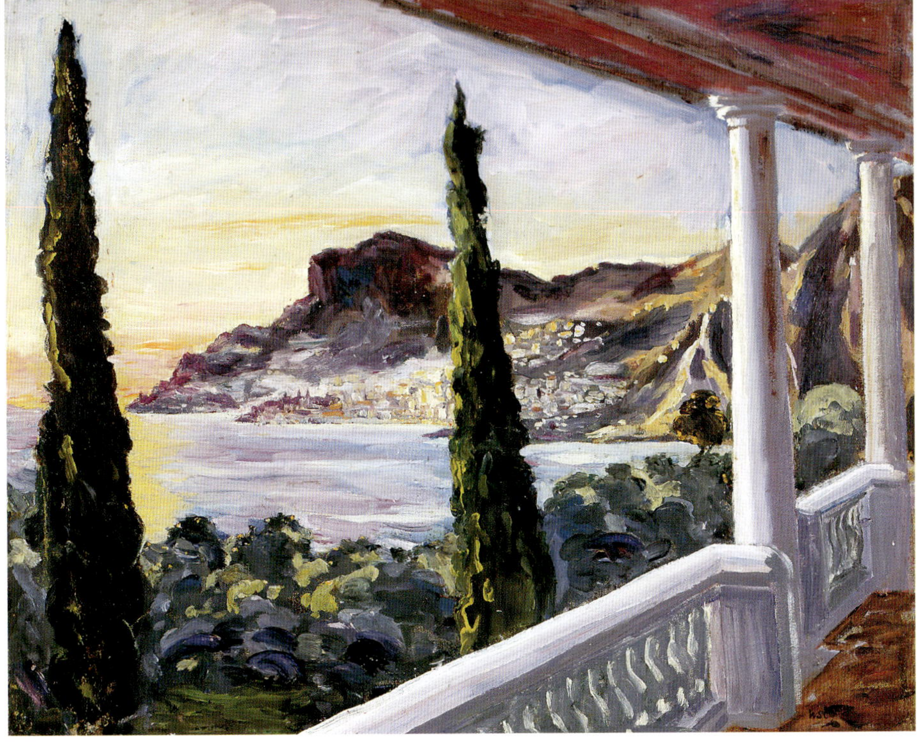

Fig 190 (C 279) left
View of Monte Carlo. As well as being attracted by the view, Churchill much enjoyed gambling at Monte Carlo's Casino.

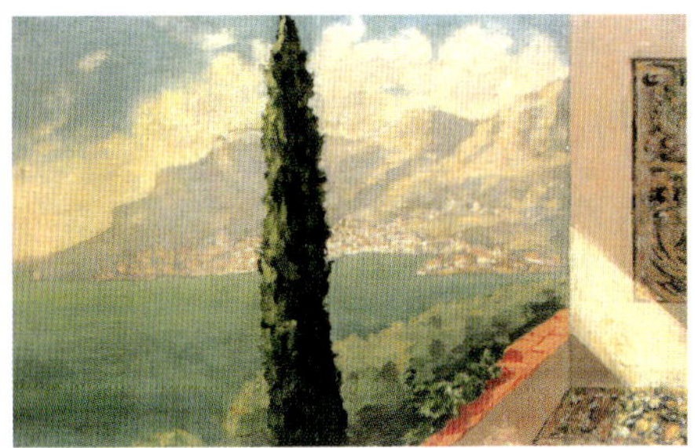

Fig 191 (C 281) above
Monte Carlo and Monaco.

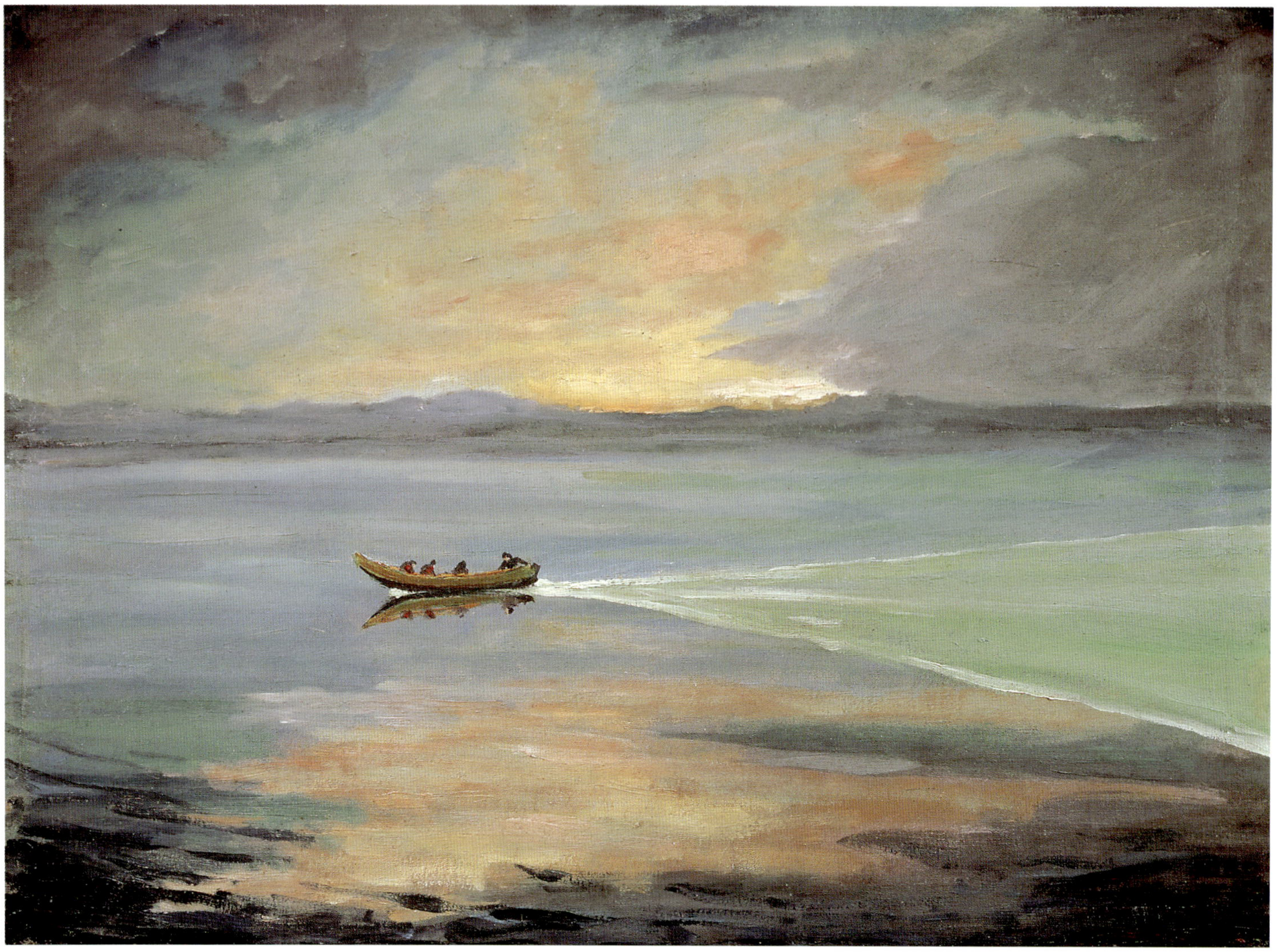

Fig 192 (C 134) above
A flat calm; the high-prowed boat is so distinctive that it might suggest the original location?

Fig 193 (C 136) right
The Firth of Forth. Perhaps painted while Churchill was staying with the Earl of Rosebery at Dalmeny House; there was a naval base nearby.

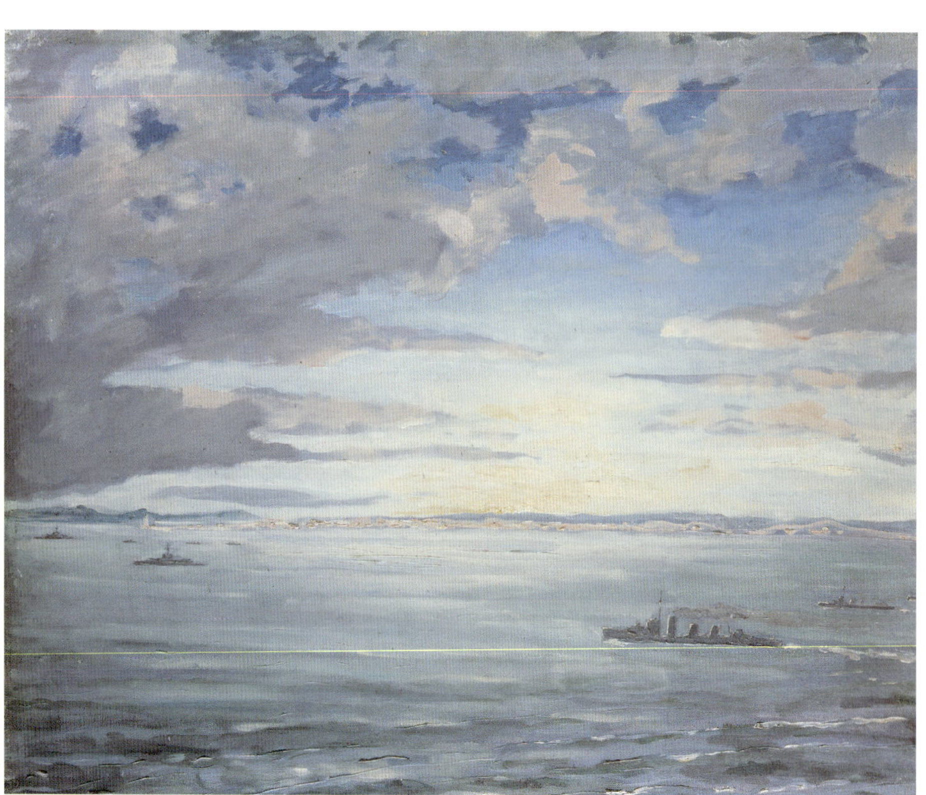

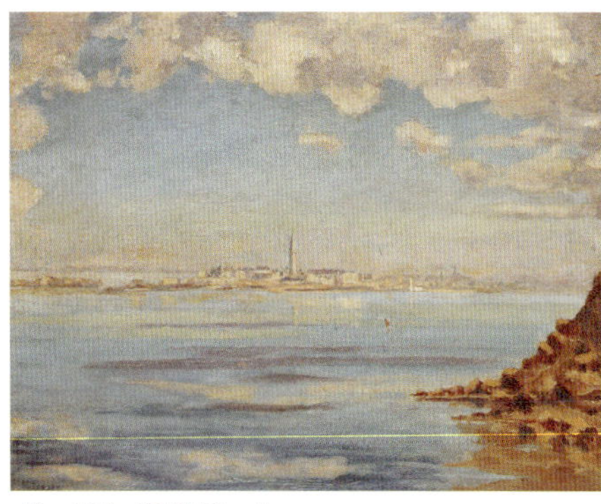

Fig 194 (C 323) above
Distant view of Venice (or St Malo). The rocks in the right foreground are likely to have been added by Churchill later.

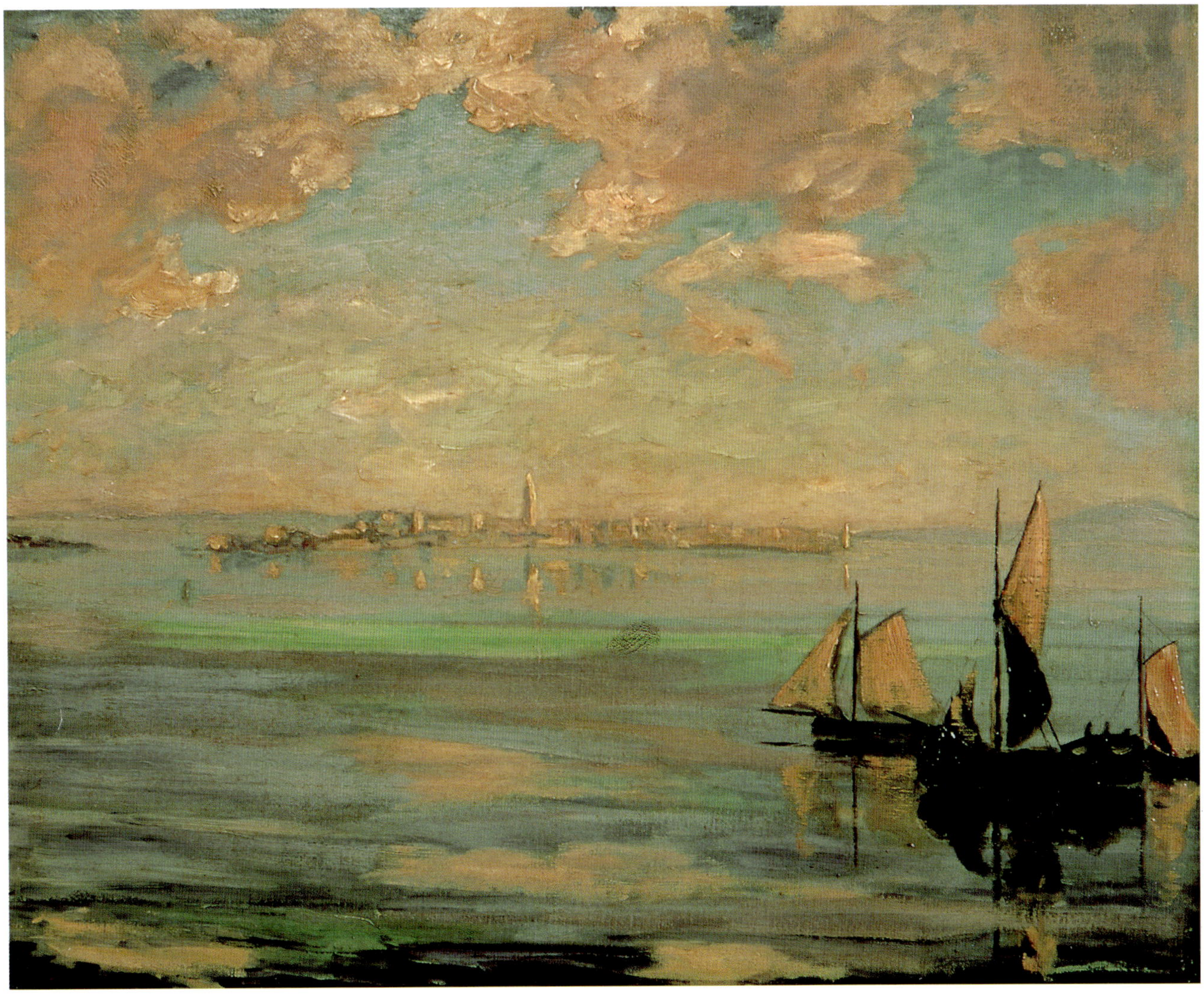

Fig 195 (C 135) above
Distant view of Venice (or St Malo). The sailing vessels in the right foreground are based on the Dutch seascape hanging in Churchill's Study at Chartwell and are likely to have been added by him later. This painting was given to Churchill's old school at Harrow by Lady Churchill after his death.

Choose well, choose wisely and choose one. Concentrate upon that one. Do not be content until you find yourself reading in it with real enjoyment. The process of reading for pleasure in another language rests the mental muscles; it enlivens the mind by a different sequence and emphasis of ideas. The mere form of speech excites the activity of separate brain cells, relieving in the most effective manner the fatigue of those in hackneyed use. One may imagine that a man who blew the trumpet for his living would be glad to play the violin for his amusement. So it is with reading in another language than your own.

But reading and book-love in all their forms suffer from one serious defect: they are too nearly akin to the ordinary daily round of the brain-worker to give that element of change and contrast essential to real relief. To restore psychic equilibrium we should call into use those parts of the mind which direct both eye and hand.

Many men have found great advantage in practising a handicraft for pleasure. Joinery, chemistry, book-binding, even brick-laying - if one were interested in them and skilful at them - would give a real relief to the over-tired brain. But, best of all and easiest to procure are sketching and painting in all their forms. I consider myself very lucky that late in life I have been able to develop this new taste and pastime. Painting came to my rescue in a most trying time. [and I shall venture in [a concluding chapter] the pages that follow to express the gratitude I feel.]

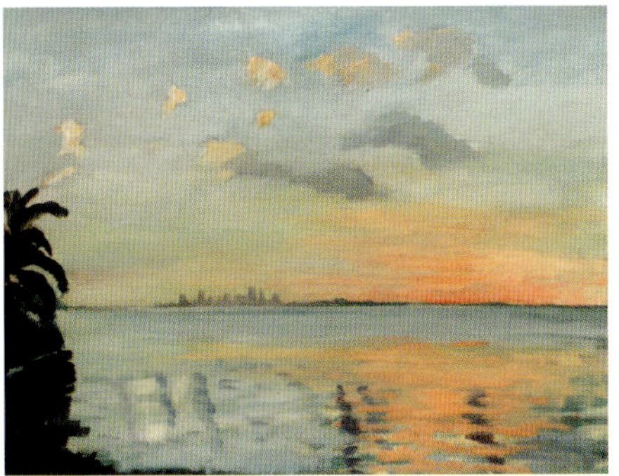

Fig 196 (C 322) above
Distant view of Venice. The foliage on the left is likely to have been added by Churchill later.

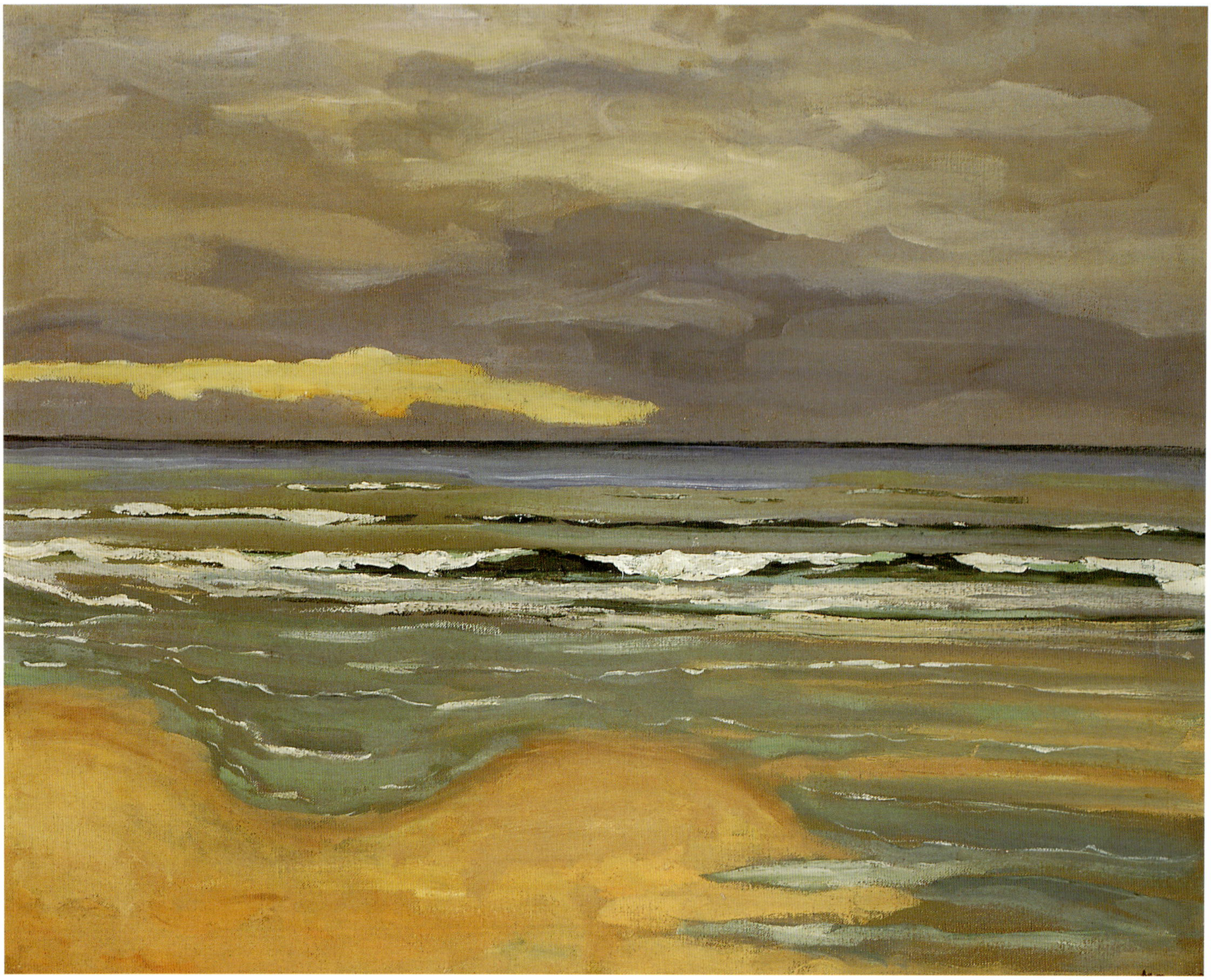

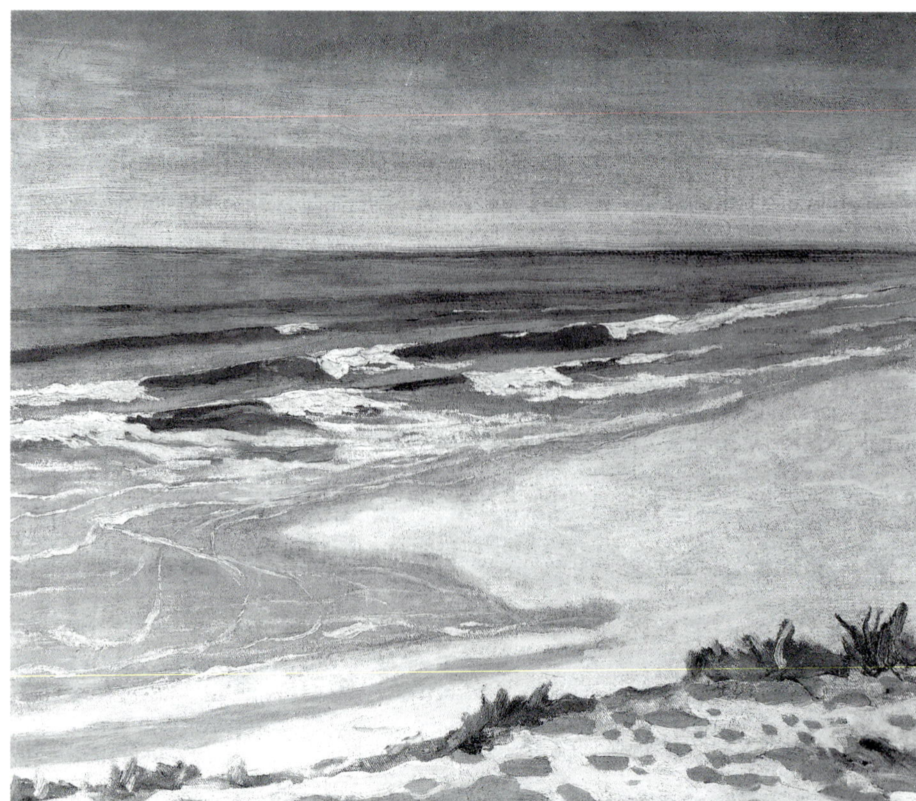

Fig 197 (C 319) above
Coast scene. The location is unknown but the surf is a reminder of how much Churchill enjoyed sea bathing.

Fig 198 (C 320) right
Coast scene. This painting was given by Churchill to his butler, Mr W. Greenshields.

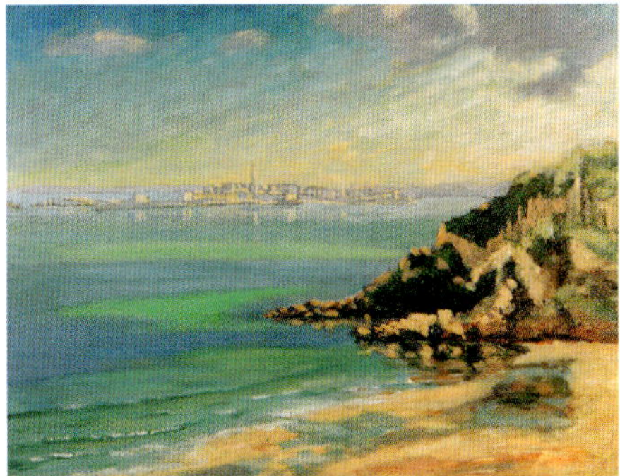

Fig 199 (C 324) above
Distant view of Venice (or St. Malo). The beach and rocks in the right foreground are likely to have been added by Churchill at a later date.

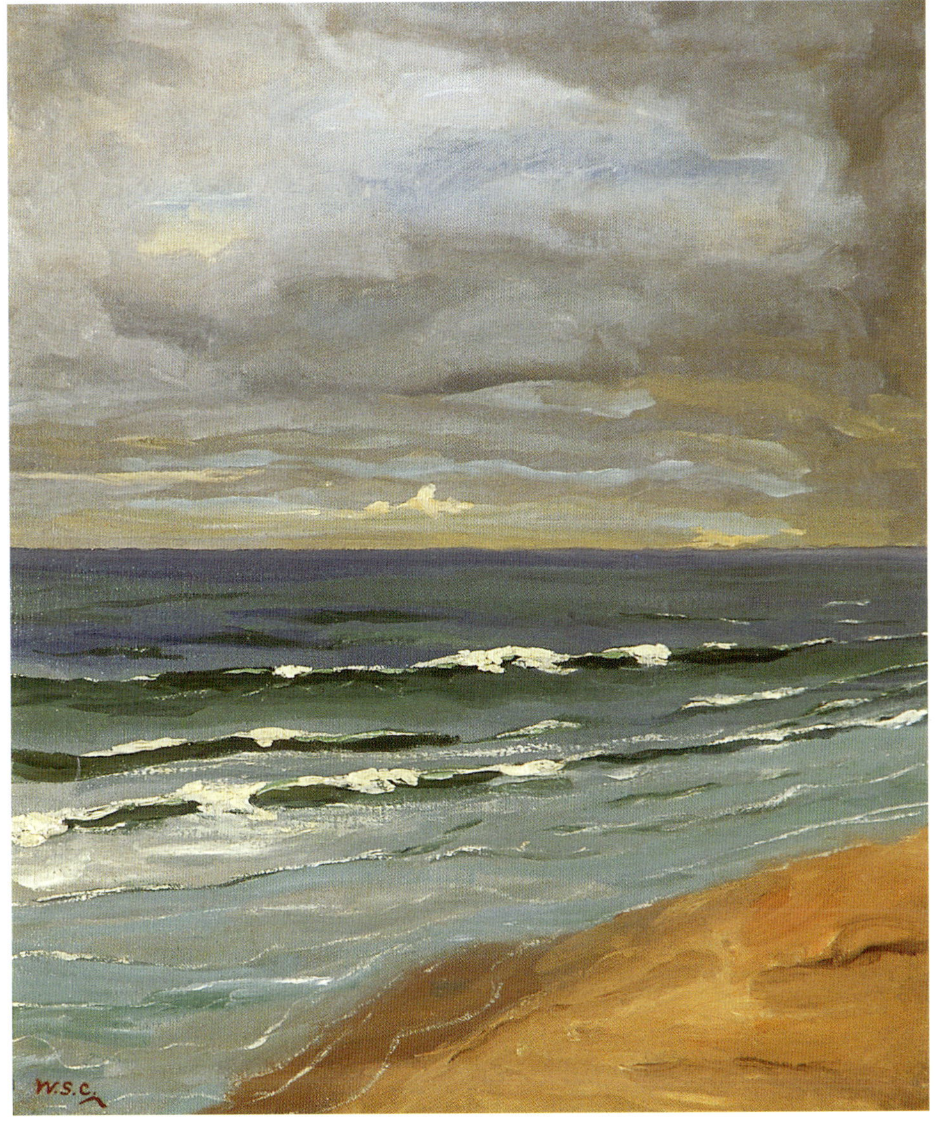

Fig 200 (C 321) left
The Atlantic near Biarritz on the south-west coast of France. Churchill gave this painting to his political colleague Brendan Bracken.

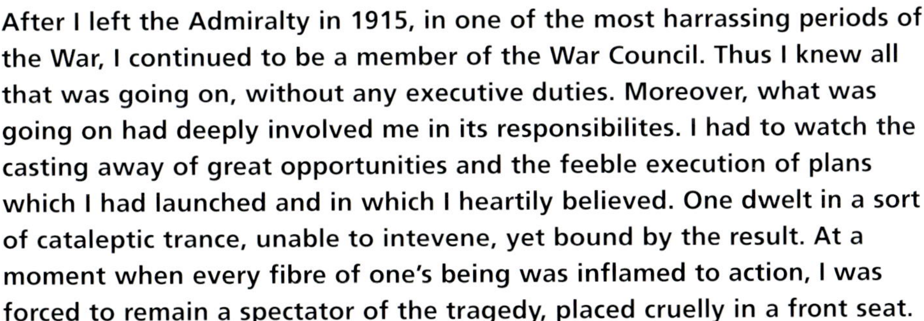

After I left the Admiralty in 1915, in one of the most harrassing periods of the War, I continued to be a member of the War Council. Thus I knew all that was going on, without any executive duties. Moreover, what was going on had deeply involved me in its responsibilites. I had to watch the casting away of great opportunities and the feeble execution of plans which I had launched and in which I heartily believed. One dwelt in a sort of cataleptic trance, unable to intevene, yet bound by the result. At a moment when every fibre of one's being was inflamed to action, I was forced to remain a spectator of the tragedy, placed cruelly in a front seat.

I do not know how I should have got through those horrible months from May till November, when I resigned from the Administration, had it not been for this great new interest which sprang up in my mind and kept my fingers busy and my eye alert. Some experiments one Sunday in the country with the children's paint-box led me to procure the next morning a complete outfit for painting in oils.

During all that summer I painted furiously. I have never found anything like it to take one's mind, for a spell, off grave matters. Golf is simply no use to me for this purpose. I find myself thinking of serious business half the time. Even between chukkas of a game of polo one's thoughts sag back occasionally to the work of the day or of the morrow. Two or three hours pass in a flash. One forgets that one is standing up or that it is luncheon time. One forgets utterly the work of the past or the worry of the future.

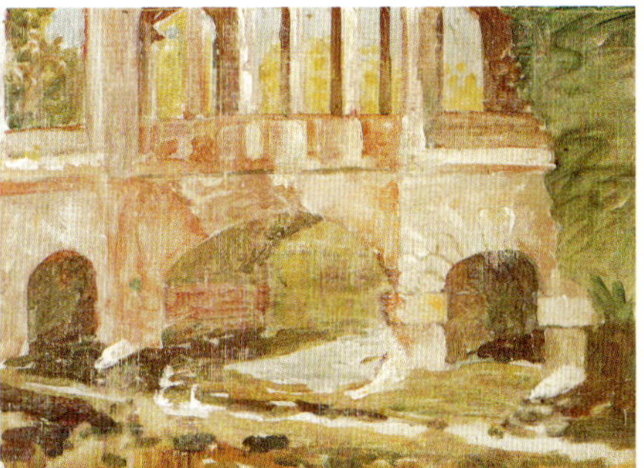

Fig 201 (C 117) above
An unfinished painting of the Palladian Bridge at Wilton.

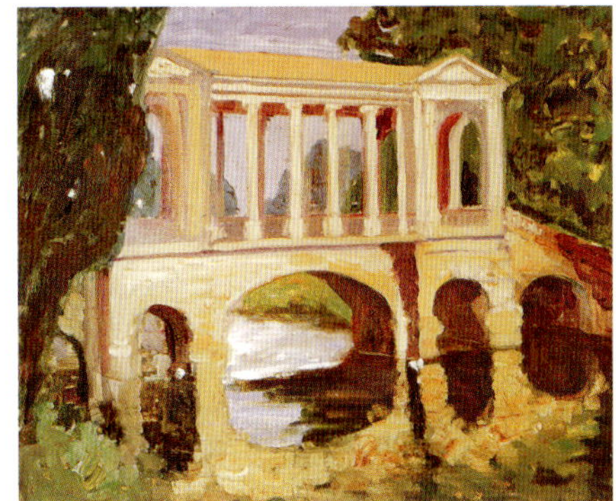

Fig 202 (C 118) above
The Palladian Bridge at Wilton: a favourite subject of Churchill's.

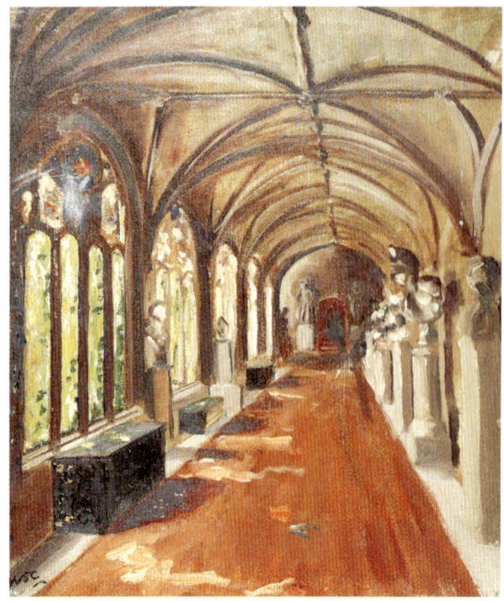

Fig 203 (C 185) above
The Long Gallery at Wilton House, near Salisbury in Wiltshire and the home of the Earl of Pembroke. Winston was such a regular visitor to Wilton that the Whitsun Bank Holiday weekend was known there as 'Winstontide.'

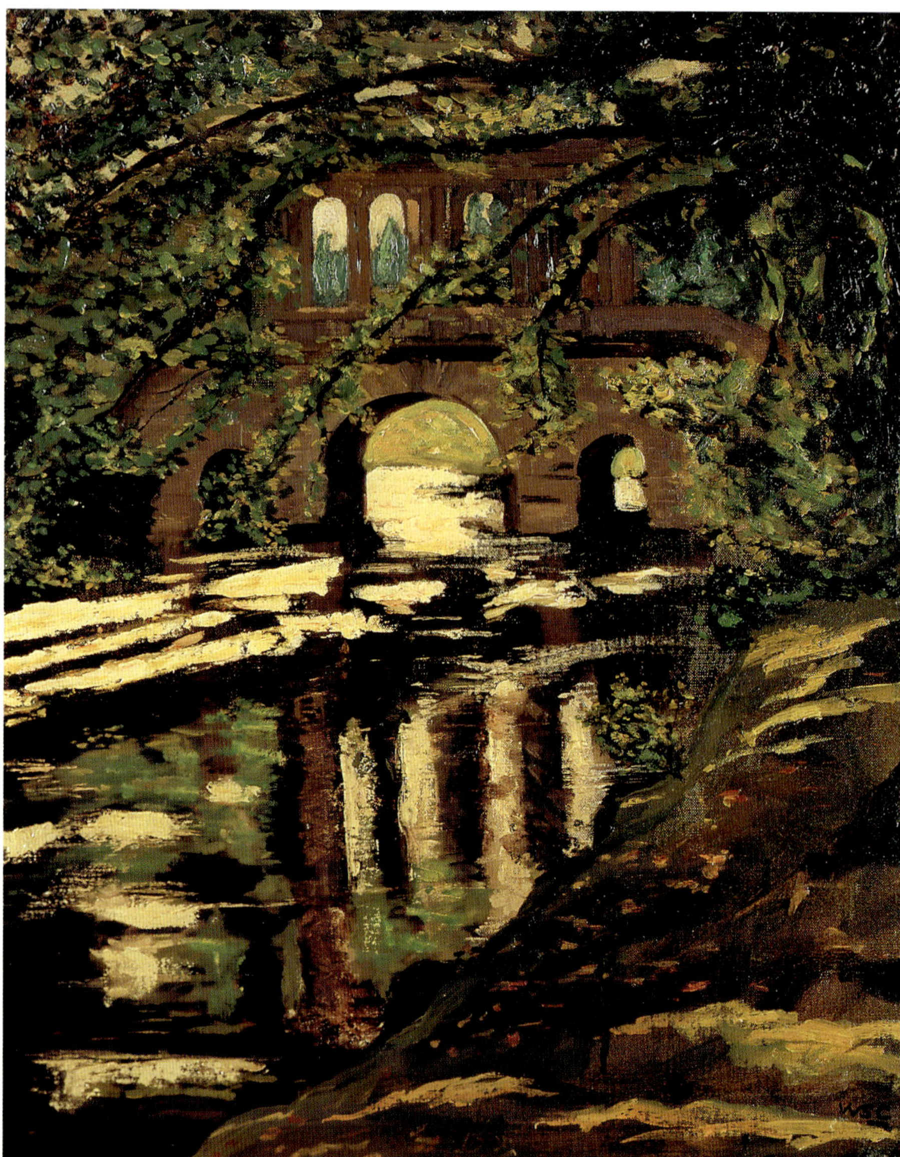

Fig 204 (C 122) right
The Palladian Bridge at Wilton is one of the architectural glories of the kingdom. Churchill was pleased enough with the quality of this painting to give it to Queen Elizabeth II in 1960.

And what fun it is! All those bright, jolly colours and their intricate relations with one another. All those nicely graded values and their reciprocal reaction upon colour and form. The whole plan of a picture built up stage by stage, from the remotest distance to the sharpest foreground, absorbs every faculty, and yet it seems a different set of faculties from those required in ordinary work. Never mind if the result is not impressive - if comprehension and aspiration have far outrun the means of execution! A few sweeps of the palette knife will clear the scene, and the canvas, all the better for past impressions, may be preserved for future enterprises.

Not only does the act of painting divert, rest and stimulate the mind, it also expands and develops the power of observation in the realms both of nature and of art. Until I began to try to paint, I had no idea how much the landscape had to show. All its colouring became more vivid, more significant, more distinguishable. I found myself instinctively as I walked noting the tint of a leaf, the reflection in a pool, the dreamy purple shades of mountains, the exquisite lacery of winter branches, the dim pale silhouettes of far horizons. These and a dozen others had been perceived and admired before in a general sense, but now they acquired a new and particular significance. The mind, led on by interest and fancy, begins to register impressions of much greater detail: and each impression carries with it a pleasure and profit of its own.

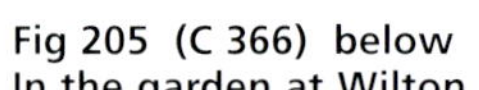

Fig 205 (C 366) below
In the garden at Wilton.

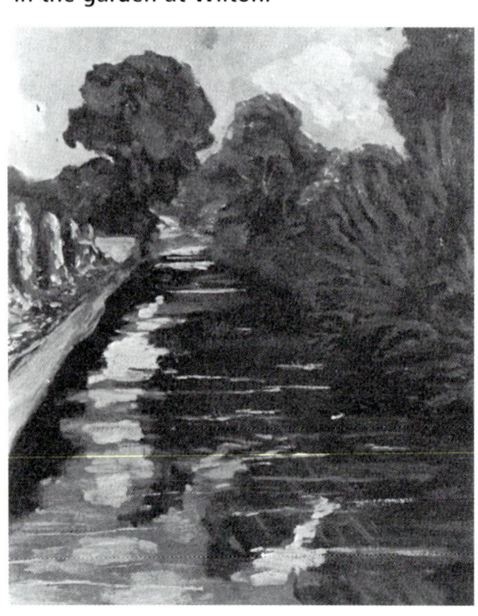

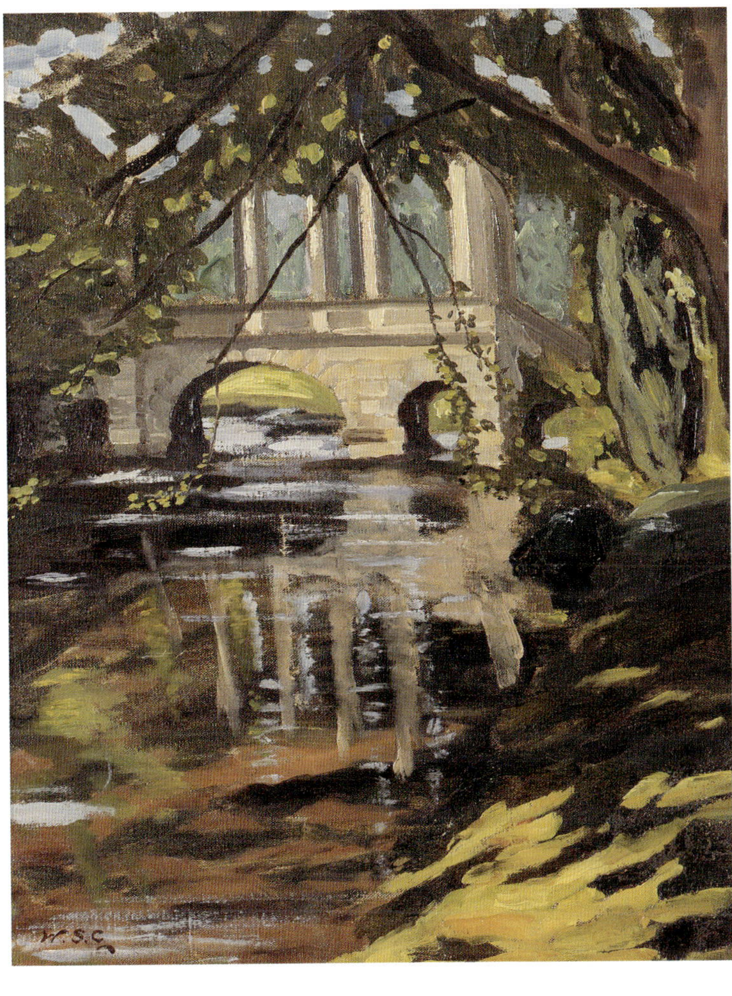

Fig 206 (C 120) left
The Palladian Bridge at Wilton, given by Churchill to his cousin Captain Oswald Frewen.

Fig 207 (C 121) below
The Palladian Bridge at Wilton. Given by Lady Churchill after Winston's death to the Earl of Pembroke.

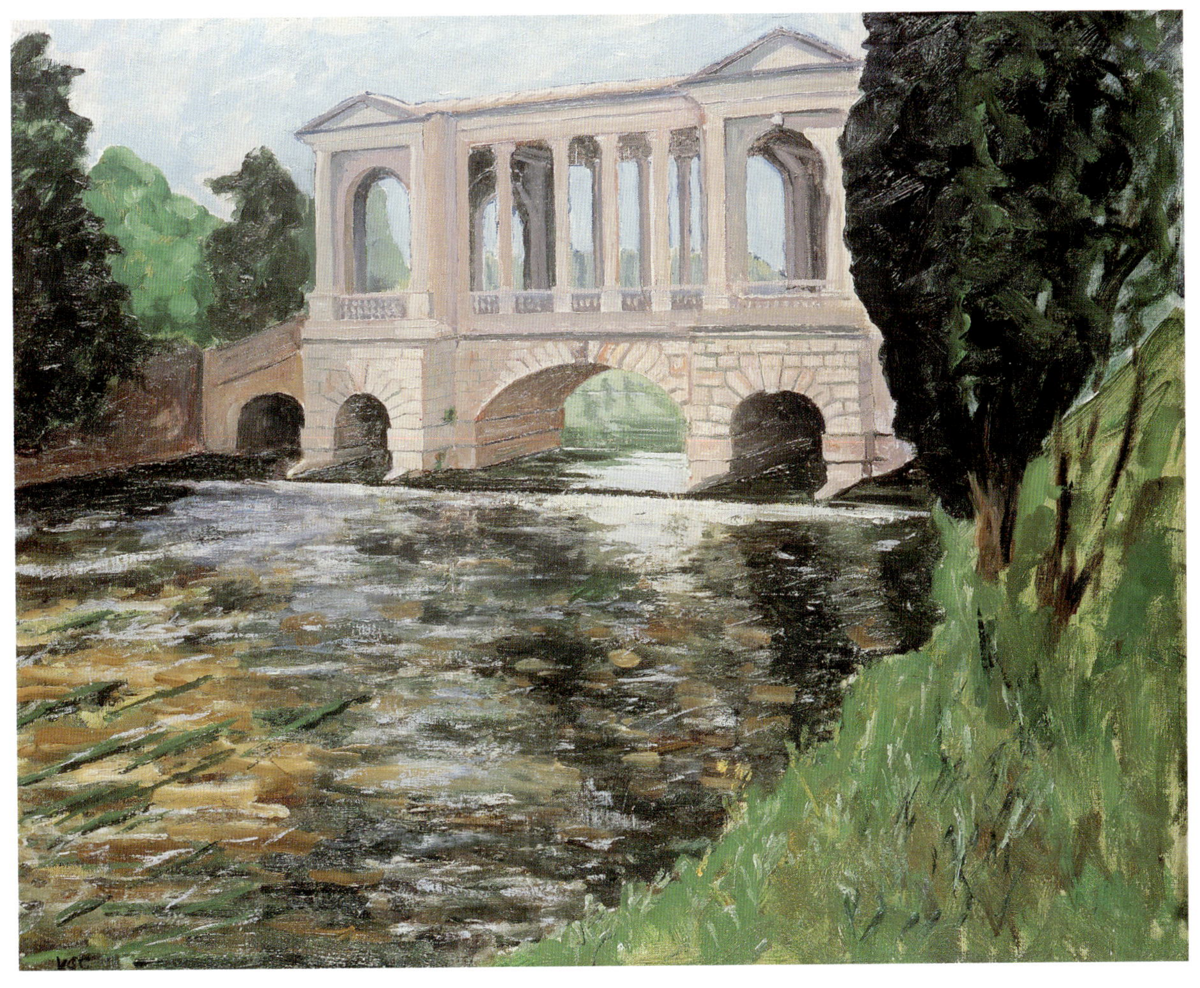

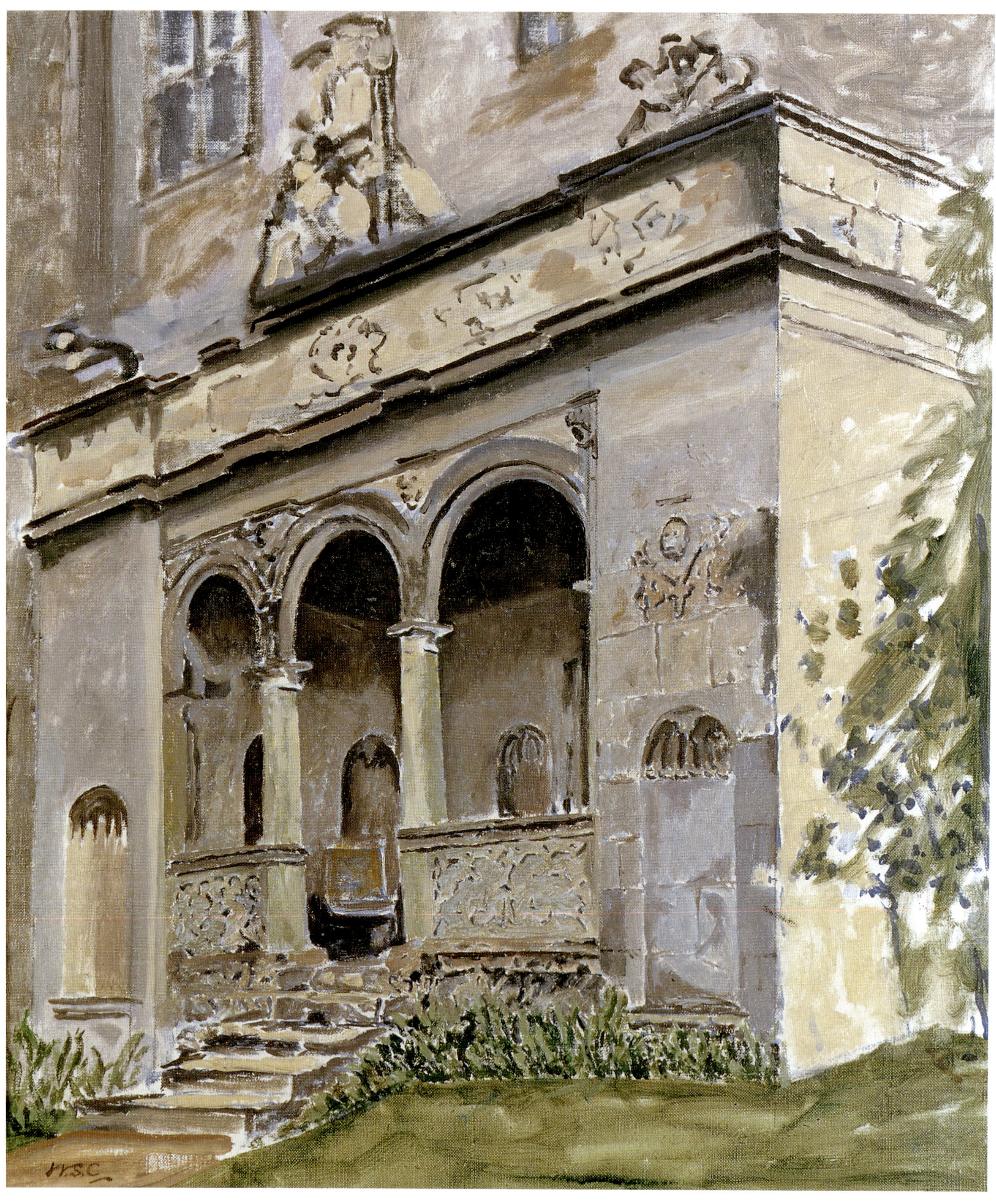

Fig 208 (C 226) above
The North Porch at the Manor House, Cranborne. Given by Churchill to the Marquess of Salisbury.

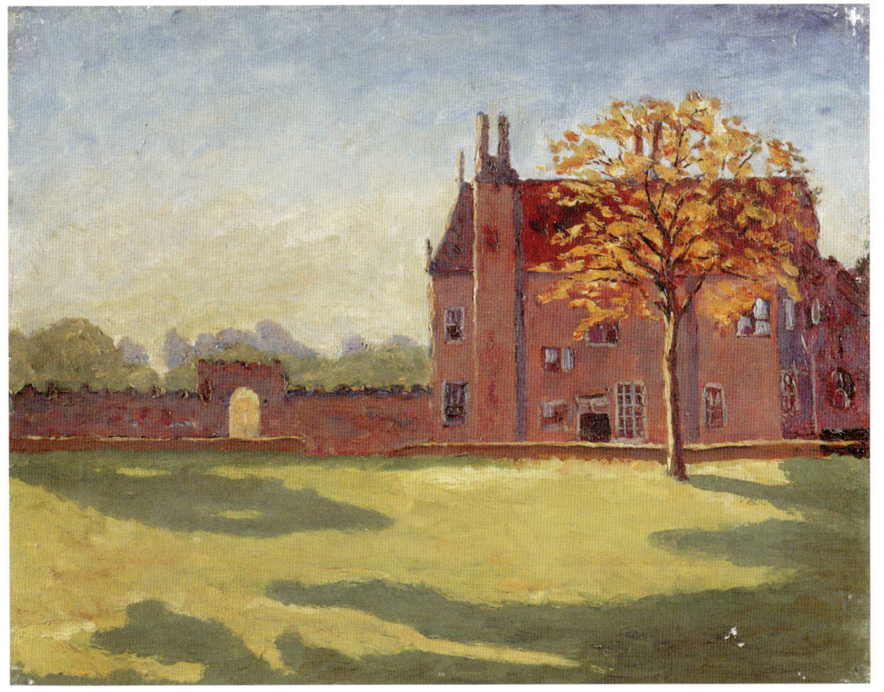

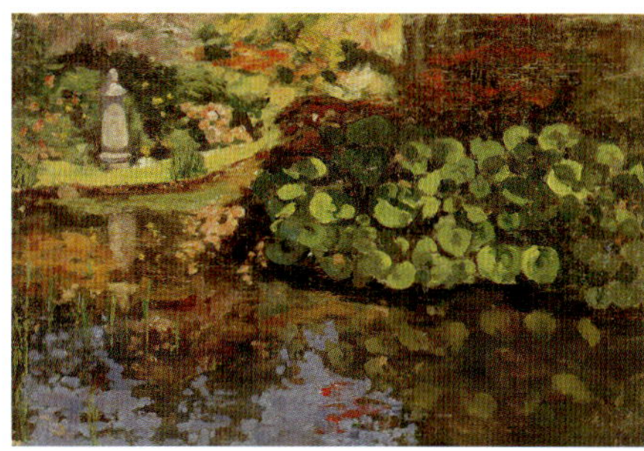

Fig 209 (C 349) above
A little sketch painting of the Lily Pond at Coombe Place in Surrey.

Fig 210 (C 145) left
Chequers on an autumn evening. An Elizabethan house, near Princes Risborough in Buckinghamshire, Chequers was given by Lord and Lady Lee to the nation as the country residence for her Prime Ministers.

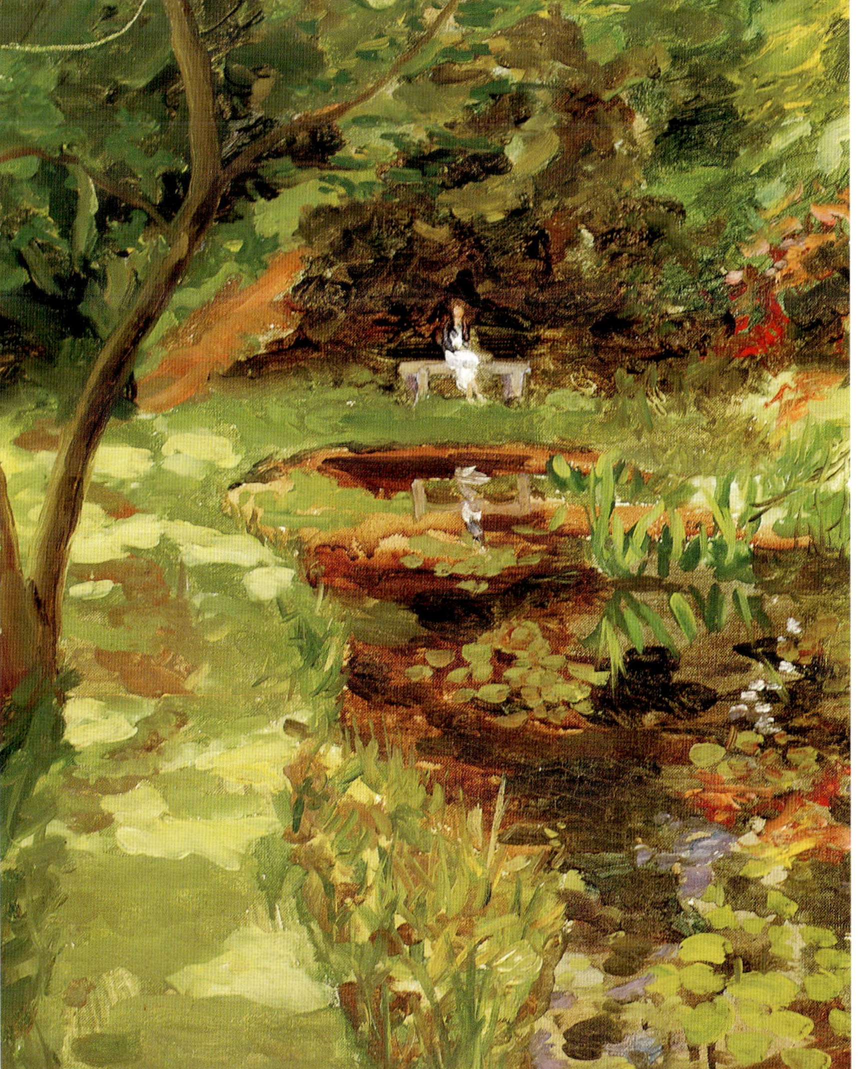

Fig 211 (C 346) left
The Lily Pond at Coombe Place in Surrey.

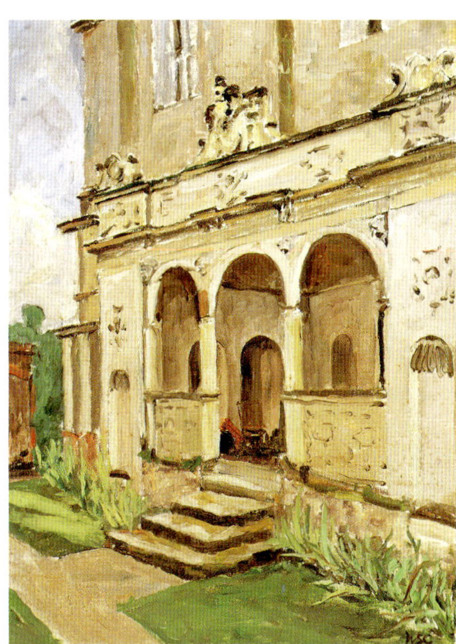

Fig 212 (C 223) above
A little painting of the Porch at Cranborne, near Wimborne in Dorset, home of Churchill's political colleague Viscount Cranborne, heir of the Marquess of Salisbury.

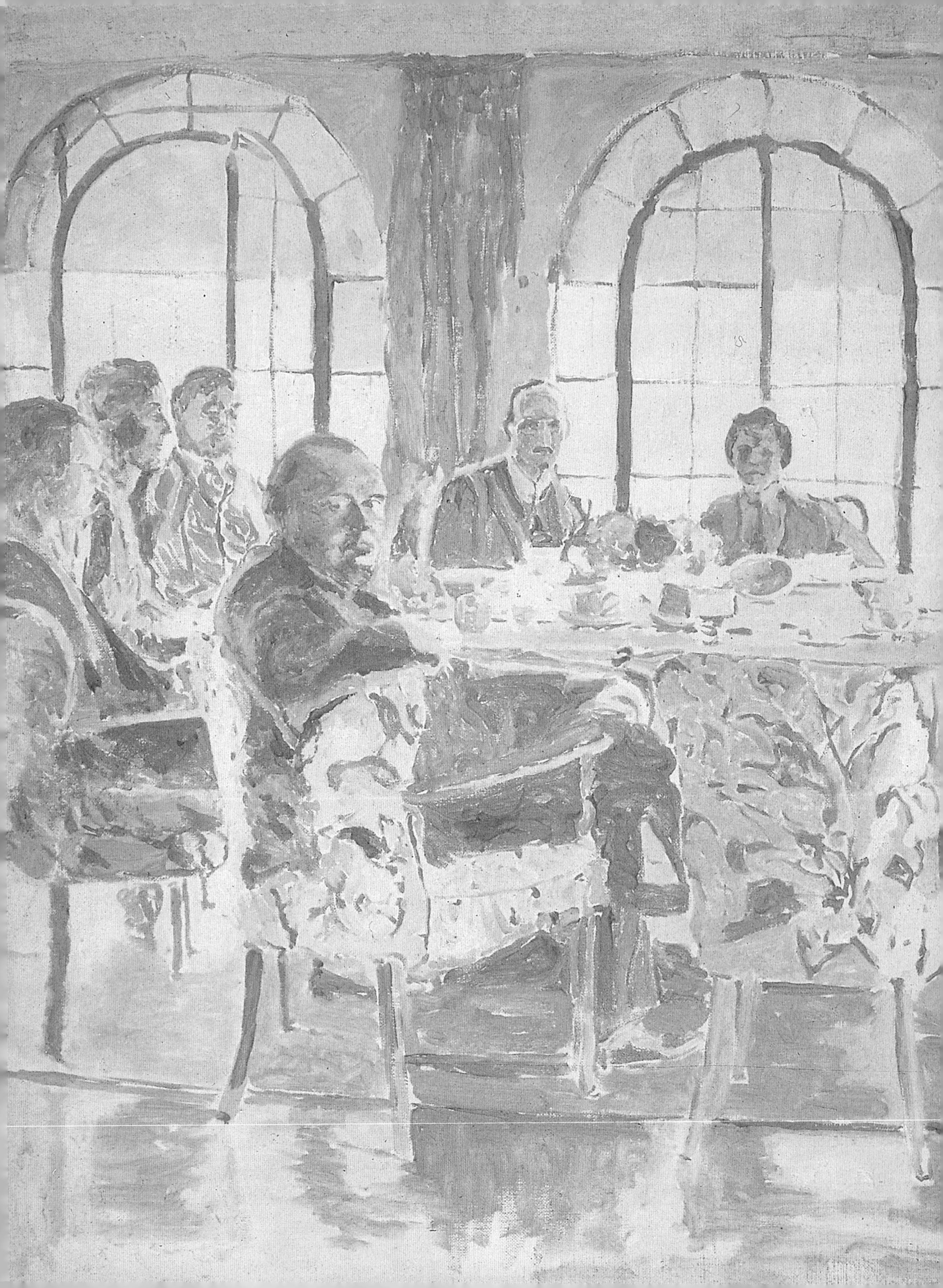

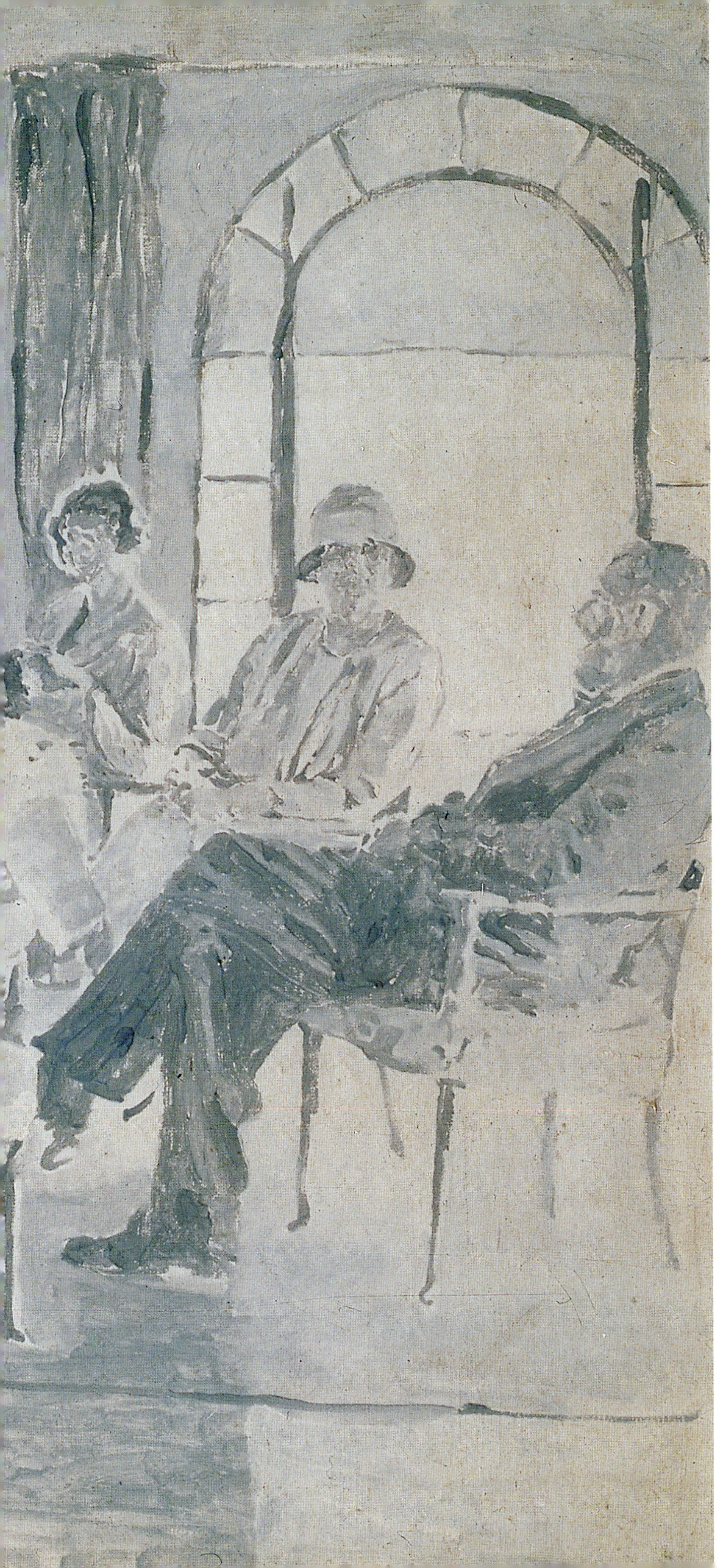

In 1927, Winston was introduced by Clementine to the artist Walter Sickert whom she had known when she was a girl living with her mother, Lady Blanche Hozier, in Dieppe. The two men struck up an immediate friendship and Sickert taught Churchill the technique of camaieu painting using a few layers of similar-coloured tones, as well as how to use a grille to transfer proportions accurately on to a canvas. He also showed Winston how photographs or newspaper cuttings, made into slides, could be projected directly on to a canvas as an aid to painting.

Fig 213 (C 36)
Tea in the Dining Room at Chartwell. Those assembled at the table are, from left to right: Therese Sickert, Diana Mitford, Edward Marsh, Winston Churchill, Professor Lindemann, Randolph, Diana and Clementine Churchill, and Walter Sickert. The photograph on which this painting was based was taken by Donald Ferguson, 29th August, 1927.

Fig 214 (C 32) right
Lord Balfour and his niece. This painting, which is probably based on a photograph, is inscribed on the back: 'Painted by my husband. Clementine S. Churchill.' Lady Churchill thus authenticated a number of Winston's paintings in his last years.

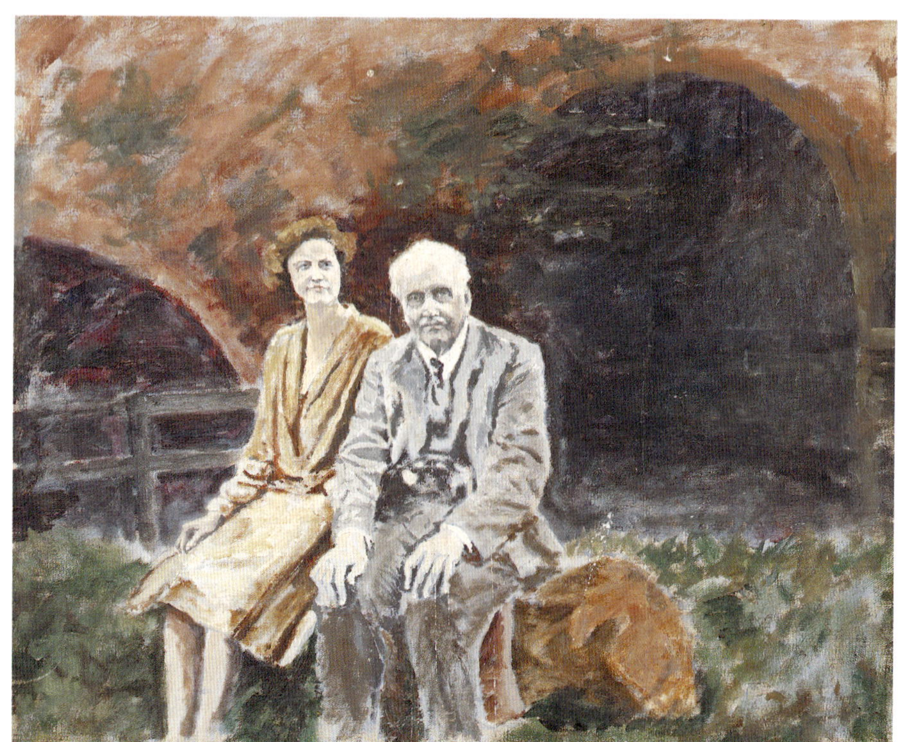

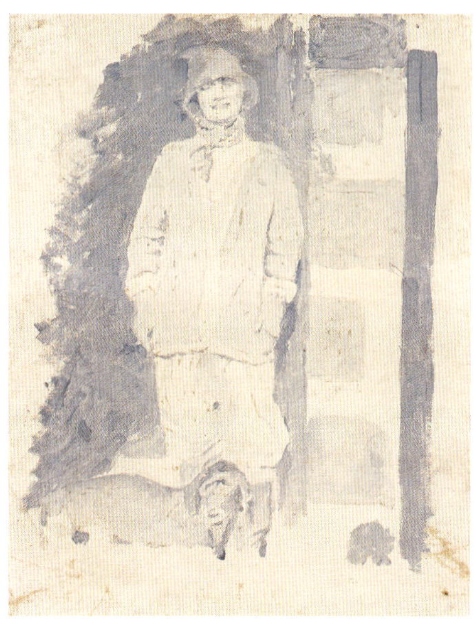

Fig 215 (C 34) above
Coco Chanel, close friend of the Duke of Westminster. This painting is based on photograph from the Studio archives at Chartwell.

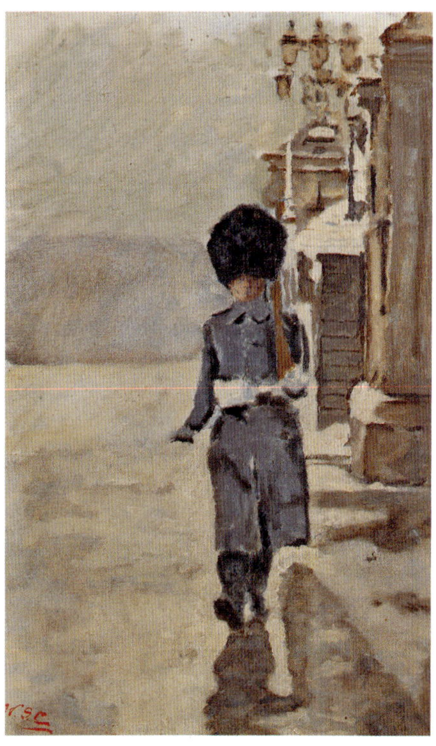

Fig 216 (C 35) above
A guardsman at Buckingham Palace. Churchill originally gave this painting to Nellie Hozier, Clementine's sister, who remained in Dieppe during the Second World War when her house was occupied by the Germans.

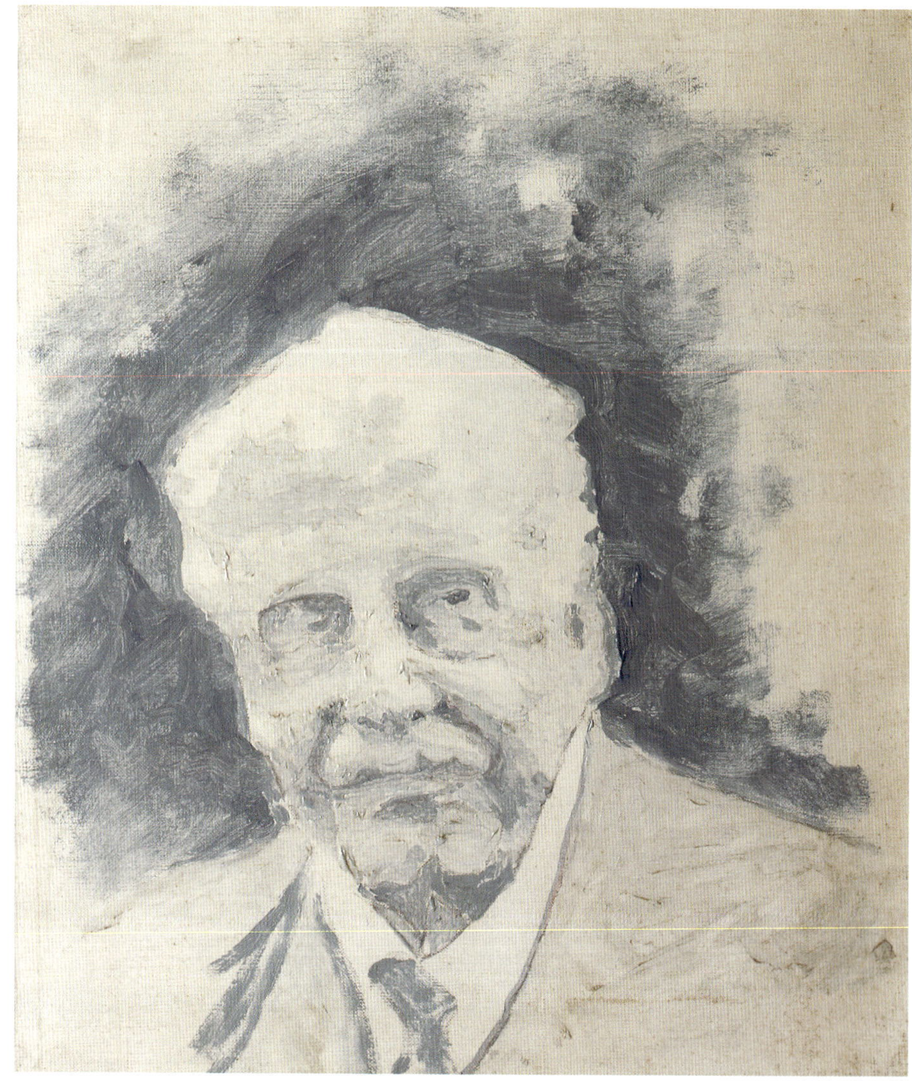

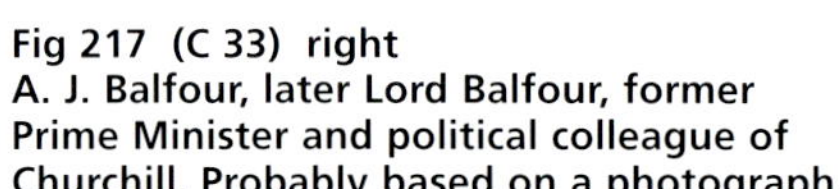

Fig 217 (C 33) right
A. J. Balfour, later Lord Balfour, former Prime Minister and political colleague of Churchill. Probably based on a photograph.

The same thing is true of looking at pictures. A general taste and unfocused admiration are sharpened and guided by an amiable jealous scrutiny and heightened interest. You look at a picture by a great artist, not only for its beauty and charm, but to notice how he did it. A single stroke of the brush may claim attention, reveal a method and suggest an imitative experiment.

Travel, too, is lightened up by a new purpose at once earnest and fascinating. Each new scene has its own story to tell in colour and shadow, in atmosphere and form. Every day and all day is provided with its expedition and its occupation - cheap, attainable, innocent, absorbing, recuperative. The vain racket of the tourist gives place to the calm enjoyment of the philospher, intensified by an enthralling sense of action and endeavour.

Painting is a companion with whom one may hope to walk a great part of life's journey,'Age cannot wither [her nor] or custom stale her [Her] infinite variety.' One by one the more vigorous sports and exacting games fall away. Exceptional exertions are purchased only by a more pronounced and more prolonged fatigue. Muscles may relax, and feet and hands slow down; the nerve of youth and manhood may become less trusty. But painting is a friend who makes no undue demands, excites to no exhausting pursuits, keeps faithful pace even with feeble steps, and holds her canvas as a screen between us and the envious eyes of Time or the surly advance of Decrepitude.

Happy are the painters, for they shall not be lonely. Light and colour, peace and hope, will keep them company to the end, or almost to the end, of the day.

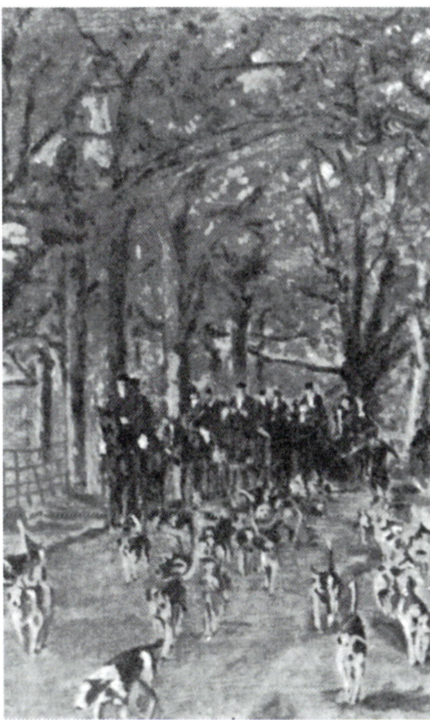

Fig 218 (C 45) above
Hunting scene. This painting is based on a photograph from the Studio archives at Chartwell.

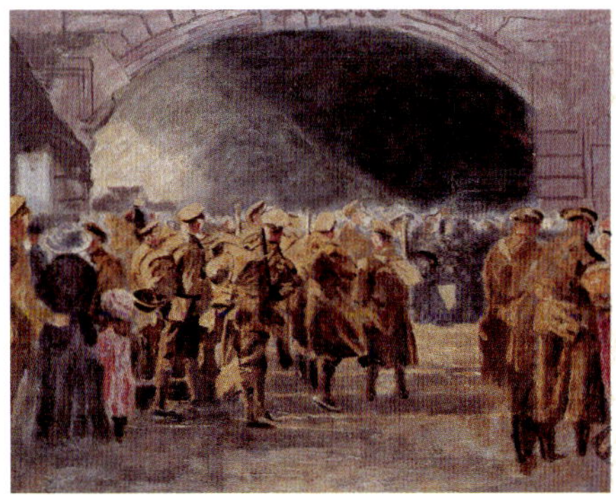

Fig 219 (C48) above
Troops going to the Front from Victoria Station, London, 1917. Based on a photograph from the Studio archives at Chartwell.

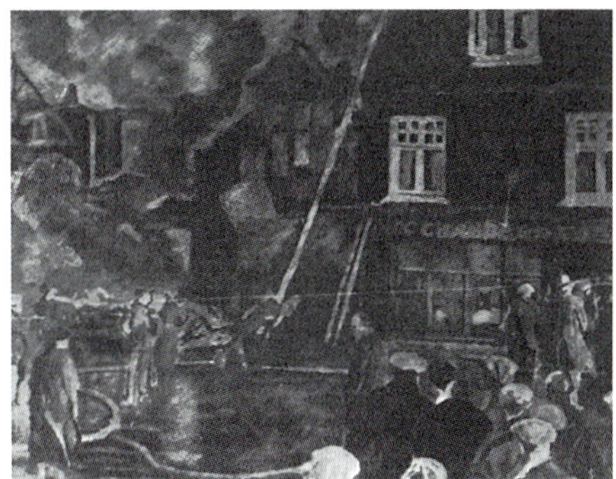

Fig 220 (C 49) above
A fire at Bures in Suffolk, based on two newspaper cuttings from the Studio archives at Chartwell.

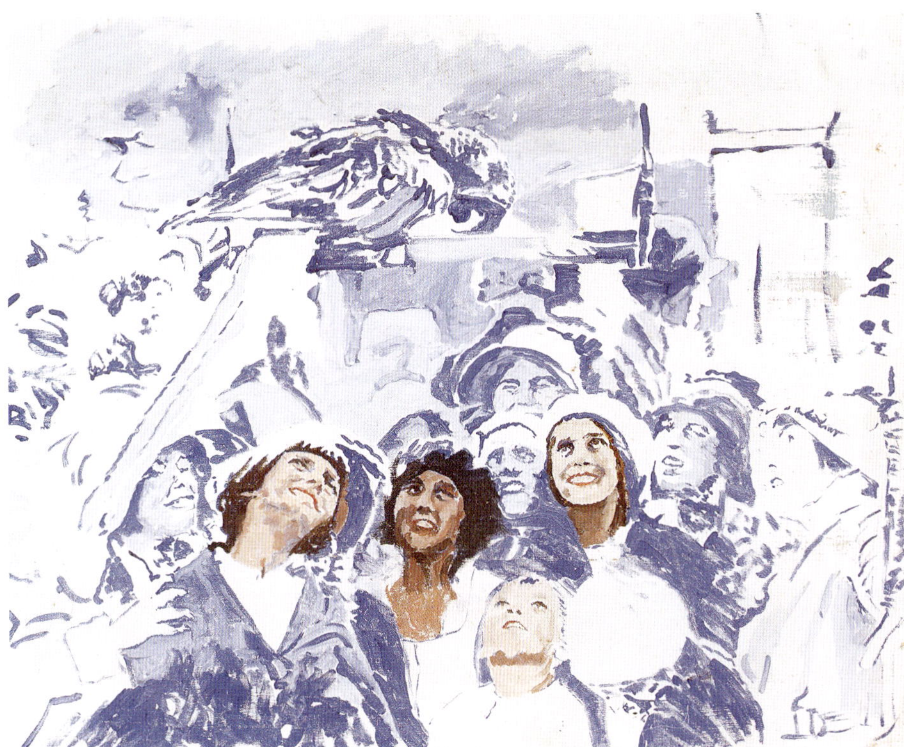

Fig 221 (C 39) left
The cockatoo. Almost certainly based on a newspaper cutting.

NOTES

(1) Churchill first wrote for *The Strand Magazine* in 1907; the articles were later published as his book *My African Journey.*

(2) Quotations from *Speaking for Themselves. The Personal Letters of Winston and Clementine Churchill.* Edited by Mary Soames, London, 1998.

(3) Hazel Lavery, an artist in her own right who worked in pastels.

(4) For example, Turner's huge painting of the Battle of Trafalgar, which measures 102 x 144 in. Now in the National Maritime Museum, it was commissioned by King George IV and given to the Royal Naval Hospital at Greenwich, where Churchill would have seen it.

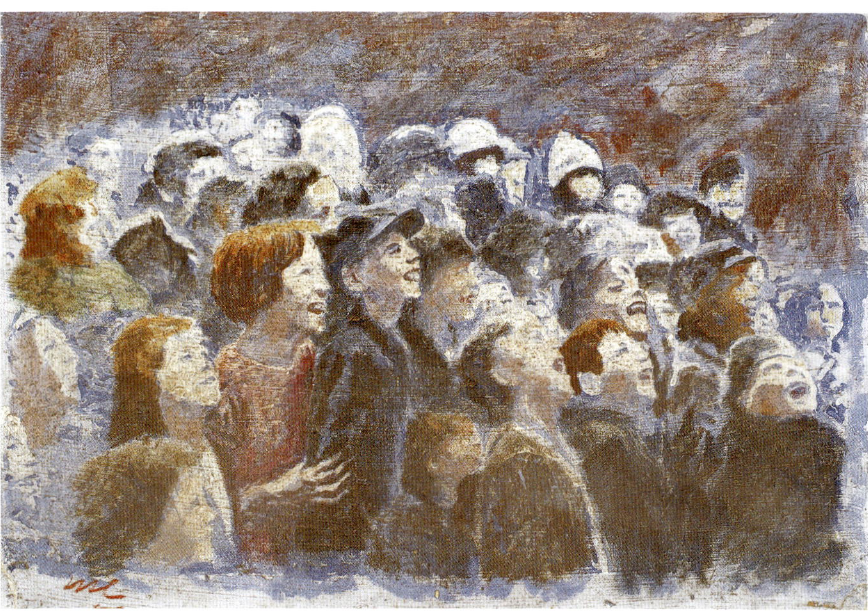

Fig 222 (C 41) above
London children enjoying a Punch and Judy show. This painting is based on a newspaper cutting from the Studio archives at Chartwell.

(5) The frequent military metaphors are unsurprising coming from a man who began his adult life as a professional soldier.

(6) John Ruskin, critic and patron who wrote extensively about Turner. His book The *Elements of Drawing* was first published in 1857. His chapter on Colour and Composition obviously greatly influenced Churchill.

(7) It is not currently known who these painters might have been; presumably they were introduced to Churchill by his friend Charles Montag.

(8) This is almost certainly Charles Montag who Churchill met in 1915, who arranged his exhibition at the Galerie Druet in Paris in 1921 and, until his death in 1956, was to be a constant painting companion of Churchill's.

(9) Churchill's ideas on this subject were admired and discussed by the art historian Sir Ernst Gombrich in his book *Art and Illusion* published in 1960.

(10) Possibly William McDougall (1871-1938) who 'held that all activity is motivated by instincts and purposive striving'.

(11) John Morley (1838-1923). Writer, editor and parliamentary colleague and close friend of Churchill's, whose most notable work was a four-volume biography of Gladstone published in 1903.

Fig 223 (C 159) below
The Waratahs playing rugby football against the South of France at Toulouse. This painting is based on a newspaper cutting from the Studio archives at Chartwell.

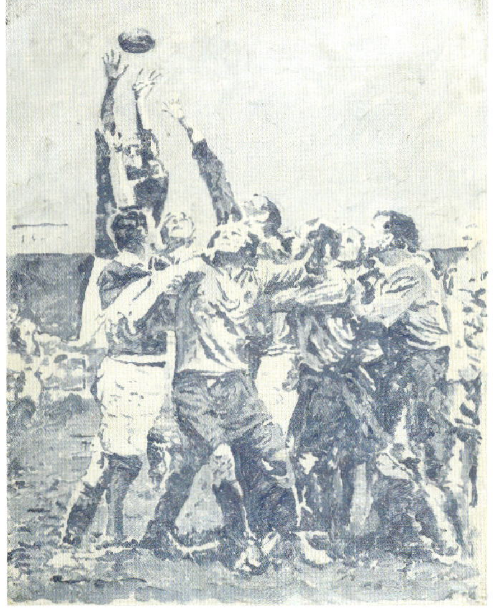

Author's Acknowledgements

Following the 1998 Sotheby's exhibition 'Painting as a Pastime' I purchased from Mark Weber copies of *The Strand Magazine* 1921/2 with Churchill's article. I quickly noticed that there were marked differences between the original text and the book published in 1948. Having bought an early edition of Churchill's book *Thoughts and Adventures* from Alan Taylor Smith, I began to seek as many other versions as I could. In this quest I was greatly helped by the publication, also in 1998, of Richard Langworth's *A Connoisseur's Guide to the Books of Sir Winston Churchill.* (Brassey's, London and Washington).

As my work progressed, I realized that the history of 'Painting as a Pastime' and of Churchill's later article 'Hobbies' had become entangled over the years and was more complex than previously thought. So I set myself the additional task of trying to work out what had happened and when.

Eventually, I was able to find the original unabridged texts as well as the later variants with the help of the British Library, the Library of Congress and the London Library. I was able to resolve the Hearst connection with the help of Susannah van Langenberg and Diane Courtney of the National Magazine Company Syndication Department.

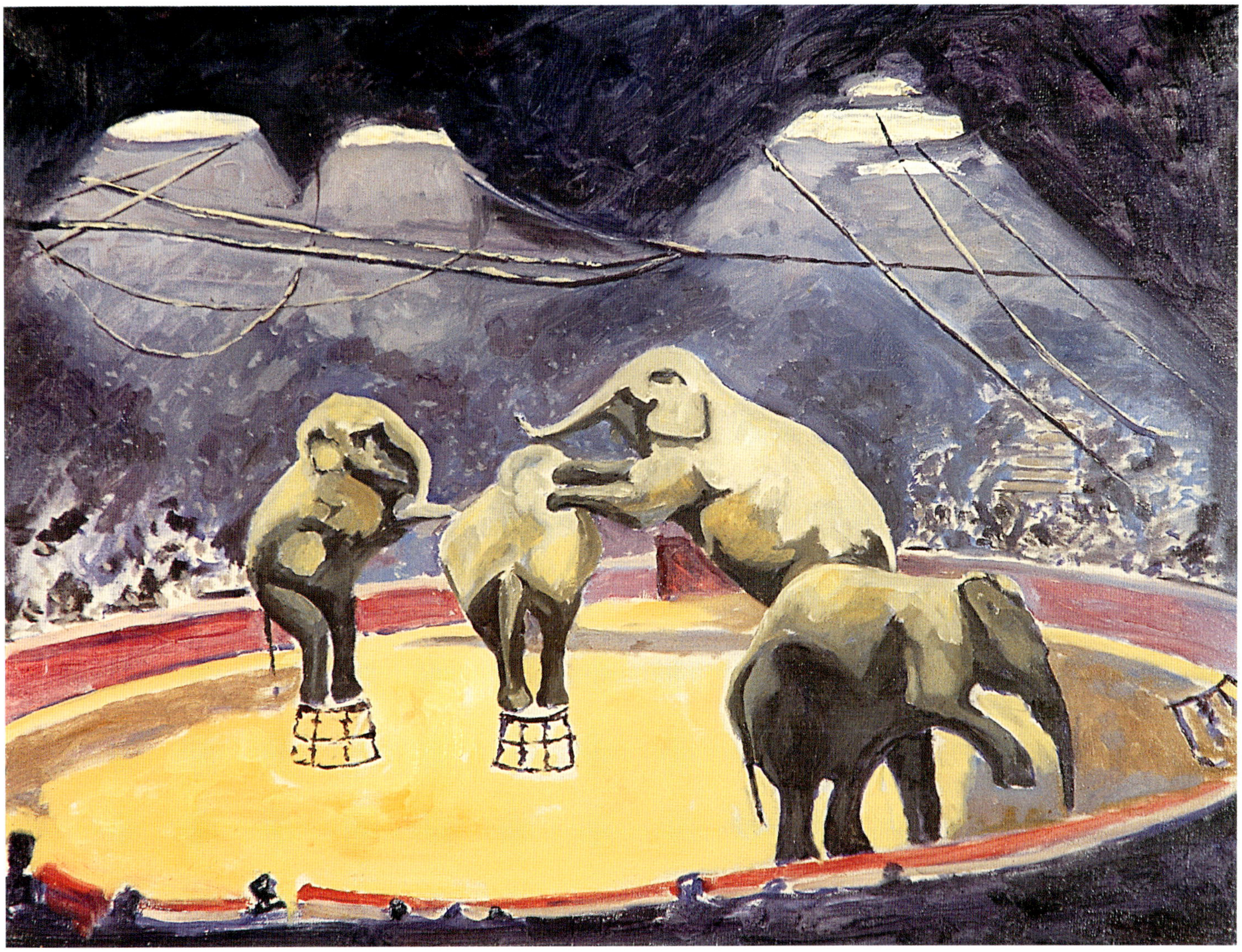

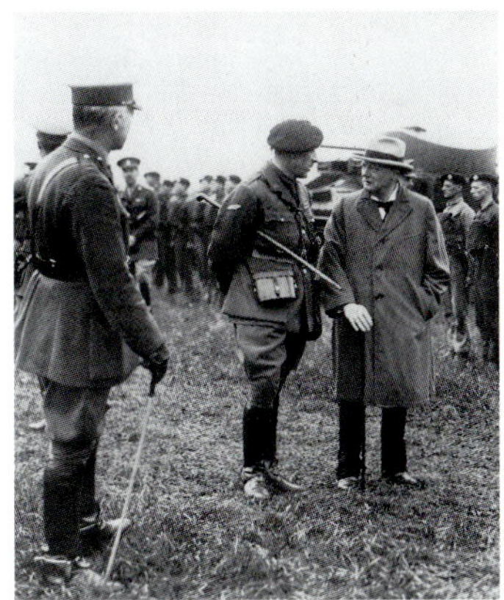

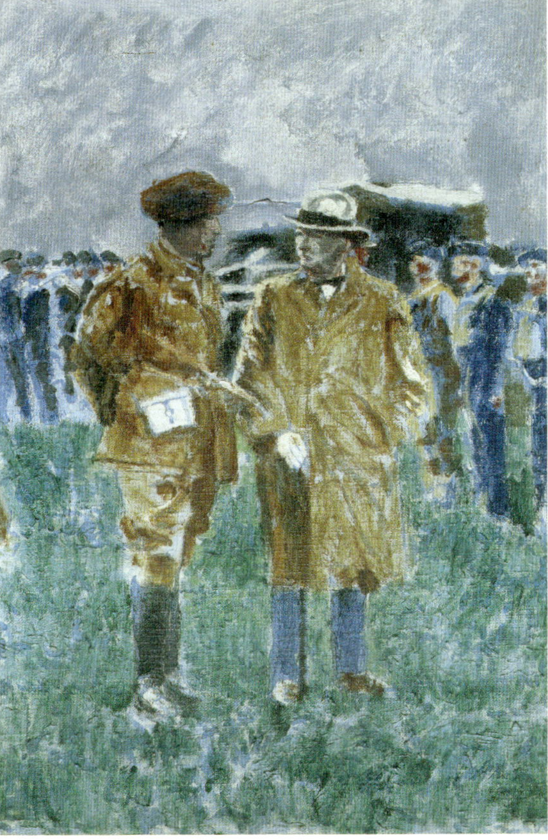

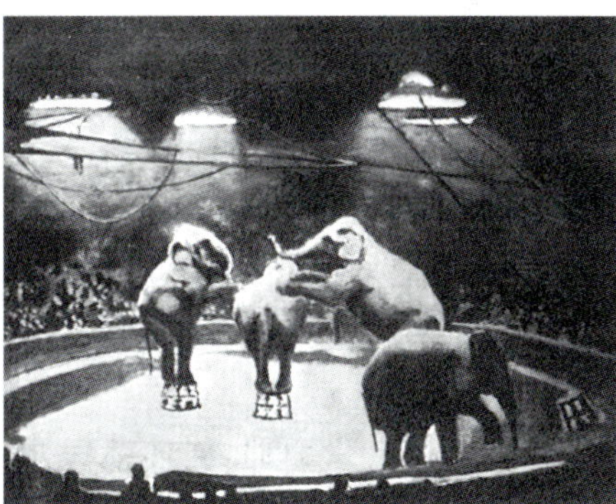

Fig 224 (C 160) above
The Circus. This painting is based on a newspaper cutting from the Studio archives at Chartwell.

Fig 225 (C 161) top of page
Bertram Mills' Circus at Olympia, London when, to the Churchill family's amusement, the elephant on the right misbehaved. This painting is based on a newspaper cutting from the Studio archives at Chartwell.

Fig 226 (C 155) left
'Painting Lesson from Mr Sickert.' This painting is based on a newspaper cutting (illustrated left above) from the Studio archives at Chartwell.

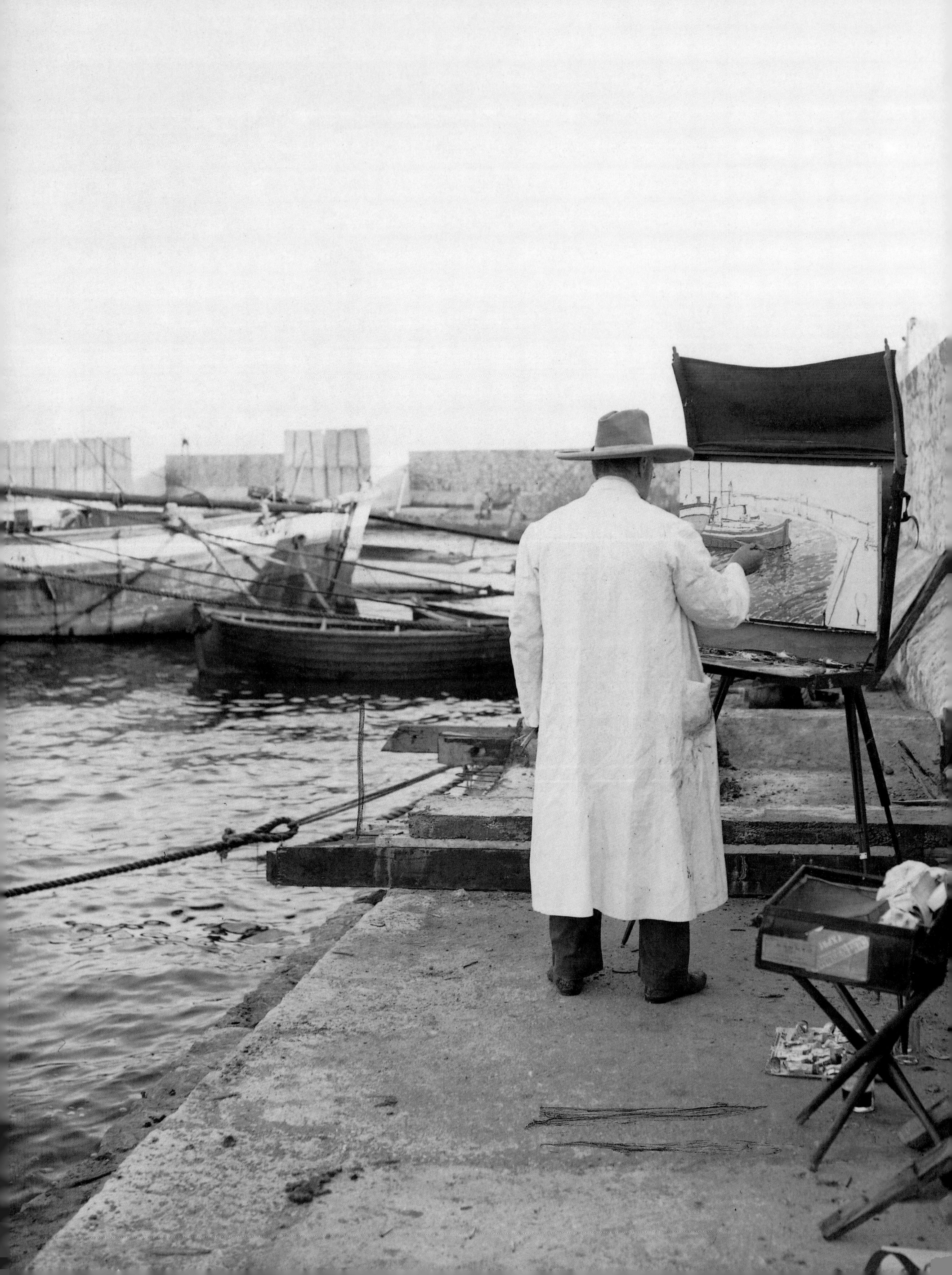

between the wars

1922 - 1939

1922 [Background] The Irish parliament voted to accept treaty with Britain; the Republicans resigned. Irish Free State Bill was introduced by Churchill in British Parliament where it was accepted. Peace agreement signed. Irish civil war after the election. Churchill defended in Parliament the government's policy of a Jewish national home in Palestine and the League of Nations voted to make this integral to Britain's Palestinian mandate. Turkish forces attacked the Greeks and occupied Smyrna in Asia Minor. British forces held the Dardanelles and war was averted. End of civil war in Russia, Stalin became General Secretary of the Communist Party. Mussolini became Fascist Prime Minister of Italy. Conservatives withdrew support from the coalition government in Britain and Lloyd George resigned as Prime Minister. Churchill lost his parliamentary seat at the subsequent general election.
The Churchills' fifth and youngest child, Mary, was born.

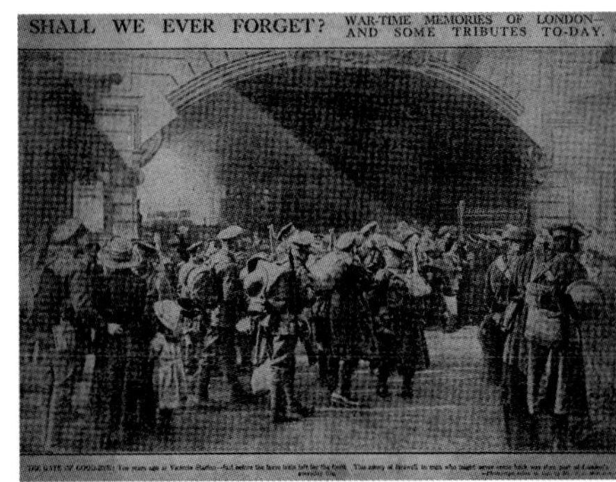
SHALL WE EVER FORGET? WAR-TIME MEMORIES OF LONDON AND SOME TRIBUTES TO-DAY.

Original newspaper cutting found in the Studio archives at Chartwell, which relates to Churchill's painting (C 48) illustrated on page 115

1922 [Painting] Churchill bought Chartwell Manor at Westerham in Kent, largely because of the view it commanded, a purchase made possible by an unexpected inheritance from a distant cousin. Over the next two years the house was rebuilt by the architect Philip Tilden.

A visit to Mimizan in the company of Edward Marsh included a trip to Biarritz, where they were joined by Charles Montag, with more painting at St Jean de Luz. At the end of the year, following his election defeat, Winston and Clementine took their family to the Riviera in the South of France, where they rented the Villa Rêve d'Or for six months. On this coast, then and often thereafter, Churchill painted many pictures.

1923 [Background] Turkish republic proclaimed. Chinese Nationalist government established. Spanish dictatorship. Independence for Transjordan. Monarchy for Egypt. France occupied the German Ruhr. British general election - the outgoing Conservative government undertook to reintroduce trade protection. Churchill invited to fight under the Free Trade banner by seven Liberal associations; he chose West Leicester but was defeated. The first two volumes of Churchill's war memoirs, *The World Crisis*, were published in Britain and the United States.

Opposite
Winston Churchill painting in the harbour at Cannes.

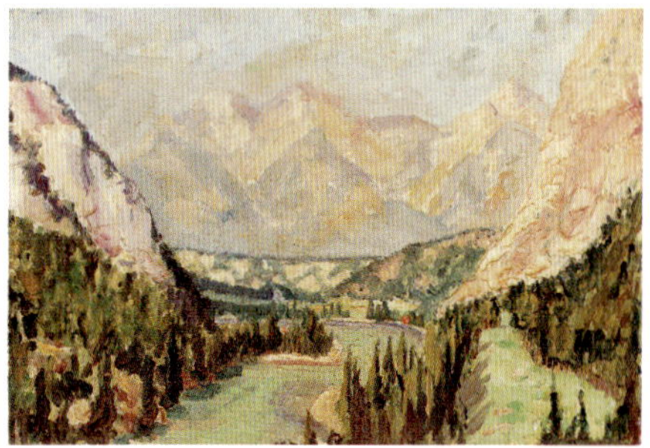

Fig 227 (C 89) above
A little painting of the Bow River, near Banff in Canada.

1920s [Painting} Many pictures record visits made by Winston and Clementine Churchill to friends and relations in these years.

Breccles in Norfolk was the home of Clementine's cousin Venetia Montagu and its wooded gardens in particular attracted Churchill's painterly eye both in this and the following decade.

Sutton Place, near Guildford in Surrey, belonged to the Duke and Duchess of Sutherland; Churchill painted the Long Gallery and the formal garden. Wilton House, near Salisbury, was the ancestral home of the Earl and Countess of Pembroke; Churchill painted the cloisters in the house and was especially inspired by the Palladian Bridge in the park.

Colonel John Astor and his wife Lady Violet lived at Hever Castle, only a few miles away from Chartwell; Churchill was much taken by its colonnaded Italian garden.

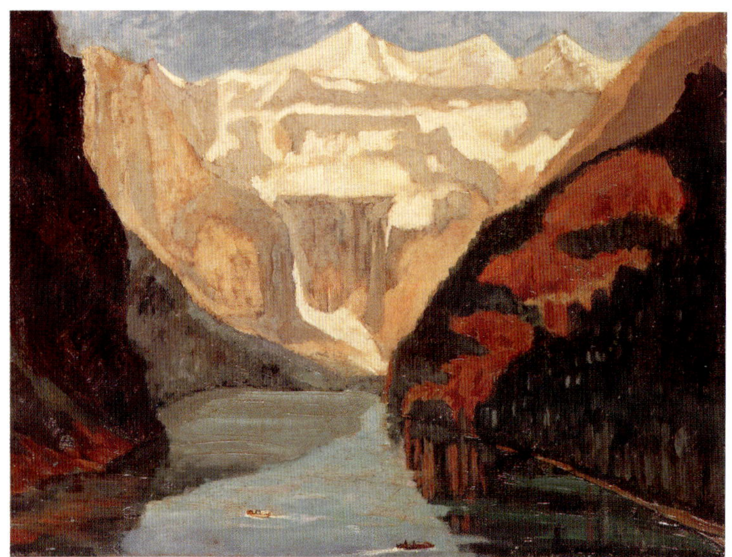

Fig 228 (C 90) above
Lake Louise. In 1929, Churchill was out of office after the General Election. He travelled to Canada and then on to the United States. In between, he spent three days in the Rocky Mountains.

After the dissolution of her marriage to Churchill's cousin the Duke of Marlborough, Consuelo Vanderbilt, with her new husband Jacques Balsan, built a house, Lou Seuil, on the French Riviera near 'the fortressed village of Eze ... Winston Churchill and his beautiful wife were among our favorite guests ... He used to spend his mornings dictating to his secretary and the afternoons painting either in our garden or in some other site that pleased him ... On his return he would amuse us by repeating the comments of those self-sufficient critics who gather round easels. An old Frenchman one day told him, "With a few more lessons you will become quite good!"'

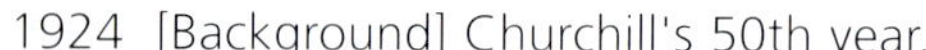

1924 [Background] Churchill's 50th year. Minority Conservative government in Britain defeated and replaced by a Labour government dependent upon Liberal support. Churchill could not endorse socialist policies in this way and, determined to return to Parliament, stood as an independent candidate in a by-election, to lose by 43 votes. At the General election later that year, he stood successfully for Epping as a Constitutionalist candidate. He was invited to become Chancellor of the Exchequer by the incoming Conservative government, so fulfilling his ambition to succeed his father in this post. Churchill's article in *The Pall Mall Gazette* on the future and frightening possibilities of war was circulated in the United States in pamphlet form; he warned therein of the intense German desire for revenge after its 1918 defeat. Lenin died.

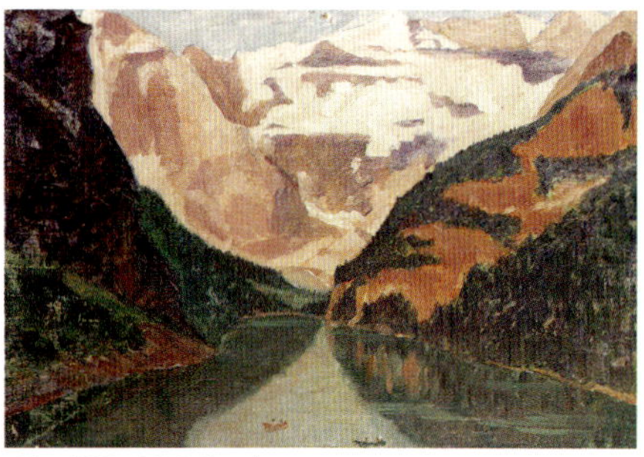

Fig 229 (C 91) above
A little painting of Lake Louise in the Canadian Rockies.

1924 [Painting] With the reconstruction of Chartwell completed, Churchill's family moved in. He drained the lake and built a dam for a swimming pool. Over the next years he personally built a series of long brick walls round the garden, which featured in several of his paintings. His new house and the marvellous views it offered often inspired his brush.

Weekend visits to his friends and relations and holidays abroad, at Mimizan in France for example, always found Churchill accompanied by the full complement of painting paraphernalia. He also took his painting gear with him on all official visits.

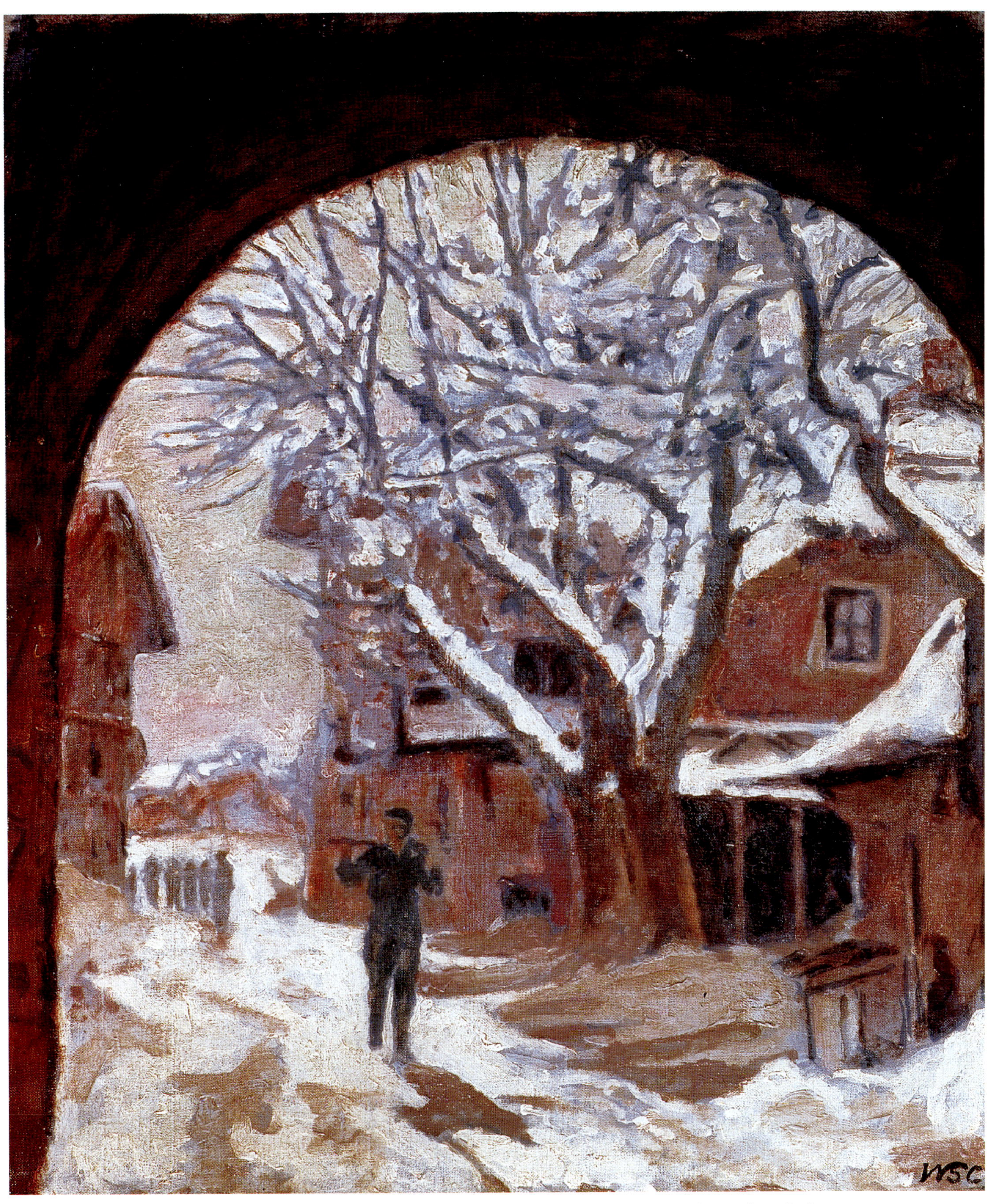

Fig 230 (C 156) above
Snow under the arch, formerly owned by Clementine Churchill who loved this picture and called it 'The Messenger.' Probably based on a photograph or newspaper cutting, the subject is unknown.

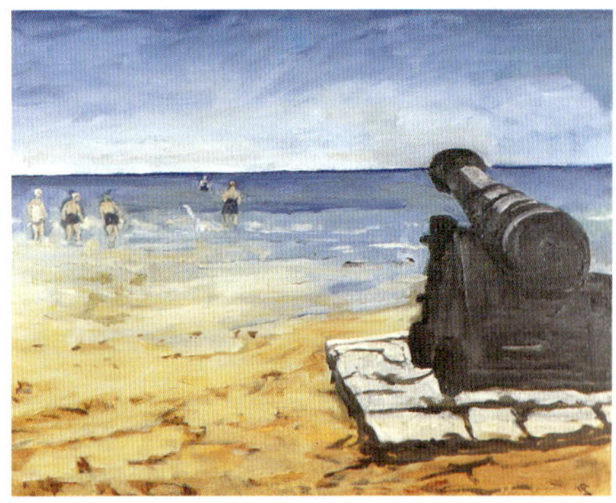

Fig 231 (C 316) above
The Beach at Walmer, overlooking the English Channel in Kent. Churchill gave this painting to General Lord Ismay, his war-time Chief of Staff.

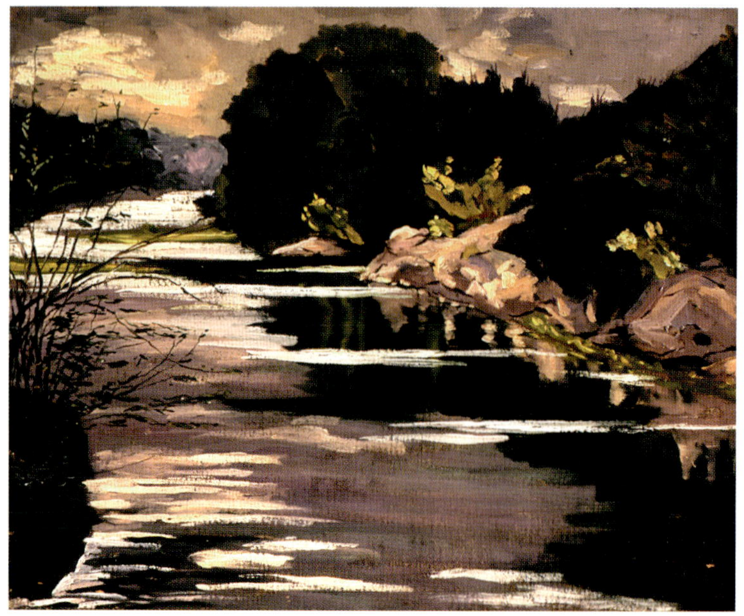

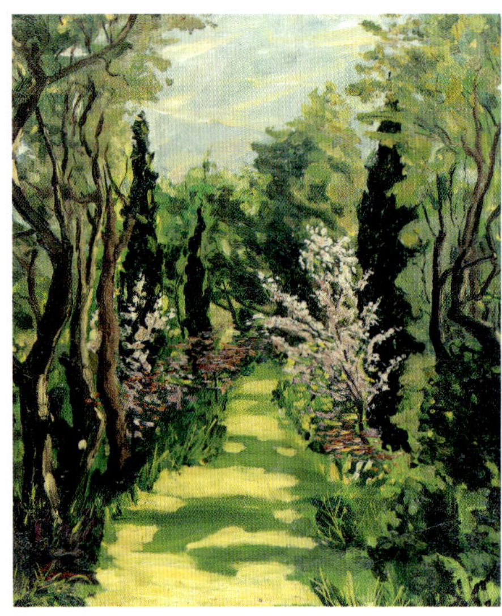

Fig 232 (C 76) above
This painting formerly belonged to Lady Lytton and may represent a view in her garden at Knebworth House.

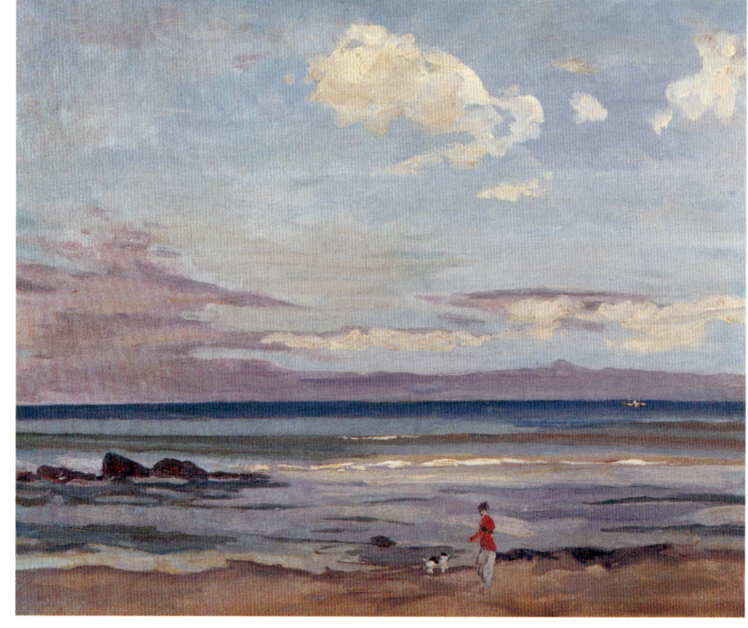

Fig 233 (C 58) above right
"Quiet Waters" given by Churchill to Lord Beaverbrook for his 80th birthday in 1959.

Fig 234 (C 102) middle right
Somewhere on the East Coast of England.

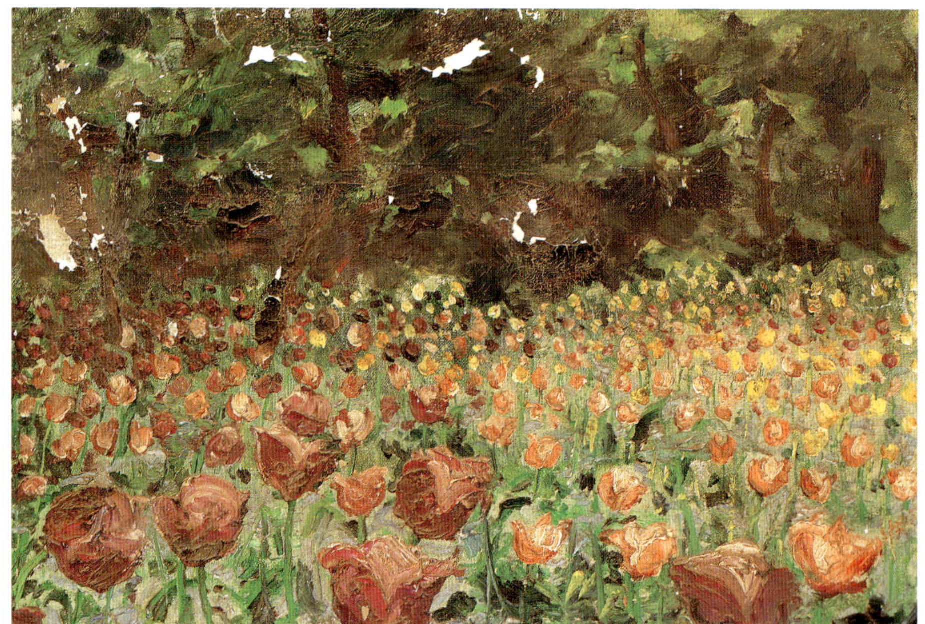

Fig 235 (C 252) right
A little painting of a field of tulips.

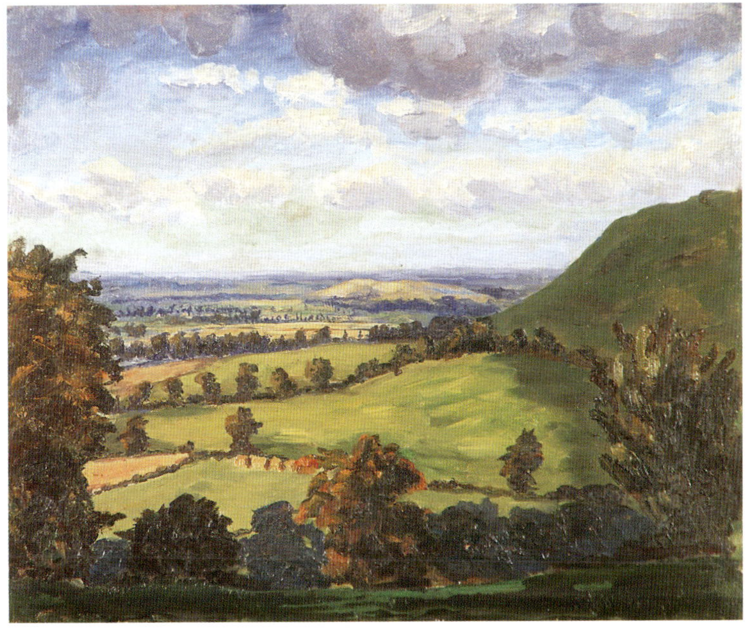

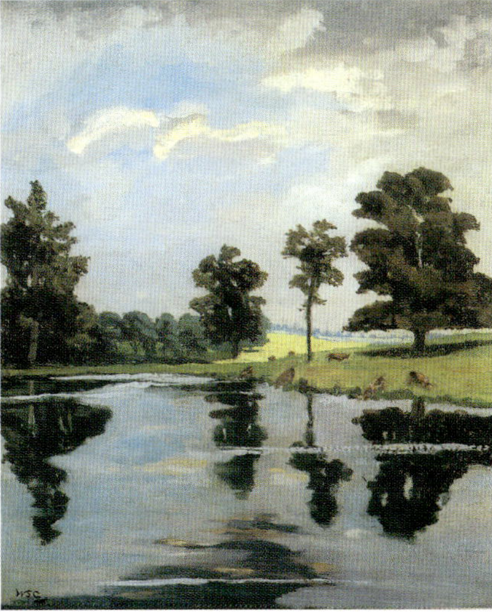

Fig 236 (C 364) above
A lake somewhere in Norfolk. This painting was formerly owned by Lady Churchill.

Fig 237 (C 285) above left
An unidentified view of an English valley.

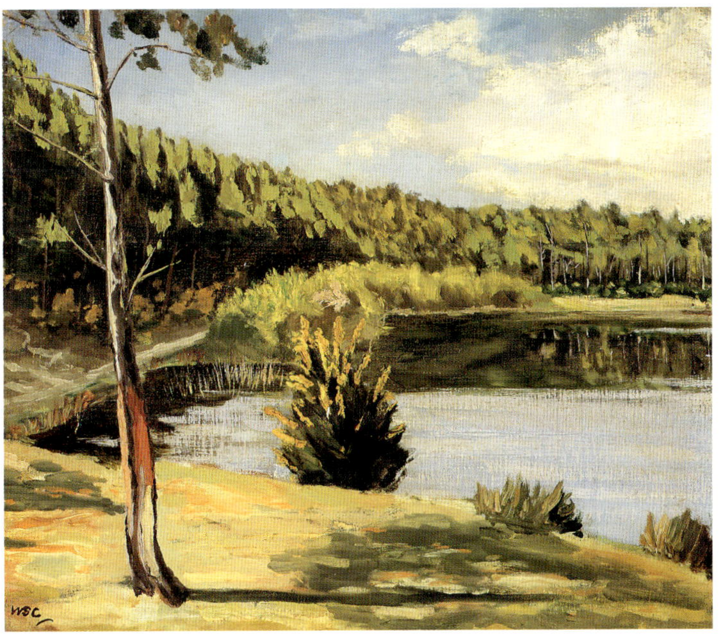

Fig 238 (C 369) left
A lake scene in Norfolk.

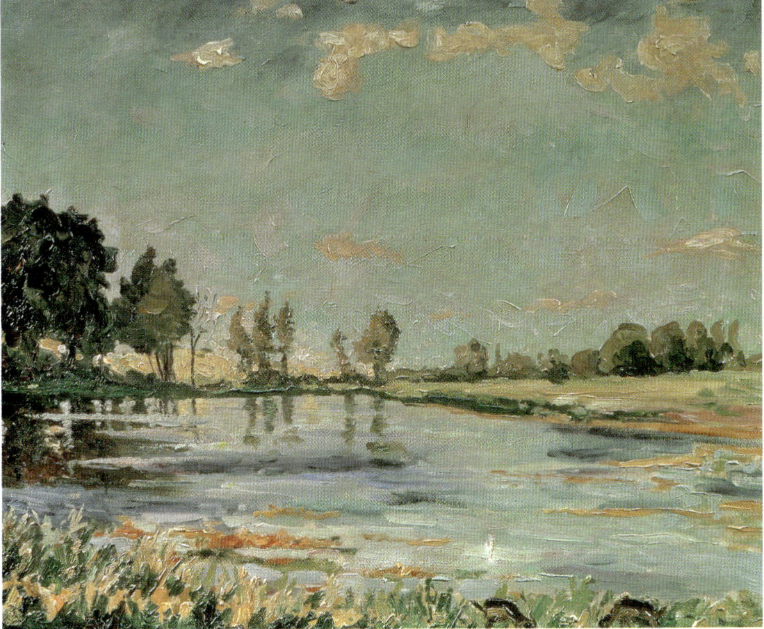

Fig 239 (C 367) left
A lake in Norfolk.

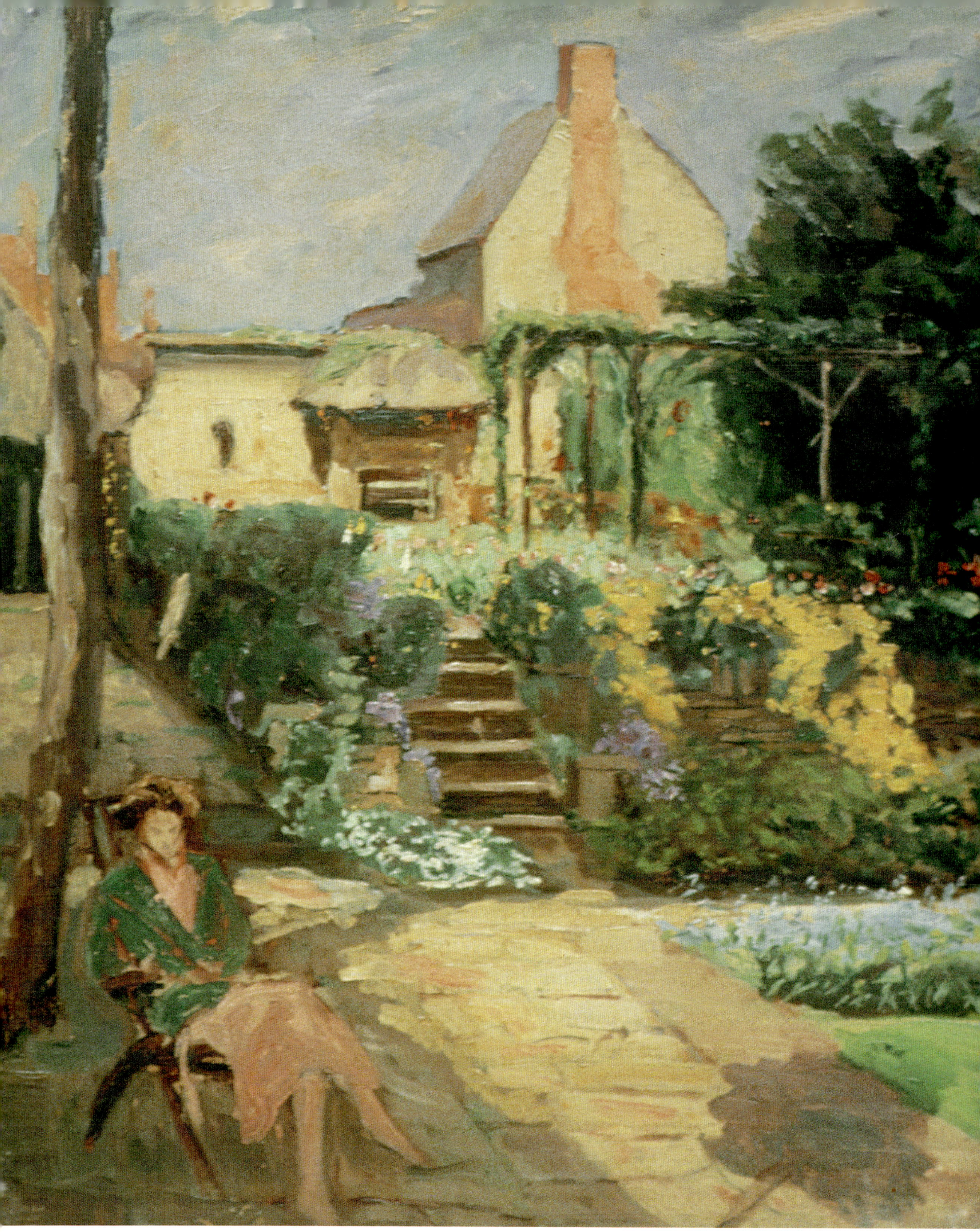

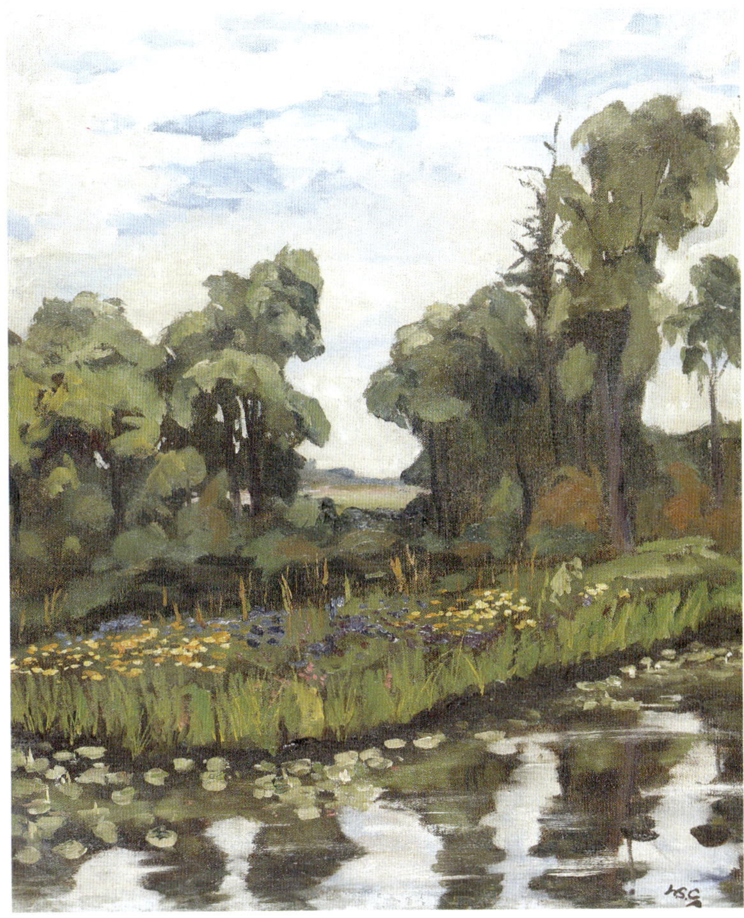

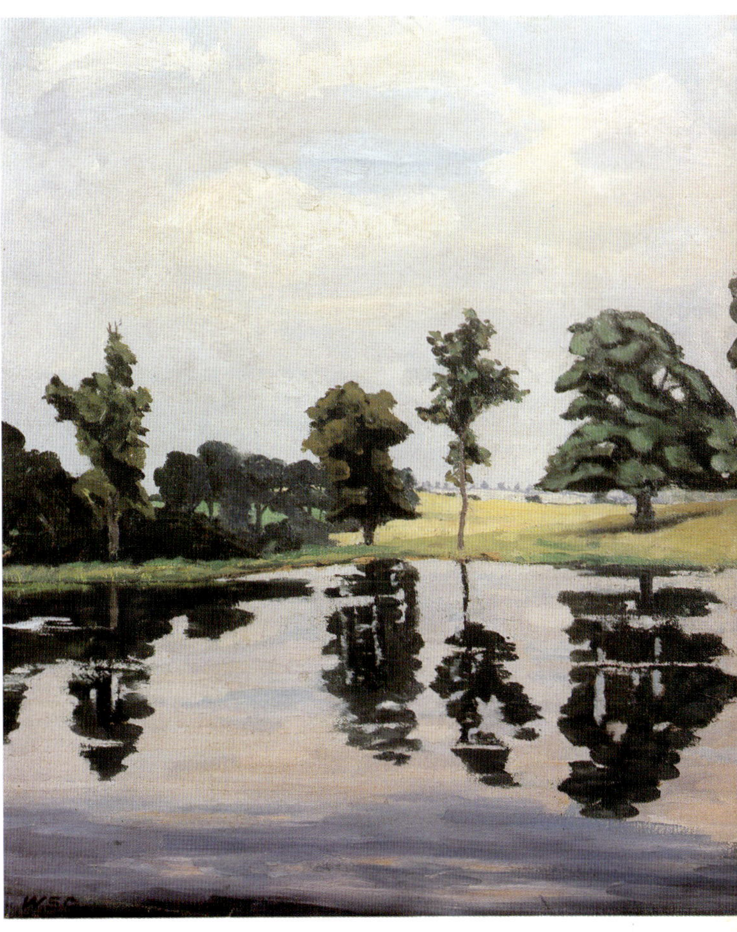

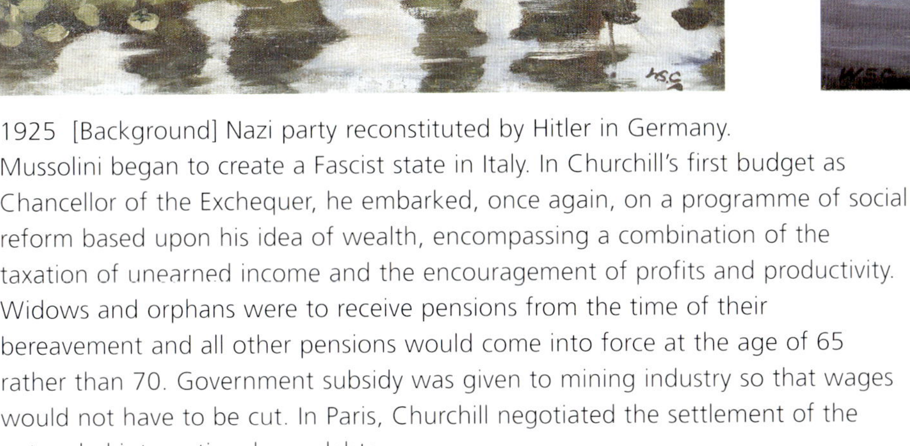

1925 [Background] Nazi party reconstituted by Hitler in Germany. Mussolini began to create a Fascist state in Italy. In Churchill's first budget as Chancellor of the Exchequer, he embarked, once again, on a programme of social reform based upon his idea of wealth, encompassing a combination of the taxation of unearned income and the encouragement of profits and productivity. Widows and orphans were to receive pensions from the time of their bereavement and all other pensions would come into force at the age of 65 rather than 70. Government subsidy was given to mining industry so that wages would not have to be cut. In Paris, Churchill negotiated the settlement of the entangled international war debts.

Fig 240 (C 356) above left
An unidentified river landscape in England.

Fig 241 (C 365) above
A Lake in Norfolk. This painting was given by Lady Churchill to her cousin Sylvia Henley.

Fig 242 (C 227) opposite page
An English garden in summer with Lady Eleanor Smith, elder daughter of Lord Birkenhead.

1925 [Painting] Churchill's painting 'Winter Sunshine, Chartwell' was exhibited anonymously at an amateur art exhibition at Sunderland House, Curzon Street, London. The competition was judged by the great patron of the arts Sir Joseph Duveen, Kenneth Clark, then a young art historian, and the portrait painter Oswald Birley. The latter chose 'Winter Sunshine' as first prize winner; Duveen disputed this as the picture was too good to be by an amateur, but Clark took Birley's side. All were delighted on being told the artist's name.

A portrait drawing by John Singer Sargent of Churchill as Chancellor of the Exchequer, wearing the same robes used by his father, hangs at Chartwell. Sargent said of Churchill's painting, 'He does what is in front of him, he doesn't shirk the difficulties and like most amateurs go wandering into distances.'

In the December 1925 edition of *Nash's Pall Mall Magazine,* Churchill's essay 'Hobbies' was published for the first time.

1926 [Background] Germany was admitted to the League of Nations. Television first demonstrated by Baird. General Strike in Britain. Churchill edited the Government's news sheet, *The British Gazette*. At the end of the Strike Churchill

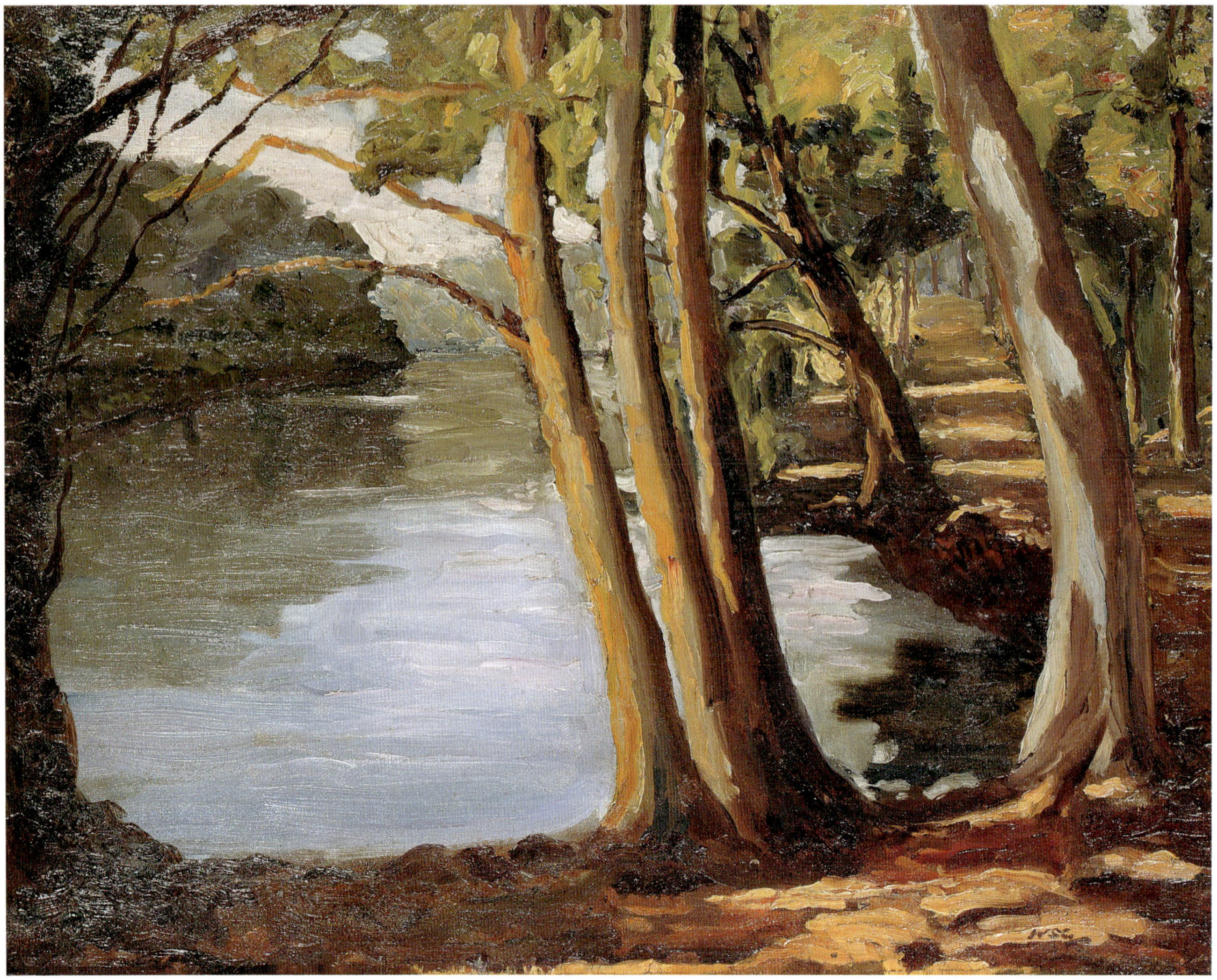

Fig 243 (C 56) above
The Thames at Taplow. Given by Churchill to Lady Juliet Duff who was a friend of both Winston and Clementine. Lady Juliet chose the painting one weekend at Chartwell with the help of Viscount Montgomery.

undertook the task of trying to conciliate between the miners and the owners. His proposal for a national minimum wage was rejected by the latter and the government withdrew from an attempt to settle the dispute.

1926 [Painting] Over many years, Churchill was a regular guest of Sir Philip Sassoon who was a considerable collector and connoisseur with two country houses, Port Lympne near Hythe on the Kent coast and Trent Park, now in Enfield, north London. Churchill painted scenes at both houses, including seascapes and interiors. Sassoon was a friend and patron of John Singer Sargent and Churchill copied, by way of self-instruction, several of his pictures including 'Two Glasses on a Verandah' and 'The Ruins of Arras Cathedral'.

Marthe Bibesco had known Churchill since her early youth. Once when they were both guests at Lympne she noticed that Winston had set up his easel under her windows 'in the first rays of the spring sun and was surrounded by paint boxes, cloths stained with all the colours of the rainbow and paint brushes set in pots ... He was completely absorbed ... wearing his immense [faded and frayed] sombrero of light felt ... painting that great expanse of marshland, spread out below the cliffs of Folkestone ...[where] according to the legend ... Julius Caesar had landed ... Four sketches were drying in the sun, propped up against the feet of the easel. He was now slashing the fifth canvas, almost throwing the paint on; he was sighing, almost out of breath with the effort of expressing his feelings.'His aunt, Leonie Leslie, tried to persuade Churchill to give Marthe one of the paintings to sell at a charity

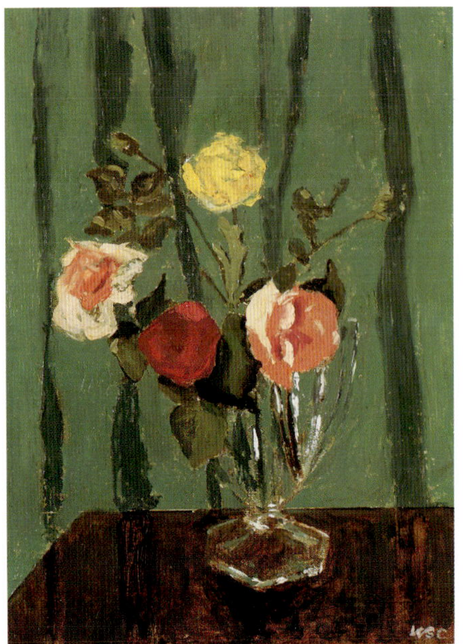

Fig 244 (C 6) above
Roses. This painting formerly belonged to Clementine Churchill.

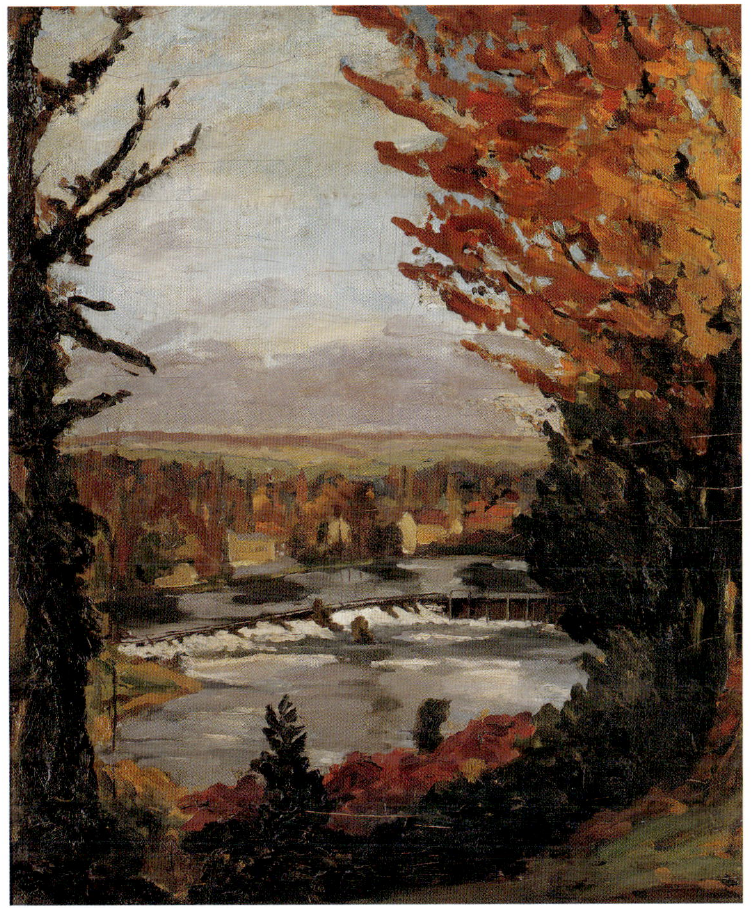

Fig 245 (C 358) left
The Thames from the grounds of Taplow Court, near Maidenhead in Berkshire, where Winston and Clementine were frequent visitors. It was the home of Lord and Lady Desborough, members of 'The Souls' an informal social and intellectual elite which included Lord Balfour. This painting was formerly owned by Lady Churchill.

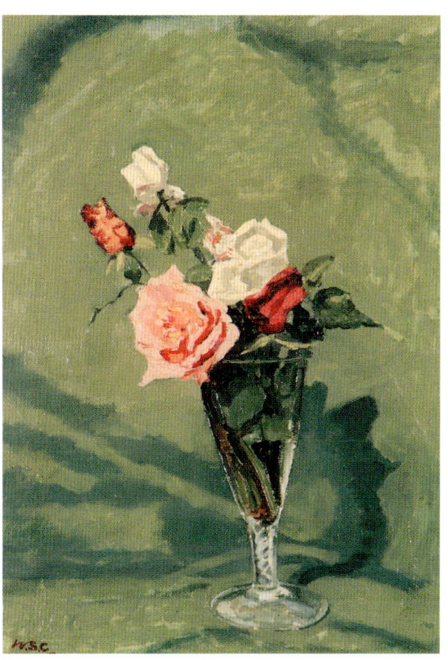

Fig 246 (C 181) above
Study of roses, given by Churchill to the actress Vivien Leigh.

Fig 247 (C 362) below left
The Thames at Taplow.

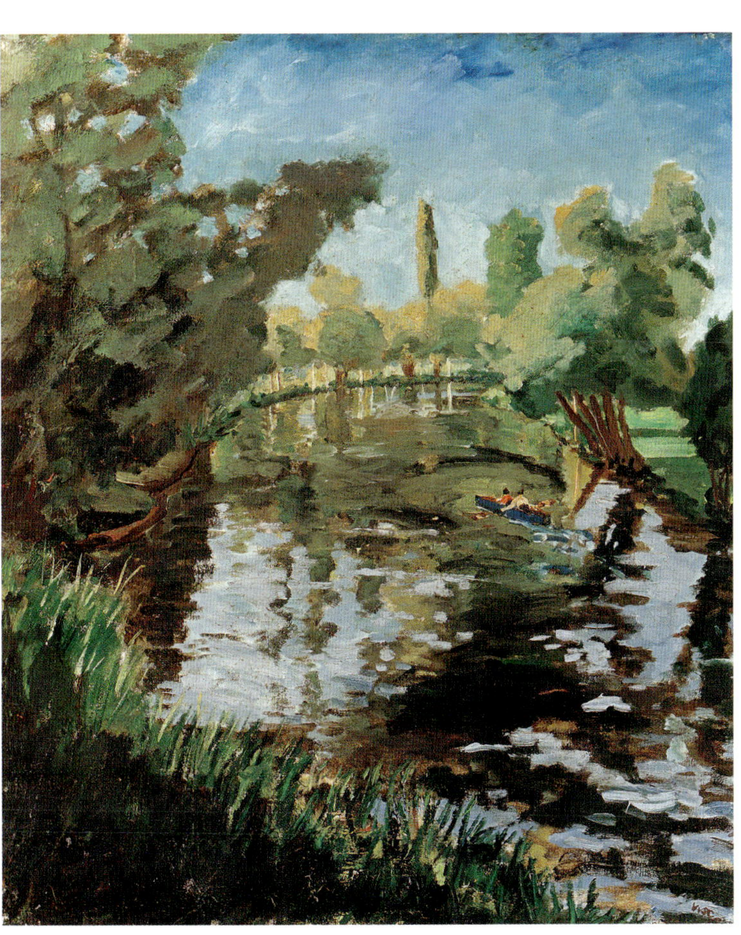

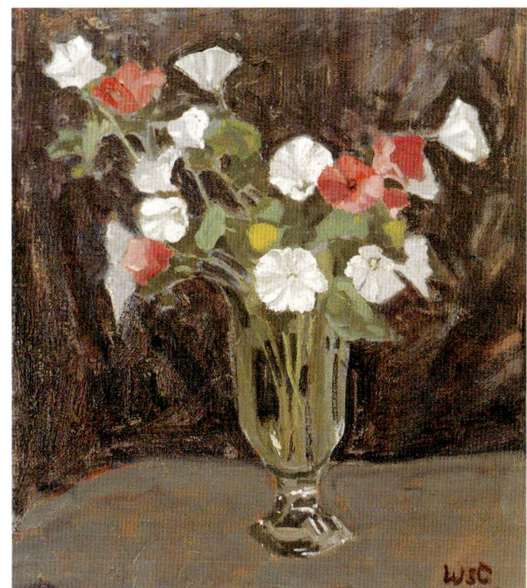

Fig 248 (C 7) above
Mallows.

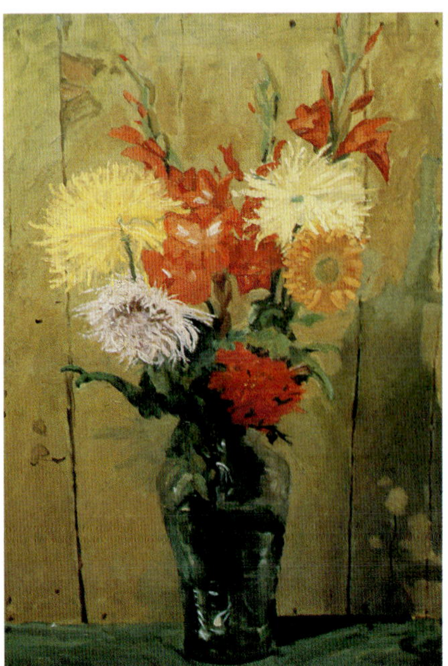

Fig 249 (C 5) above
Flowers in a green glass vase.

In total, Churchill's still life paintings show his determination to tackle difficult subjects - not always with success. His liking for flowers may have been furthered by making the garden at Chartwell from 1924 onwards; and the visits there of the artist Sir William Nicholson in the 1930s must have helped develop Winston's interest in the problems of painting objects of similar tones. Still life subjects also provided Churchill with opportunities for painting, at Chartwell or elsewhere, when the weather prevented him from working out of doors.

bazaar in Paris, 'as you have painted the same landscape five times this morning'. Winston demurred: 'They are too bad to sell and too dear to me to give!'

1927 [Background] First solo Atlantic flight by Lindbergh. British Broadcasting Corporation (BBC) founded. British army gave up the lance as a weapon. Churchill urged the right of individuals to contract out of a trade union's compulsory political levy. Met Mussolini in Rome and approved of his struggle against Leninism. Holidays with the Balsans at Lou Seuil. The third volume of his war memoirs was published. Devoted much attention to a scheme to abolish local rates in an effort to stimulate industry. Embarked upon an autobiography of his young days entitled *My Early Life*.

1927 [Painting] Clementine Churchill was knocked down by a bus in London's Brompton Road. Newspaper reports of this accident brought the artist Walter Sickert to the Chancellor's official residence, No. 11 Downing Street. More than 25 years before, Sickert had been friends with Clementine Churchill's mother, Lady Blanche (who had died in 1925), when she was living with her two daughters in Dieppe. On one occasion Sickert had taken Clementine on a day's gallery visiting in Paris, which included a meeting with Camille Pissarro in his studio.

Churchill and Sickert took to each other, talking often and at length during the next two years about painting. Sickert taught Churchill the *camaïeu* way of preparing canvas using an under-painting of several layers, usually of two colours; he explained the method in two detailed letters. Sickert also taught him how to use photographs as aids towards painting and the use of a grille to transfer proportions accurately on to a canvas. Sickert visited Chartwell and worked with Churchill on many pictures. Later, Churchill told Sir John Rothenstein, 'Sickert imparted to me all his considered wisdom about painting. He had a room specially darkened to work in, but I wasn't an apt pupil, for I rejoice in the highest lights and the brightest colours.'

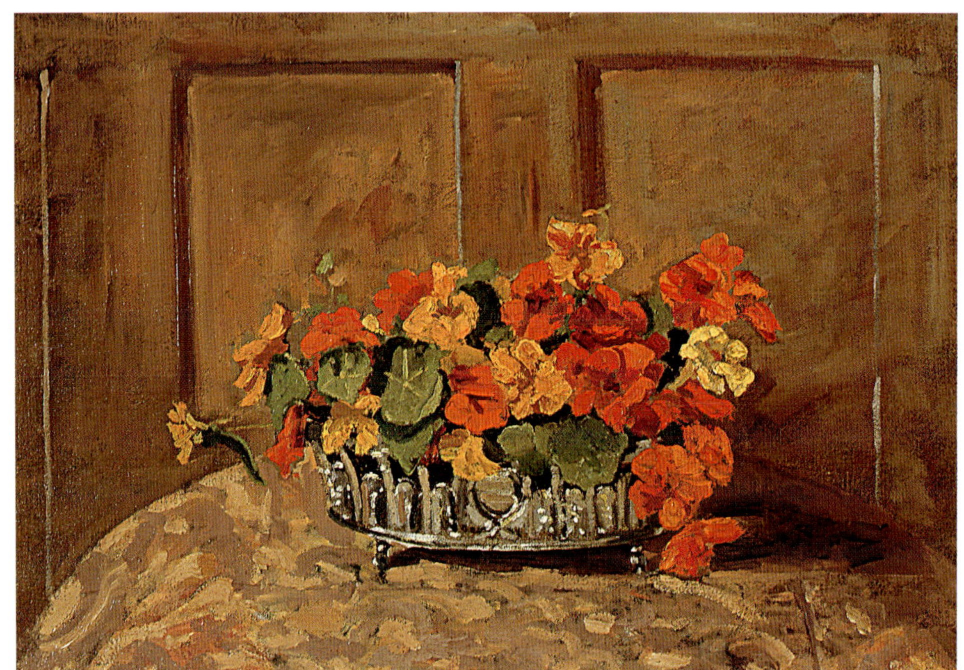

Fig 250 (C 172) above
Nasturtiums in a silver presentation bowl. The flower arrangement was made by Churchill's secretary, Grace Hamblin. This painting formerly belonged to Clementine Churchill.

Frederick Lindemann, Professor of Experimental Philosophy at Oxford, who was a lifelong friend, presented Churchill with a camera to help with his painting. Churchill went with Lindemann to Venice to join Clementine where she was convalescing with their eldest daughter, Diana. Stopping in Paris on the way he bought a lantern with a lens that could project a photograph directly on to a canvas to the exact size needed. From then on Churchill used this method regularly so as to overcome his lack of expertise as a draughtsman - although he continued to sketch the outline of subjects in charcoal working direct on to canvas when out of doors.

Churchill went to stay with King George V at Balmoral in Scotland and while there worked on a painting based on a photograph of the churchyard of St Paul's Cathedral, London. The King asked Churchill to donate this painting to a local

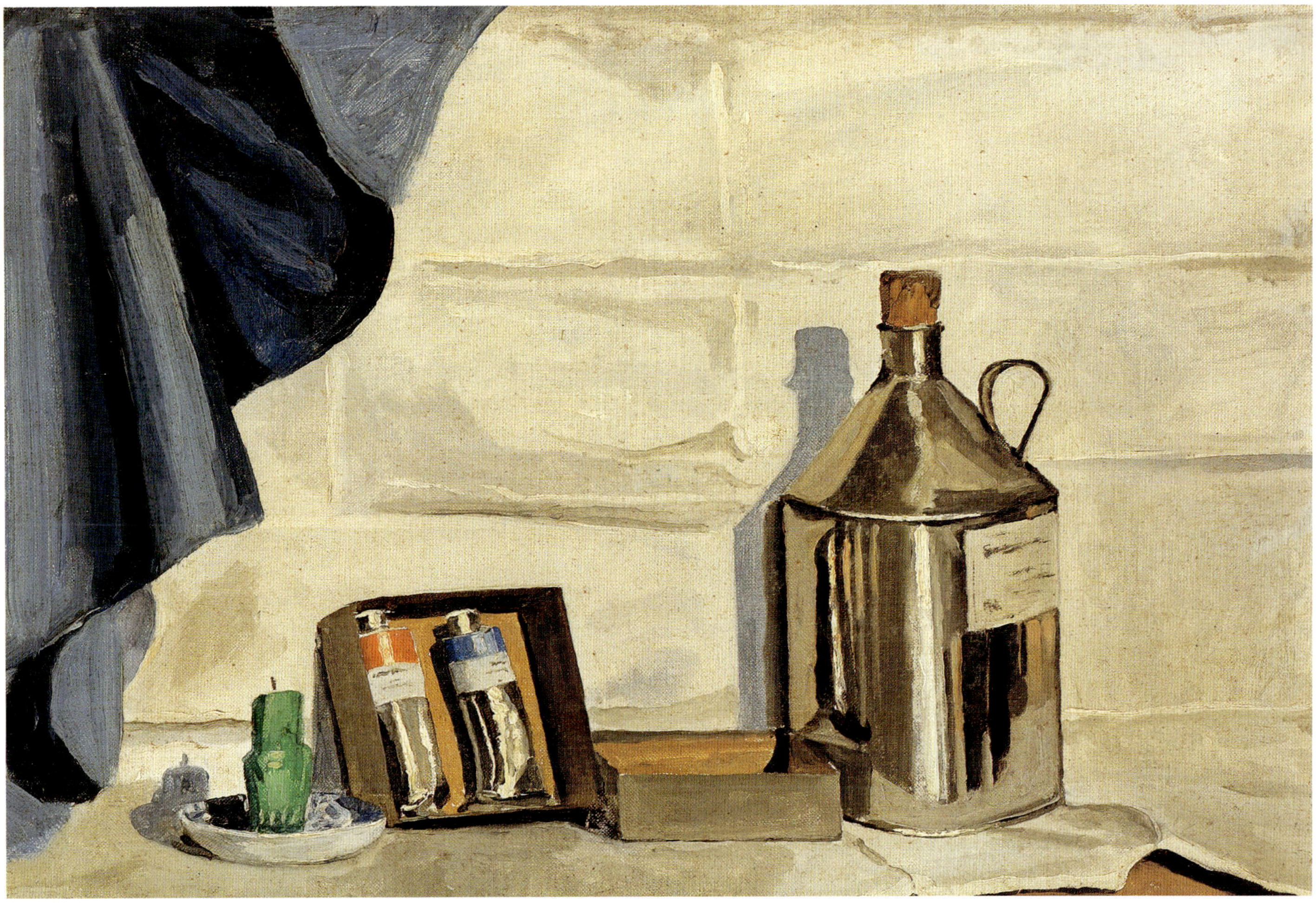

Fig 251 (C 166) above
Studio still life. This painting formerly belonged to Clementine Churchill.

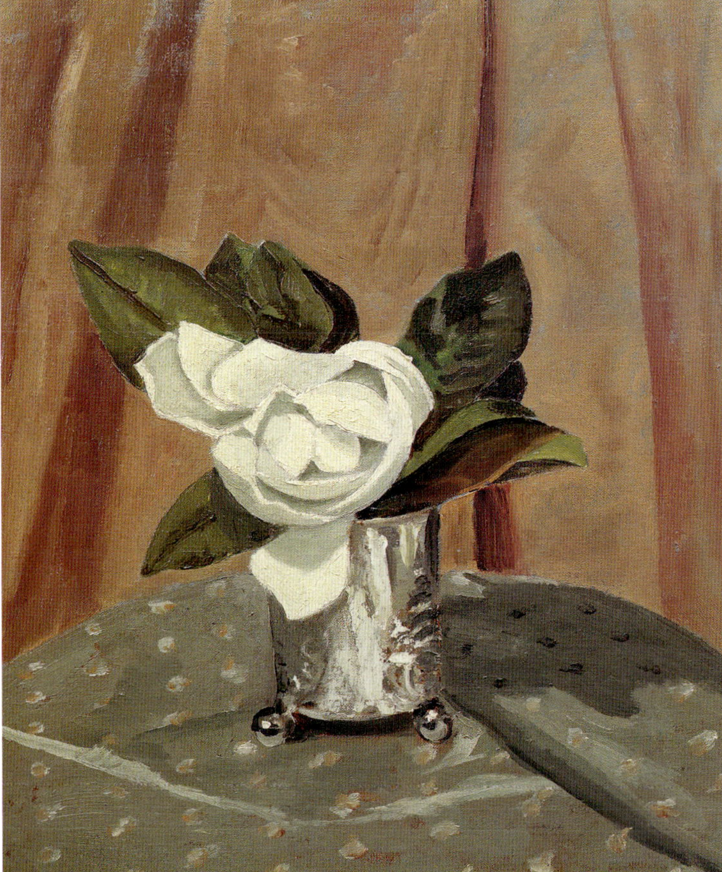

Fig 252 (C 154) left
Magnolia. A bloom from the tree planted by Clementine under Winston's bedroom window at Chartwell.

Fig 253 (C 8) below
Flowers in the Studio at Chartwell. This painting formerly belonged to Clementine Churchill.

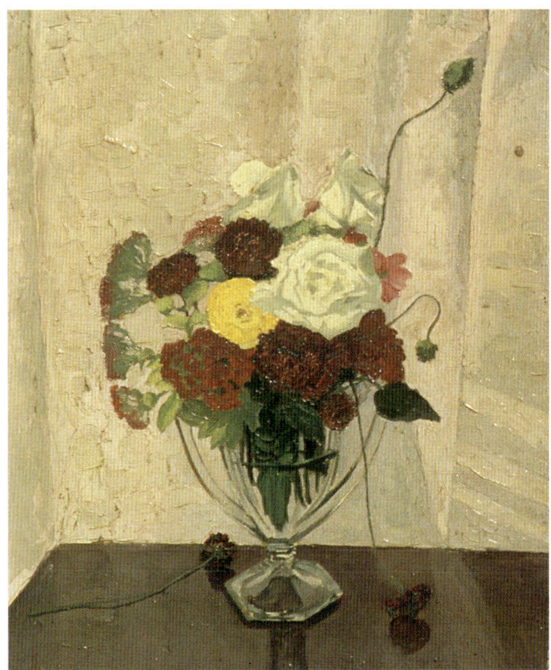

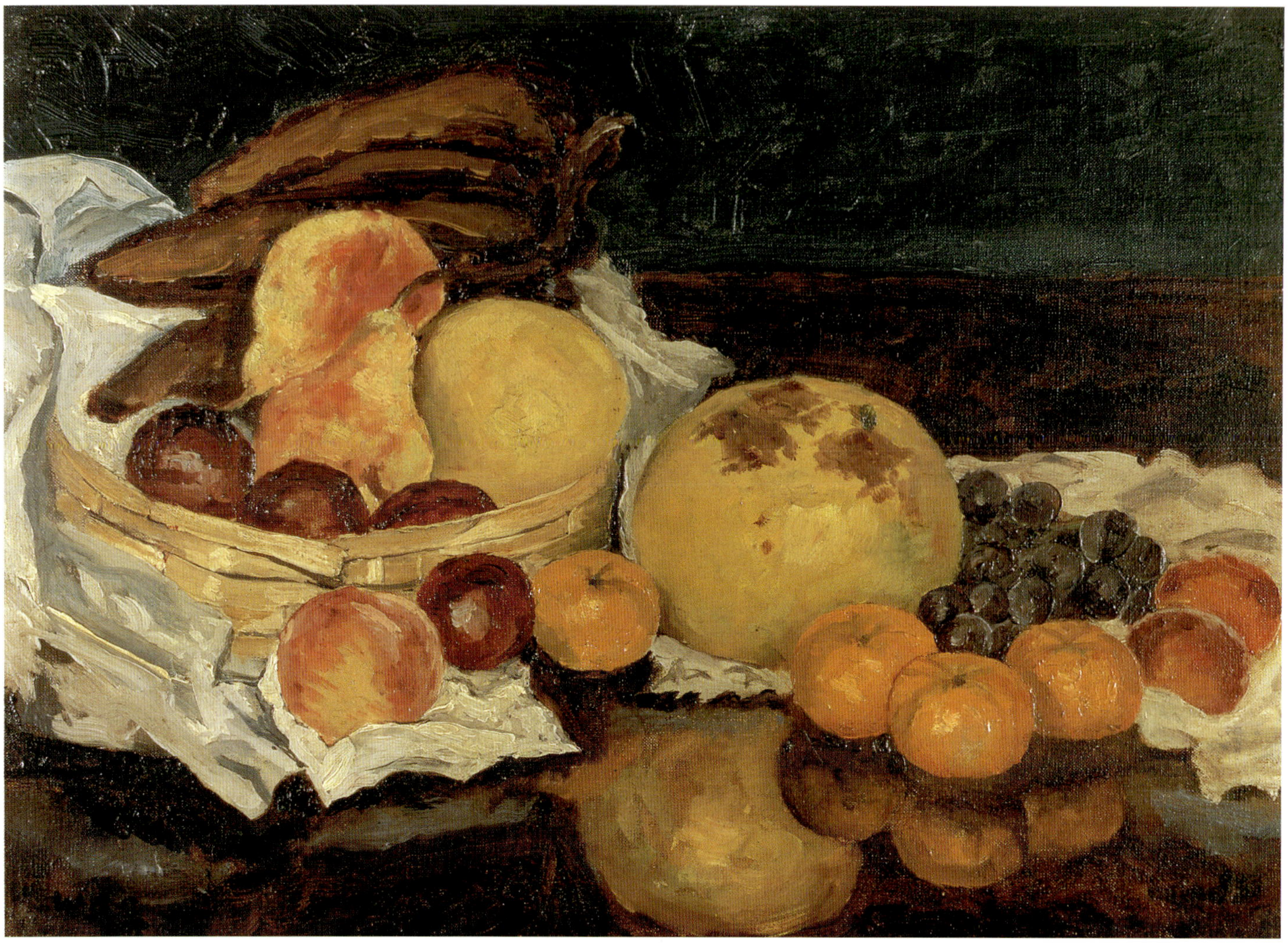

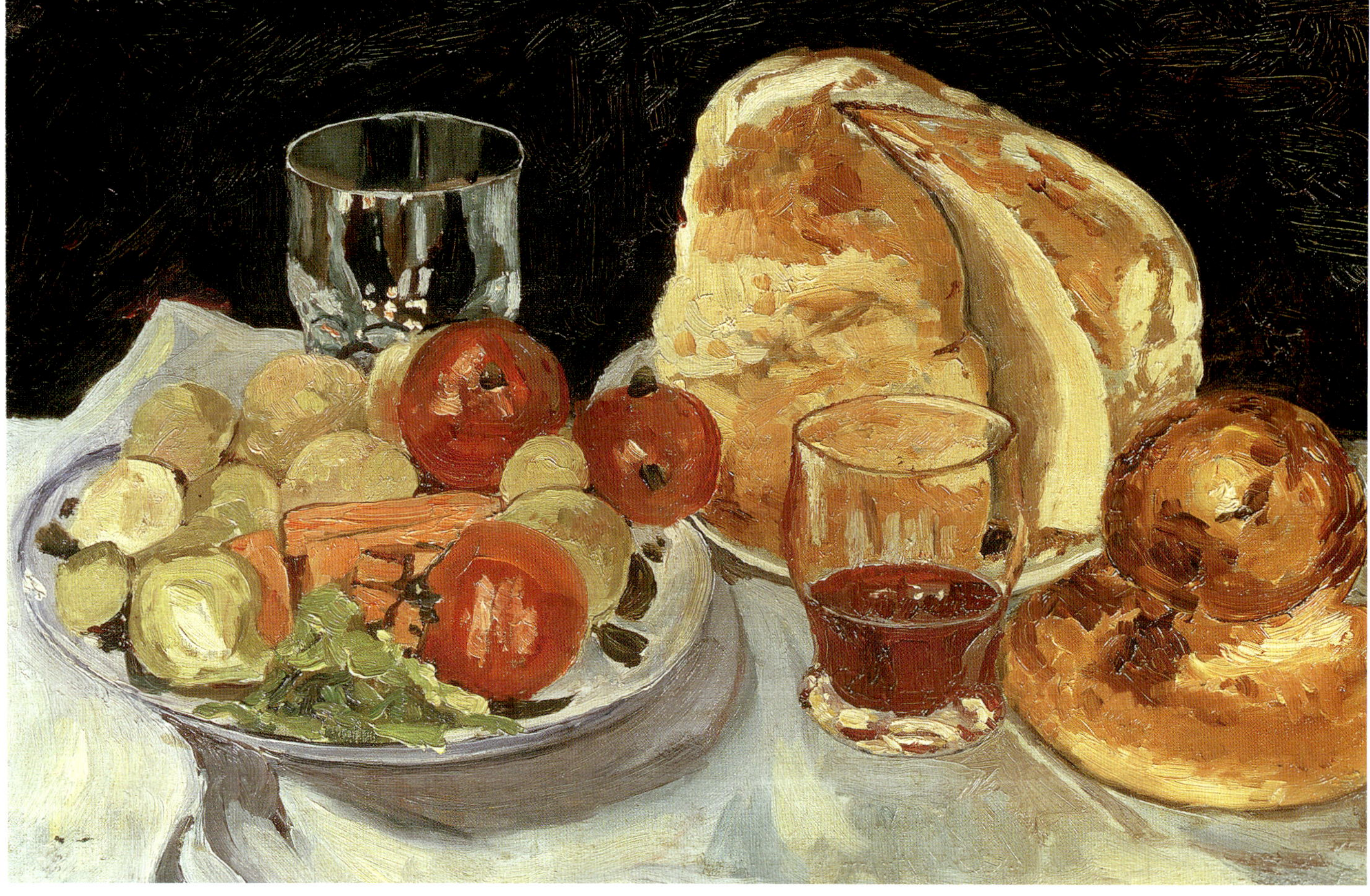

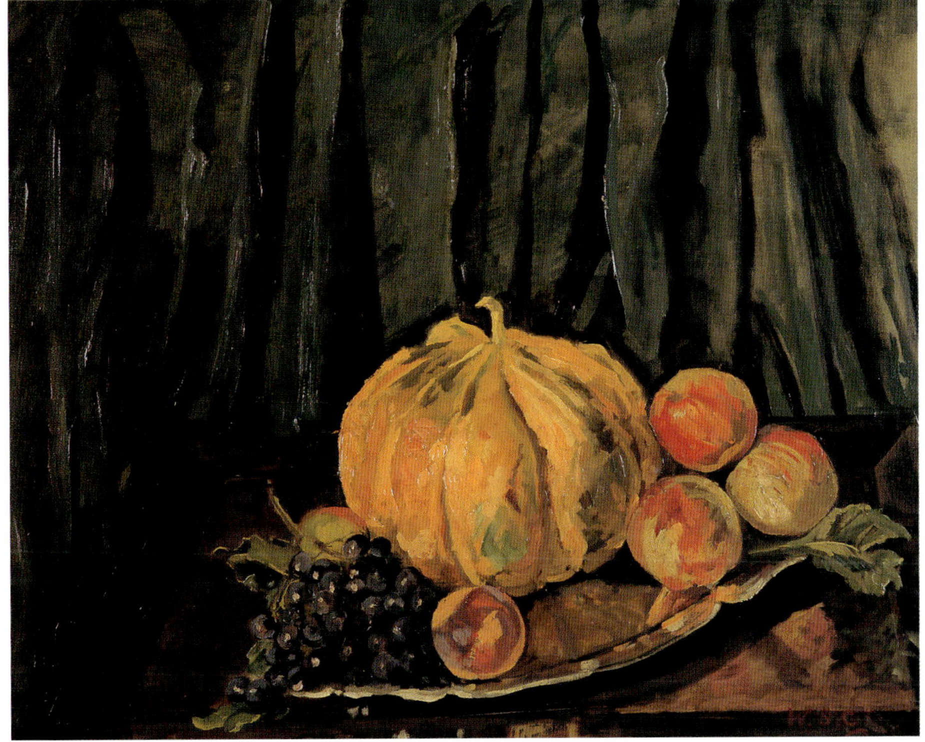

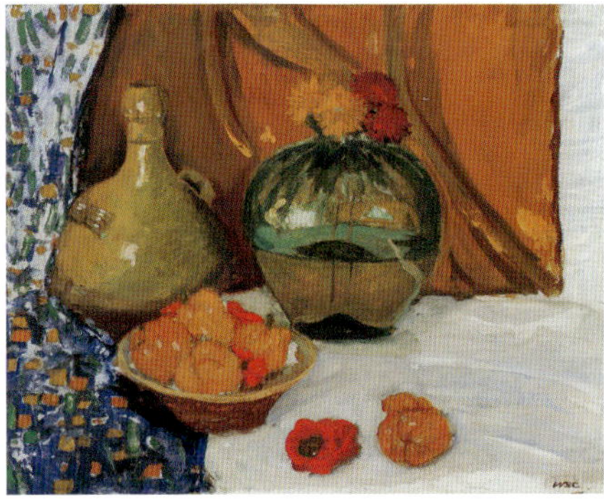

Fig 254 (C 9) above
Fruit and two jars. This painting formerly belonged to Clementine Churchill.

Fig 255 (C 169) left
Still life of fruit. This painting is based on photograph from the Studio archives at Chartwell.

charity sale where it was auctioned by Sir Frederick Ponsonby, Keeper of the Privy Purse, for 115 guineas (£120.75).

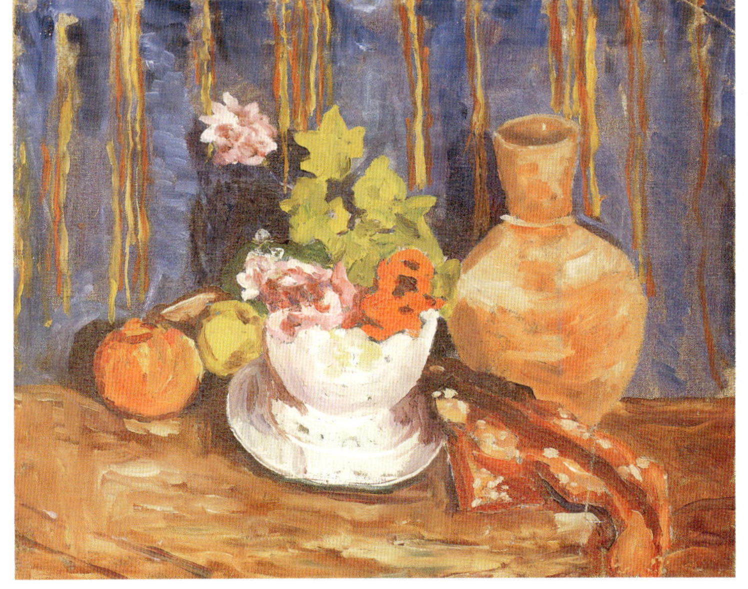

Fig 256 (C 170) above
Flowers in a white bowl.

Fig 257 (C 167) opposite above
Fruit and reflections.

Fig 258 (C 168) opposite below
A loaf of bread.

1928 [Background] Russia's first five-year plan. Penicillin discovered by Fleming. Votes for women in Britain, on the same terms as men. Churchill's fourth budget included an almost 100 per cent rise in children's allowances; his derating scheme was introduced with the aim of reviving industry and creating new jobs. At Chartwell, Churchill worked on the fourth, post-war volume of his memoirs and built a cottage for his daughter Mary. At Balmoral he met the King's granddaughter, the two-and-half-year-old Princess Elizabeth (Queen Elizabeth II).

1928 [Painting] During this period, Churchill painted several successful portraits using Sickert's painting techniques and glass slides projected by lantern. Examples from this time include portraits of Lord Balfour and his niece; the Duke of Westminster with his dog; and a large picture of teatime at Chartwell where the guests included Therese and Walter Sickert, Eddie Marsh and Professor Lindemann.

1929 [Background] German airship *Graf Zeppelin* circumnavigated the earth. Collapse of the New York stock exchange and beginning of world economic depression. Anti-British riots in Palestine. In his fifth budget, Churchill abolished the duty on tea imposed since the time of Queen Elizabeth I. General election in Britain. Churchill made his first broadcast urging his listeners to avoid class warfare and violent political strife. Labour government elected and Churchill, out of office, began work on his four-volume biography of his ancestor John, Duke of Marlborough, published between 1933 and 1938.

1929 [Painting] Churchill travelled to Canada and the United States where he visited William Randolph Hearst at San Simeon. Hearst invited him to write for his newspapers. During a three-day trip in the Rocky Mountains, Churchill painted at

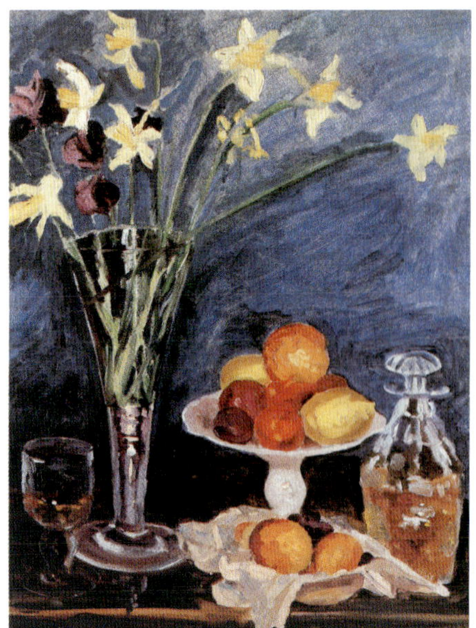

Fig 259 (C 180) above
Daffodills and tulips.

Fig 260 (C 171) right
Flowers in a blue vase.

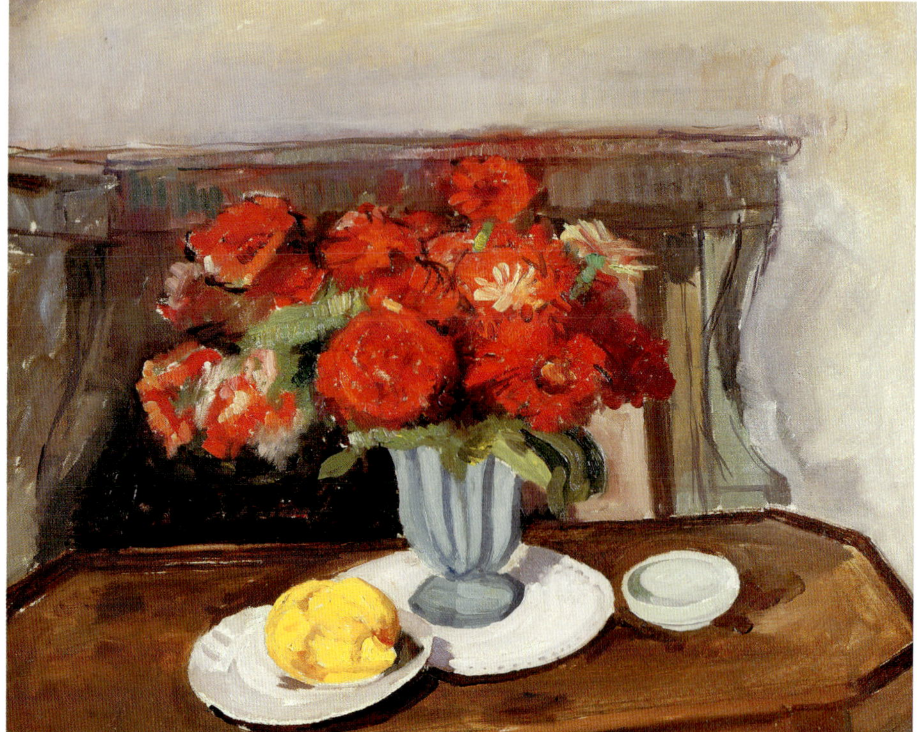

Lake Emerald and Lake Louise. He was in New York at the time of the collapse of the stock market in which he lost a substantial amount of capital. Through his journalism he was able to keep up his income but his style of life was much reduced. For a while, there were to be no further travels abroad for painting or pleasure.

Churchill's article 'Painting as a Pastime' was re-published in *The Hundred Best English Essays*, edited by the Earl of Birkenhead.

1930 [Background] Allied troops ended their occupation of Germany. Collective farms established in Russia. First non-stop flight from Paris to New York. Whittle's first experiments with gas turbines for jet propulsion. Churchill's autobiography, *My Early Life*, published and translated into many languages.

1930s [Painting] Churchill was without official national political responsibilities for most of the decade and around half of his extant pictures were painted during this period. Many paintings from this and the previous decade, such as the pictures of his goldfish pond, are reminders of the pleasure and contentment that Churchill found at Chartwell. He enjoyed painting the flowers from Clementine's now maturing garden - in particular the magnolia that she had planted beneath his bedroom window. When bad weather forced him indoors Churchill turned his attention to still-life subjects: a range of bottles, a group of silver and other more traditional subjects.

Grace Hamblin, who lived locally, went to work for Churchill at Chartwell as a secretary in 1932. Nearly 70 years later she told me how the still life of nasturtiums in a silver basket came to be painted: (C 172). 'they're very graceful and they have that very pretty leaf, but they've got an awful smell. Nobody would ever use them for flower arranging ... If you put them into a container, by the morning they've gone their own way. As I was walking through the garden to work one morning I saw a lovely bed of nasturtiums ... the colours were beautiful. And I thought to myself, "The Churchills have this presentation silver basket, which was more often than not on the dining table at Chartwell." They were having a luncheon party and I thought, "Wouldn't they look lovely with the

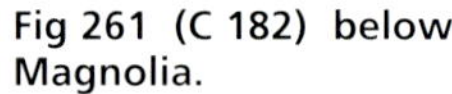

Fig 261 (C 182) below
Magnolia.

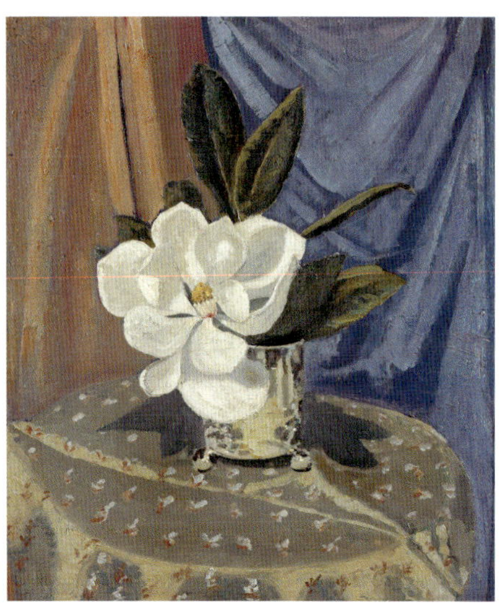

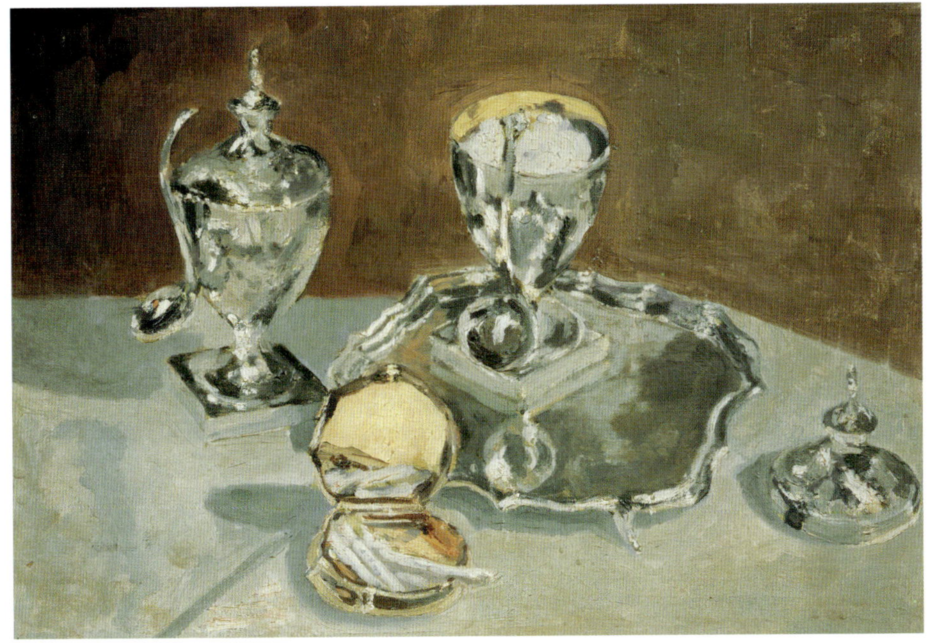

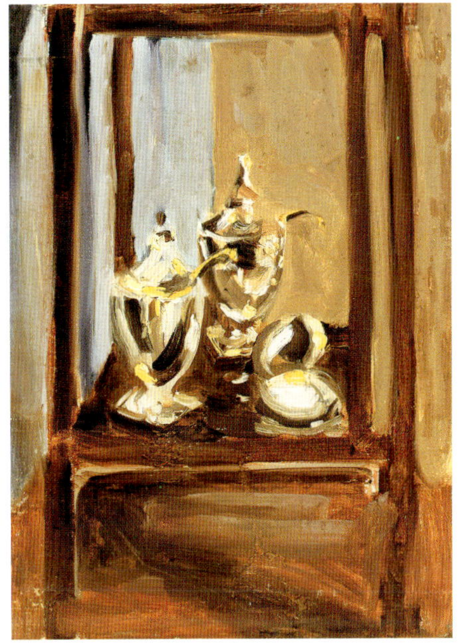

Fig 262 (C 174) above
Silver life.

Fig 263 (C 173) above left
Still life, silver. This painting was given by Churchill to his political colleague Sir Anthony Eden, who succeeded him as Prime Minister and later became Lord

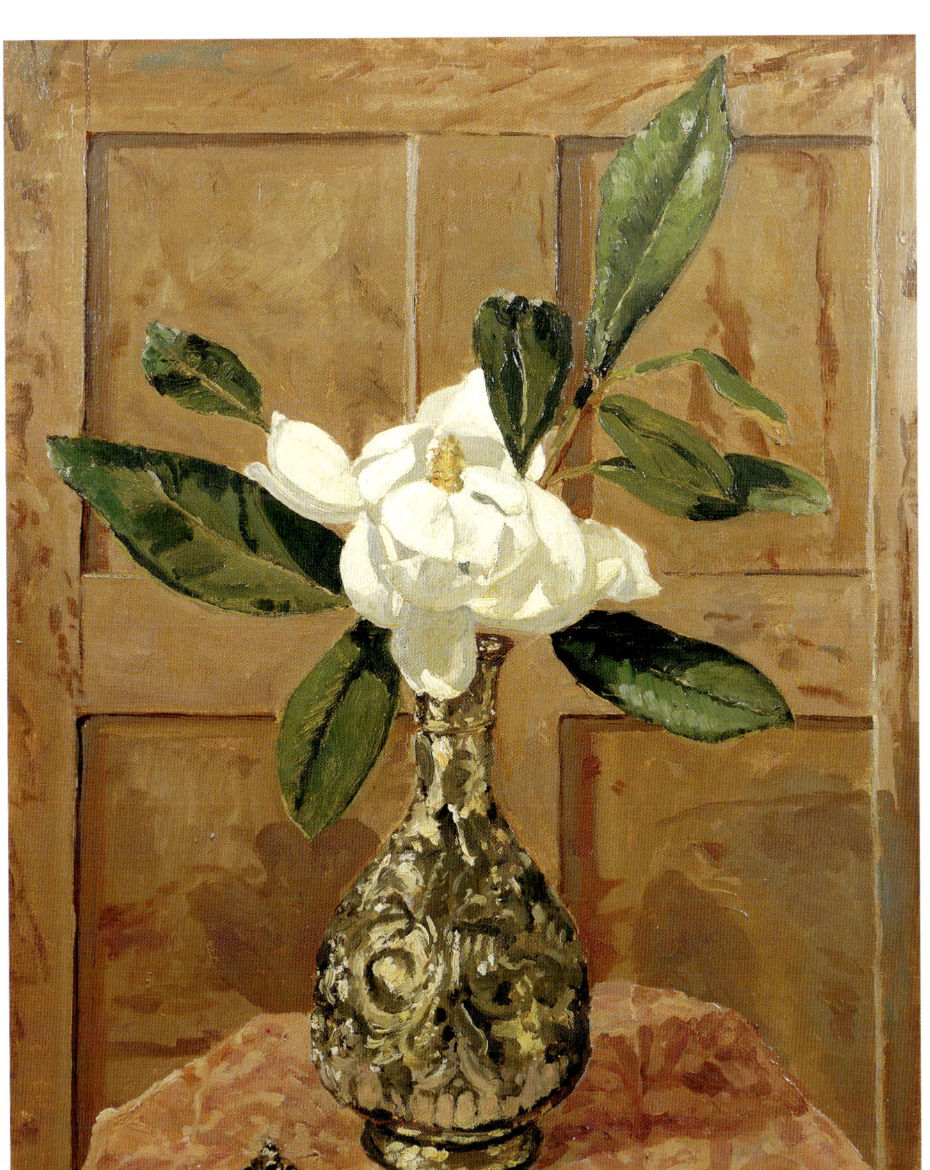

Fig 264 (C 183) left
Magnolia. Given by Churchill to his youngest daughter, Mary.

Fig 265 (C 175) below
Silver life, painted in January 1937.

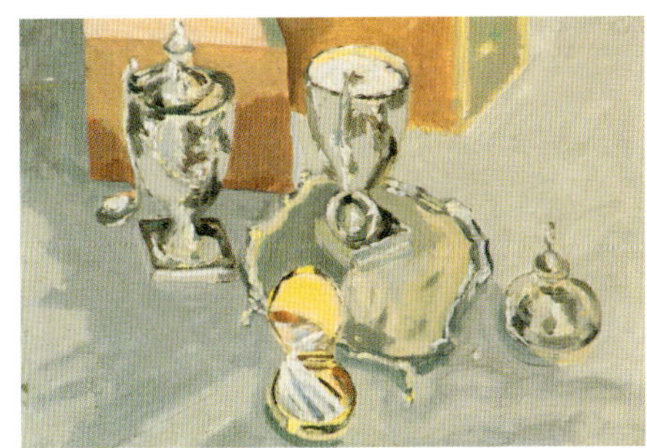

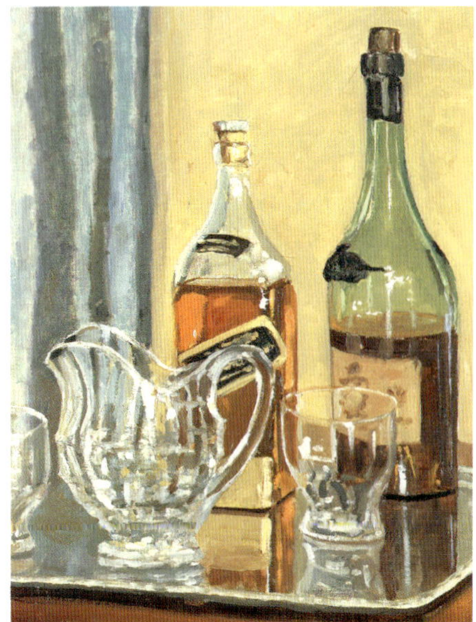

Fig 266 (C 176) above
Jugs and bottles. Given by Churchill to Mr and Mrs Averell Harriman

silver?" Sir Winston fell in love with the arrangement. He thought how lovely they looked. Which they did for that moment.'

On a later occasion, in London, Churchill brought home the Prince of Wales (later King Edward VIII) after a dinner. Grace Hamblin was on duty and had to give him a message. Churchill said to the Prince, 'Oh Sir, may I present my secretary? She's very uneducated.' Miss Hamblin, then a young woman and very conscious of her background, felt humiliated by this unkind remark. 'I was uneducated and I was very much aware of it. Then I think [Sir Winston] saw something was wrong and he said to the Prince, "But she arranges flowers quite beautifully."And then he painted the picture.'

From 1920, Churchill had had a personal armed police bodyguard, Sergeant Walter Thompson, who later recalled, 'I have been with [Churchill] on various painting holidays and the intensity with which he has thrown himself into the task has amazed me. He would start painting in the early morning and continue with work until 7 o'clock in the evening with only a short break for lunch ... He would frequently call upon my services to supply him with a dab of this or that. At the end of a long day, I would take it upon myself to clean his palette, which always looked like fifty rainbows.

'When I finished my first tour of duty with Churchill in 1931, I plucked up my courage and asked ... "Would you be willing to give me a painting, Sir?" I have only known him to give away his work on two occasions ... He replied, 'You pick whatever you like, Thompson, and you can have it.' ... Eventually I decided upon a picture that I had seen him paint while he was staying with Sir Philip Sassoon at his house in Barnet ... I asked him if he would sign the picture for me. He answered ... "I have never signed one, Thompson, but I will initial this for you."'

1931 [Background] Financial crisis in Britain. Salaries cut by 10 per cent. Taxes on imported fruit and vegetables. Revolution in Spain. Grain shortages in Russia. Japanese invaded Manchuria. Failure of banks in Austria and Germany. First German pocket battleship launched. Labour government resigned in Britain and National government formed. General election. London conference on future of India. Churchill resigned from the Conservative shadow cabinet because of his

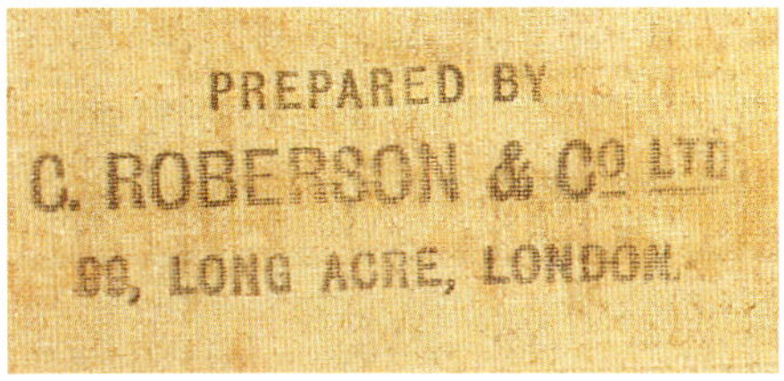

PREPARED BY
C. ROBERSON & Co LTD
99, LONG ACRE, LONDON.

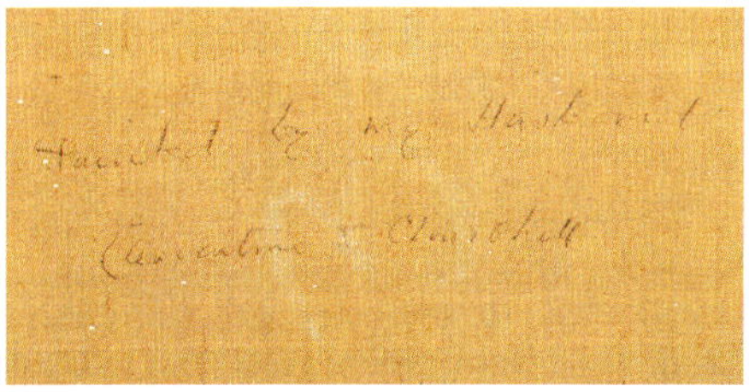

Many of Winston Churchill's canvases carry the stamp of Roberson, Long Acre, London, as shown top.

In Sir Winston's later years, Clementine Churchill inscribed the back of some of his canvases with: 'Painted by my husband. Clementine S. Churchill.' (See above)

Fig 267 (C 178) opposite page
Mallows. This painting formerly belonged to Clementine Churchill.

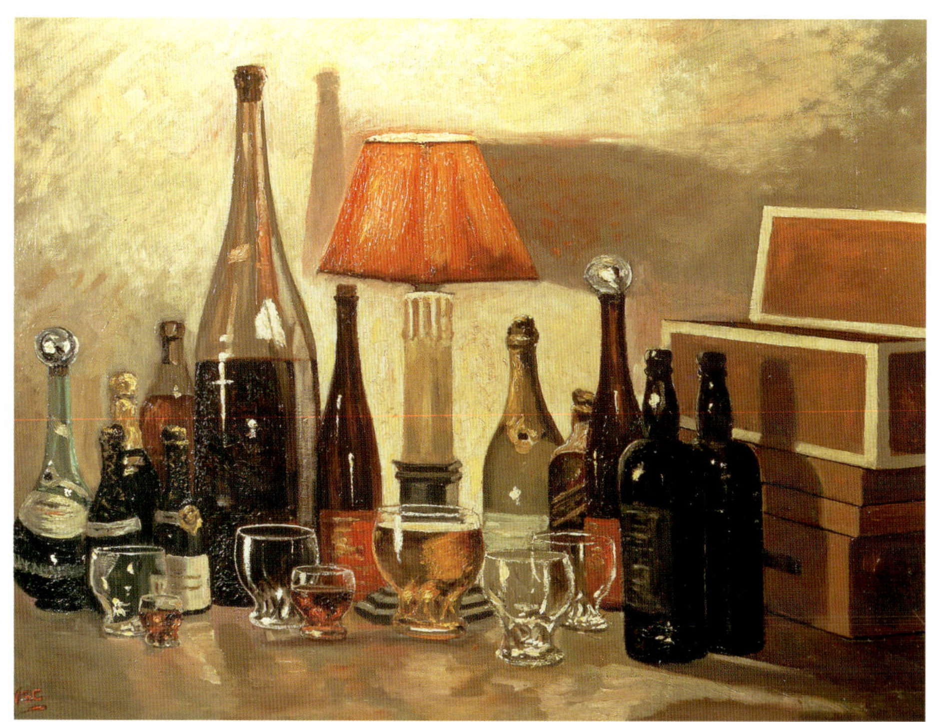

Fig 268 (C 177) right
Bottlescape. Painted in 1926. Churchill is said to have sent his children round the house at Chartwell to collect the items he showed in the picture.

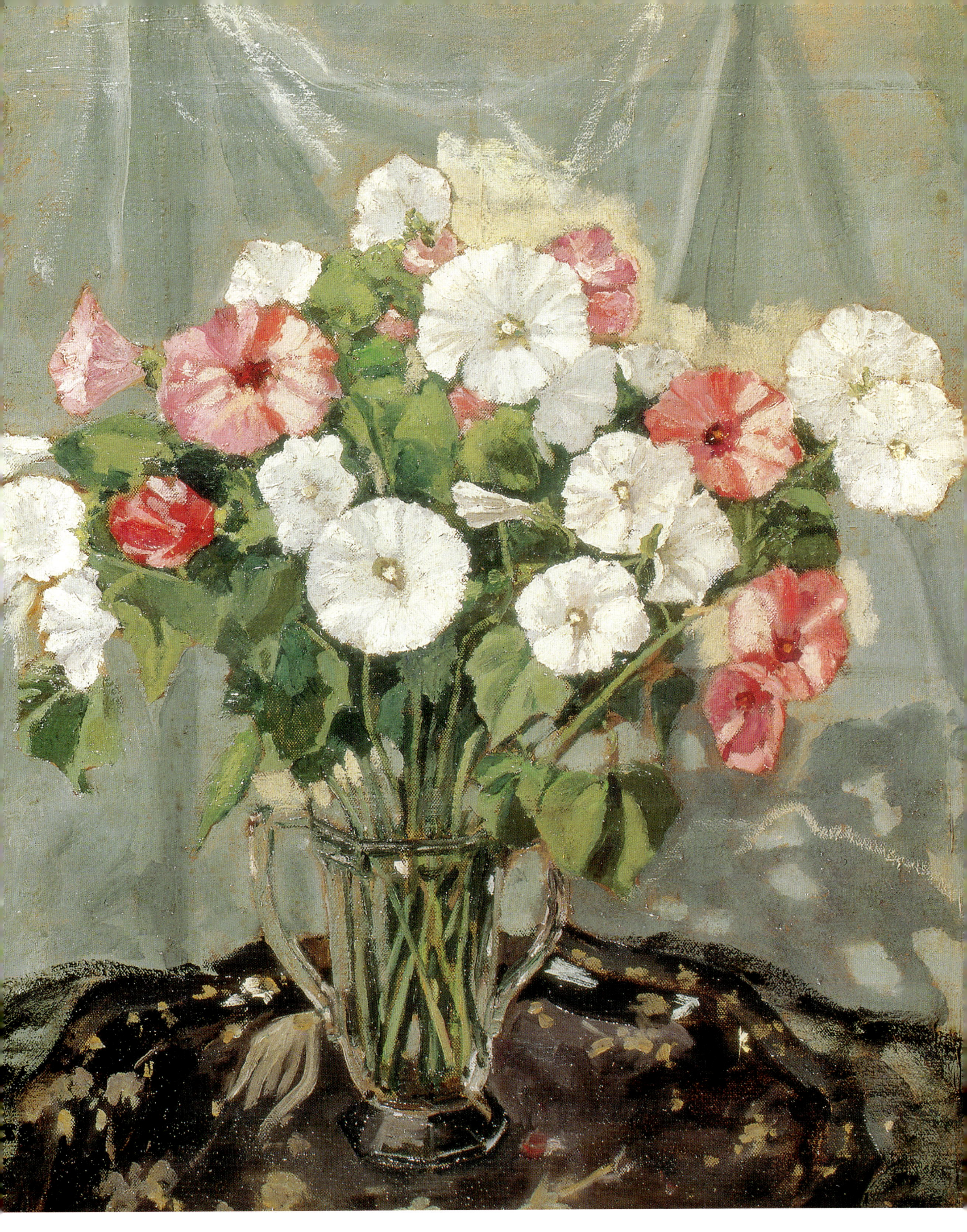

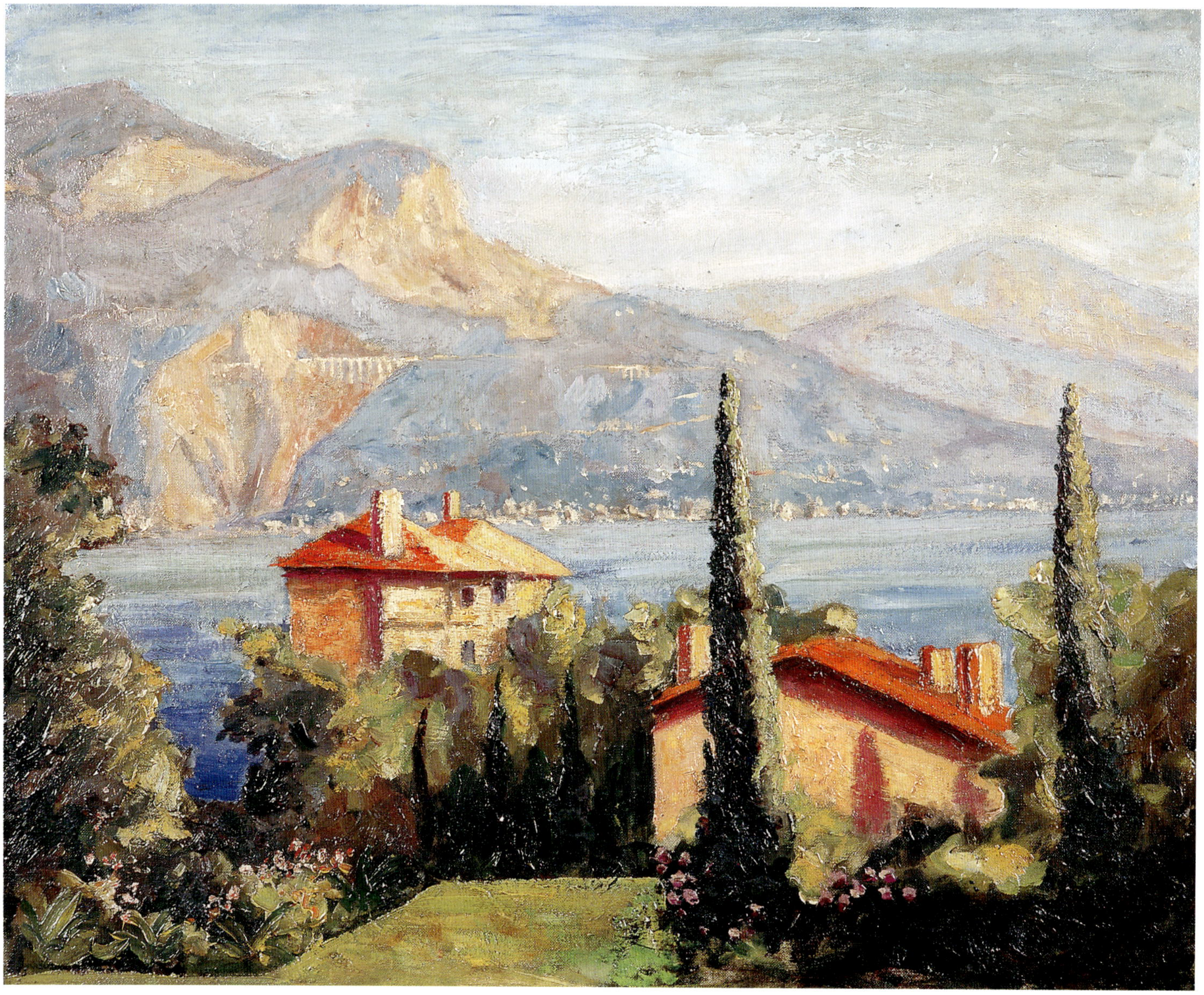

Fig 269 (C 199) above
Coast scene on the Riviera.

The South of France in general and the Riviera in particular were often visited by Churchill. After he began to paint they had a special interest for him, as these pictures show.

opposition to current national policy on Indian self-government, which he insisted would lead to the domination by Hindus of Muslim and other minorities. The final, fifth volume of his war memoirs was published.

1931 [Painting] The Churchills went on a driving holiday through France, visiting Biarritz, Avignon and Juan-les-Pins, and as always he took his painting equipment with him. Churchill went on a lecture tour in the United States to recoup some of his financial losses. He was knocked down by a car on New York's Fifth Avenue on the way to see his friend the financier Bernard Baruch and was badly hurt. Following his accident he went to Nassau in the Bahamas to recover and was upset to find himself too weak to paint.

While on his lecture tour in the United States and after his accident, Churchill employed Miss Phyllis Moir as his secretary. She noticed 'his exceptionally keen visual sense. He takes an artist's delight in beauty of line and colour. When he sees a beautiful woman, his face lights up with pleasure and admiration.'

Later she recalled a long weekend spent at Bernard Baruch's 'vast plantation' in South Carolina, 'situated on an island some miles up the James River from Georgetown ... It was a haven of peace ...' Baruch felt that his old friend needed a holiday and should not bring Miss Moir with him, but Churchill countered by explaining that he needed her to help him with a series of articles he was writing

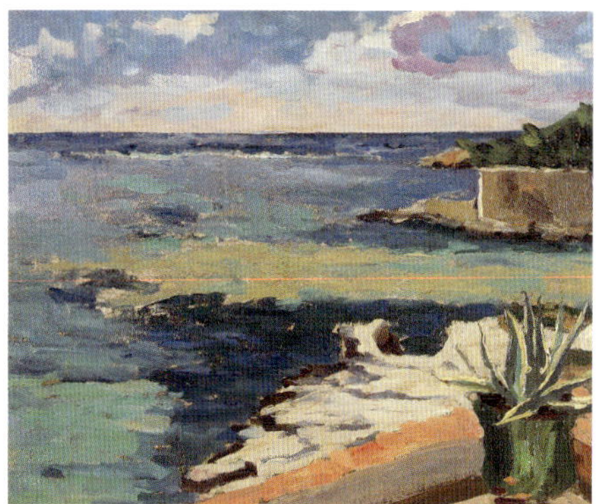

Fig 270 (C 93) above
A cactus on the coast somewhere in the south of France.

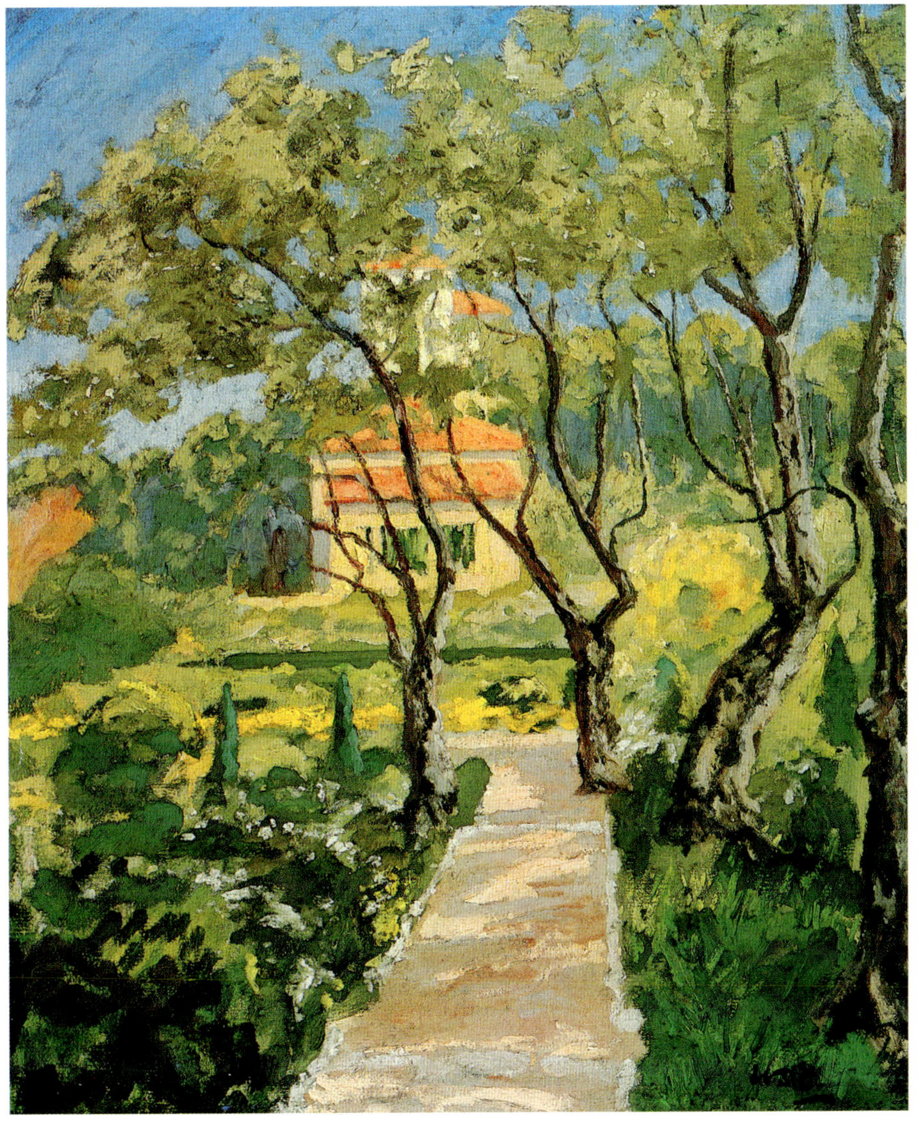

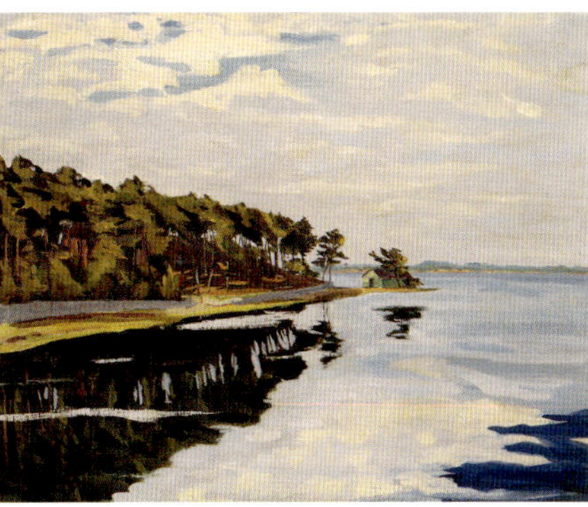

Fig 271 (C 132) above
The coast on the Antibes peninsular. Given by Churchill to his bodyguard, Detective Sergeant R. E. Golding

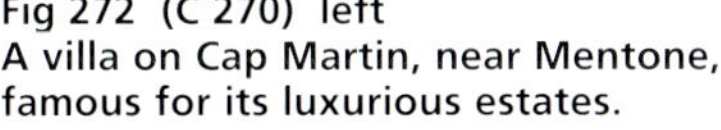

Fig 272 (C 270) left
A villa on Cap Martin, near Mentone, famous for its luxurious estates.

Fig 273 (C 201) below left
The Villa Gardens at Mentone in the south of France.

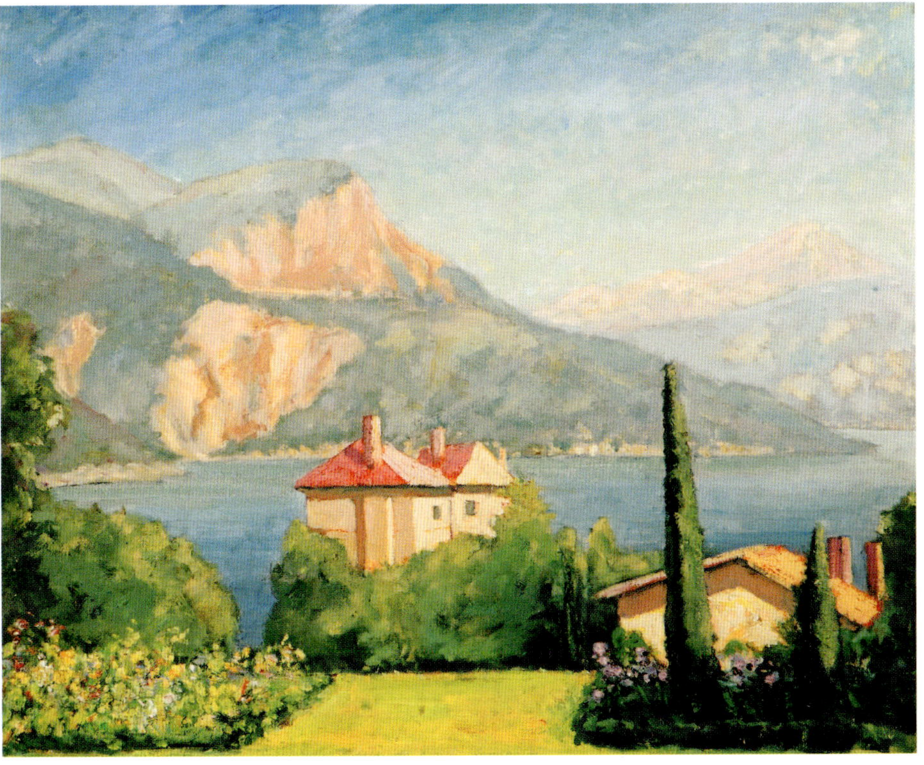

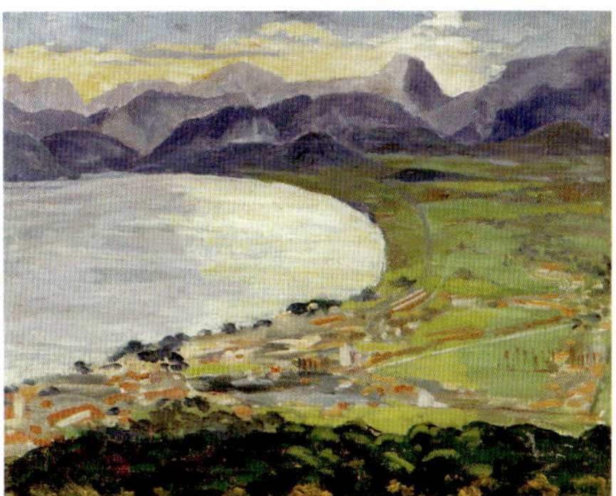

Fig 274 (C 295) above
A coast scene somewhere on the Riviera.

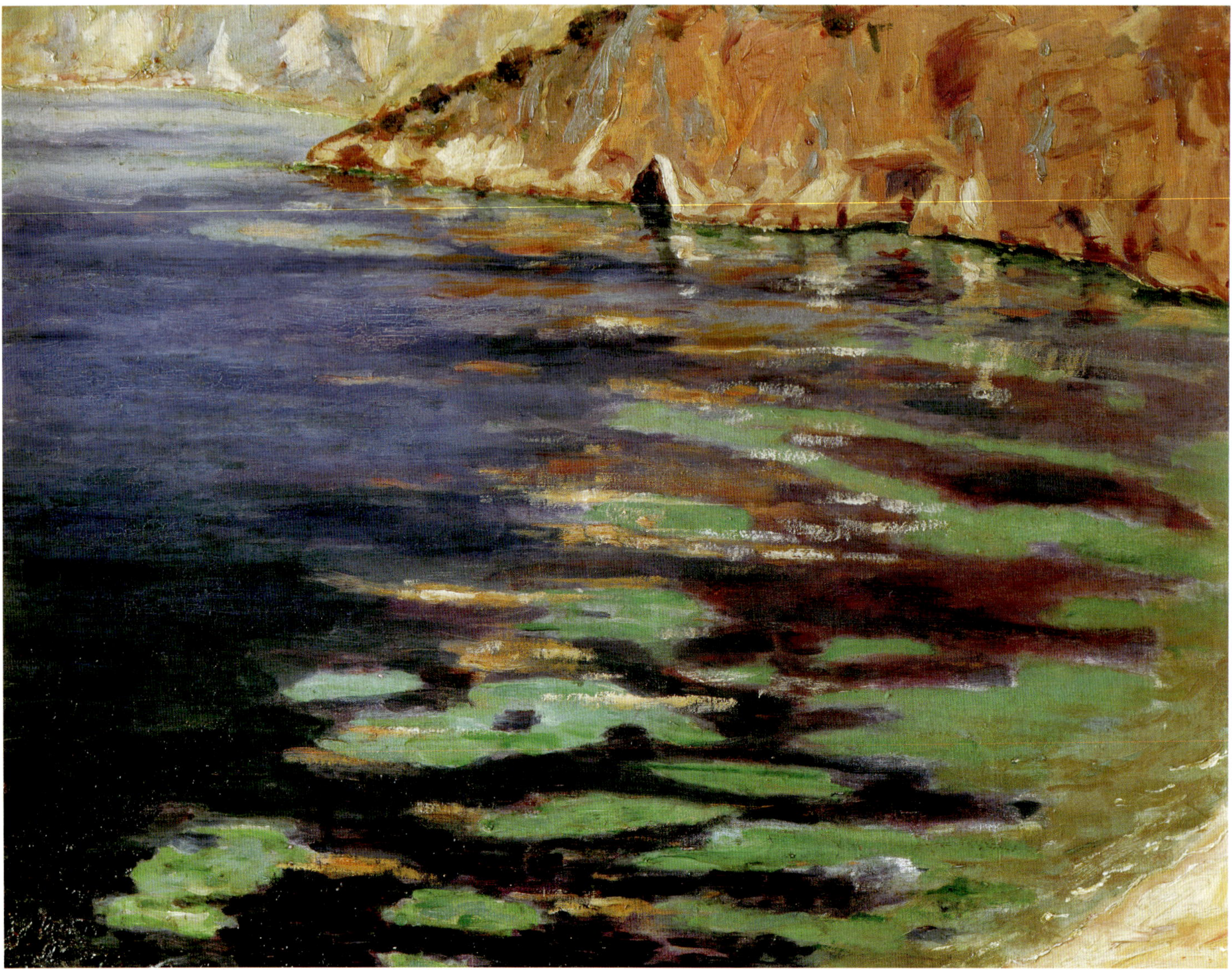

Fig 275 (C 325) above
The coast near Cannes. On loan to the Palace of Wesminster.

Fig 276 (C 291) opposite page above left
The coast somewhere on the Riviera.

Fig 277 (C 299) opposite page above right
A harbour scene with yachts.

Fig 278 (C 298) opposite page right
A study of boats. This painting formerly belonged to Clementine Churchill.

for Collier's, which work he found relaxing and that 'a secretary was as necessary to him as a fountain pen'. To which remark Miss Moir added one of her own: 'As a matter of fact, a secretary is the same thing to him as a fountain pen!' Over the weekend, as well as drafting his series of articles and dashing off another for a British newspaper, 'Mr Churchill did, as a matter of fact, manage to modify somewhat his normal busy routine. He went crabbing with his host, spent part of the morning discussing world affairs ... [and] painted several landscapes.'

1932 [Background] Free Trade abandoned by Britain and import duties imposed. Unemployed hunger march to London. British Union of Fascists founded. Roosevelt elected President of the United States. Nazi power grew in Germany. Civil disobedience in India. World Disarmament Conference in Geneva. Oxford Union supported the motion 'That this House refuses in any circumstances to fight for King and Country'. In the British Parliament and through newspaper articles, Churchill warned against German military ambitions and its wish for revenge. Successful lecture tour in the United States. Completed first half of the first volume of his life of Marlborough and began to plan a four-volume history of the English-speaking peoples.

When touring the battlefields of the Duke of Marlborough in Belgium, Holland and Germany, Churchill became ill with paratyphoid and spent two weeks in a sanatorium in Salzburg. Returning to Chartwell he tried to make up for lost time on his biography of Marlborough and suffered a relapse. A collection of his

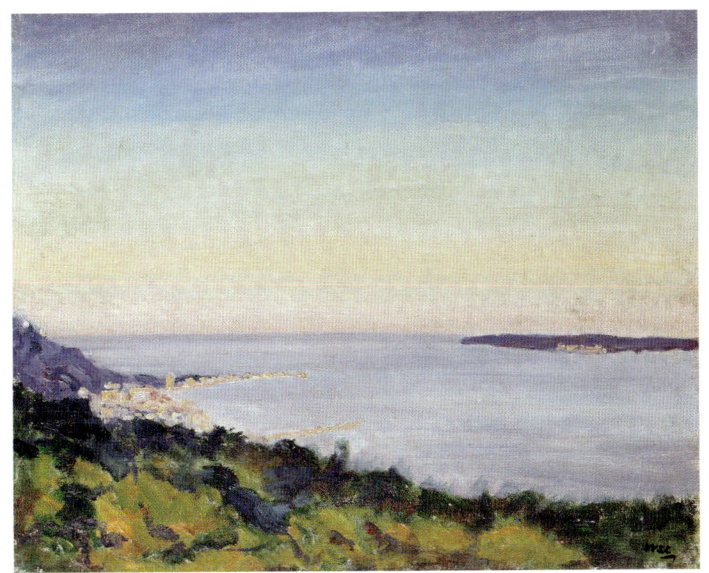

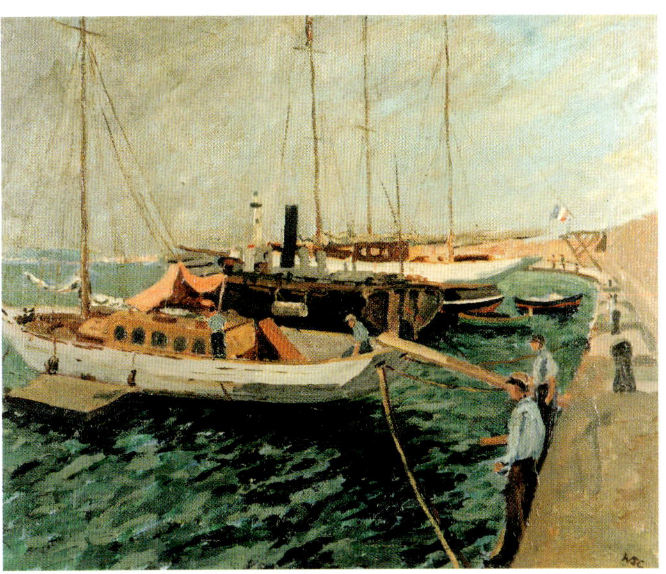

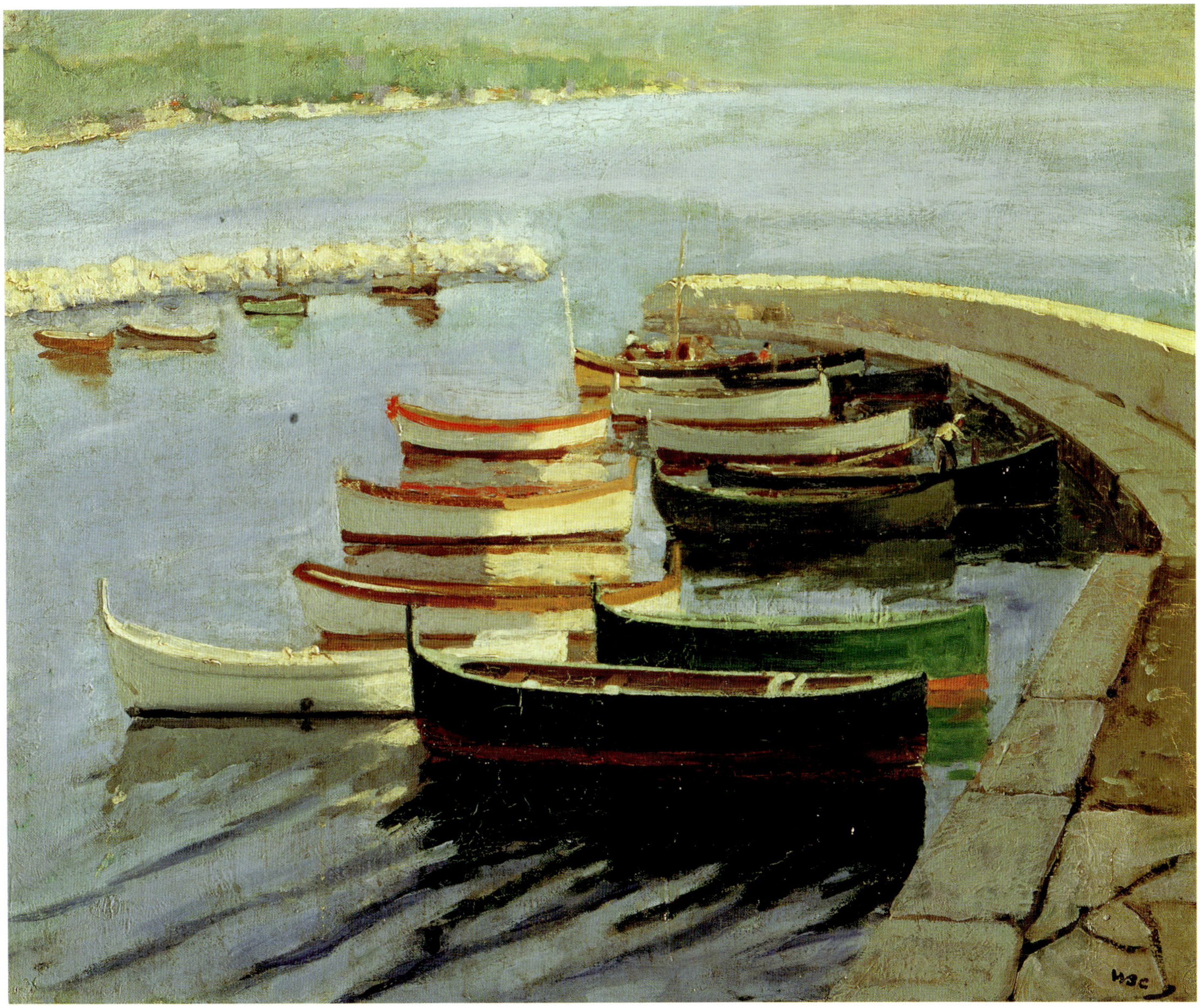

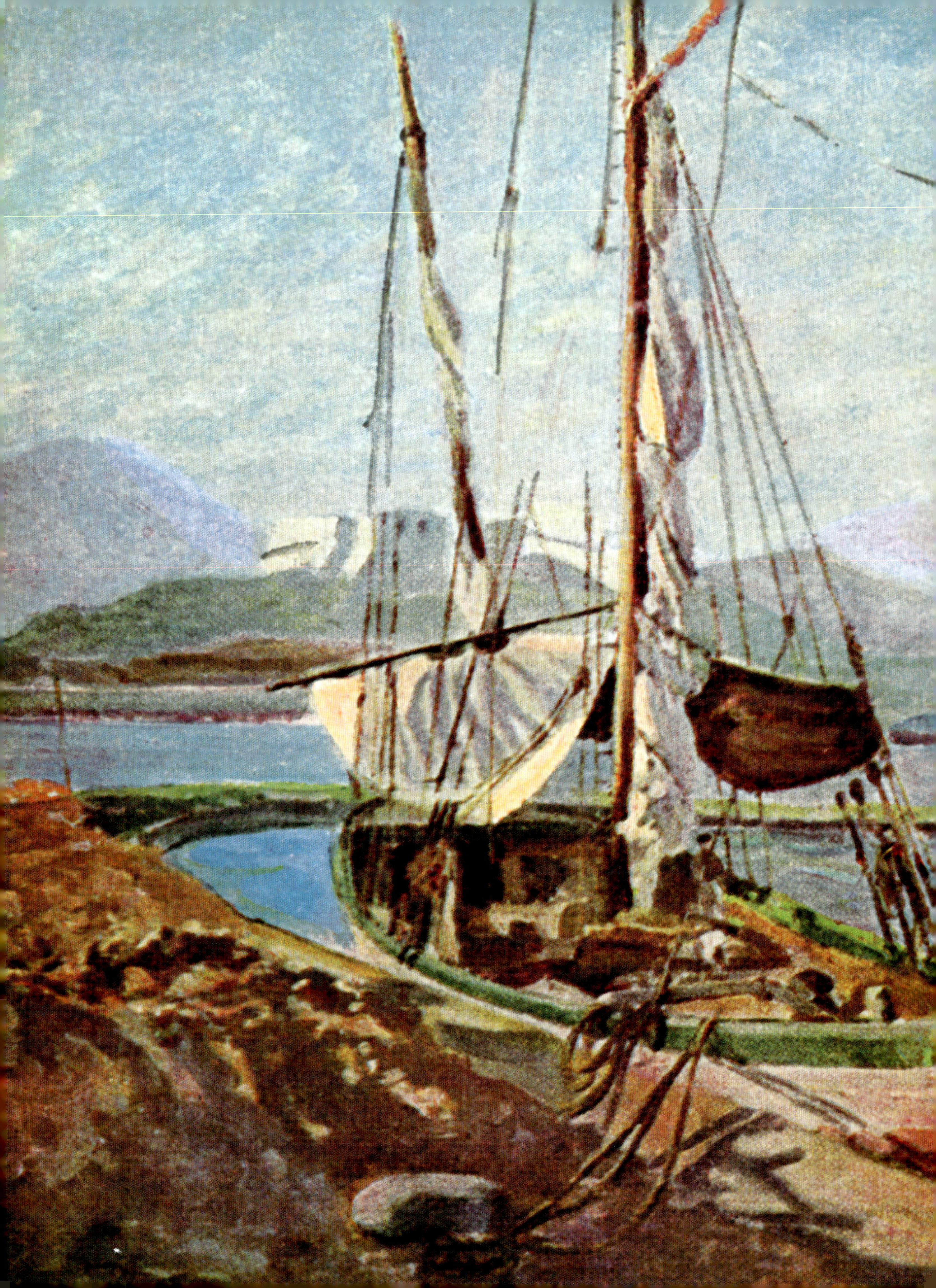

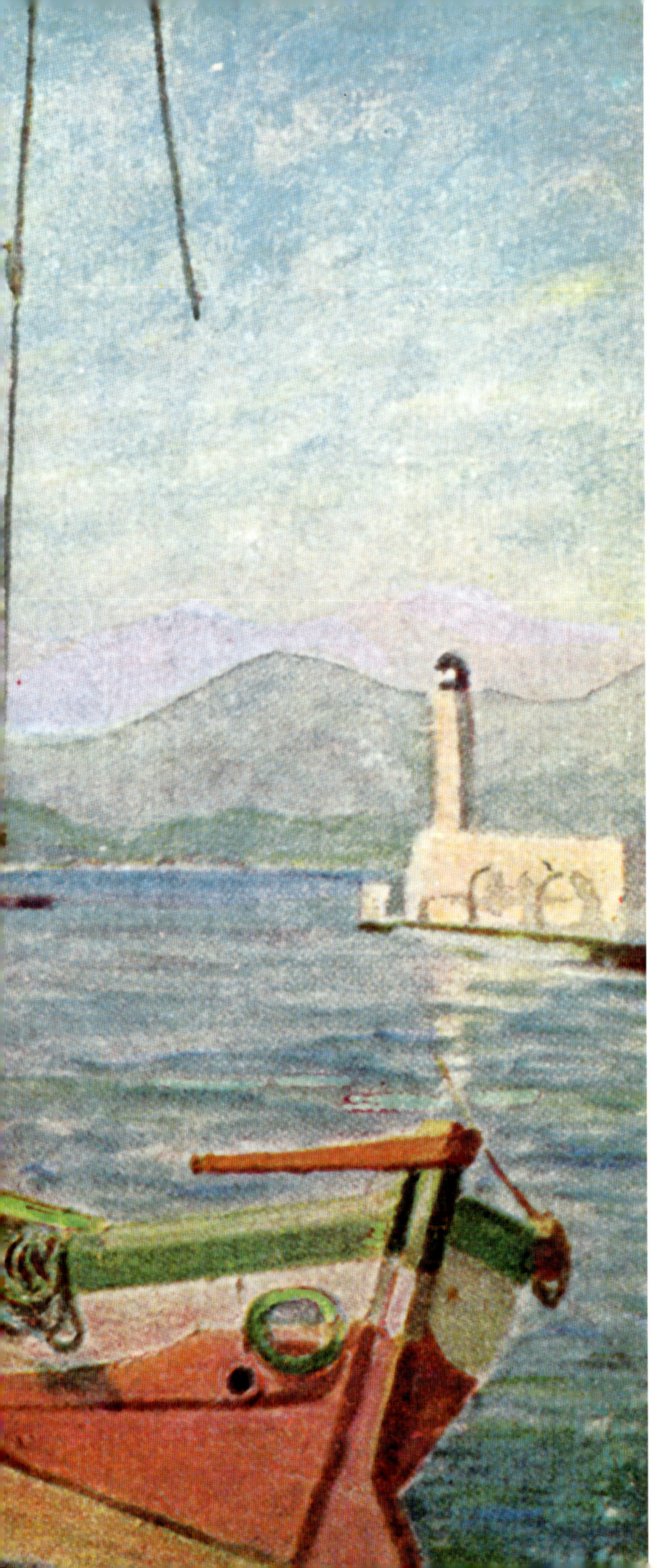

Fig 279 (C 301)
Sailing boat in harbour at Antibes. Churchill gave this painting to Sir Robert Menzies, former Prime Minister of Australia.

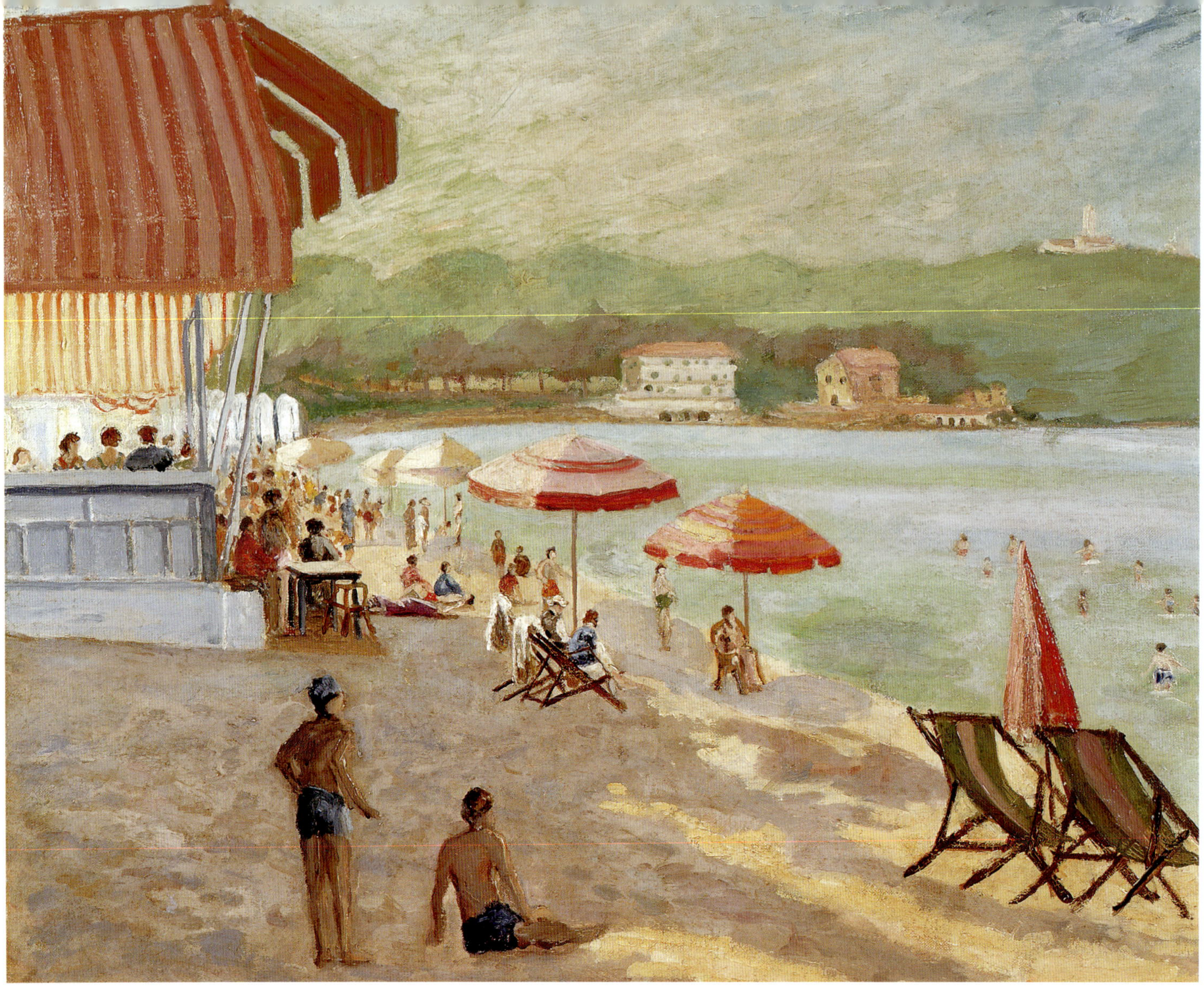

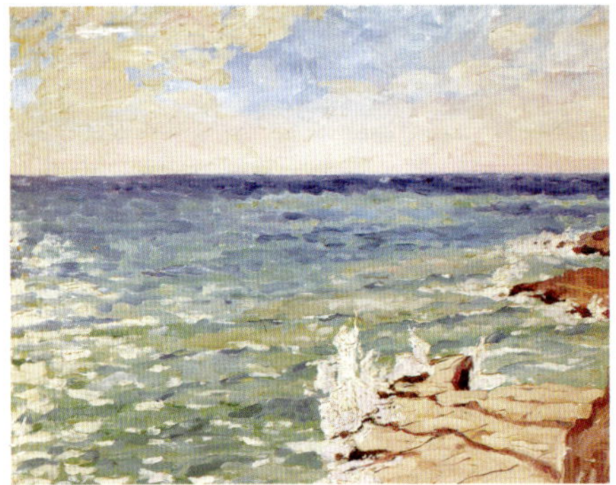

Fig 280 (C 326) above
Coast scene near Cannes.

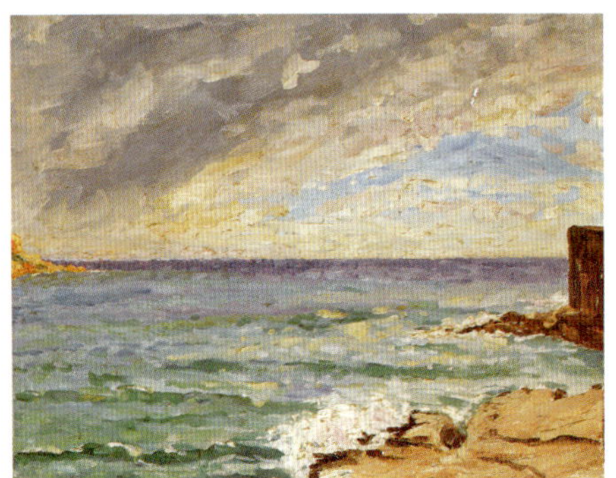

Fig 281 (C 327) above
Coast scene somewhere on the Riviera.

writings, *Thoughts and Adventures*, was published including shortened versions of his two essays, 'Painting as a Pastime' and 'Hobbies'.

1932 [Painting] Churchill spoke at the Royal Academy of Arts dinner and wrote a long review of the Summer Exhibition for *The Daily Mail* to which he was already contributing articles on matters of national and international concern. He knew the paper's proprietor, Lord Northcliffe, and was a friend too of his younger brother, Lord Rothermere, who had a villa in the South of France, La Dragonnière on Cap Martin, where Churchill stayed and painted.

Careful reading of *The Daily Mail* review shows most of the text to lack the elegance and drive so characteristic of Churchill's prose, as seen, for example, in his 'Painting as a Pastime'. Is this because of some felt diffidence in the task of art criticism? His papers in the archives at Churchill College reveal a much more interesting story.

The pressure on Churchill's time was such that he asked his close friend Sir Edward Marsh, a notable patron of artists and poets, to draft the review for him. Handwritten text in his grasp, Winston visited the exhibition with Clementine and Eddie. He scribbled on the back of the manuscript several catalogue numbers and names: 'Smuts, Glyn Philpot, The Beach by Arnesby-Brown, Var Valley, Oliver Hall'. However, the last four paragraphs of the article are Churchill's own - as the quality of the prose suggests.

'The general and final impression of this year's Royal Academy is most pleasing. There is an almost complete absence of slovenly or impudent work. Care and

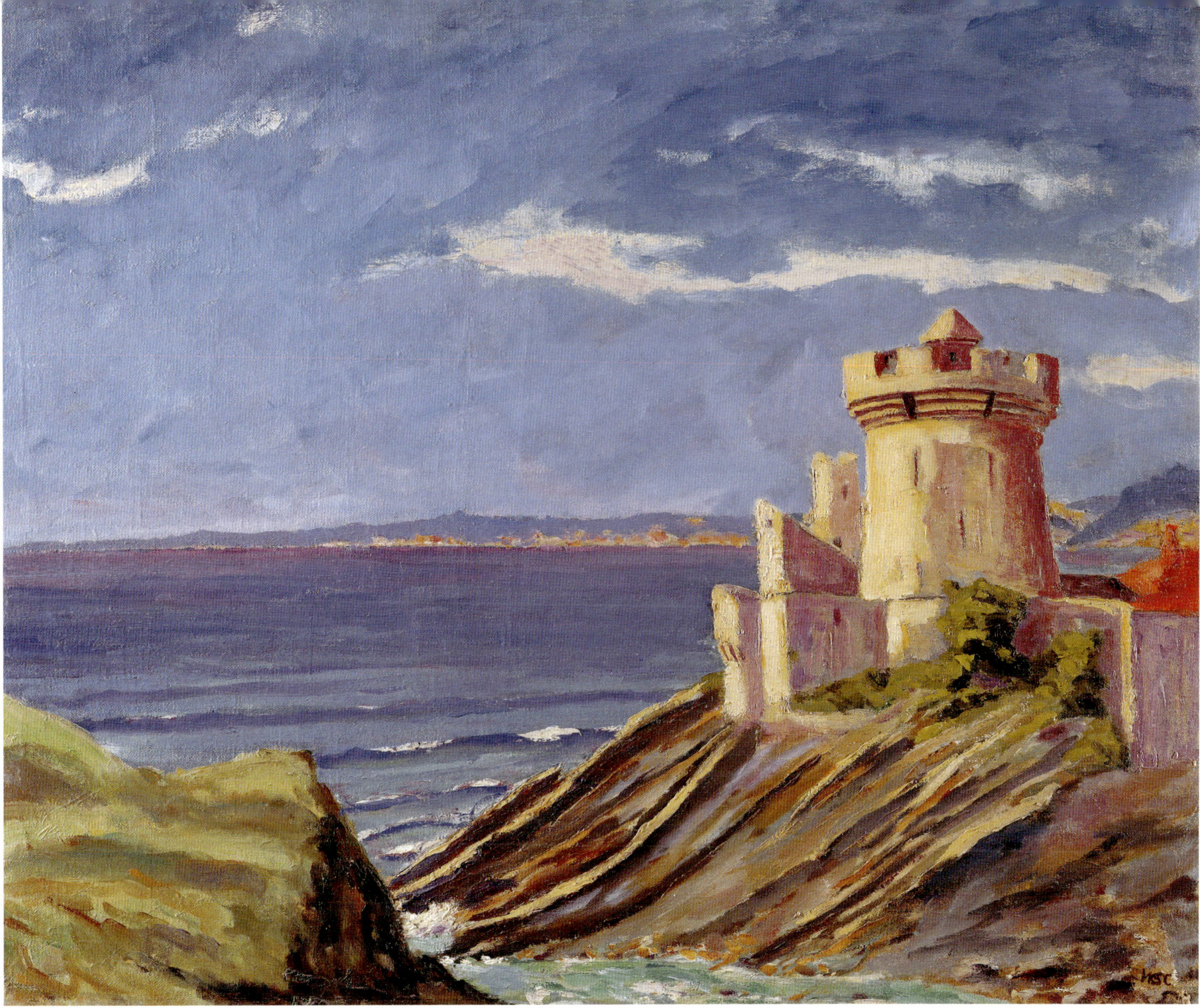

Fig 282 (C 328) above
This castle on the Riviera, probably dates from the time when the coast and its rich hinterland were prey to marauders.

Fig 283 (C 318) opposite page top
Beach scene on the Riviera. This painting is based on photographs from the Studio archives at Chartwell; characteristically for Churchill, the figures are not too successful.

fidelity in definition and value are distinguished throughout the galleries. Aspiring painters are taught that a high level of technical proficiency with brush and pencil is one of the criteria by which they will be judged.

'Excursions into bizarre impressionism may be accepted from those who have proved their credentials. But slap-dash and short cuts to Fame or notoriety are evidently, and rightly, discouraged. My other prevailing impression is the gaiety and love of colour which characterise our art at the present time.

'We do not have much sunshine in our island, but the English people in every walk of life delight in flowers and gardens, and greet our grey skies with more flowers than any other people grow.

'This year's Royal Academy reflects with remarkable, if unconscious truth this English and island taste.'

1933 [Background] Hitler became Chancellor of Germany; concentration camps were set up. Spanish Fascist party founded. Roosevelt's 'New Deal' in the United States. Britain continued to pursue a policy of disarmament. Pacifist candidate returned to Parliament at a by-election. The first volume of Churchill's *Marlborough: His Life and Times* published.

1933 [Painting] Winston and Clementine Churchill paid their first visit to Château de l'Horizon, the newly completed house of Maxine Elliott at Golfe-Juan near Cannes.Clementine did not enjoy the Riviera life and Winston subsequently went there regularly on his own, staying and painting either with Maxine or at

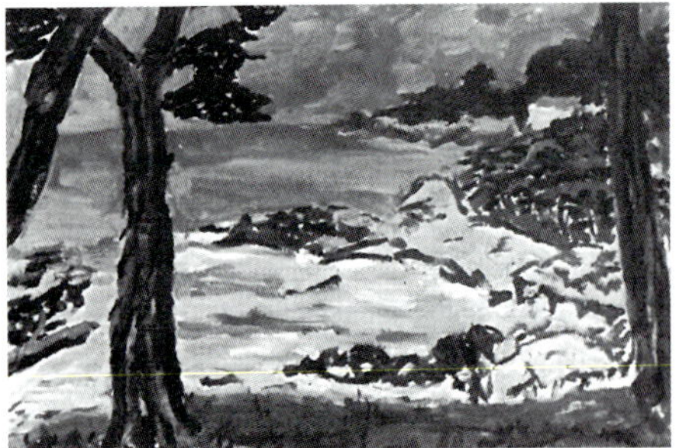

Fig 284 (C 347) above
A sketch of a scene probably on the Riviera.

Fig 285 (C 335) right
The coast near Cap d'Ail, south-west of Monaco.

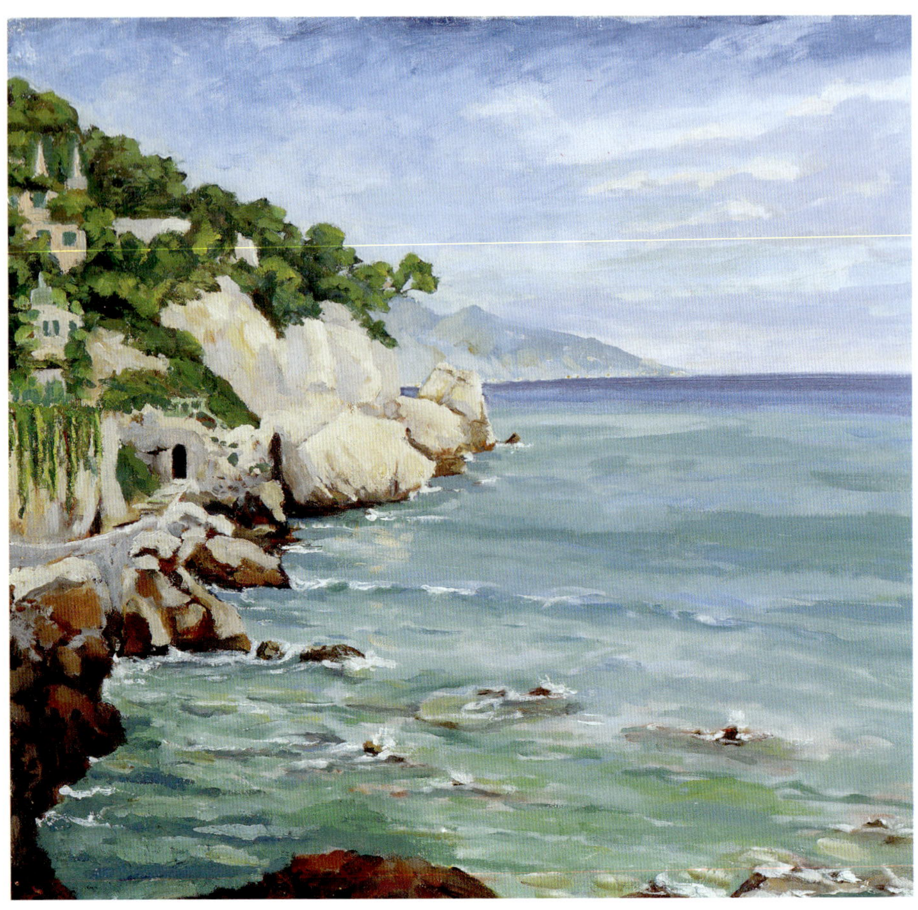

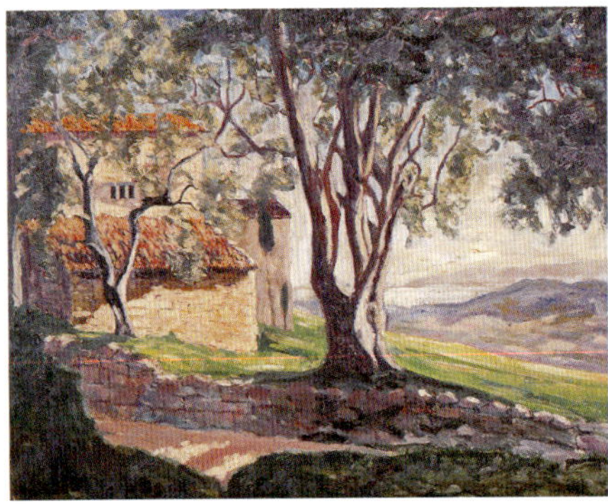

Fig 286 (C 497) above
Scene in the South of France. This painting was given by Churchill to the widow of the chairman of his constituency party, Sir James Hawkey.

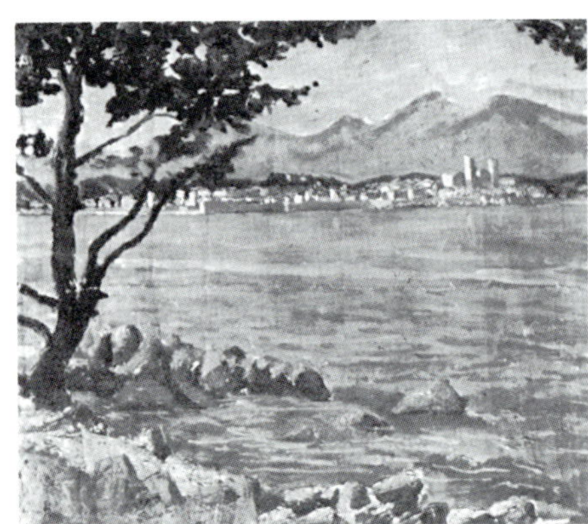

Fig 287 (C 336) above
View of the resort town of Antibes, at the foot of the Alpes Maritimes. This painting was given by Churchill to his butler, Mr W. Greenshields.

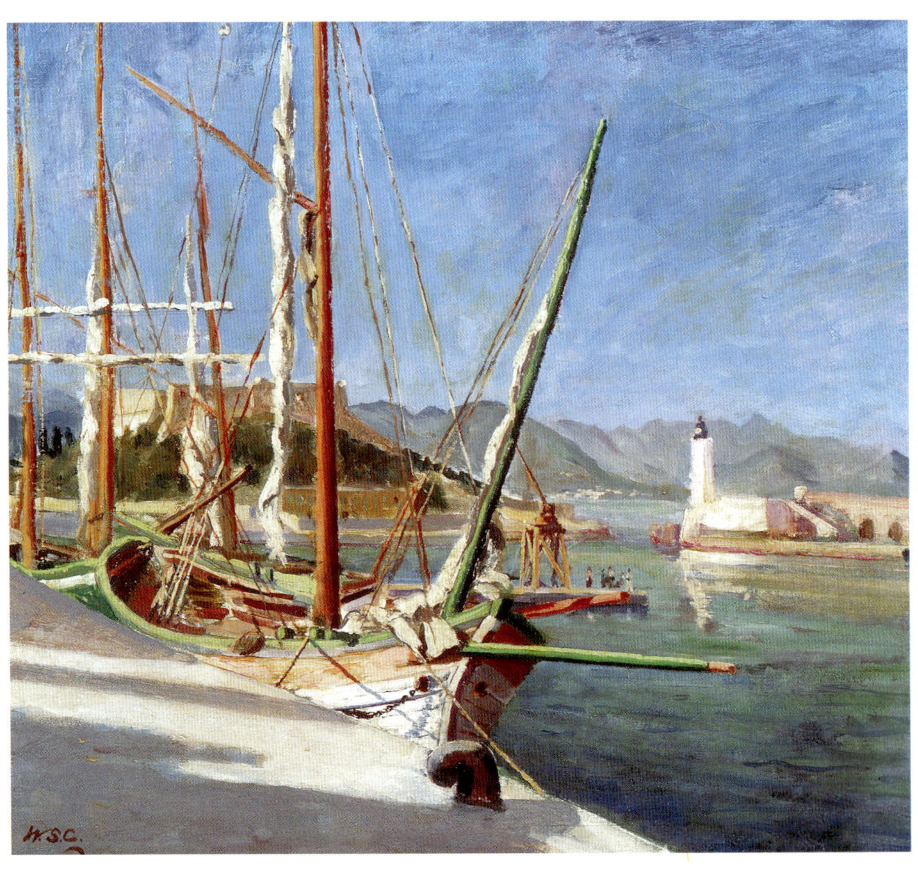

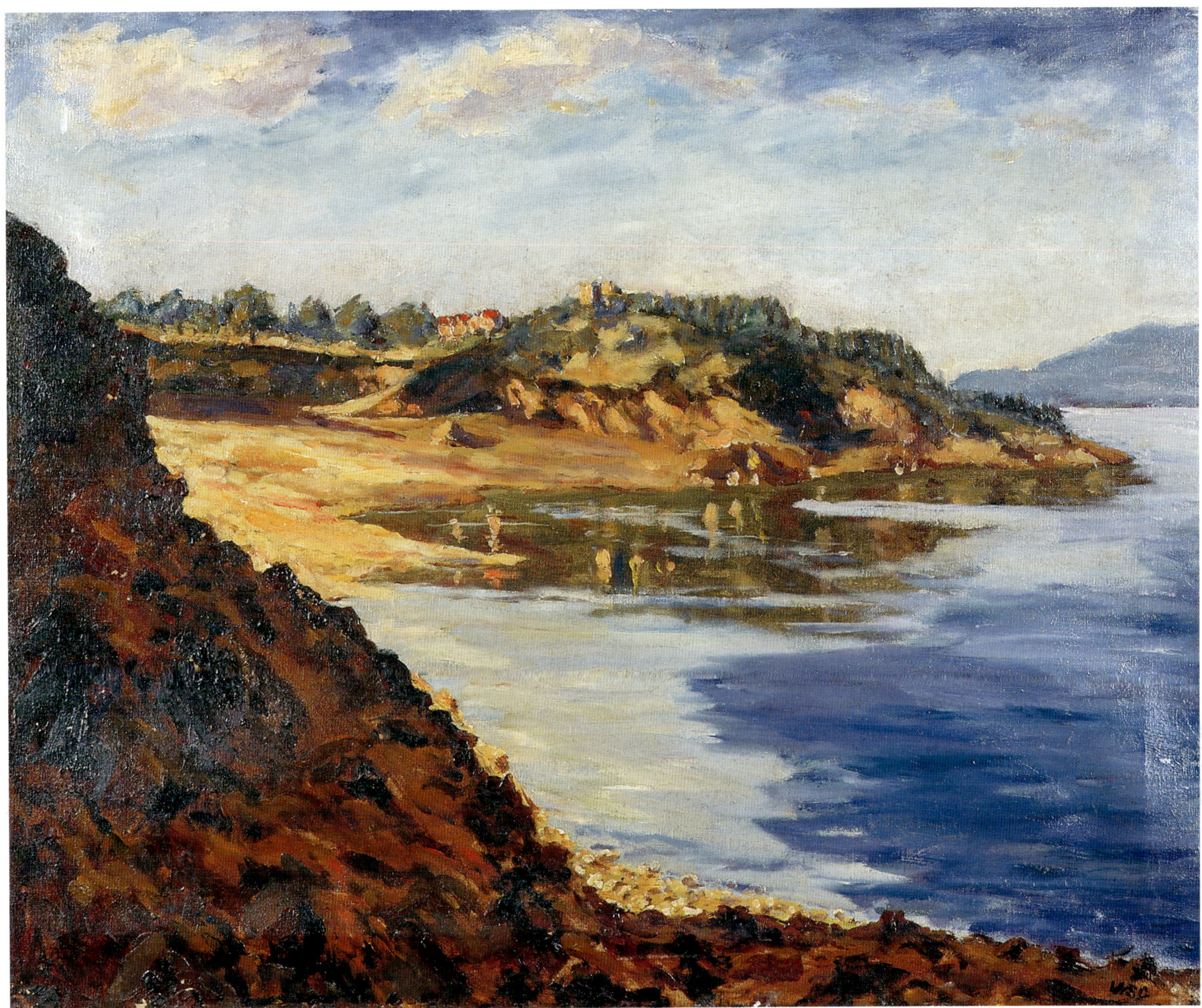

Fig 288 (C 329) above
Somewhere on the Riviera coast.

Fig 289 (C 500) opposite page near left
Sailing boat in harbour at Antibes. This painting was given by Sir Winston Churchill to Mr Antonio Giraudier, a rich Cuban who kept him supplied with cigars and brandy.

other villas on the coast: with Daisy Fellowes, wife of his kinsman Reginald, at Les Zoraides or at La Dragonnière also at Cap Martin. At the latter Churchill found inspiration in the olive groves and garden.

Maxine Elliott was American-born, an immensely successful actress and a considerable socialite, who entertained famously and lavishly. She was 'a considerable social snob', remembered her niece Diana Forbes-Robertson. Before the First World War she held court at Hartsbourne Manor, near Bushey Heath in Hertfordshire, and had many friends, social as well as political, in common with the Churchills. In her later years she decided to settle on the Riviera and, failing to find a house to her liking, decided, characteristically, to build one. She chose a narrow site that 'seemed an impossibility ... with on the ocean side ... a sheer drop over vicious rocks ... on their top was poised a swimming pool that had a water chute down which you simply slid into the sea.' Maxine 'knew perfectly well that [Churchill], though out of office, towered above the familiars of the Château who came and went. He was the only person [Diana] saw permitted to be late for meals, and the only one who could leave the Château to paint at Saint Paul de Vence all day without being scolded as a "gadabout".'

In the summer, Sir William Nicholson came to Chartwell to paint a conversation piece of Winston and Clementine Churchill commissioned by a group of their friends to mark their Silver Wedding anniversary. Nicholson became a friend of the Churchill family. 'He stayed many months to paint,' recalled Sarah Churchill later, 'and left innumerable funny little drawings about the house ...' One bought by her mother had the caption: 'Necessity, Endeavouring to Recollect Who Was the Father of Invention'. Nicholson greatly influenced Churchill in respect of his general style and his move towards a quieter palette of colours. Churchill told Sir John Rothenstein, 'I think the person who taught me most about painting was William Nicholson.'

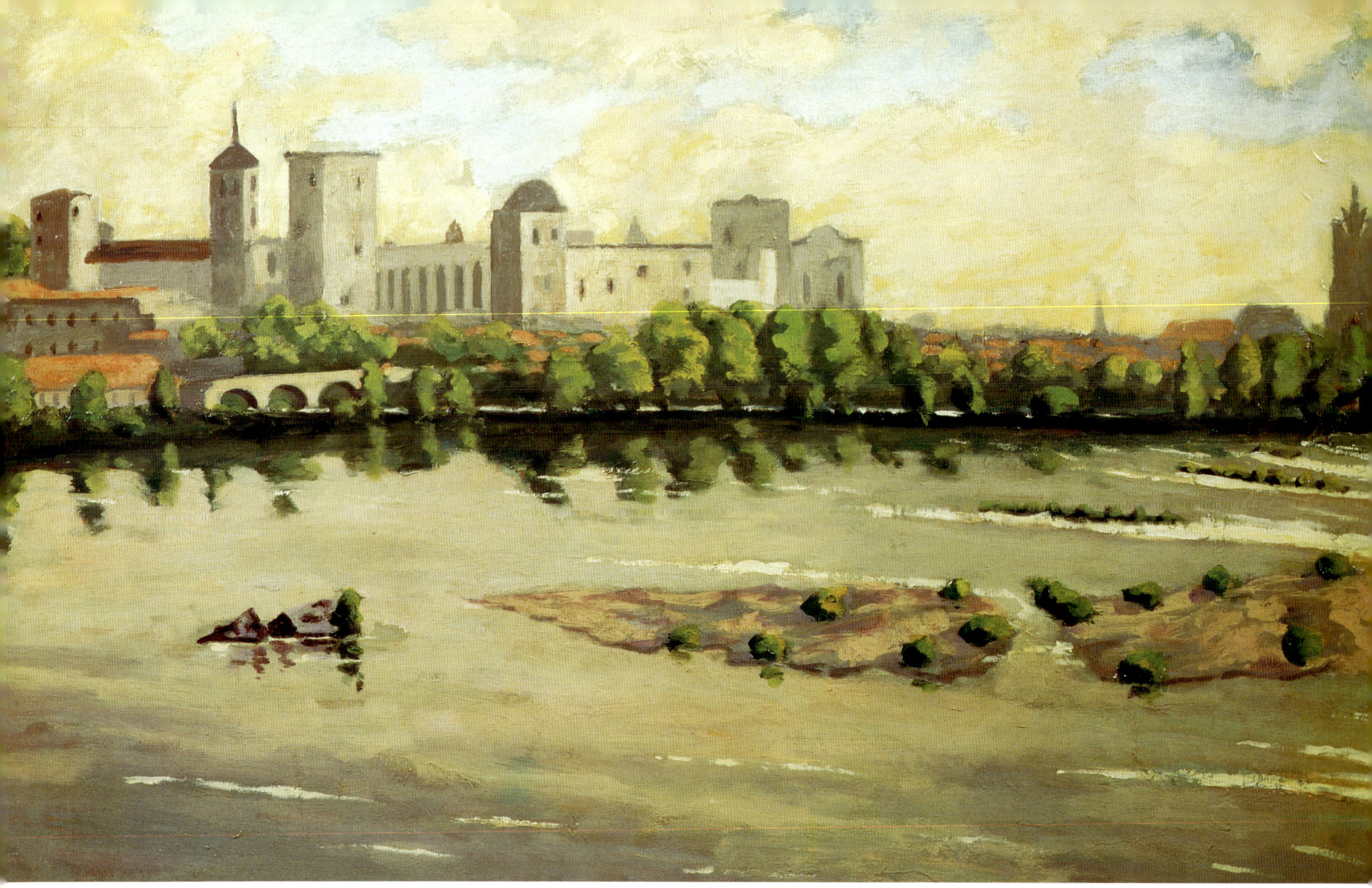

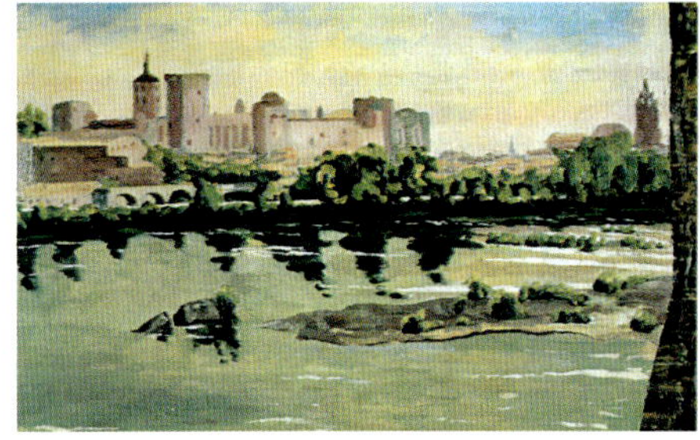

Fig 290 (C 94) above
View of Avignon, in southern France.

1934 [Background] Churchill's 60th year.
Hitler became President of Germany and murdered his rivals. Stalin established 'treason trials' in Russia. King Alexander of Yugoslavia assassinated. British government subsidy for building the Atlantic liner *Queen Mary*. Means tests for unemployment relief. Britain and France began to oppose German rearmament. Churchill urged the reorganization of factories so that they might be transferred quickly to war production and proposed doubling the size of the Air Force because of the threat of aerial bombardment. Broadcast about his fears of German intentions. The second volume of his life of Marlborough was published.

1934 [Painting] The French painter Paul Maze asked Churchill to write the introduction to his war memoirs. They had first met in 1916. Paul Maze had served during the First World War as a non-commissioned liaison officer with the British Expeditionary Force, using his sketching skills with great bravery to document landscape details in advance of action. In his introduction Churchill wrote that in Maze's work 'we have the battle-scenes of Armageddon recorded by one who not only loved the fighting troops and shared their perils, but perceived the beauties of light and shade, of form and colour, of which even the horrors of war cannot rob the progress of the sun.' Maze subsequently made his home in Britain and he and Churchill came to know each other well: Winston enjoyed his company and valued his advice on painting.

Fig 291 (C 101) top of page
During the 14th century, Avignon was the residence of successive (French) popes who built the ramparts that still protect its historic core. The light there was especially attractive to painters and Churchill went there specifically in 1931.

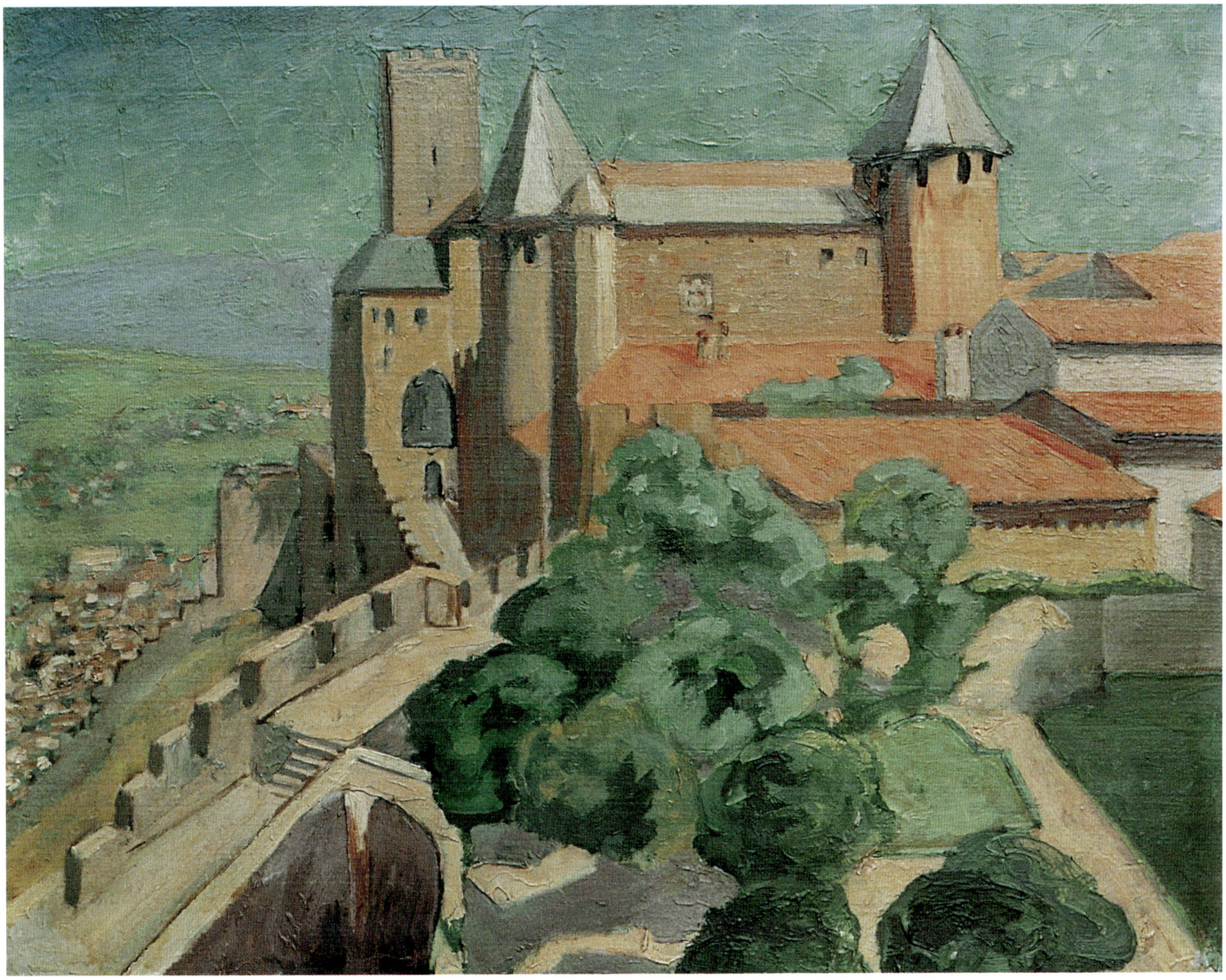

Fig 292 (C 205) above
View of Carcassonne, fortified in the 13th century by King Louis IX.

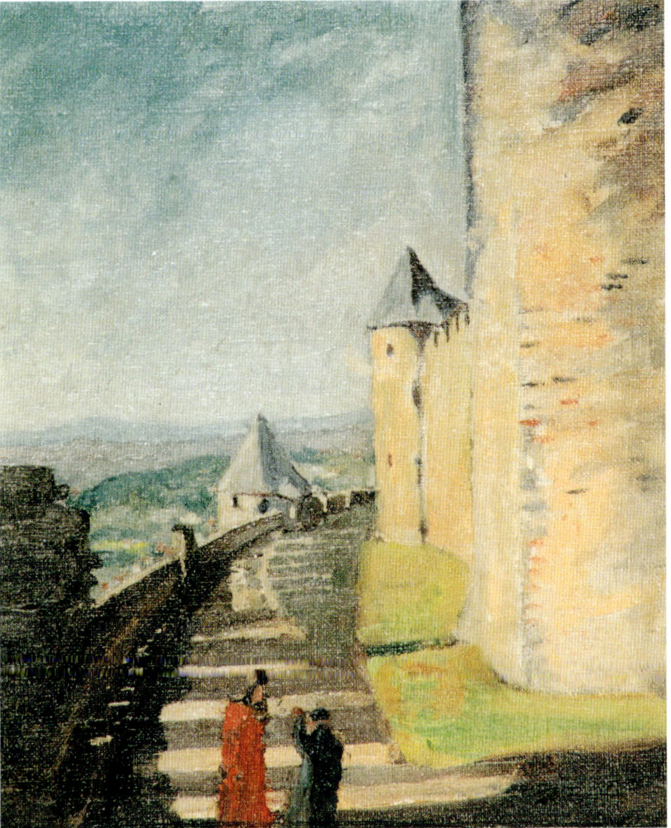

Fig 293 (C 206) left
The medieval battlements at Carcassonne. Churchill gave this little painting to his youngest daughter Mary: 'The first picture papa gave me when I was a child.'

During the 1930s they would meet at St Georges-Motel near Dreux north of Paris, the summer home of Consuelo and Jacques Balsan. 'Here,' wrote Consuelo, 'we were privileged to become hosts to a number of friends to whom we lent small houses on the estate. This group of artists, musicians and writers centred round Paul Maze ... an artist not only in oils and pastels, but also in his truely Bohemian mode of life ... he lived gaily with his Scottish wife at the Moulin ... One weekend ... a unique picture was made ... signed by five artists ... Winston was painting on the lawn in front of the house ... I had invited Paul Maze and three fellow artists to luncheon ... Undaunted by such critical observers he drew four brushes from his stock and handing them round said, "You Paul shall paint the trees - you Segonzac the sky - you Simon Lévy the water and you Marchand the foreground, and I shall supervise."'

Over the same weekend 'Winston decided he wanted to paint our moat,' recalled Consuelo Balsan. 'After careful thought he made up his mind that he preferred the water rough to smooth. Sending to Dreux for a photographer, he placed two gardeners in a boat and told them to create ripples with their oars ... With characteristic thoroughness Winston persisted until all possibilities had been exhausted ...'

Fig 294 (C 208) below
A distant view of Carcassonne. In the far south of France, the city had important strategic significance for many centuries.

Churchill wrote a second review for *The Daily Mail* of the Royal Academy's Summer Exhibition. The archives at Churchill College apparently contain nothing

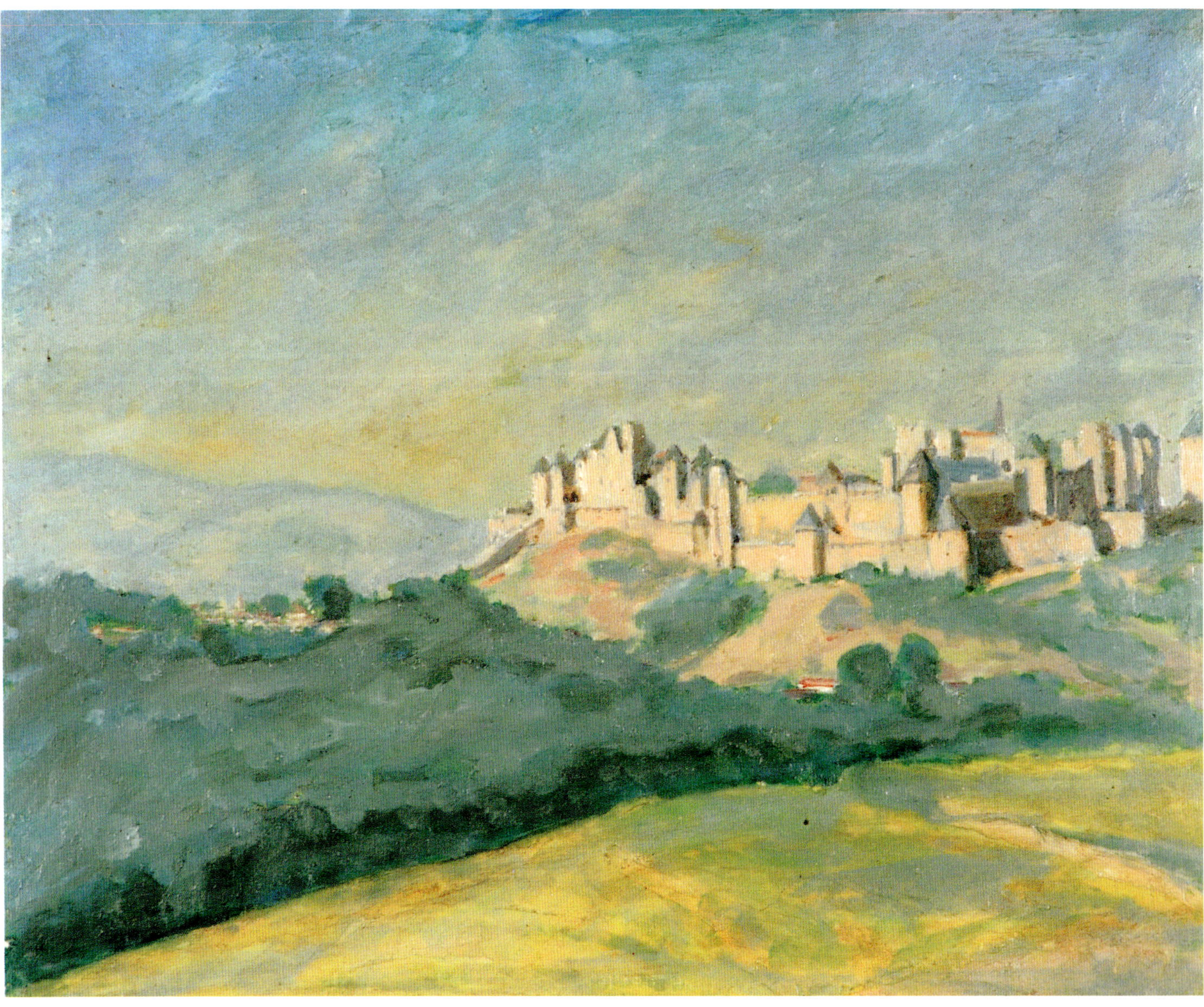

bar the printer's galley proof of the text, of which most is in the recognizable style of the Churchill-pastiche adopted by Edward Marsh. But there are some short passages unmistakably by Churchill himself that provide fascinating evidence of his thoughtful and informed knowledge of the work of living painters.

'I cannot understand why no greater fuss is made about the noble scenes that M. Oliver Hall tinges with a consistency of tenderness and melancholy which never degenerate into monotony. In each of his pictures, as the eye reaches them, it finds a point of rest and satisfaction. Mr Terrick Williams is another artist who paints from one palette, of greys and blues and greens, but every time with a new delicacy and delight. His loveliest piece here is "Sun and Mist, Mousehole", which gives the essence of all fair-weather dawns on boat-ridden harbours ... and Mr Algernon Newton, in his "Townscape", suffuses a dreary scene with the consecration of serene light which is his secret magic.'

Winston and Clementine Churchill sailed with Lord Moyne on his yacht, *Rosaura*, through the eastern Mediterranean. Paintings of Greek temples and the battlements at Rhodes resulted.

1935 [Background] Silver Jubilee of King George V and Queen Mary. Military conscription in Germany. Persecution there of the Jews. Mussolini's Italy invaded

Fig 295 (C 215) below
This view of Carcassonne shows the Lower Town to where the inhabitants were banished for failing to resist a siege in the 13th century.

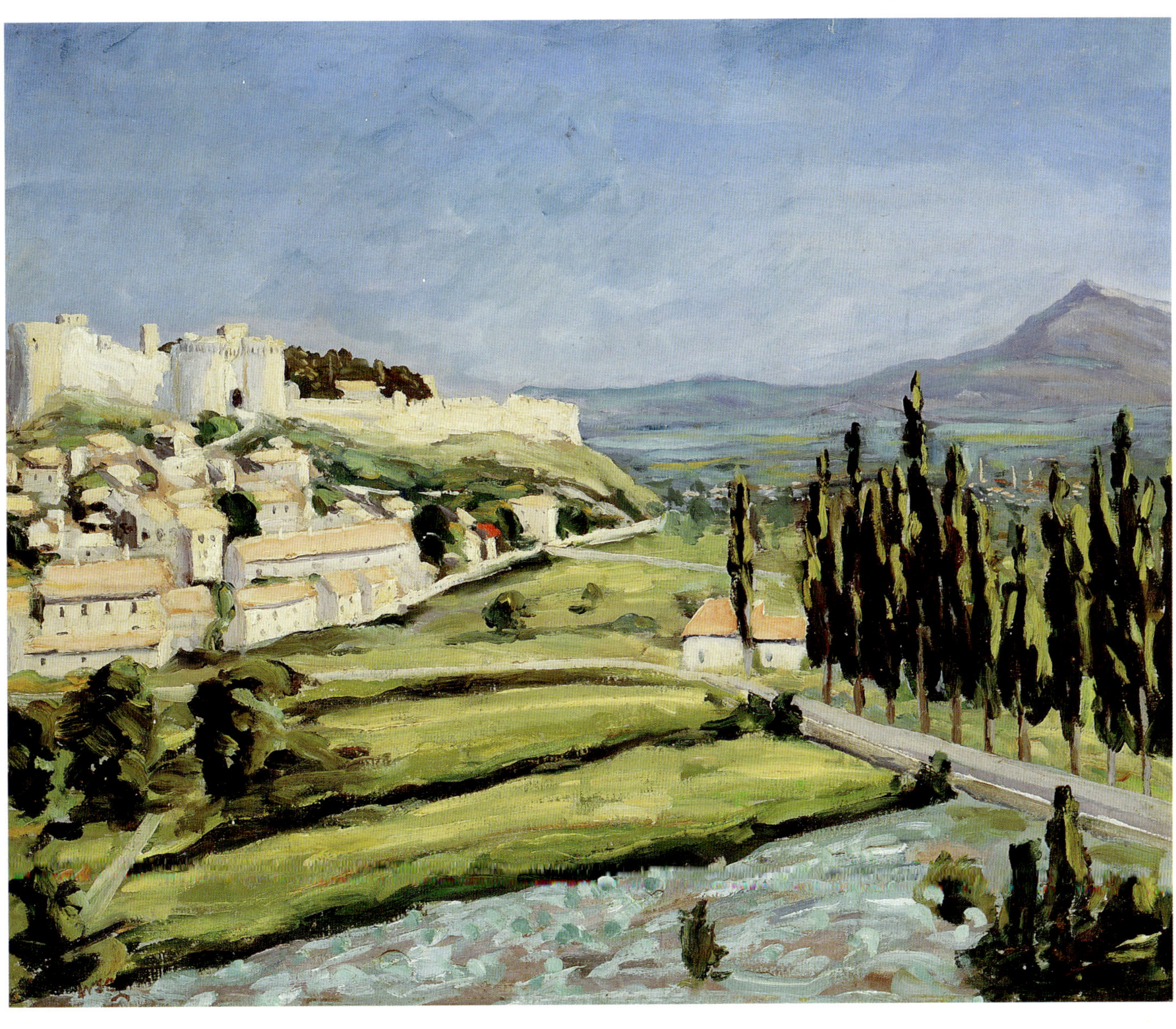

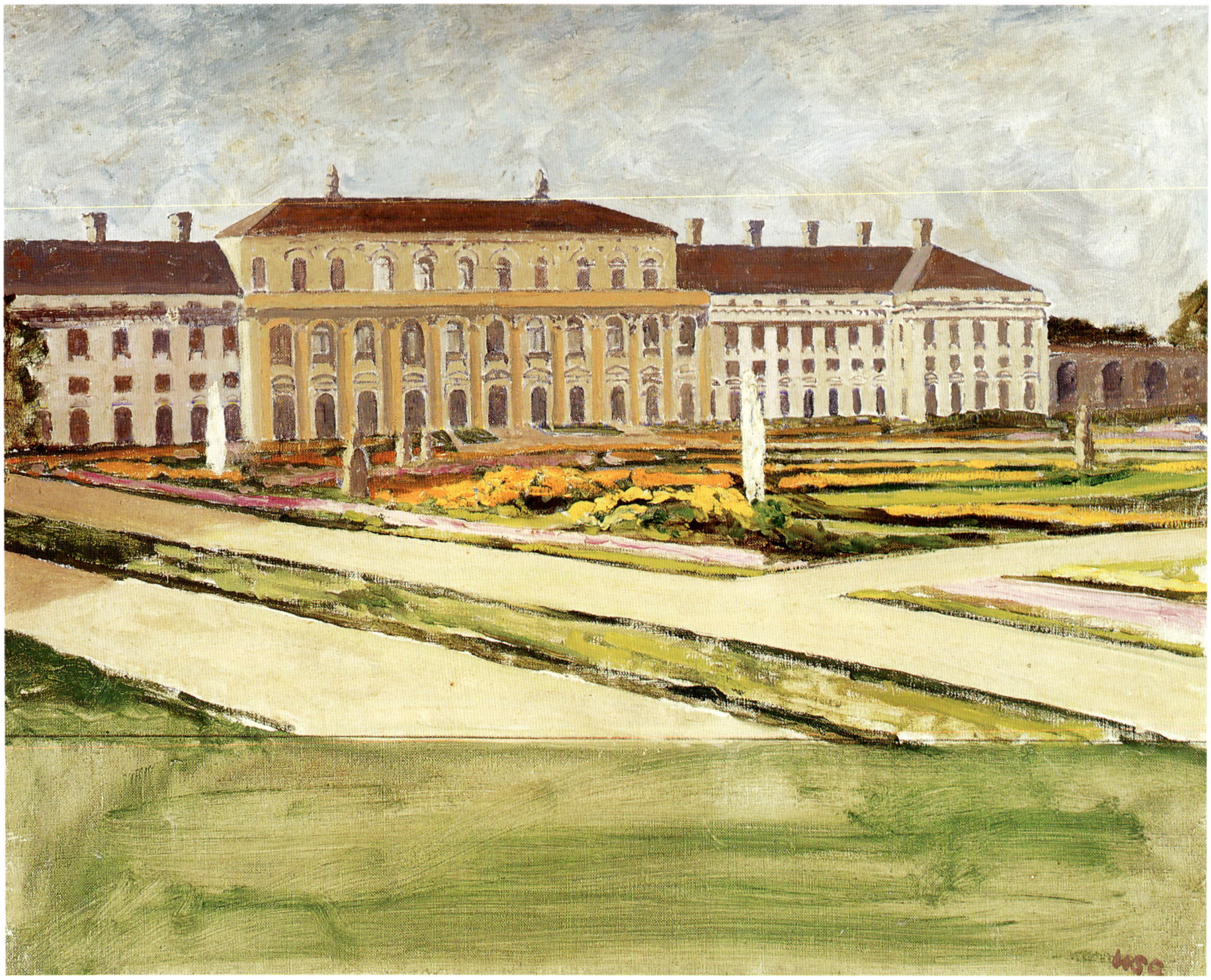

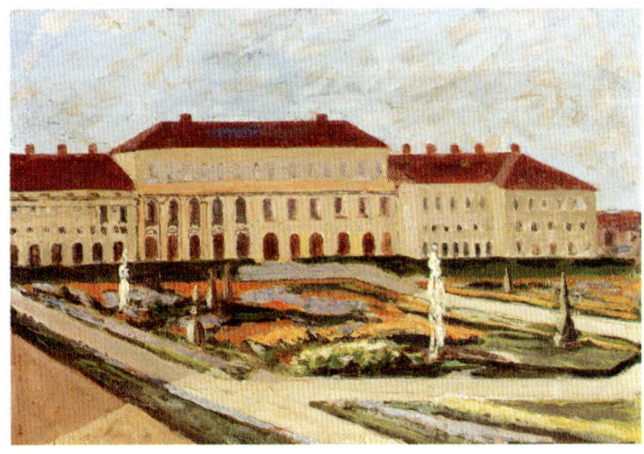

Fig 296 (C 139) above
The Schloss Schleissheim near Munich.

Fig 297 (C 138) top of page
In 1932 Churchill was working on the biography of his great ancestor, the first Duke of Marlborough. Before exploring the site of the Battle of Blenheim he spent three days in Munich, when these views of the 17th-century Baroque palace of Schloss Schleissheim may have been painted.

Abyssinia. Principles of radar formulated by Watson-Watt. General election in Britain and defeat of the National government by Conservatives. To general surprise, and his own mortification, Churchill was not offered a post.

1935 [Painting] Churchill went on holiday to the South of France to paint at Maxine Elliott's chateau near Cannes. Having failed to gain a government position, Churchill went on a long working and painting holiday; he took Clementine to Majorca via Barcelona and, after her return to England, went on to North Africa in the New Year.

1936 [Background] Germany reoccupied the Rhineland without allied protest. Civil war in Spain. Former Bolshevik leaders executed in Russia. British government embarked on defence reforms. Churchill became the focus of national anxiety about Nazi intentions and his speeches and writings about the urgent need for rearmament commanded great influence. On the death of King George V his eldest son, Edward VIII, succeeded to the throne, but a constitutional crisis caused by his marriage intentions forced him to abdicate in favour of his brother George VI. The third volume of Churchill's biography of Marlborough was published.

1936 [Painting] In North Africa Churchill wanted to explore the painting possibilities recommended by Lavery and other friends. He went first to Tangier and then to Marrakech, where he stayed at the Mamounia Hotel, as he was to

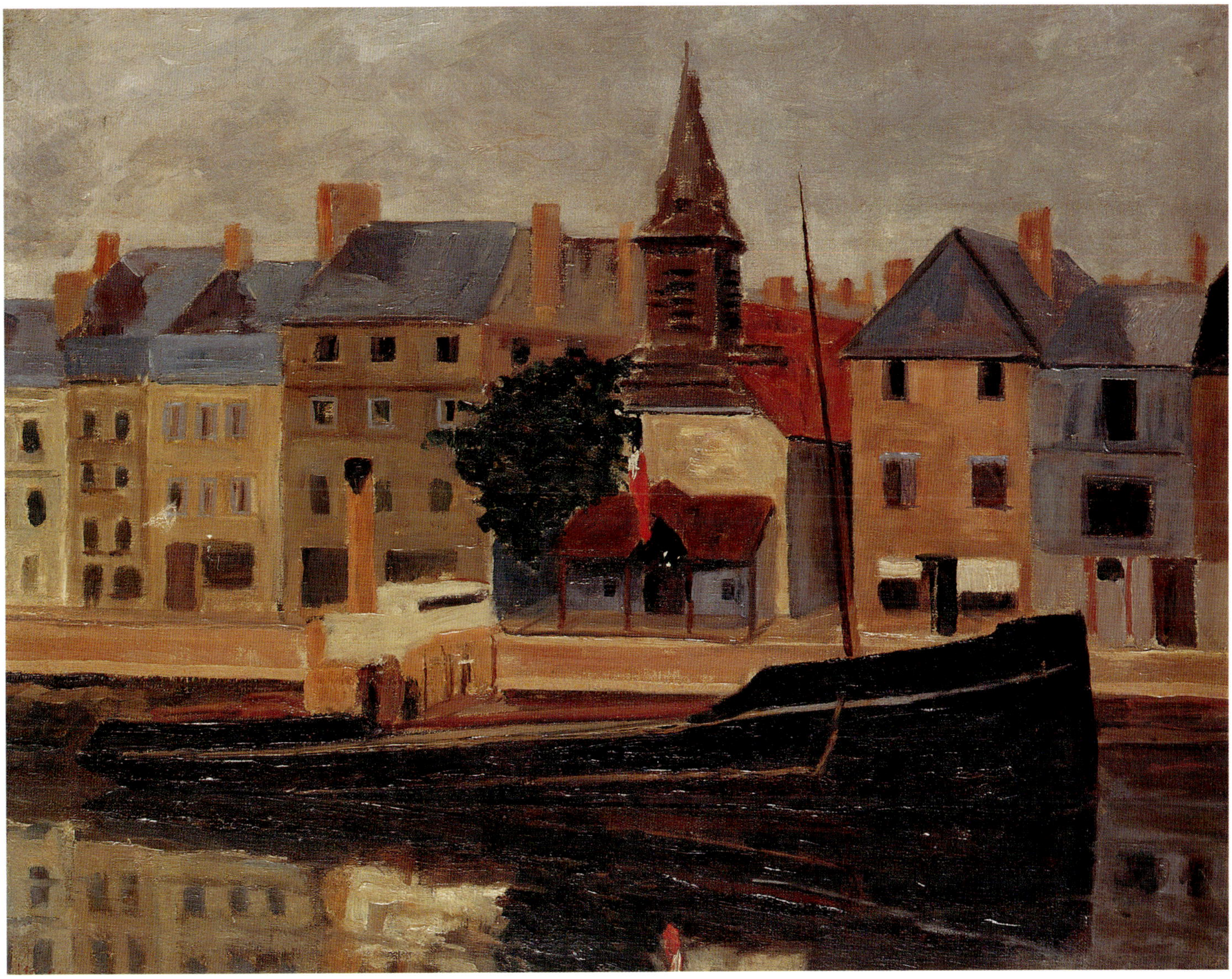

Fig 298 (C 302) above
Canal scene. Given by Churchill to Mr Vic Oliver, husband of his second daughter, Sarah.

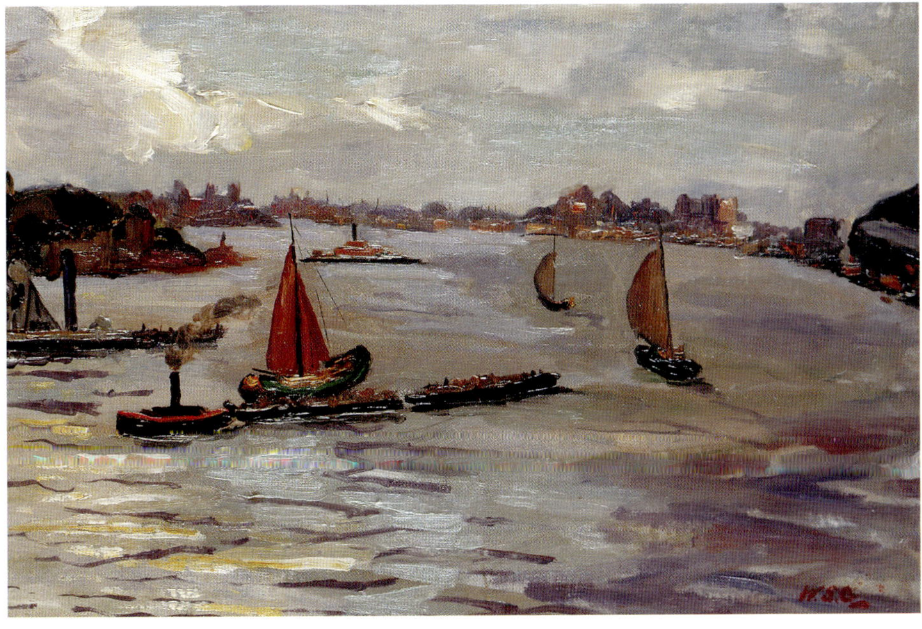

Fig 299 (C 296) left
Amsterdam Harbour from Lord Beaverbrook's yacht, given by Churchill to Mr Walter Graebner, Time-Life representative in London after the Second World War.

Fig 300 (C 250) below
A view on the Rhine, a little painting done perhaps when Churchill visited Germany in 1932.

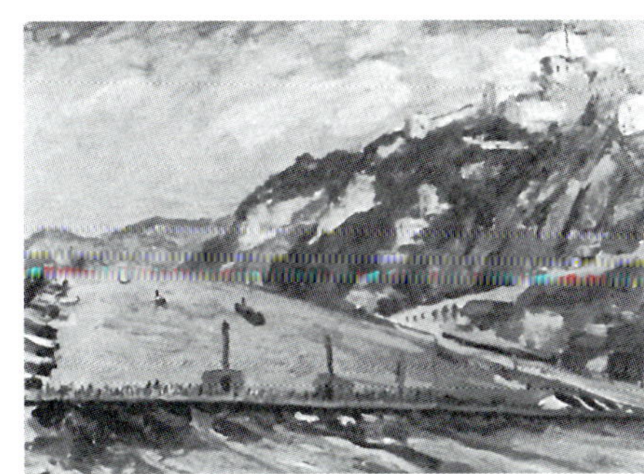

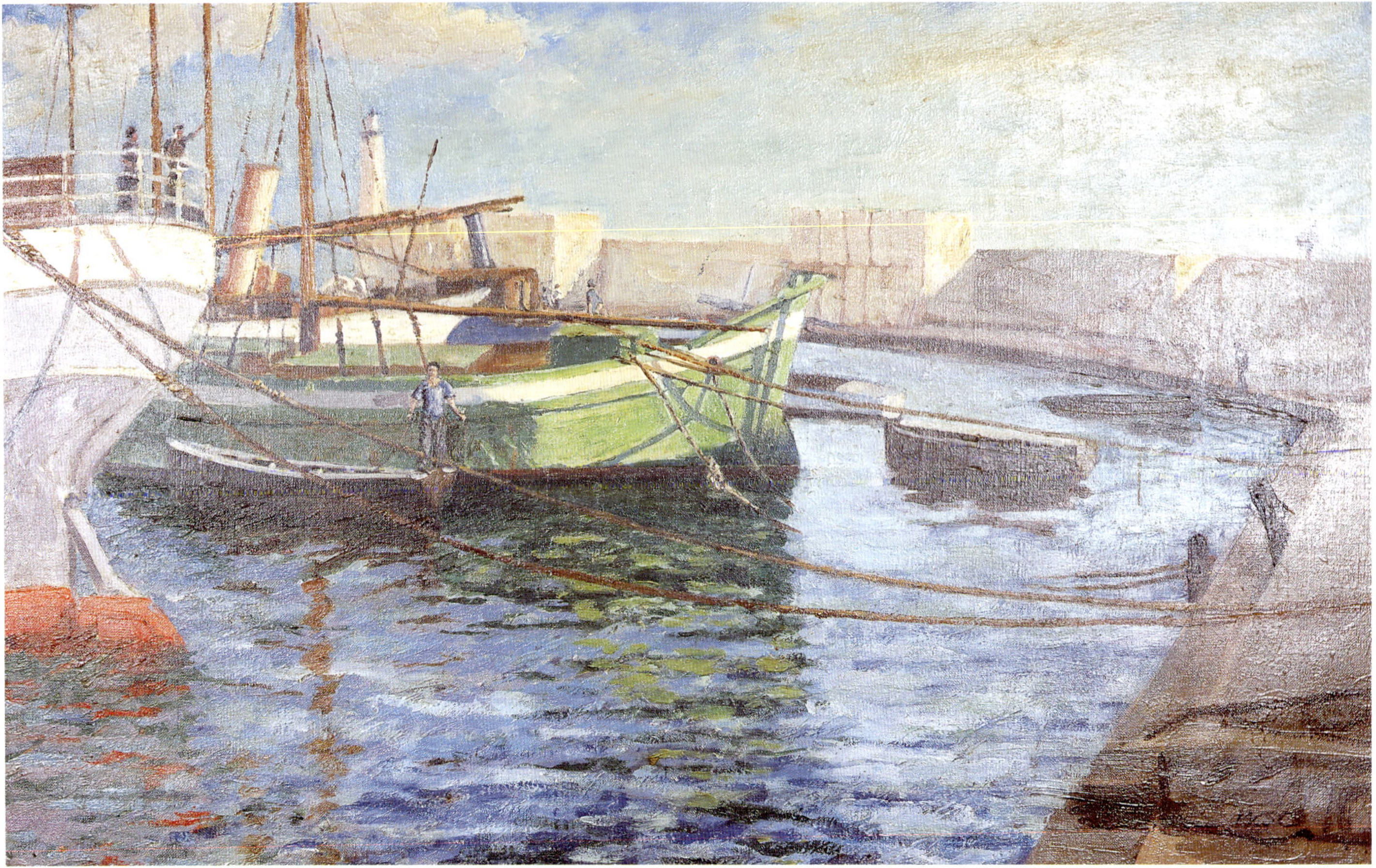

Fig 301 (C 300) above
Boats in Cannes Harbour. This painting is based on a photograph from the Studio archives at Chartwell.

Cannes, at the heart of the French Riviera and as celebrated for its climate as for its setting, inspired Churchill to paint some of his best pictures.

do many times. He found the views of the city and the Atlas mountains seen from the balcony of the hotel particularly attractive.

Later, Churchill went to stay with the Balsans at St Georges-Motel and then on to Maxine Elliott where he discovered and was inspired by the clear water of the river Loup.

Throughout this decade, his visits provided him with painterly inspiration for his brush, notably at Blenheim, where he was particularly attracted by the Marlborough tapestries.

He stayed at Knebworth House with Lord and Lady Lytton (the latter was his first great love, Pamela Plowden), where he painted the Great Hall, and at Taplow Court in Buckinghamshire, the home of Lord and Lady Desborough, where the waters of the Thames fascinated him.

Grace Hamblin, his secretary, recalled one occasion when she accompanied Churchill to Hever. 'I think he did like someone with him when he was actually painting ... in the same way that he liked someone there when he was working. Although I was young, I quite had the feeling that he liked an audience. Not to show off, he just liked someone there. I just sat there and waited. Occasionally, he would say, "Hand me the cobalt blue", or something like that. He wouldn't like you to talk though ...'

1937 [Background] Guernica in Spain bombed by German planes. Persecution of Jews, Protestants and Catholics in Germany. Italian-German axis formed. War between China and Japan. King George VI crowned. Churchill continued to speak and write about the dangers facing Europe. His views became internationally known through a new literary agent, Emery Reves, a Hungarian Jew based in Paris with extensive newspaper connections. Driven by the constant

Fig 302 (C 311) below.
Sunset at Cannes harbour. This painting was given by Churchill to his son, Randolph.

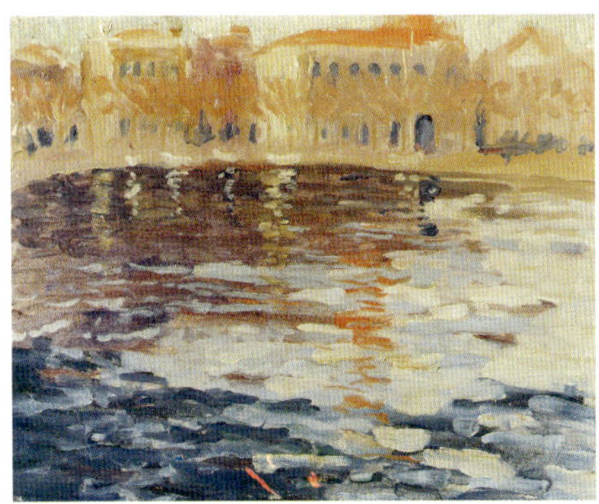

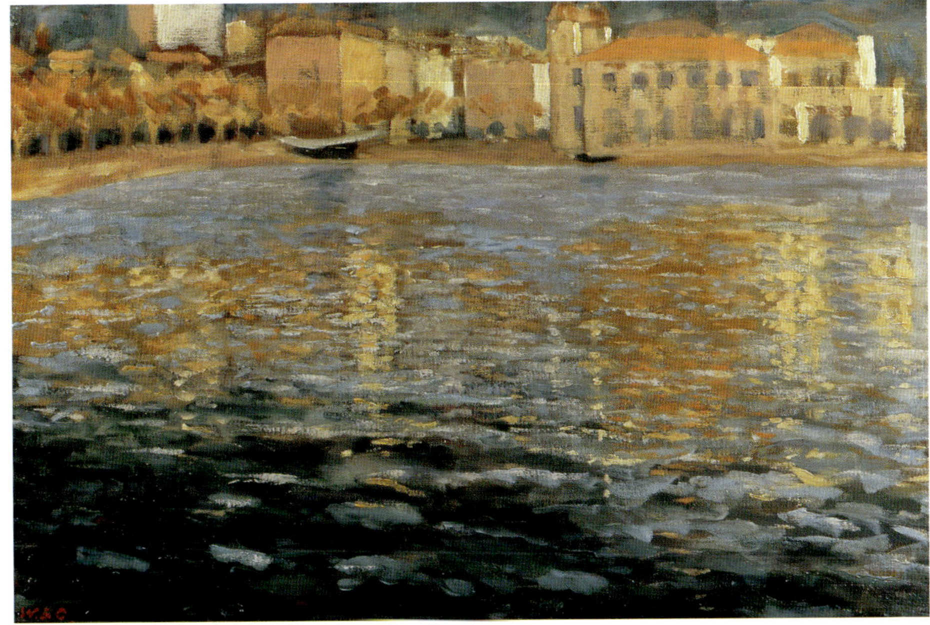

Fig 303 (C 305) left
Sunset, Cannes. This painting formerly belonged to Clementine Churchill.

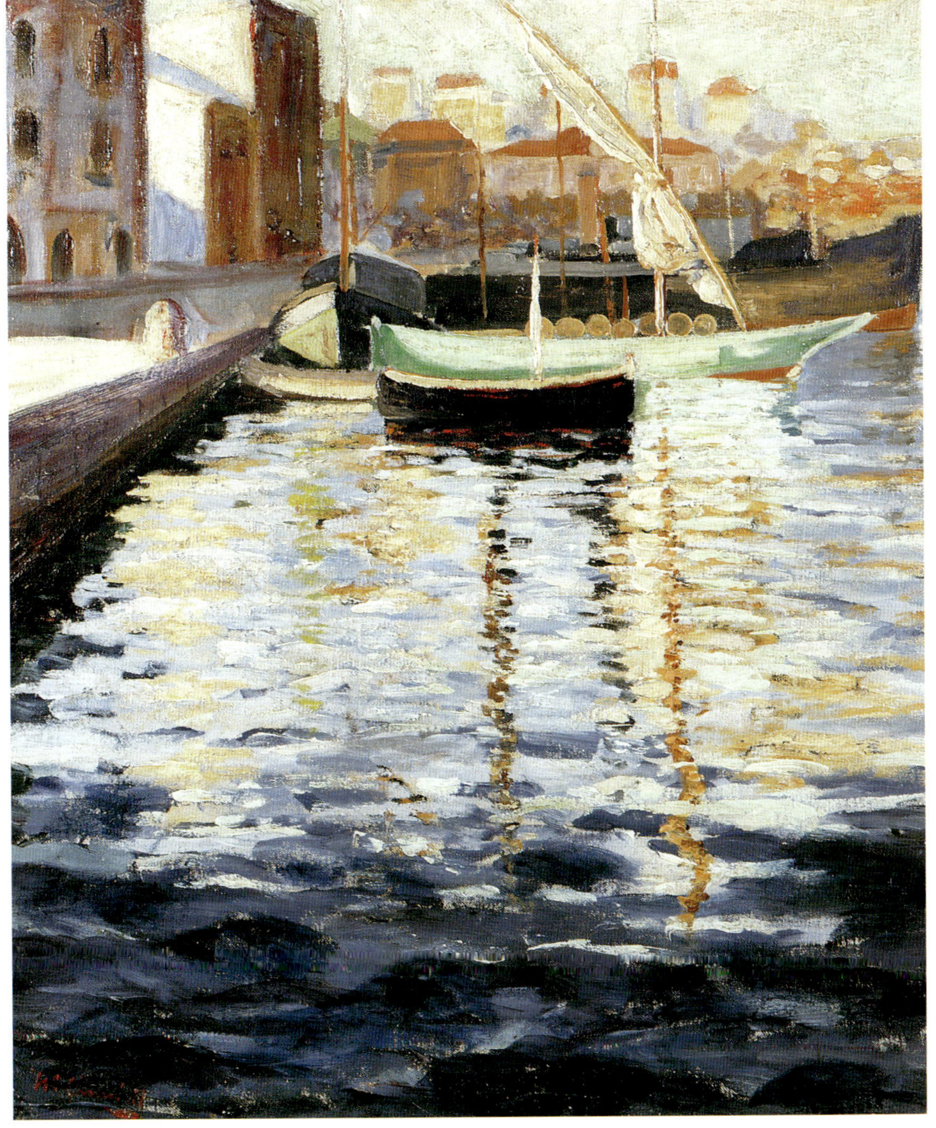

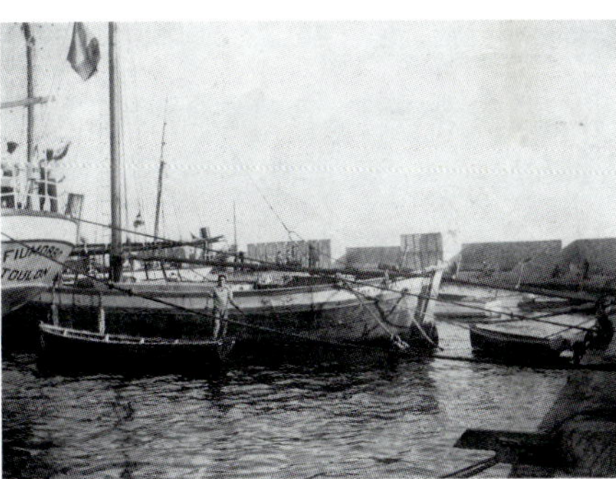

This photograph from the Studio archives at Chartwell relates to the painting shown on the facing page.

On the back of the photograph are the rough sketches by Churchill illustrated on page 244.

Fig 304 (C 304) left
Boats in Cannes harbour.

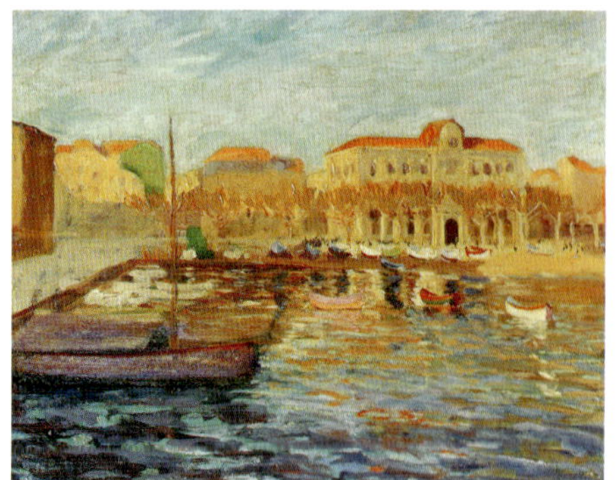

Fig 305 (C 310) above
Harbour, Cannes. This painting formerly belonged to Clementine Churchill.

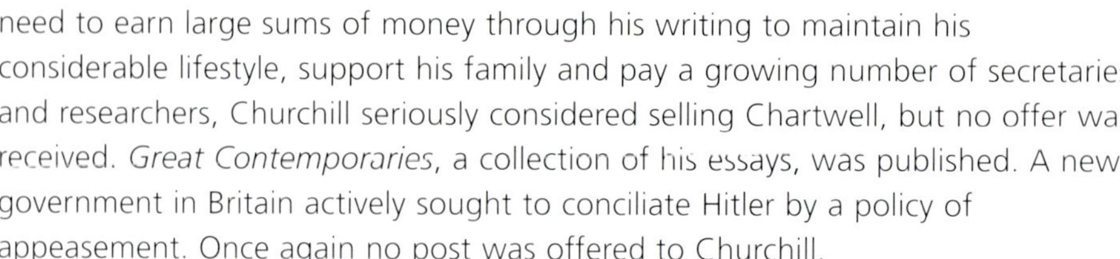

need to earn large sums of money through his writing to maintain his considerable lifestyle, support his family and pay a growing number of secretaries and researchers, Churchill seriously considered selling Chartwell, but no offer was received. *Great Contemporaries*, a collection of his essays, was published. A new government in Britain actively sought to conciliate Hitler by a policy of appeasement. Once again no post was offered to Churchill.

1937 [Painting] Churchill paid one short visit to Lord Rothermere's house, La Dragonnière on Cap Martin, to paint. Sir John Lavery asked if he would lend a picture to an exhibition at the New Burlington Galleries, 'Sea Power - The King's Ships and the Merchant Navy'. Churchill refused, saying that he 'does not consider any one of his paintings good enough'.

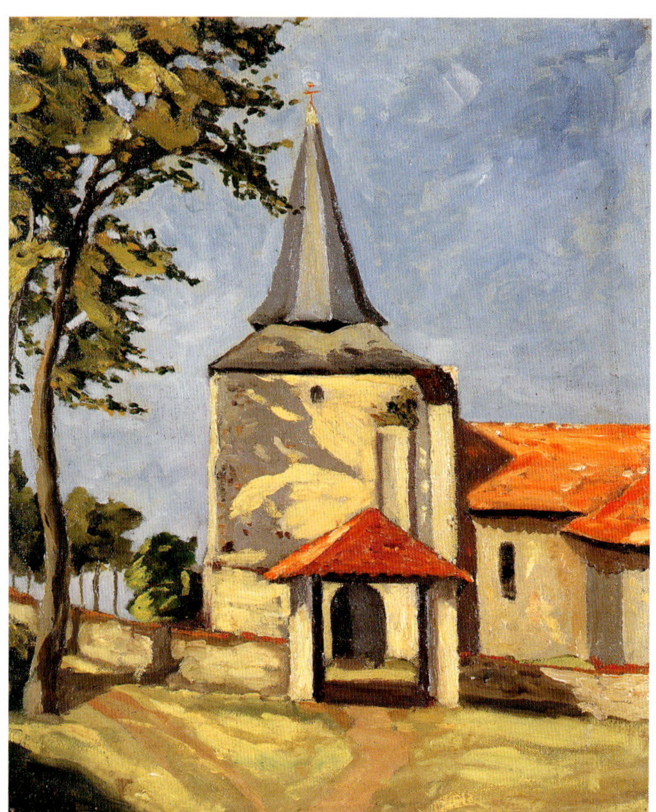

Fig 306 (C 240) above
A church, somewhere in the South of France.

1938 [Background] Hitler annexed Austria and, through the Munich pact, the European powers agreed to his seizure of the Sudetenland in Czechoslovakia. Much rejoicing in Britain at a perceived victory for its government's policy of appeasement. Civilians were issued with gas masks and trenches dug in parks as an air-raid precaution. Kristallnacht: co-ordinated anti-Jewish violence in Germany, Austria and the Sudetenland. Hitler attacked Churchill publicly; the latter's allies grew in number and influence in Parliament and elsewhere. Churchill's fourth and final volume of his biography of Marlborough was published and the first volume of his *History of the English-speaking Peoples* completed.

1938 [Painting] Churchill visited Maxine Elliott at the Château de l'Horizon in the South of France but was too tired to paint there. On the same trip he stopped briefly with Daisy and Reginald Fellowes at Les Zoraides.

Taplow Court near Maidenhead was often visited by Churchill, as several of his paintings commemorate. It was the home of Lord and Lady Desborough, members of 'The Souls', an informal social and intellectual elite which included Churchill's friend Lord Balfour. The Desboroughs' elder sons Julian, the poet, and Billy Grenfell had been killed on active service during the First World War. The Cedar Walk was a feature of the garden at Taplow Court, many of its trees being dedicated to special visitors. In 1938, Churchill planted a Weeping Cedar, insisting on this unusual variety because it expressed his feelings about the future of Europe at the time.

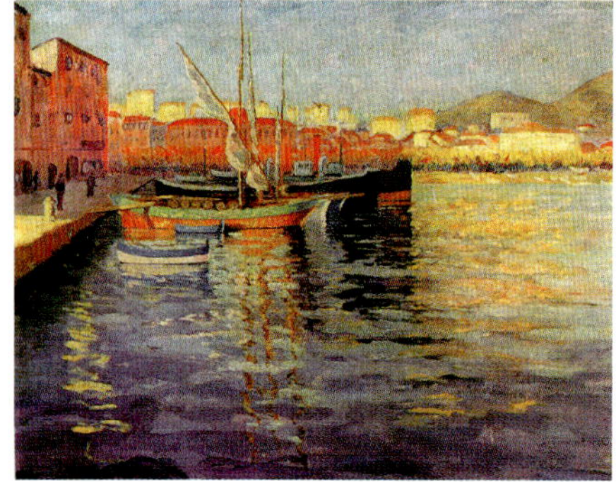

Fig 307 (C 306) above
Harbour scene, Cannes. This painting formerly belonged to Churchill's second daughter, Sarah.

1939 [Background] Churchill was criticized in his own constituency for his hostility towards the Munich agreement. Germany invaded Czechoslovakia. Italy invaded Albania. End of Spanish Civil War. National service register introduced in Britain. Churchill condemned the government's decision to curtail Jewish immigration into Palestine. He broadcast to the United States about his fears of forthcoming war. Growing public calls for Churchill to be included in the government. Russia made agreement with Germany. Britain signed treaty of alliance with Poland. British fleet ordered to war stations. Hitler invaded Poland. Britain and France declared war. Churchill joined the War Cabinet as First Lord of the Admiralty. This news inspired the signal to the Fleet: 'Winston's back.' Russia invaded Poland and Finland. British Expeditionary Force landed in France. Churchill made his first wartime broadcast. German submarines began to sink

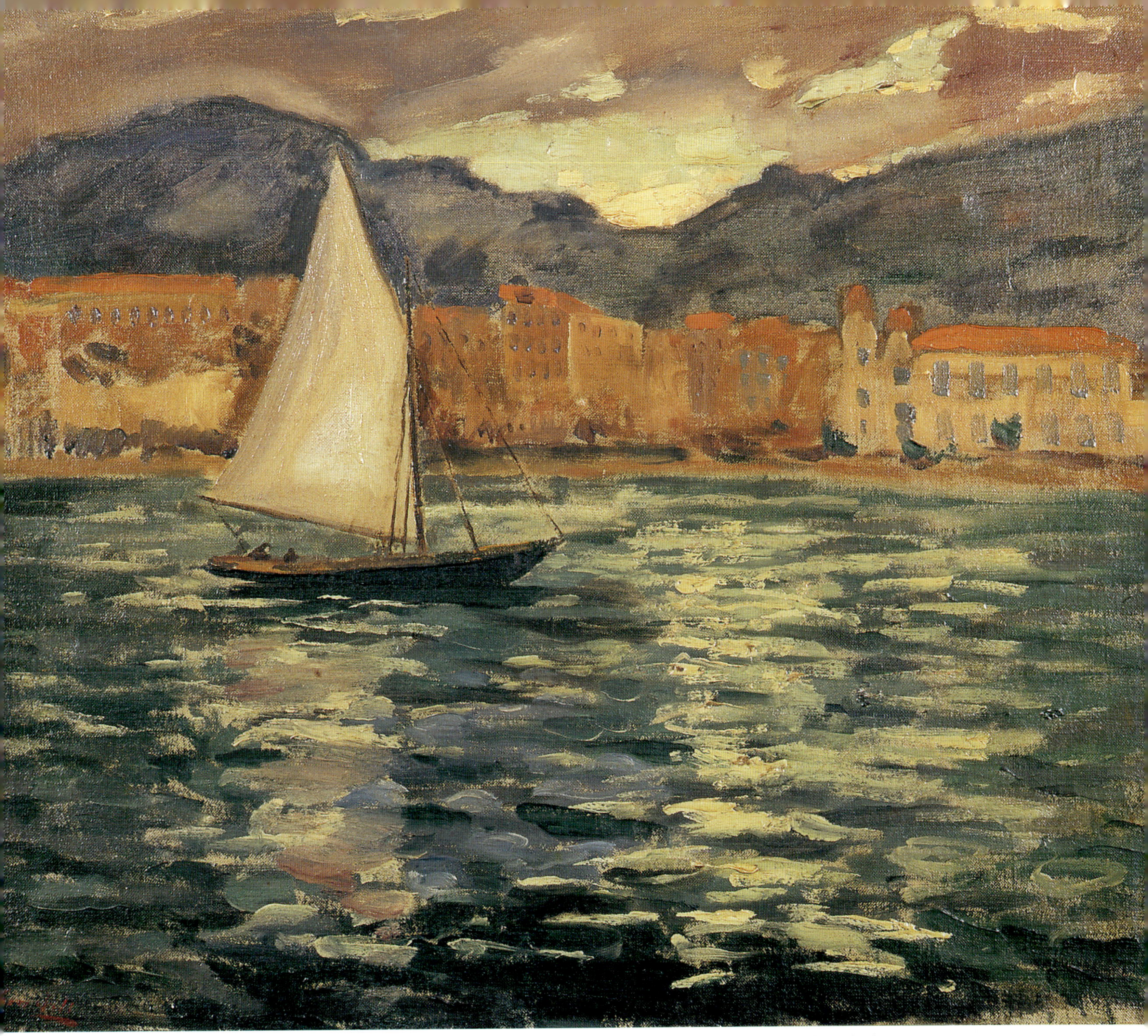

Fig 308 (C 308) above.
Boats in Cannes Harbour. This painting formerly belonged to Churchill's eldest daughter, Diana.

British merchant vessels. Battleship *Royal Oak* sunk at Scapa Flow. German battleship *Graf Spee* blew herself up after being caught by British cruisers.

1939 [Painting] That summer Churchill paid what were to be his last visits to Maxine Elliott at the Château de l'Horizon, who died the following year, and to Consuelo and Jacques Balsan at St Georges-Motel, near Dreux in Normandy. At the latter, he painted in the company of Paul Maze who had a studio in the chateau's mill, the Moulin de Montreuil. On August 27, Maze recorded Churchill's remark in his diary : 'This is the last picture we shall paint in peace for a very long time.' War was declared on September 3rd.

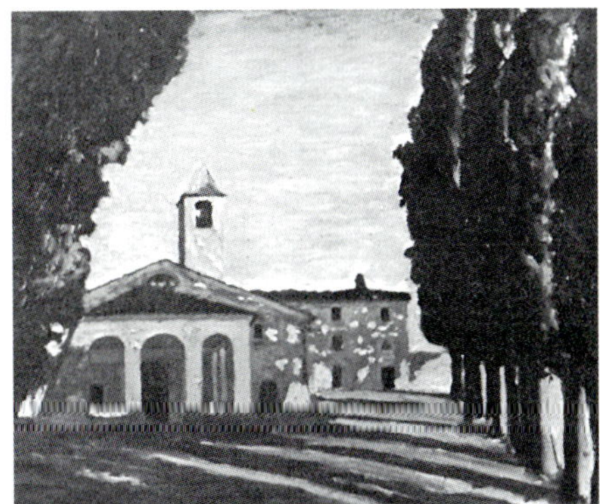

Fig 309 (C 238) above
St Jean de Vie. between Cannes and Grasses.

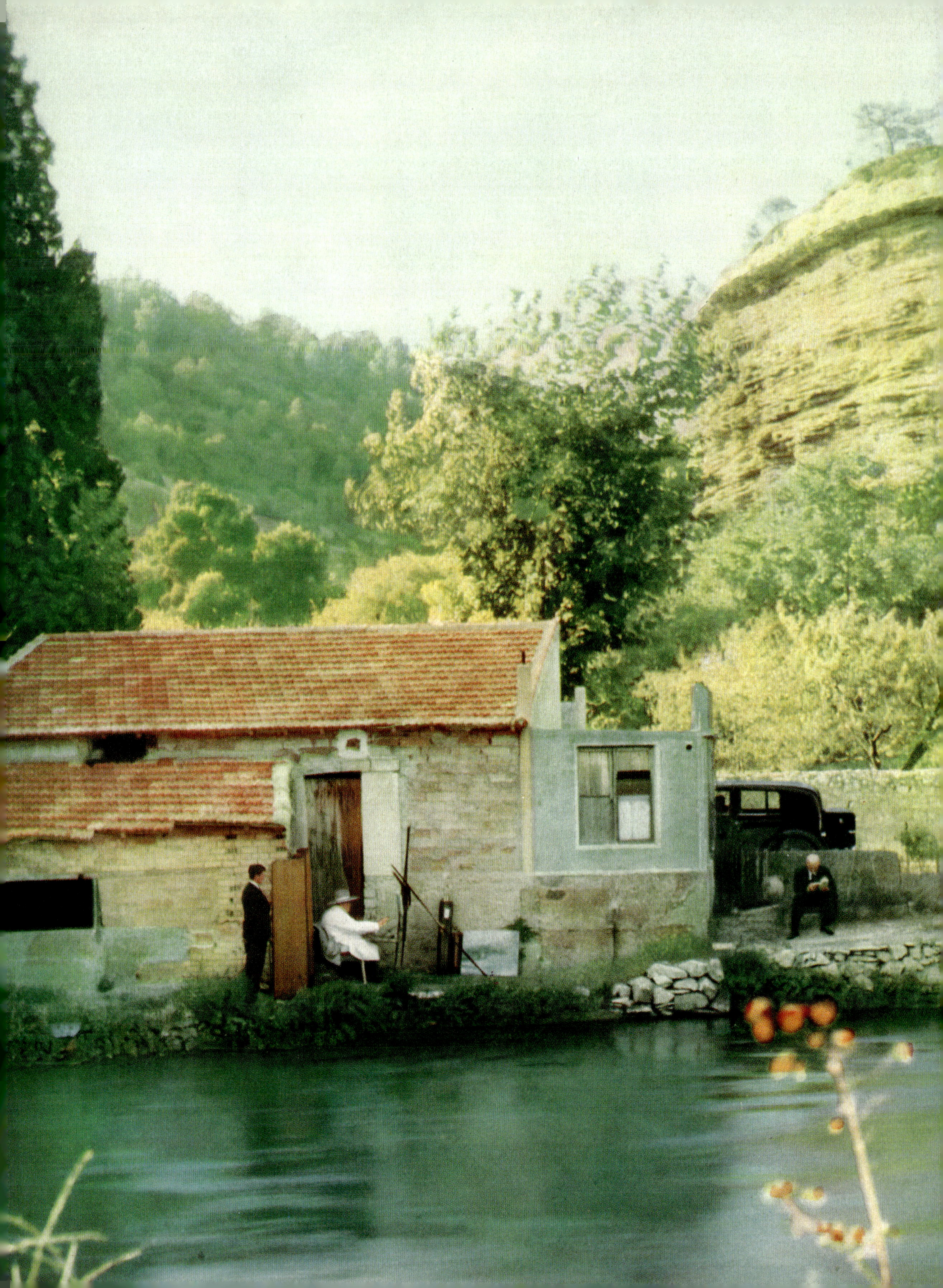

later years
1940 - 1965

1940 [Background] Churchill's 65th year.
Germany invaded Norway and Denmark. British forces' landing in Norway repulsed. Germany invaded Holland, Belgium and France. Churchill became Prime Minister of an all-party government. He told Parliament, 'I have nothing to offer but blood, toil, tears and sweat ... without victory there is no survival.' Churchill said in Parliament, 'We shall go on to the end ... we shall fight on the seas and oceans [and] in the air ... we shall defend our island, whatever the cost may be ... we shall never surrender.' German troops captured Paris. French armistice. President Roosevelt re-elected in United States. Italy invaded France and Greece. German aircraft bombed Britain with increasing ferocity. Invasion appeared imminent. British and other forces evacuated from Dunkirk. Battle of Britain won by fighter aircraft. Berlin and Hamburg bombed. British troops attacked Italian forces in the North African desert and torpedo aircraft sank Italian battleships at Taranto.

1940 [Painting] With the threat of invasion, the Director of the National Gallery in London, Kenneth Clark, suggested sending its most important paintings to Canada. Churchill replied, 'No, bury them in caves and cellars. None must go. We are going to beat them.'

1941 [Background] German submarine successes during the Battle of the Atlantic threatened Britain's supplies. British forces overcame Italian troops in Somalia. Germany invaded Yugoslavia, Greece and Russia. Bombing in Britain and Germany. Italy bombed Malta. Churchill crossed the Atlantic by battleship to meet Roosevelt: the resulting Atlantic Charter proclaimed the right of 'all peoples to choose the form of government under which they live'. Russian and British forces occupied Persia. Italian and German forces landed in Egypt. Japan attacked United States fleet in Pearl Harbor. United States declared war. Italy and Germany declared war on the United States. Churchill sailed for a second time for discussions with Roosevelt, and suffered a mild heart attack during their conference in Washington. Travelled to Ottawa to address the Canadian Parliament. Japan invaded Philippines. Hong Kong surrendered.

Opposite
Sir Winston Churchill painting on the Sorgues River, Vaucluse. His valet stands behind him and Lord Cherwell is reading a book on the right. From The Illustrated London News, 1954.

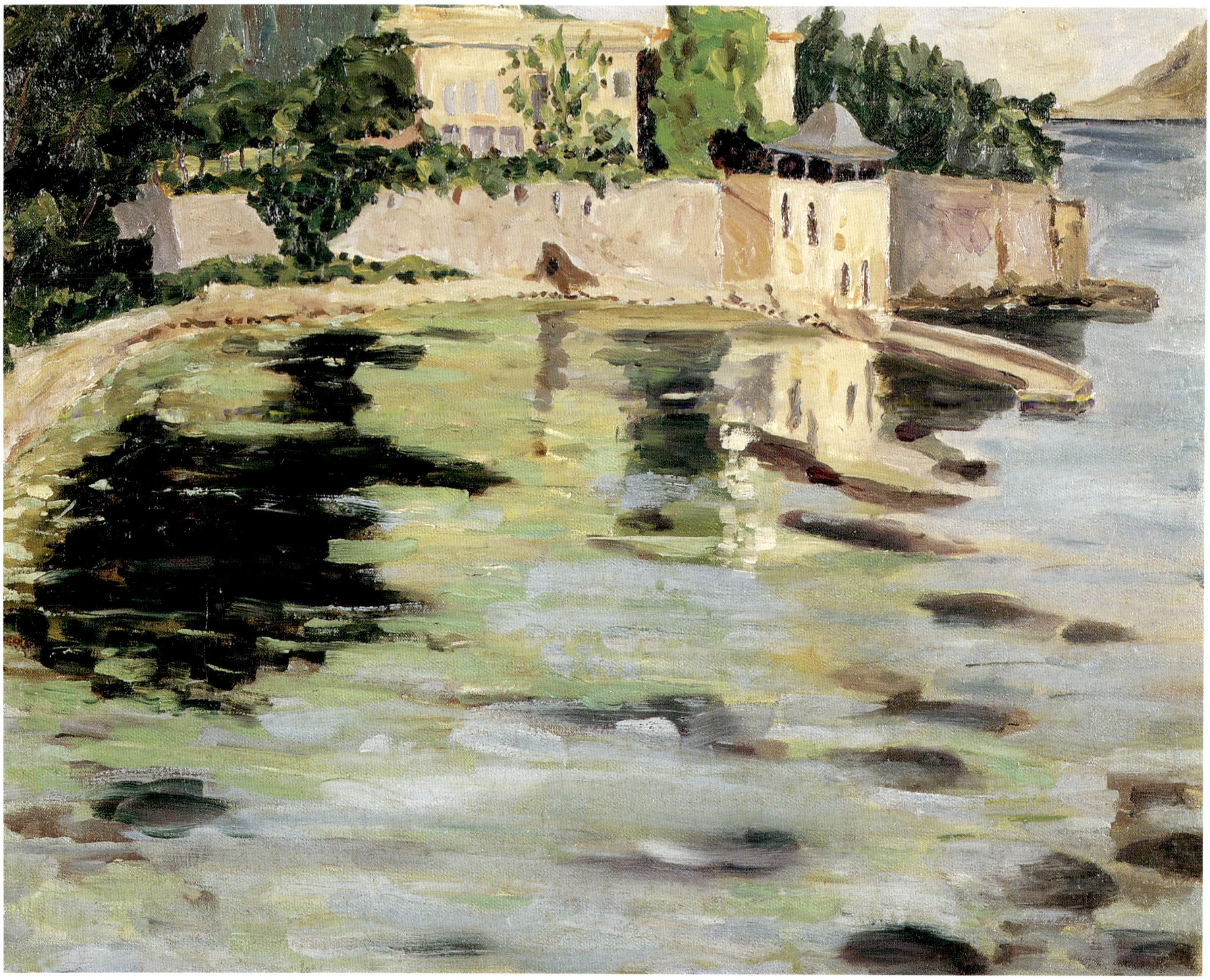

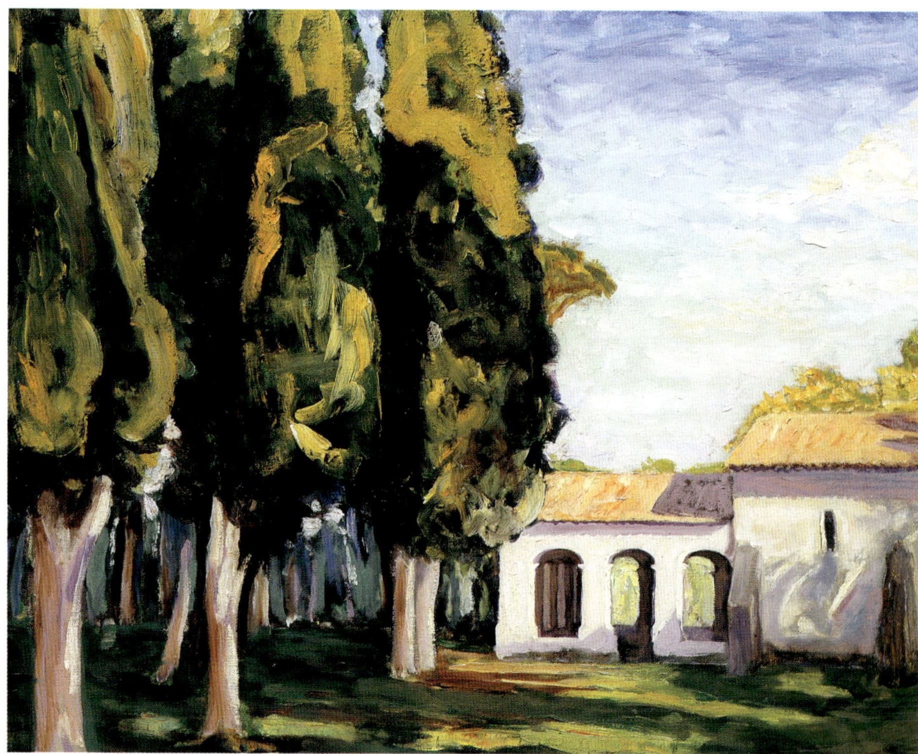

Fig 310 (C 96) above
Coast scene near Cannes.

Fig 311 (C 244) right
Notre Dame de Vie above Cannes.

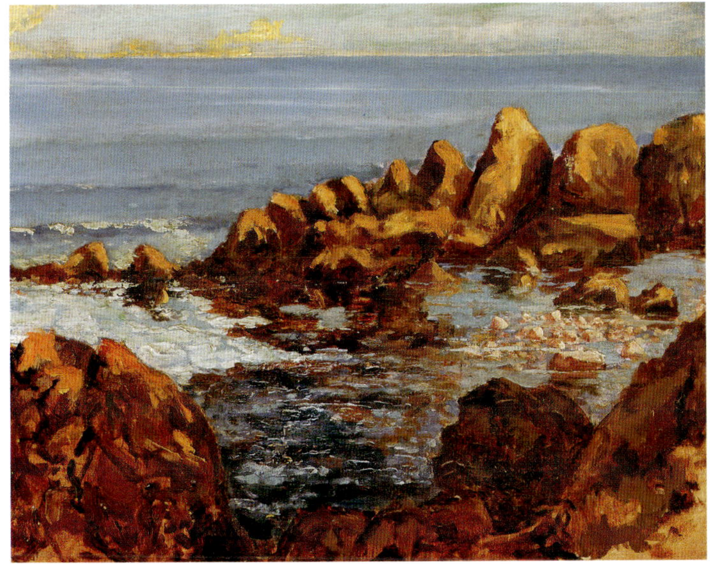

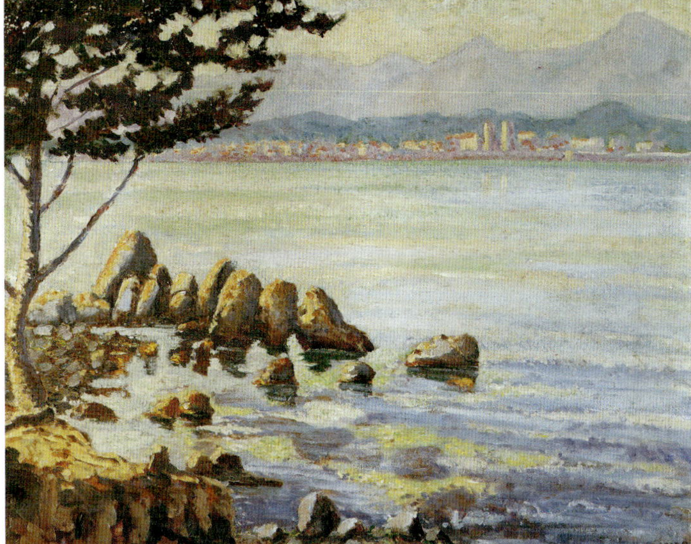

Fig 312 (C 337) above
Coast scene near Antibes, north-east of Cannes.

Fig 313 (C 338) top of page left
Rocks near Cannes. These porphyry rocks are a feature of the Esterel region.

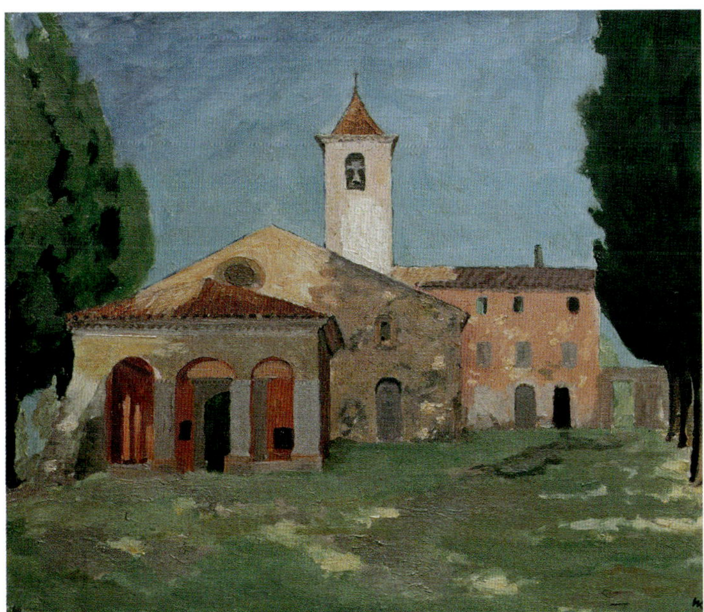

Fig 314 (C 241) left
St Jean de Vie, between Cannes and Grasses.

1941. [Painting] First exhibition at the National Gallery in London of 'Recording Britain': watercolours commissioned from professional artists of buildings and landscapes threatened by war damage. John Piper painted a series of views of Windsor Castle for King George and Queen Elizabeth.

1942 [Background] Churchill went from Washington to Florida to recuperate after his minor heart attack and returned to England by flying boat via Bermuda. Singapore was captured by the Japanese who then invaded Java and subsequently Burma. American forces defeated in the Philippines. First thousand-bomber raid by British aircraft against Germany. Japanese invasion fleet defeated by Americans at Midway Island. Germans captured Tobruk from the British in the Western Desert. Churchill flew once again across the Atlantic to meet Roosevelt. British arctic convoys to Russia temporarily suspended because of heavy losses. Churchill flew to Egypt to encourage the British forces. Then he flew to Moscow for discussions with Stalin. Churchill was criticized in the British Parliament for his direction of the war. British troops defeated German-Italian armies in the Western Desert. British and American forces landed in North Africa and engaged German army in Tunisia. Russian army encircled the German forces besieging Stalingrad. King George VI awarded the George Cross to the island of Malta. London/Washington/Moscow declaration denounced the mass murder of Jews.

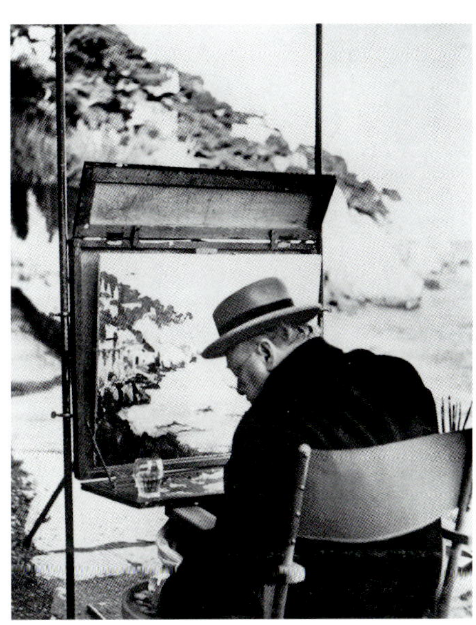

Winston Churchill painting near Cap d'Ail. For the picture, see Fig. 285, page 144.

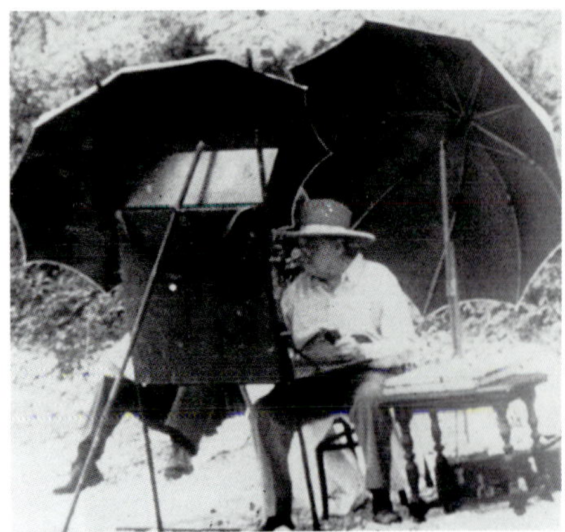

Winston Churchill, protected from the strong sun by two umbrellas paints at an unidentified location.

1942 [Painting] This was the most uncertain year of the war for Britain and its allies. Frank Salisbury determined to paint Churchill's portrait as a 'personal expression of sincere admiration'. There being no occasion for private sittings, Salisbury was given the opportunity of sketching Churchill in the House of Commons. Several versions were painted including one that hangs in the library at Chartwell showing Churchill in his celebrated 'siren' suit.

1943 [Background] Churchill and Roosevelt met at Casablanca in North Africa to agree Anglo-American strategy: they publicly declared that the war would be continued until the unconditional surrender of both Germany and Japan was achieved. British troops captured Tripoli. Allied forces defeated Germans to take control of North Africa. Sicily was invaded and then Italy, where incoming German forces resisted fiercely. Churchill sailed to the United States to meet Roosevelt and addressed Congress. Subsequently he made a second transatlantic journey to the Quebec conference after which he rested at a fishing camp in the Laurentian mountains. Mussolini resigned and Italy surrendered. Conference in Cairo with Roosevelt. Both flew to Tehran to meet Stalin. Churchill's exhaustion forced him to rest a little in Marrakech, but he was too tired on this second visit to paint.

Fig 315 (C 339) below.
Red rocks near Theoule, south-west of Cannes.

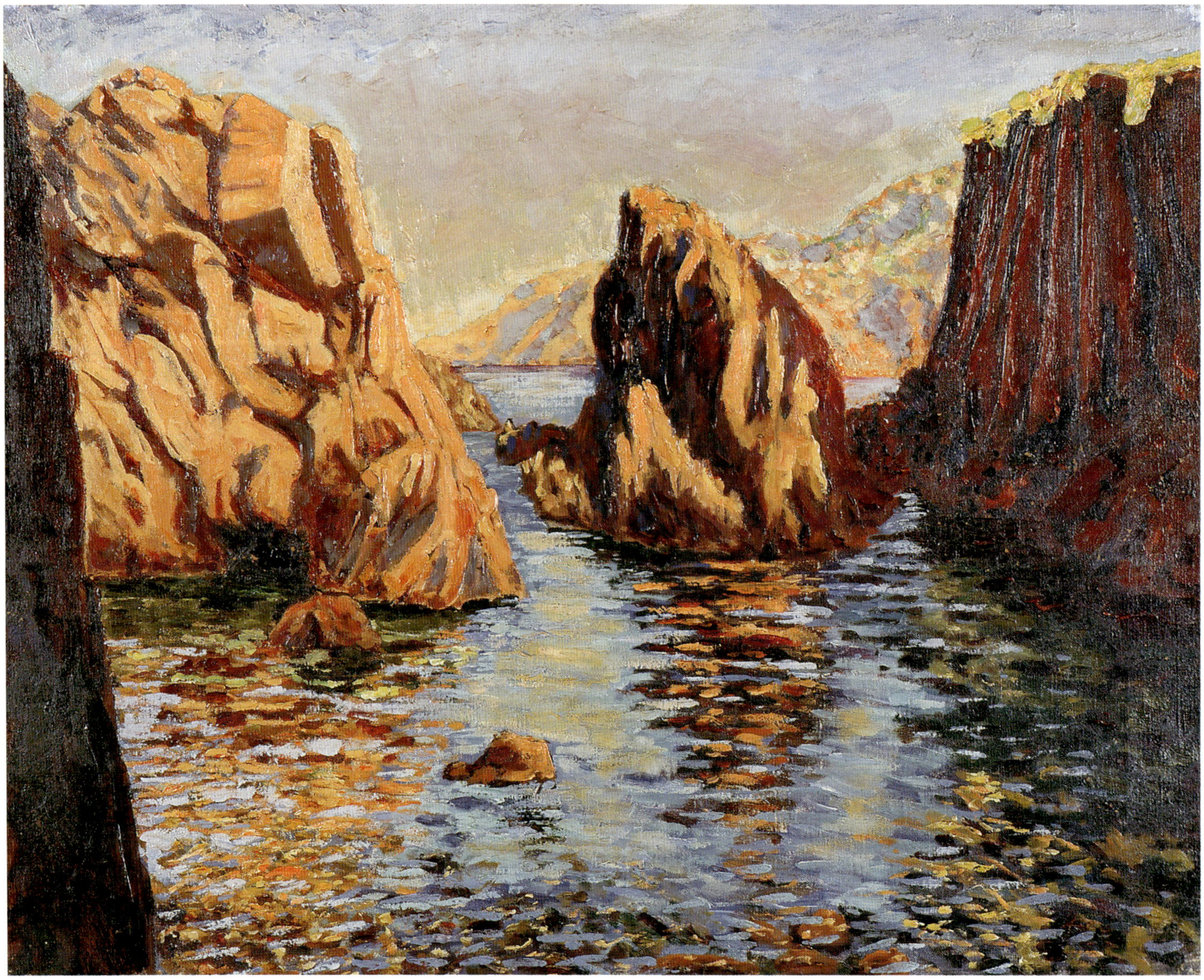

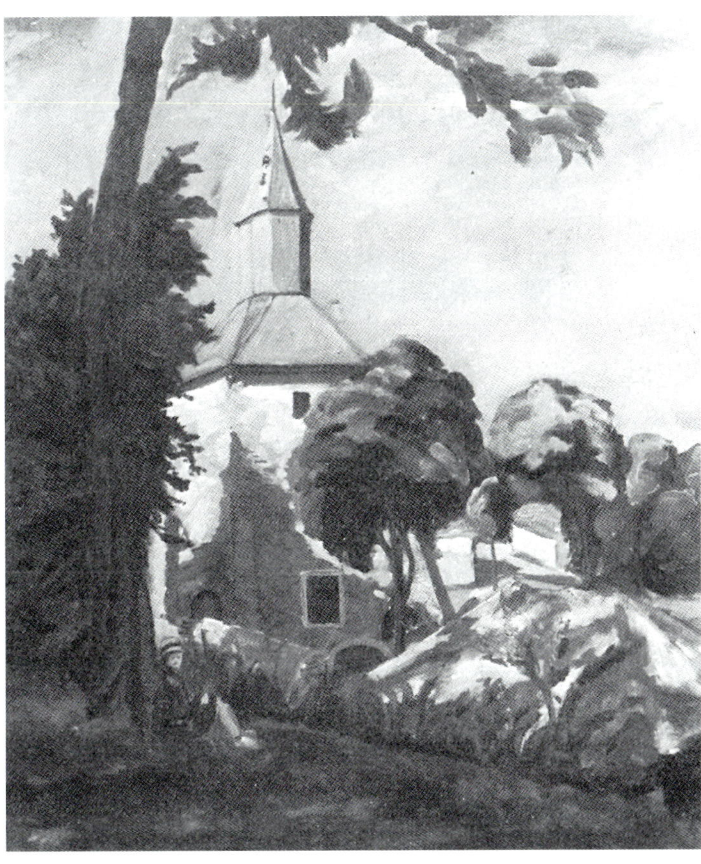

Fig 316 (C 242) left
A church, somewhere in the South of France. Winston gave this painting to Marryott Whyte, Clementine's cousin, who in 1921 came to supervise their children and then to look after their youngest daughter, Mary.

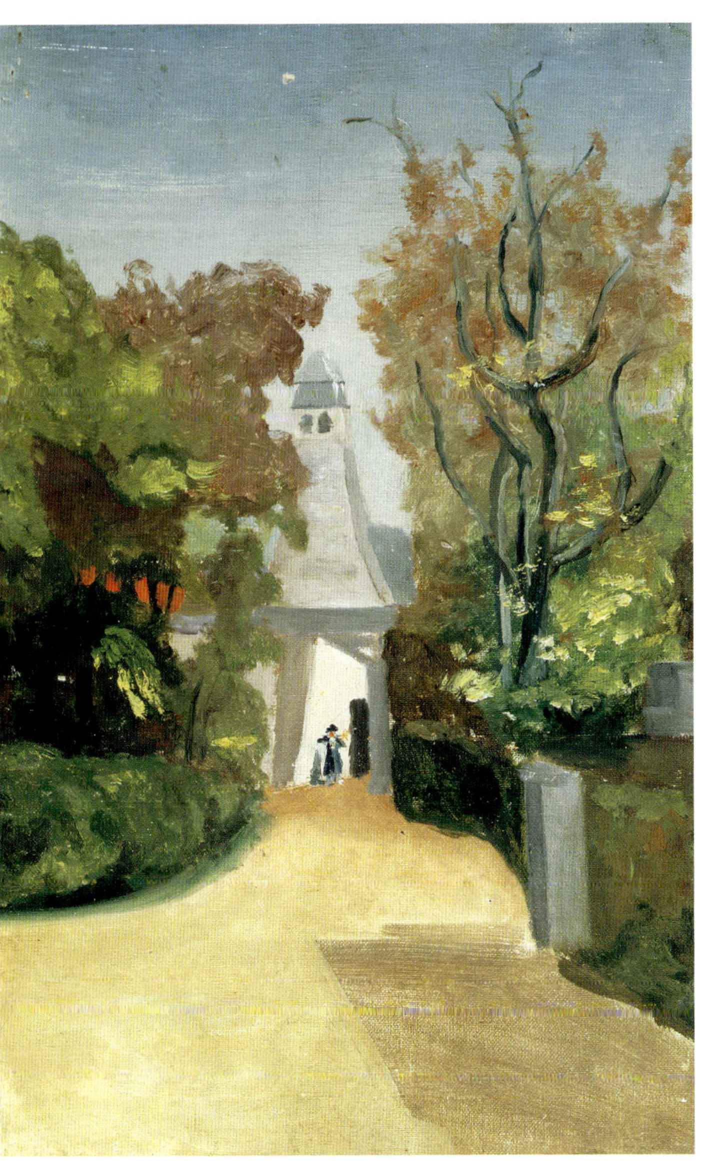

Fig 317 (C 243) below left
A painting of a scene somewhere in the South of France.

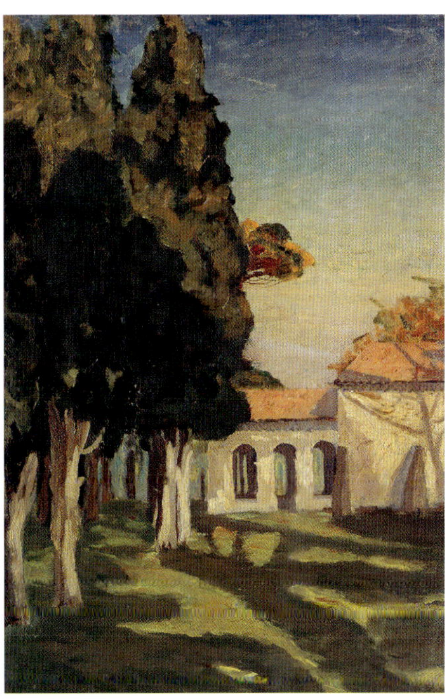

Fig 318 (C 245) above
The Porch of Notre Dame de Vie.

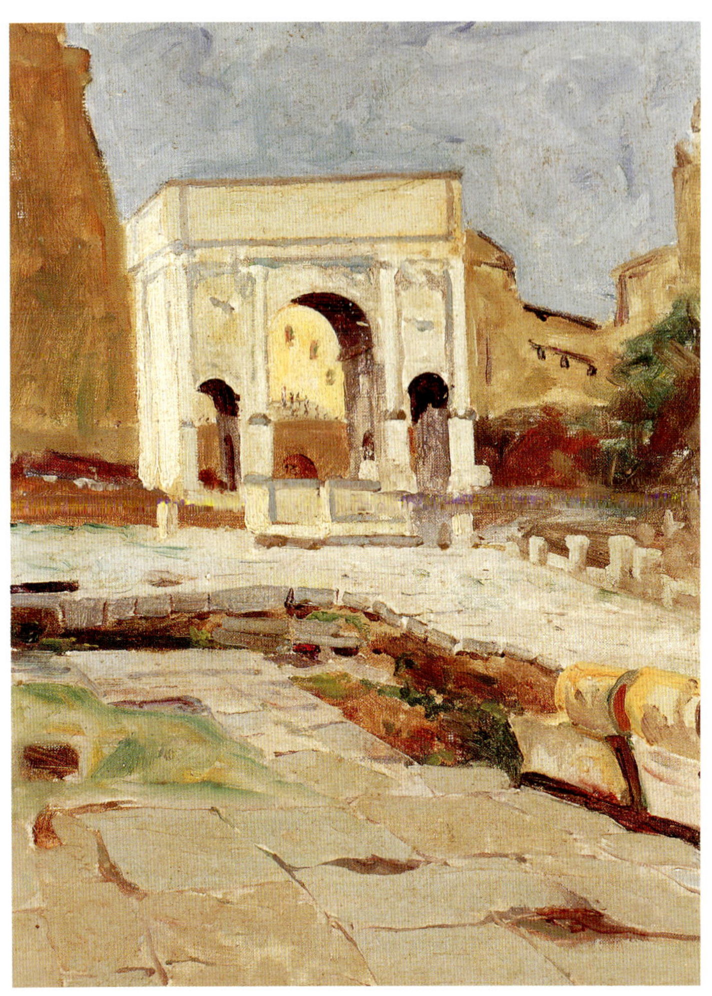

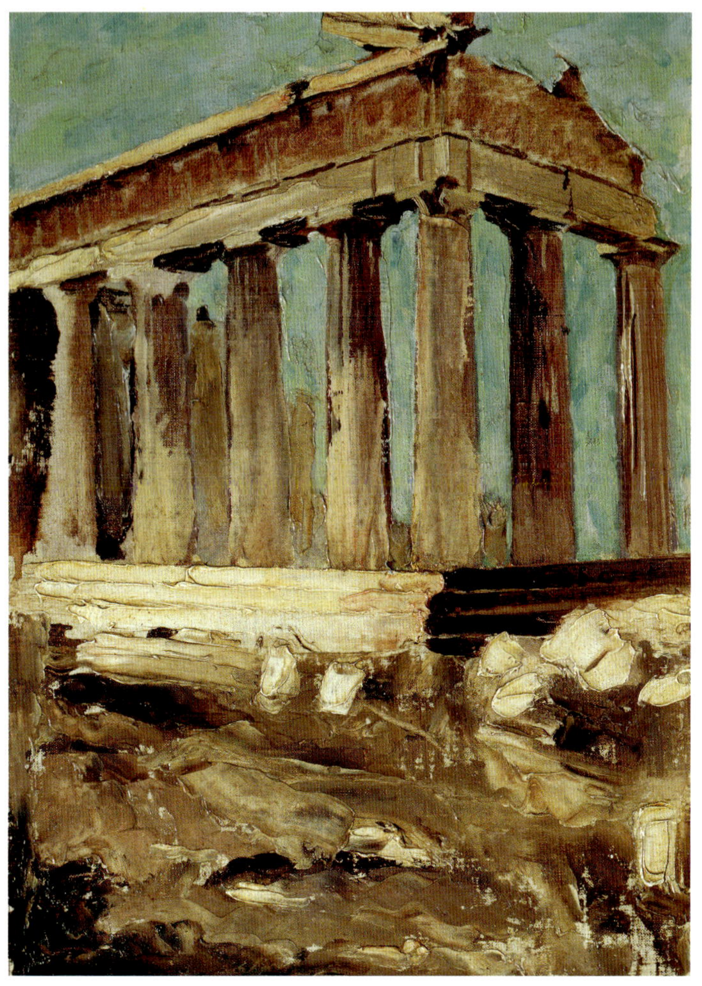

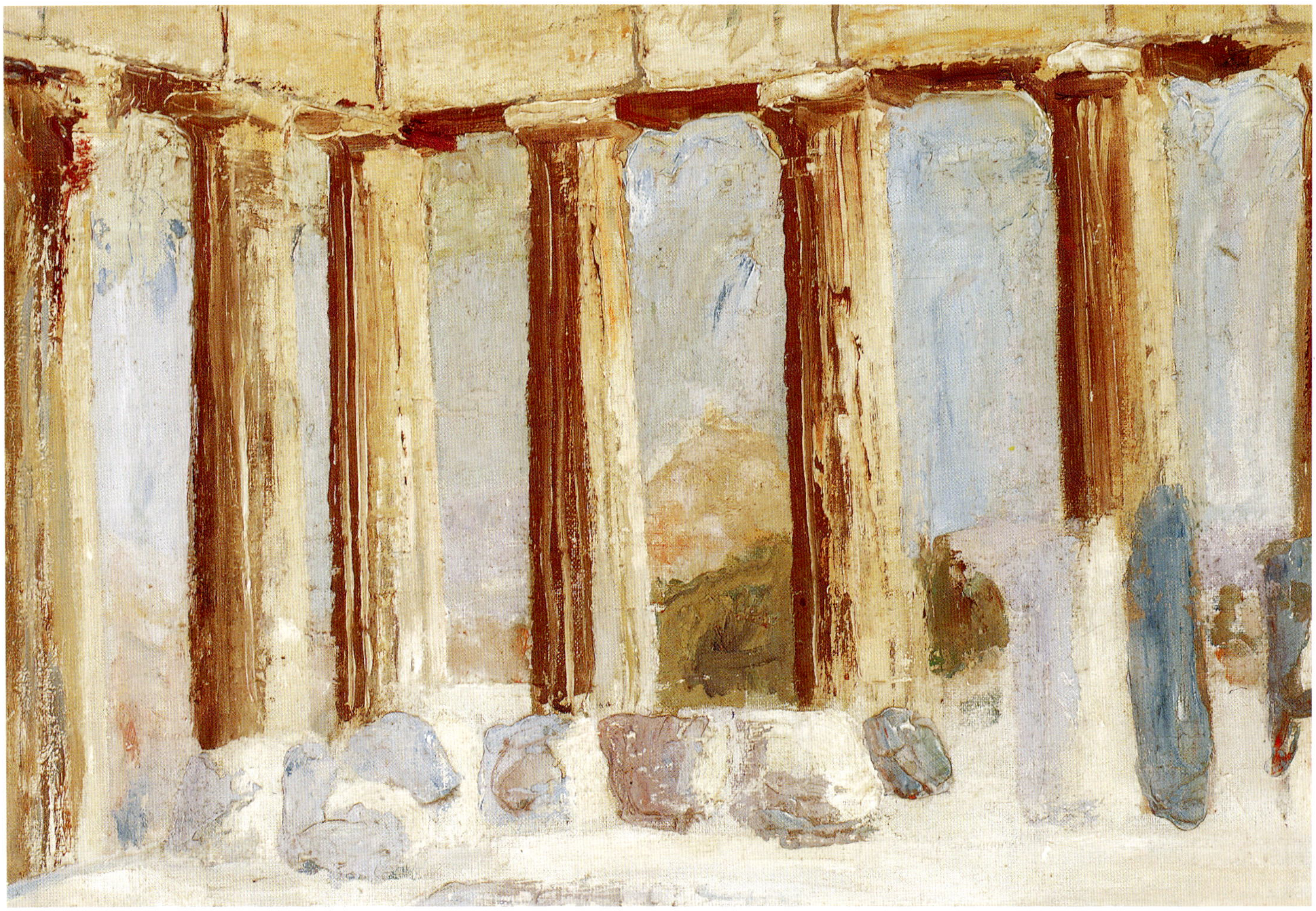

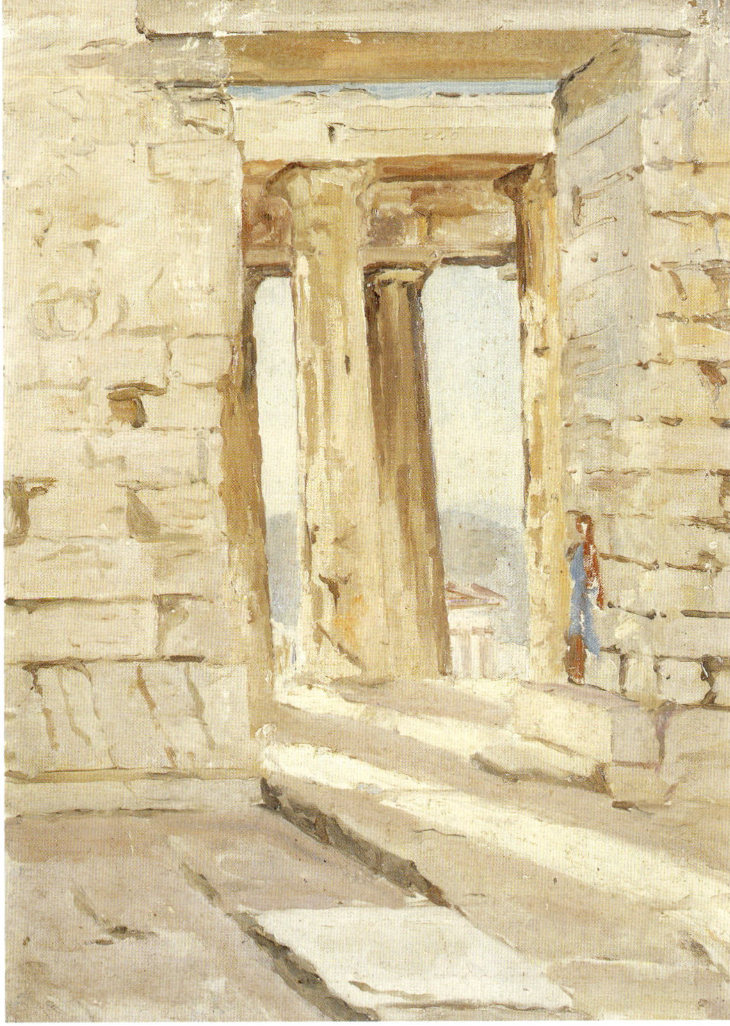

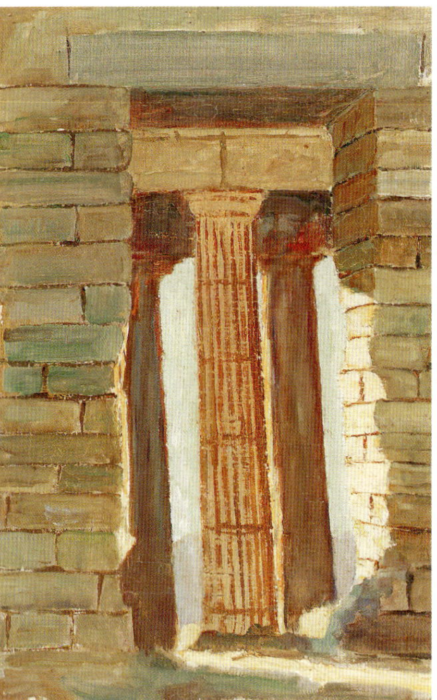

Fig 319 (C 114) above
Doorway and pillars in shadow.

Fig 320 (C 113) left
Greek temple.

In 1934, Winston and Clementine sailed with Lord Moyne on his yacht through the eastern Mediterranean. Churchill's paintings of temples and the battlements at Rhodes are likely to date from that time.

Fig 321 (C 95) opposite page top left
The Forum in Rome.

Fig 322 (C 97) opposite page top right
A ruined Greek temple.

Fig 323 (C 115) opposite page bottom
A little painting of the pillars within a ruined Greek temple.

1943 [Painting] After the Casablanca conference, Churchill insisted on taking Roosevelt to visit Marrakech. 'You cannot come all this way to North Africa without seeing Marrakesh ... I must be with you when you see the sun set on the Atlas Mountains', Churchill later recounted in his *History of the Second World War*. They stayed at the Villa Taylor, the house of the American Vice-Consul, from where, after Roosevelt's departure, Winston 'spent two days in correspondence with the War Cabinet ... and painting from the tower the only picture I ever attempted during the war.' He gave the completed painting, a view of the city and the Atlas Mountains, to the President as a memento. After the Cairo conference later in the year, Churchill took Roosevelt to see the Sphinx and the Pyramids.

Churchill's personal police bodyguard, Walter Thompson, had rejoined his staff in 1940. 'During the War,' he recalled, 'the Prime Minster took with him his painting box and a canvas on many of his journeys. He was a little optimistic ...' Of Churchill's single wartime picture at Marrakech, Mr Thompson wrote, 'No more suitable place for Mr Churchill to be at his painting could be imagined, for the whole scene was a riot of the colour from which he draws his inspiration.'

1944 [Background] Churchill's 70th year.
Rome captured. Allied forces landed in France and began to advance against German armies. Flying bombs and then rockets launched against Britain. Russian forces advanced on the Eastern Front. News of mass murders of Jews at Auschwitz. American forces regained the Philippines. Failure of Allied parachute attack on Arnhem. Churchill angered by Russian refusal to help Poles fighting German forces that were encircling Warsaw. Wearied by many flights to

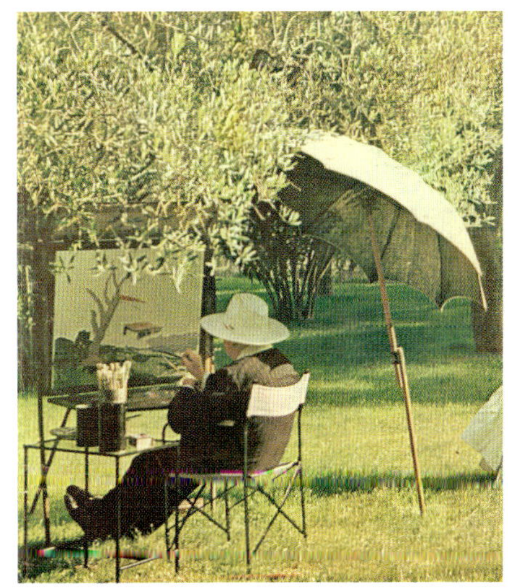

Sir Winston Churchill painting on the French Riviera in the 1950s.

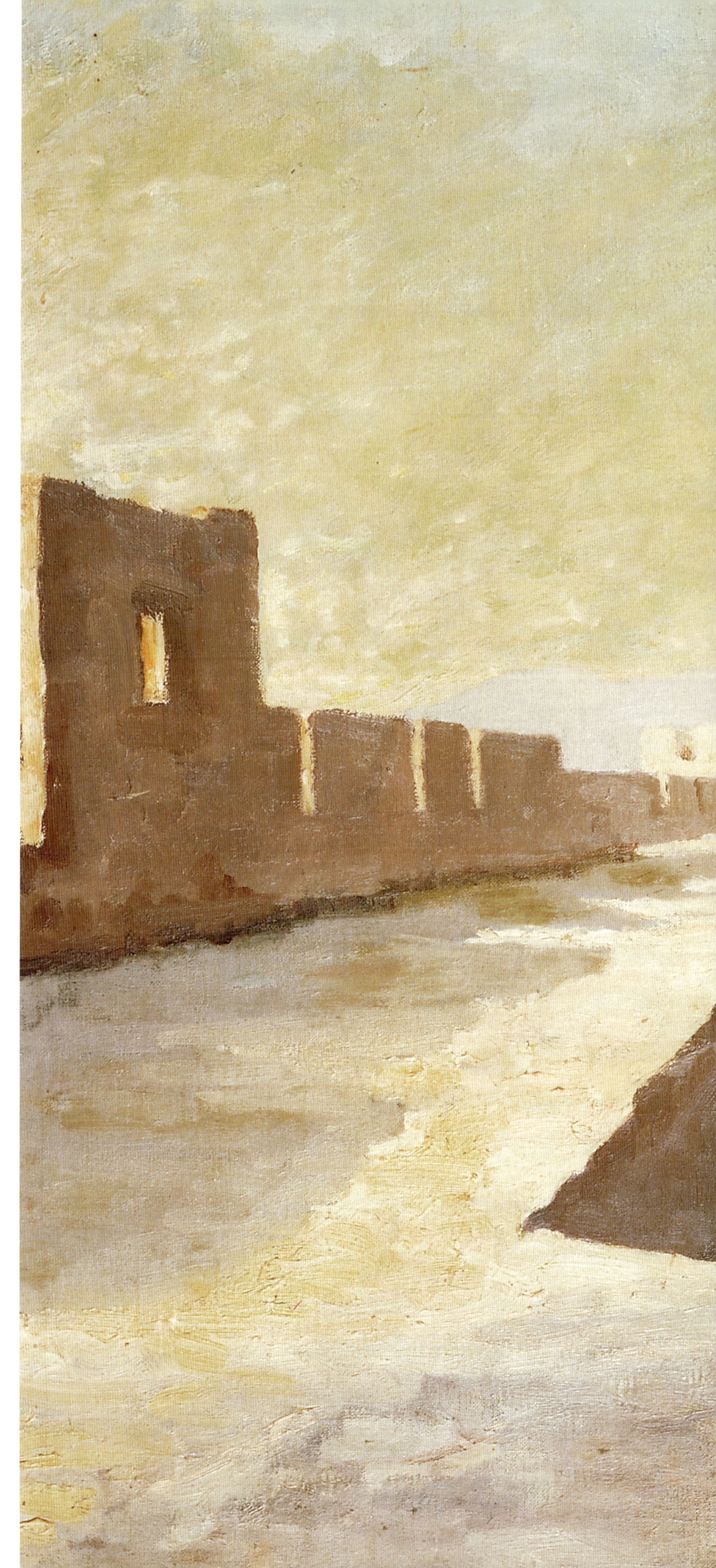

Fig 324 (C 216)
The Battlements at Rhodes. One of the largest of the Greek islands, it was the headquarters of the Knights Hospitallers of St John from the 14th to the 16th centuries. This picture may well have been painted by Churchill in his Studio after his return from his 1934 Mediterranean voyage with Lord Moyne.

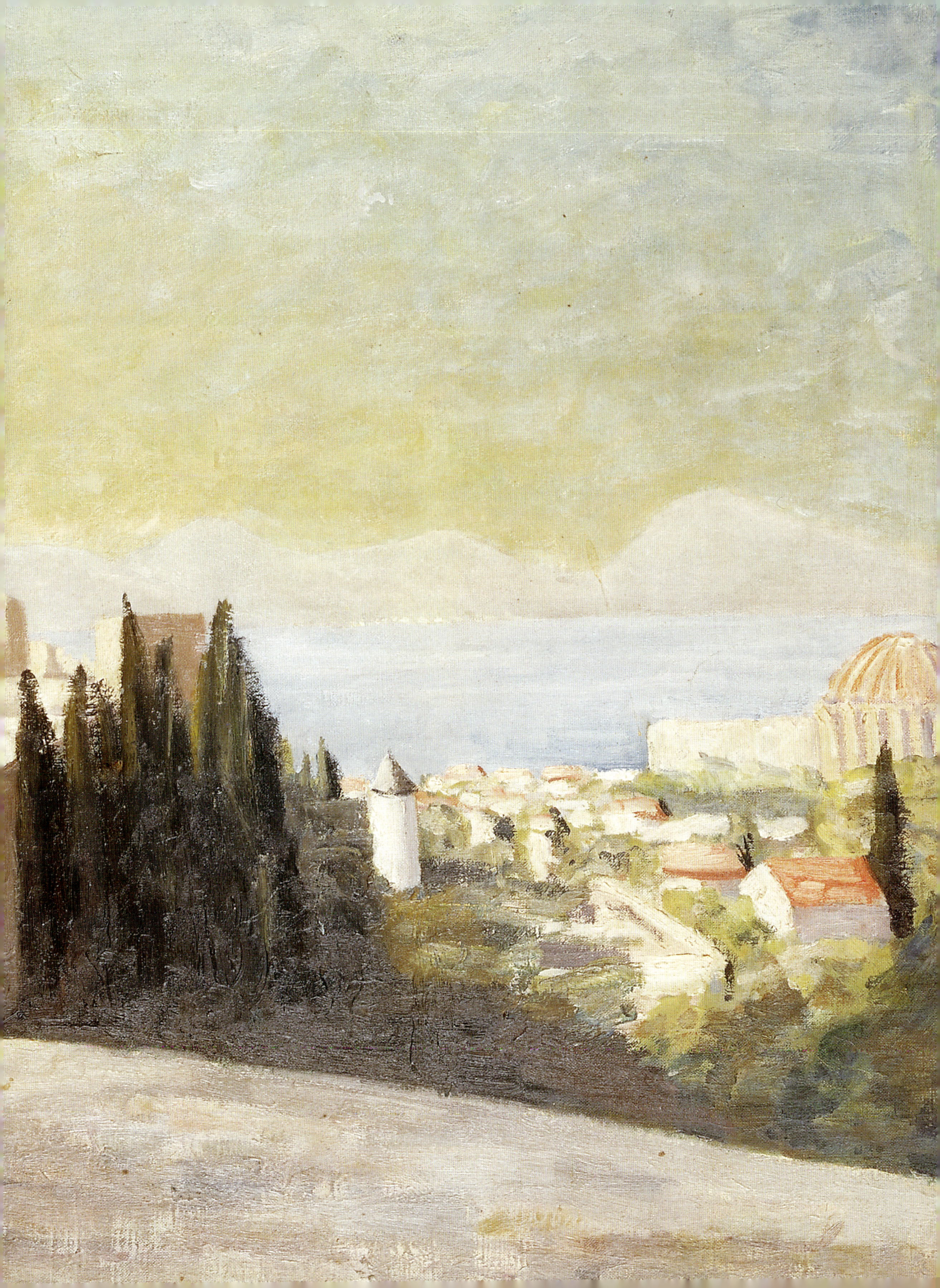

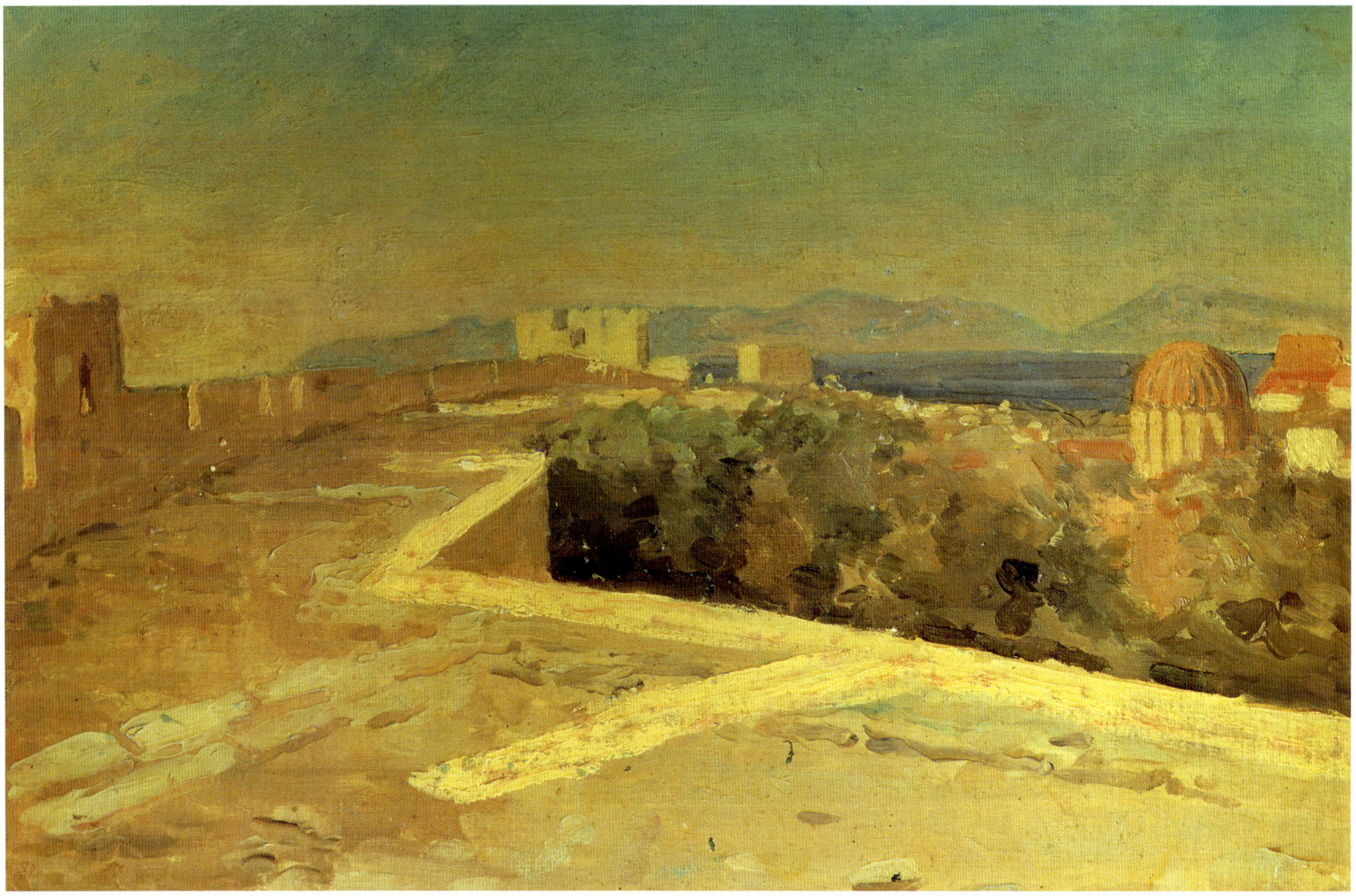

Fig 325 (C 212) above
Ramparts at Rhodes. This painting was given by Churchill to his grandson, Winston.

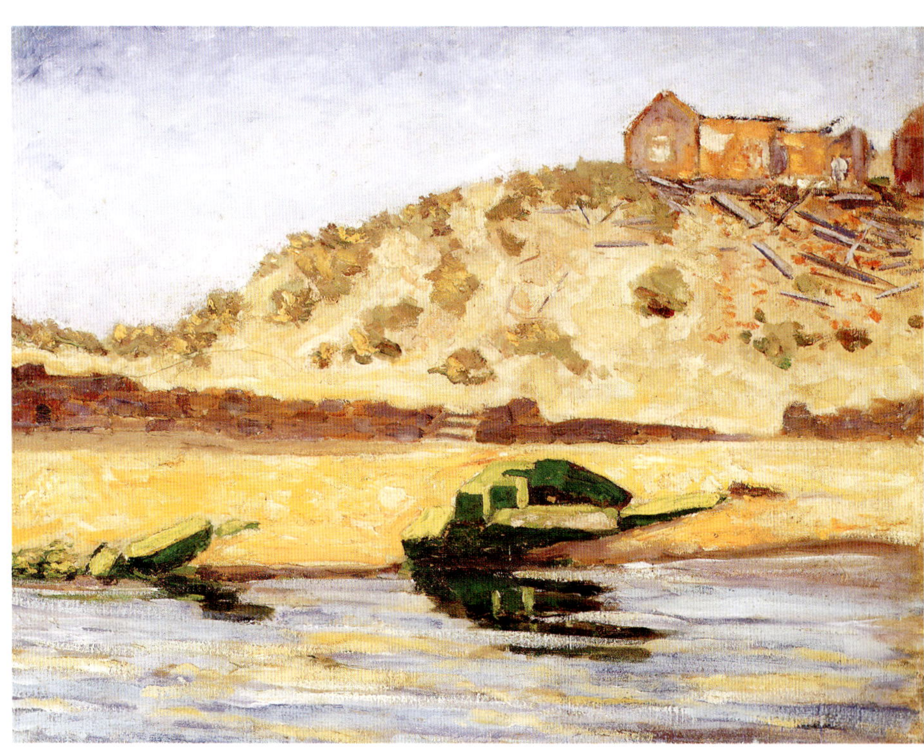

Fig 326 (C 88) right
An unidentified coast scene.

European theatres of war, Churchill was increasingly troubled by ill health. Flew to visit Roosevelt. Flew to Moscow to meet Stalin. Joined General de Gaulle in Paris to celebrate its liberation. National Health Service proposed in Britain.

1944 [Painting] Invited to have his portrait painted, Churchill replied, 'I'm afraid I can make no promise in wartime, and will hardly be worth painting unless the war stops soon.' Visited Capri and was entranced by the waters of the Blue Grotto.

1945 [Background] Conference with Roosevelt and Stalin at Yalta in the Crimea. Free elections promised by Russia for Poland. British and Canadian troops crossed into Germany. British and American bombing of Dresden. American forces crossed the Rhine. Roosevelt died and Truman became President of the United States. German armies in Italy surrendered. American and Russian forces met in Germany at River Elbe. Hitler committed suicide. Germany surrendered. Peace in Europe. Germany partitioned by the Allies.

Coalition government resigned in Britain: general election. Potsdam conference with Truman and Stalin during which the British election results showed Churchill to have been defeated. Labour government formed. American atom bomb dropped on Hiroshima. Russia declared war on Japan. Atom bomb dropped on Nagasaki. Japan surrendered. United Nations formed. Out of office, Churchill began to work on his war memoirs. Truman invited him to lecture at Westminster College, Fulton, Missouri. Churchill addressed the Belgian Parliament calling for a United States of Europe 'within which all its peoples may dwell together in prosperity, in justice and in peace'.

1945 [Painting] In the interval between polling day and the Potsdam conference with Truman and Stalin, during which the results of the election would be declared, Winston and Clementine took a short holiday in France, at the Château de Bordaberry, near St Jean-de-Luz, overlooking the Bay of Biscay. It was owned by a Canadian, Brigadier-General Brutinel, owner of the Château Margaux vineyard and a leading member of the Resistance during the late war. Other members of the party included Mr Bryce Nairn, British Consul in Bordeaux, and his wife Margaret, who had been a professional painter before her marriage. She encouraged Winston to take up his brush again and they painted together at St Jean-de-Luz, at Hendaye and on the river Nivelle.

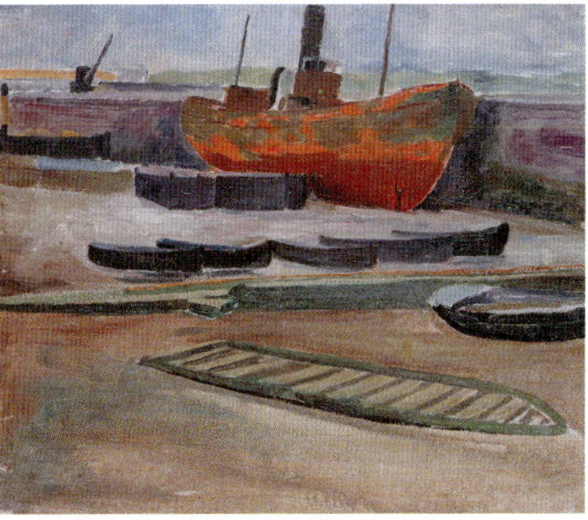

Fig 327 (C 307) above
A harbour scene somewhere in the South of France

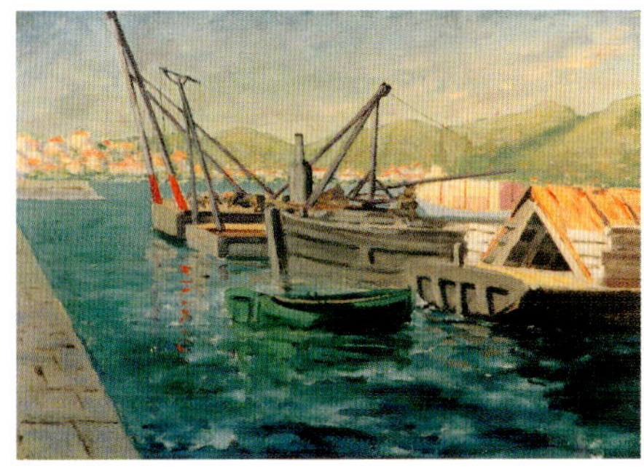

Fig 328 (C 303) above
A harbour somewhere in the South of France: Churchill was obviously fascinated by the cargo derricks. After Winston's death Clementine gave this painting to Lady Margaret Colville.

Illustration below
Winston Churchill and Doris Castlerosse on the rocks below Maxine Elliott's Chateau de l'Horizon. This photograph has been squared up for use in a painting. Detail, from the Studio archives at Chartwell.

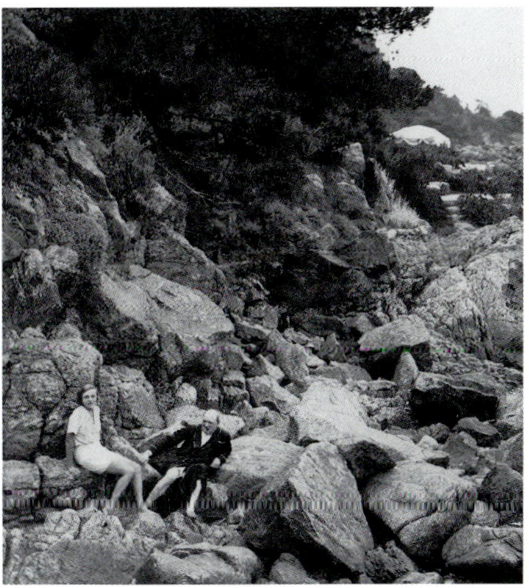

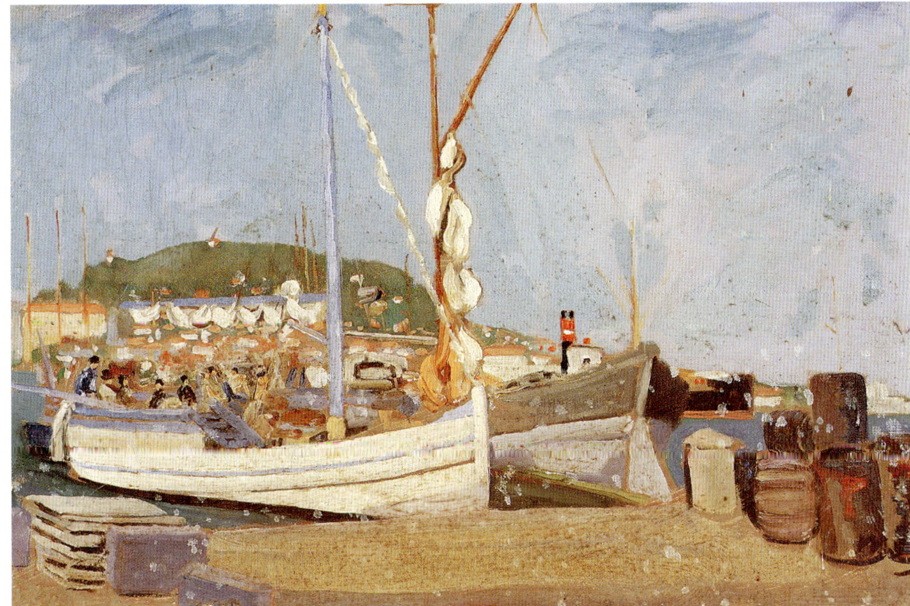

Fig 329 (C 131) left
A little painting of boats in a harbour somewhere in the South of France.

Fig 330 (C 312) right
St-Jean-Cap-Ferrat. This quiet Mediterranean resort on a peninsular, east of Nice was a favourite of the Churchills.

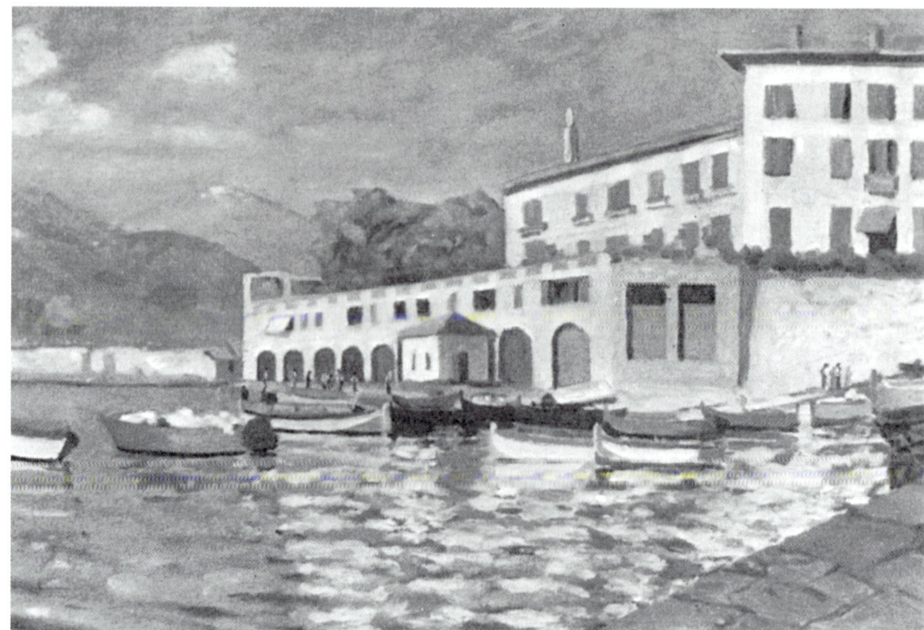

Fig 331 (C 313) right
St-Jean-Cap-Ferrat. Churchill gave this painting to his London neighbour Dr S. Leonard Simpson.

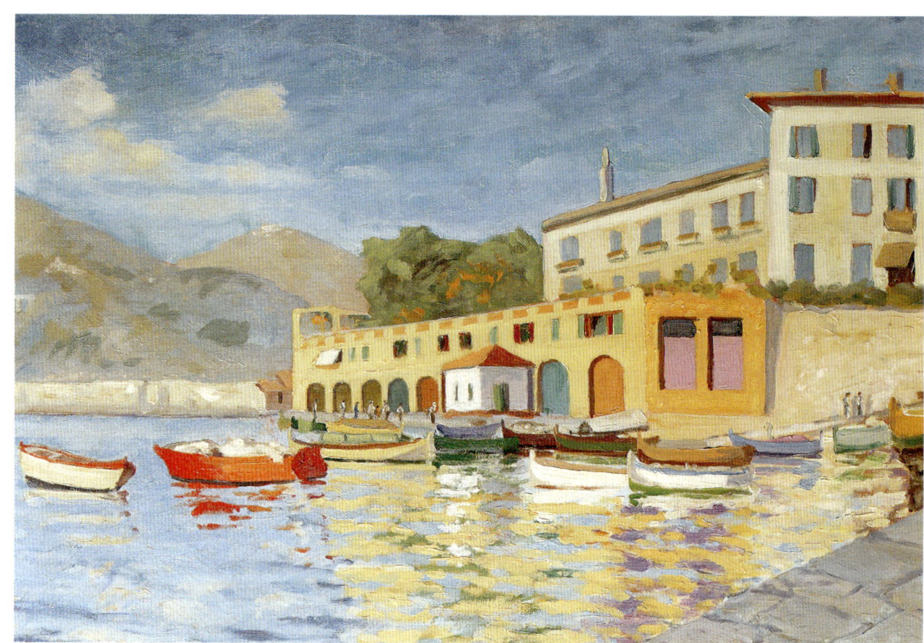

Fig 332 (C 81) right below
A little painting of Marrakech.

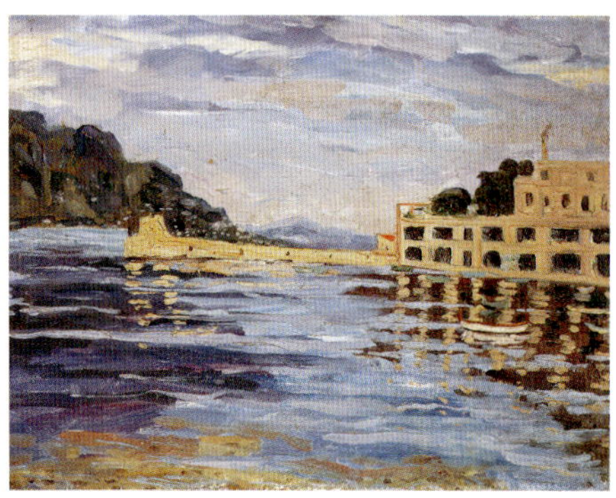

Fig 333 (C 314) above
The Club House and Jetty at St-Jean-Cap-Ferrat.

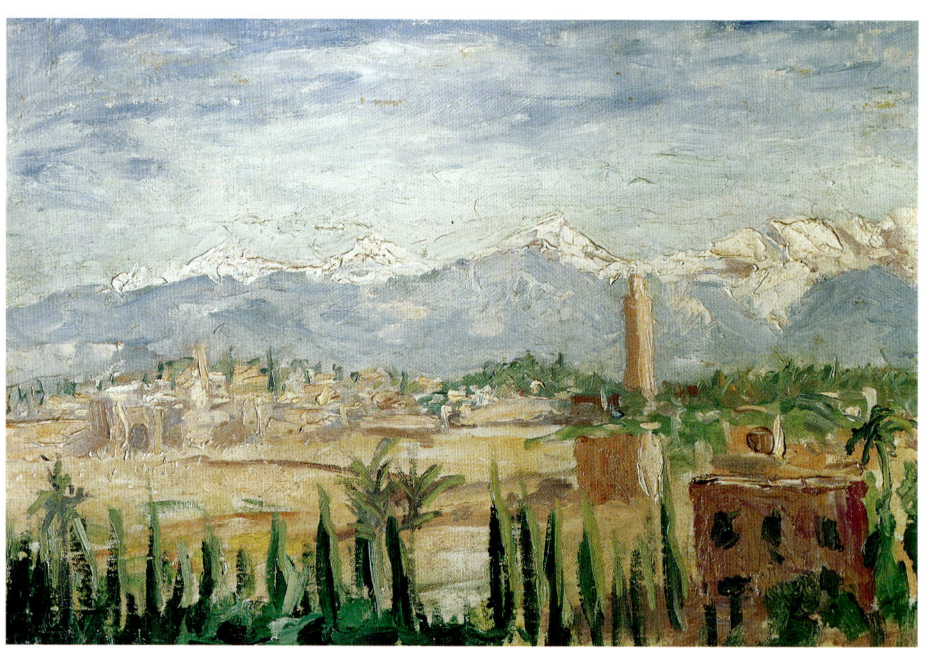

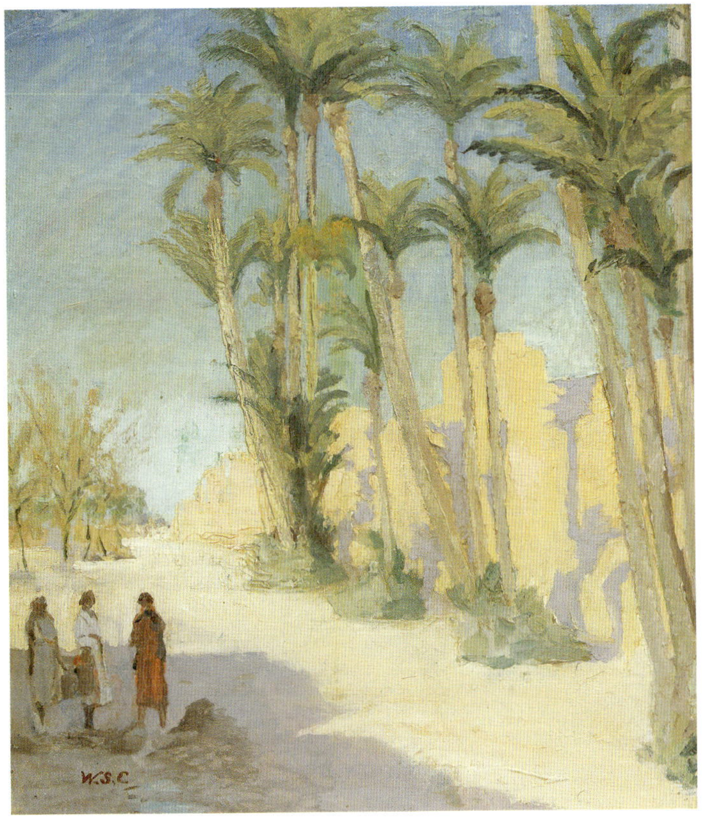

Fig 334 (C 124) left
This painting of Marrakech was a gift by Churchill to the Hudson's Bay Company, in recognition of his appointment in 1956 as the first 'Grand Seigneur of the Company of Adventurers of England Trading Into Hudson Bay.'

In the winter of 1936 Churchill travelled for the first time to Morocco in North Africa to where he had been recommended by Sir John Lavery and other artist friends.
He was clearly fascinated by Marrakech (the spelling he preferred) and its people and gathered a large number of photographs on this and subsequent visits, which still remain in the Studio archives at Chartwell. All three of these pictures showing a group of palm trees in Marrakech can be related directly to photographs (see example below) found in the Studio archives at Chartwell.

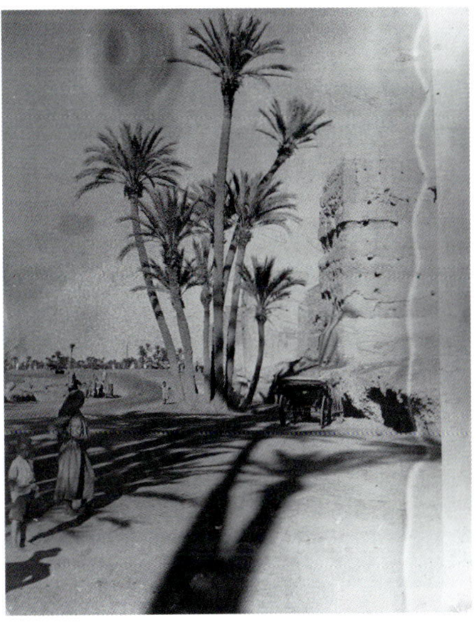

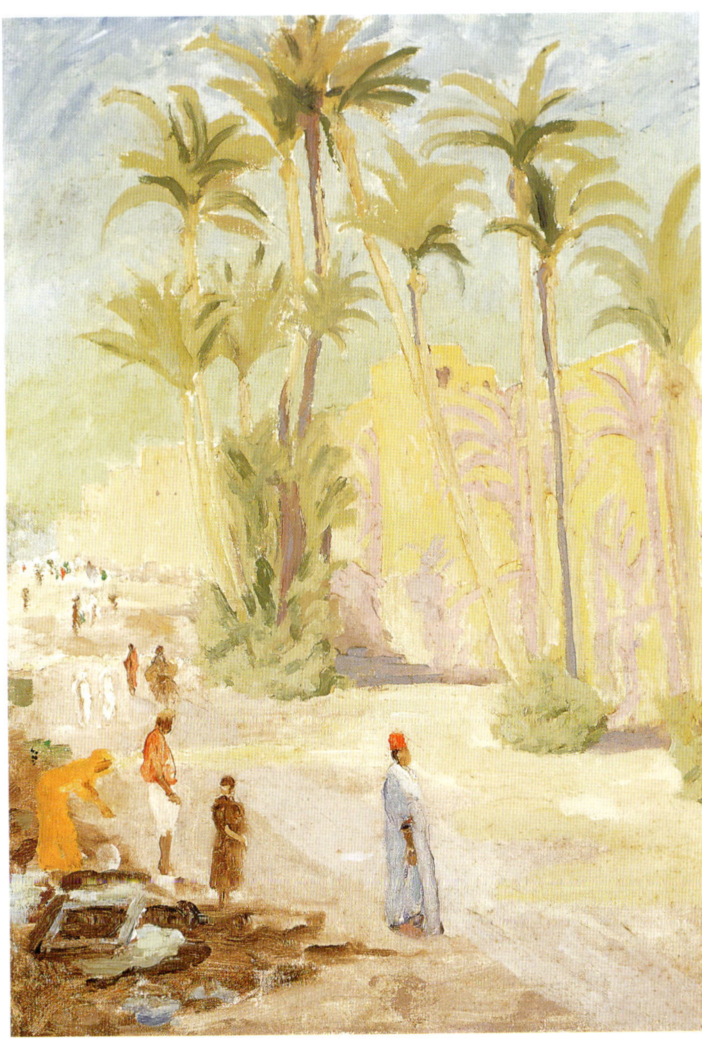

Fig 335 (C 128) left
Palm trees in Marrakech.

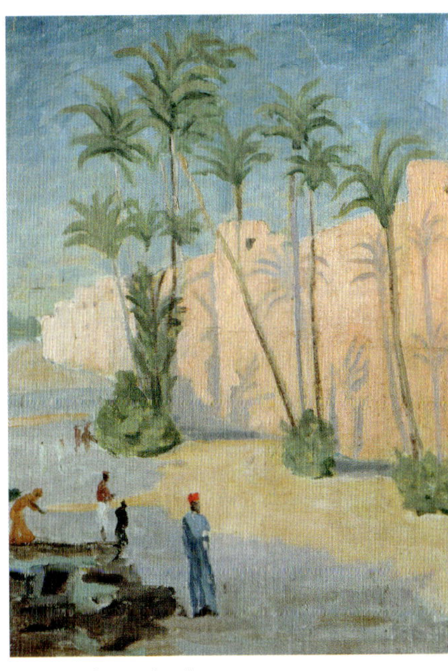

Fig 336 (C 127) above
A little painting of palm trees.

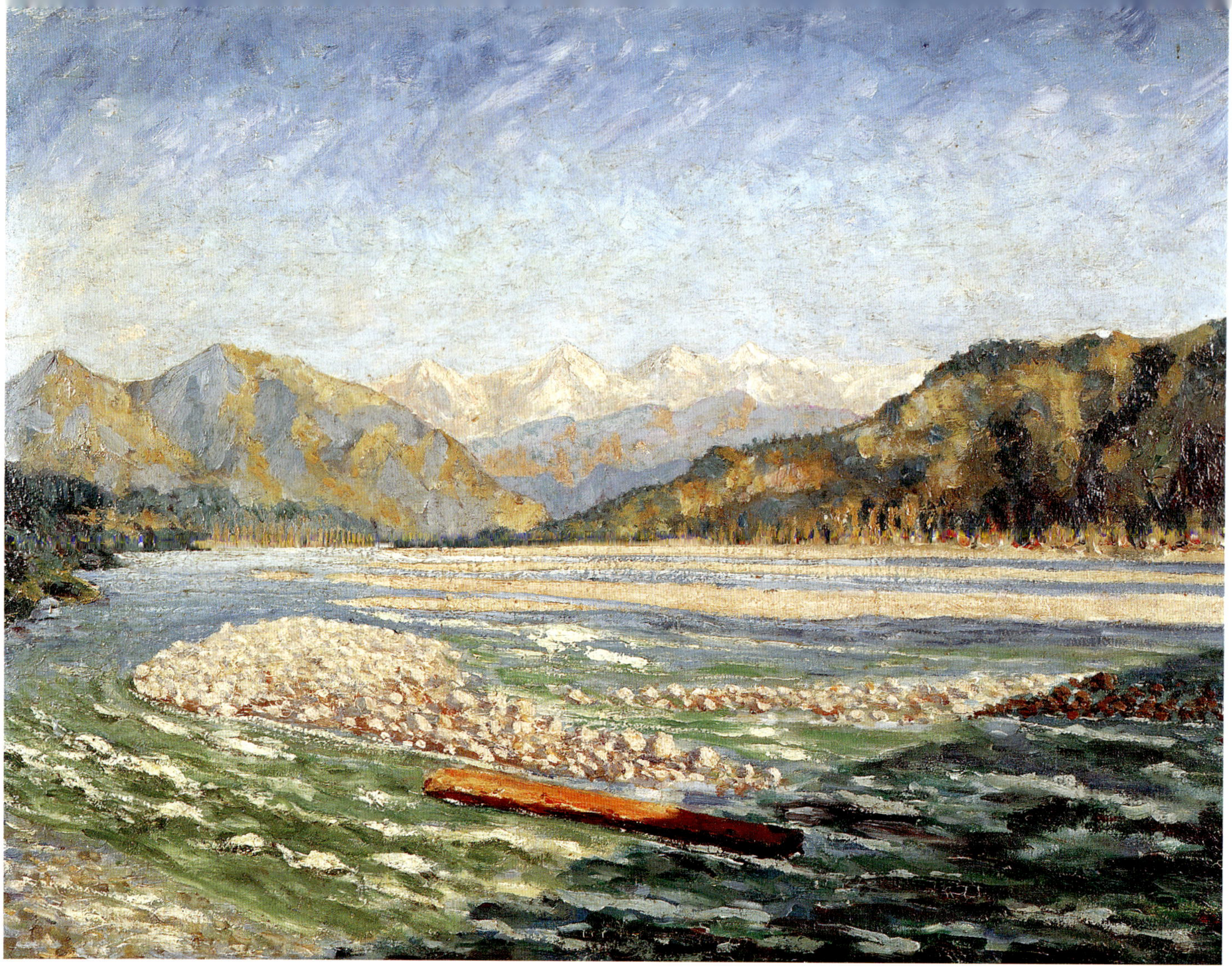

Fig 337 (C 196) above
The Valley of the Ourika, in the desert near Marrakech. This painting formerly belonged to Clementine Churchill.

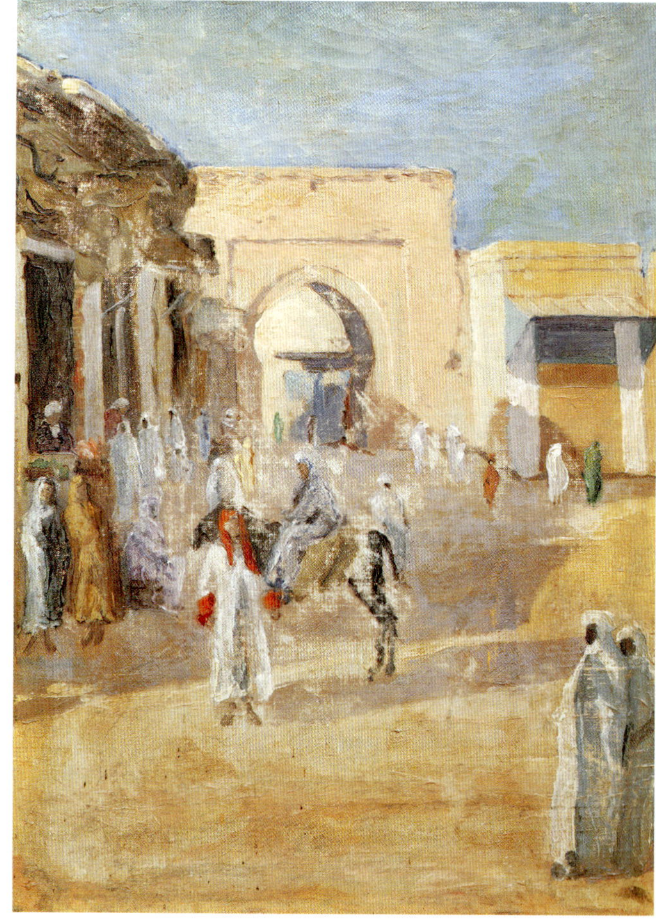

Fig 338 (C 217) right
A little sketch probably in the souk (the market) in Marrakech, perhaps as early as the winter of 1935/6.

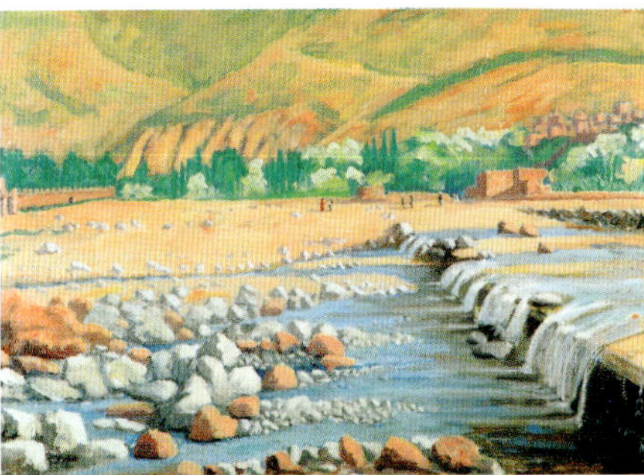

Fig 339 (C 213) above
Churchill subsequently gave this painting of a scene near Marrakech to Field Marshal Viscount Montgomery of Alamein.

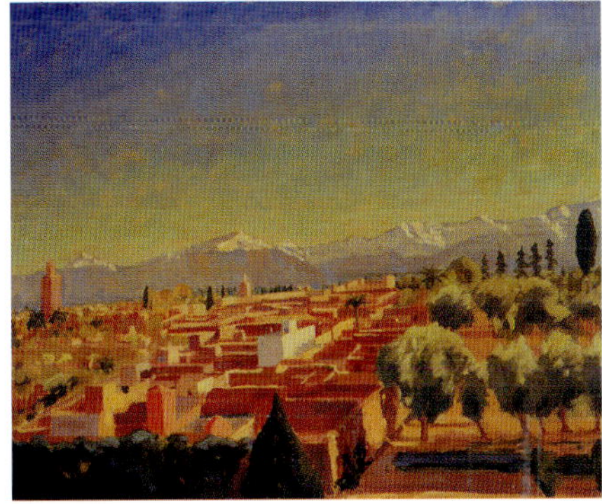

Fig 340 (C 214) above
Churchill gave this painting of Marrakech to former Prime Minister David, later Earl, Lloyd George, when they were both staying there at the Mamounia Hotel in 1936.

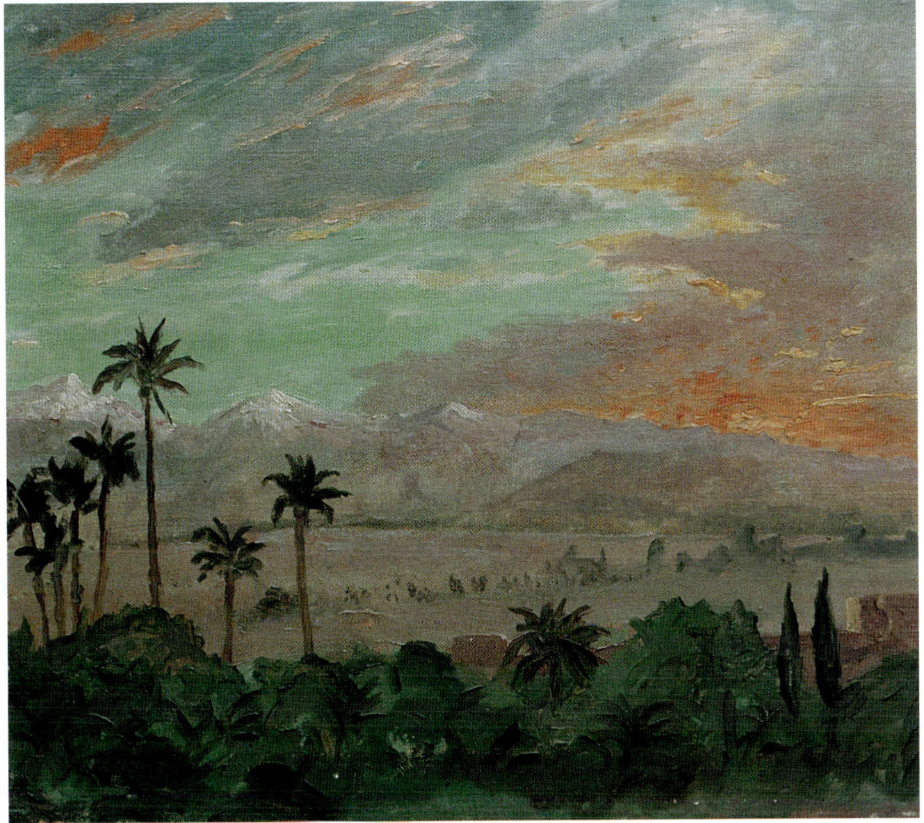

Fig 341 (C 211) above left
Sunset over the Atlas Mountains. This spectacular scene so attracted Churchill that he insisted on bringing President Roosevelt to witness it after the Casablanca Conference in 1943.

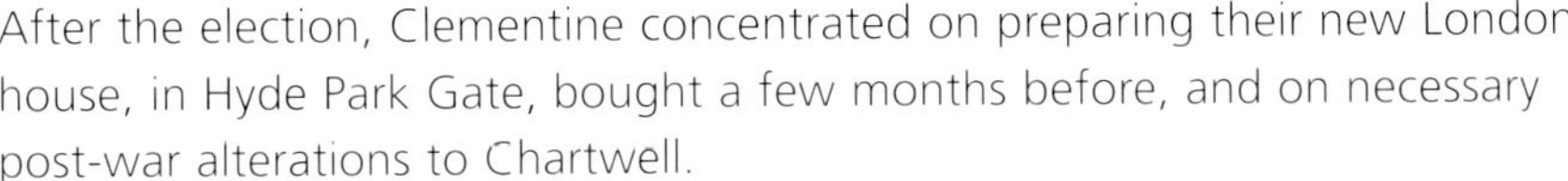

After the election, Clementine concentrated on preparing their new London house, in Hyde Park Gate, bought a few months before, and on necessary post-war alterations to Chartwell.

Churchill's family decided he needed a long painting holiday. Field Marshal Alexander, Supreme Allied Commander for the Mediterranean, offered Winston his former wartime headquarters, the Villa delle Rose on the shores of Lake Como. 'I purposely avoided interfering with his holiday,' Alexander wrote later, 'though I did stay with him for just one week-end, when we spent the Sunday painting. At one point [Churchill] turned to me and said, "You know, when I was turned out of office, I felt it to be a very hard thing after all I had done." Then with a smile, and waving his hand to the scene he was painting, he added, "But life has its compensations, you know - if I was still in office I wouldn't be here to enjoy this lovely climate and marvellous landscape."'

Churchill's old friend and mentor Charles Montag came down from Paris to stay at the Villa and paint. Sarah Churchill was of the party and later recalled, 'The days are filled with painting and picnics ... There were some perfectly frightful pictures in the house, and one above all he sat and stared at every evening.' Eventually, and despite Montag's and Sarah's protestations, her father decided to repaint the offending picture. The result 'was breathtaking, it was enchanting, it was lovely. The whole thing accomplished and back in its frame and back on the wall inside half an hour.' The next morning, Churchill decided to undo what he described as his 'act of artistic rape' and the picture 'was once more carried upstairs to the bathroom ... which was being used as a studio ... to have its face washed'.

During this time Churchill also painted on Lake Lugano. Churchill and his party returned home by car along the Italian and French Rivieras. Their first stop was at Villa Pirelli, east of Genoa. Near here at Recco, Churchill began to paint a scene of a bombed viaduct and houses but his tactless action attracted a hostile crowd.

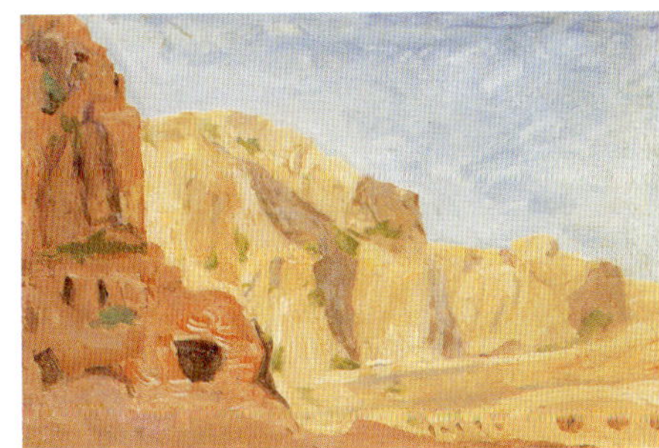

Fig 342 (C 83) above
The entrance to the Gorge at Todhra, some distance east of Marrakech. This painting formerly belonged to Clementine Churchill.

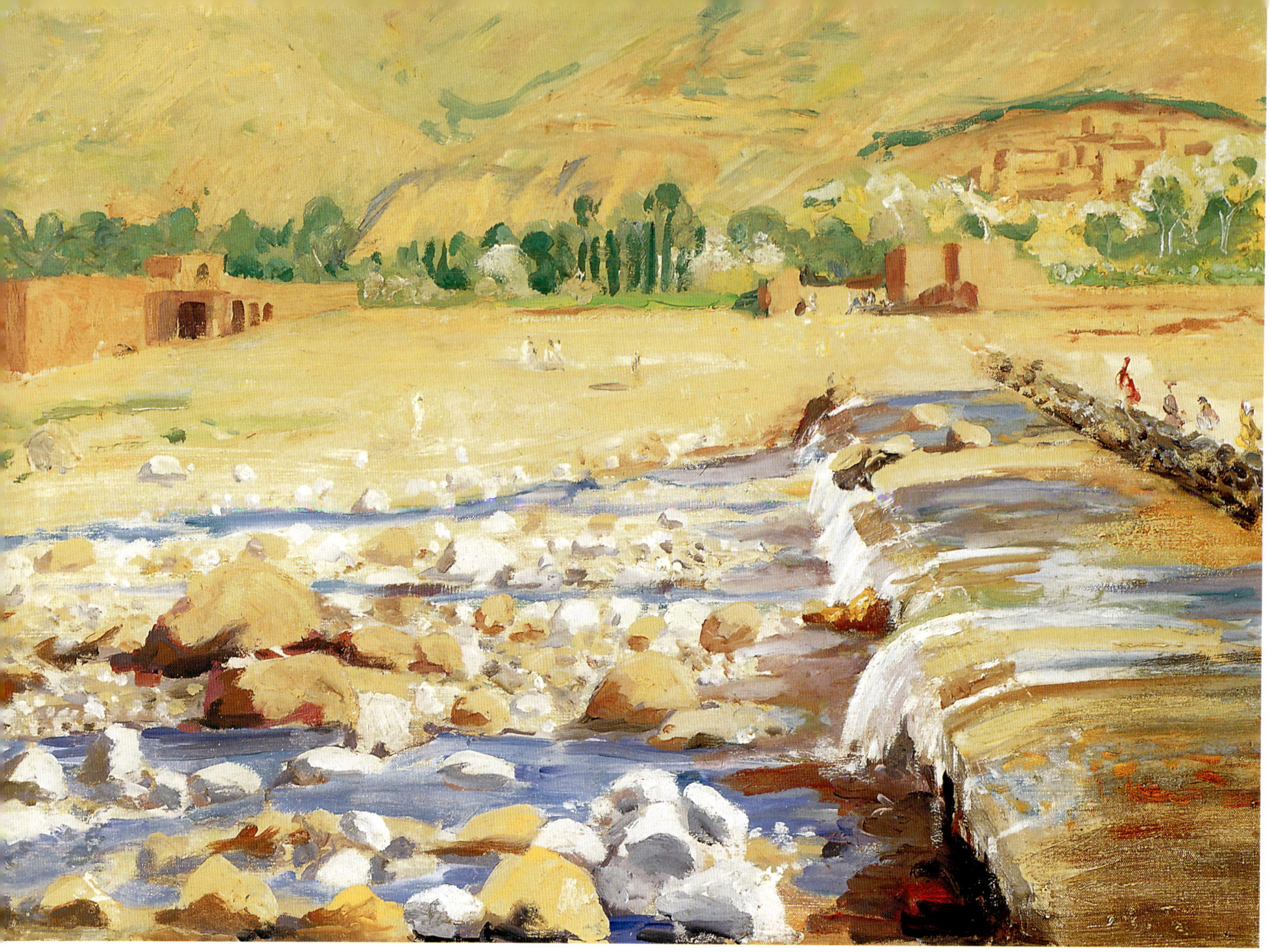

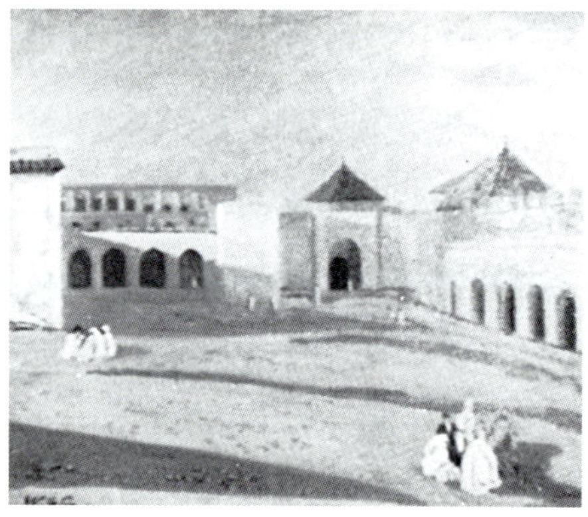

Over the border in France he revisited pre-war haunts at Monte Carlo and Antibes where he stayed in a villa loaned him by General Eisenhower. At Cap Martin he went again to the olive grove at La Dragonnière. He returned to London having painted 15 pictures in 25 days of sunshine. Churchill went to Paris where he was taken round the Louvre by its director. The wife of the British Ambassador, Lady Diana Cooper, wrote to a friend that Churchill 'revelled in the pictures, touching their surfaces gently, with his delicate hand'.

1946 [Background] The King awarded Churchill the Order of Merit in the New Year's Honours List. Churchill visited the United States with Clementine and at Miami Beach discussed with his agent Emery Reves the future international circulation and translation of his war memoirs. In his speech at Fulton, Churchill spoke of the descent of an Iron Curtain across the continent of Europe and of the need of a settlement with Russia, which, he was convinced, did not want war so much as 'the fruits of war'. Speaking later at the University of Zurich, he declared that the first step in the re-creation of the European family must be a partnership between France and Germany. Bank of England, civil aviation and coal industry nationalized in Britain.

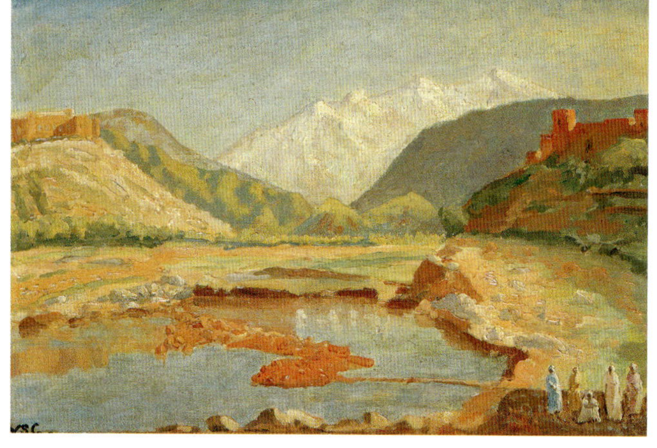

Churchill became worried that his income would not be sufficient to maintain Chartwell, and his friend Lord Camrose proposed that he and a group of wealthy individuals buy it and present it to the National Trust on condition that Churchill and his wife could live there for their lifetimes. Churchill established a team of researchers and secretaries to help him with his war memoirs.

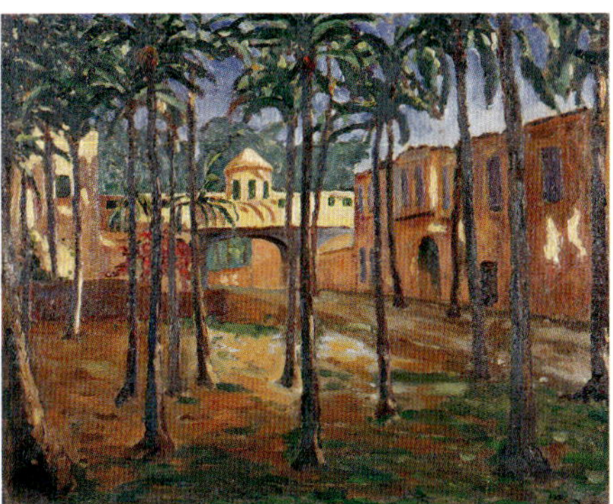

Fig 343 (C 273) above
An unidentified town in North Africa.

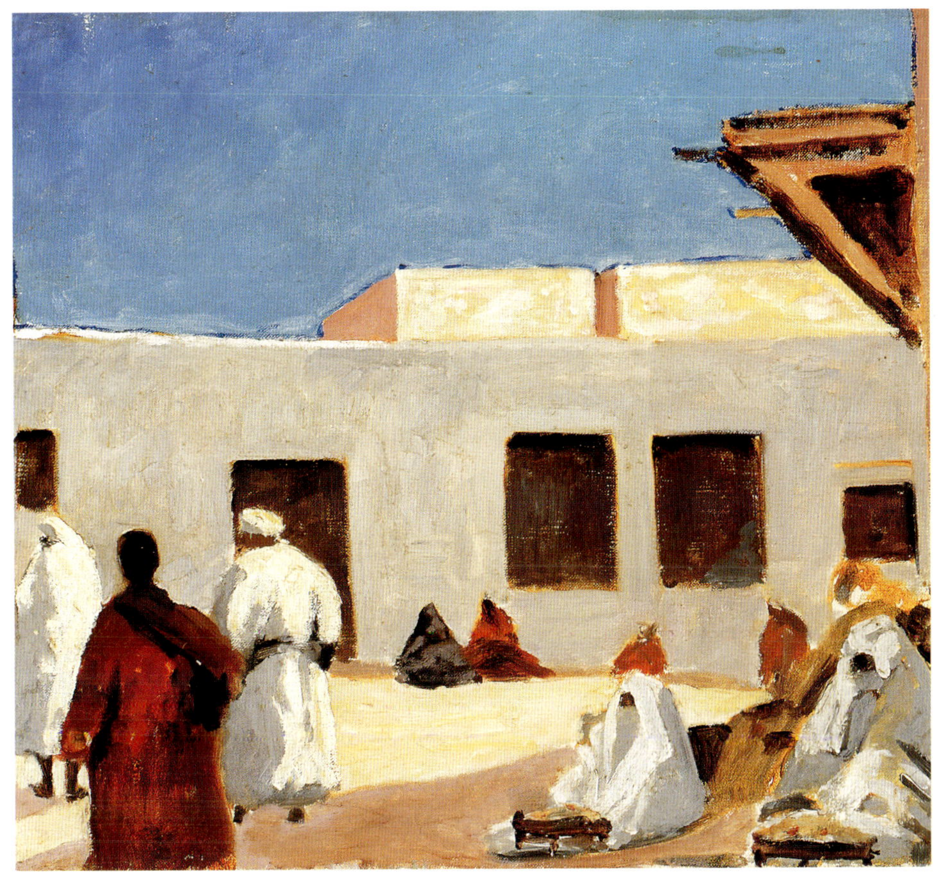

Fig 344 (C 219) left
A scene in Marrakech.

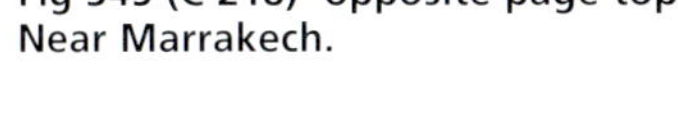

Fig 345 (C 218) opposite page top
Near Marrakech.

Fig 346 (C 220) opposite page centre
In Marrakech.

Fig 347 (C 197) opposite page below
The Ourika Vallery near Marrakech with the Atlas Mountains in the background. Clementine Churchill gave this painting to her cousin Sylvia Henley.

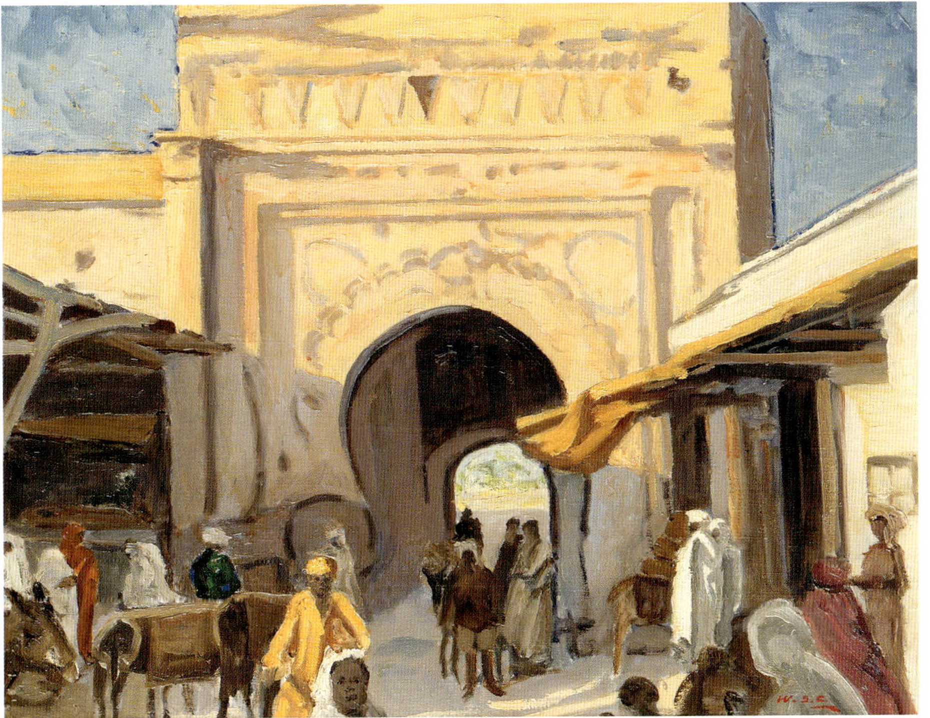

Fig 348 (C 224) left
A busy scene in front of one of the Gates in Marrakech.

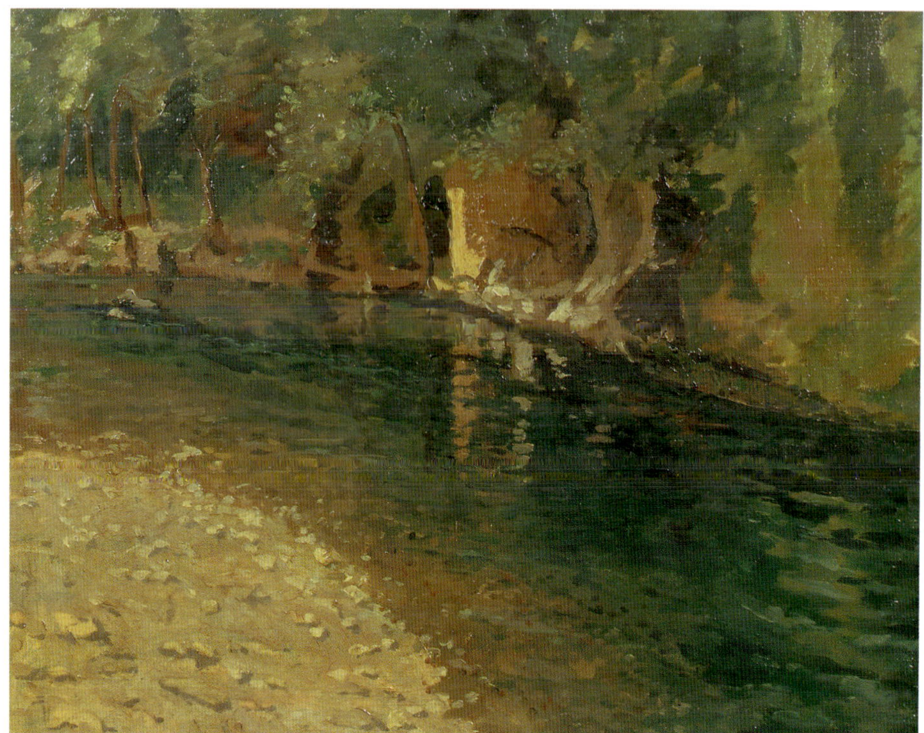

Fig 349 (C 352) above
The Loup River in the Alpes Maritimes. The painting was one of two successfully entered by Churchill under the pseudonym of David Winter for the Royal Academy's Summer Exhibition in 1947. In 1955 Churchill presented it to the Tate Gallery at the request of the Trustees.

1946 [Painting] In January colour reproductions of Churchill's paintings appeared in *LIFE Magazine* in the United States. This had been arranged by Walter Graebner, the London representative of Time-Life, who earlier approached Churchill about writing a series of three articles for which the editors were offering $75,000. Churchill declined: 'That was a very good offer you made me - very flattering – It's the best offer I've ever had ... But I'm not in a position to write anything now ... ' Instead Churchill pointed to a series of pictures displayed on the chairs and sofas in the room: 'I've been on holiday in Italy and the South of France ... and while there made these paintings ... Do you think your people might like to publish them - that is take them in place of one of the articles?' Walter Graebner 'congratulated him on the excellence of his pictures, expressing surprise that he could find the time to take up painting on top of all his other work. Behind an enormous grin [Churchill] murmured, "Genius has many outlets."'

Winston and Clementine visited the United States and went to Miami Beach to stay with a wartime Canadian friend, Colonel Frank Clarke. They then visited Jacques and Consuelo Balsan who had moved to the United States from France. Churchill painted in Miami and at Havana: it was his first visit to Cuba since 1895.

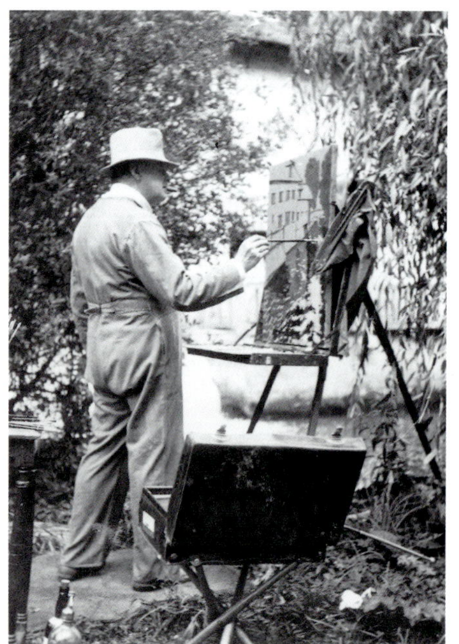

Winston Churchill painting, in 1939, the Mill at the Chateau St-Georges-Motel in Normandy - the home of Consuelo and Jacques Balsan.

In the summer the Churchills became friends with Sir Oswald Birley and his wife, Rhoda; Birley had been commissioned to paint Churchill's portrait by the Speaker of the House of Commons. Birley reminded Churchill that he had never claimed his prize for winning the 1925 painting competition - a picture by Oswald Birley - and suggested that he paint one of his youngest daughter, Mary.

In August a group of Swiss individuals offered Churchill a house for a holiday on Lac Léman, the Villa Choisi, owned by a banker, M. Alfred Kern. During this time he experimented in tempera and with working on very large canvases. Churchill presented Mme Kern with a still life of fruit on a silver dish, painted on a wet day.

In November Churchill paid an official visit to Belgium. At Dinant he painted the Meuse on a large canvas and in Bruges painted in the garden of a convent, the Béguinage.

1947 [Background] India partitioned into two nations. Electricity supply, railways, canals and road transport nationalized in Britain. Marshall Plan provided US aid for the post-war recovery of Europe. Communist government in Poland.

1947 [Painting] The President of the Royal Academy, Sir Alfred Munnings, tried to persuade Churchill to enter some of his paintings for the Academy's Summer Exhibition. 'Unless you treat me as an outsider and put my work in with the rest ... I do not wish to send,' Winston asserted. 'I don't trust you a yard, Alfred. Whatever happens you'll pass them because they are mine.' Churchill finally agreed but only under the pseudonym David Winter. His old friend Edward Marsh helped him select the pictures, finding Churchill to be 'very choosy and resolute' and willing to send forward only two: 'Winter Sunshine' and 'The Loup River, Alpes-Maritimes'. Both were accepted and hung.

In the winter Churchill returned to the sunshine of Marrakech to work on his war memoirs and to paint - from the balcony of his hotel, the Mamounia and at the Ouriki gorge.

1948 [Background] Communist coup in Czechoslovakia. Gandhi assassinated in India. Communist forces invaded China. Communist republic in North Korea. Terrorism in Malaya. Russian blockade of West Berlin: Allied airlift. British health service nationalized. *LIFE Magazine* and *The Daily Telegraph* began to serialize Churchill's war memoirs, attracting a huge public readership. Churchill spoke at the inaugural meeting of the Congress of Europe and later supported the French proposal for a European assembly. In Parliament he demanded that Britain recognize the new state of Israel. The first volume of Churchill's *History of the Second World War* was published.

1948 [Painting] In his will, General Sir Ian Hamilton left his old friend Churchill a figure of a black buddha. Churchill painted the buddha with a scarlet hippeastrum, which had been a get-well present from Princess Marina, Duchess of Kent, after he caught bronchitis in Marrakech.

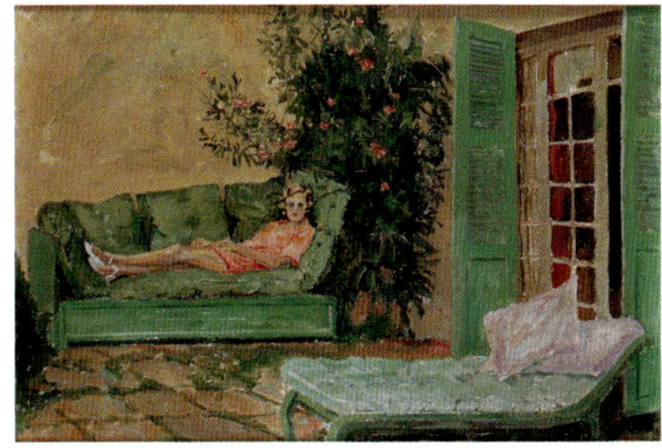

Fig 350 (C 158) above
Viscountess Castlerosse on the Terrace at the Chateau de l'Horizon.

The Chateau de l'Horizon was built in the early 1930s at Golfe Juan near Cannes, by the actress Maxine Elliott, whom the Churchills had known for many years. She was a famous hostess and her visitors included many celebrated socialites of the day such as Doris Castlerosse. Clementine didn't enjoy this company so Winston would go there to paint on his own. He was the only one of Maxine's guests able to come and go as he pleased and on one such venture he discovered the attractions of the Loup River.

Illustration below
The painting above is based on this photograph from the Studio archives at Chartwell.

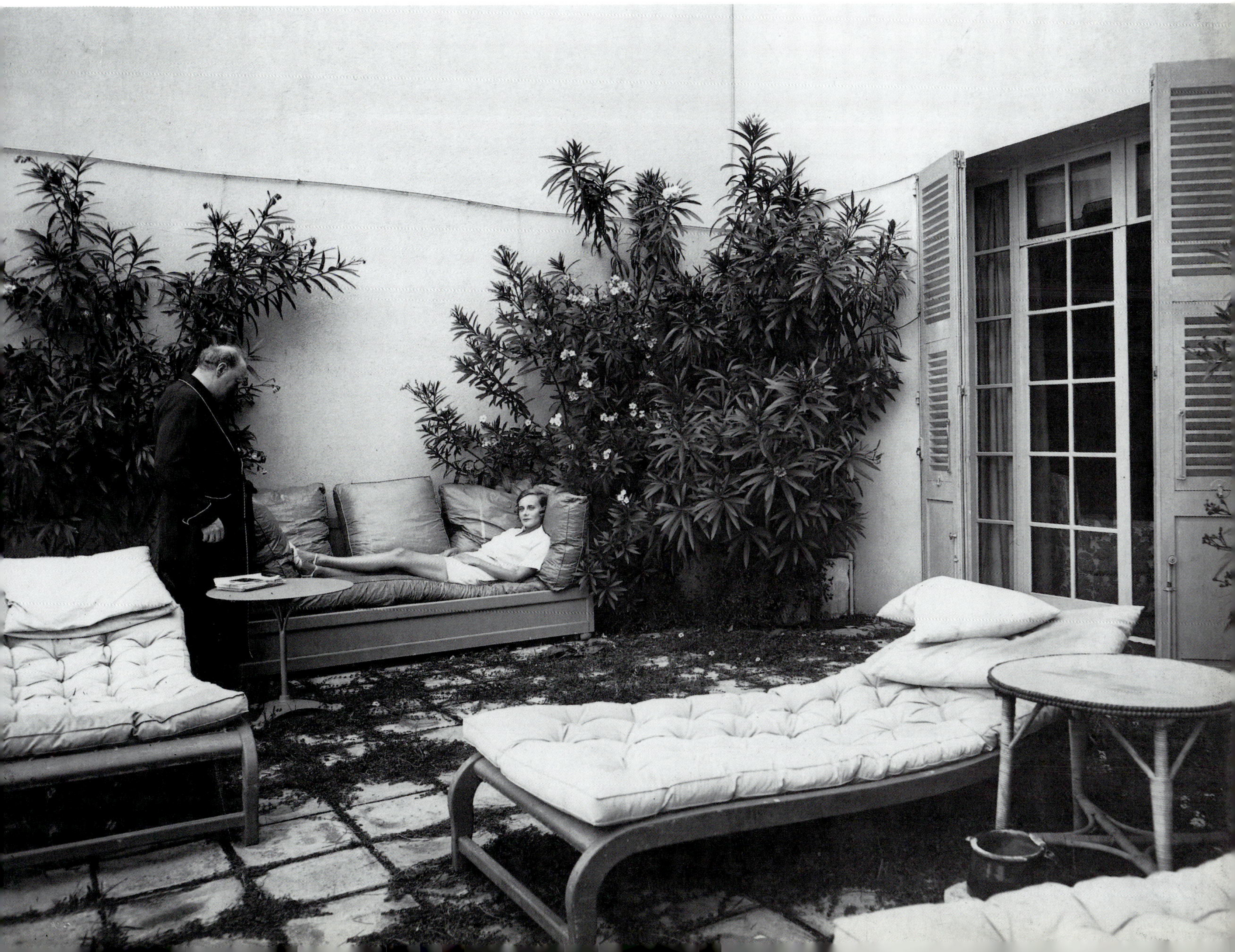

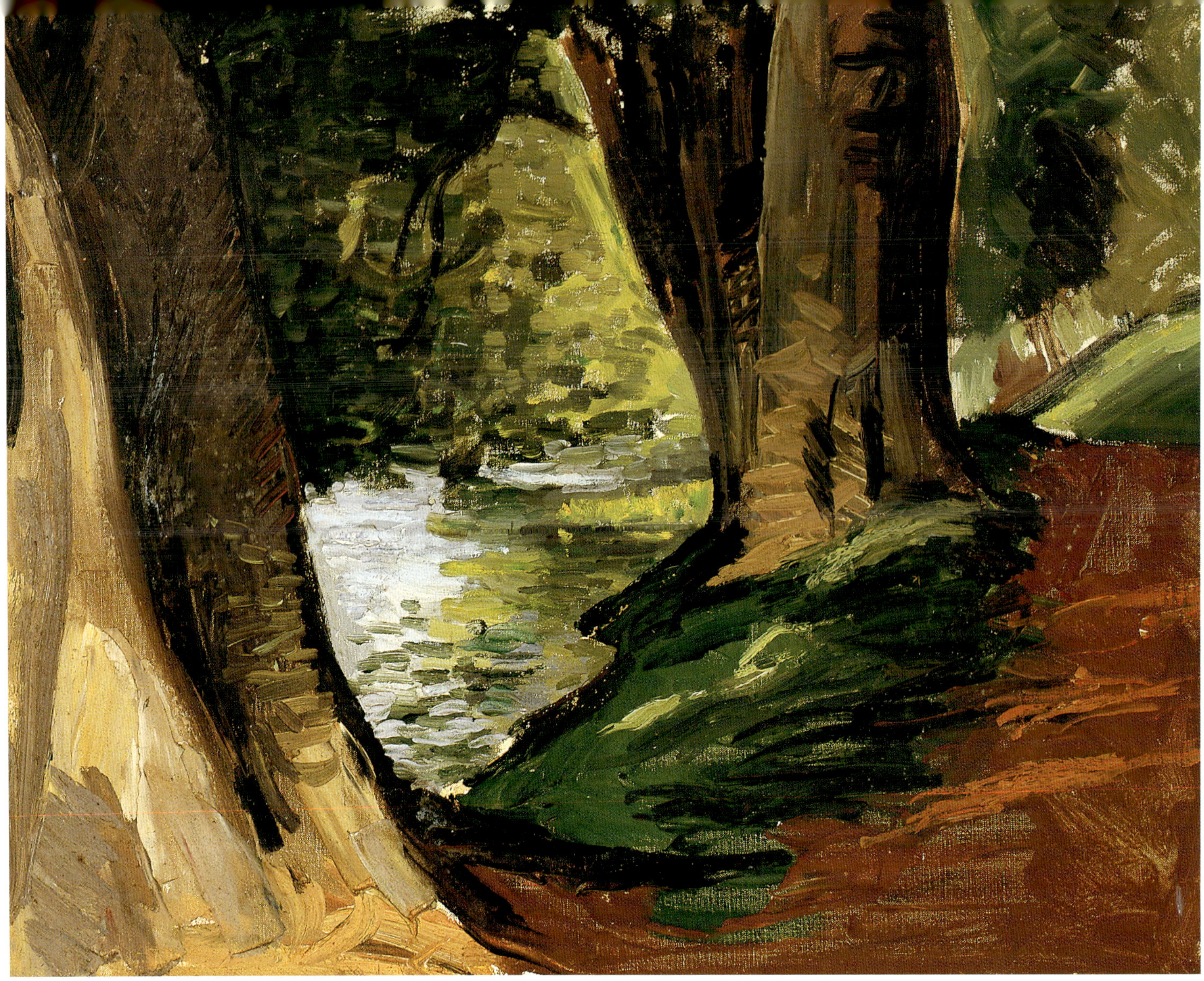

Fig 351 (C 360) above
As this and the facing illustration (C 363) clearly show, Churchill felt relaxed and confident enough when painting on the Loup to experiment with different techniques.

Churchill's essays forming *'Painting as a Pastime'* were first published in book form and swiftly reprinted. Overseas editions appeared in many countries including the United States, Finland, France, Germany, Holland, Italy and Japan.

The English art critic Eric Newton reviewed 'Painting as a Pastime' for the *New York Times Magazine.* Praising Churchill's combination of self-confidence and modesty and admitting that such a notice 'is not a proper place for an art critic's estimate of what he has painted', Newton went on to discuss the paintings reproduced in the book: 'each one of the plates is solid proof that every word in the essay is serious. No one who was not in furious earnest could paint as competently as this.'

A standard work on The Goldfish was published with technical illustrations. The publisher, Mr W. S. Shears, could find no 'worthy modern representation of the goldfish in Western European painting - even with the help of Sir Robert Witt' and asked permission to include Churchill's 'The Goldfish Pool, Chartwell'. Permission was readily granted.

Churchill began to receive many requests from Britain and overseas to loan pictures for exhibition or to reproduce his paintings, including one for decorating silk scarves. These were generally refused.

Count Michael de la Bedoyere sent a copy of his review of *'Painting as a Pastime'* with the recommendation that Churchill might like to try working in pastel. Churchill's secretary replied, 'He wonders whether your attention has been drawn

Fig 352 (C 368) below
A Pool on the Loup River.

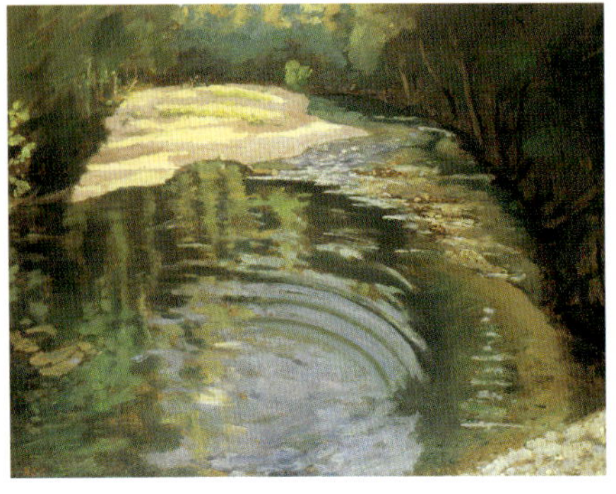

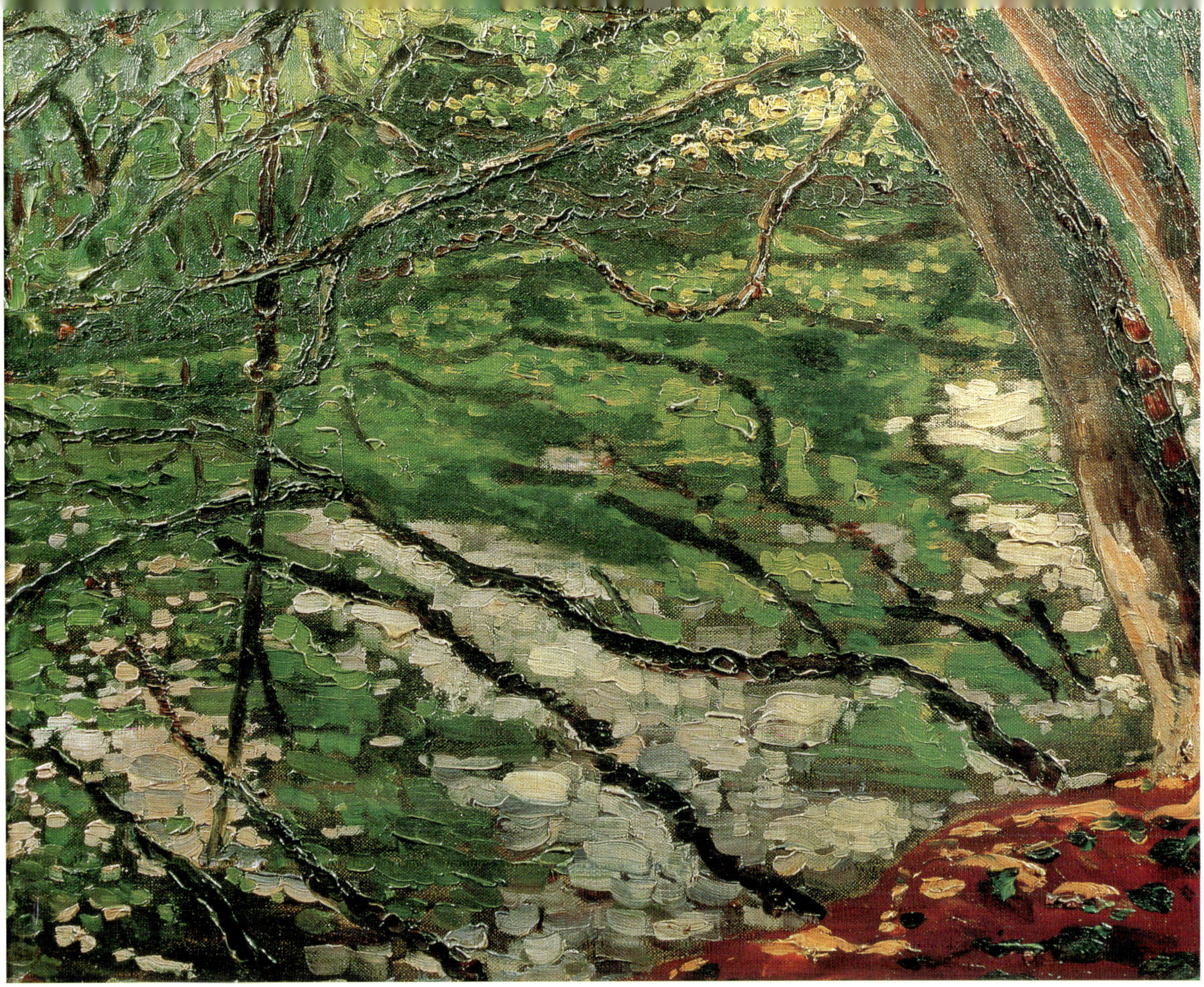

Fig 353 (C 363) above
Another successful experiment when painting on the River Loup. (See C 360)

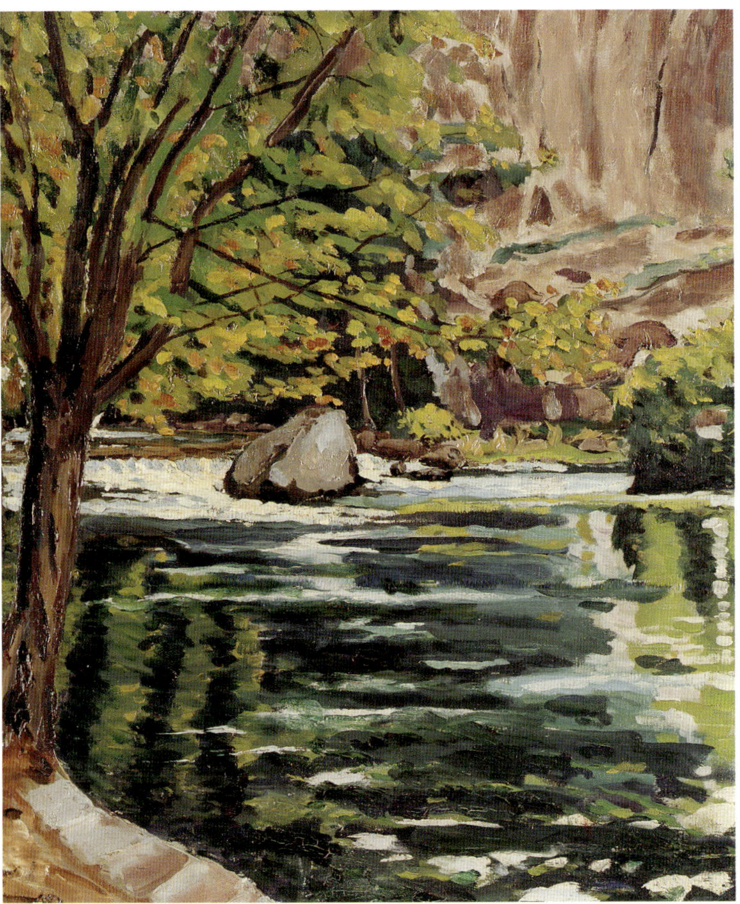

Fig 354 (C 361) left
Scene on the Loup River.

Fig 355 (C 152) below
Lady Castlerosse.

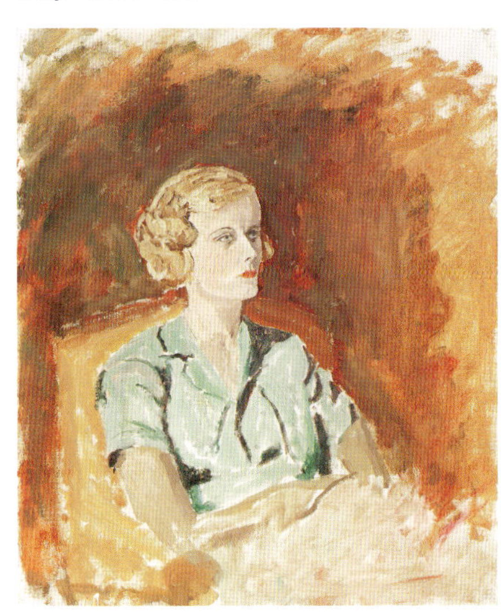

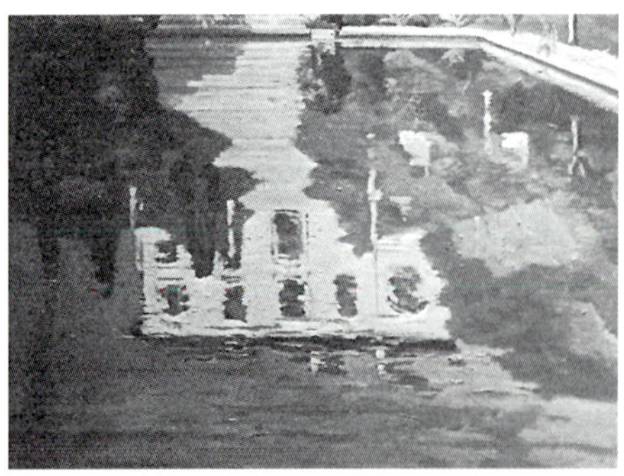

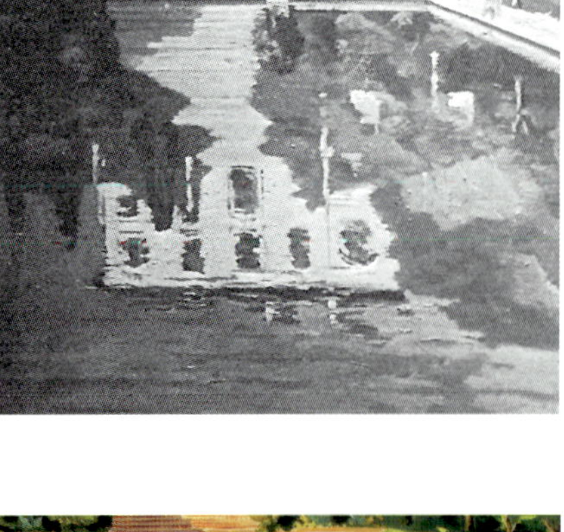

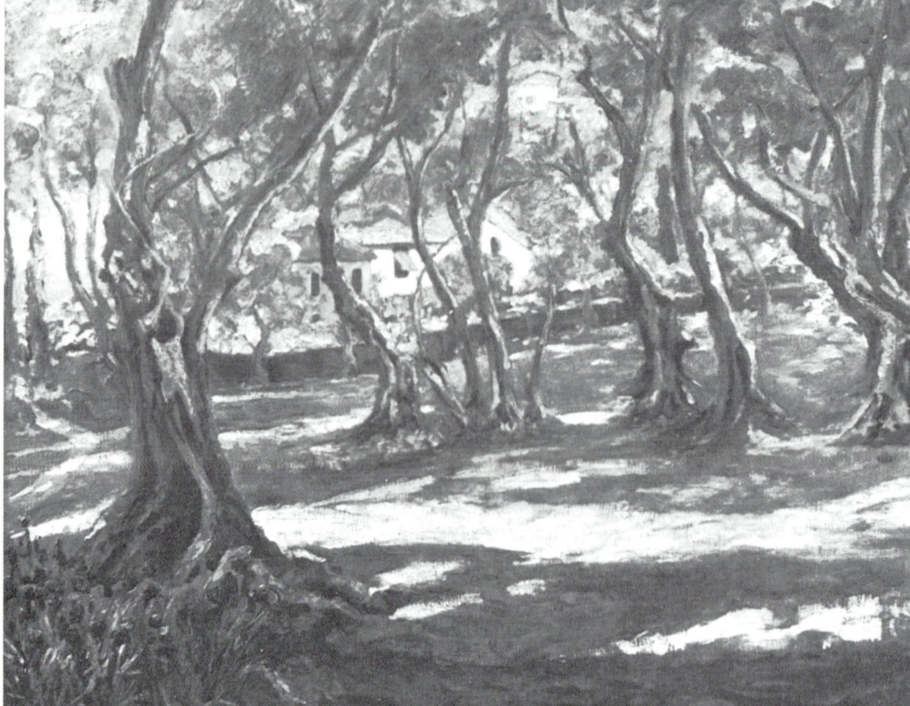

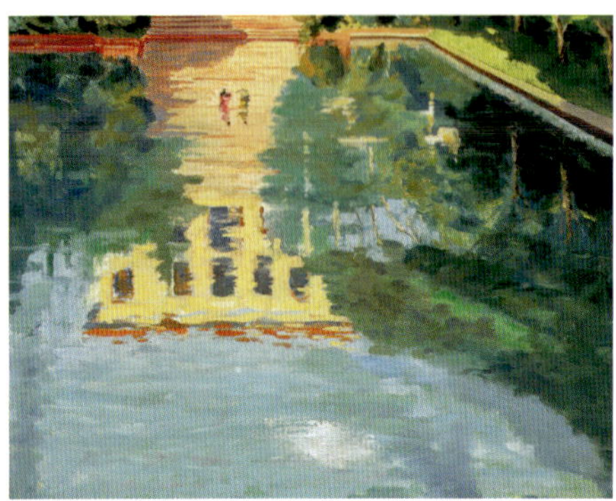

Fig 356 (C 350) above
Les Zoraides on Cap Martin, near Menton was the Riviera villa of Daisy Fellowes, wife of Winston's cousin Reginald. Churchill gave this painting to Rhoda Birley, wife of the portrait painter Sir Oswald.

Fig 357 (C 351) top of page
This view of Les Zoraides, like the one immediately above (C 350) is based on photograph from the Studio archives at Chartwell. (See right) This painting formerly belonged to Clementine Churchill.

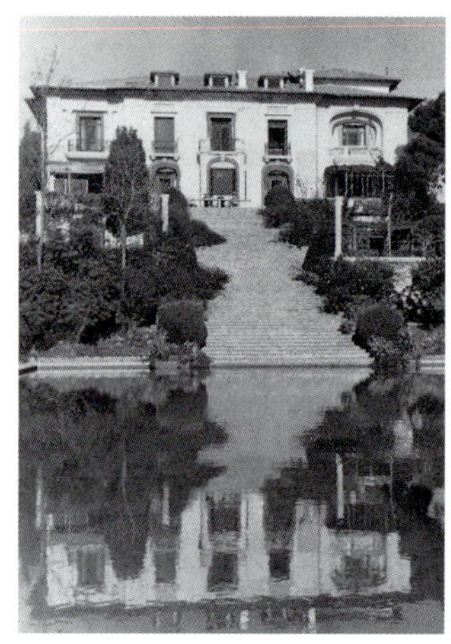

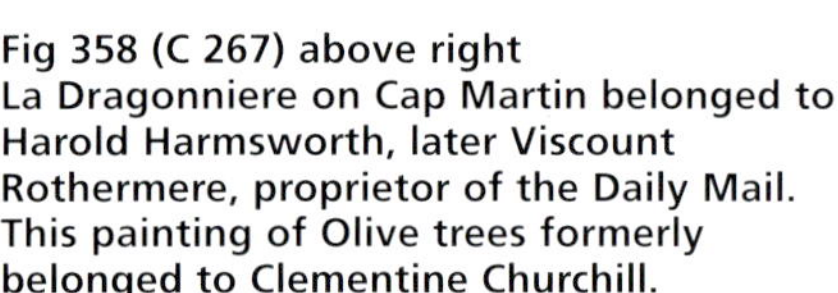

Fig 358 (C 267) above right
La Dragonniere on Cap Martin belonged to Harold Harmsworth, later Viscount Rothermere, proprietor of the Daily Mail. This painting of Olive trees formerly belonged to Clementine Churchill.

Fig 359 (C 268) opposite page above
The famous olive groves on Cap Martin enhance its exclusive appeal.

Fig 360 (C 271) opposite page below
The sunken garden at La Dragonniere.

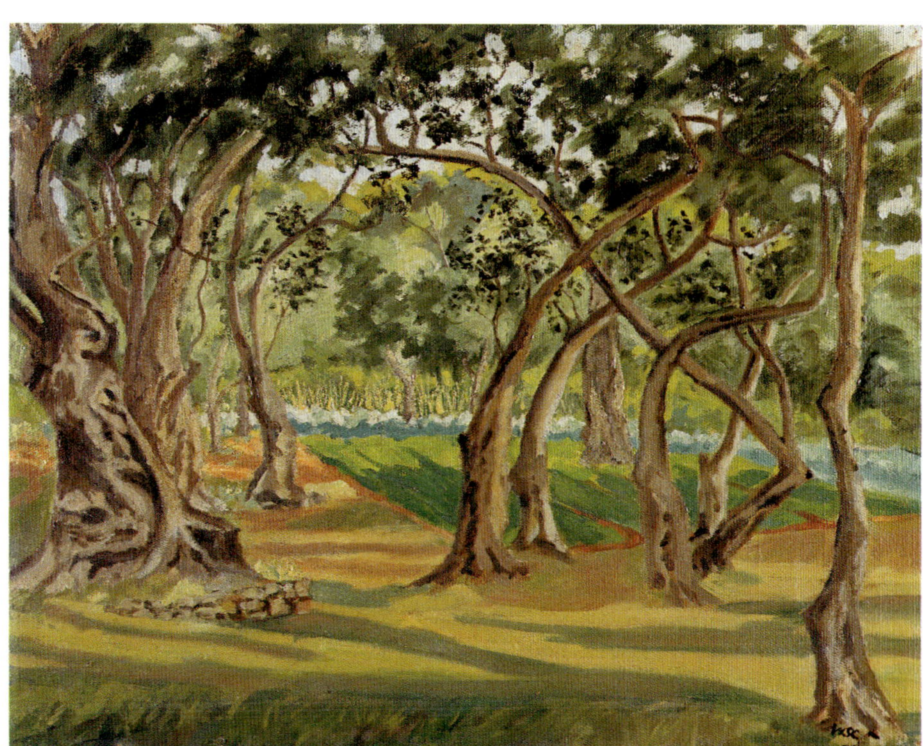

Fig 361 (C 272) right
Olive grove at La Dragonniere. Churchill gave this painting to his grandson Winston.

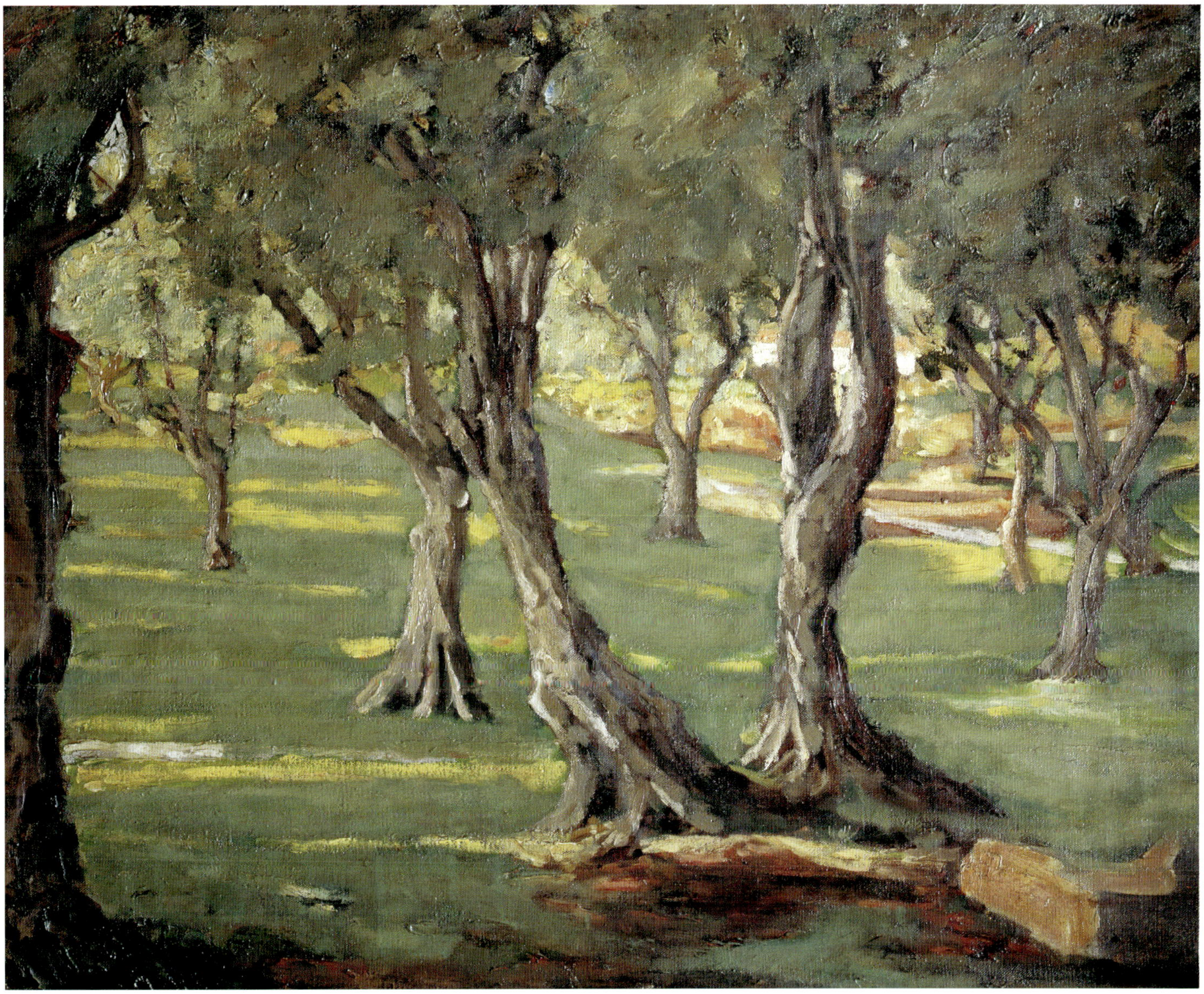

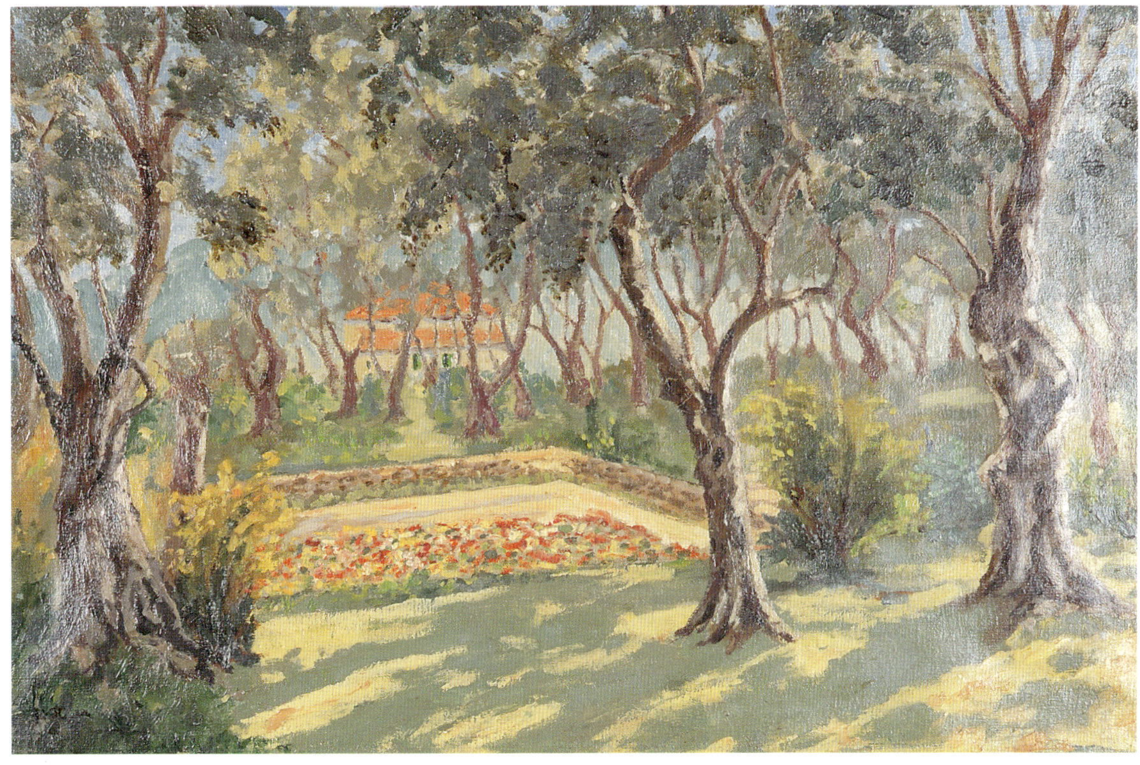

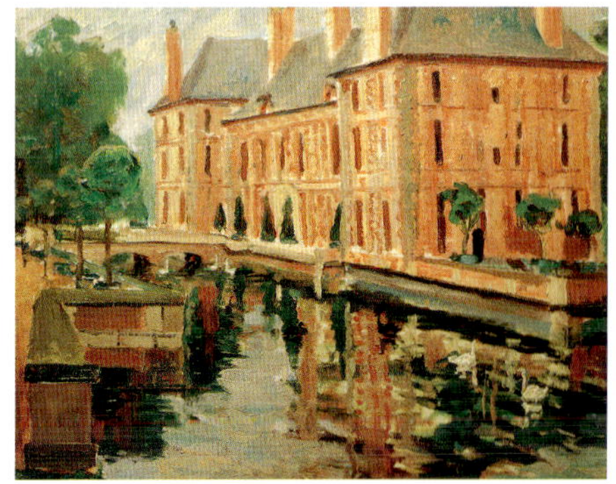

Fig 362 (C 230) above
The Chateau St-Georges-Motel at Dreux in Normandy was the summer home of Consuelo Balsan and her husband Jacques. Consuelo, who was one of the American Vanderbilts, was unhappily married previously to Churchill's cousin Sunny, Duke of Marlborough. The Balsans entertained lavishly and widely and were especially interested in artists, writers and musicians. One of these was the painter Paul Maze to whom they loaned the Moulin, or mill, on the estate; he and Churchill became close painting companions. In August 1939 when they were working together at St-Georges-Motel, Churchill remarked that was likely to be his last opportunity for painting before war; this was declared the next month.

to tempera in its modern form. He gets a great deal of enjoyment out of using this medium, in addition to oils.'

The Royal Academy of Arts unanimously appointed Churchill as Honorary Academician Extraordinary. His certificate of membership, his Diploma, signed by the King as the Academy's Patron and Protector, proclaimed that this appointment was made, 'in consideration of your eminent services to our Realm and People, and of your achievements in the Art of Painting'. From 1948 until his death, Churchill's paintings hung as of right as a member at the Royal Academy's annual Exhibition.

Winston and Clementine Churchill went to stay at the Hôtel du Roy Pené in Aix-en-Provence. There were many ideal locations for painting: Les Calanques, near Cassis on the coast, Les Baux, St Rémy with its Roman arch, and La Fontaine de Vaucluse. Cézanne's Mont St Victoire also attracted him. From Aix he went on to La Capponcina, the villa on the Côte d'Azur owned by his friend Lord Beaverbrook, proprietor of *The Daily Express*. This villa was to become a favourite painting place for Churchill.

1949 [Background] Churchill's 75th year.
North Atlantic Treaty signed. Ireland became a republic outside the British Commonwealth. Communists gained control of Hungary. Communist republic in China. West German republic. East German Communist republic. Gas industry nationalized in Britain. Speaking in Brussels, Churchill supported a European Court of Human Rights. At the first meeting of the Council of Europe in Strasbourg, Churchill urged that West Germany be invited to attend. He took up horse racing as an owner. The second volume of Churchill's *History of the Second World War* was published.

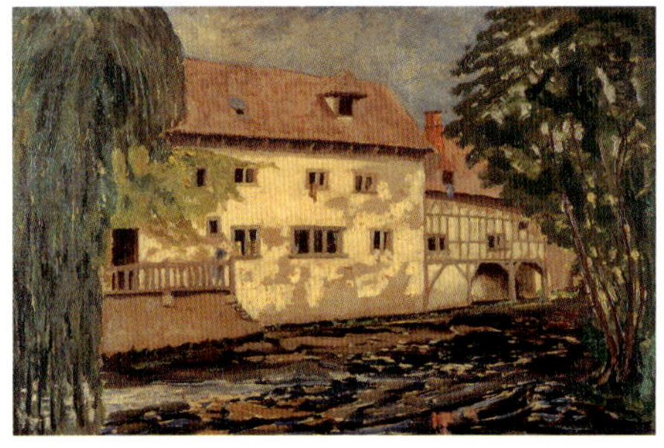

Fig 363 (C 234) above
The Mill at St-Georges-Motel.

1949 [Painting] Churchill stayed with Clementine on Lake Garda and Lake Carezza before travelling to Strasbourg. Going on thereafter to paint at La Capponcina, he suffered a mild stroke.

Clementine persuaded Winston to give a picture of 'The Blue Room at Trent Park' to be sold at auction in aid of the Young Women's Christian Association. It fetched 1,250 guineas (£1,312.50) at Christie's; its Brazilian buyer presented it to the Art Museum at São Paulo. Sir John Rothenstein, Director of the Tate Gallery, met Sir Winston at a Royal Academy function given to celebrate the presentation of his Diploma and was invited to lunch at Chartwell: 'I'd like you to see my daubs.' After visiting his studio, Churchill said, 'If it weren't for painting, I couldn't live; I couldn't bear the strain of things.'

Fig 364 (C 249) below
A village fete at St-Georges-Motel. This painting formerly belonged to Clementine Churchill.

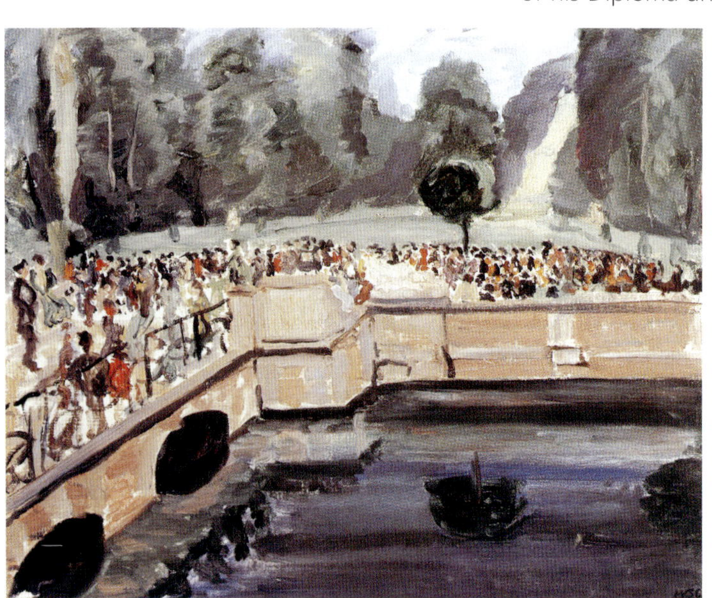

1950 [Background] War between North Korea, supported by Chinese Communists, and the United Nations. Indian republic. General election in Britain. Labour returned again. British steel industry nationalized. Churchill supported the plan for a Western European coal and steel pool and spoke in Strasbourg to the Council of Europe of the need for a European army. The third volume of Churchill's *History of the Second World War* was published.

1950 [Painting] Winston and Clementine travelled to Madeira to visit Bryce and Margaret Nairn whose company

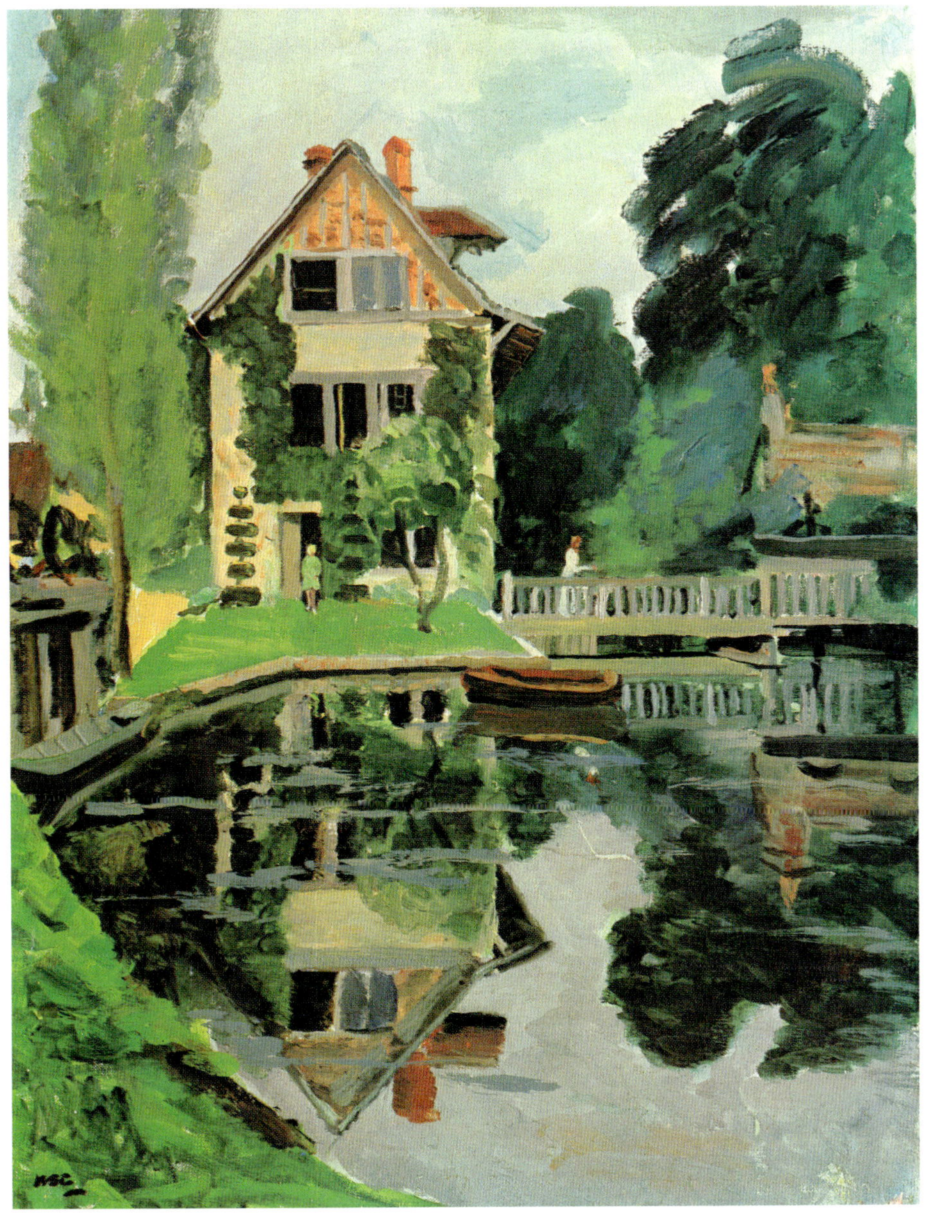

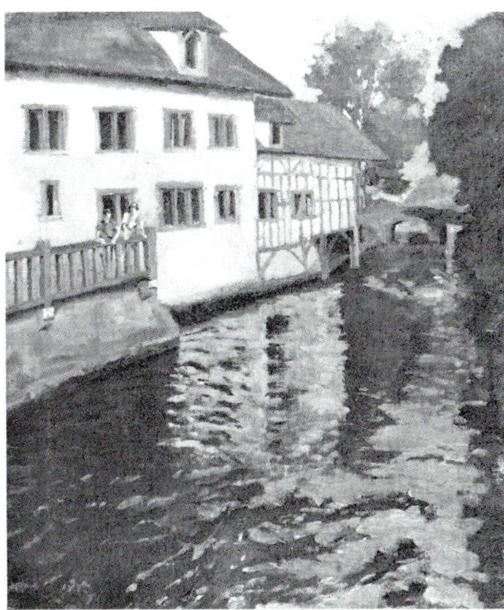

Fig 365 (C 231) above
The Mill at La Colle with Sarah and Randolph Churchill looking over the pool. Churchill gave this painting to Maxine Elliott.

Fig 366 (C 140) left
The Moulin at St-Georges-Motel. This painting formerly belonged to Clementine Churchill.

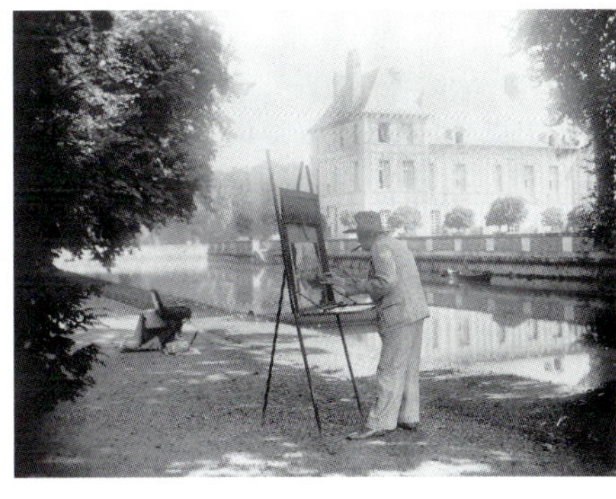

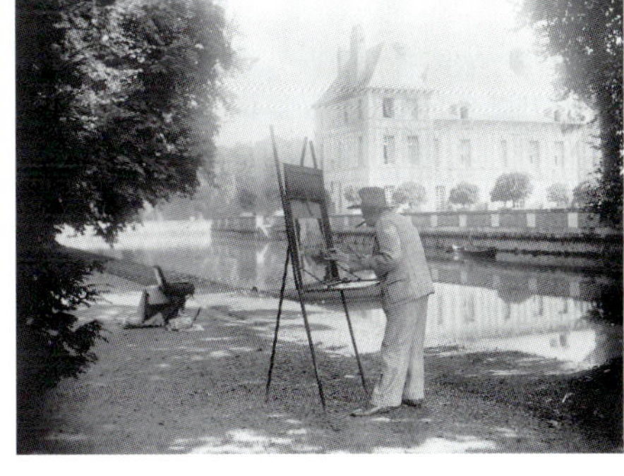

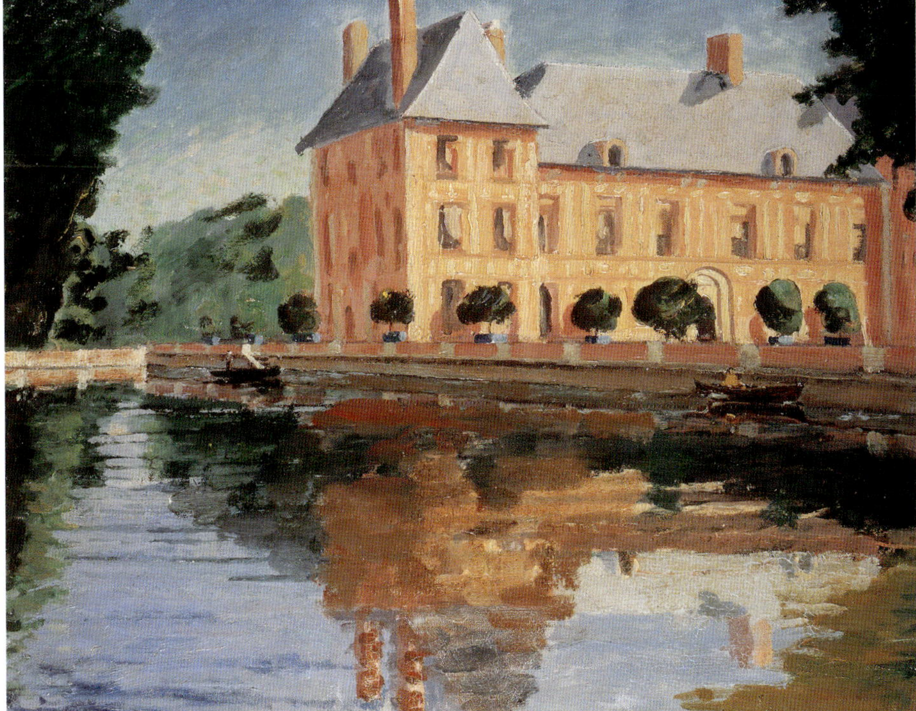

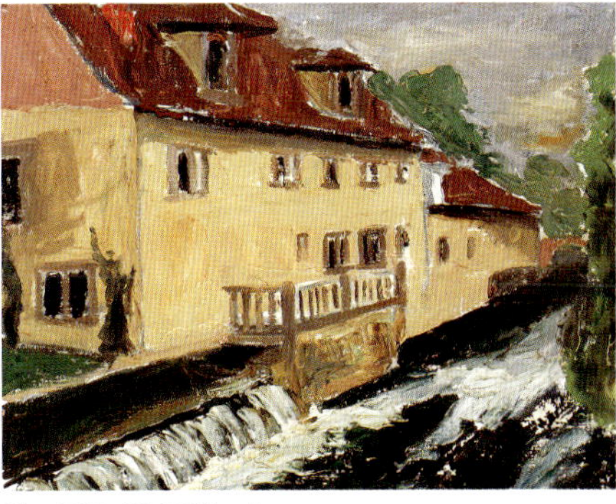

Fig 367 (C 233) above
The Mill at St-Georges-Motel.

Fig 368 (C 232) left
The Chateau St-Georges-Motel. The painting was given by Winston to his youngest daughter Mary. It is based on a photograph from the Studio archives at Chartwell. (See above centre)

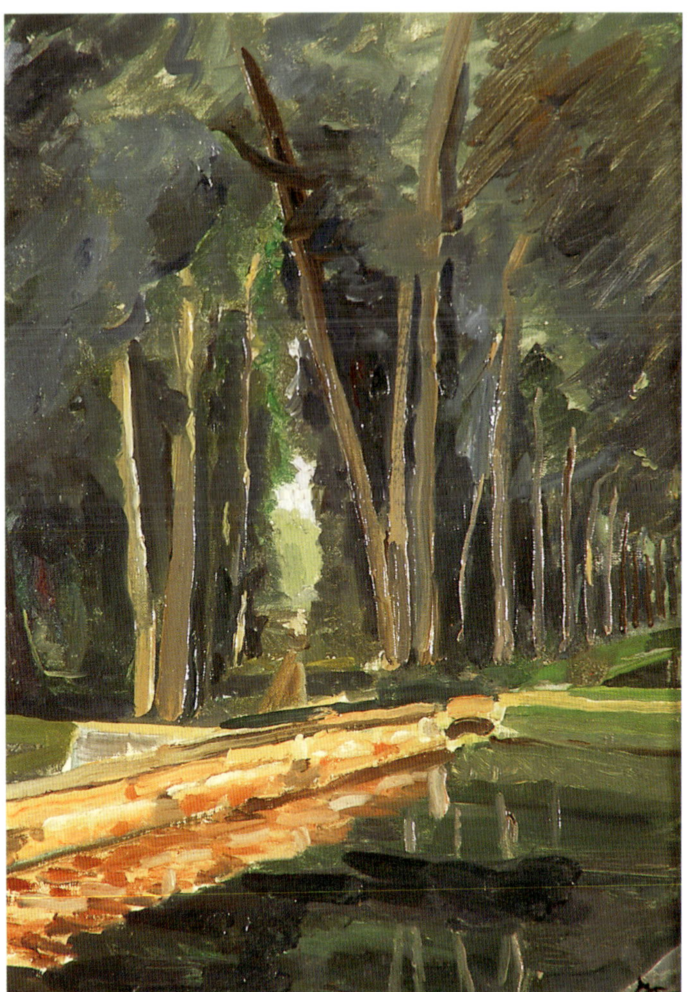

they had enjoyed in France in 1945. Here he painted the fishing port but had to cut short his visit because of the general election. Churchill returned to Marrakech that winter to complete the fifth volume of his war memoirs and to paint. He made the acquaintance there of the painter Jacques Majorelle, and was particularly interested in his use of tempera.

In 1950, Norman McGowan became Churchill's personal valet. On the second day of his employment at Chartwell, Churchill announced, 'Norman, I want to show you how to look after my paints and brushes. It will be an important part of your duties.' They were in the Studio together. Churchill's paintings leaned one against the other round the walls. This 'seeming untidiness was in fact an orderly array in my Guv'nor's mind. He would go straight to a cluster of four or five and withdraw a half-completed canvas which he had that afternoon decided to work on again.'

In the years that followed, Norman McGowan recalled that 'One of my jobs on holiday was ... to photograph the scene Mr Churchill was painting. He would also buy the high-quality glossy photographs sold in France and Italy, as a reference of the buildings, trees and so on. We also took colour pictures ... so that on some dull, wintry day in England these could be projected and he could thus recapture the general colour atmosphere. Many of the pictures painted on holiday were little more than outlines with perhaps a section coloured until their completion weeks or months later in the studio.'

Fig 369 (C 353) above
The Canal at St-Georges-Motel. Churchill gave this painting to his successor as Prime Minister, Sir Anthony Eden, later the Earl of Avon.

Fig 370 (C 355) opposite page
This little painting of a scene in the park of the Chateau St-Georges-Motel is signed by several artists including Paul Maze, Andre de Segonzac and Winston himself, who supervised the making of this joint work. Churchill gave this picture to his butler, Mr H. J. Chamberlain.

Fig 371 (C 354) below
The Avenue and Formal Pool at St-Georges-Motel.

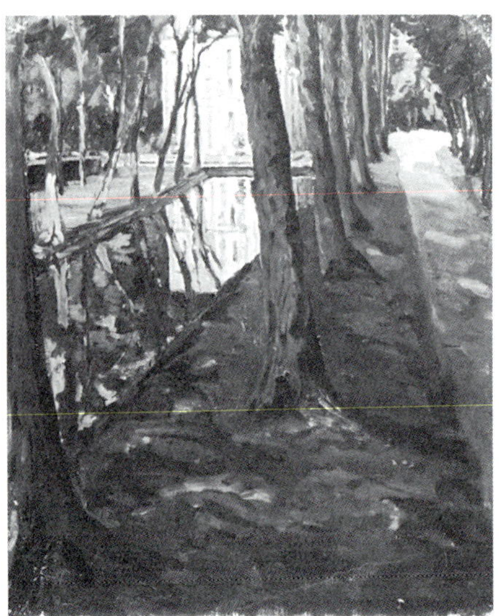

Joyce C. Hall had 'For many years ... dreamed of having Winston Churchill's paintings on our greetings cards. It was an unlikely possibility.' Following an approach to Churchill's solicitor, Mr Anthony F. Moir, the idea was accepted and twelve paintings were chosen. None was signed and all were shown over Sunday brunch to the members of the [American] Association of Art Museum Directors for their opinion. 'After carefully examining each painting,' one of them said: "Well, one thing is certain. Whoever the artist is, he's more than a Sunday painter." The others reflected his judgment.' On learning the name of the artist, 'They were greatly surprised and agreed that it had been important to see the paintings without prejudice.' The few Churchill paintings some had seen reproduced in magazines 'had not done them justice. Now confronted with the actual work, they were amazed by his ability.'

Joyce C. Hall visited Churchill at Chartwell and told him of the museum curators' reaction. 'He became quite emotional. Some time later, his daughter Sarah told [Mr Hall] that a compliment about his painting pleased him more than anything said about his writing or even his statesmanship.'

1951 [Background] Japanese peace treaty. Introduction of Health Service charges split Labour party. Dock strike in Britain. General election in Britain won by the Conservative party. Churchill became Prime Minister. The fourth volume of Churchill's *History of the Second World War* was published.

1951 [Painting] At Marrakech, Churchill discovered a new subject, Tinerhir, on the far side of the Atlas mountains. President Truman's daughter Margaret visited Chartwell and Churchill gave her a picture of the panorama of the Atlas

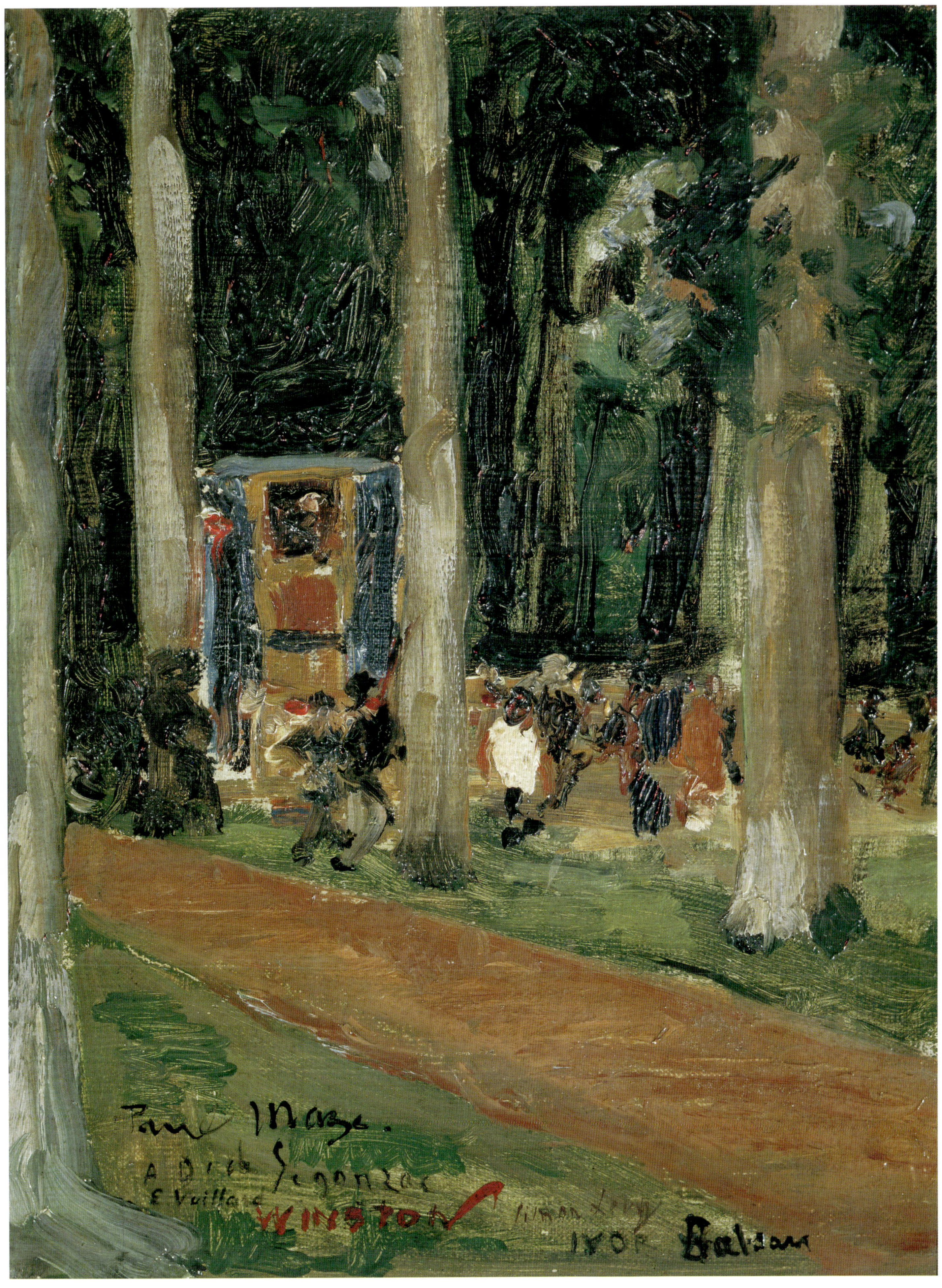
Paul Maze.
E Vuillard
WINSTON
Balsan

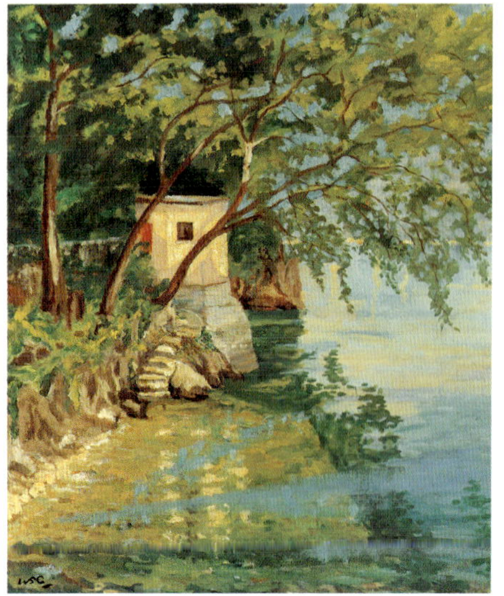

Fig 372 (C 383) above
Scene on Lake Como, painted in 1945. This painting formerly belonged to Clementine Churchill.

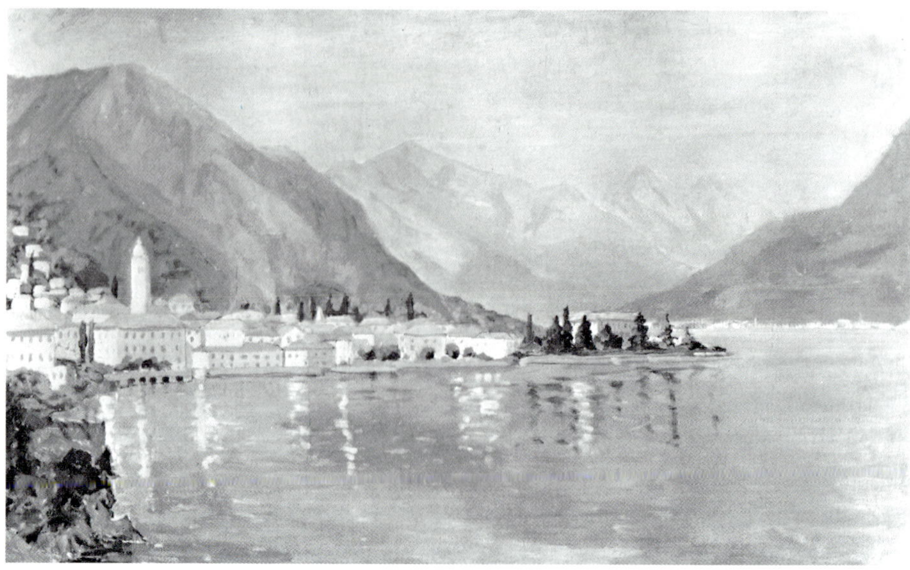

Fig 373 (C 405) above right
Lake Menaggio on Lake Como, painted in 1945

mountains from Marrakech to take to her father. Churchill went to Venice where he painted the great staircase of the Doge's Palace, the Colleoni statue, the Rialto Bridge and a scene on the island of Torcello.

Churchill admired the acting of Laurence Olivier and Vivien Leigh who returned the compliment, with the practical result that once at the end of a heavy season, 'we prescribed for ourselves a painting holiday ... We had both read Churchill's book on painting and this had inspired us,' Olivier recalled. 'He shrewdly explains that anybody can paint, and that the exercise is of exceptional benefit to those whose minds are filled with their work and the worries attendant upon it.' In 1951 both went to have Sunday lunch at Chartwell. 'He was obviously most taken with Vivien, and he gave her one of his paintings. We were assured that this was the only picture of his that he had been known to give away.'

1952 [Background] King George VI died and his daughter succeeded as Queen Elizabeth II. Churchill went to Washington to meet President Truman. Apartheid in South Africa. America tested the hydrogen bomb and Britain an atomic bomb. Churchill's increasing physical frailty and deafness became a matter of concern: his mental faculties were not impaired but he began to consider resignation. Eisenhower elected President of the United States. The fifth volume of Churchill's *History of the Second World War* was published.

1952 [Painting] Churchill went to Beaverbrook's villa, La Capponcina. A picture painted then of Cap d'Ail was deposited at the Royal Academy in 1958 as Churchill's Diploma Work. This followed an approach by its President, Sir Charles Wheeler, who told Churchill that 'every Academician since the time of Sir Joshua Reynolds' had provided such an example of his abilities.

Earlier in the year, Churchill wrote to Wheeler's predecessor, Sir Gerald Kelly, 'I have received the notice from the Academy about sending in some pictures for this year. I do not think on any account I could send more than one or two at the outset. Perhaps you could come down one day and pick them out from what I have ... I should of course be very glad to send none at all. On the other hand I must apprise you of the fact that Lord Alexander has a whole flock of really fine pictures far better than any I have painted, especially in still life, and I am sure it would be a feature in the Royal Academy if you persuaded him to send you a few. I will help you with him if you decide to make an approach.'

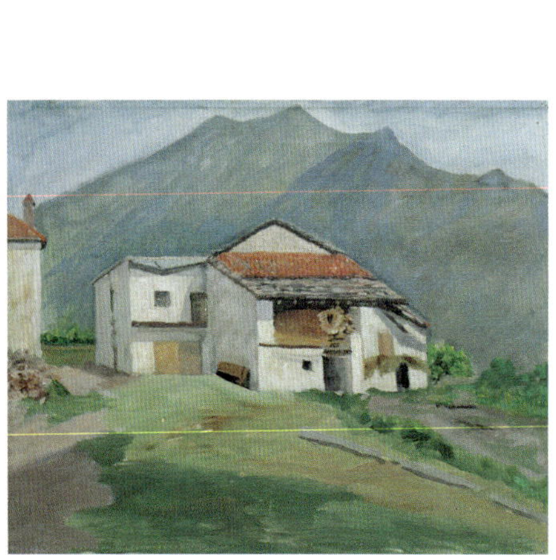

Fig 374 (C 229) above
A farm at the head of Lake Como, painted in 1945.

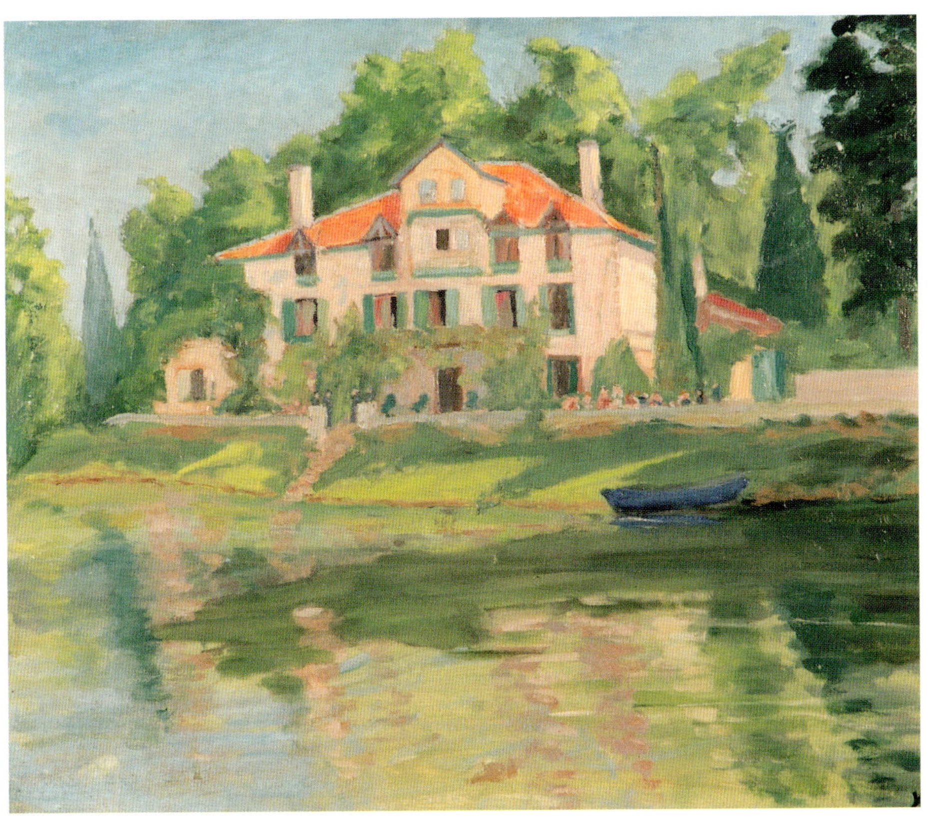

Fig 375 (C 474) left
A villa on the River Nivelle. This was painted in 1945 between the parliamentary elections held in the United Kingdom after the successful end of the war with the Nazis and before the Potsdam Conference. Many votes had to be counted from those serving in the British forces overseas which meant a delay before the results could be declared. In between, the Churchills took a short holiday in France, near St-Jean-de-Luz, south of Bordeaux, where this picture of Mrs Cunliffe-Owen's house was painted.

Fig 376 (C 381) below
This view of Marrakech, showing the Tower of the Katoubia Mosque on the right, was painted by Churchill in 1943 after the Casablanca Conference. It was the only picture he felt able to paint during the Second World War when he was otherwise totally absorbed - physically, mentally and emotionally. Churchill gave this painting to President Roosevelt whom he insisted on taking to Marrakech after the Conference for them both to enjoy the spectacle of the sun setting on the snow of the Atlas Mountains. The picture was painted from the tower of the Villa Taylor after the President's departure, from where both had viewed the scene the previous evening.

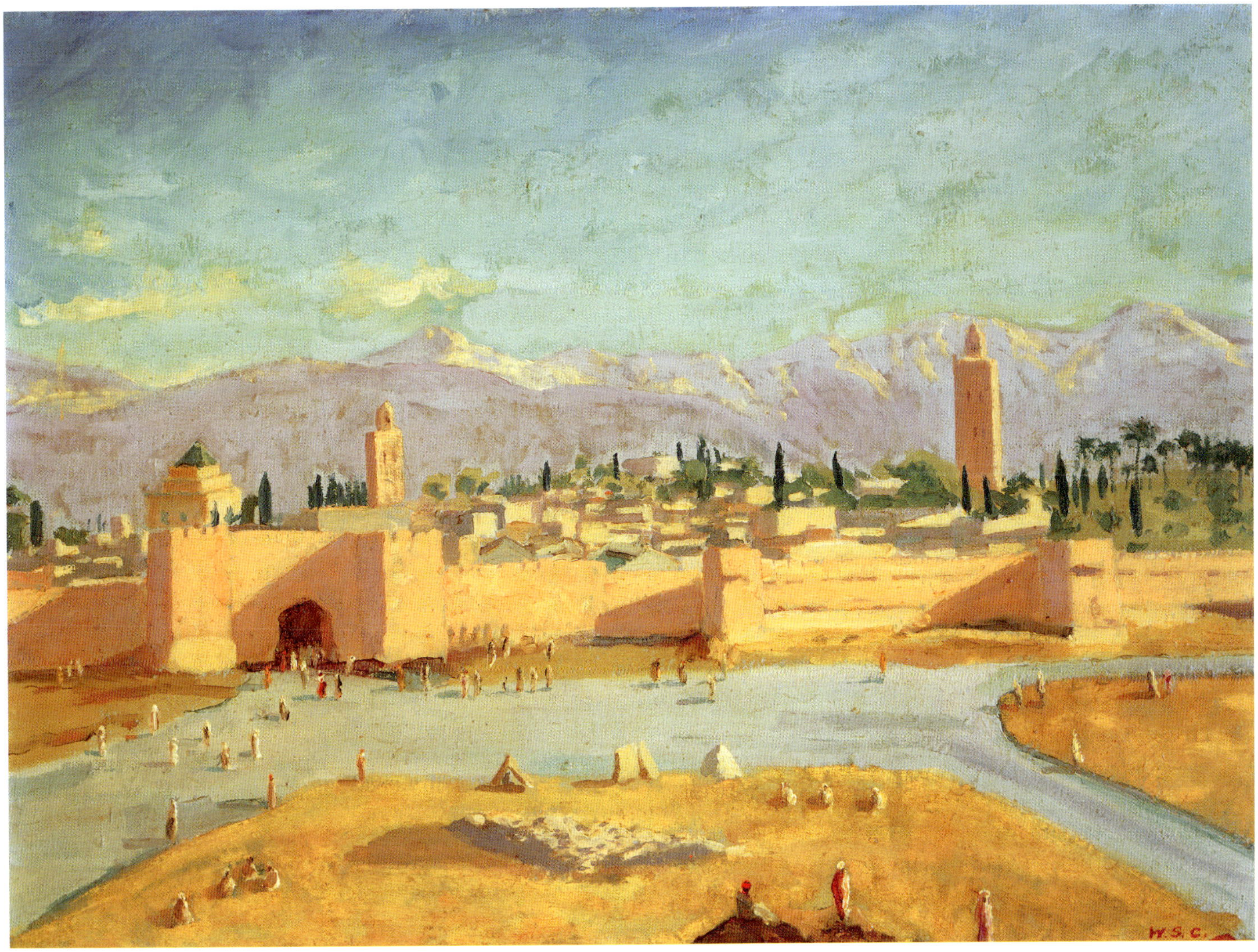

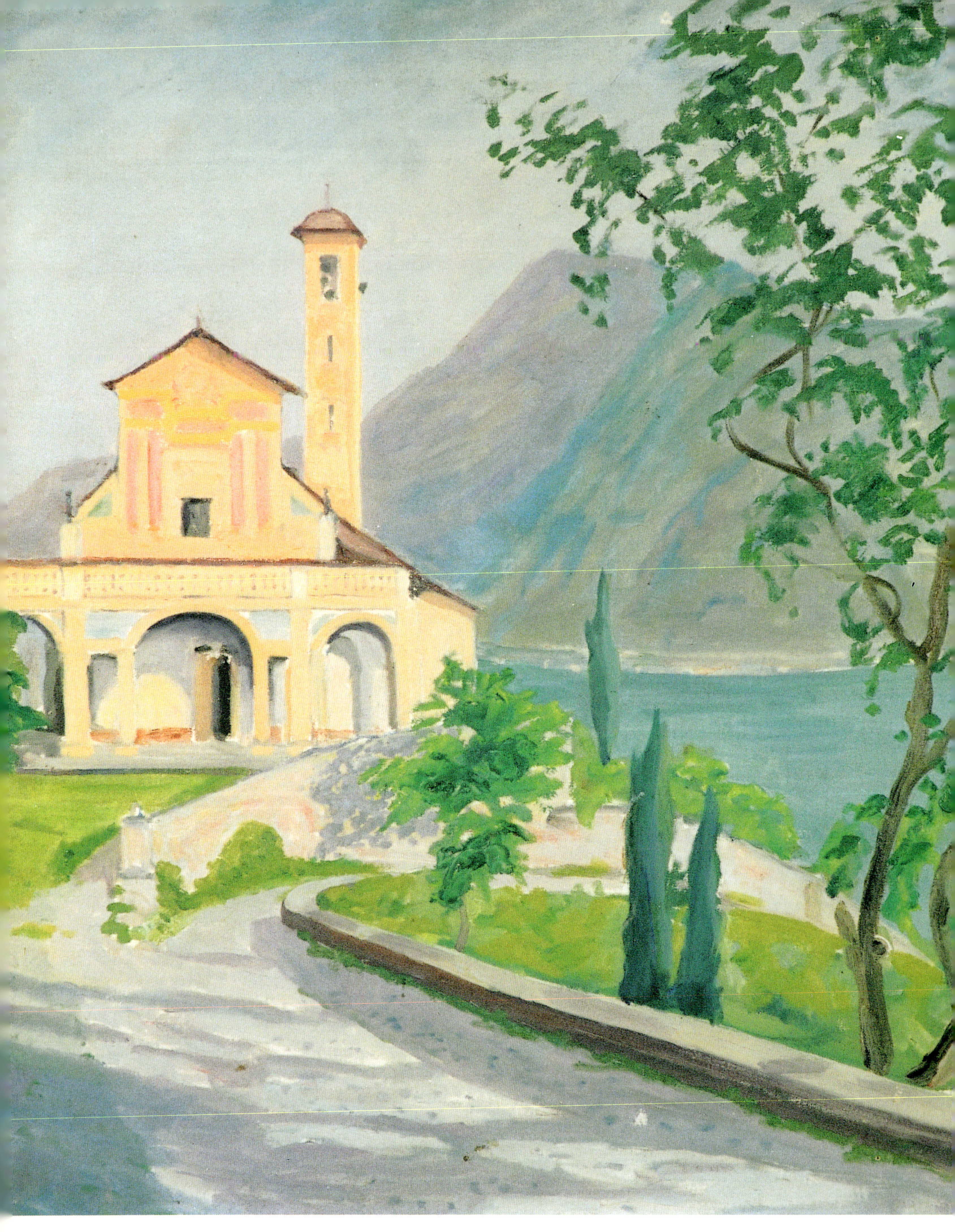

The Queen commissioned Oscar Nemon to sculpt a bust of her Prime Minister for Windsor Castle. Painter and sculptor became friends. During the sittings Churchill attempted to sketch Nemon but tore up the results on being asked to show them: nonetheless Nemon managed to rescue one.

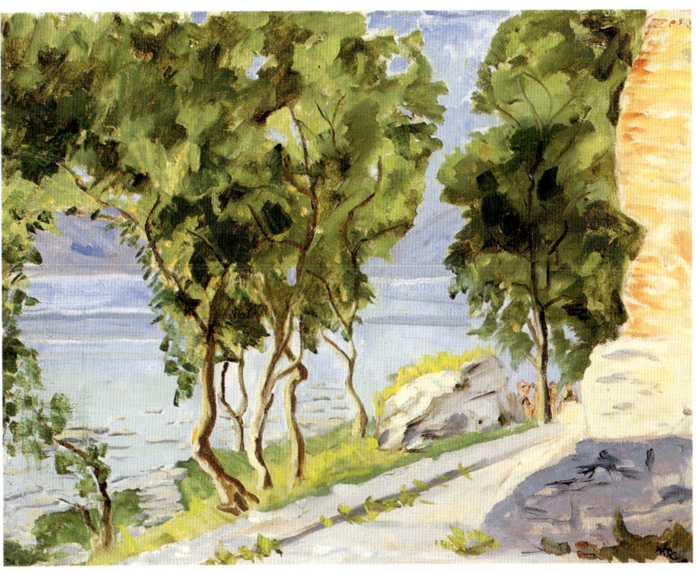

Fig 377 (C 394) above
This scene on Lake Como was painted in about an hour and formerly belonged to Clementine Churchill. It may date from 1948.

1953 [Background] Churchill flew to Washington to meet Eisenhower and urged a meeting with the Russians. Stalin died. As a newly created Knight of the Garter, Churchill attended the Queen's coronation. Suffered another and severe stroke. Armistice in Korea. Egyptian republic. Churchill completed the sixth volume of his war memoirs and began to rework his *History of the English-speaking Peoples*. Churchill was awarded the Nobel Prize for Literature. Attended the Bermuda conference of American, British and French leaders.

1953 [Painting] After his visit to President Eisenhower, Churchill went to Jamaica, where he painted at Prospect, the house near Ocho Rios owned by Sir Harold and Lady Mitchell. Churchill later gave one of the paintings of Jamaica Beach (C 424) to Mr Joyce C. Hall because of his kindness to his daughter Sarah and his help in furthering her career.

Fig 378 (C 416) opposite page
Church by Lake Como. Painted in September 1945, this picture formerly belonged to Clementine Churchill and is based on photographs from the Studio archives at Chartwell.

Churchill made a speech at the Royal Academy dinner where he declared that 'The arts are essential to any complete national life. The nation owes it to itself to sustain and encourage them ... The controversies in the field of art are at least as vigorous as those in politics.' Churchill's painting of 'Tapestries at Blenheim', which had been exhibited at the Royal Academy in 1948, was included, with pictures loaned from the Royal Collection, in the Arts Council's Coronation exhibition, 'British Life: Elizabeth I to Elizabeth II'.

Churchill was always modest about his pictures and 'so hates to part with his work that he might fairly be described as a collector of it', Professor Thomas Bodkin wrote. He added, 'A striking characteristic of his pictures is their quite extraordinary decisiveness ... His drawing makes factual statements, though these may not always be quite accurate in detail ... [the details] are never of substantial importance.'

Following his stroke and initial recuperation at Chartwell, Churchill went to find sun in the South of France at Beaverbrook's villa, La Capponcina, where he painted the rocks and pine trees.

Fig 379 (C 395) below
Scene on Lake Como. This painting may date from 1945 or from 1946 when Churchill experimented with working on larger-sized canvases.

1954 [Background] Churchill's 80th year.
Growing calls for Churchill's resignation in Britain. In Parliament he declared with regard to Russia that 'Peace is our aim, and strength is the only way of getting it.' Churchill flew to Washington to discuss cooperating on the peaceful use of atomic energy and to urge once again the need for detente with Russia. The sixth and final volume of Churchill's *History of the Second World War* was published.

1954 [Painting] Oscar Nemon sculpted Churchill again, for a statue for the Guildhall in the City of London; this time Churchill was inspired to try his hand at sculpting a bust of Nemon and a unique plaster work was the result.

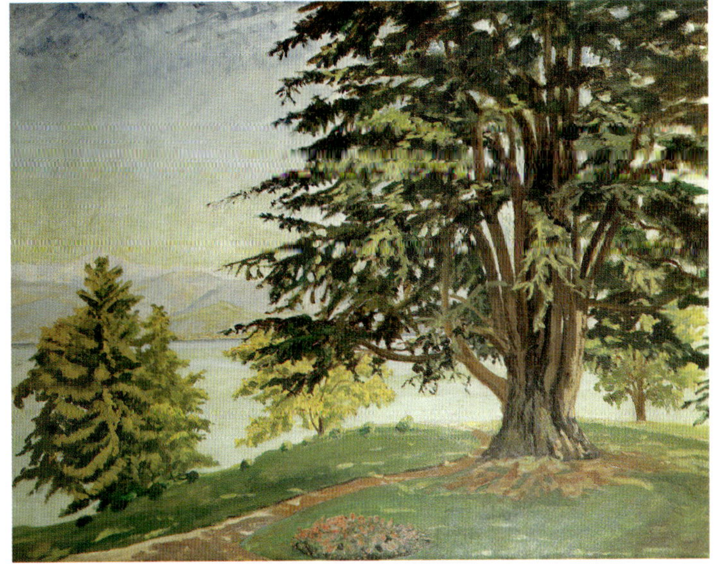

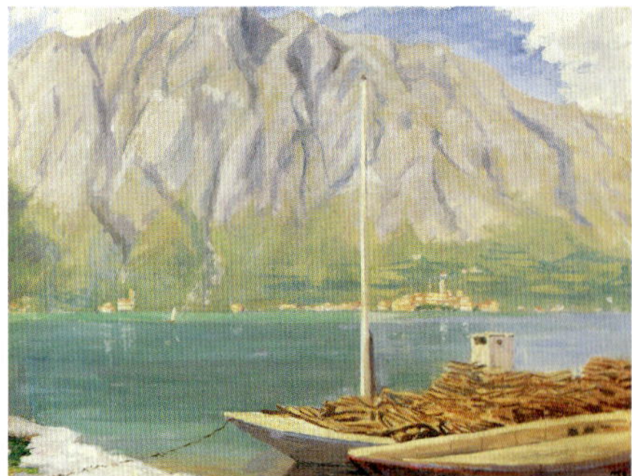

Fig 380 (C 413) above
By Lake Lugano, painted in 1945.

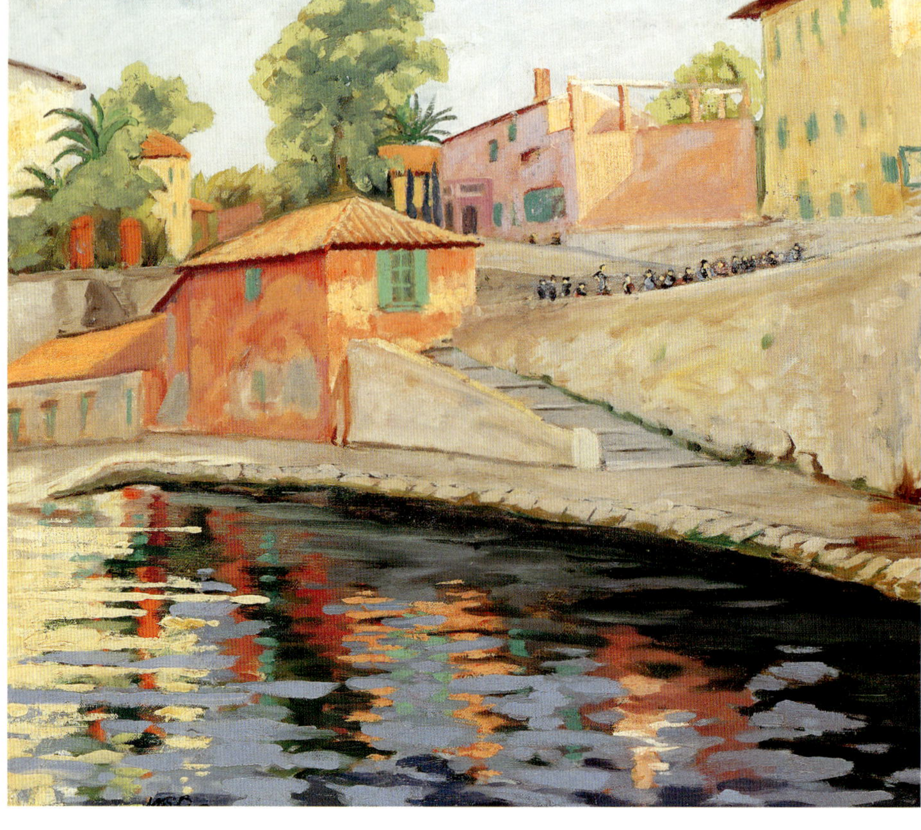

Fig 381 (C 415) right
At St-Jean-Cap-Ferrat, painted in 1945. This picture was composed from three small photographs in the Studio archives at Chartwell.

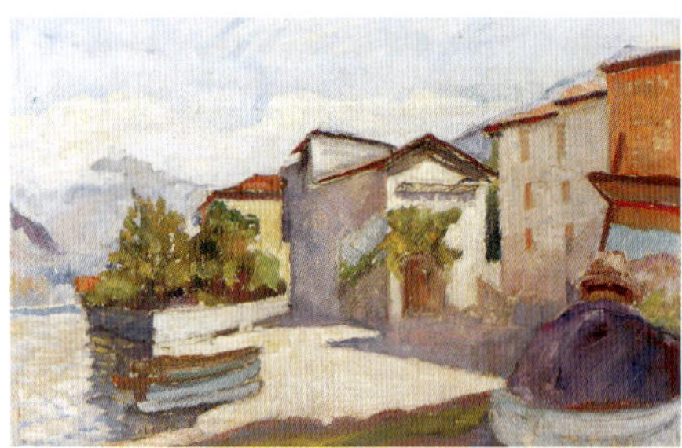

Fig 382 (C 420) above
A little picture of a village near Lugano with the artist at his easel. Painted in 1945.

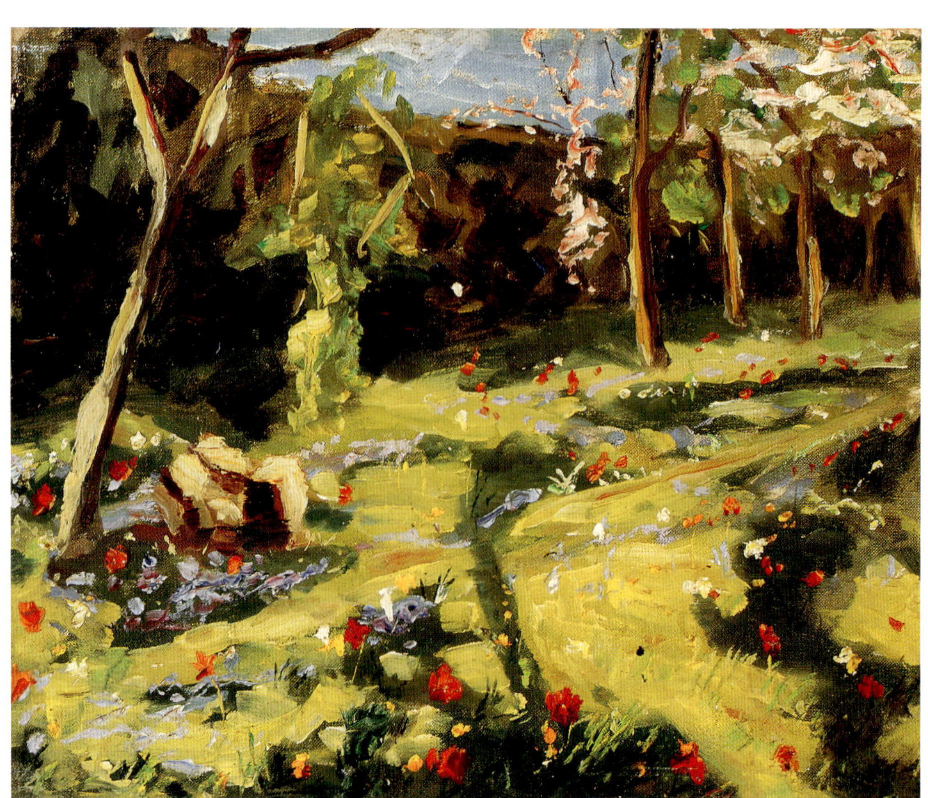

Fig 383 (C 441) right
A scene on Cap Martin, done in the 1940s.

In celebration of Churchill's 80th birthday, the two Houses of Parliament commissioned Graham Sutherland to paint his portrait. Both Winston and Clementine grew to like the artist and his wife. Churchill much admired the power of Sutherland's drawing and Sutherland in his turn wrote later to the Earl of Birkenhead, Winton's godson, of Churchill's 'extraordinary talent as a painter, particularly when he was not under the influence of some artist or other.'

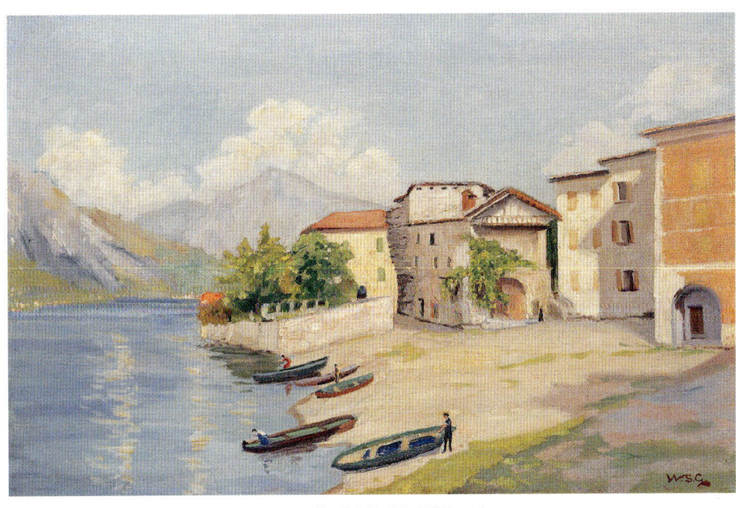

Fig 384 (C 419) above
Village scene on Lake Lugano, painted in 1945. Churchill gave this picture to his solicitor, Anthony F. Moir.

In the event, Churchill took a violent dislike to the finished portrait, which he nonetheless described courteously in his acceptance speech as 'a remarkable example of modern art. It certainly combines force and candour. These are qualities which no active Member of either House can do without or should fear to meet.' Churchill's sense that Sutherland's painting showed him to be both ruthless and senile came to be shared by Clementine, who destroyed the portrait in about 1955/6.

1955 [Background] Britain announced decision to build the hydrogen bomb. Violence in Cyprus. Rebellion in Argentina. West Germany joined NATO. Allied occupation of Austria ended. Communist purge in China. Warsaw treaty linked Russia and Eastern Europe. Churchill resigned as Prime Minister. General election and Conservatives returned again. Churchill continued to work on his *History of the English-speaking Peoples* and, speaking at the Guildhall, said, 'I am on the side of the optimists. I do not believe that humanity is going to destroy itself. I have for some time thought it would be a good thing if the leaders of the great nations talked privately to one another.' [See also below.]

Fig 385 (C 421) below
At St-Jean-Cap-Ferrat, painted in 1946. Churchill gave this painting to his grandson, Winston.

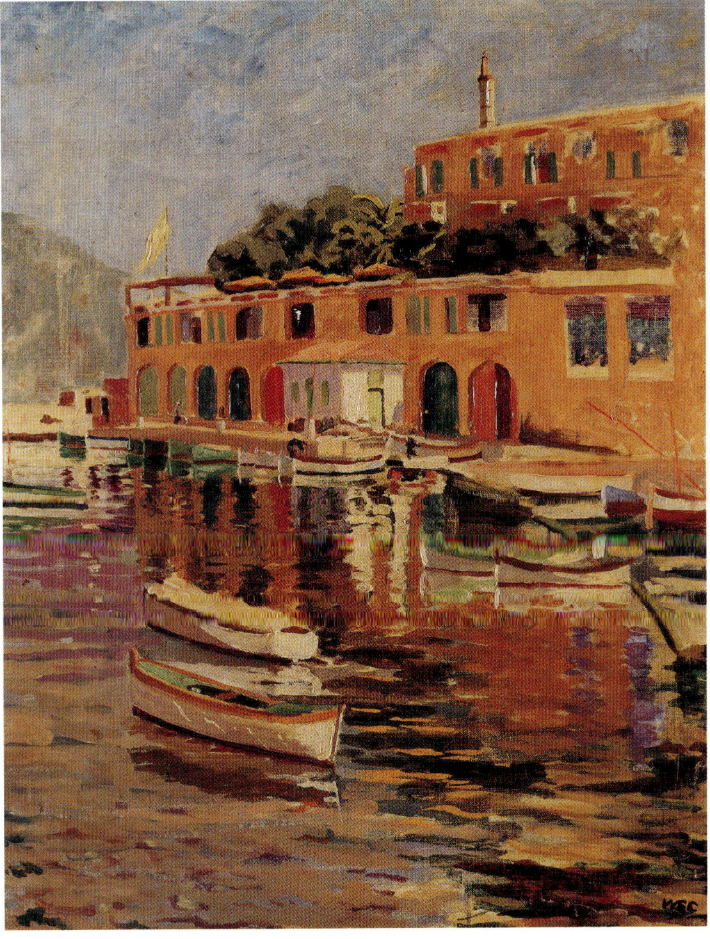

1955 [Painting] After his resignation Churchill went on holiday to Sicily where he stayed at the Villa Politi in Syracuse. Here he painted the cavern's mouth at the Grotto of the Ropemakers. Later, at Chartwell, Winston painted a portrait of Clementine based on a photograph of her at the launch of HMS *Indomitable* in 1940.

Attending the unveiling of his statue by the Lord Mayor at the Guildhall in the City of London, Churchill said, 'I must admit that I think that the House of Commons has made a good rule in not erecting monuments to people in their lifetime. But I entirely agree that every rule should have an exception. The fact that you have done so in my case will both prove the rule and emphasize the compliment. I greatly admire the art of Mr Oscar Nemon whose prowess in the ancient realm of sculpture has won such remarkable modern appreciation. I also admire this particular example... because it seems to be such a very good likenes. But on this point ... I cannot claim to be either impersonal or impartial. I am indeed an interested and biased party.'

The Trustees of the Tate Gallery asked Churchill for one of his pictures for the national collection. Its director, Sir John Rothenstein, was of the opinion that such an acquisition would be 'fascinating in the way, for instance, a landscape by the elder Pitt would be, but the chief consideration was that if one of the very best could be secured, it would be an

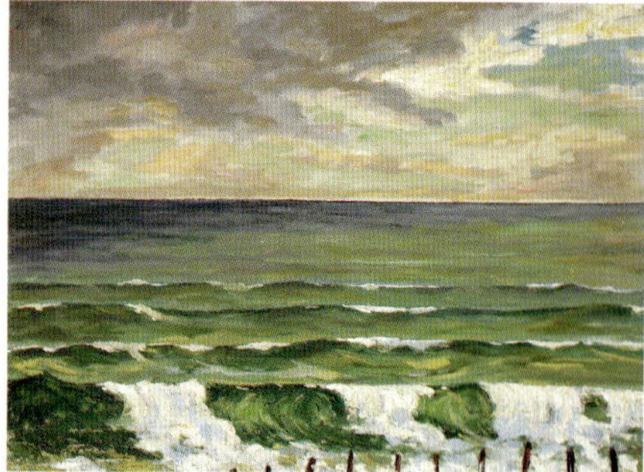

Fig 386 (C 317) above
The Surf Club at Miami, painted in 1946.

Churchill was advised by his doctor to spend the winter months away from Britain and so embarked on a long and relatively leisurely trip to the United States. In Florida, Winston and Clementine were the guests of Colonel Frank Clarke, a Canadian industrialist, who in 1943 had been Churchill's host during a short rest in the Laurentian Mountains after the Quebec Conference. Also in 1946, Churchill flew from Miami to revisit Cuba where he painted - but no extant pictures are known.

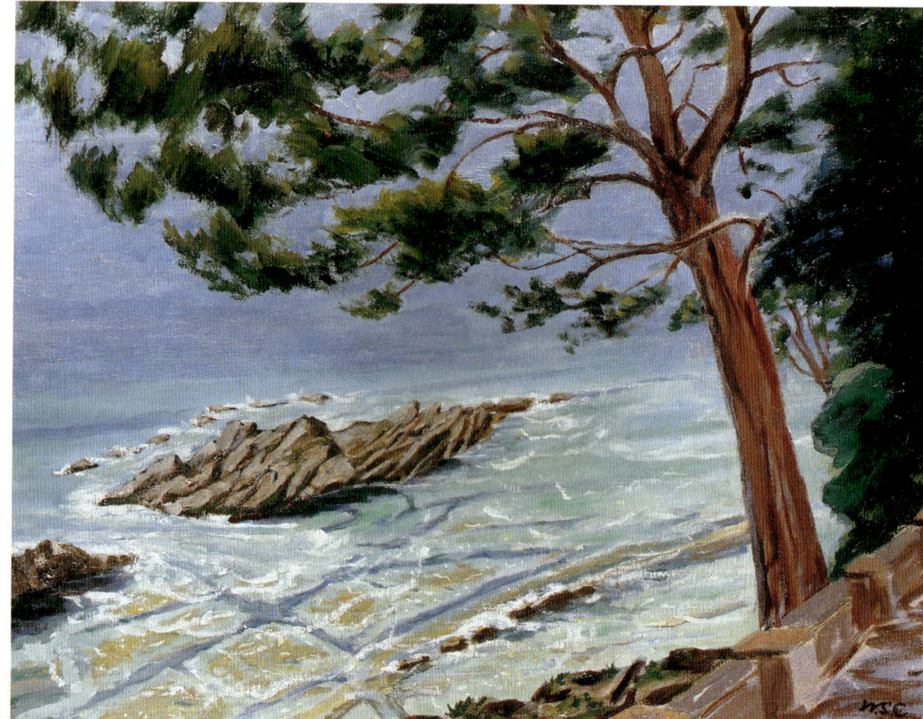

Fig 387 (C 425) right
A view of the Mediterranean from the Villa Pirelli, near Genoa painted in 1945. This picture formerly belonged to Clementine Churchill.

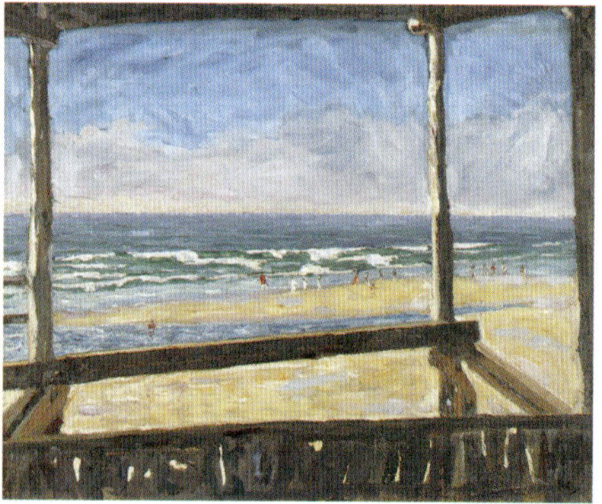

Fig 388 (C 345) above
View from a bathing hut at the Miami Surf Club, painted in 1946.

Fig 389 (C 422) opposite page below
Scene from the Venetian Causeway, Miami Beach, Florida. Based on a photograph from the Studio archives at Chartwell. Churchill gave this picture to Colonel and Mrs Frank W. Clarke.

acquisition worthy in its own right.' Rothenstein, who had advised Churchill often on what pictures to show at the Royal Academy exhibitions, came to Chartwell to help select a picture. The painting chosen was executed by Churchill in 1936 and shows the Loup River in the French Alpes Maritimes.

Sir John Rothenstein had advised the Parliamentary Press Gallery that, for their 80th birthday gift, they commission Edward Ardizzone to draw Sir Winston speaking in the House of Commons. (The picture hangs at Chartwell.) Prior to that presentation, Churchill told Sir John in regard to the Sutherland portrait, 'I think the time has come for an artist to give some consideration to the subject of a portrait, instead of looking over the wilderness of his subject hoping to discern there some glimmer of his own genius.' On another occasion, also recorded by Rothenstein, Churchill said of Sutherland's portrait, 'Haven't you noticed that the pain one suffers is by no means necessarily proportionate to its cause?'

The Prime Minister of Australia, Sir Robert Menzies, went to lunch at Chartwell. Since 1948 he had being trying to obtain a painting by Churchill whom he had known since 1935.

'I must say that I had offered to buy or borrow ... But it was in vain ... ' Suddenly Winston said, "By the way, you must have one of my pictures." I spun round rather more nimbly than I had for years,' Menzies recalled. The process of choice was complicated by the presence of the President of Royal Academy who was selecting pictures for the next exhibition and it seemed as if Sir Robert was going to have to be satisfied with a painting he didn't much like. Then Churchill's son-in-law, Christopher Soames, noticed the look in Menzies's eye and remarked, 'But that is not good enough for your old friend. What about one of these on the wall?' He pointed to the Antibes picture. 'I at once expressed warm approval ... quickly embraced the family, and departed with remarkable speed! There was no sign of pursuit. I had the picture.'

By contrast with Menzies's lengthy campaign, when Sir Robert and his wife Dame Pattie were lunching at Chartwell some years later, she wanted to take a photograph of Churchill and nervously asked him, 'May I take your picture?' To

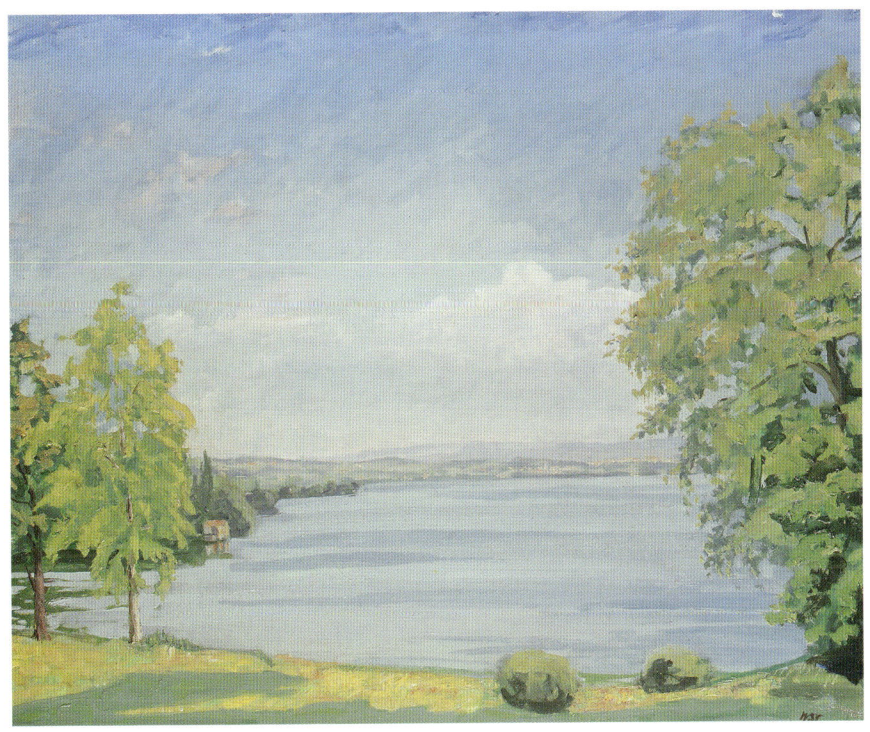

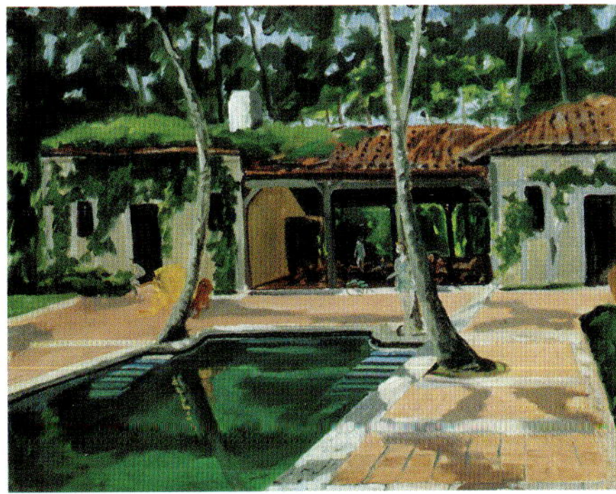

Fig 390 (C 126) above
The Swimming Pool at Casa Alva painted in 1946. This was the Florida home of Jacques and Consuelo Balsan who, after the Nazi invasion of France, made a daring and dangerous escape south into Spain before deciding to settle permanently in the United States.

Fig 391 (C 397) left
Lake Geneva. Painted in Switzerland in 1946, Churchill's executors later gave this picture to the Trustees of Chequers - the official country home for Britain's Prime Ministers.

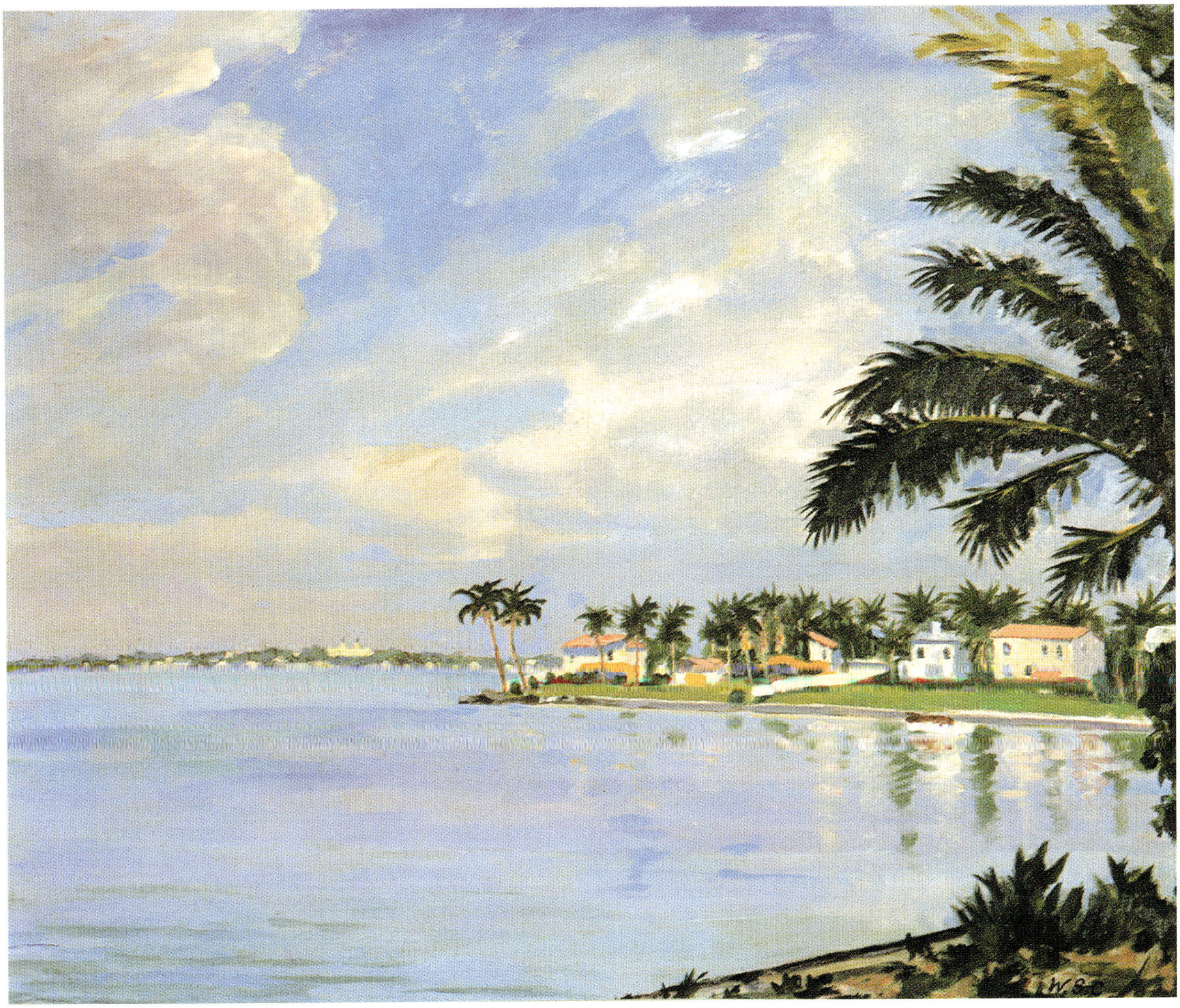

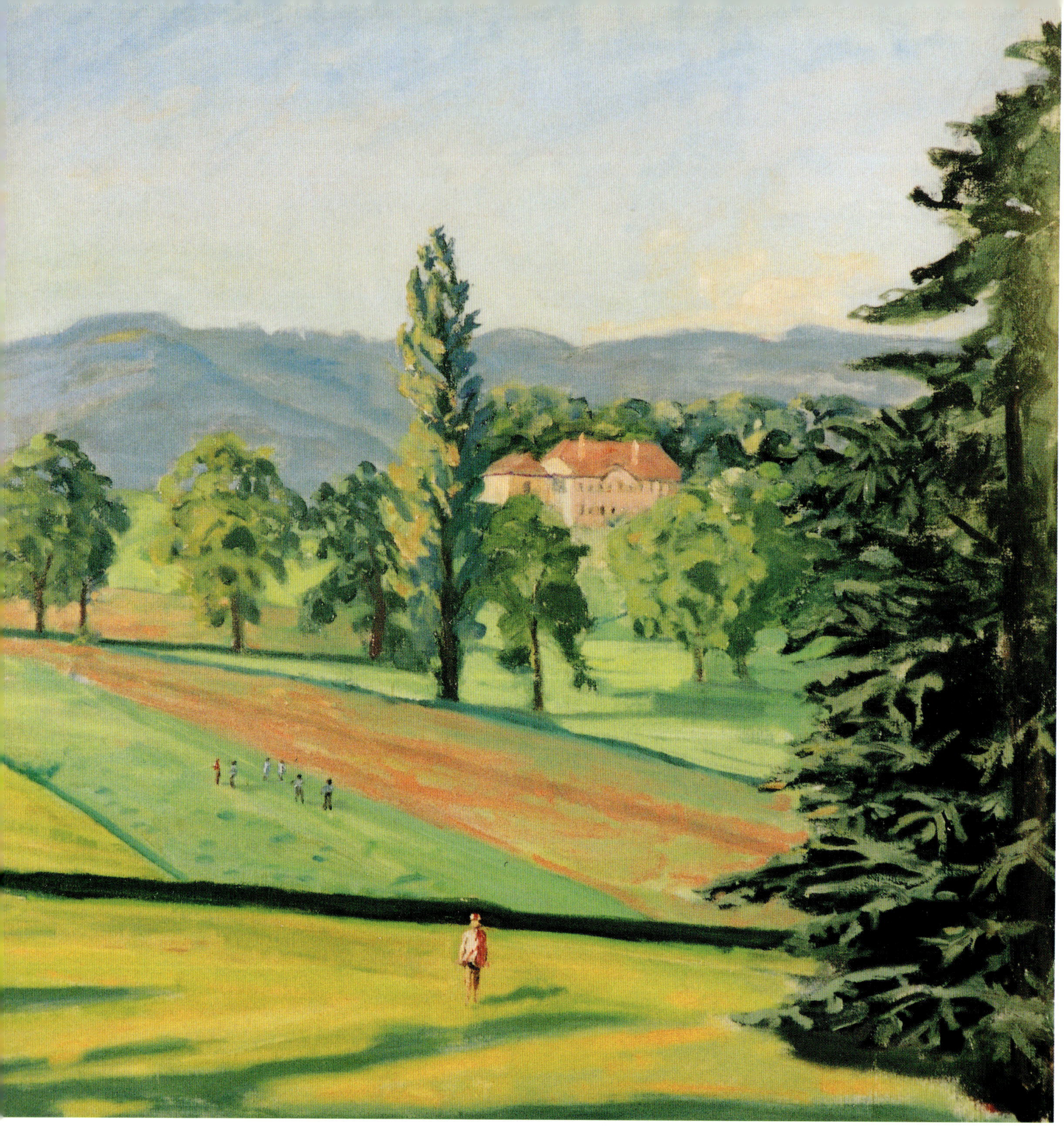

Fig 392 (C 444) above
Inland view from Choisy.

In the summer of 1946, an informal group of Swiss private citizens offered the Churchill family the chance of a holiday in Switzerland on the shores of Lake Geneva - Lac Leman - at the Villa Choisi, the home of a banker Alfred Kern.

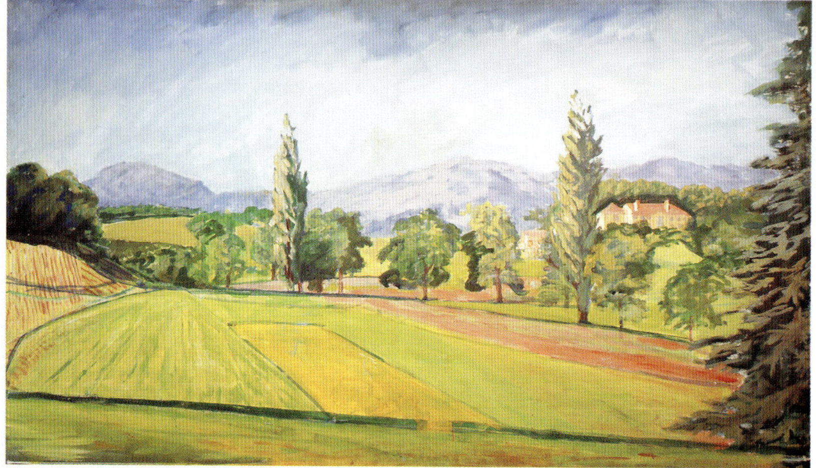

Fig 393 (C 447) right
A large unfinished painting of a landscape near Choisy.

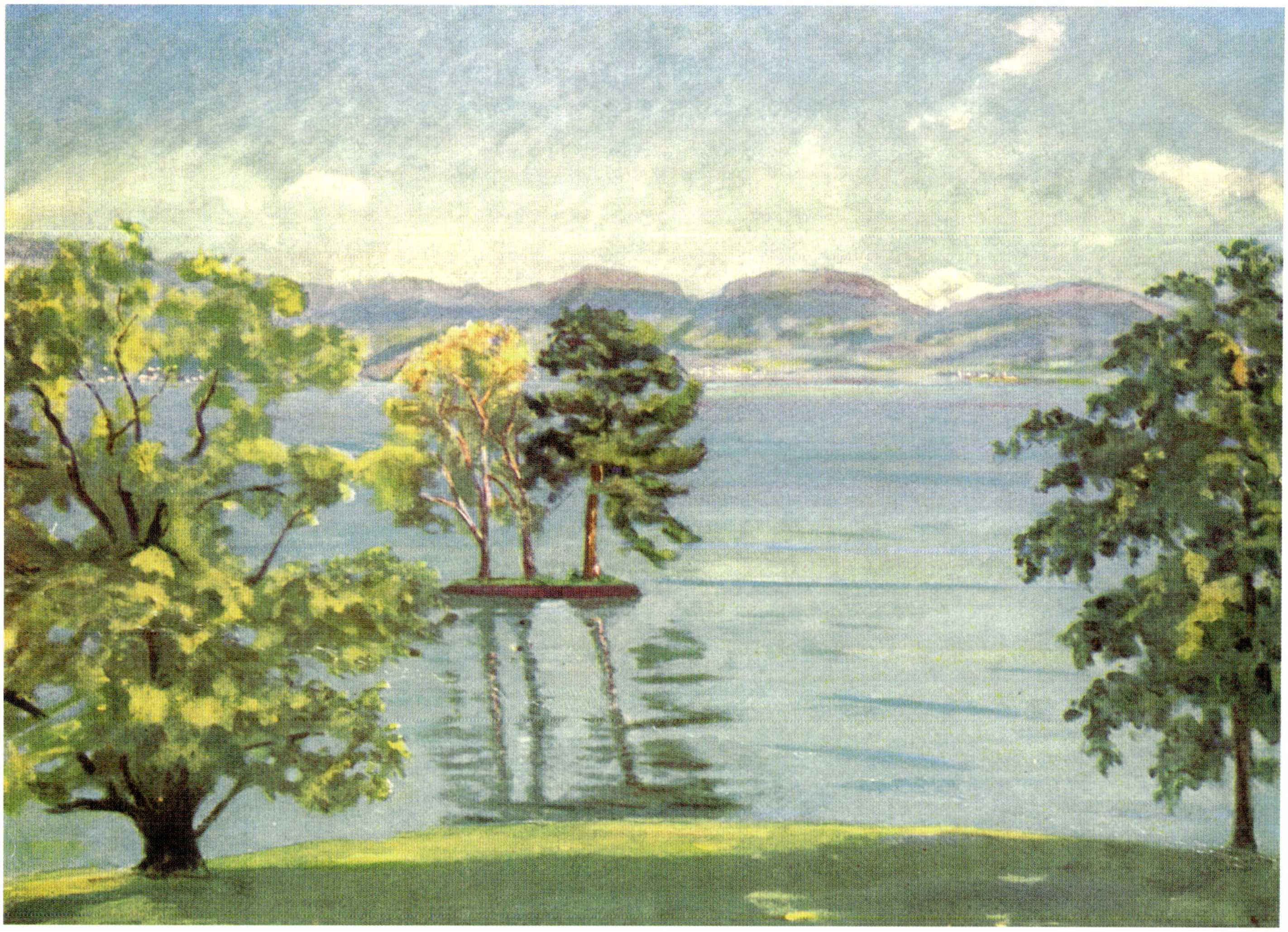

Fig 394 (C 398) above
Lake Geneva and Mont Blanc. Churchill gave this painting to his doctor, Lord Moran.

the astonishment of both, as Menzies wryly recalled, 'Winston replied, "that's all right, Clemmie has it ready!" ... she took the photograph, and walked out with one of Winston's paintings already crated up for delivery.'

Winston and Clementine went to find sunshine at Beaverbrook's villa, La Capponcina, which was to become an increasingly favourite haven in his last years for painting, writing and resting.

1956 [Background] Russian leaders visited Britain and met Churchill. Suez crisis: Egypt seized the canal. Israel attacked Egypt, Britain and France sent troops and ships. Russia threatened intervention. United Nations exacted a cease-fire. Russia crushed revolution in Hungary. Revolt against France in Algeria. Eisenhower re-elected President of the United States. The first two volumes of Churchill's *A History of the English-speaking Peoples* were published. He suffered another stroke.

1956 [Painting] In January Churchill made the first of many long visits to La Pausa, a villa near Roquebrune amid olive groves above Cap Martin, which was the French home of Emery and Wendy Reves. Churchill loved staying with the Reveses who had a collection of Impressionist pictures that included work by Monet, Manet and Cézanne. He painted often at La Pausa, exterior views and still lifes, and copied some of the pictures in the house. Reves gave him a Monet painting of the Thames, which included an impression of the Houses of Parliament. This still hangs at Chartwell.

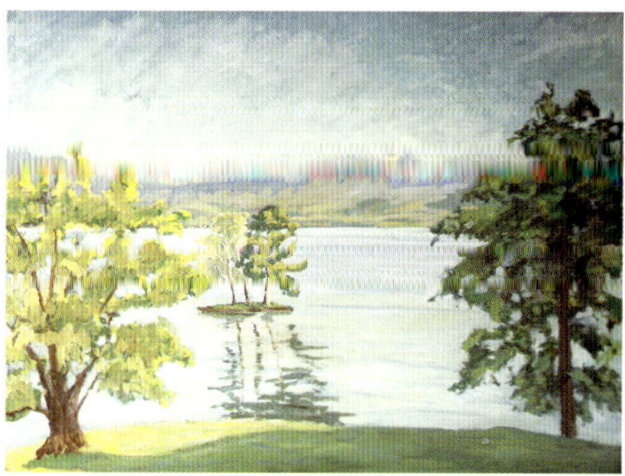

Fig 395 (C 399) above
This large painting of the view from Choisy of the island on Lake Geneva with Mont Blanc in the background was, like the picture above, based on a photograph from the Studio archives at Chartwell.

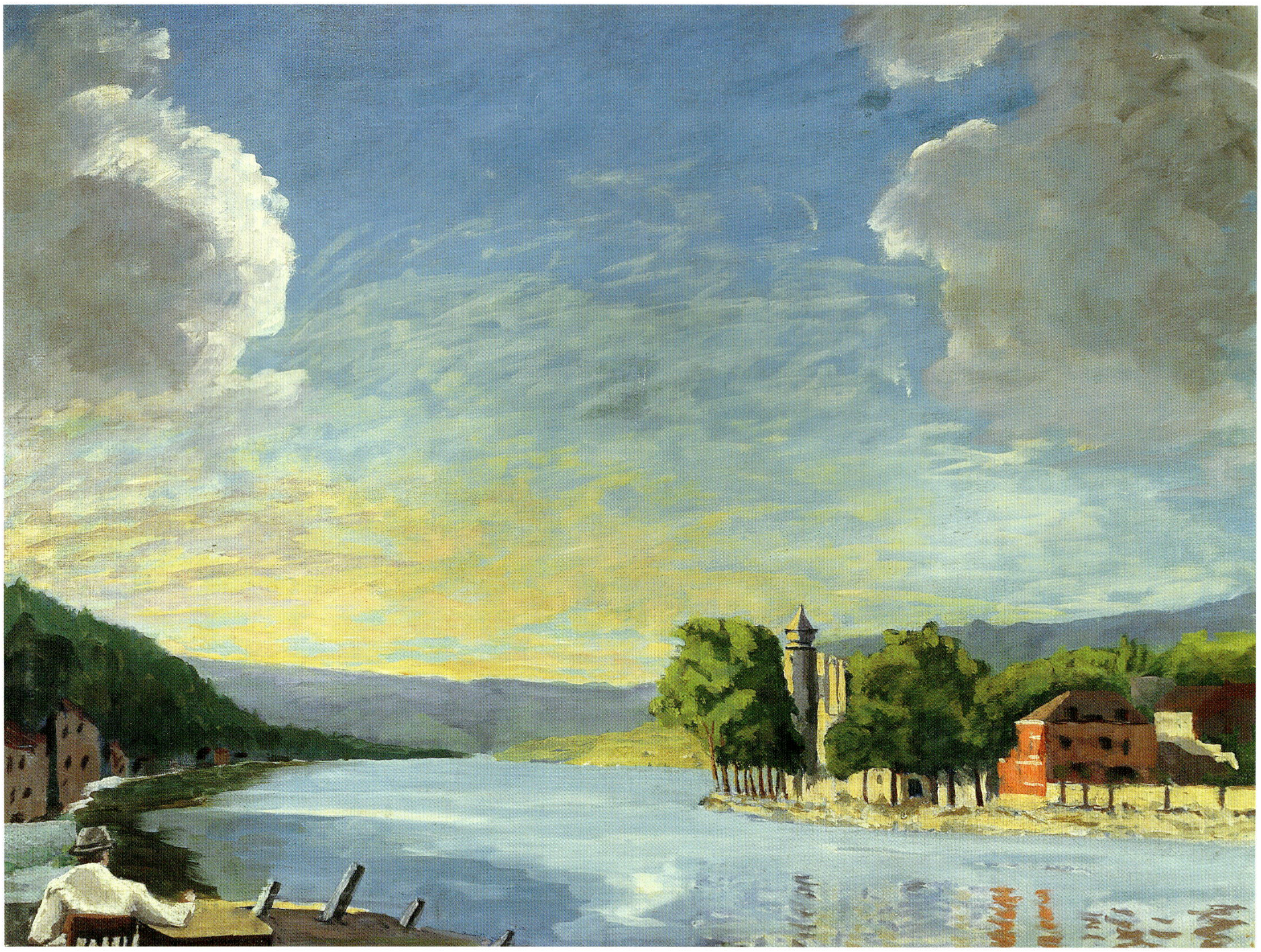

Fig 396 (C 400) above
Scene on the River Meuse at Dinant. Late in 1946, Churchill was invited to make a private visit to Belgium by its Prince Regent; these views of the Meuse and Bruges were the result.

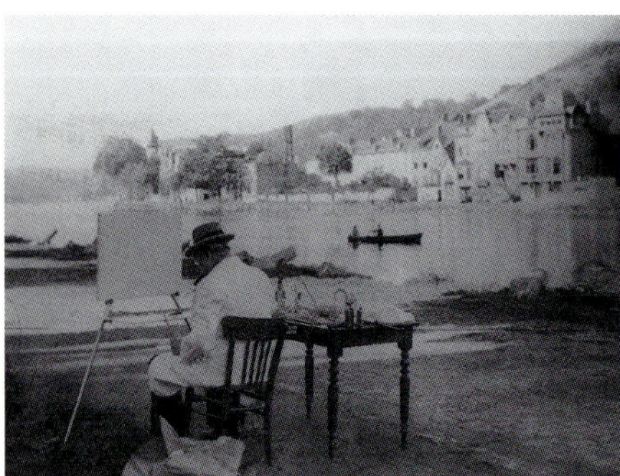

Winston Churchill painting at Dinant on the river Meuse in 1946. This photograph, marked up by Churchill, is from the Studio archives at Chartwell.

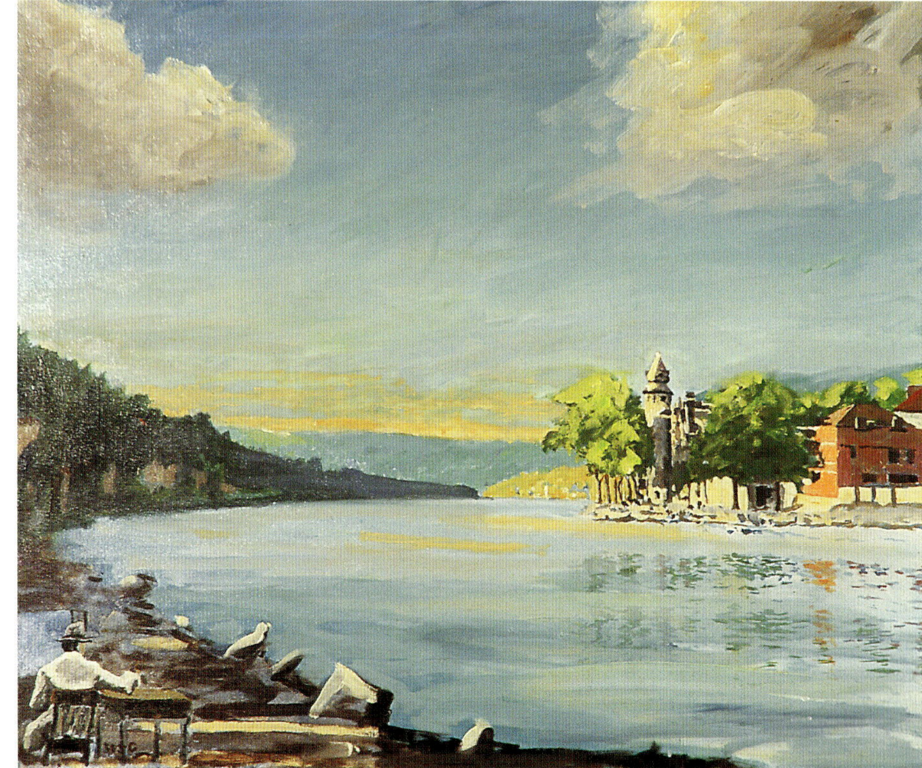

Fig 397 (C 396) right
This scene on the Meuse with the artist at his easel was based, like the others here, on a series of small photographs from the Studio archives at Chartwell.

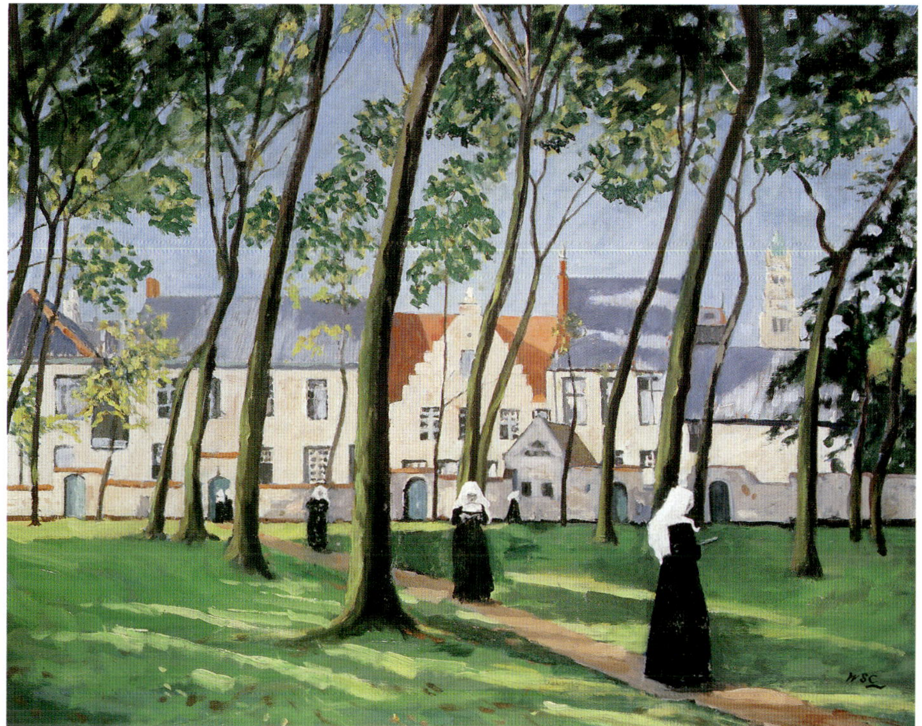

Fig 398 (C 443) left
Le Beguinage in Bruges. A 16th century convent, the Begijnhof (in Flemish) is occupied by Benedictine nuns. Churchill based this painting on a series of small photographs of the nuns walking round their shady oasis; he had enlargements made of some of the figures so that he could place them exactly where he wanted in the painting. The original photographs are in the Studio archives at Chartwell. See example below centre. Churchill gave this picture to his secretary, Grace Hamblin.

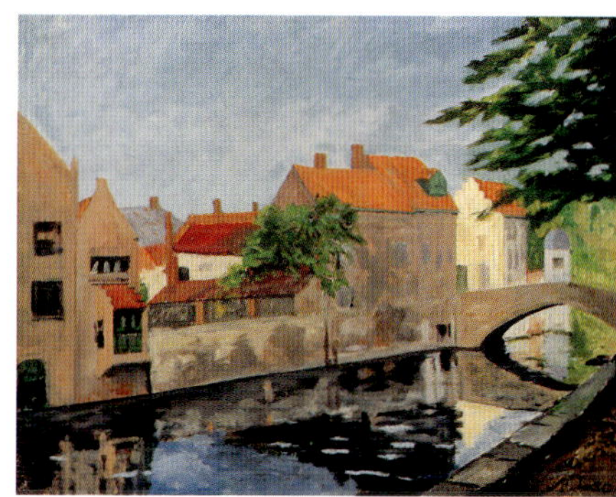

Fig 399 (C 414) above
Canal scene at Bruges, based on a series of small photographs from the Studio archives at Chartwell.

About this time, Arthur Sulzberger was to celebrate his 20th anniversary as publisher of *The New York Times*. His wife Iphigène wanted to give him 'something special ... He had once told me he would love to own a painting by Winston Churchill ... but knew his work was unobtainable.' Gladwyn Jebb, the British Ambassador in Paris, advised Iphigène to contact Christopher Soames who replied, 'I know how fond my father-in-law is of Arthur. But, he'd rather part with one of his children than with one of his paintings.' ... 'The next thing I knew the painting was on its way.' (C 297).

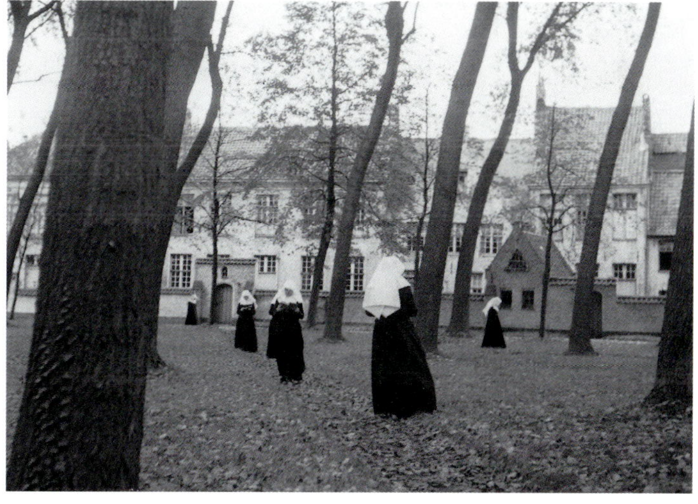

1957 [Background] British Home Guard disbanded and armed forces reduced. European Economic Community established by the Treaty of Rome. Rebellion in Iraq. Race riots in the US. Churchill suffered two small strokes. Flew to visit Eisenhower in Washington. Russia launched the first earth satellite. The third volume of Churchill's *A History of the English-speaking Peoples* was published.

1957 [Painting] Churchill paid three long visits to the Reveses' villa, La Pausa, where he painted constantly indoors and out.

From 1932, Grace Hamblin worked as secretary first for Sir Winston and then for Lady Churchill. After the war, Miss Hamblin recalled, Churchill's 'paintings were stored in the drawing room at Chartwell, which wasn't being used. Sir Winston loved days of hanging pictures ... he'd say in the morning to his secretary, "I'll hang pictures today" and this meant getting the carpenter along who would follow him round and see where he wanted the paintings put. He liked a secretary or someone with him to help to line them up.'

One day at Chartwell, Churchill brought one of his paintings in to the office. 'He put it up and then he said, "What do you think of it?" It was one of his most terrible paintings. And he must have seen my expression, because I wouldn't dare to

Fig 400 (C 401) below
Scene on the Meuse.

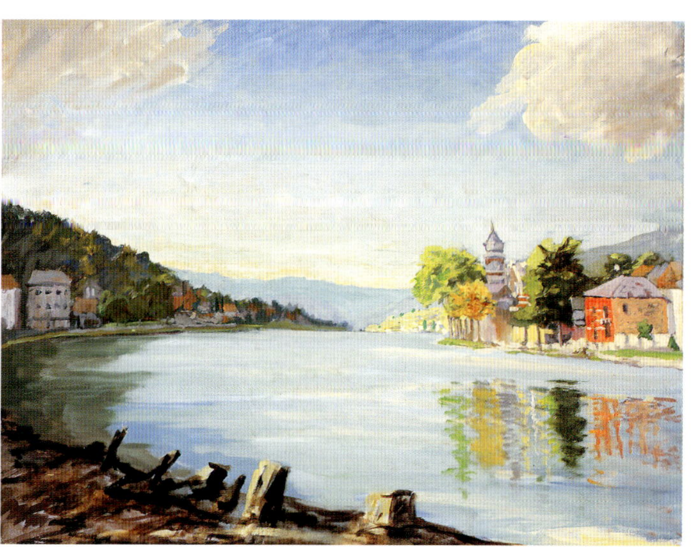

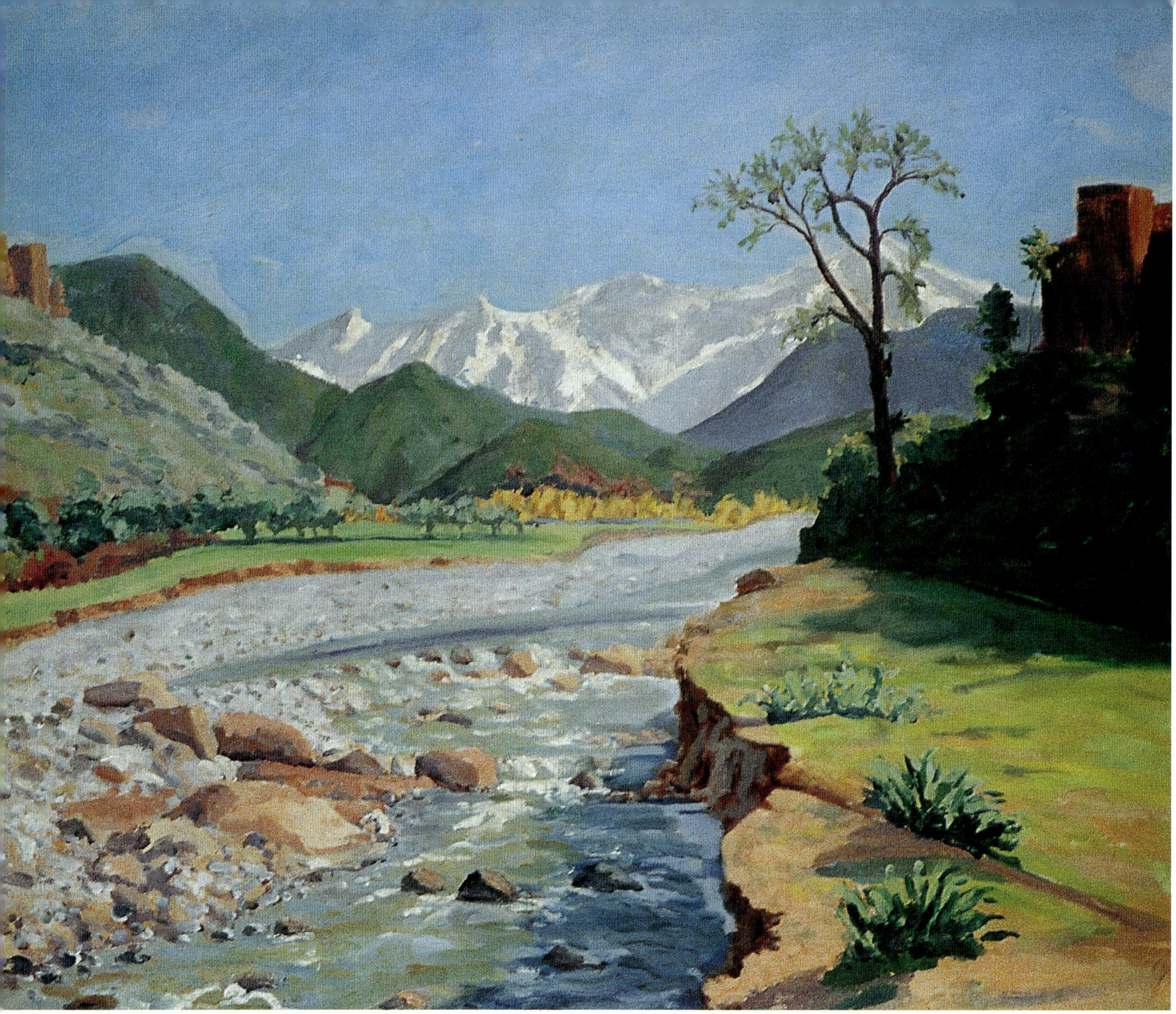

Fig 401 (C 431) above
The Valley of the Ourika and the Atlas Mountains. Painted in 1948, Churchill gave this picture to President Eisenhower in 1958. It was at the President's invitation that a large exhibition of Sir Winston's paintings toured the United States in that year.

In 1947, Churchill travelled once again to Marrakech in Morocco which he regularly visited from then until 1959, attracted as much by the warm climate as by the variety of the subjects offered by the city and its desert location. Within the city's walls Churchill was clearly fascinated, for example, by its gardens, the great Mosque, and the colourfully garbed peoples; for the latter he sometimes used photographs as an aid to accuracy. In 1950 he discovered the special delights of Tinerhir, in the Sahara desert on the far side of the Atlas Mountains from Marrakech. During that same visit Churchill met the artist Jacques Marjorelle who introduced him to painting in tempera, rather than oil; Winston was fascinated by this new technique and experimented with it subsequently but no extant examples are known.

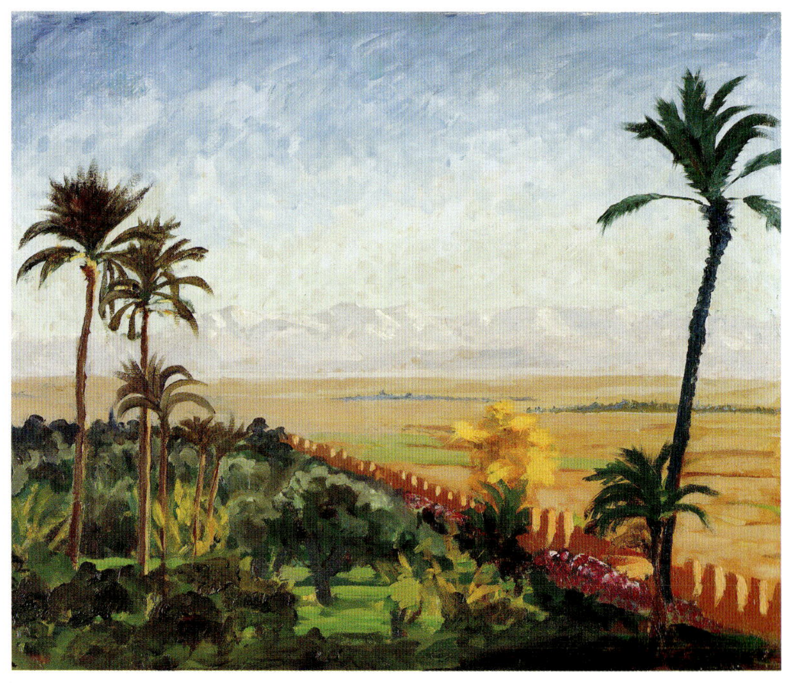

Fig 402 (C 430) right
Marrakech, painted in 1947. Churchill gave this painting to his grandson, Winston.

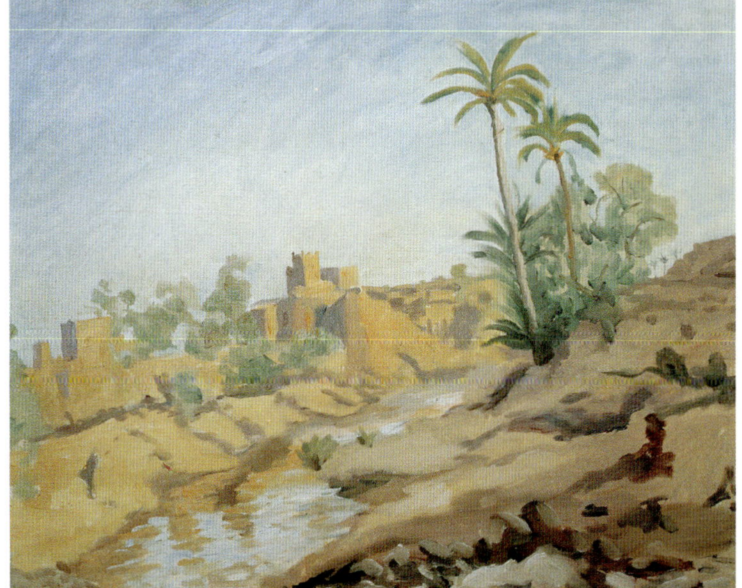

Fig 403 (C 433) left
The valley of the Ourika near Marrakech. This painting formerly belonged to Clementine Churchill.

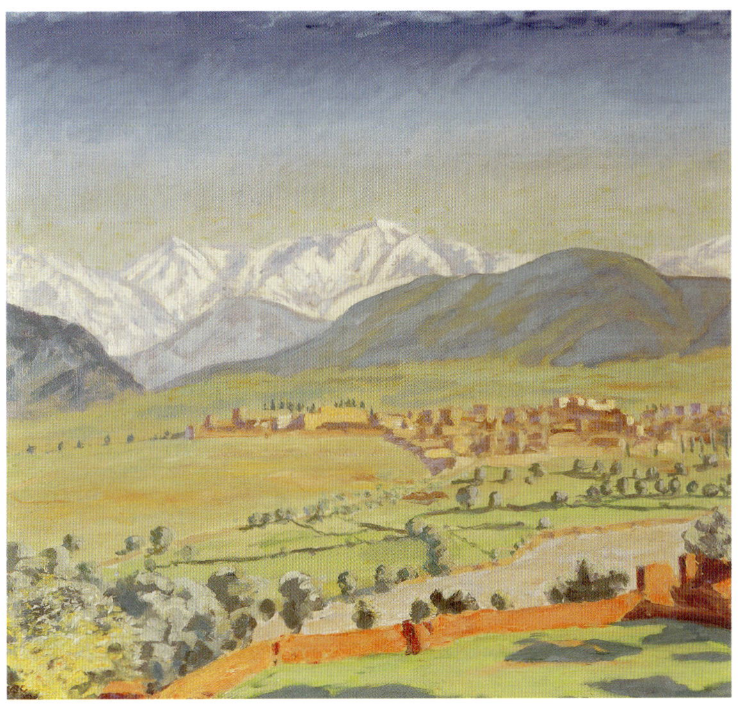

Fig 404 (C 428) left
Marrakech.

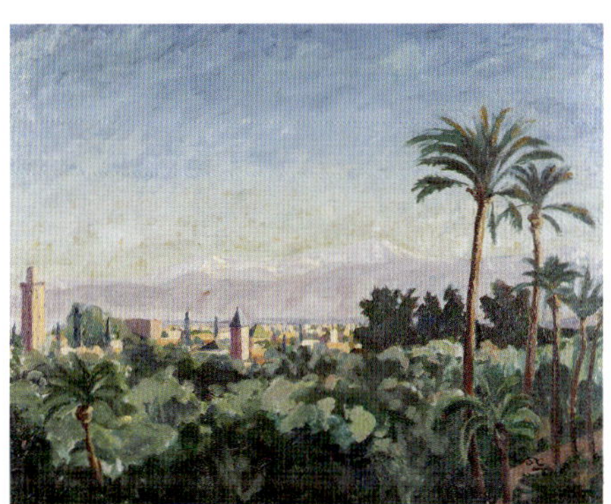

Fig 405 (C 429) above
This painting of Marrakech is based on a photograph from the Studio archives at Chartwell.

criticize it, I promise you, I know nothing about painting. I said, "Well, it's not my favourite." And he said, "Which is your favourite?" And I said, "Well, I love the Béguinage." So he said, "Oh, well, we'll put that here." Some years later it went on exhibition with others to New York. When it came back and I was helping him unpack it, he said, "This is yours. Take it home." That's all there was to it. Just like that ... enough to kill anybody. I couldn't believe it ... to receive one of his paintings, and from him!' (C 443)

'Sir Winston didn't care to give his pictures away, but after the war he gave away quite a lot ... as acknowledgement of something that had been done for him ... They were mostly particular friends.' His frame maker Frank Patrickson would pack them up and send them away. 'Sir Winston and he would sit down and initial a batch. He wouldn't do it on the way.'

'I adored Lady Churchill, but not for a long time ... she needed a lot of knowing ... she knew exactly what she wanted. Inside herself she was an extremely good woman. She took a great interest in [Sir Winston's] painting ... and she could

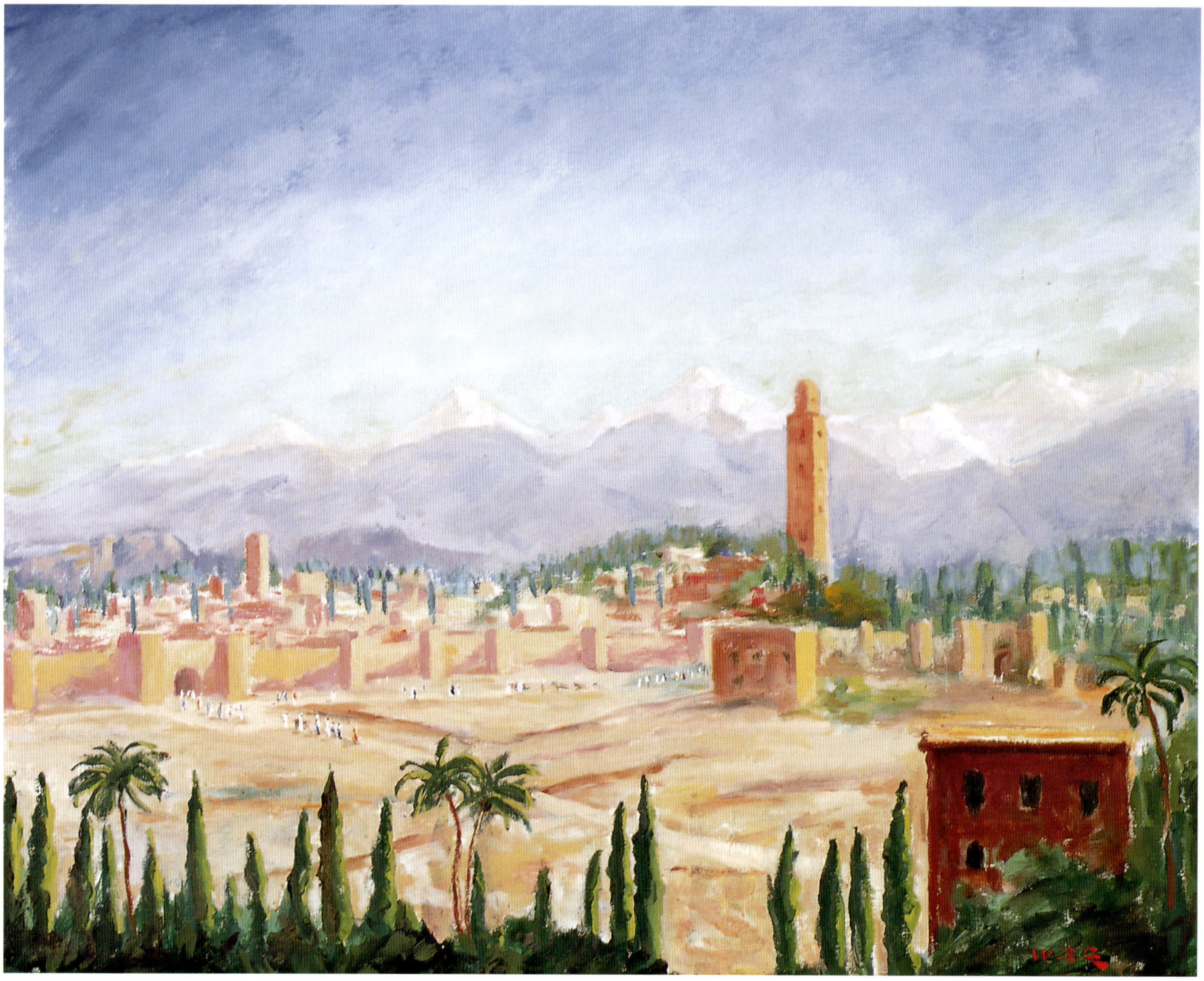

Fig 406 (C 432) above
This view of Marrakech formerly belonged to Clementine Churchill.

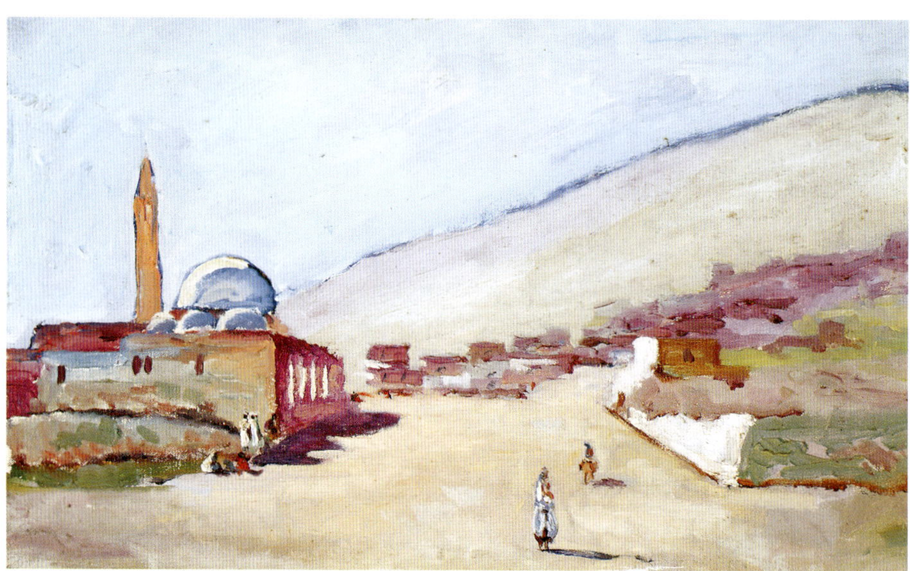

Fig 407 (C 437) right
A village near Marrakech.

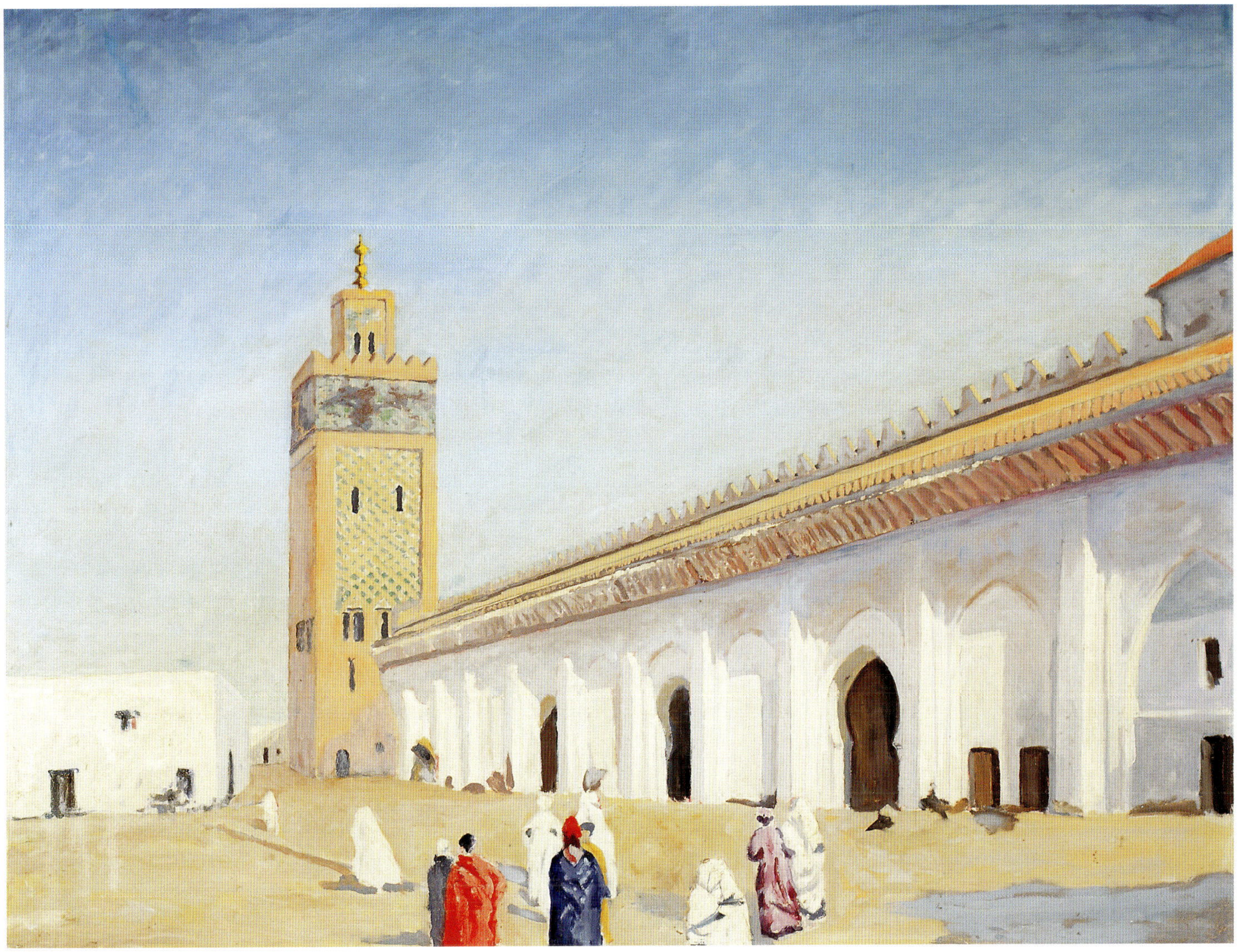

Fig 408 (C 435) above
The Mosque at Marrakech.

criticize, she was very, very good. He took notice, he might not appear to, but he did. They loved each other dearly. It was extraordinary and it remained.'

1958 [Background] Military coup in Iraq. Fifth Republic in France. French troops left Tunisia and Morocco. Churchill decorated in Paris by President de Gaulle with the Croix de la Libération. In his reply Churchill said, 'I have often made speeches in French, but that was wartime, and I do not wish to subject you to the ordeals of darker days.' Race riots in Britain. First US earth satellites. Churchill College for science and engineering founded at Cambridge University. Winston and Clementine celebrated their Golden Wedding in the South of France at Beaverbrook's villa, La Capponcina. Churchill began a series of cruises as the guest of Aristotle Onassis on his yacht *Christina*. The fourth and final volume of Churchill's *A History of the English-speaking Peoples* was published.

1958 [Painting] Churchill paid two long visits to the Reveses at La Pausa. Although his interest remained, he began to feel less and less inclined to paint as his physical strength began to fail.

Churchill received a letter from President Eisenhower who wrote, 'a travelling exhibition of your paintings in the United States would not only attract a good deal of attention among all the people here interested in painting; but I am certain it would serve in a very definite way to strengthen the friendship between our two countries ... The tour would create a wave of good will across our country that would be both exciting and valuable.' Despite many doubts,

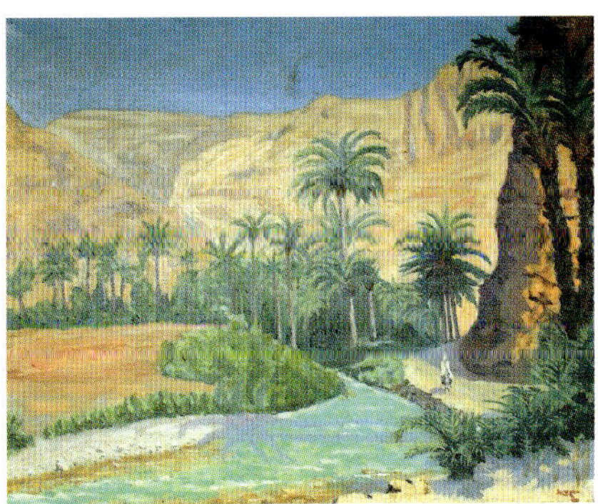

Fig 409 (C 436) above
Churchill gave this painting of a view near Marrakech to his accountant, James Wood.

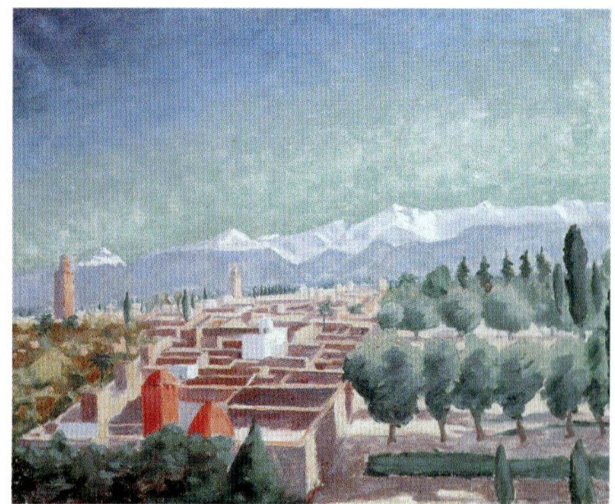

Fig 410 (C 466) above
Marrakech and the Atlas Mountains.

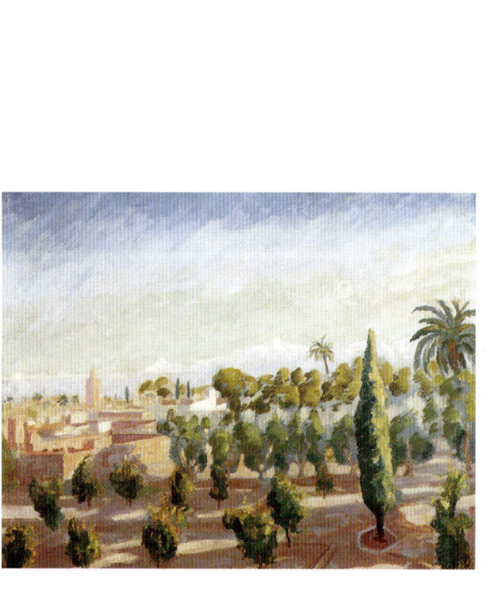

Fig 411 (C 465) above
Garden at Marrakech.

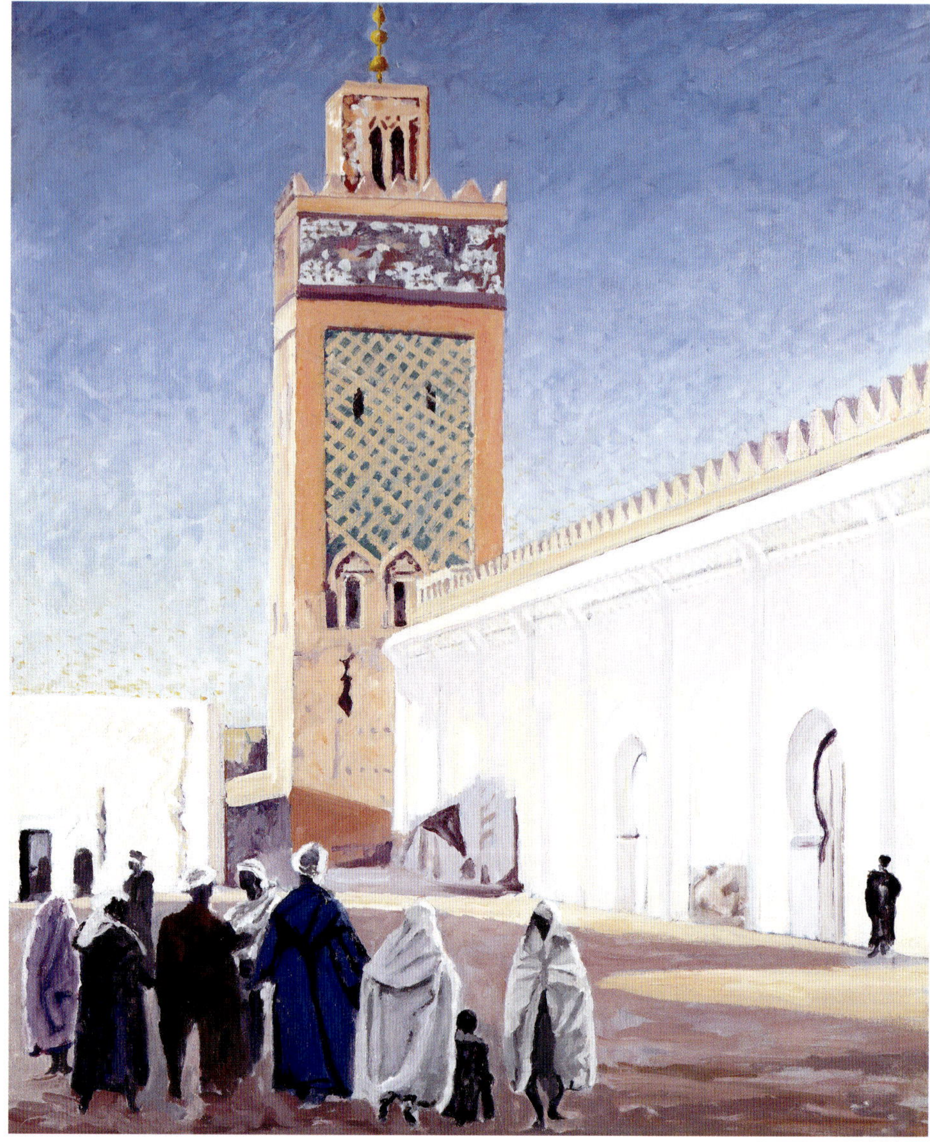

Fig 412 (C 438) above right
The Mosque at Marrakech.

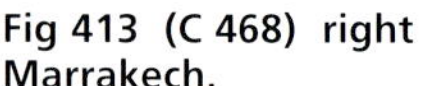

Fig 413 (C 468) right
Marrakech.

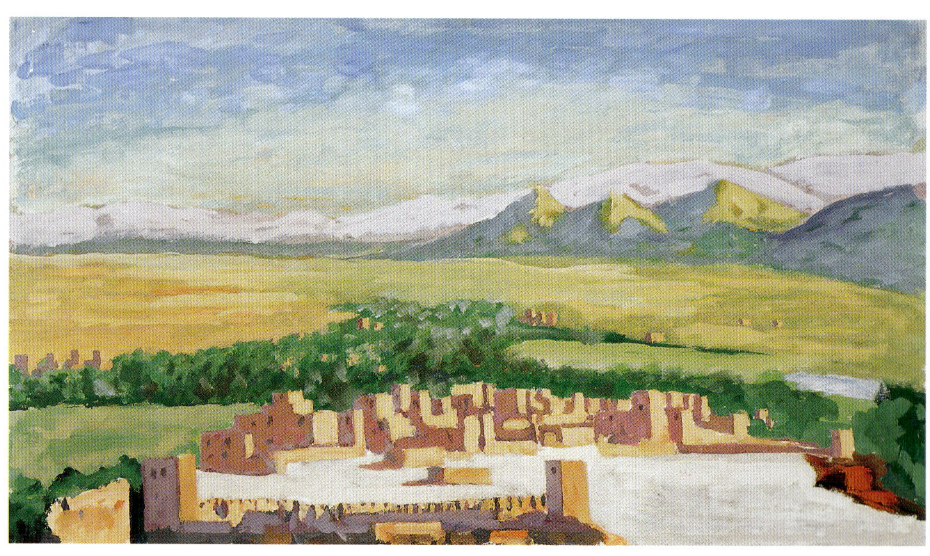

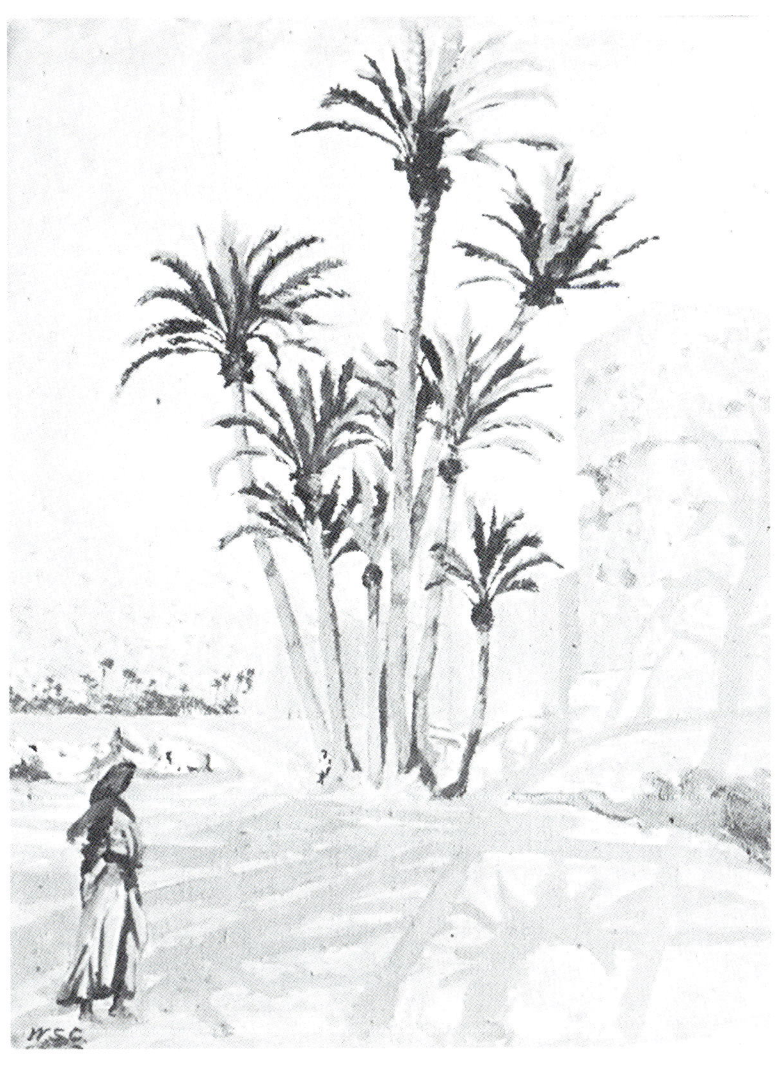

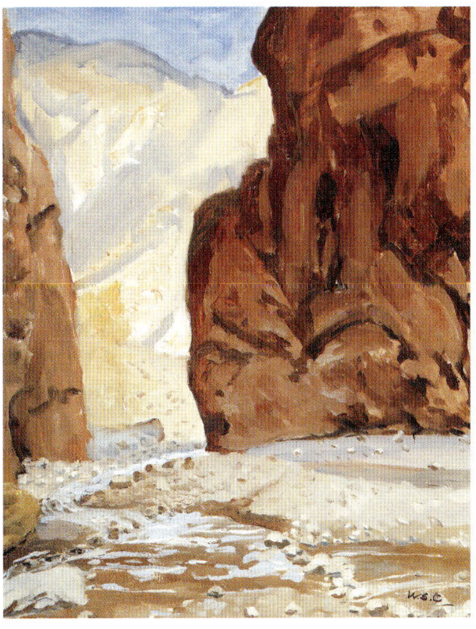

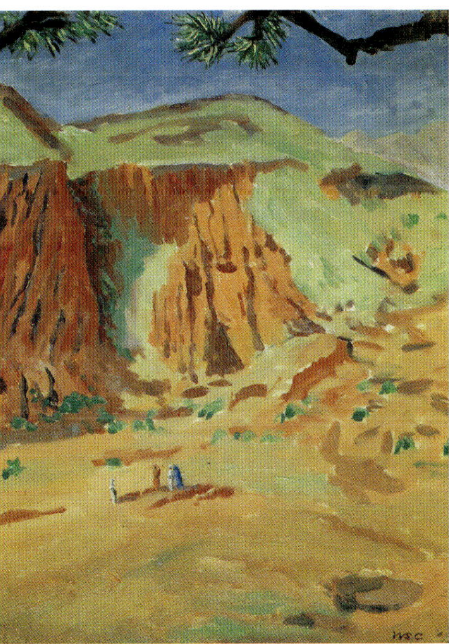

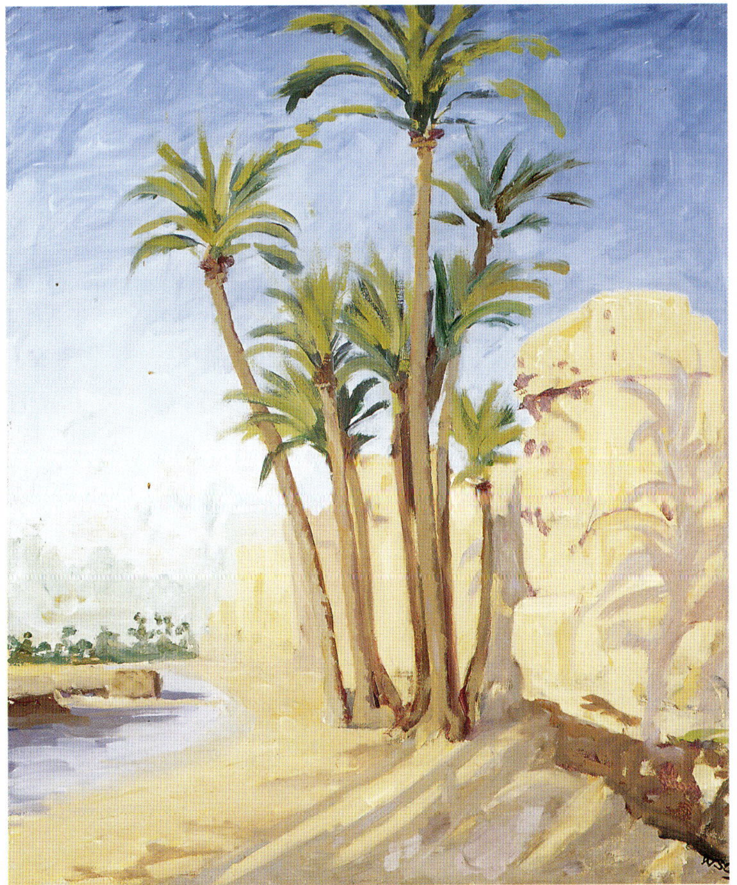

Fig 414 (C 458) above top
The Todhra Gorge. This painting is based on a pair of photographs, joined horizontally, from the Studio archives at Chartwell.

Fig 415 (C 459) above
The Gorges at Todhra are near Tinerhir. The painting formerly belonged to Clementine Churchill.

Fig 416 (C 464) above left
Palms near Marrakech. This painting, like the one below, is based on a photograph from the Studio archives at Chartwell.

Fig 417 (C 463) left
Group of palm trees near Marrakech.

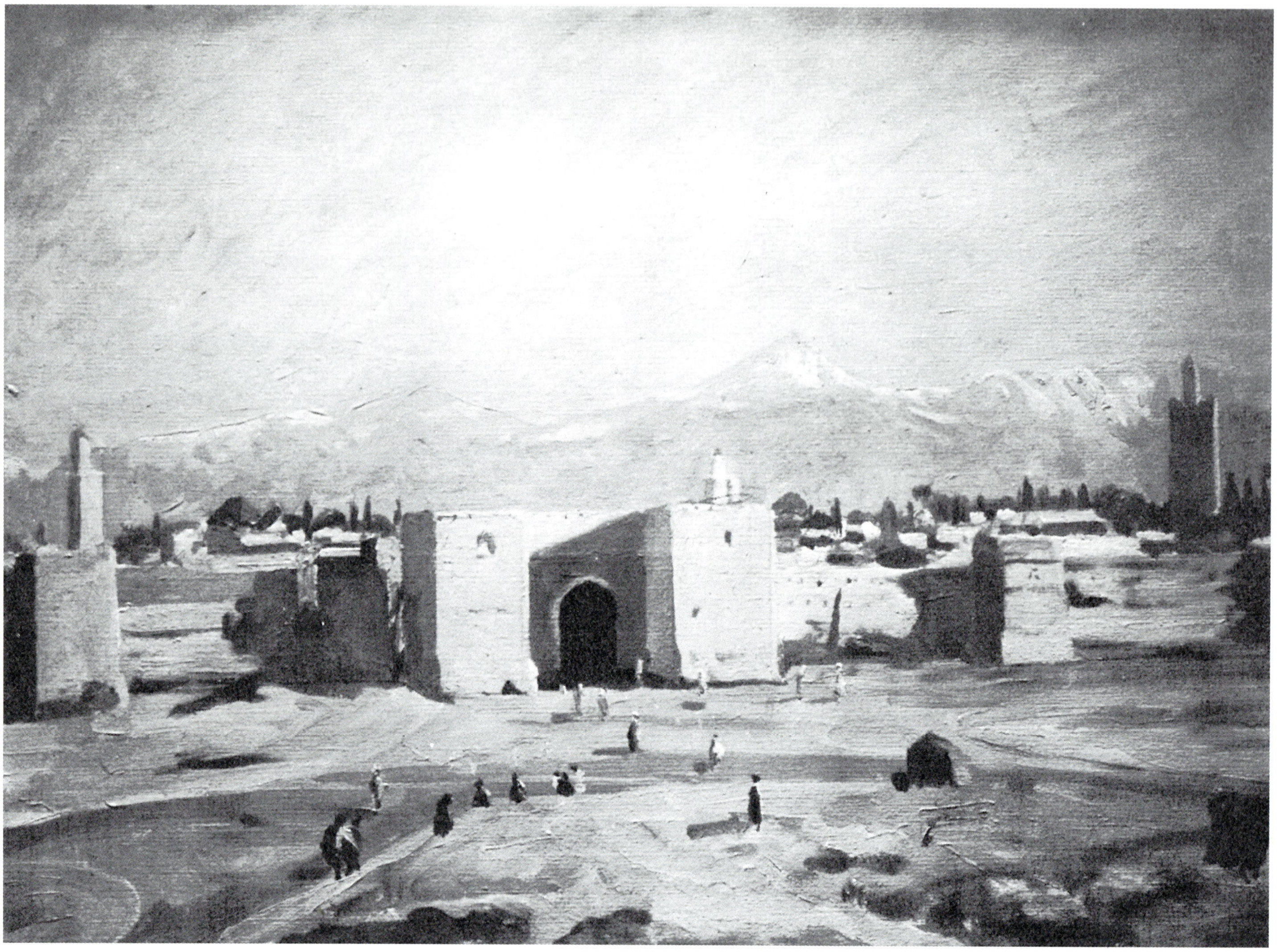

Fig 418 (C 434) above
Churchill gave this view of Marrakech to President Harry S.Truman.

Churchill agreed to the idea, in part because of the enthusiasm of his daughter Sarah. The exhibition, containing 35 paintings, was conceived and arranged by Joyce C. Hall of Hallmark Cards, who had reproduced some of Churchill's pictures on greetings cards. Opening in Kansas City, it was visited by President Truman who pronounced the pictures 'Damn good. At least you can tell what they are and that is more than you can say for a lot of these modern painters.'

This was the first exhibition solely devoted to Churchill's paintings and it attracted enormous public interest with more than half a million visitors. That it had been mounted in the United States first was pronounced 'a signal compliment' by President Eisenhower, who concluded his foreword to the catalogue, 'A very well known and great friend of his and mine, the late Sir Oswald Birley, recognized as one of the most distinguished of twentieth-century painters, once remarked to me, "If Sir Winston had given the time to art that he has given to politics, he would have been by all odds the world's greatest painter."'

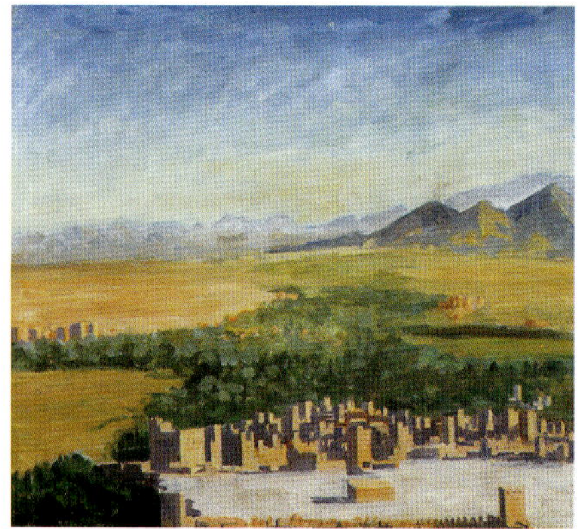

Fig 419 (C 469) above
The Plain of Tinerhir. This painting was presented by Lady Churchill to the Queen's Royal Hussars 'as a token of gratitude for the part played by the Regiment during the funeral of Sir Winston Churchill. 30th Jan. 1965.'

The pictures were shown in Kansas City, Detroit, New York, Washington, Providence, Dallas, Minneapolis and Los Angeles. Thereafter, because of the wide enthusiasm it had aroused, the exhibition travelled to Canada, visiting Toronto, Montreal, Fredericton and Vancouver; and then to Australia, where it was seen in Canberra, Sydney, Brisbane, Melbourne, Hobart, Adelaide and Perth; followed by the cities of Dunedin, Christchurch, Wellington and Auckland in New Zealand. The exhibition of Churchill's paintings came to London in the following year, in response to an earlier approach from the President of The Royal Academy.

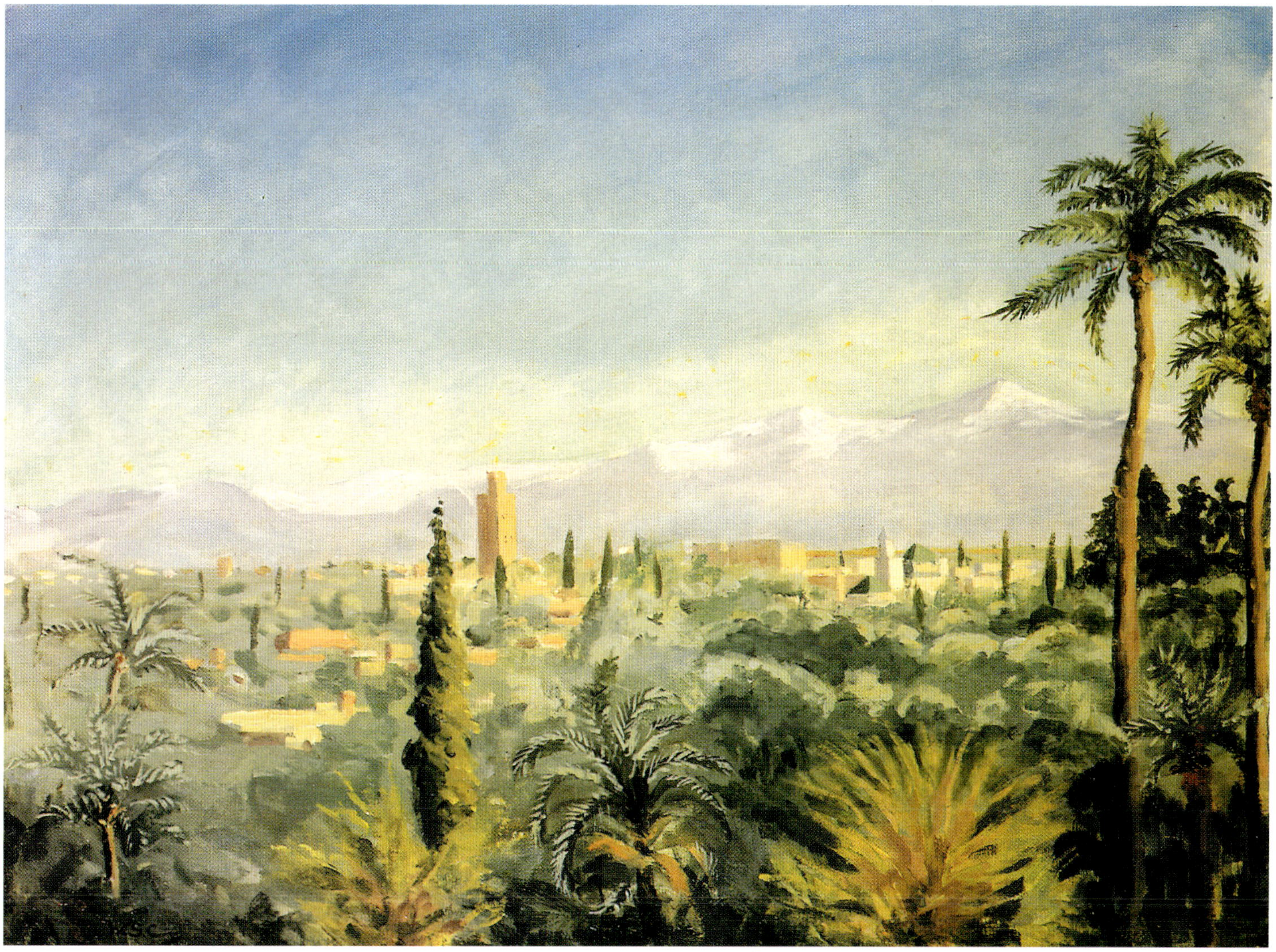

Fig 420 (C 501) above
Churchill gave this view of the Atlas Mountains from Marrakech to Antonio Giraudier.

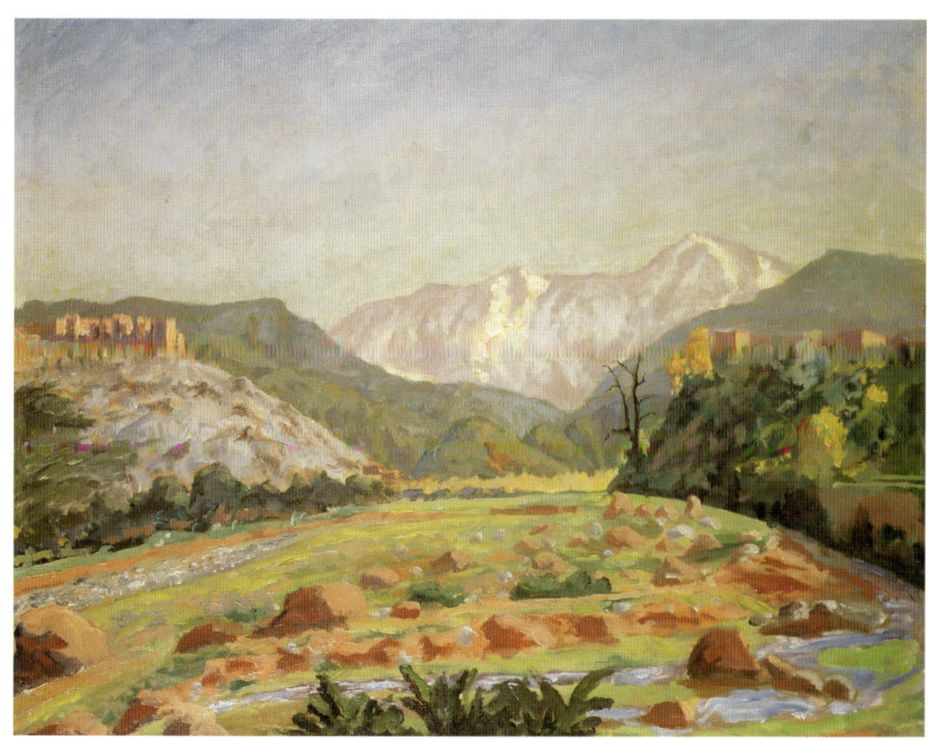

Fig 421 (C 470) left
The valley of the Ourika. This painting is based on photographs from the Studio archives at Chartwell.

Fig 422 (C 460) right
A gate in Marrakech. This painting and those illustrated on the following pages are likely to have been painted in the course of Churchill's last visits to Marrakech in the late 1950s.

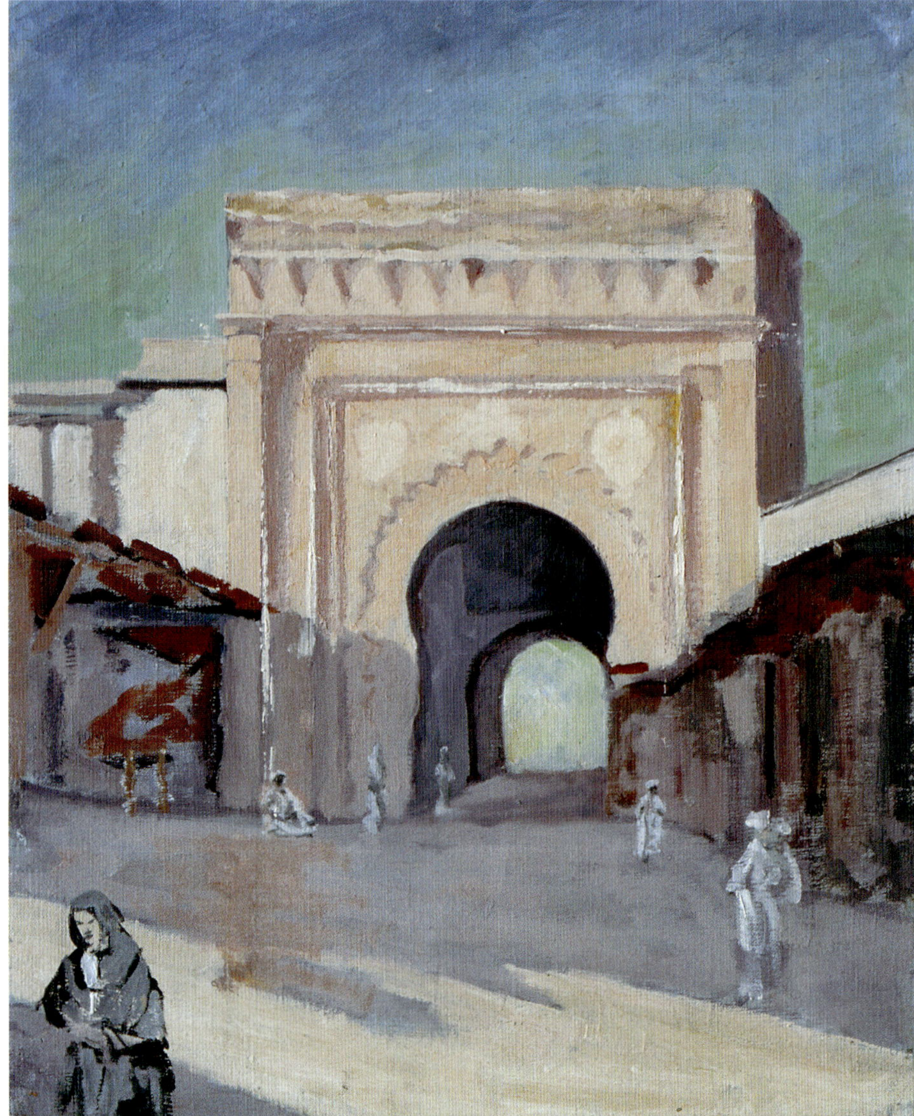

Winston Churchill painting at Marrakech in the 1950s.

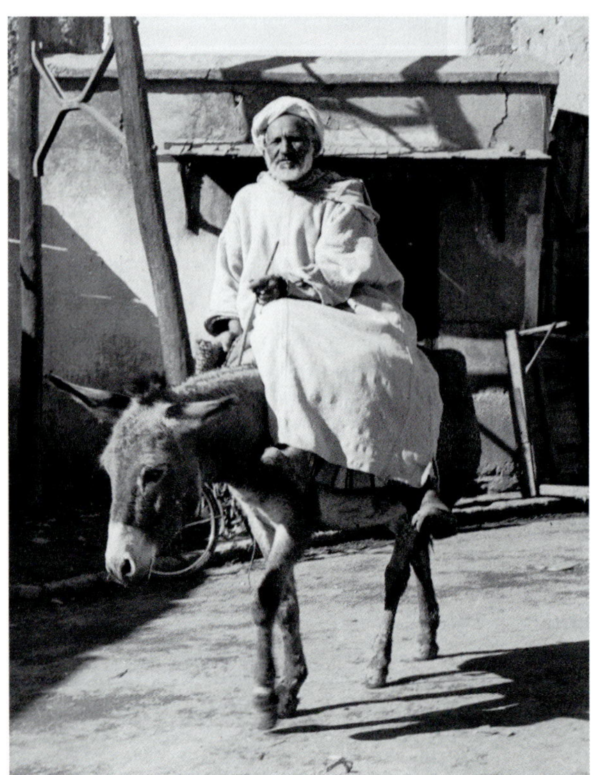

Right
This photograph from the Studio archives at Chartwell, showing an Arab on a donkey, was used by Churchill in his painting illustrated on the facing page.

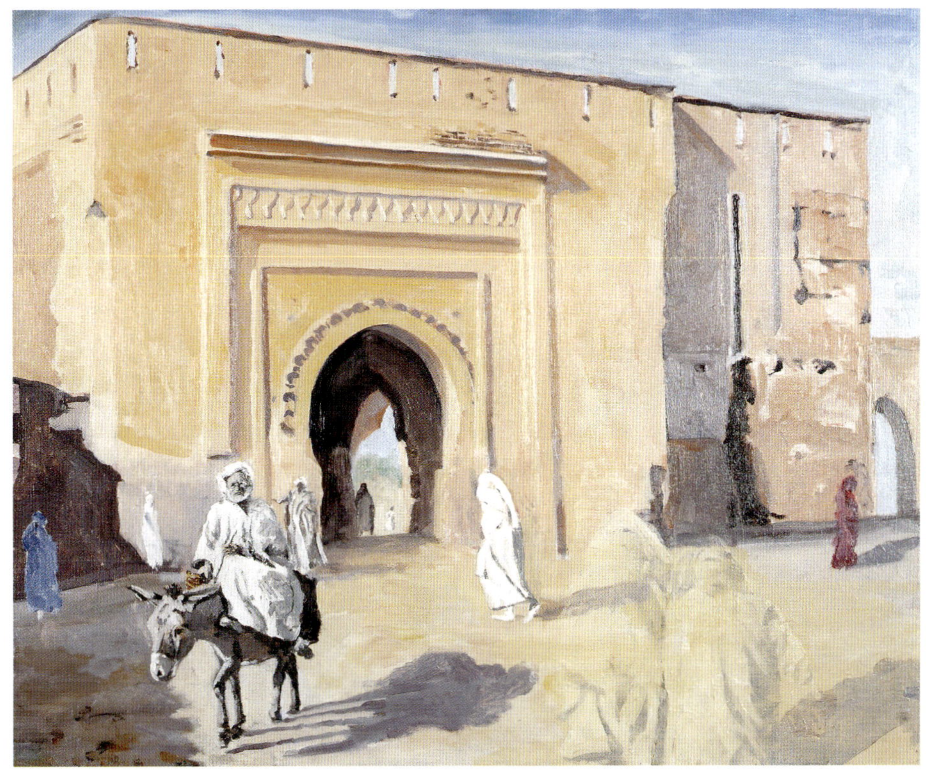

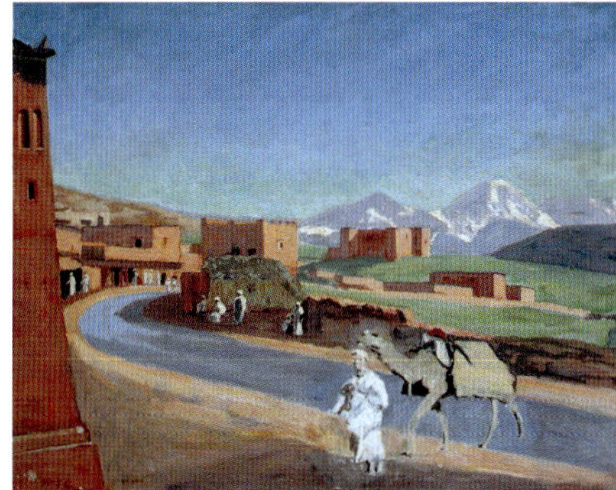

Fig 423 (C 457) above
In this scene at Marrakech, the man leading a camel is based on a photograph from the Studio archives at Chartwell.

Fig 424 (C 462) left
This scene at Marrakech shows another of its famous gates. The man on a donkey is based on a photograph from the Studio archives at Chartwell.

1959 [Background] Churchill's 85th year.
General election in Britain. Churchill elected once again as the Member for Woodford. Uprising in Tibet against Chinese rule. Revolution in Cuba. US launched first atomic-powered submarine.

1959 [Painting] Churchill visited President Eisenhower in Washington and gave him one of his paintings, 'The Valley of the Ourika and Atlas Mountains', chosen by the President at Churchill's repeated insistence: 'I hope that when the [touring] exhibition is over you will select a picture to retain for yourself as a token of my continuing respect and affection.'

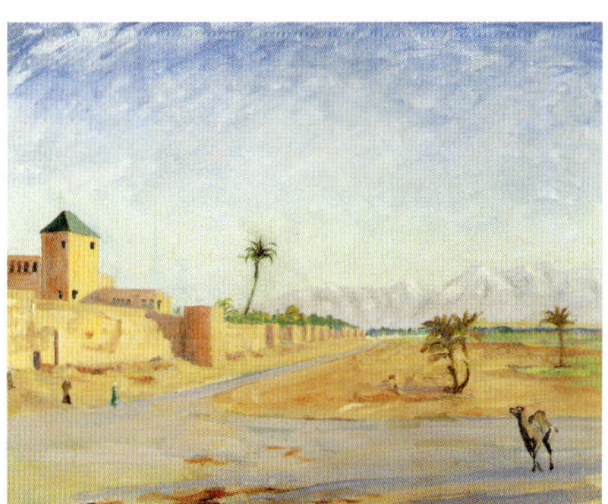

Fig 425 (C 453) above
The walls at Marrakech with a camel. This painting is based on a series of photographs from the Studio archives at Chartwell.

In their letters to each other the topic of painting was often mentioned. In 1950 Eisenhower wrote, 'I have had a lot of fun since I took up, in my somewhat miserable way, your hobby of painting ... I like it tremendously and, in fact, have produced two or three little things that I like well enough to keep.' Then late in 1954, Eisenhower wrote from the White House, 'As you know, I occasionally flatter myself by attempting to paint likenesses of friends ... I would be tremendously intrigued by the effort to paint one of you. Would it be an intolerable burden on you to allow an artist friend of mine [Thomas Stephens] to visit you long enough to take a few photographs and draw a few hasty color sketches that I could use in such an attempt? The final result would, of course, not be good but also it might not be so bad as to be unendurable.'

Churchill replied from No. 10 Downing Street the following January, 'I need hardly say I shall be greatly honoured to be one of your subjects in an artistic sense. Although my experiences as a model have not been altogether agreeable lately I submit myself with great confidence to your well-balanced love of truth and mercy.' Later on Churchill asked, 'How are you getting on with the portrait? I hope you will show it to me when it is finished and I warn you I shall claim full rights of retaliation.'

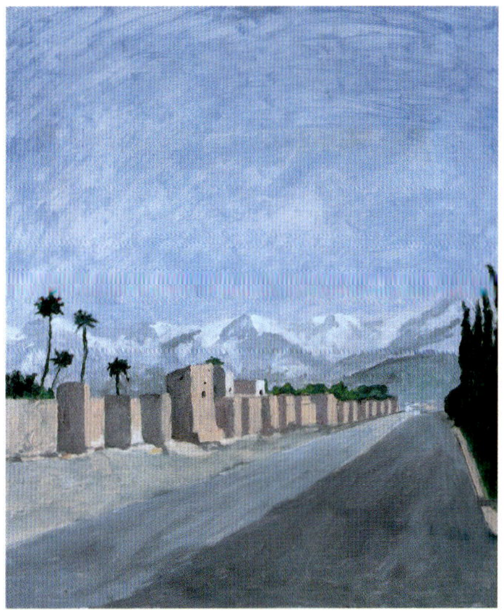

Fig 426 (C 452) above
The walls at Marrakech. Painted in 1959 during Churchill's last visit when in his 85th year.

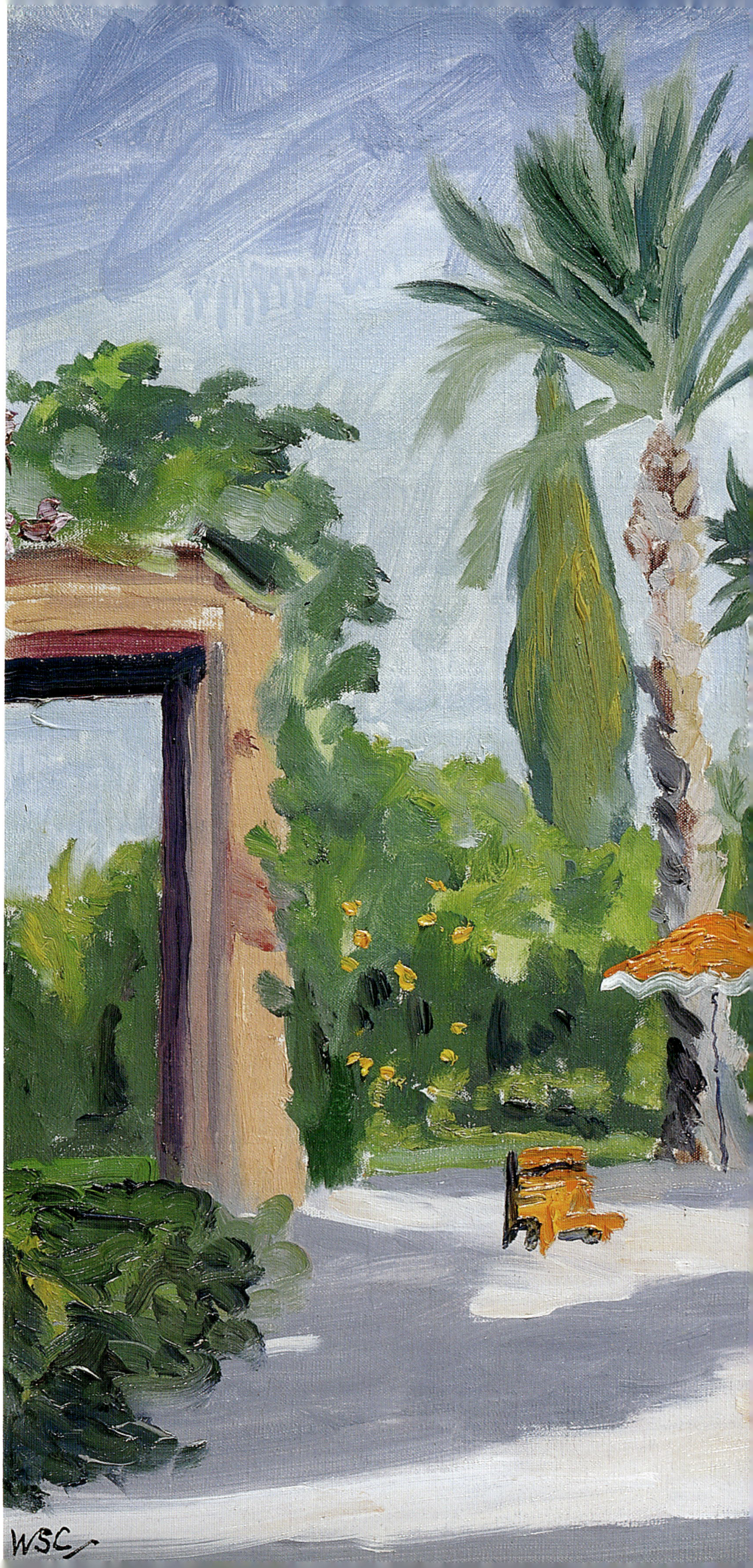

Fig 427 (C 467)
The garden at the Mamounia Hotel. This hotel is where Churchill invariably stayed from his first visits to Marrakech in the 1930s until his last in the 1950s.

Illustration below
Photograph of the garden at the Mamounia Hotel from the Studio archives at Chartwell.

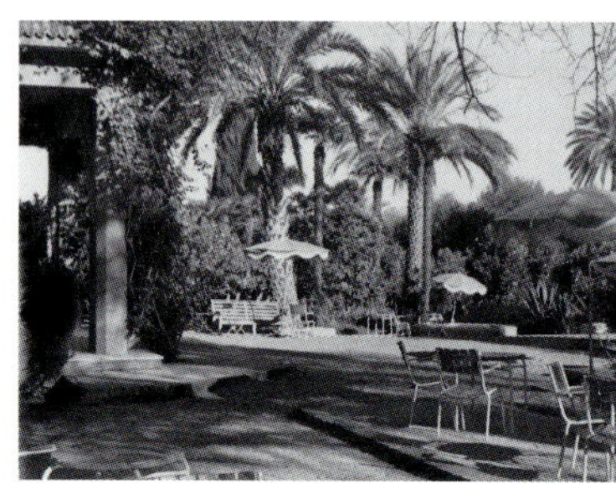

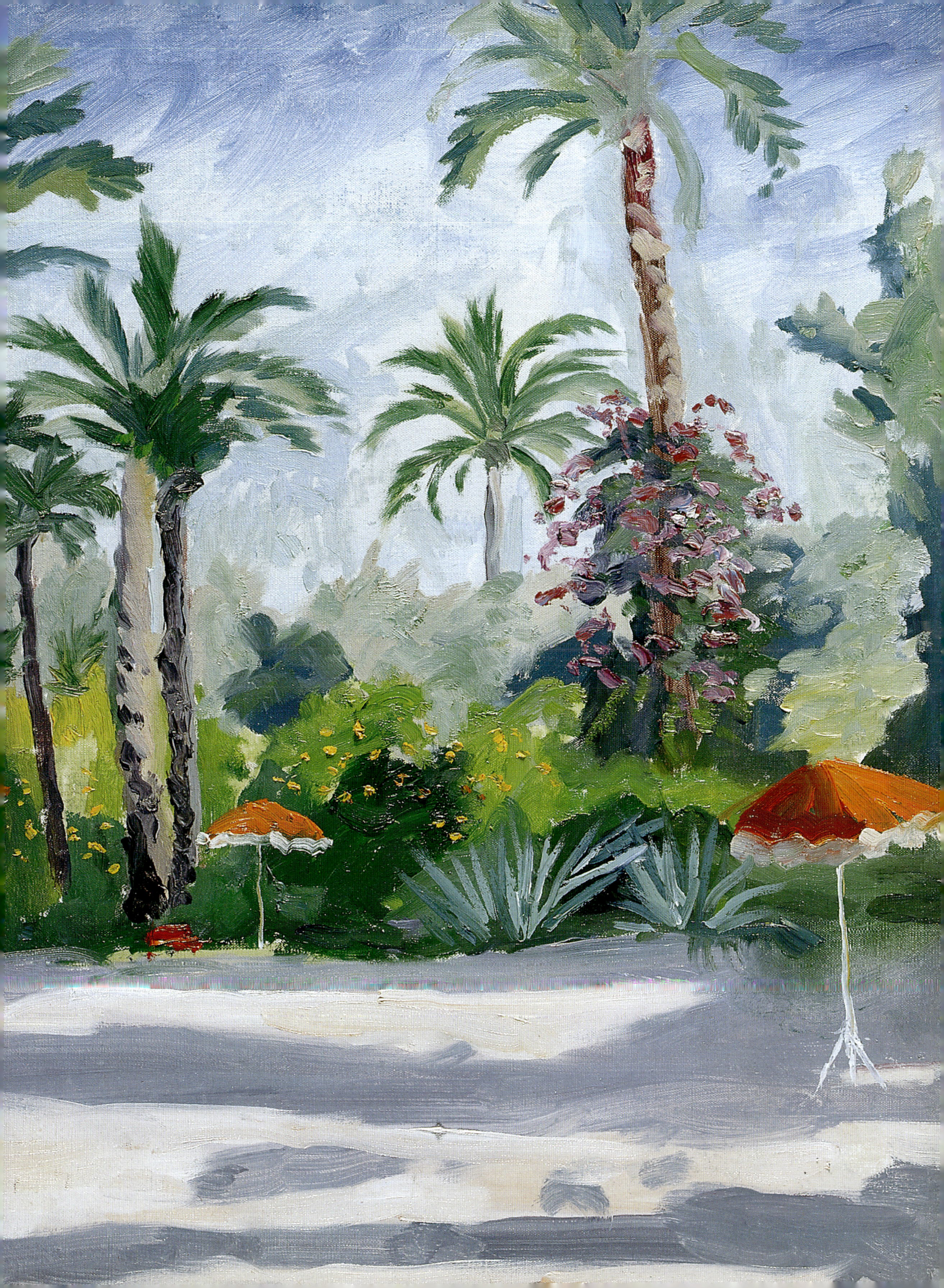

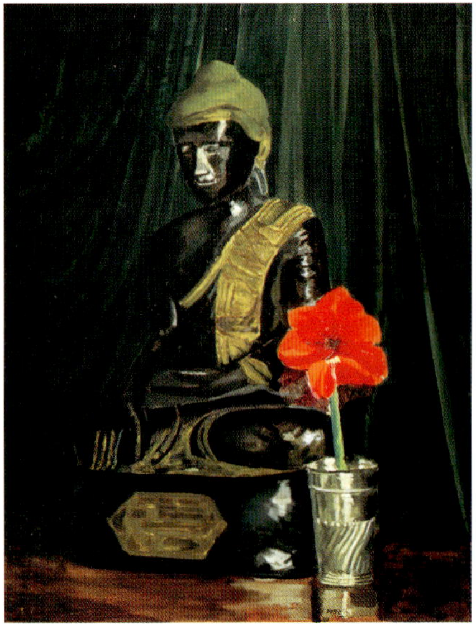

Fig 428 (C 382) above
Buddha and lily. The Buddha was left to Churchill in the will of his old friend Sir Ian Hamilton; the hippeastrum lily was a gift from Princess Marina Duchess of Kent when Winston caught bronchitis staying out too late painting in Marrakech in 1947.

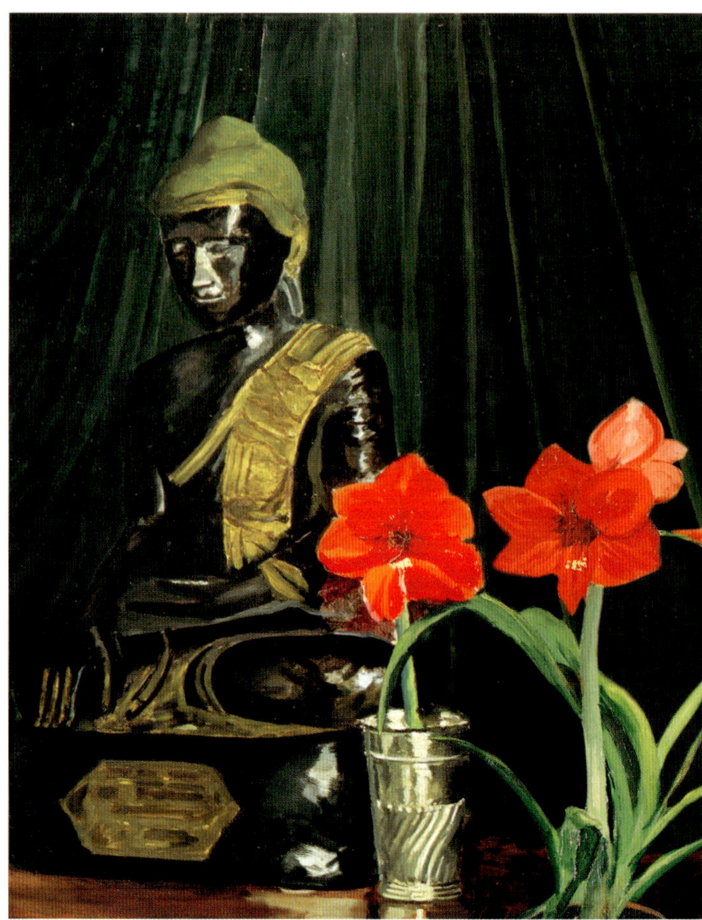

Fig 429 (C 377) right
Buddha and lilies.

In 1946 Churchill once again became worried by his financial situation. Lord Camrose suggested that he and a group of friends purchase Chartwell anonymously and present it to the National Trust on the understanding that Winston and Clementine should live there undisturbed, which they did with increasing contentment for the rest of their lives.

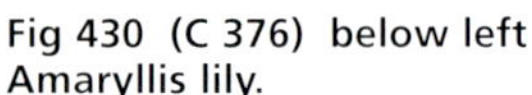

Fig 430 (C 376) below left
Amaryllis lily.

Fig 431 (C 378) below right
Orchids. Winston gave this painting to Churchill College in Cambridge.

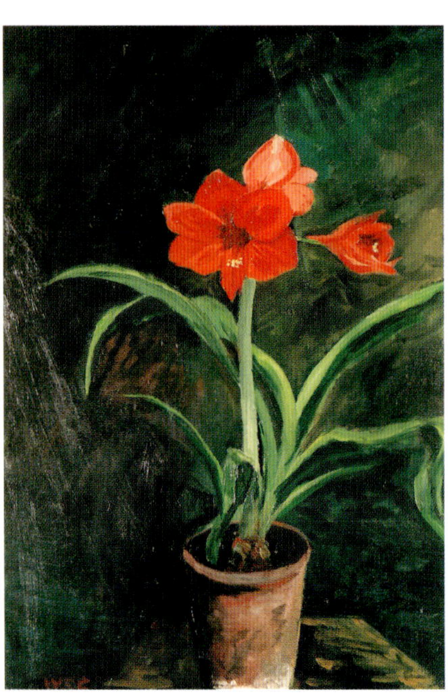

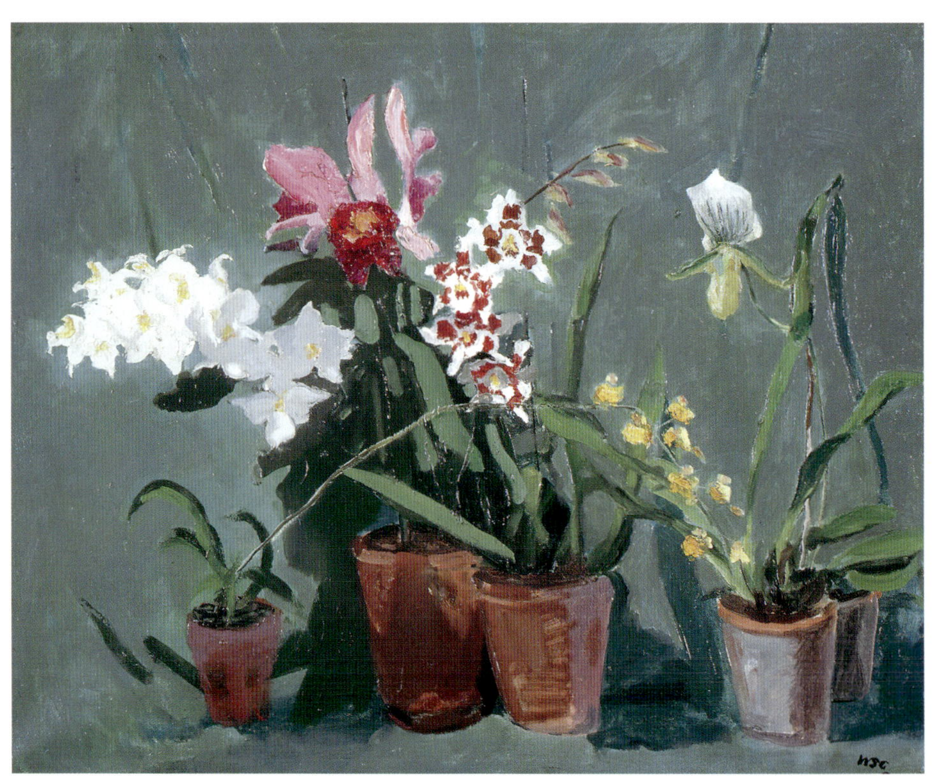

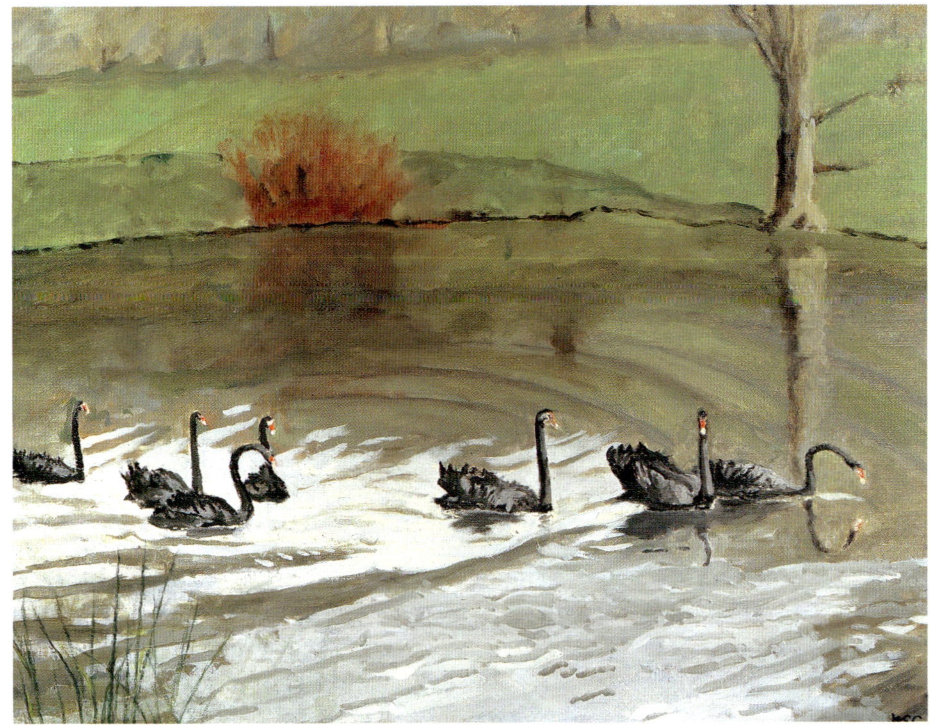

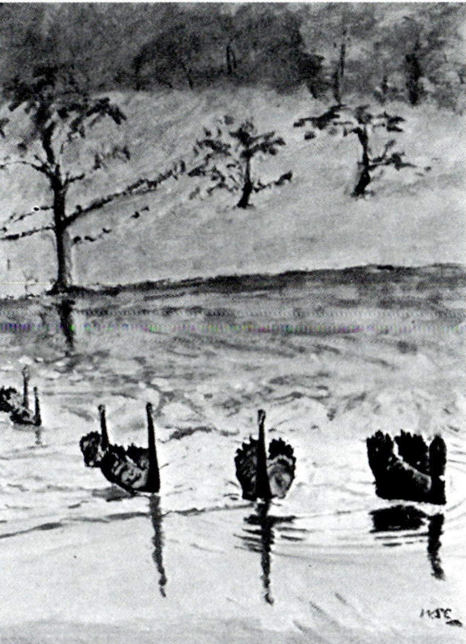

Fig 432 (C 379) above
Black swans on the lake at Chartwell. These were the gift of the Government of Western Australia.

Fig 433 (C 384) left
Black swans. Winston gave this painting to his son, Randolph. Both paintings are based on a series of small photographs from the Studio archives at Chartwell.

Churchill went once again to Marrakech where he painted on his balcony at the Hotel Mamounia. It proved to be his last visit there. During another long sojourn to paint and read in the sunshine at La Pausa, Churchill was visited by his artist friend Paul Maze and his wife.

The Royal Academy of Arts in London held a one-man exhibition comprising 62 of Churchill's paintings including the 35 that had been on the 1958 world tour. The Academy exhibition attracted 141,000 visitors during the five months of the show and, because of the numbers, had to be rehung in three galleries rather than the original two.

The President of the Academy, Sir Charles Wheeler, told Churchill on a visit to his studio at Chartwell, 'I can't think how you have found time in your life to do anything else but paint.' Of the exhibition, 'a well-known' artist remarked to the Royal Academy's Secretary, Sidney Hutchison, 'There are things here that only an amateur would let out of his studio but there are at least a dozen of these pictures which any professional would have given his ears to have painted.'

David Carritt reviewed the exhibition for the London *Evening Standard*. After reminding us that Sir Winston's first cousin Lord Ivor Spencer-Churchill was the most serious English collector of Impressionists and Post-Impressionists after the late Samuel Courtauld, he stated, 'There is nothing intellectual in Sir Winston's art, but there is nothing stupid either ... Sir Winston actually paints like a painter ... They are not merely bold and colourful, an extension of his personality as we know it from his achievements in other fields. Many of them are gentle and contemplative and painted with a total absence of flourish ... one is struck by his willingness to learn from others in a field where he is, by necessity, an amateur.'

The anonymous art critic of *The Times* commented, 'Water, indeed, seems to fascinate him, not only for the Impressionist painter's beano that can be had with broken reflections but also for the far more exacting tonal exercise - that which engaged the ageing Monet to the exclusion of all else - set by a surface which is partly transparent.'

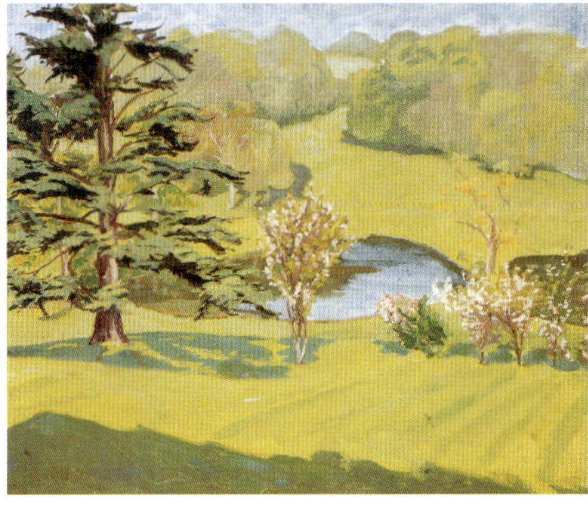

Fig 434 (C 482) above
The lakes at Chartwell, which were considerably enlarged by Churchill in the 1920s and 1930s.

Fig 435 (C 380) below
Cecily Gemmell, one of Churchill's post-war secretaries.

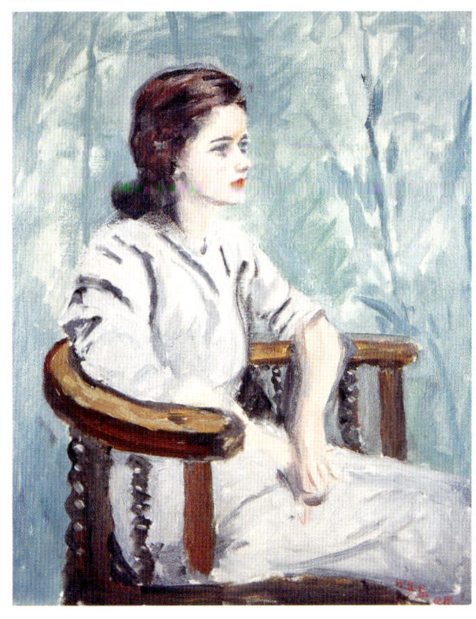

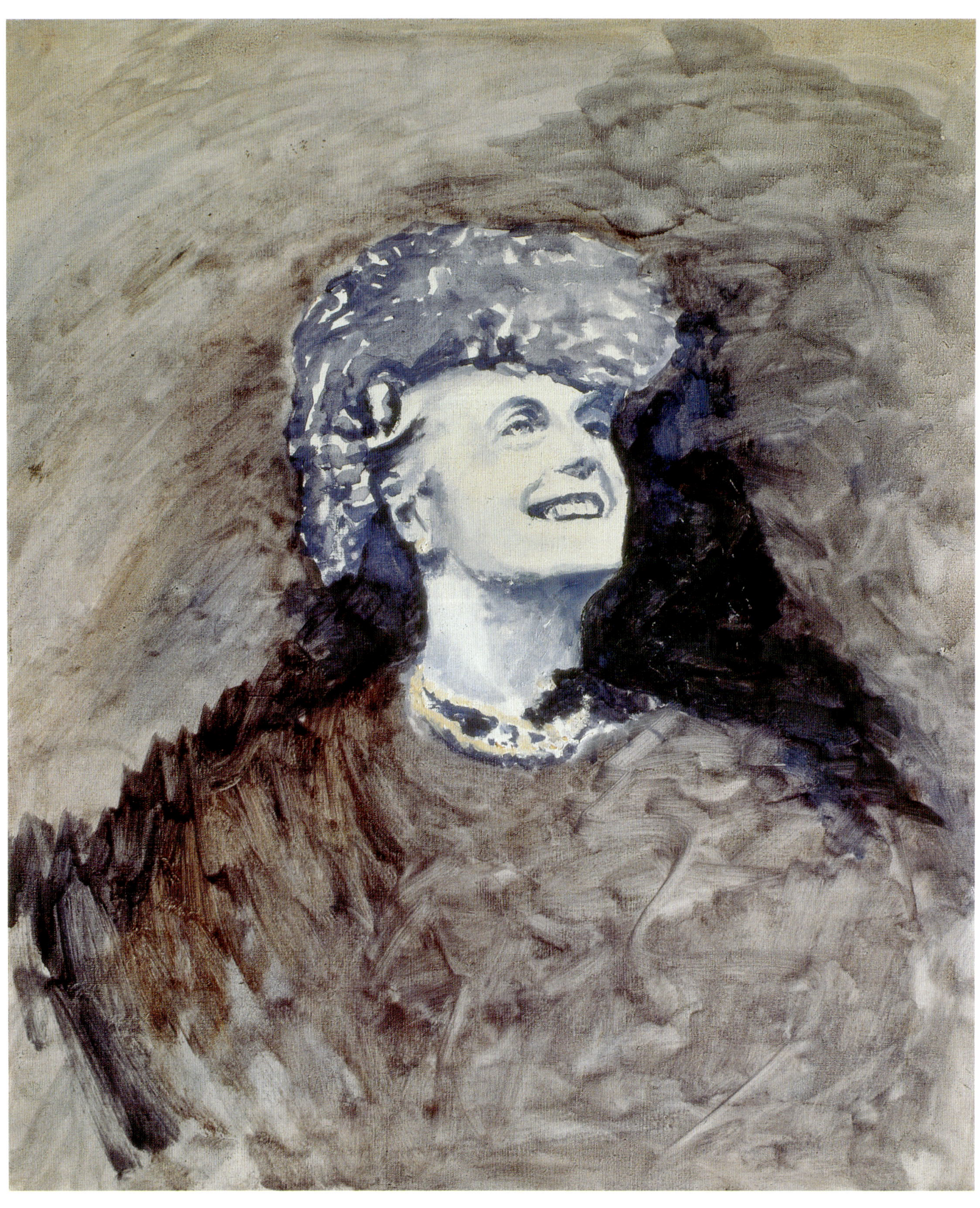

Fig 436 (C 456) above
Clementine Churchill at the launching of HMS Indomitable in 1940. Winston based this painting, done in 1955, on a favourite photograph that still stands on his desk in the Study at Chartwell.

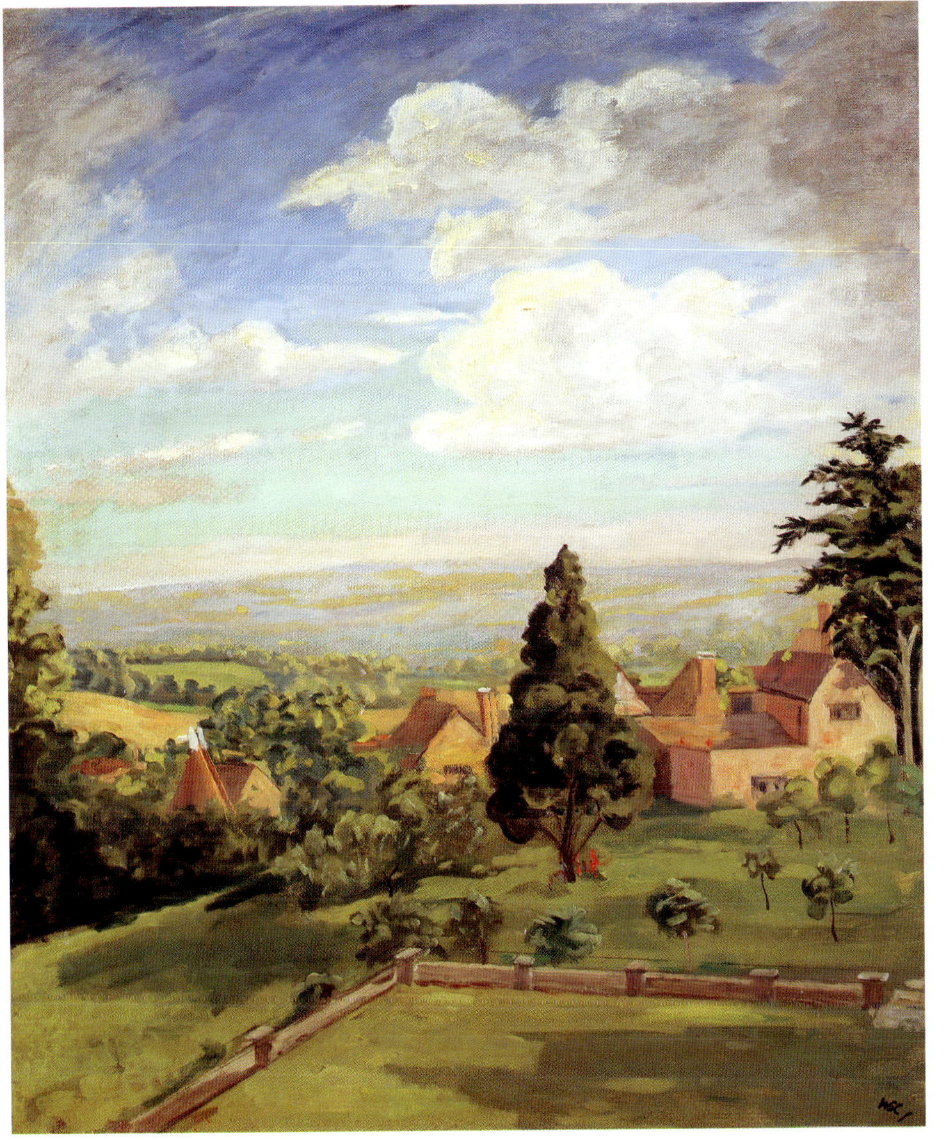

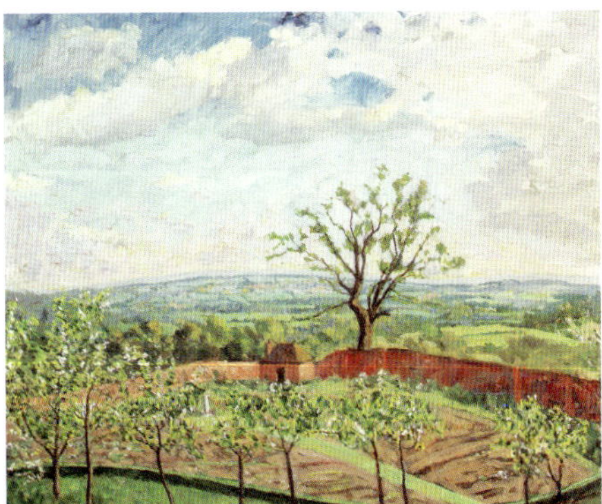

Fig 437 (C 446) above
The kitchen garden at Chartwell showing some of the walls built before the war by Churchill himself.

Fig 438 (C 445) left
View from Chartwell showing Winston's Studio in the centre foreground. This painting formerly belonged to Clementine Churchill.

Fig 439 (C 442) below
Landscape at Chartwell. The sheep are based on a photograph from the Studio archives at Chartwell; more were added by Churchill after the painting was first illustrated in Strand Magazine, 1946.

John Russell in *The Sunday Times* wrote, 'In all of them, without exception, the tone is one of such infectious enjoyment ... This headlong quality runs through all his work. Among the classic hazards which beset the amateur painter, for instance, moving water, light reflected through foliage, and sunshine on the far side of shadow must always rank high. Sir Winston delights in tackling all three at once, as in the picture done at Wilton in the 1920s ... but it is above all in the South of France that Sir Winston's love of life comes through most palpably ... in the paintings done in his eighty-second and eighty-third years there is a feeling of abandon, a free-flying delight in the world around him, which must communicate itself even to the most difficult visitors.'

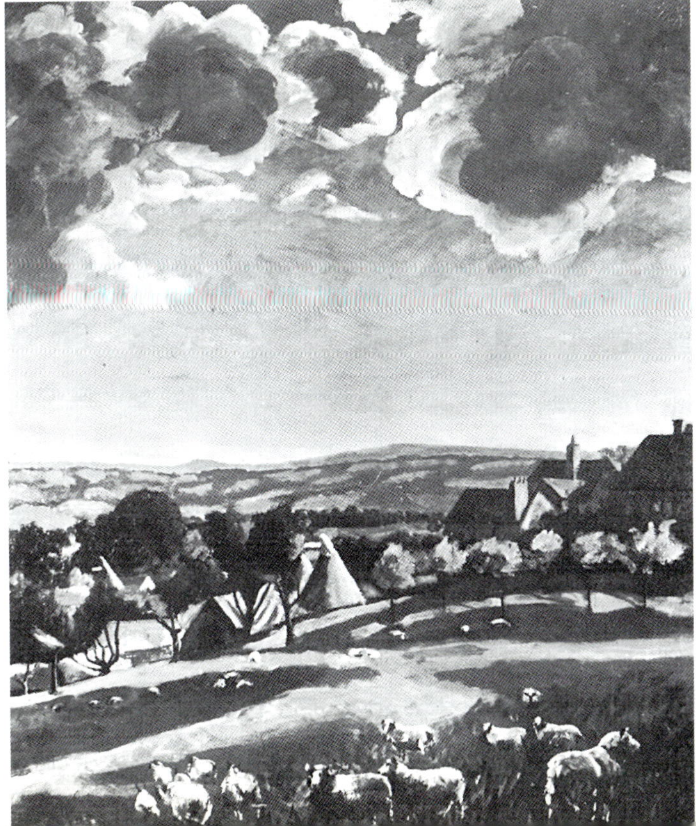

Churchill found himself no longer able to paint, even on his visits to the sunny clime of the South of France. He gave the Queen one of his pictures for her private collection, a view of 'The Palladian Bridge at Wilton'. Another painting, 'Cork Trees at Mimizan', was auctioned at Sotheby's for £7,400 in aid of the World Refugee Fund, for which Clementine had made a broadcast appeal. In his book *Art and Illusion* Professor Ernst Gombrich quoted several times from 'Painting as a Pastime' by way of illustrating Churchill's acute appreciation of the mystery of 'the part that memory plays in painting'.

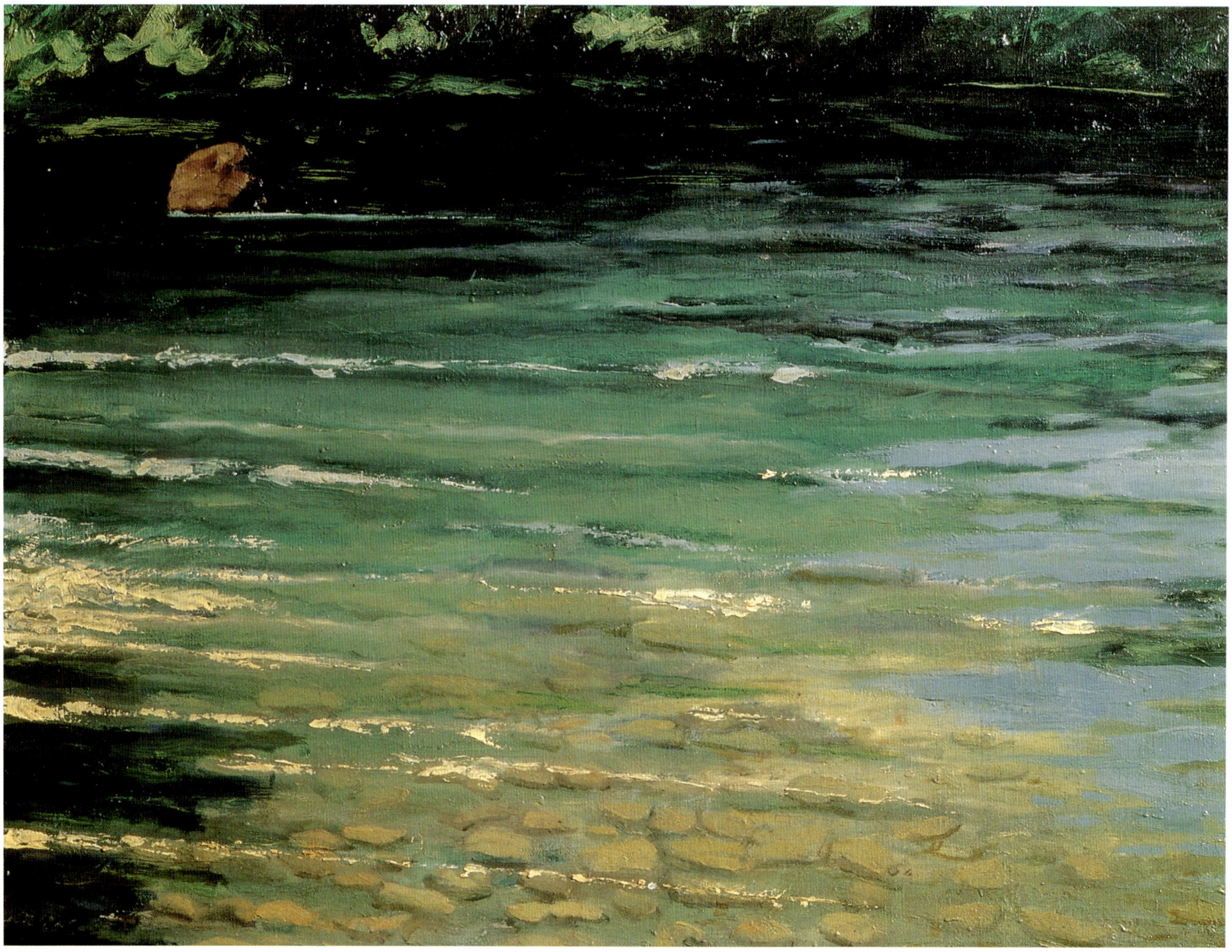

Fig 440 (C 385) above
Water, Vaucluse. This painting formerly belonged to Clementine Churchill.

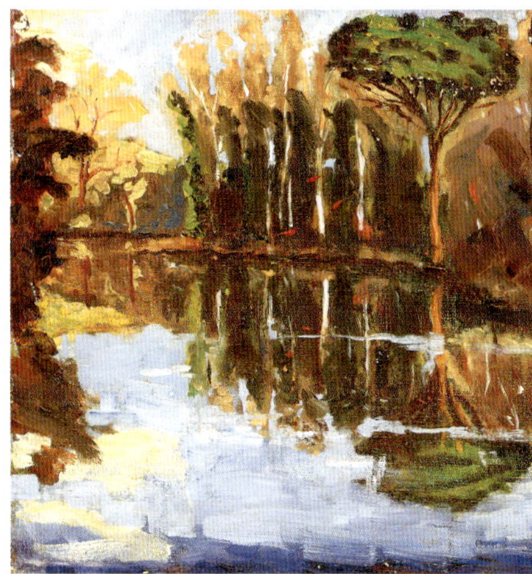

Fig 441 (C 389) above
Water, Vaucluse.

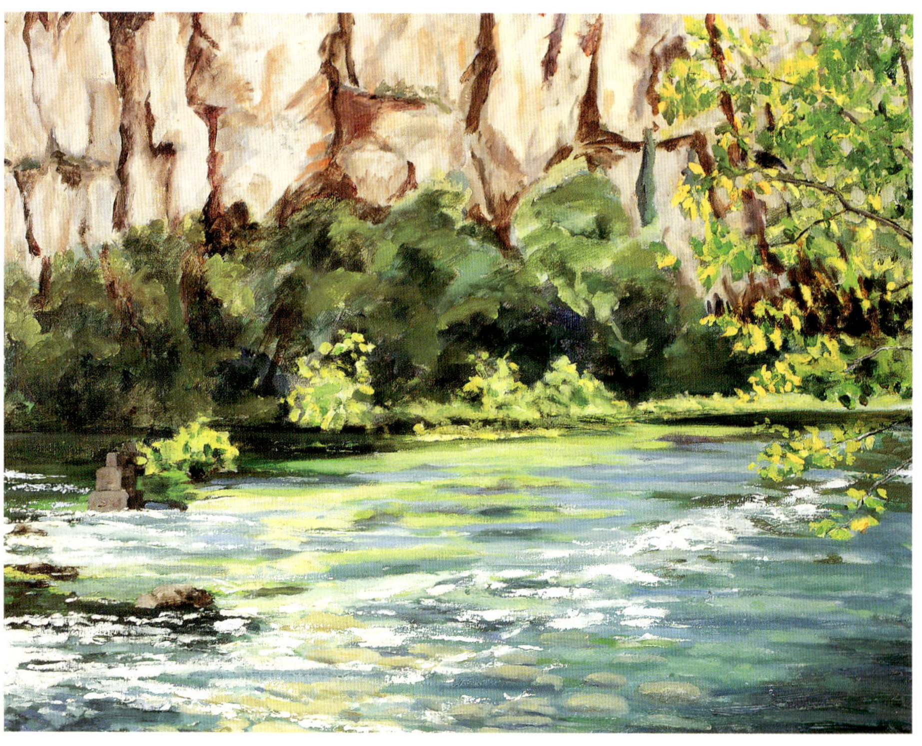

Fig 442 (C 387) right
Fontaine de Vaucluse. This painting formerly belonged to Clementine Churchill.

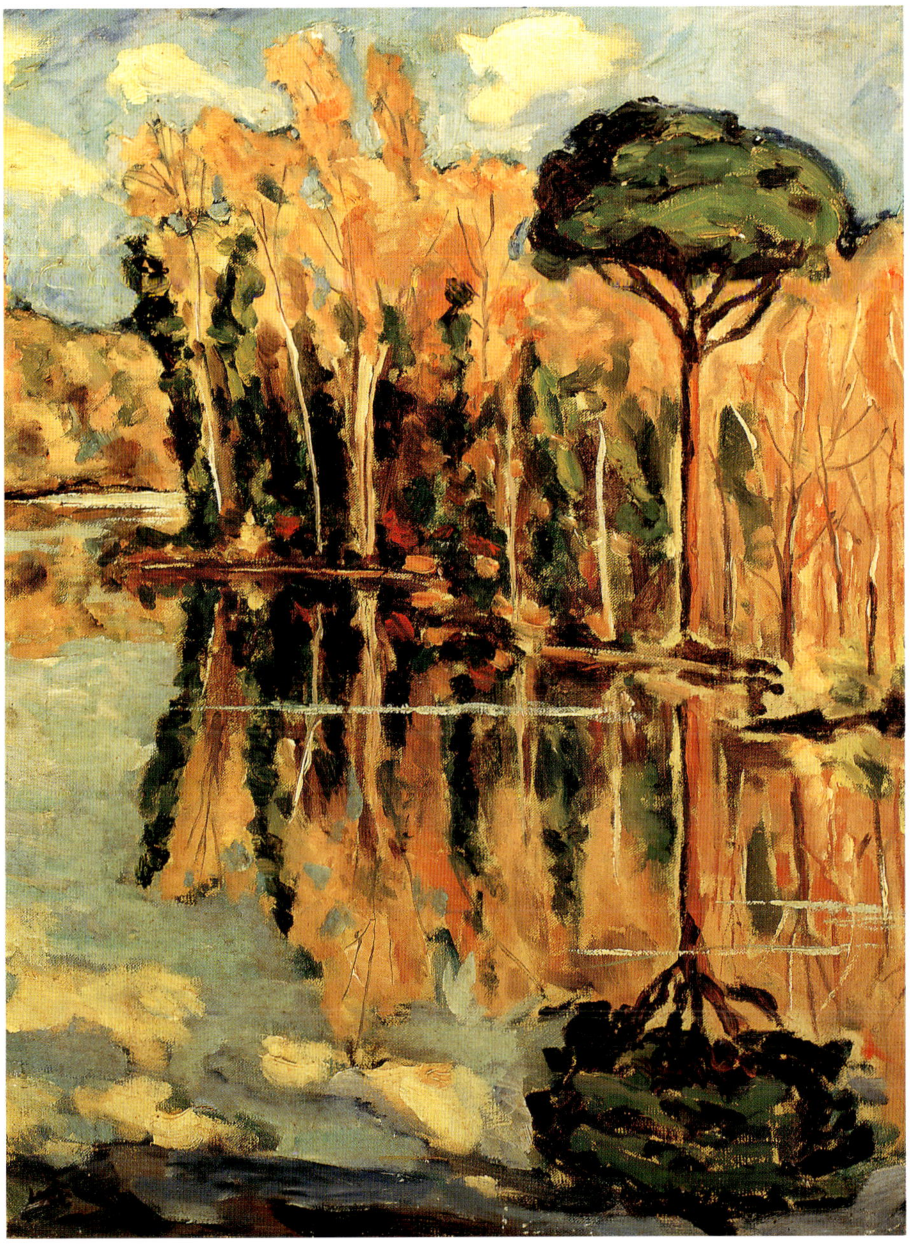

Fig 443 (C 390) left
Water, Vaucluse. This painting formerly belonged to Clementine Churchill.

In 1948, whilst on holiday in France at Aix-en-Provence, in southern France, Churchill visited and became entranced by La Fontaine de Vaucluse, a dark spring and glittering river associated with the 14th century poet Petrarch. During this same long summer break with his wife and family, Churchill also painted Mont St Victoire, so often celebrated in the works of the modern French artist Cezanne. Then, and in the succeeding decade, Winston revisited favourite places such as Les Calanques near Cassis on the coast, as well as others of his haunts further along the Riviera.

Fig 444 (C 386) below
Fontaine de Vaucluse. This painting formerly belonged to Clementine Churchill.

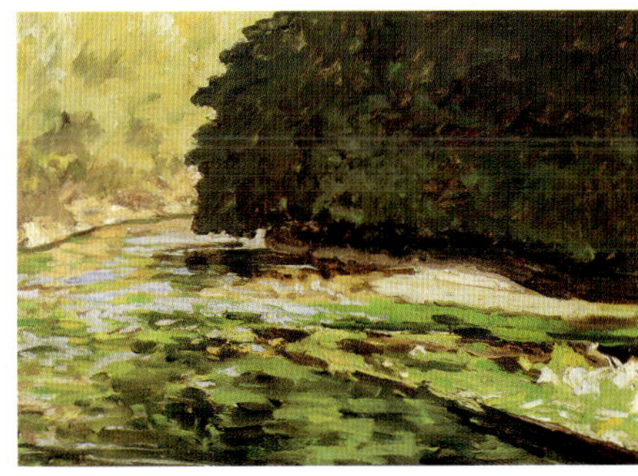

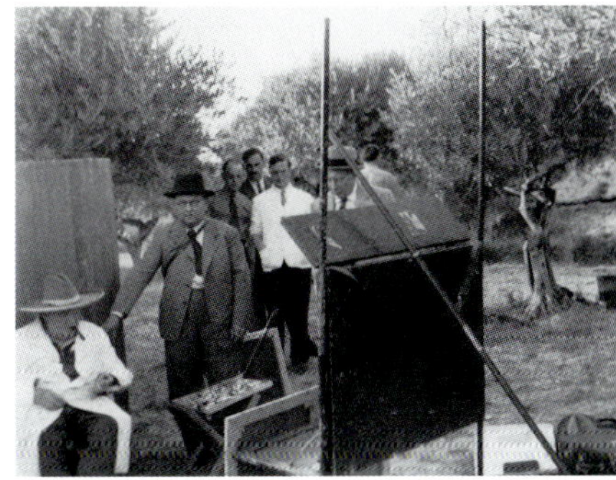

Sir Winston Churchill painting probably on Cap Martin in the 1950s.

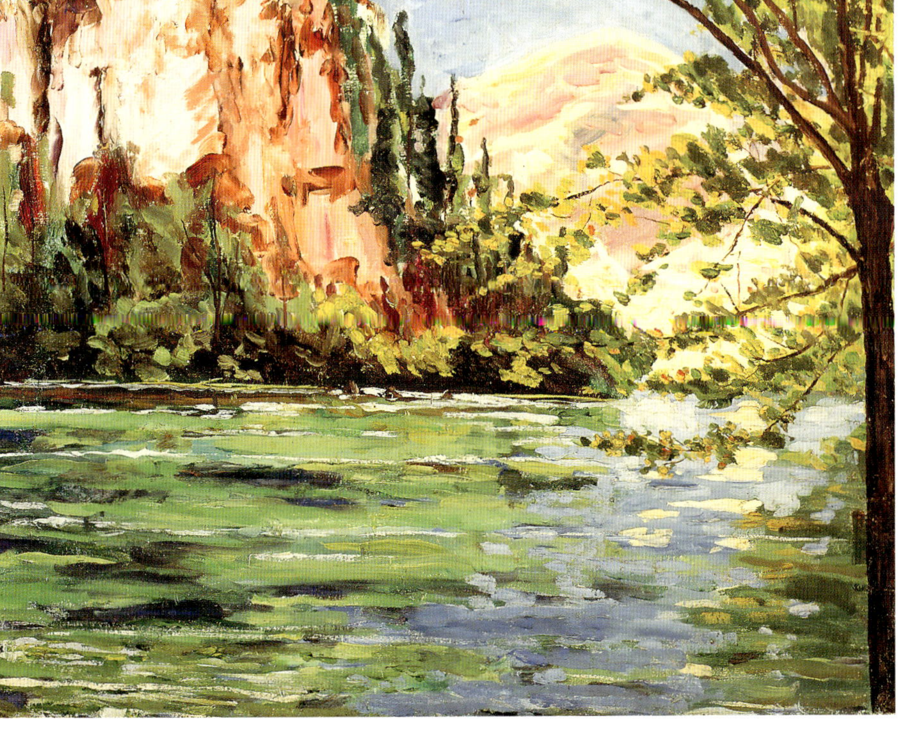

Fig 445 (C 388) left
Fontaine de Vaucluse. This painting formerly belonged to Clementine Churchill.

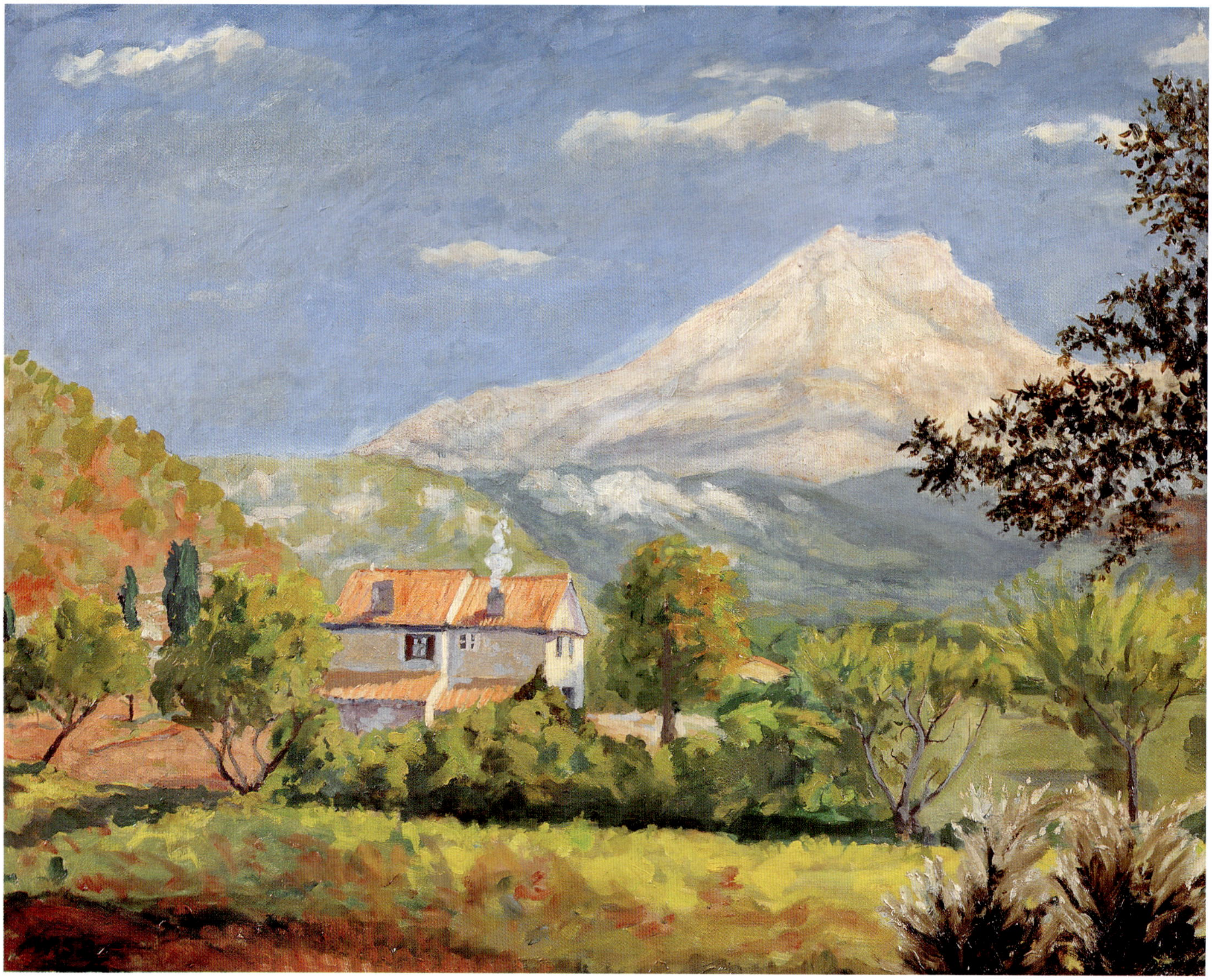

Fig 446 (C 202) above
La Montagne, St Victoire. Painted in 1948 and based on two photographs from the Studio archives at Chartwell.

1963 [Background] Churchill was proclaimed an Honorary Citizen of the United States.

1963 [Painting] Mrs Julia Tickner, the former housekeeper at Hoe Farm in Hascombe near Godalming and the widow of its head gardener, wrote to say that she was still carefully looking after two of Churchill's paintings, which had been left with her to dry when the family stayed at the farm in 1915. 'How very kind of you to have looked after my paintings so faithfully for all these years and to have kept them in such excellent condition,' wrote Sir Winston, enclosing an inscribed copy of 'Painting as a pastime' by way of thanks.

Fig 447 (C 407) below
Coast scene near Marseilles.

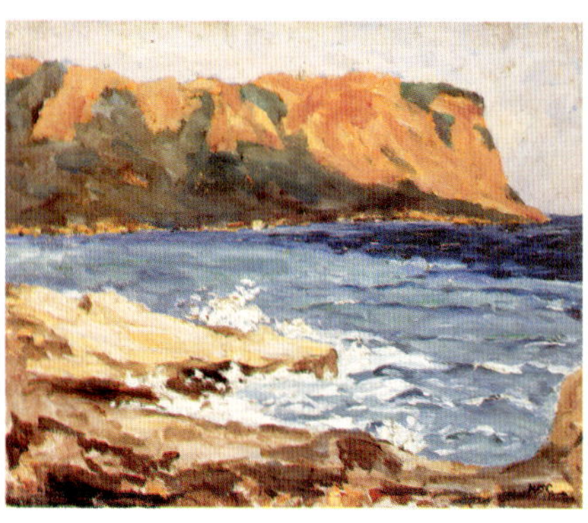

1964 Churchill's 90th year.
Joyce C. Hall was 'determined to do a television special on some aspect of Sir Winston's life ... as a tribute to the man on his ninetieth birthday - November 30th, 1964. But there were options on just about everything Sir Winston had ever written [except] "Painting as a Pastime".' Based on this, he commissioned the film producer Jack Le Vien, who had already made two TV documentaries based on Churchill's war memoirs, to make *The Other World of Winston Churchill*. In the same year, for Hallmark's 'People to People' exhibit at the New York World's Fair, 'we were loaned more than 40 of Churchill's paintings ... The great Oscar Nemon bust ... as well as a sculpture Churchill did of Nemon.'

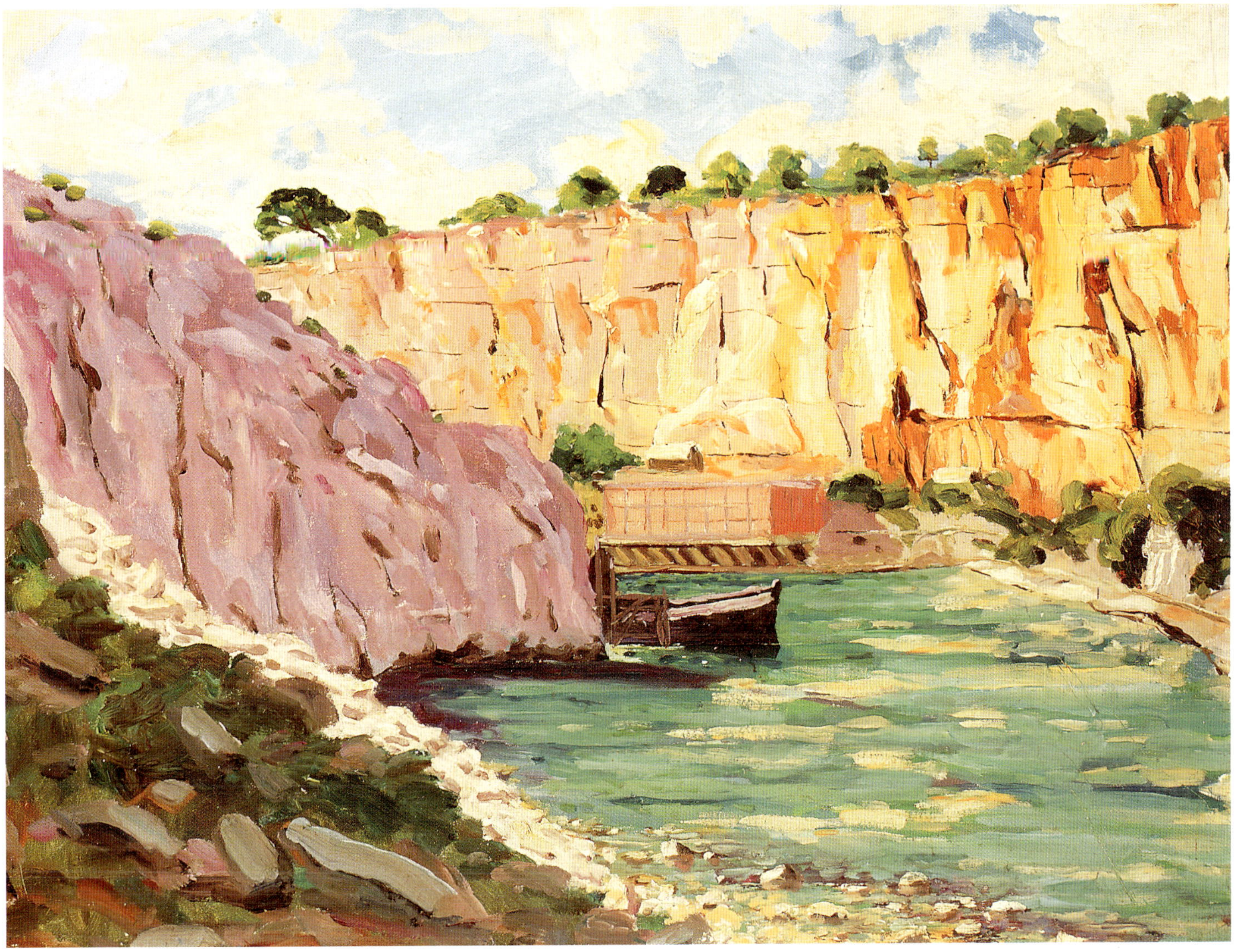

Fig 448 (C 248) above
The Calanques, a series of rocky inlets on the coast near Marseilles.

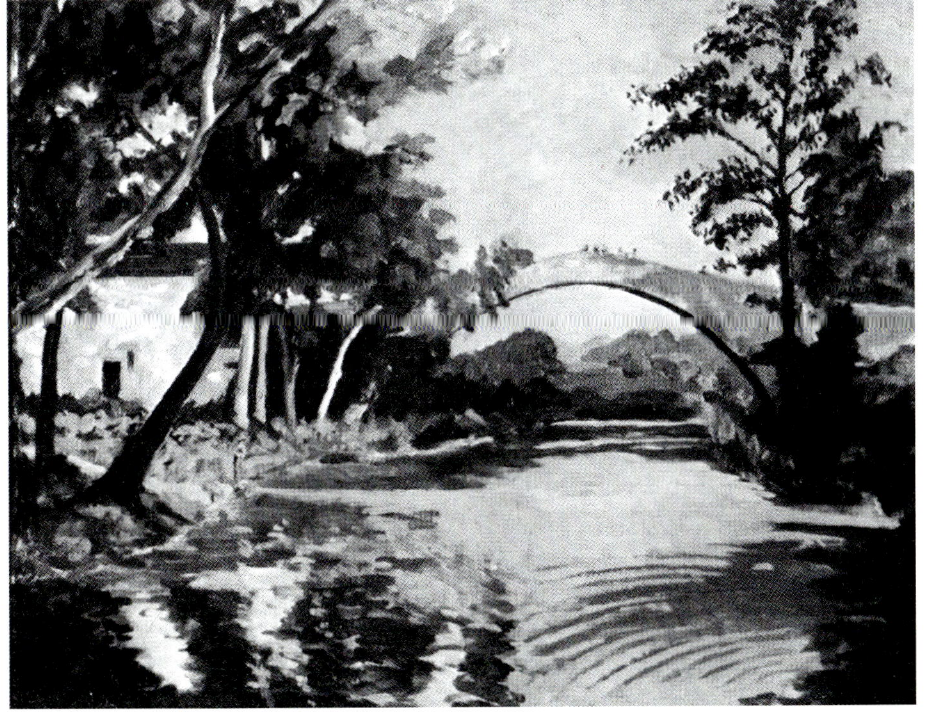

Fig 449 (C 392) left
Bridge near Aix-en-Provence.

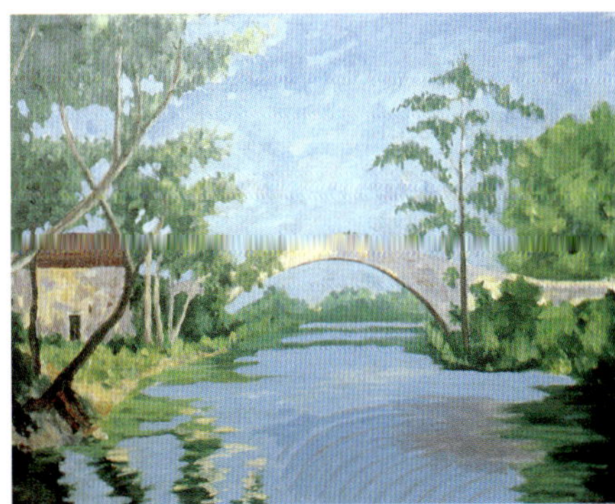

Fig 450 (C 393) above
Churchill gave this painting of the bridge near Aix-en-Provence to the artists' paint manufacturer Willi Sax.

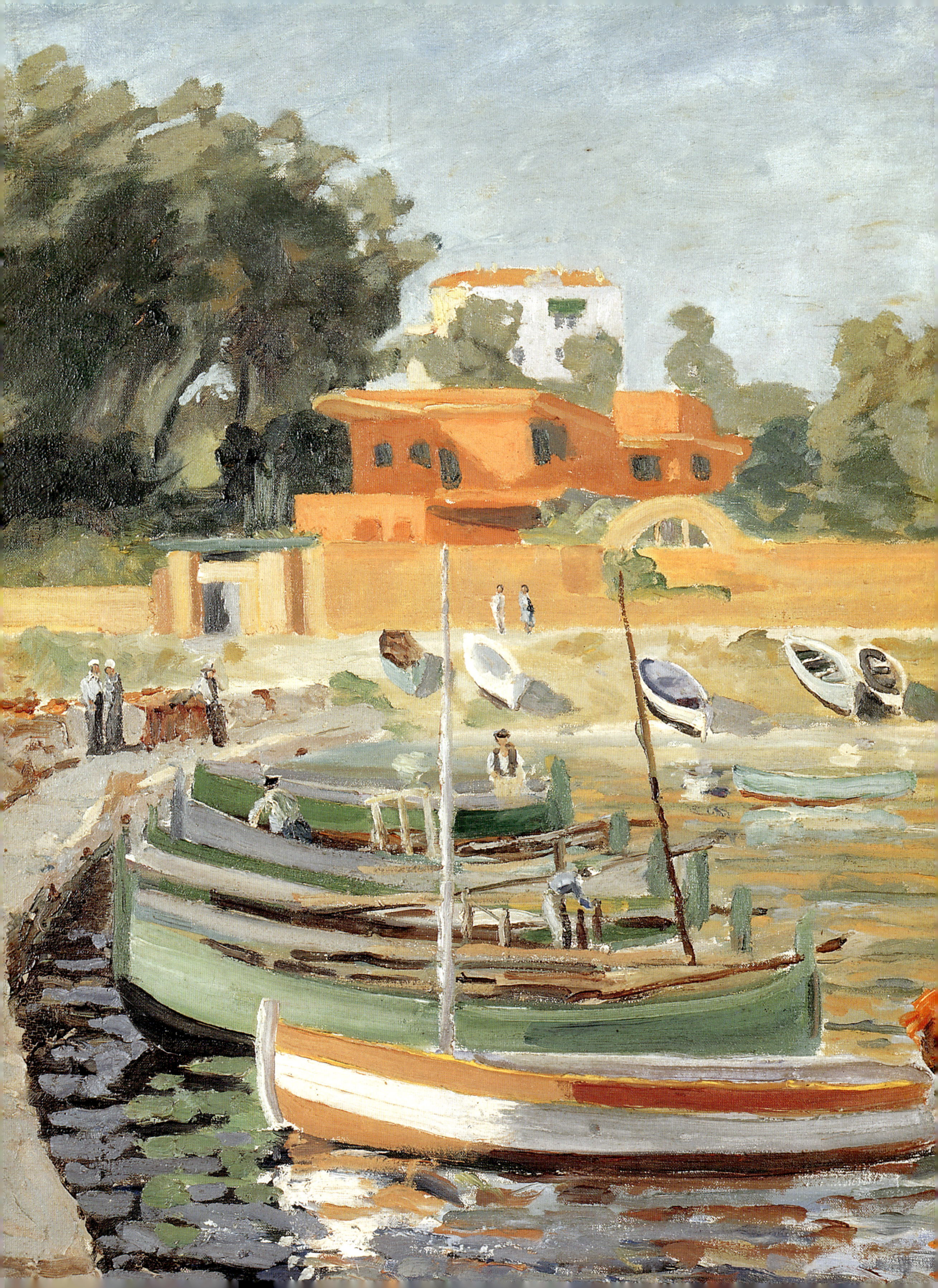

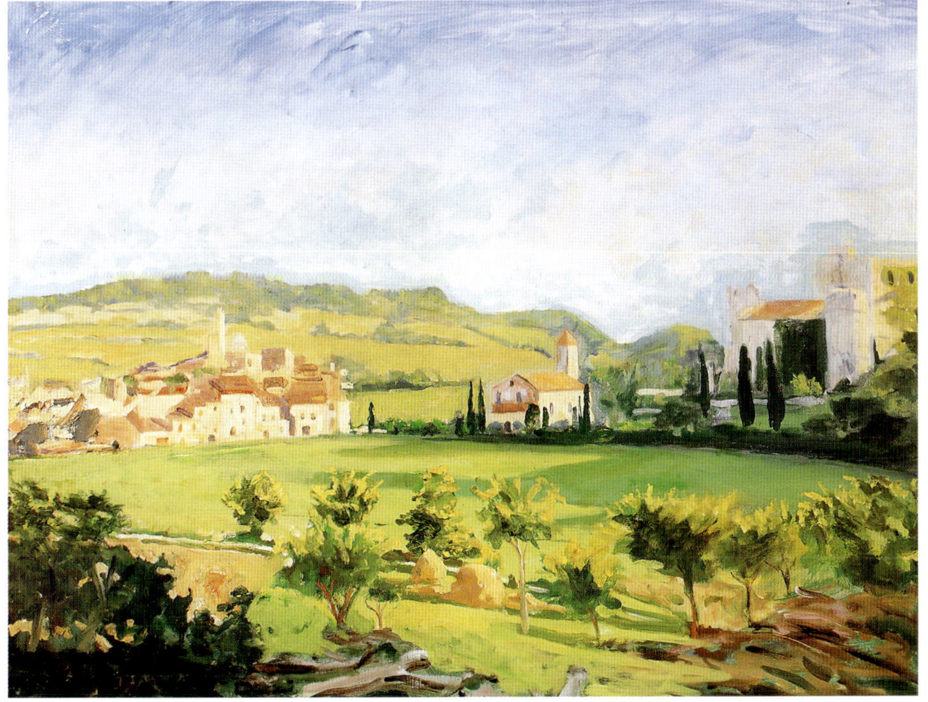

Fig 451 (C 417) opposite page
A harbour scene somewhere on the French Riviera. This painting formerly belonged to Clementine Churchill.

Fig 452 (C 210) left
The Chateau de Lour Mairin, near Aix-en-Provence.

Fig 453 (C 404) below
Beaches near Antibes on the French Riviera.

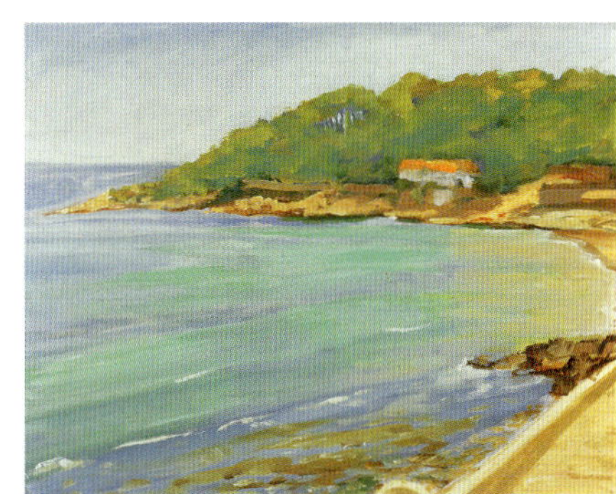

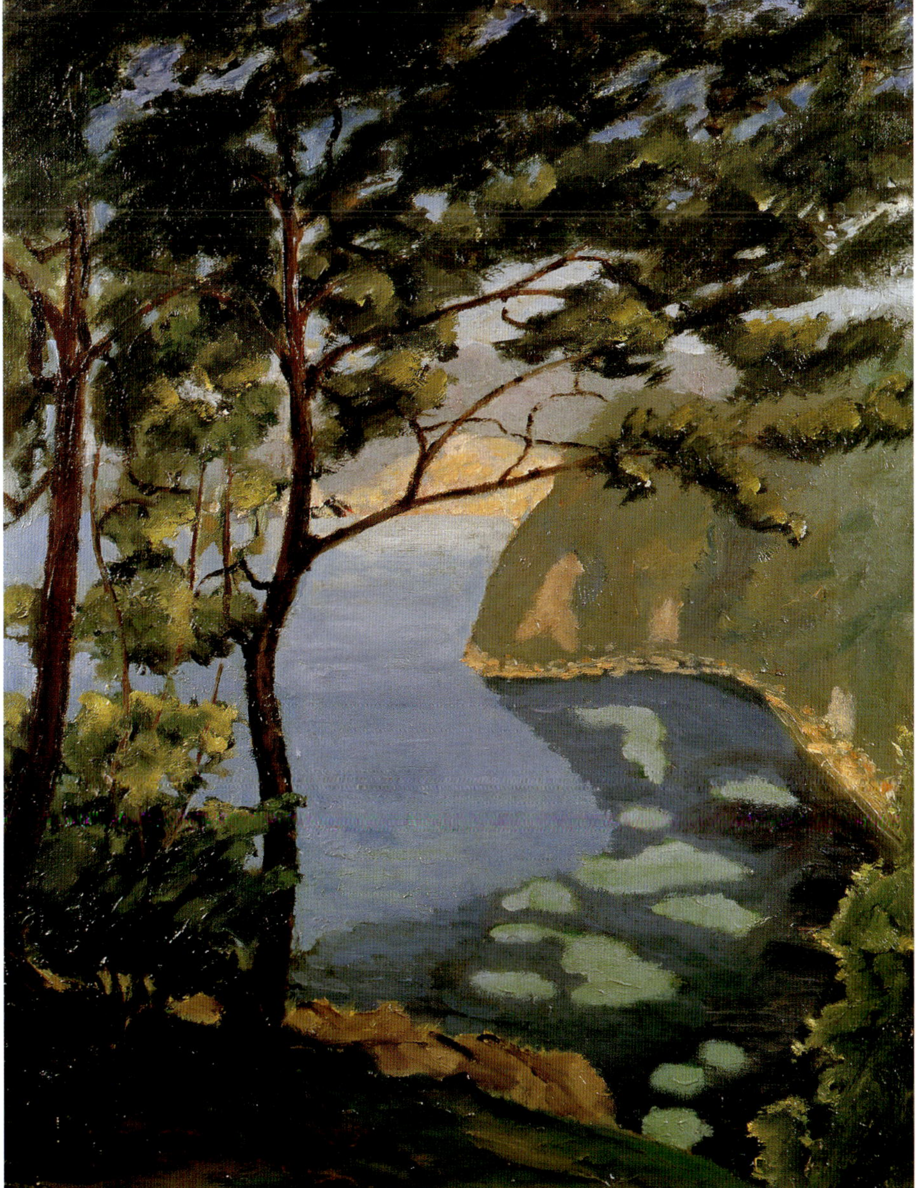

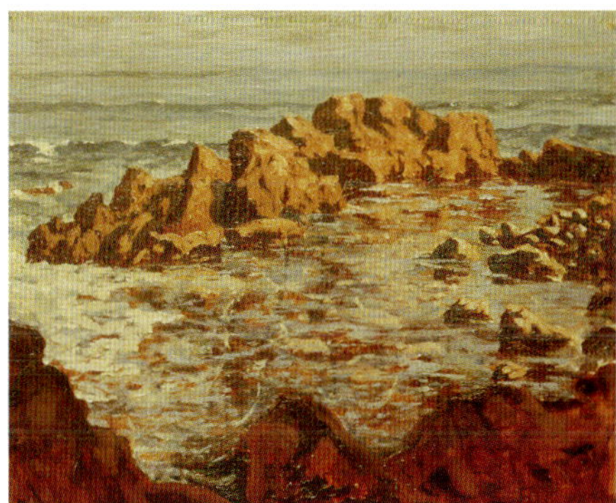

Fig 454 (C 427) above
Rocks near Cannes. After Sir Winston's death, Lady Churchill gave this painting to the University of Bristol of which he had been Chancellor since 1929.

Fig 455 (C 490) left
A view somewhere on the French Riviera.

Fig 456 (C 403) below
Churchill gave this view of beaches near Antibes to Horatia Seymour who had been one of Clementine's bridesmaids at their wedding in 1908.

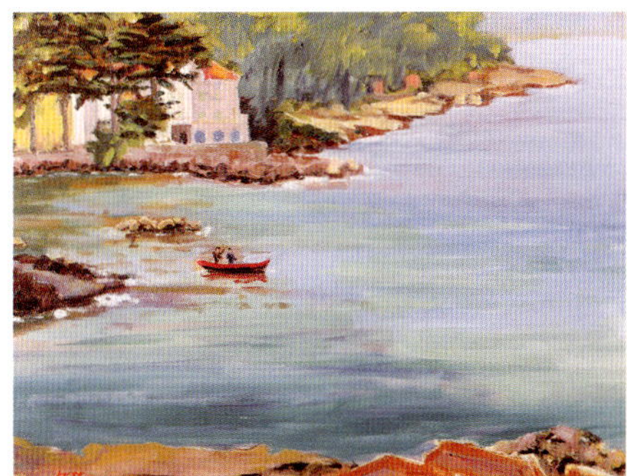

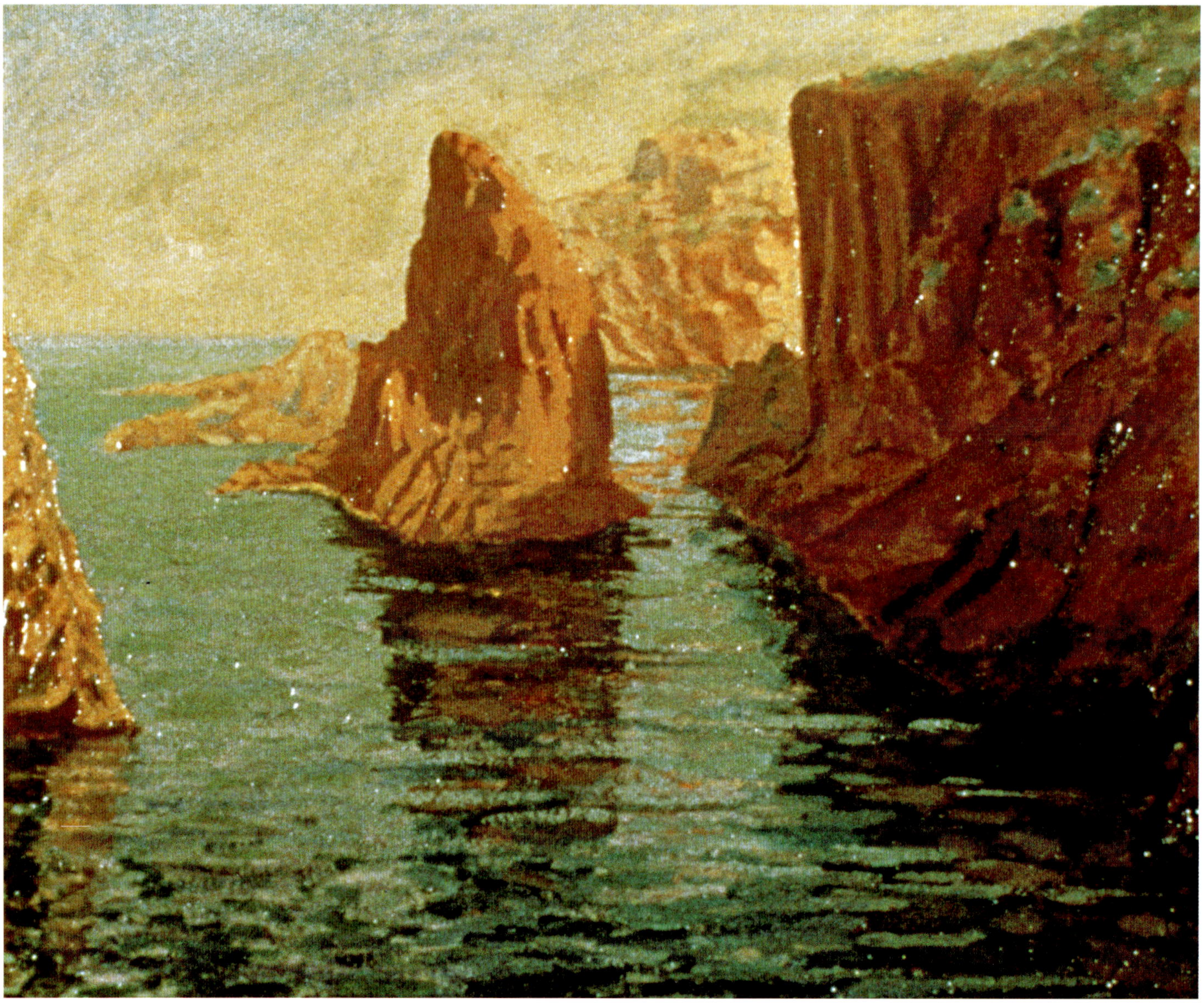

Fig 457 (C 485) above
Red Rocks.

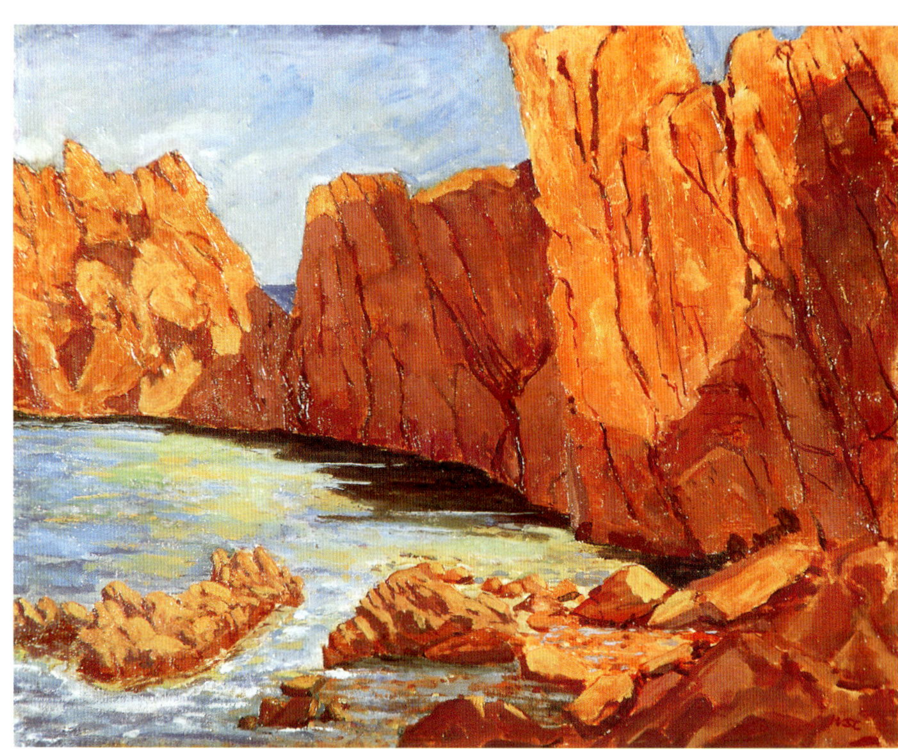

Fig 458 (C 486) right
Red Rocks, characteristic of the Riviera near Cannes where the coast is dominated by outcrops from the Esterel mountains.

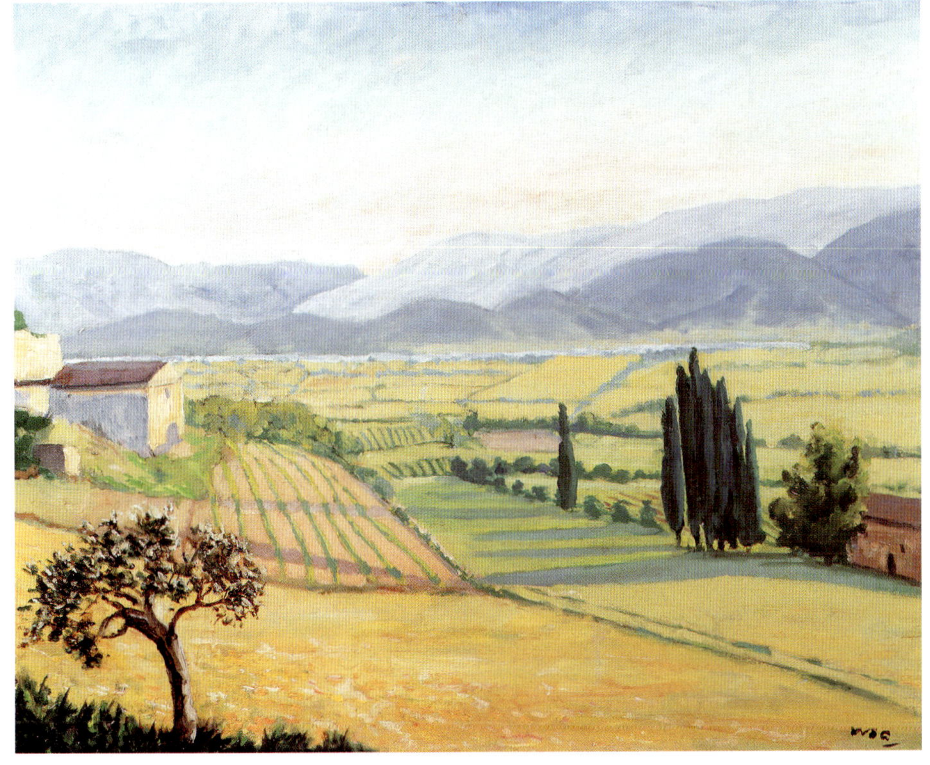

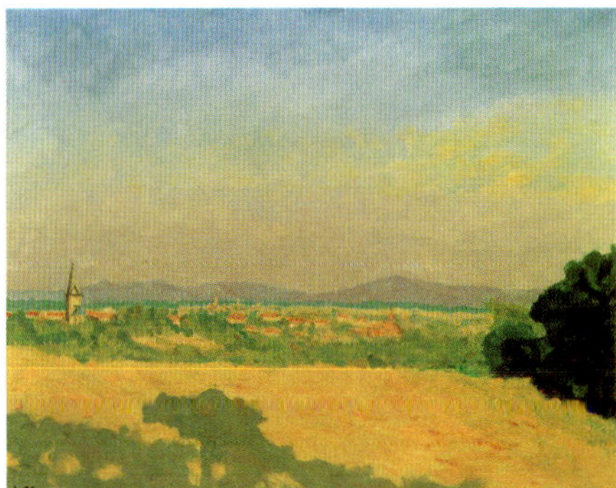

Fig 459 (C 448) above
Distant view of a town in the south of France.

Fig 460 (C 449) left
Churchill gave this view of a landscape in Provence between Aix and Arles to Sir Edward Heath, his parliamentary Chief Whip.

1965 Churchill died on 24th January. After a State Funeral at St Paul's Cathedral in the presence of the Queen, he was buried beside his parents, and next to his brother Jack, in Bladon churchyard within sight of his birthplace, Blenheim Palace.

Postscript. In 1968, following the publication the previous year of my first book of Churchill's paintings, Sir John Rothenstein, by then retired as Director of the Tate Gallery, was commissioned to make a short film by the government's Central Office of Information.

In the course of his commentary, held in the Tate Archives, Sir John Rothenstein remarked, 'Because of Churchill's towering achievements in other spheres, some people have acclaimed him as a great painter. Others, because he was an amateur, have dismissed him as a mere dabbler. I'm convinced that both opinions are wrong. Without training or leisure he couldn't have been a great painter. Because of these two appalling obstacles much of his work has little value. But a just assessment of any artist must be made on the basis of his best work, not his failures.

'The astonishing fact about Churchill the painter is that in spite of obstacles that would have prevented other men from painting at all, he painted a number of pictures of rare beauty.'

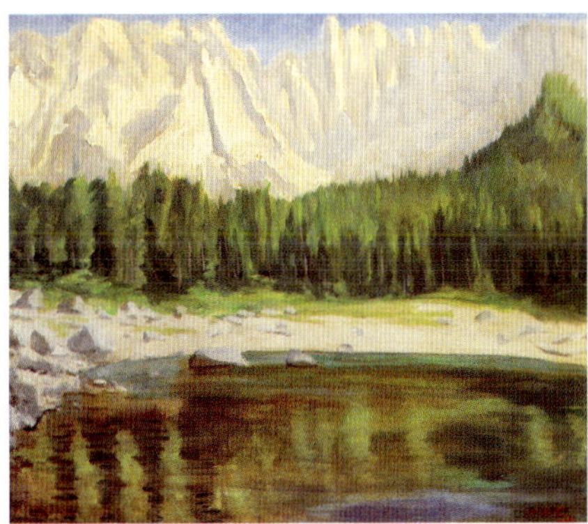

Fig 461 (C 410) above
Lake Carezza in the north Italian Dolomite mountains. Churchill gave this painting to his political colleage Lord Normanbrook.

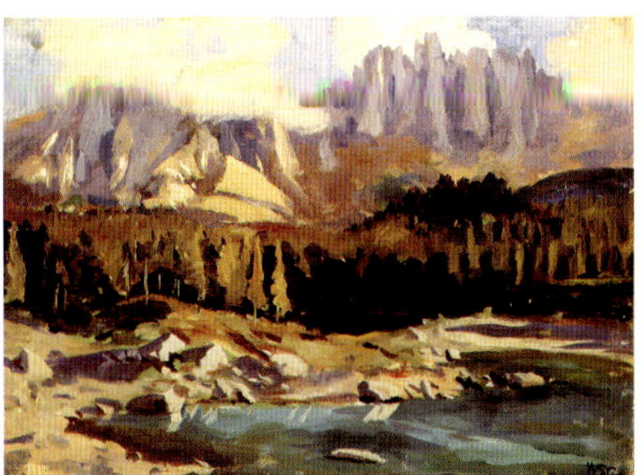

Fig 462 (C 409) above
This painting of Lake Carezza, like the others in the series, is based on photographs from the Studio archives at Chartwell.

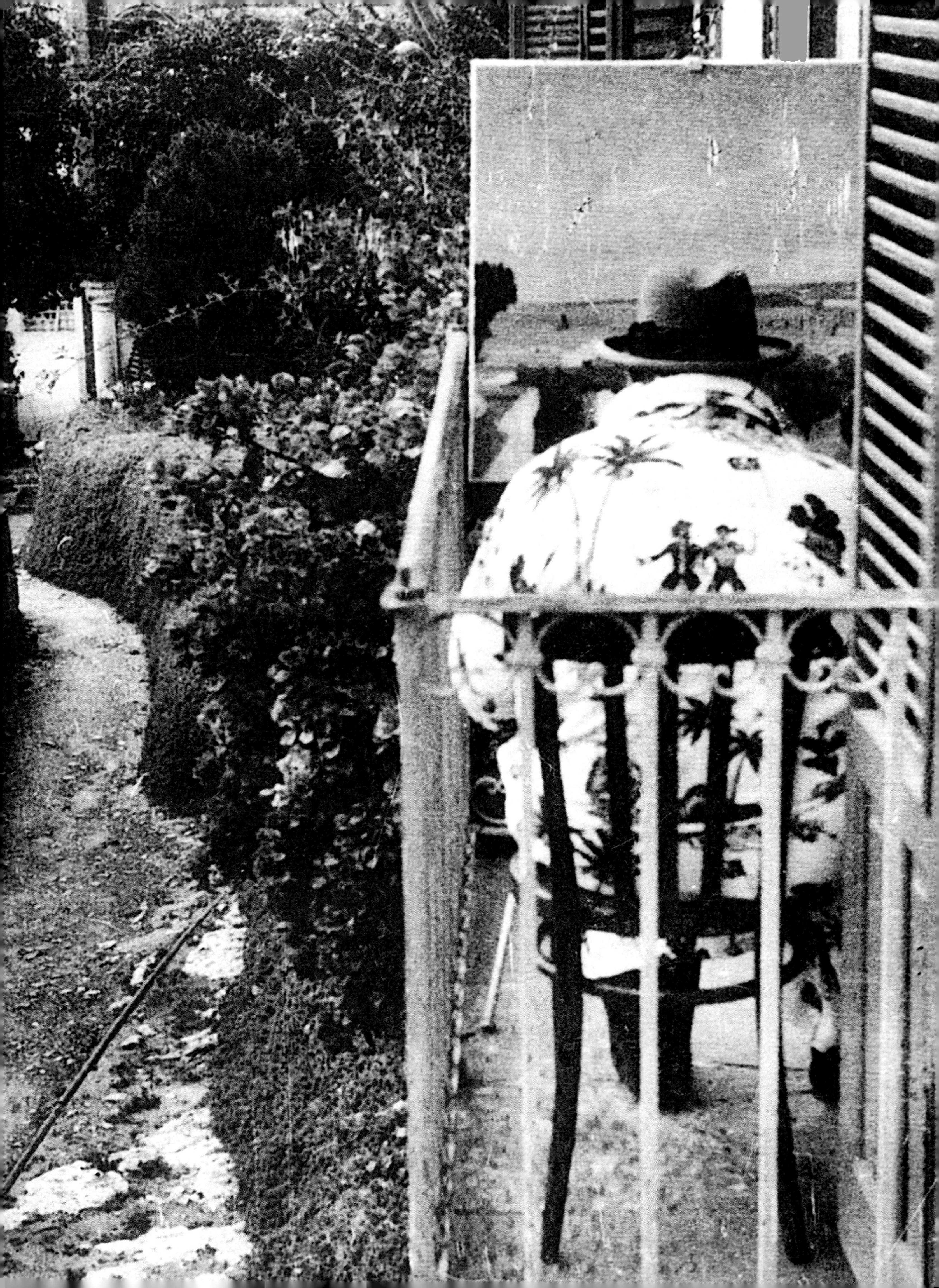

discoveries and mysteries

In Churchill's bedroom at Chartwell a painting of the London dining room of his beloved mother Jennie hangs over his bed. Signed by the Scottish artist P. M. Adam and dated 1919, it is characteristic of the interior scenes in which he specialized. How and when the picture came into Winston's possession was unknown, until a visit to Chartwell by Mr and Mrs Tim Doheny from California unexpectedly resolved the mystery. They brought with them a photograph of a hitherto unknown painting of 'La Lieutenance, Honfleur' with the familiar 'WSC' initials (See page 238. Fig. 506. (C 515)). They showed this to Sue Medway who recognized the scene as being near to the Château St Georges-Motel in Normandy, owned by Consuelo Balsan, where Churchill often painted.

The painting certainly looked from the photograph as if it could be by Sir Winston Churchill, although there was no other known example by him of the same view. There followed lengthy correspondence with Mrs Doheny during which I prompted her to try to find details of the provenance of the painting, for this was going to be the only way that its authenticity might be confirmed.

After a great deal of work, Anita Doheny was able to discover that her mother-in-law, Mrs Leigh Battson, had bought the Honfleur painting from the Wildenstein Gallery in New York in 1967. It came with a photocopy of a handwritten letter by Churchill, dated February 10th, 1928, when he was Chancellor of the Exchequer.

'My dear Mr Adam,' it read. 'After many hesitations & vacillations I have at last decided upon a picture to send you ... I hope you may find something to like in it, & will accept with it the last of my apologies for the delay in this acknowledgement of yr kindness in giving me yr beautiful picture of my Mother's diningroom, which is a constant source of pleasure to me.'

Mary Soames immediately recognized the reference to the painting of her grandmother's dining room in her father's bedroom at Chartwell and so two mysteries were resolved simultaneously.

Opposite
Sir Winston Churchill painting on the balcony of the Villa Politi, Sicily, 1955.

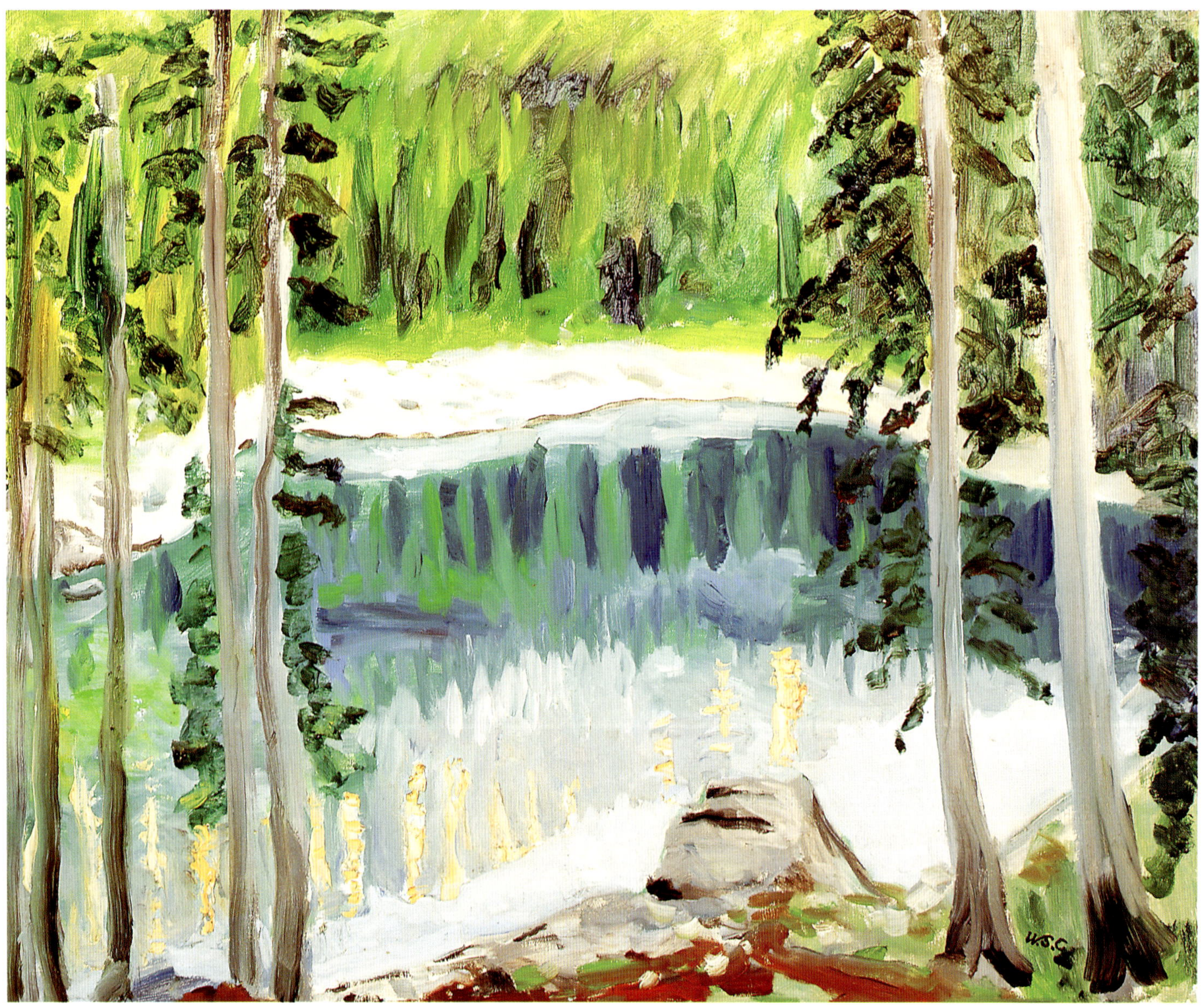

Fig 463 (C 391) above
Winston painted this sketch of Lake Carezza in 20 minutes. The picture formerly belonged to Clementine Churchill.

This little story contains all or most of the elements that have to be present before a hitherto unknown painting attributed to Sir Winston Churchill can be accepted as genuine.

Pointers towards Authenticity

First: the painting has to look like a Churchill. In other words, the subject, style, colouring and technique all have to be represented in others of his known work. But this is essentially subjective, sometimes dangerously so.

Second: the size and support, i.e. the canvas or (smaller) canvas board or, more rarely, the wooden panel has to be typical of those used by Churchill. Many but not all of his canvases are stamped on the back with the name of his London supplier, Roberson; a few have the stamp of a Parisian maker, Blanchet.

Third: the signature. Only two or three paintings are signed 'W. Churchill'. Most signatures take the form of his initials 'WSC' only. Relatively few of Churchill's paintings are signed, however, and some of these were initialled on his behalf by his London framemaker, Frank Patrickson, who used, he told me, a cut-out brass pattern. The paintings involved were those sent as gifts by Churchill in his later years.

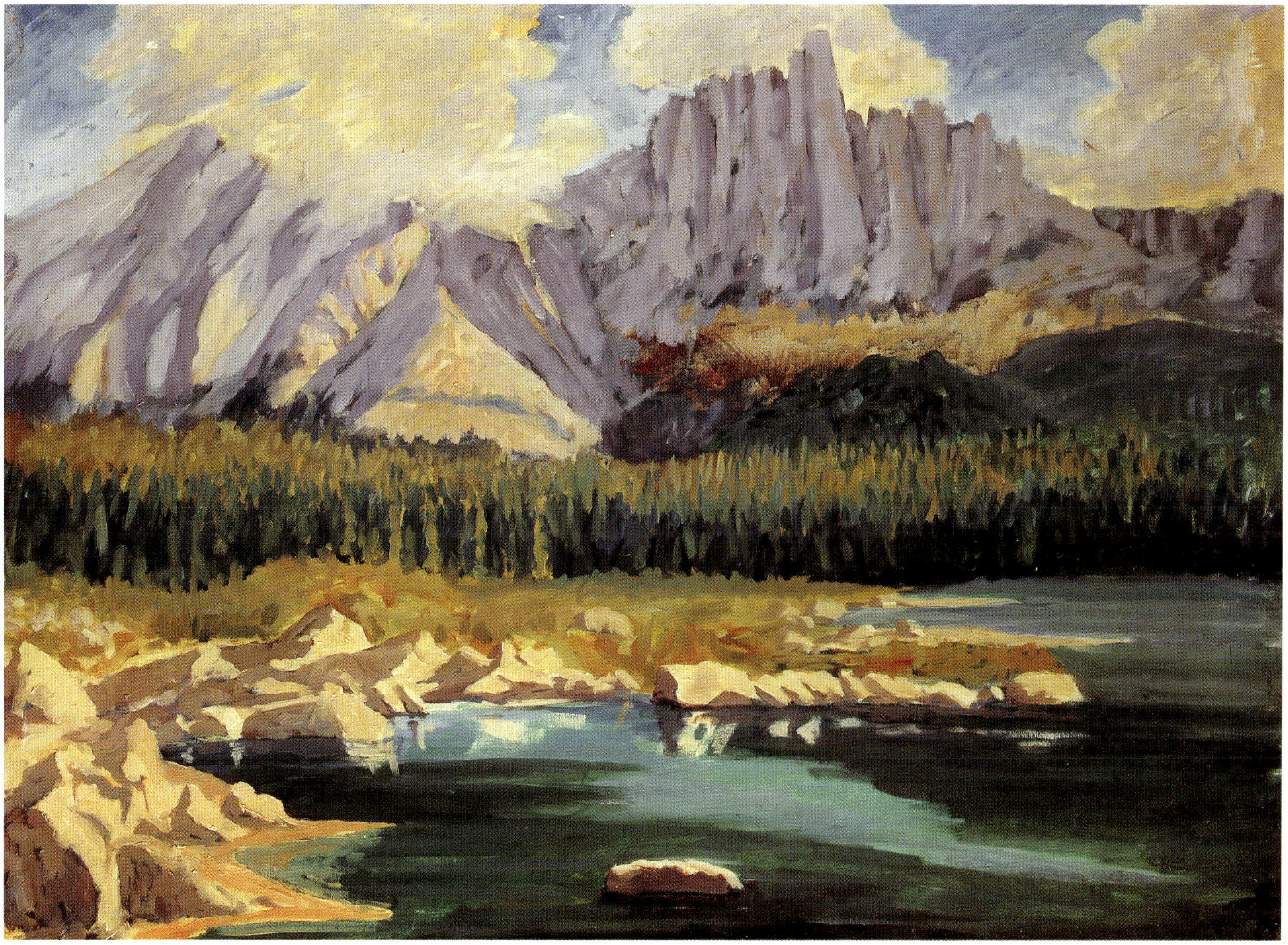

Fig 464 (C 408) above
Lake Carezza in the Dolomites.

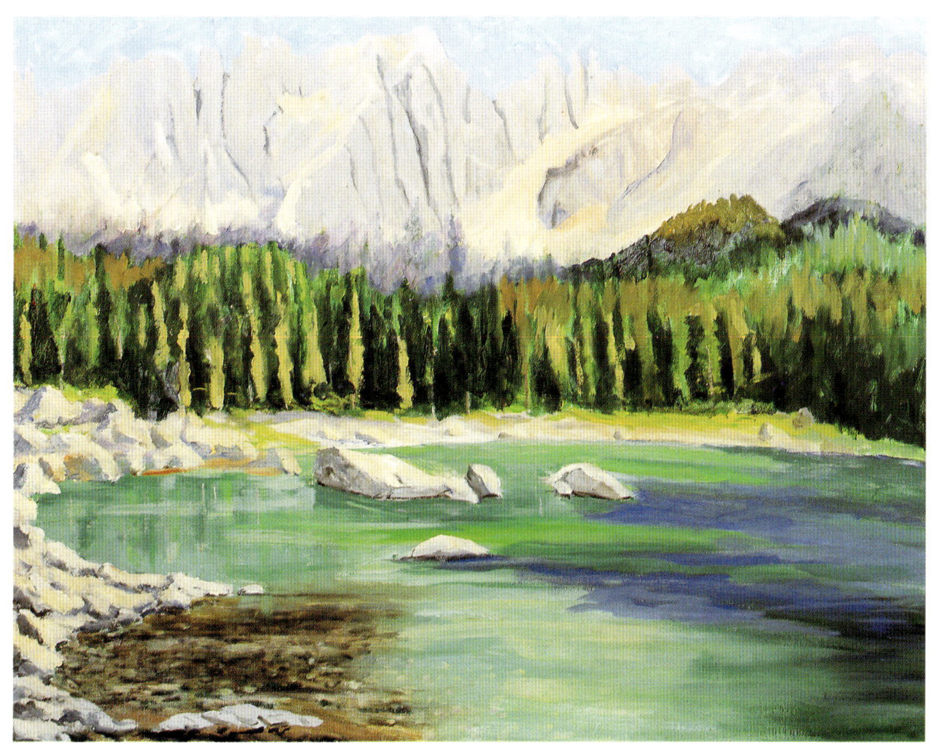

The first meeting of the Council of Europe was held at Strasbourg in 1949. Churchill, now in his 75th year, was to make a major speech. Beforehand, he and Clementine went to stay at Lake Garda in the Dolomite mountains of northern Italy, from where the party moved on to the much smaller, more mountainous, Lake Carezza, which Winston found much more to his liking in terms of its 'paintitious' subjects.

Fig 465 (C 411) left
Lake Carezza.

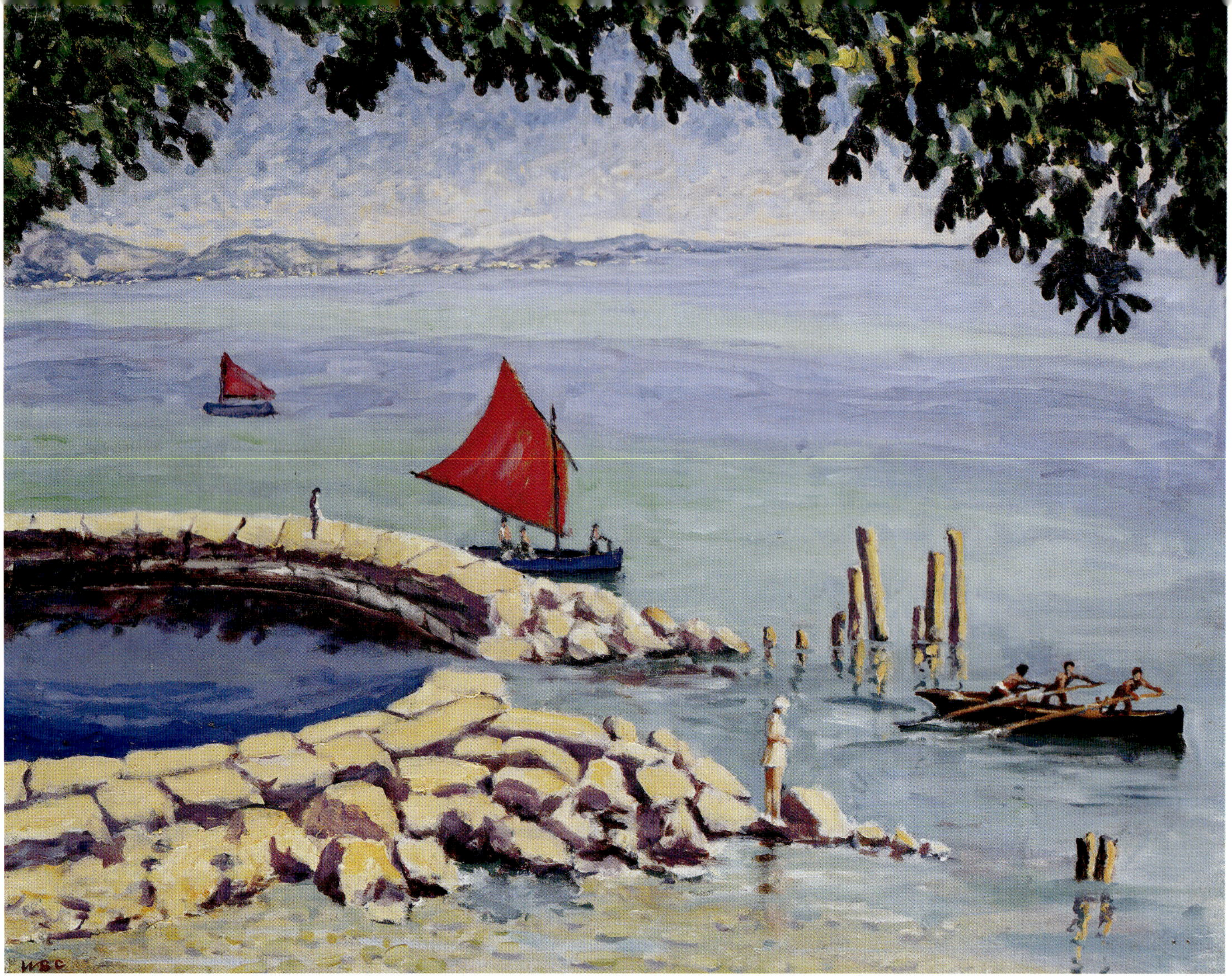

Fig 466 (C 423) above
San Viglio on Lake Garda. This painting is based on photographs from the Studio archives at Chartwell.

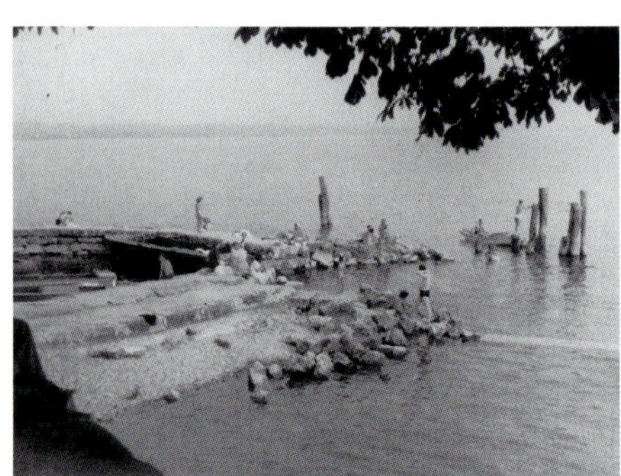

This photograph from the Studio archives at Chartwell, relates to the painting of Lake Garda shown above. It has been marked up by Churchill.

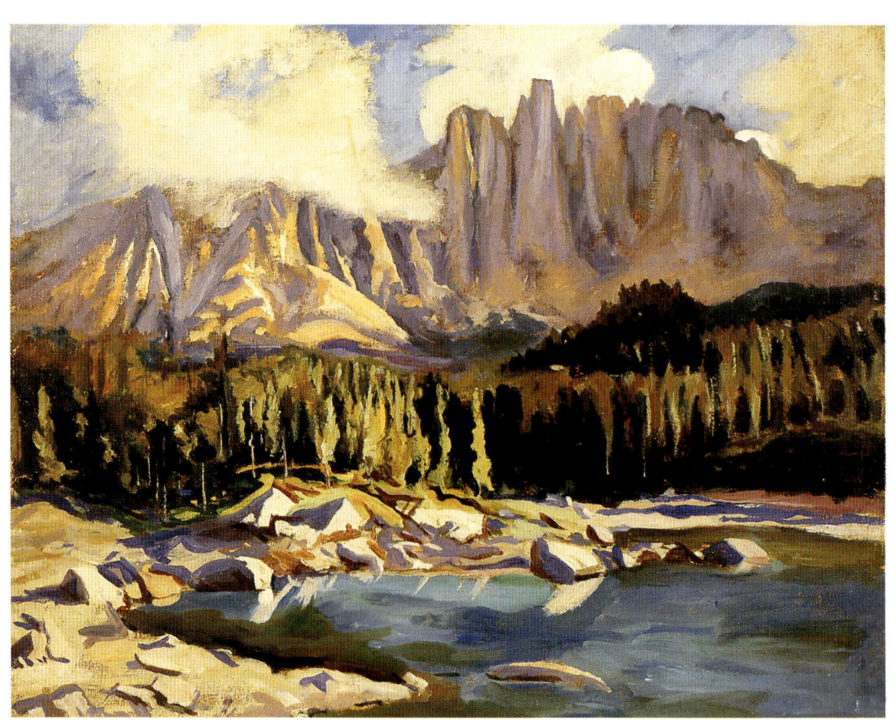

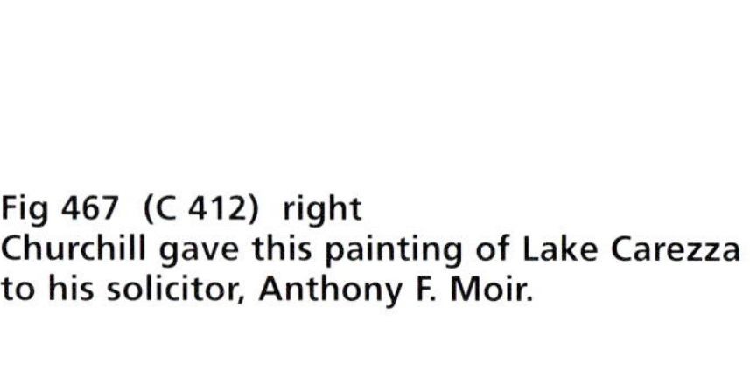

Fig 467 (C 412) right
Churchill gave this painting of Lake Carezza to his solicitor, Anthony F. Moir.

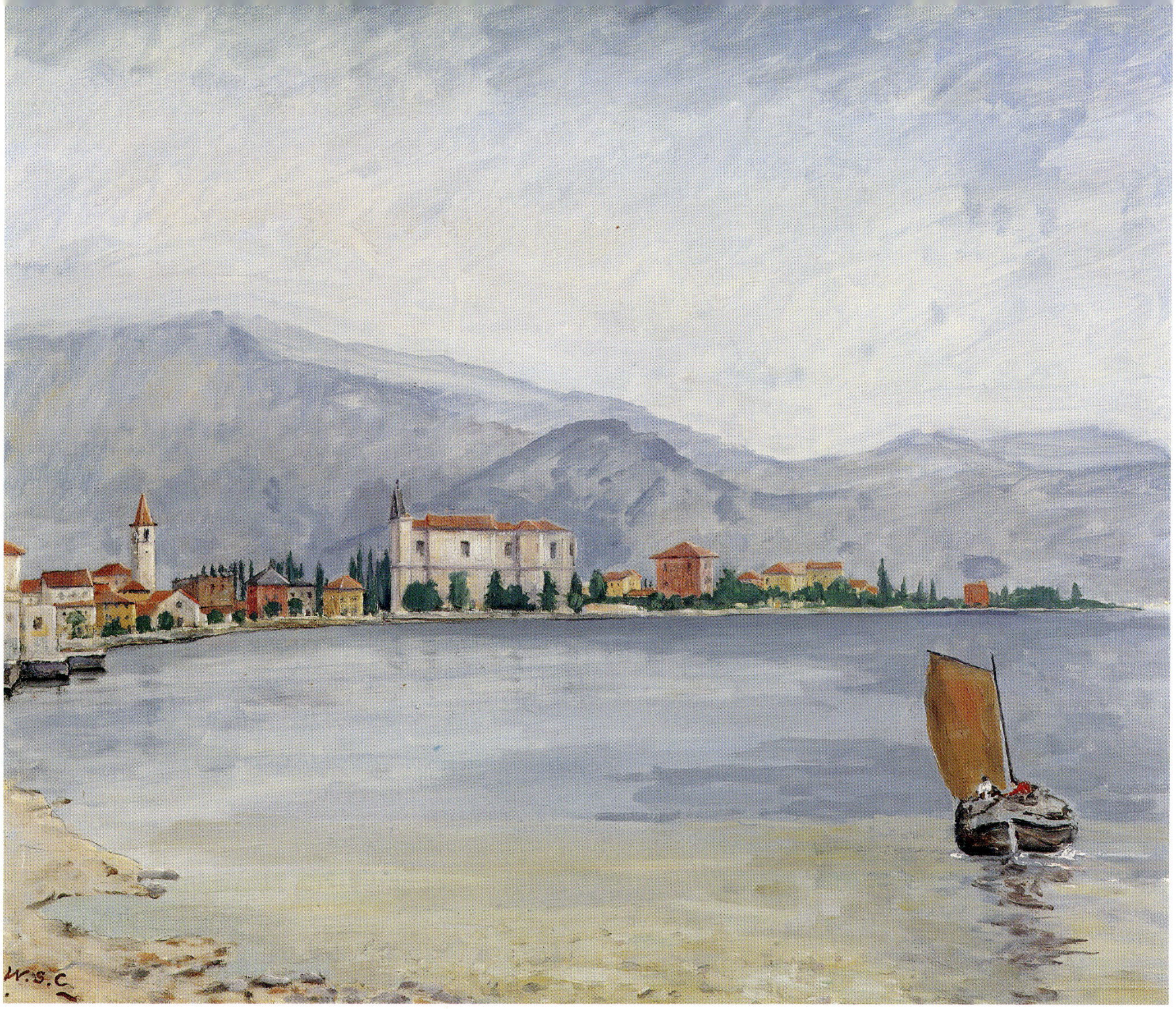

Fig 468 (C 402) above
Churchill gave this view of Lake Garda to Viscount Camrose.

Fourth: the provenance. This is the most important, indeed the imperative point. Technically, 'provenance' is the history of ownership of the picture. In Churchill's case, this means that there has to be a provable or very likely history of ownership from the time Churchill painted the picture to the present. His fame was such and his reluctance to part with his paintings so firm that there is no exception to the rule that the circumstances of his sale or gift of a picture will be known or can be discovered.

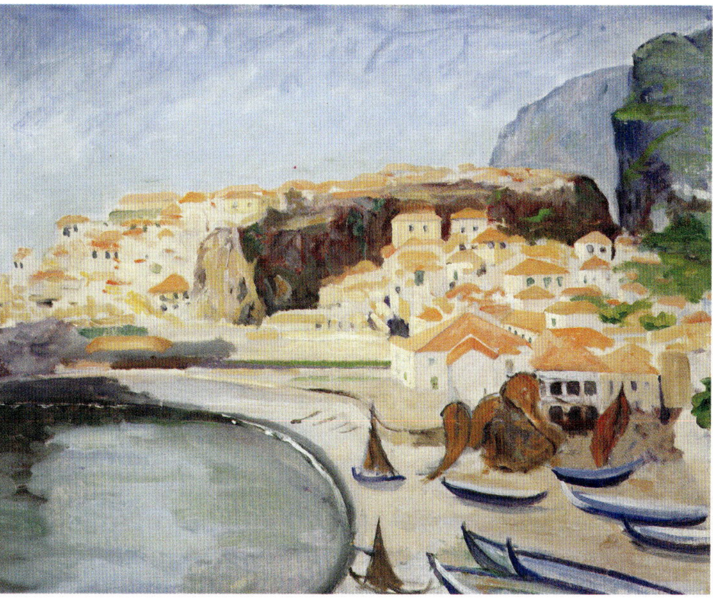

Fig 569 (C 294) above
A winter holiday in Madeira in 1950 was interrupted by the calling of a general election in Britain and Churchill had to hurry back home. This was the only painting he had time to complete in the warmth of the Atlantic island.

At the time of the Churchill exhibition at Sotheby's in 1998, Hugo Swire heard from I. R. S. Bond that he was the owner of Churchill's painting of St Paul's churchyard (C 512). This was a fascinating discovery, for the picture had been missing since its sale in a charity auction at Balmoral Castle in 1927 where Churchill, as Chancellor of the Exchequer, was the guest of King George V and Queen Mary.

Mr Bond subsequently told me that Churchill's painting had been bought at the Balmoral fete by his father, Mr Stanley Shaw Bond, for 115 guineas (£1.75), the bidding having started at £10; and that his father was duly presented with the picture by the Queen.

Again, by way of the National Trust at Chartwell, this time from Carole Kenwright, there came a letter and photographs of another hitherto unknown Churchill painting, 'Landscape with Two Trees' (C 511). The owner was Michael Donaldson, who on visiting Chartwell and speaking to John Brunsden had learnt that a new catalogue of Churchill's paintings was being prepared. The picture had been given to Mr Donaldson's mother, Miss Maud Elgie, who, before

Fig 470 (C 297) right
Near Venice. Churchill gave this painting to Arthur Hays Sulzberger of The New York Times.

In his 77th year and hard at work on the fifth and penultimate volume of his wartime memoirs, Churchill took his family in 1951 to stay in Venice where in the afternoons he was able to swim in the Lagoon and to complete a number of paintings.

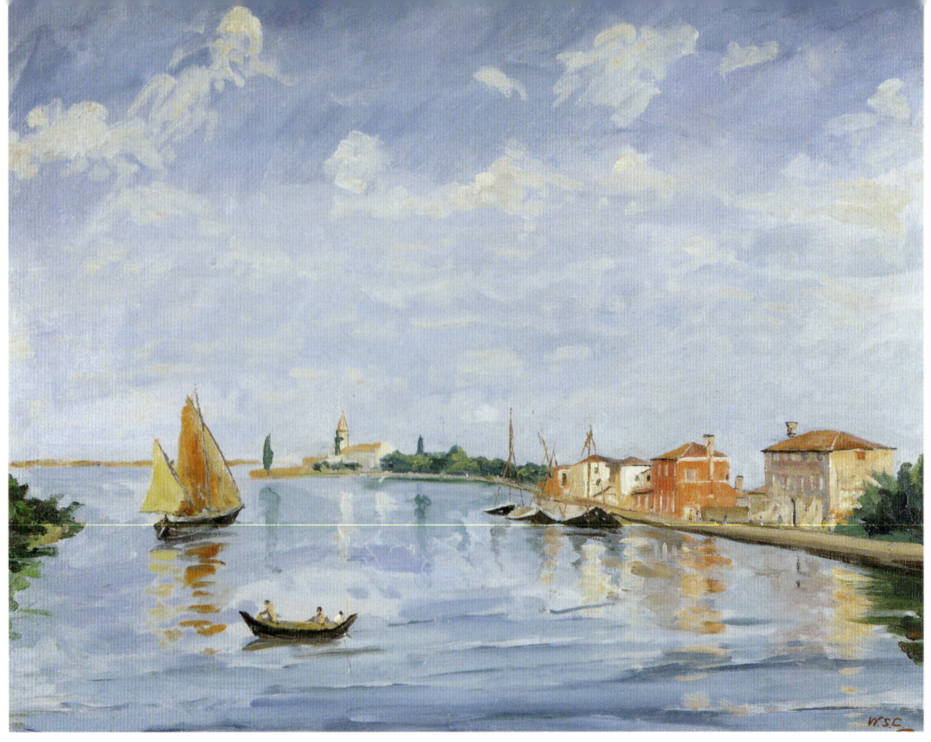

Fig 471 (C 439) below right centre
The Scuola di San Marco in Venice.

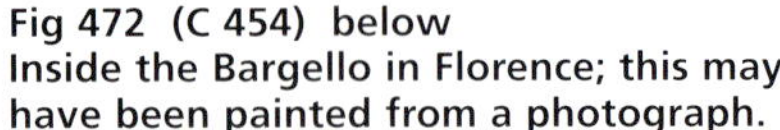

Fig 472 (C 454) below
Inside the Bargello in Florence; this may have been painted from a photograph.

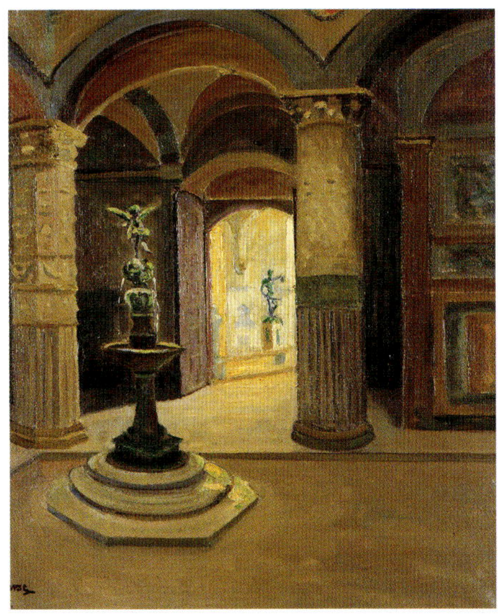

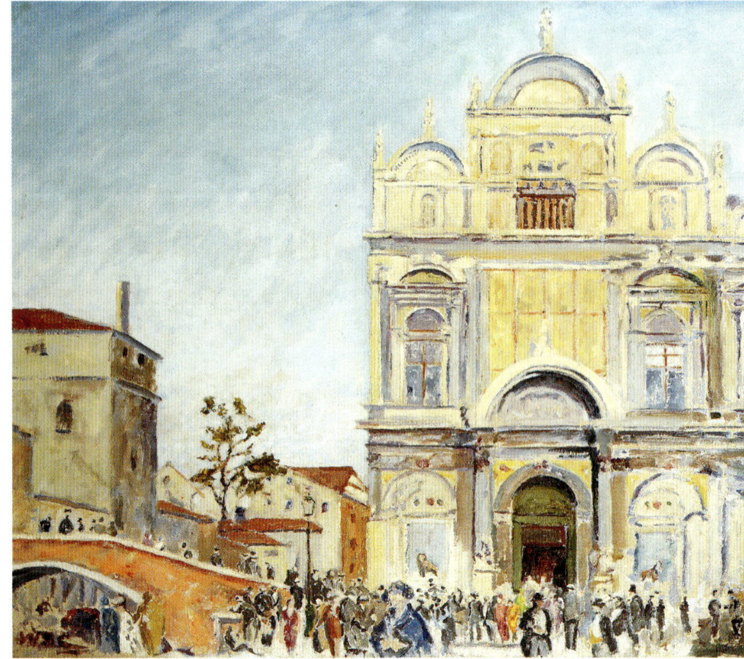

Fig 473 (C 479) below right
Near Venice.

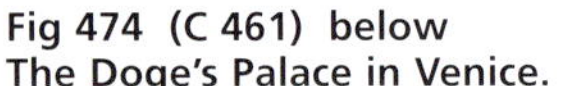

Fig 474 (C 461) below
The Doge's Palace in Venice.

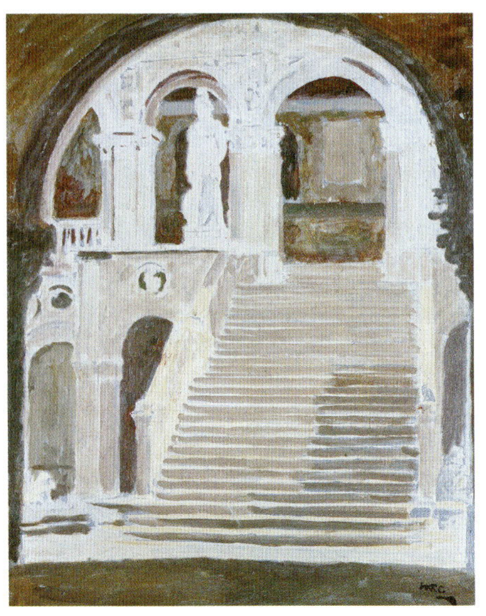

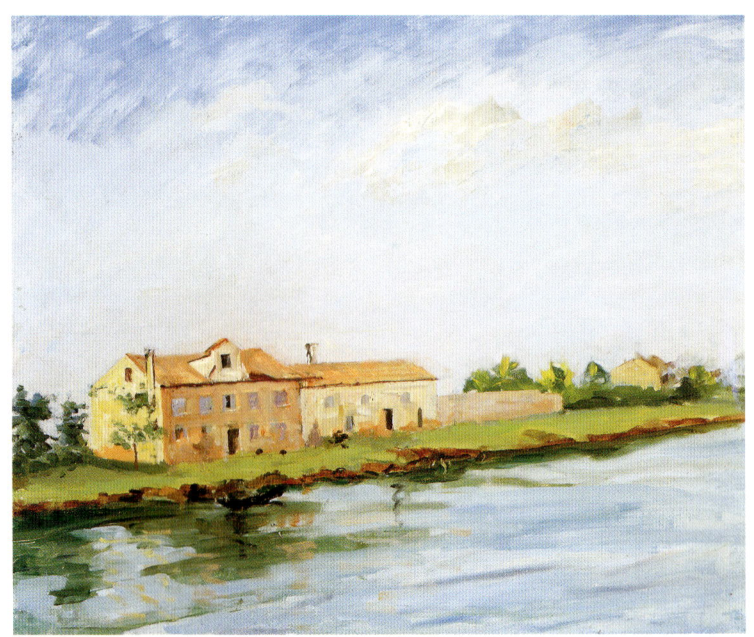

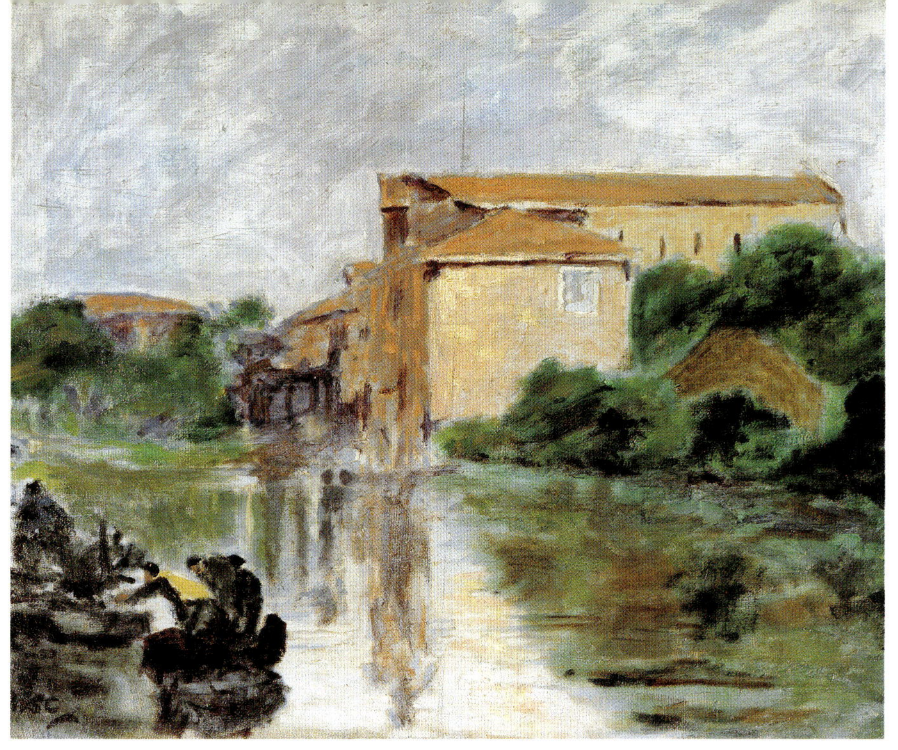

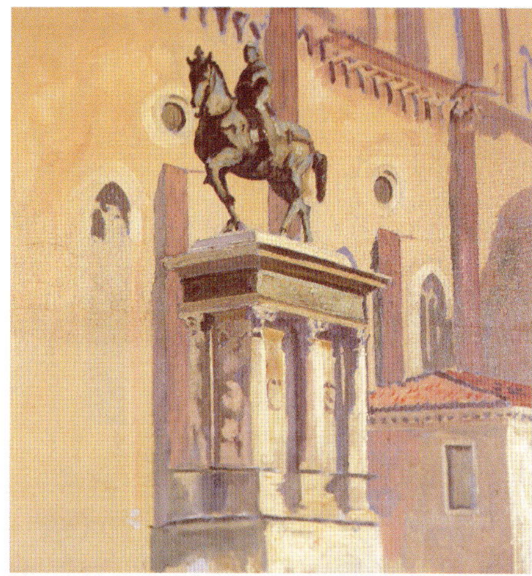

Fig 475 (C 451) above
The Colleoni Memorial in Venice.

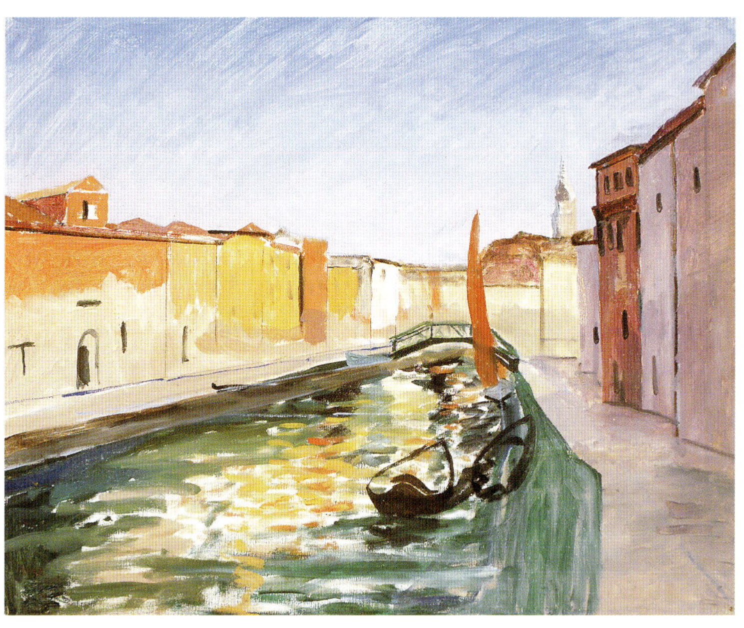

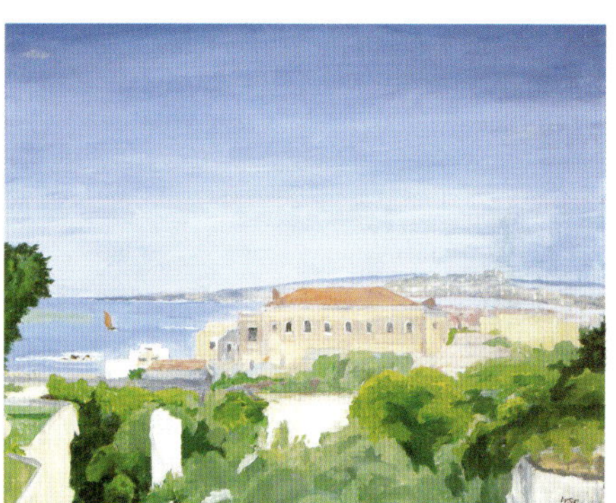

Fig 476 (C 480) above
Scene near Venice.

Fig 477 (C 418) top left
Torcello, one of the islands in the Venetian Lagoon. This very sensitive painting formerly belonged to Clementine Churchill.

Fig 478 (C 478) left centre
An unfinished painting of a canal scene in Venice is based on photographs from the Studio archives at Chartwell.

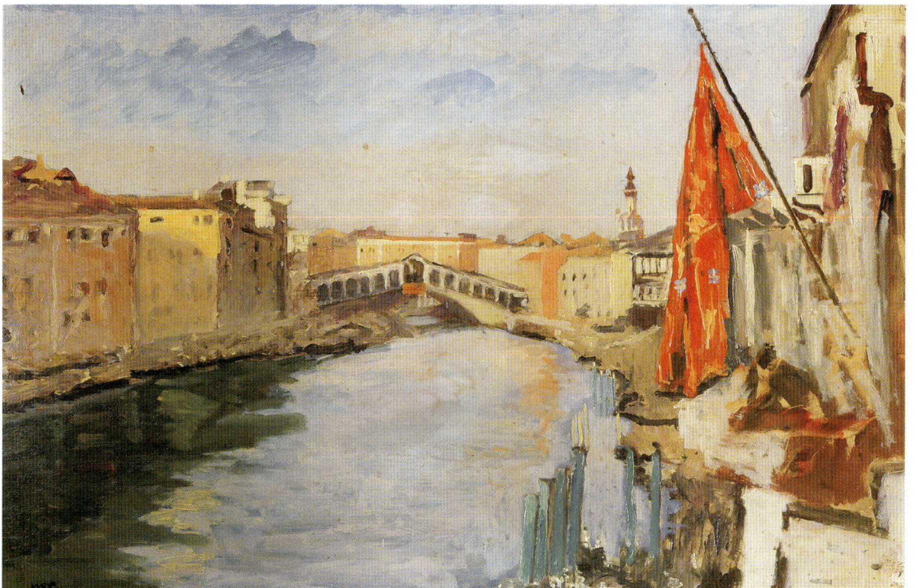

Fig 479 (C 476) left
This painting of the Grand Canal in Venice with the Rialto Bridge was presented to the Palace of Westminster, seat of Britain's Parliament, by Clementine Churchill after Sir Winston's death in 1965. The picture is based on a sketch and photograph from the Studio archives at Chartwell.

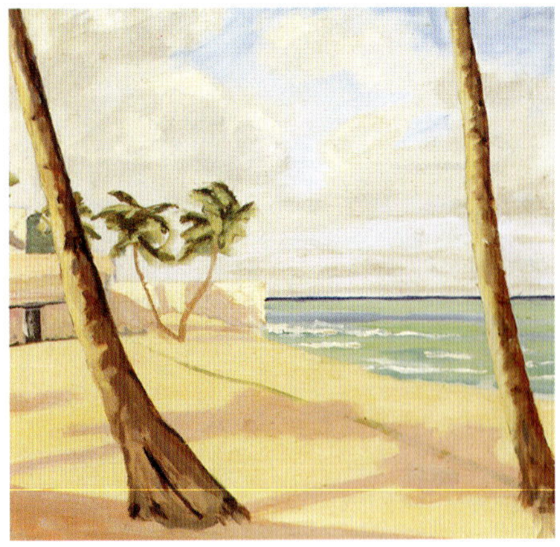

Fig 480 (C 484) above
Jamaican beach.

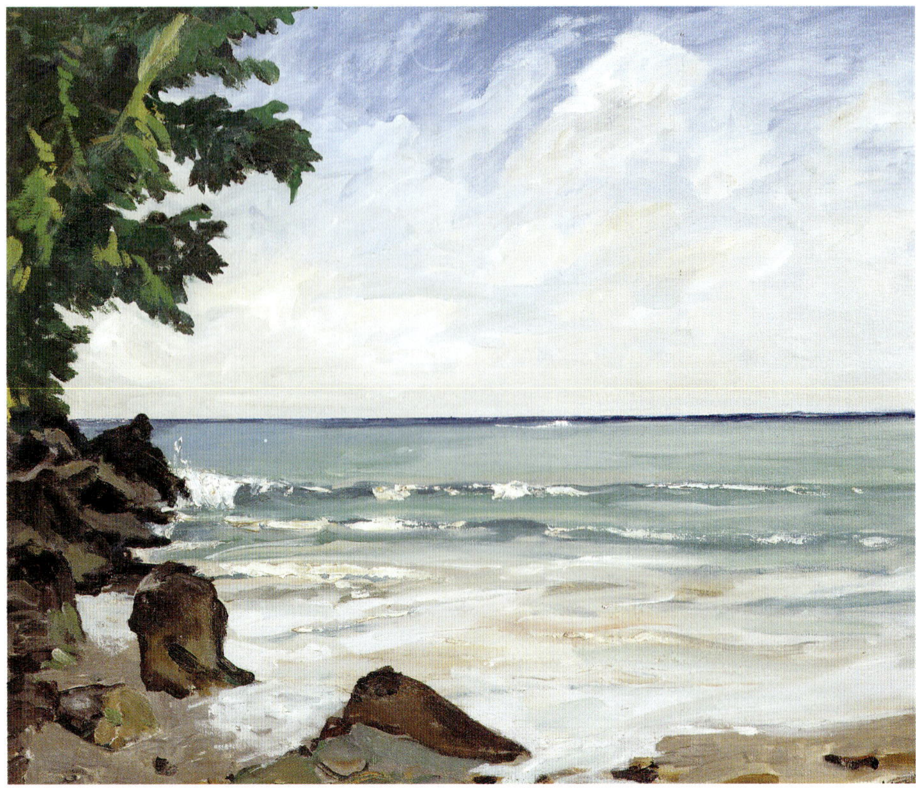

Fig 481 (C 424) right
Frankfort Beach. Churchill gave this painting to Joyce C. Hall of Hallmark Cards.

After winning the general election in 1951 Churchill became Prime Minister again in his 77th year and office once again gave him little time for painting. Following a visit to President Eisenhower in 1953 he flew to Jamaica for a holiday and to work on the last volume of his wartime memoirs. His hosts were Sir Harold and Lady Mitchell who loaned him their house, Prospect, near Ocho Rios; Frankfort Beach was on their estate.

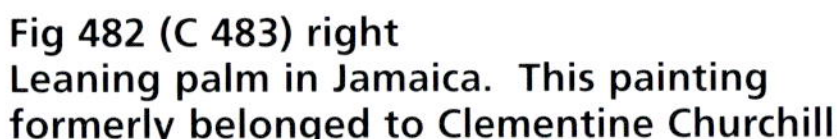

Fig 482 (C 483) right
Leaning palm in Jamaica. This painting formerly belonged to Clementine Churchill.

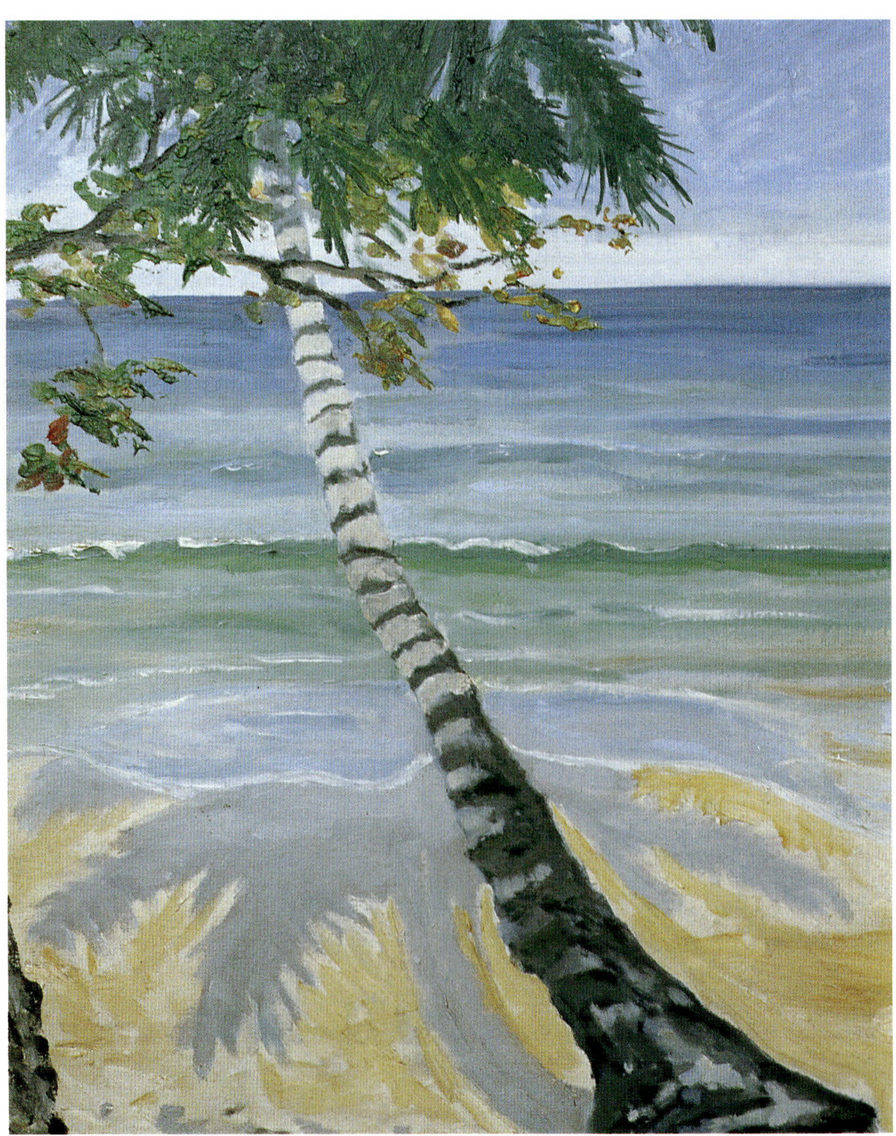

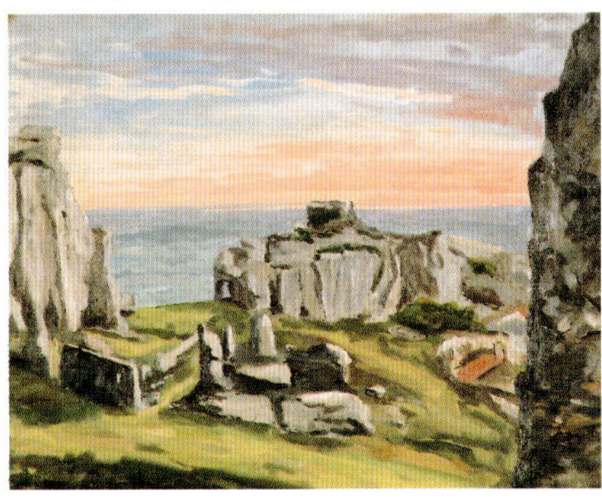

Fig 483 (C 340) above
Rocky scene in Sicily. After resigning as Prime Minister in 1955 in his 80th year, Churchill went on holiday to Sicily where two pictures, this and the other of the Grotto of the Ropemakers, on the facing page were painted.

Fig 484 (C 426) below
Churchill gave this painting of Frankfort Beach, Jamaica, to his political colleague Earl Woolton.

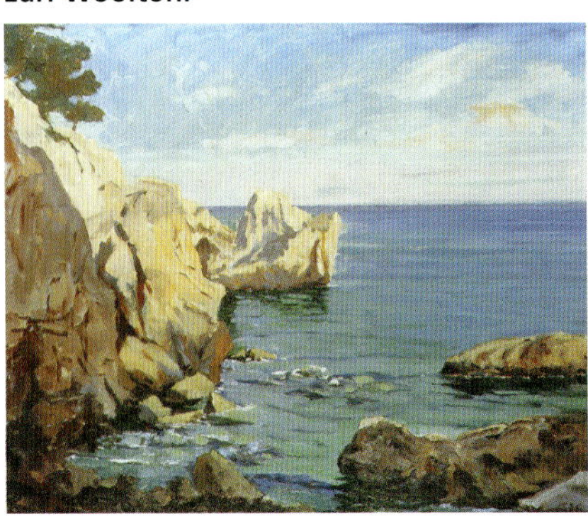

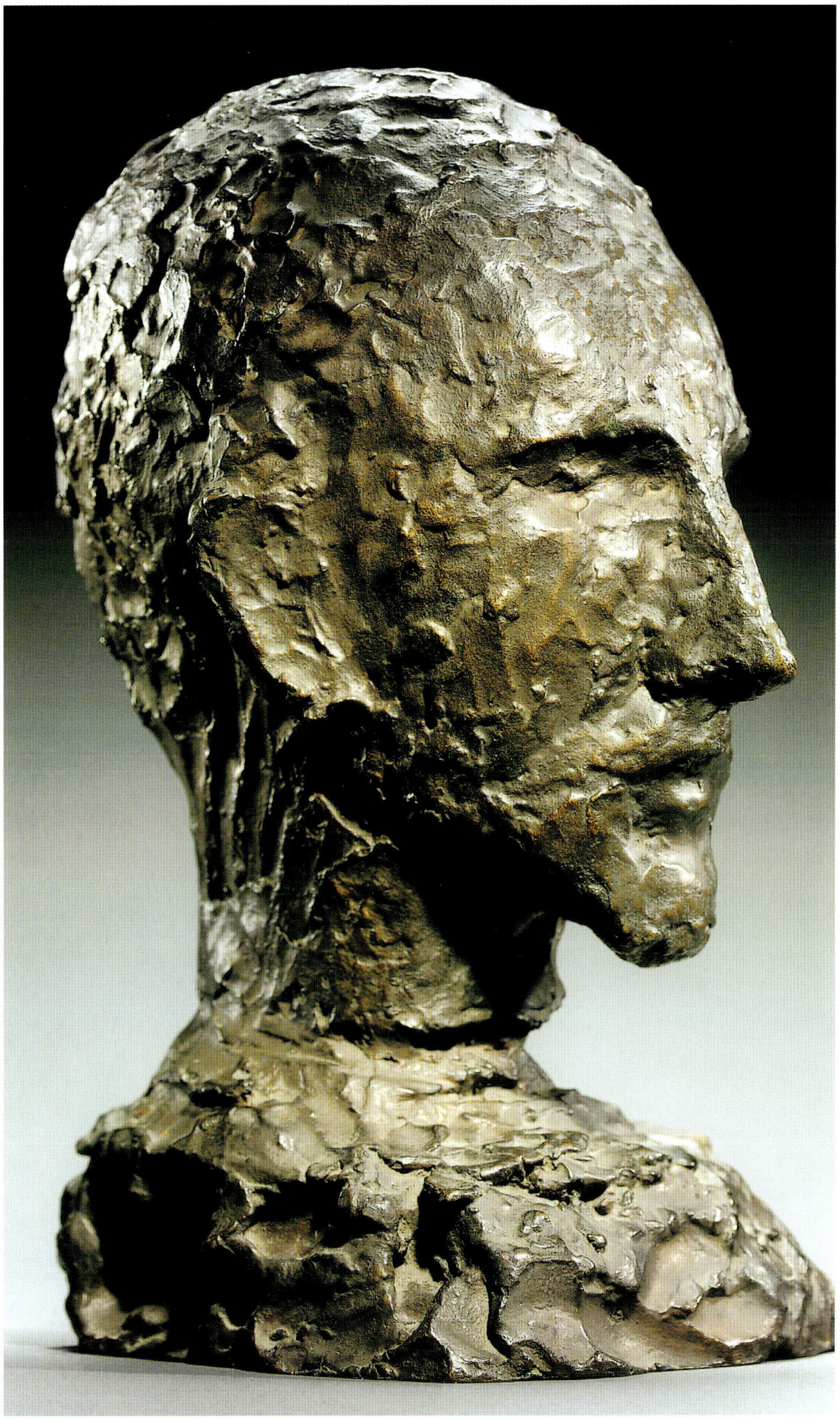

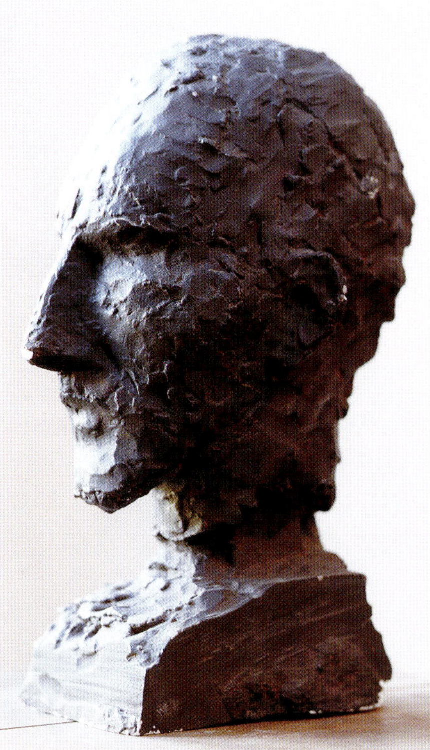

Fig 485 (C 495) above
Churchill allowed Nemon to cast a unique bronze from his plaster cast.

Fig 486 (C 496) left
Whilst sitting in 1954 to Oscar Nemon for a sculpture for the Guildhall in the City of London, Churchill was persuaded by that most charming of artists to try his hand at portraying Nemon; and this unique plaster cast was the result.

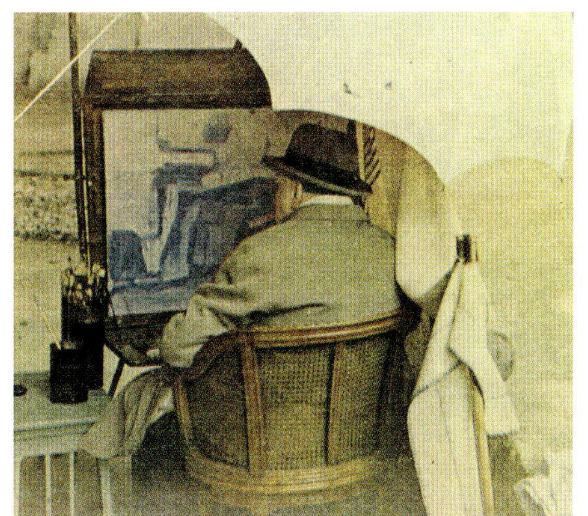

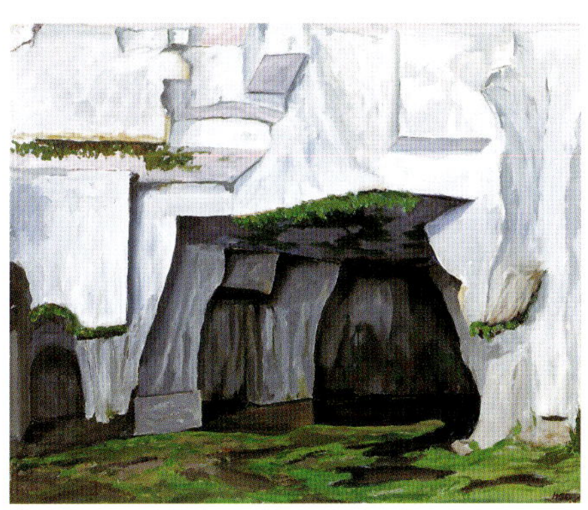

Fig 487 (C 487) above
The Grotto of the Ropemakers at Syracuse in Sicily, which Churchill is seen painting in the photograph.

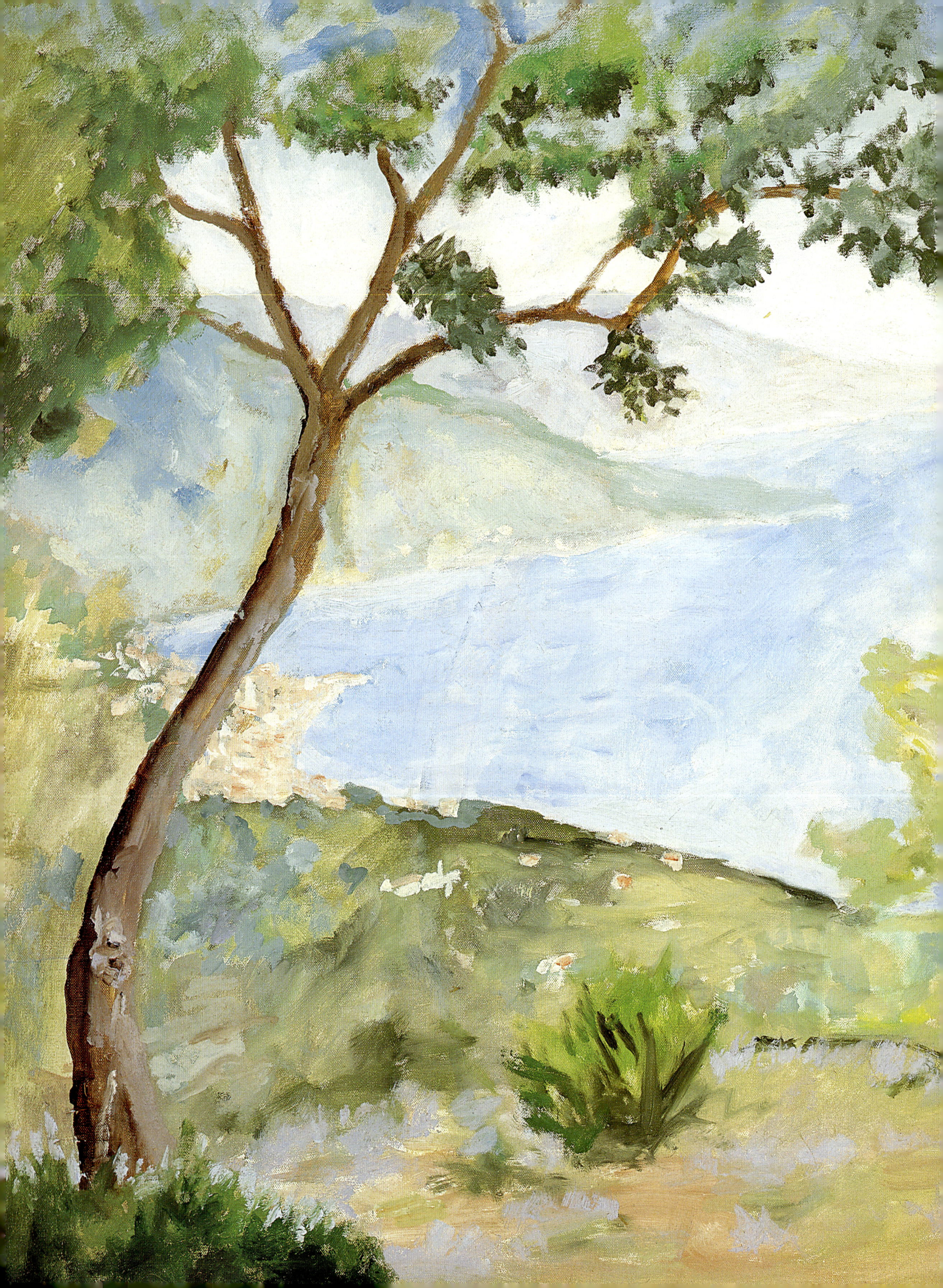

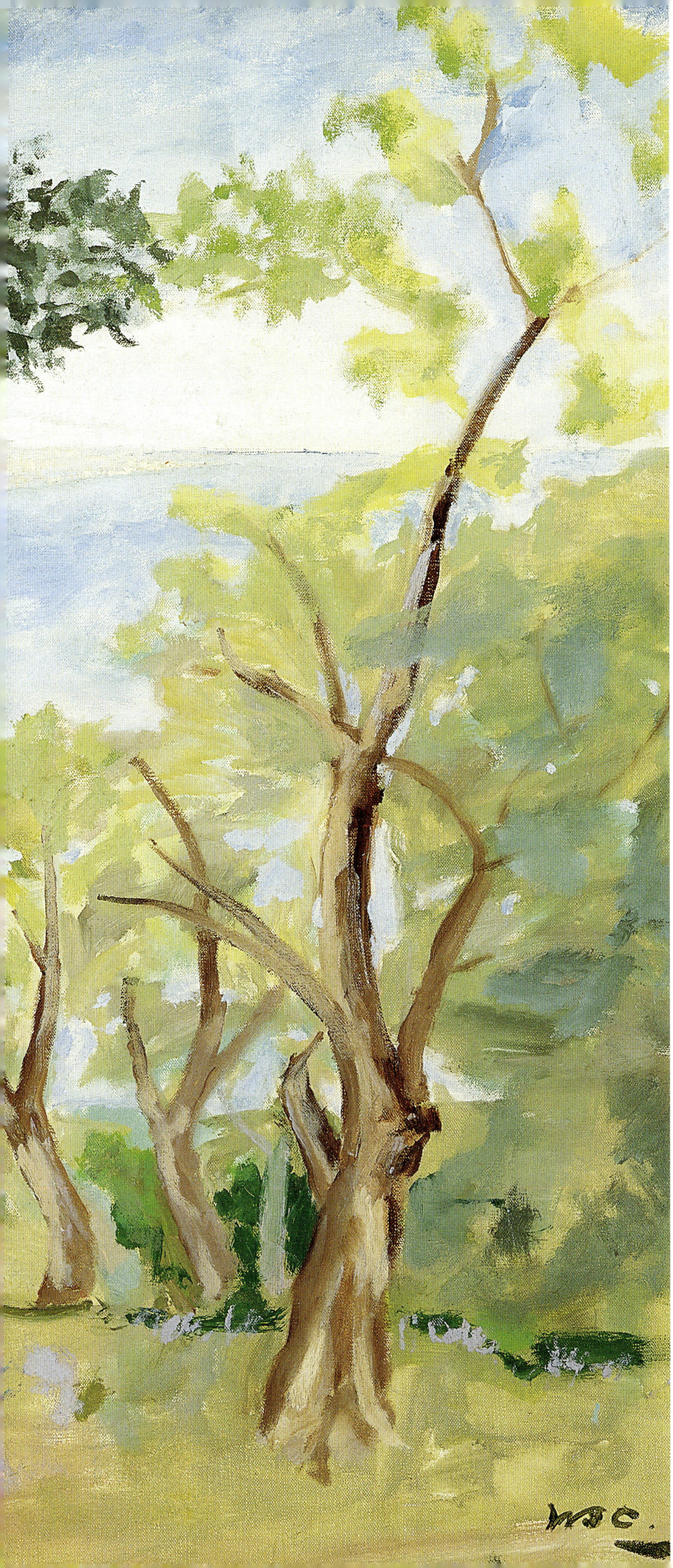

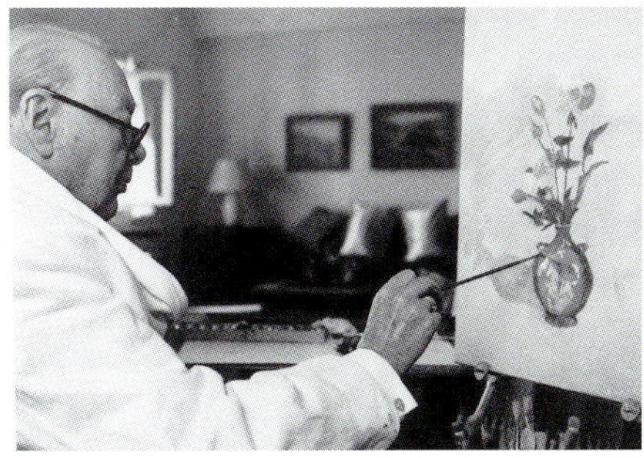

Winston Churchill at La Pausa in the 1950s, copying a painting by Cezanne of a vase of tulips. (See following page)

Fig 488 (C 494)
View from La Pausa of Menton in the south of France with Italy in the distance. La Pausa, near Roquebrune above Cap Martin, was the Riviera villa of Emery Reves, who handled the overseas rights for Churchill's writings. Here he and his young wife Wendy, in particular, spoiled and cossetted Winston in the course of four long visits between 1956 and 1958. The Reveses had an exceptional collection of Impressionist and Post-Impressionist paintings including two by Cezanne, which Churchill copied. He gave this painting of the view from La Pausa to Emery and Wendy Reves.

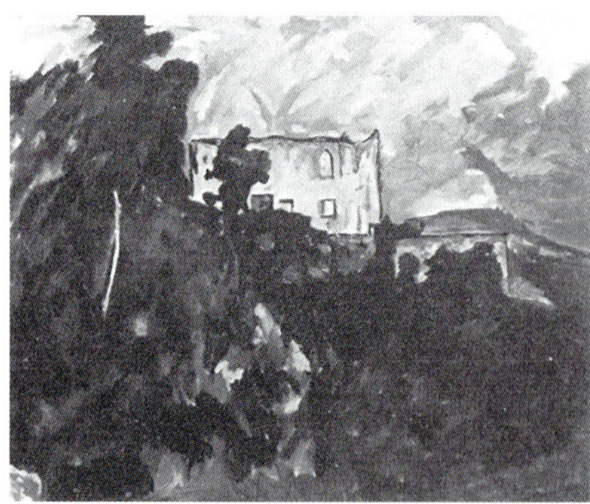

Fig 489 (C 477) above
Copy of Cezanne's painting of La Maison Rouge near Aix-en-Provence.

Fig 490 (C 450) right
Copy of Cezanne's painting of a Vase of Tulips.

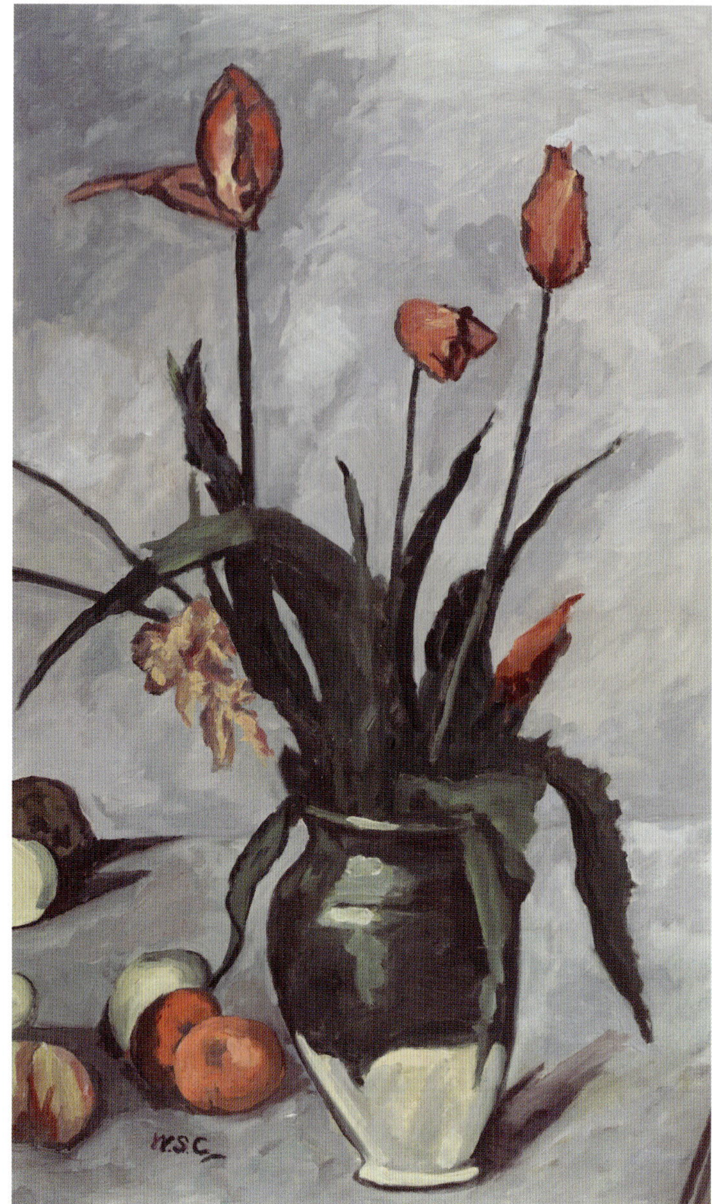

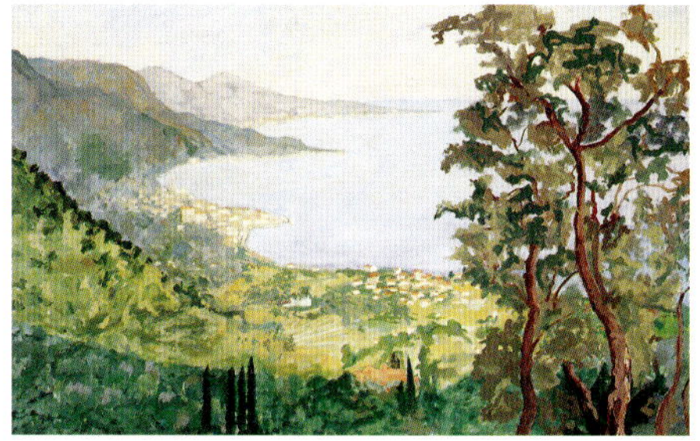

Fig 491 (C 493) above
View of Menton from La Pausa.

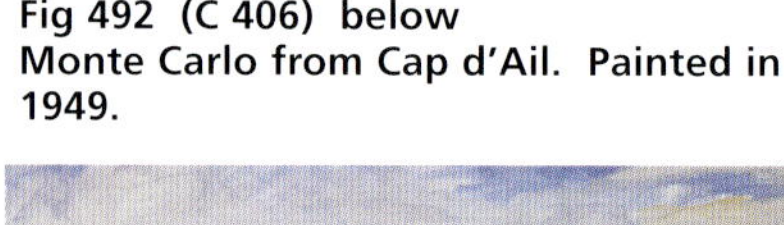

Fig 492 (C 406) below
Monte Carlo from Cap d'Ail. Painted in 1949.

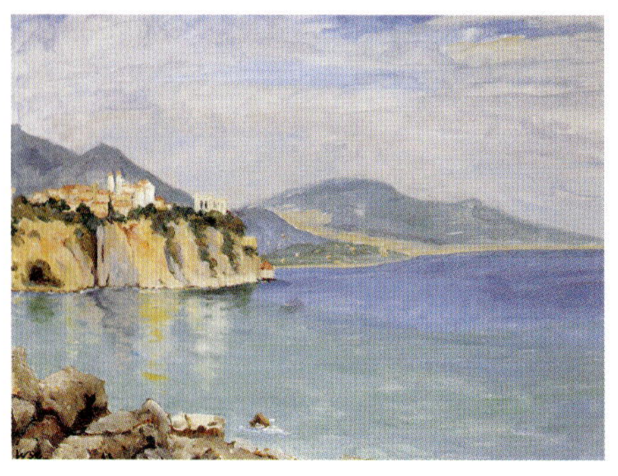

her marriage had been employed by the Churchills between 1919 and 1921 to look after their two elder children, Diana and Randolph. The exact subject remains unknown and although his mother thought it to have been Mimizan, Michael Donaldson, who lives in the South of France, points out that this cannot have been the case as his painting shows a hilltop town and Mimizan, in Les Landes, near Bordeaux, is flat.

Sometimes research into the lives of Churchill's friends can throw light on his pictures. For example, one of Churchill's most beautiful paintings is of Ightham Mote in Kent (C 235). When it was sold at Sotheby's in 1966, it came from the collection of Sir Winston's old friend General Sir Ian Hamilton but its true and much more interesting history has been only recently discovered by Celia Lee. When working on the life of the General Hamilton's beautiful wife, Jean, Mrs Lee found in her diary details of several mutually encouraging painting expeditions in Churchill's company. Jean Hamilton worked in pastel and one of her pictures is very similar to Churchill's 'Olive Trees, Cap Martin' (C 268).

In her book *Jean, Lady Hamilton 1861-1941* (London, 2001), Celia Lee quotes from Lady Hamilton's diary of November 1920. 'Sir John Lavery advised me to buy one of Winston's pictures ... I thought them really lovely ...' In June the following

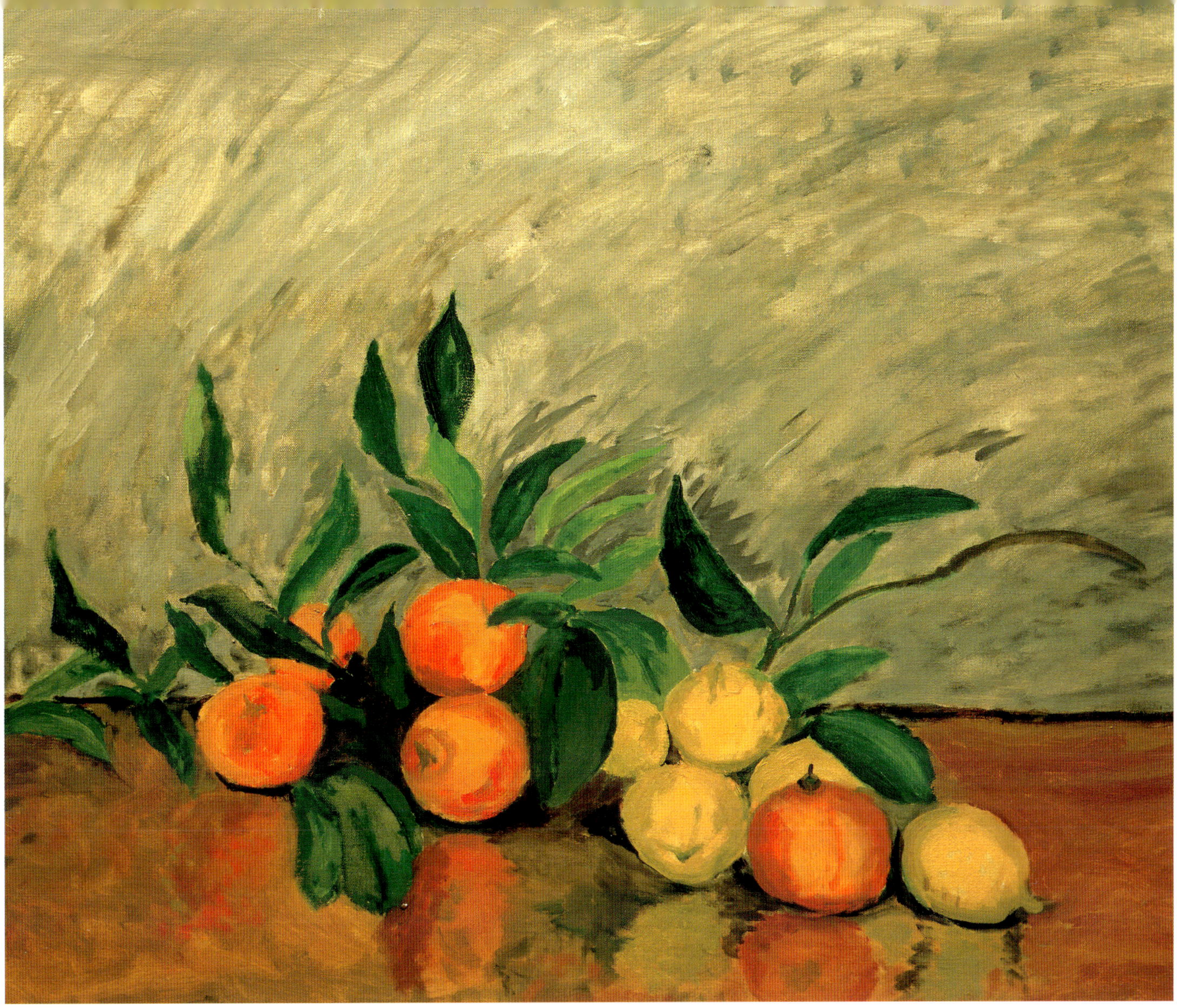

Fig 493 (C 455) above
Oranges and lemons: an arrangement made by Wendy Reves for Winston to paint at La Pausa.

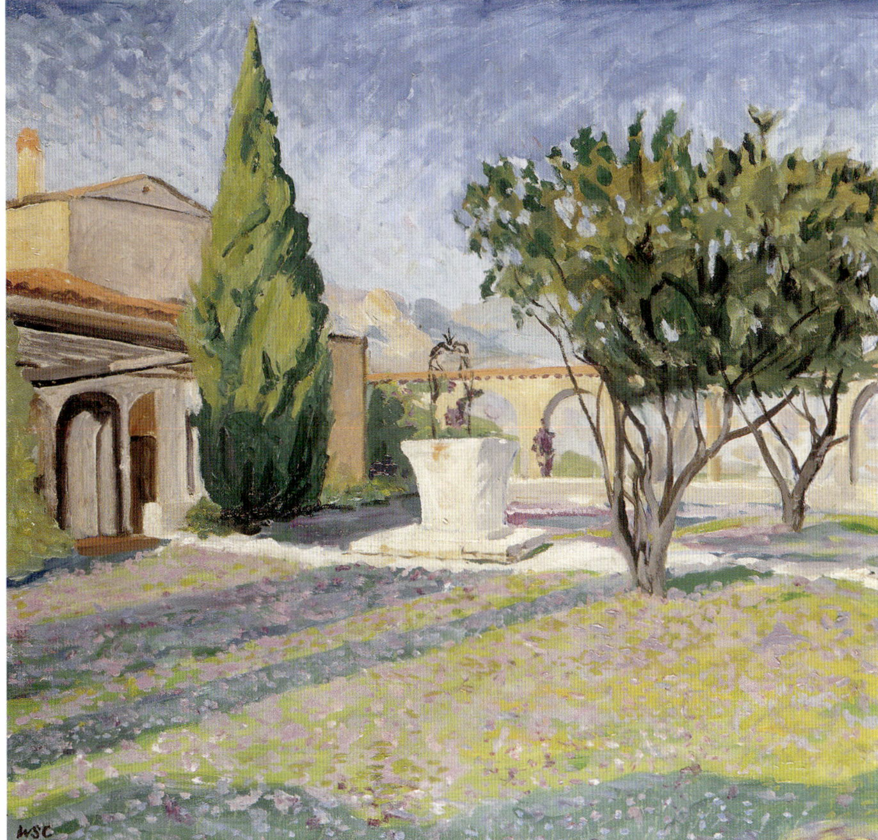

Fig 494 (C 471) left
Blue Grass at La Capponcina. This painting is based on a series of photographs mounted together from the Studio archives at Chartwell.

Fig 495 (C 481) below
View of Monte Carlo from Cap d'Ail.

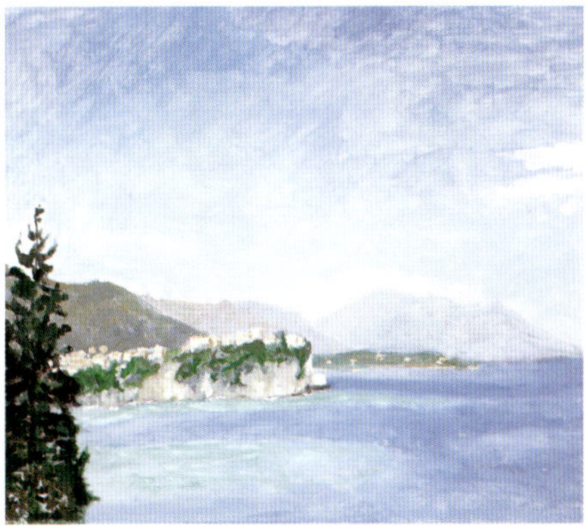

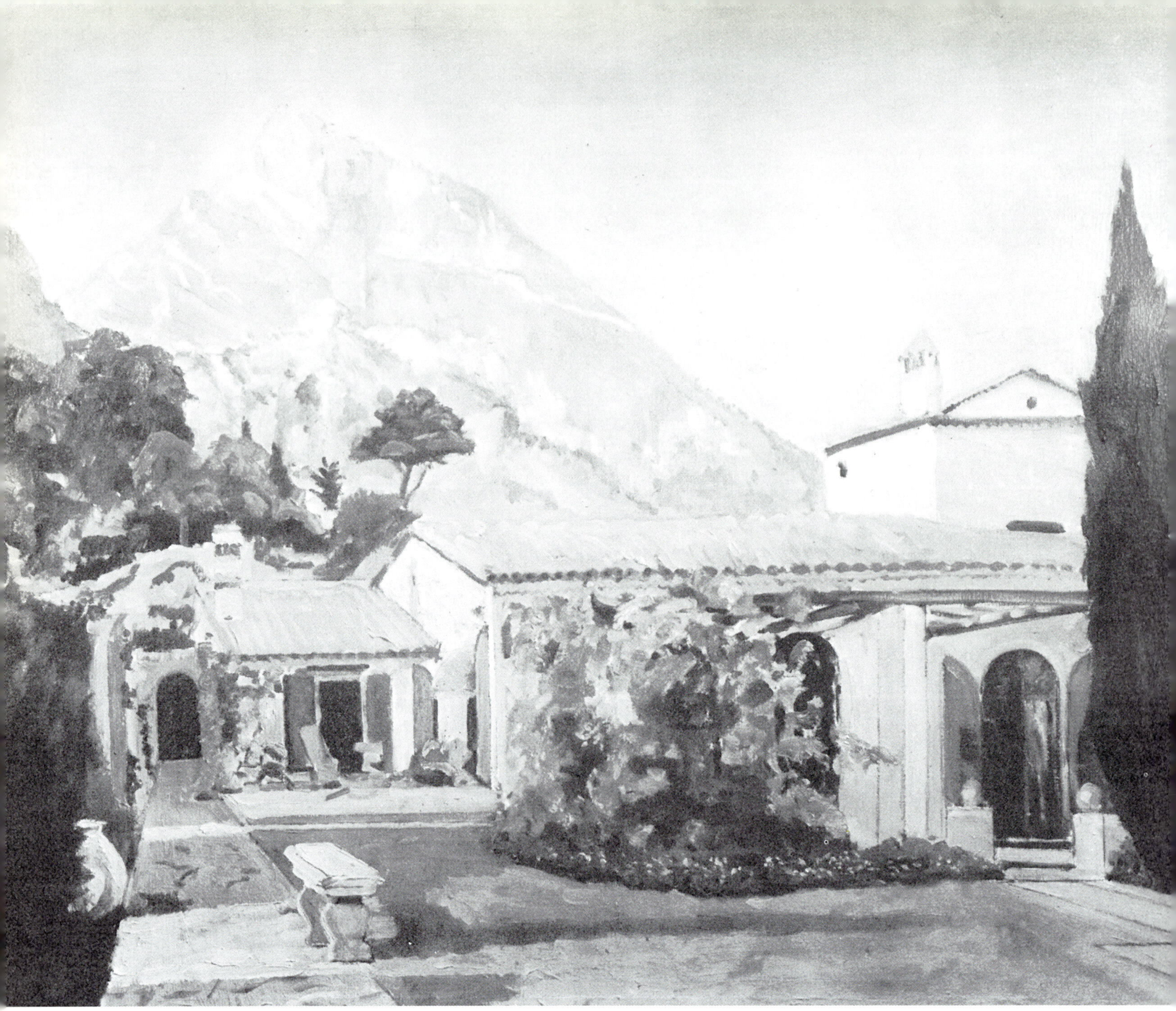

Fig 496 (C 472) above
Churchill gave this painting of La Capponcina to Lord Beaverbrook.

year, Winston wrote to Jean, 'You expressed a wish to buy one of my pictures ... I have been doubtful about selling any of them because I don't think they are good enough and also because I am steadily improving. Nevertheless as several people have been asking to buy, I have said that I will sell them at £50 a piece this year ... I am genuinely reluctant to sell these daubs - particularly to a friend.' In October the same year, Winston carried down to Lullenden (which the Hamiltons had bought from the Churchills) Jean's choice, 'Ightam Moat' (this was the spelling she used, as also in *The Strand Magazine* reproduction).

The 1927 Balmoral auction was, as far as is known, the first public auction of a Churchill painting. In 1921, his friend and long-time painting companion Charles Montag organized an exhibition at the prestigious Galerie Druet in the rue Royale, Paris, of a number of Churchill's paintings shown under the pseudonym 'Charles Morin'. Professor Thomas Bodkin in his contribution to *Churchill: By His Contemporaries* stated, without quoting his source, that six of Churchill's paintings were sold in Paris. Assuming this to be correct, then their present whereabouts is a mystery.

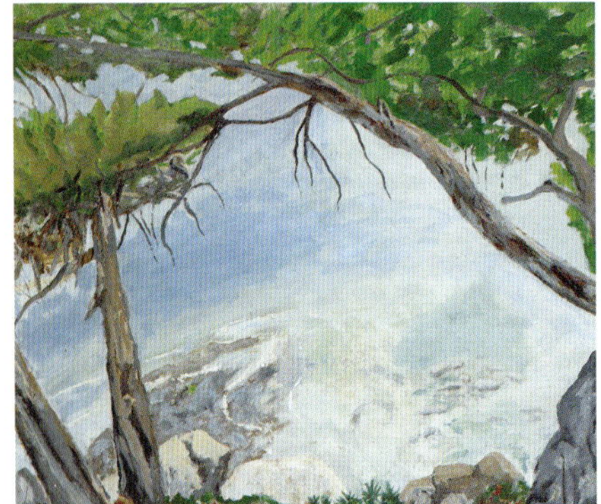

Fig 497 (C 488) above
The sea from La Capponcina.

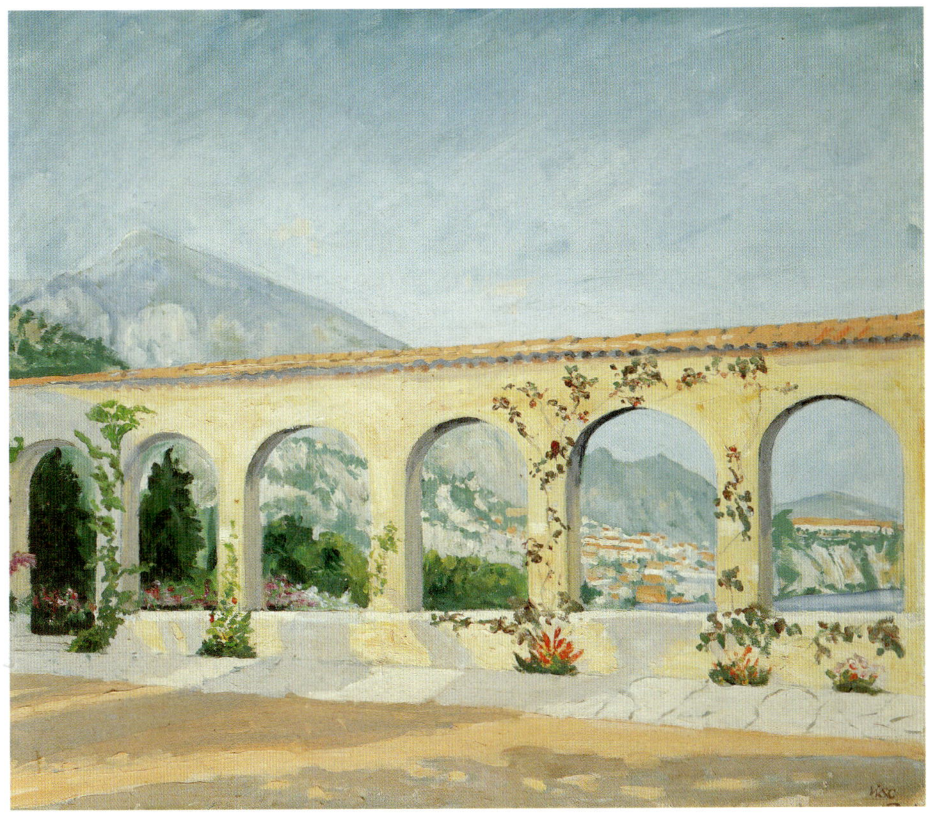

In 1948 Churchill paid his first visit to La Capponcina, Lord Beaverbrook's Riviera villa on Cap d'Ail near Monte Carlo. Mary Soames describes the property as 'an oasis of privacy... with lovely views.' Winston and Clementine became increasingly regular visitors at La Capponcina where Churchill found much to paint until 1960 when this was no longer physically possible. After his resignation as Prime Minister, Winston seriously considered the idea of buying a Riviera villa for himself but, apart from the great expense, his increasingly lengthy visits to La Pausa and La Capponcina proved both comfortable and satisfying for himself and his family.

Fig 498 (C 475) left
The Walled Garden at La Capponcina.

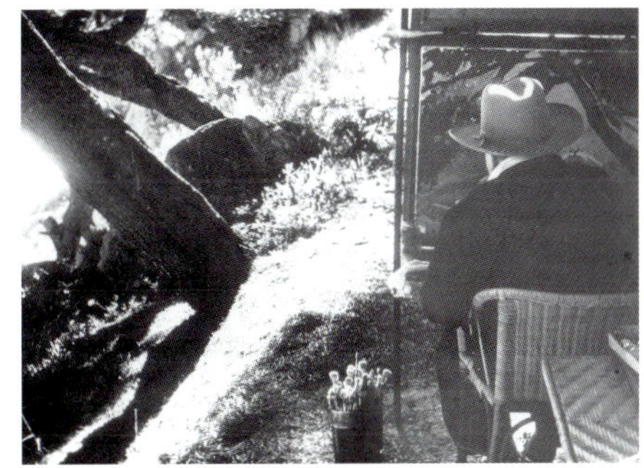

Sir Winston Churchill painting at La Capponcina in the 1950s.

A surprising number of Churchill's paintings that were reproduced during his lifetime have yet to be found. These include pictures shown in the *The Strand Magazine*, 1921/2 (C 519, C 520, C 521); *The Strand Magazine*, 1946 (C 522); *The Illustrated London News*, 1954 (C 523); and, most surprising of all perhaps, two paintings illustrated in the catalogue of his Royal Academy exhibition, 1959 (C 516, C 524).

Further light on several paintings by Churchill, including some that have appeared at auction but whose present whereabouts is unknown, has been shed by the large cache of his Studio photographs in the National Trust's archives at Chartwell. Three of these in particular show scenes with the dazzling socialite Lady Castlerosse at the time when both were guests at Maxine Elliott's Riviera villa in the South of France (C 158, C 517, C 518).

Three possible Churchill paintings are also included in this new catalogue. Two of them, 'Gardens at Port Lympne' (C 533) and 'Lake Carezza' (C 509), have provenances that have yet to be verified and so their authenticity remains in doubt. The third, 'The Gallery, Esher Place' (C 526), is of unusual interest. I was t

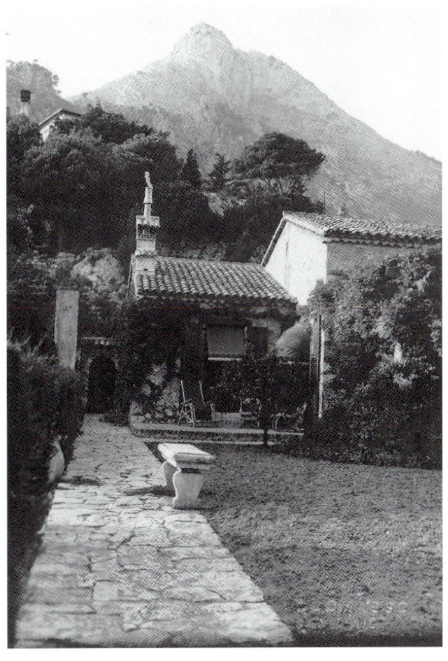

Photograph of La Capponcina from the Studio archives at Chartwell. It relates to Churchill's painting on page 237.

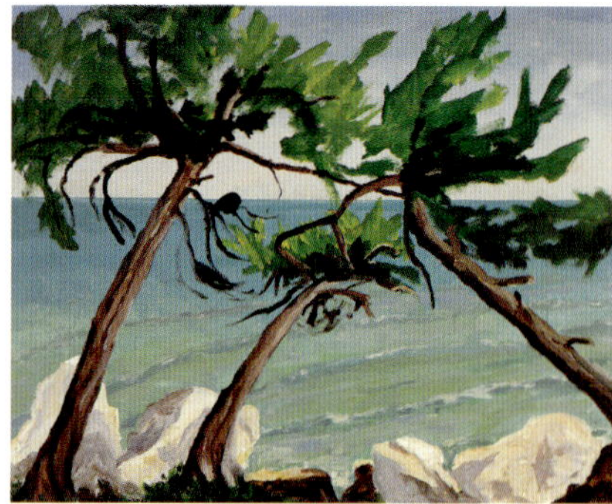

Fig 499 (C 491) above
The Custody of the Child. Churchill gave this painting to Emery and Wendy Reves.

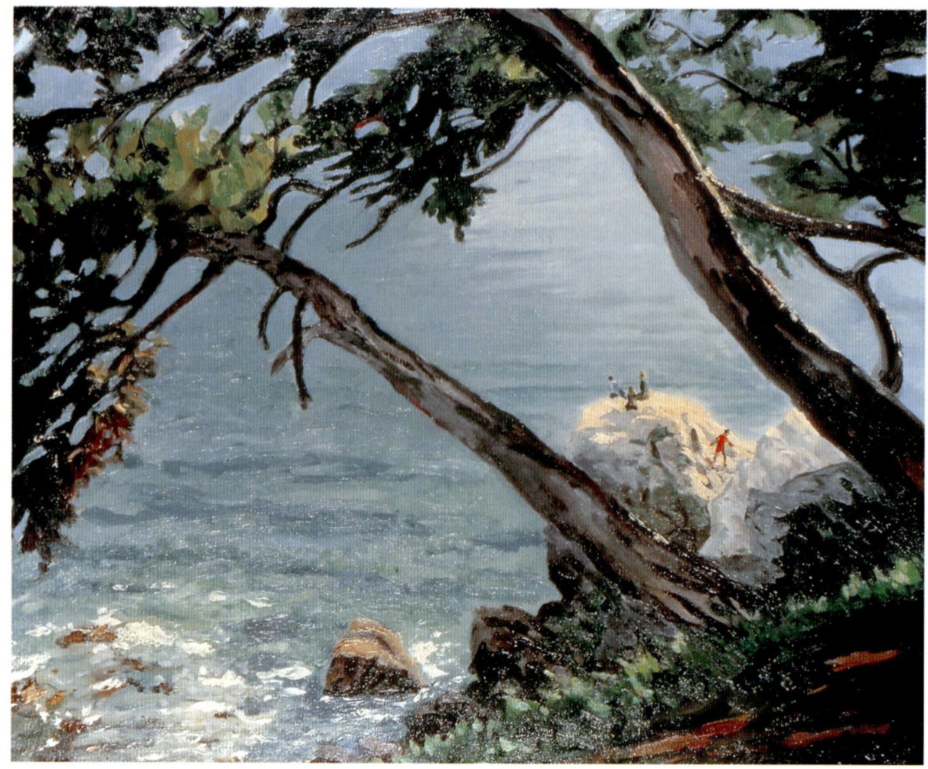

Fig 500 (C 489) right
Cap d'Ail, Alpes Maritimes, from La Capponcina. Churchill gave this painting to the Royal Academy of Arts in London following his election as Honorary Academician Extraordinary; every member of the Academy since its foundation in 1768 is bound to deposit a work for its permanent collection. This picture was painted in 1952.

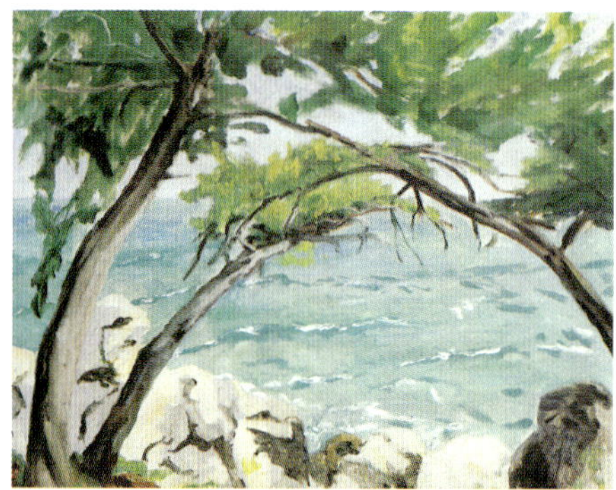

Fig 501 (C 503) above
The Sea from La Capponcina. Painted in 1955 and presented to Lord and Lady Beaverbrook by Churchill on the occasion of their marriage in 1963.

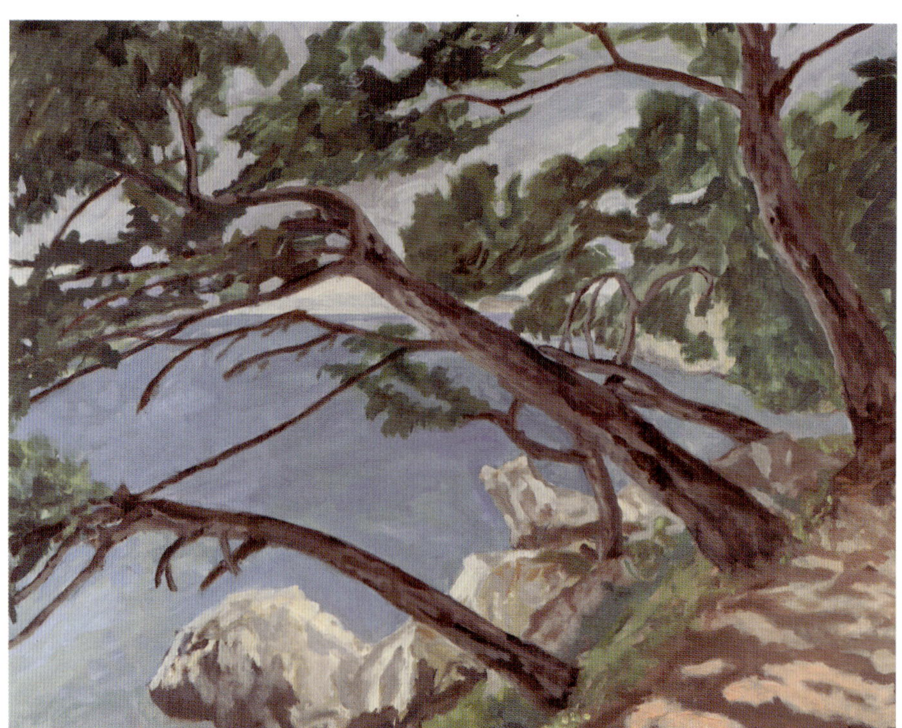

Fig 502 (C 492) right
Sea and pine trees at Cap d'Ail.

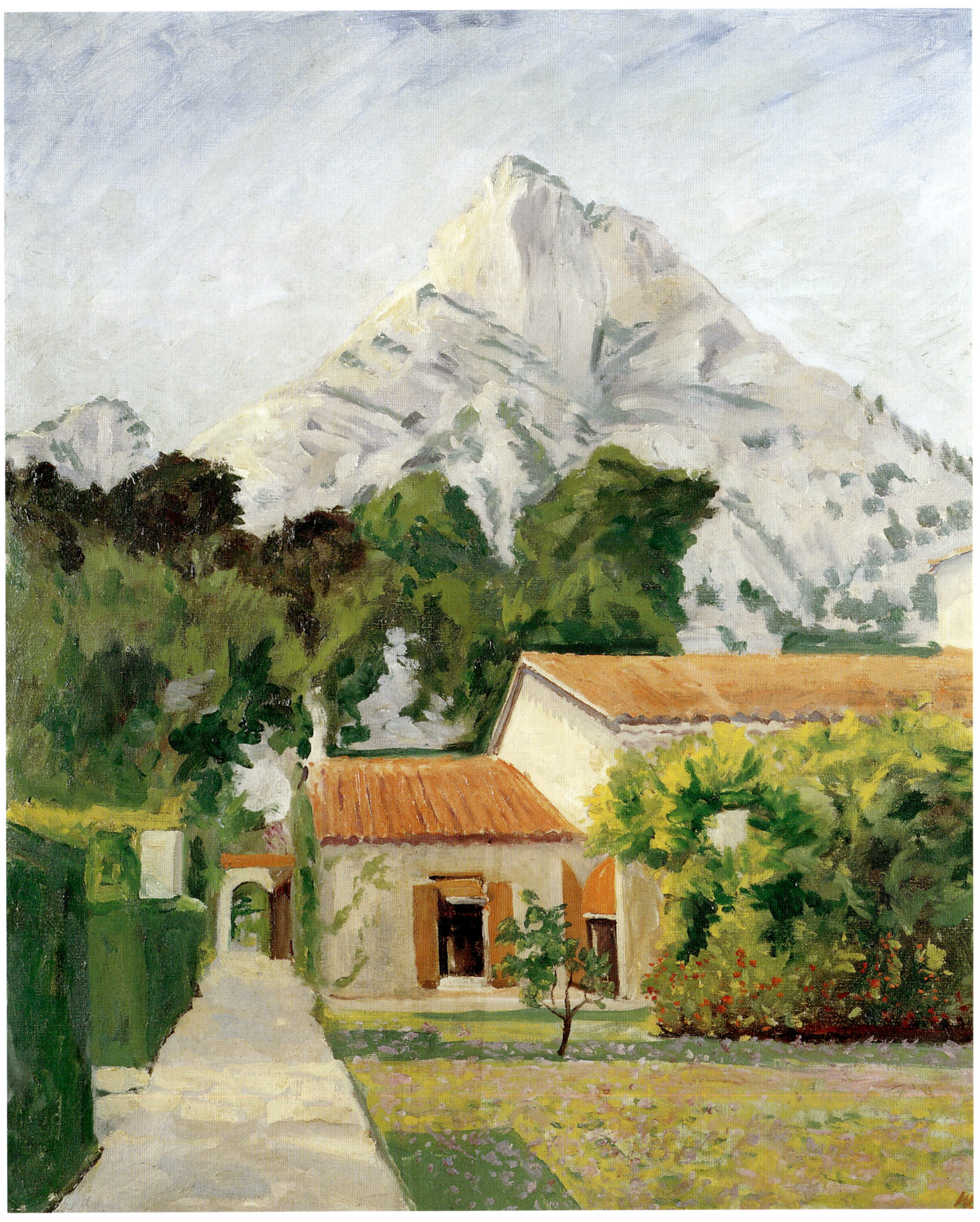

Fig 503 (C 473) above
This view of the villa at La Capponcina is based on a photograph from the Studio archives at Chartwell in which Clementine is clearly seen in the shadow within the open door on the left.

On these and the following pages are illustrated paintings and sketches by Churchill that have been discovered since his death in 1965, plus others that were illustrated in his lifetime but are currently missing. Three paintings are of uncertain provenance and so cannot be formally authenticated yet.

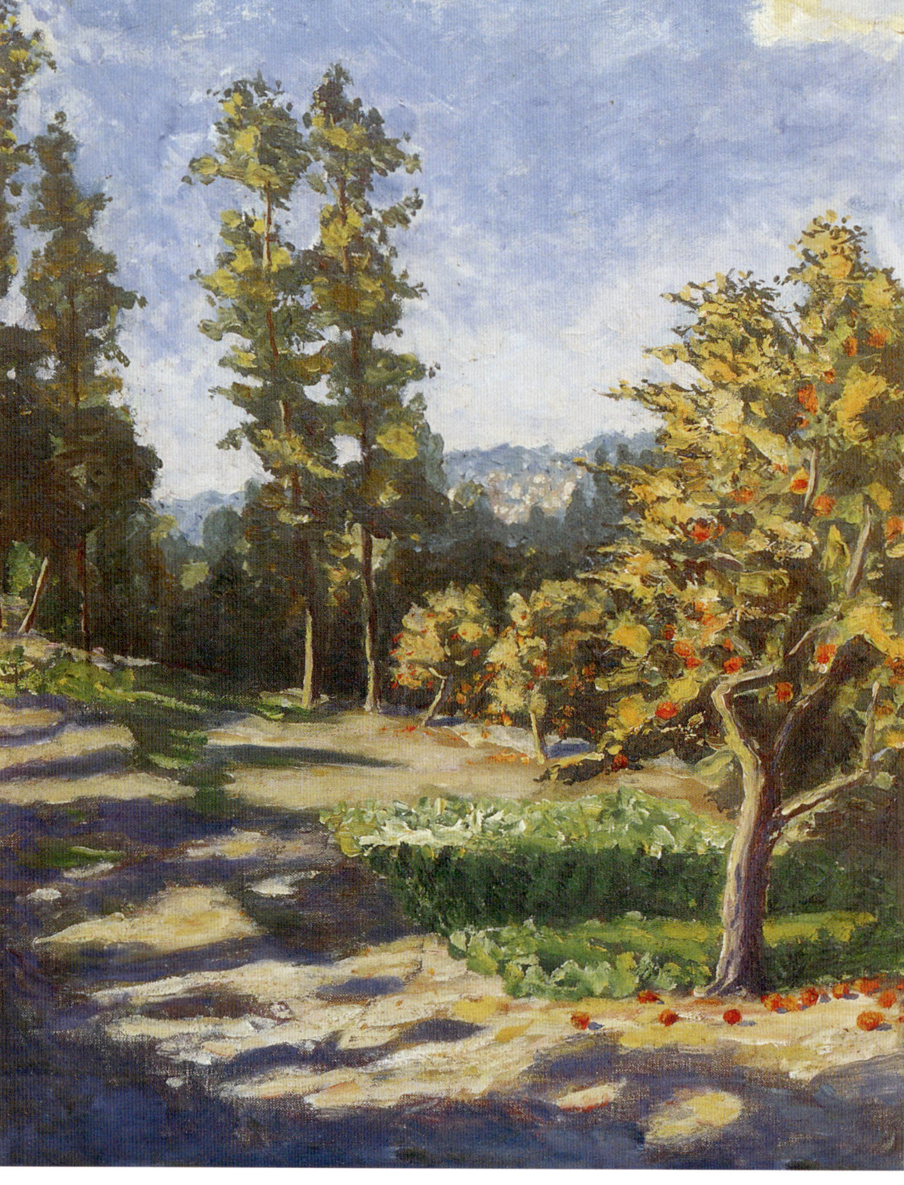

Fig 504 (C 511) right
Landscape with two trees. Given by Churchill to Maud Elgie who between 1919 and 1921 was employed by Clementine to look after their children.

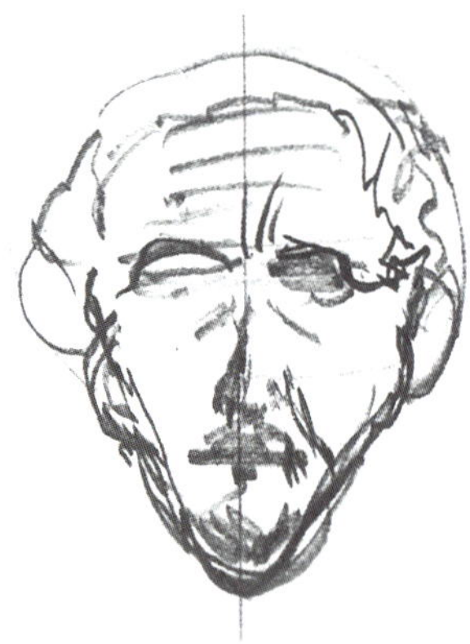

Fig 505 (C 527) above
Sketch of the sculptor Oscar Nemon done by Churchill in 1952 while sitting at Chequers for his bust commissioned by Queen Elizabeth II for Windsor Castle.

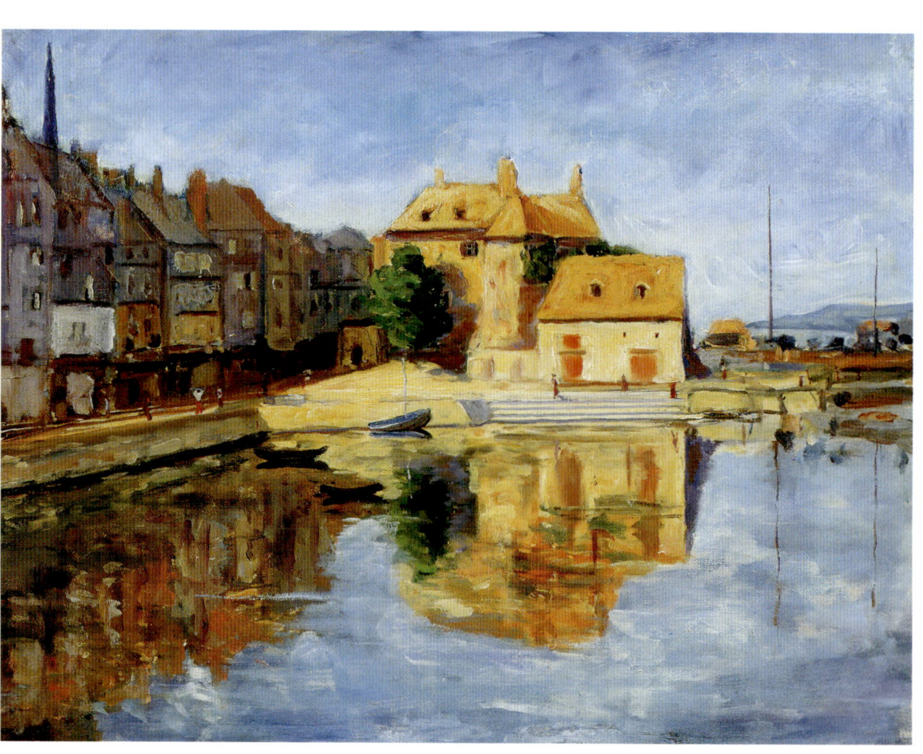

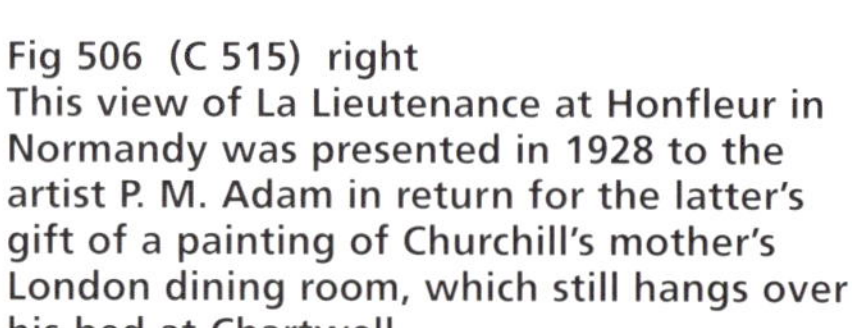

Fig 506 (C 515) right
This view of La Lieutenance at Honfleur in Normandy was presented in 1928 to the artist P. M. Adam in return for the latter's gift of a painting of Churchill's mother's London dining room, which still hangs over his bed at Chartwell.

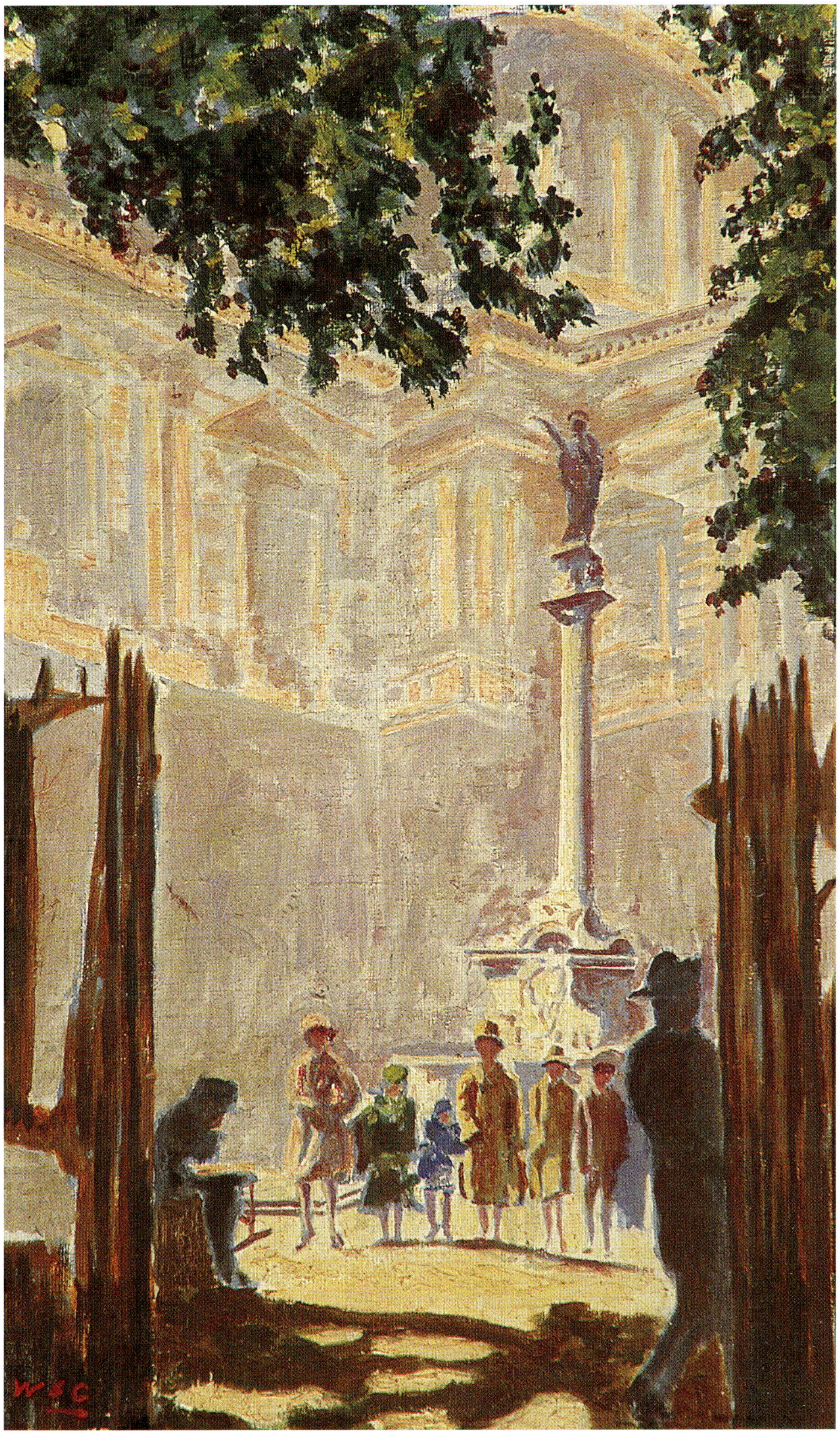

first shown it by Edward Maggs, of the booksellers Maggs Bros in London. Dated on the stretcher 1915, it has every appearance of being an early painting by Churchill but lacks any helpful provenance; and despite lengthy research commissioned by Mr Maggs, a definite connection has yet to be discovered. Nonethess, its American owners, Eric and Rosalyn Anderson, are certain that it is a genuine Churchill and their conviction must be honoured until their painting's authenticity has been confirmed. It is certainly possible that the artist left the painting behind him, expecting, perhaps, to finish it on another visit; or he may simply have forgotten it, as was the case with two of his paintings of Hoe Farm, done in 1915.

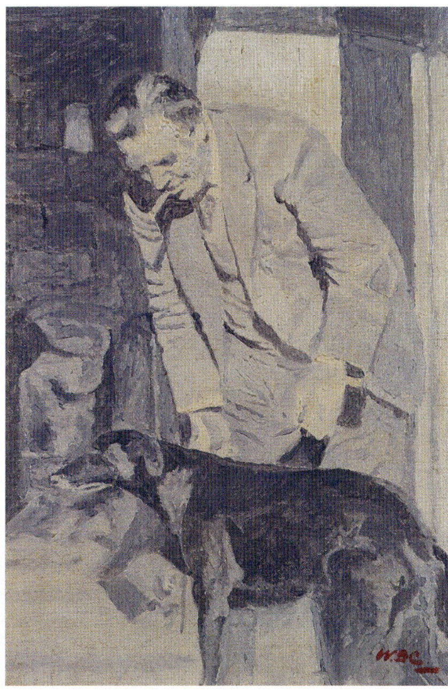

Fig 507 (C 508) above
Bendor, Duke of Westminster with his lurcher Sam. Doubtless painted from a photograph while Churchill was under the influence of the artist Walter Sickert from about 1927.

Fig 508 (C 512) left
St Paul's Churchyard. In 1927 Queen Mary persuaded Churchill to donate this painting to a charity auction held at Balmoral Castle in Scotland where it was sold for 115 guineas (£120.75)

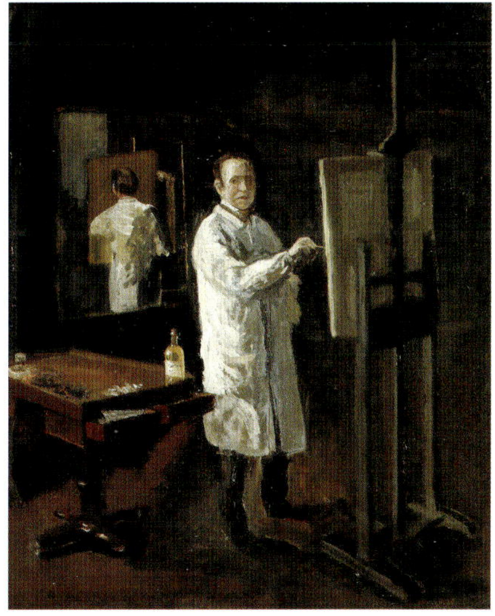

Fig 509 (C 507) above
Sir John Lavery in his Studio, painted in 1915. Churchill gave this portrait to Sir John who showed it in the Royal Society of Portrait Painters exhibition in 1919. This was the first known public exhibition of one of Churchill's works.

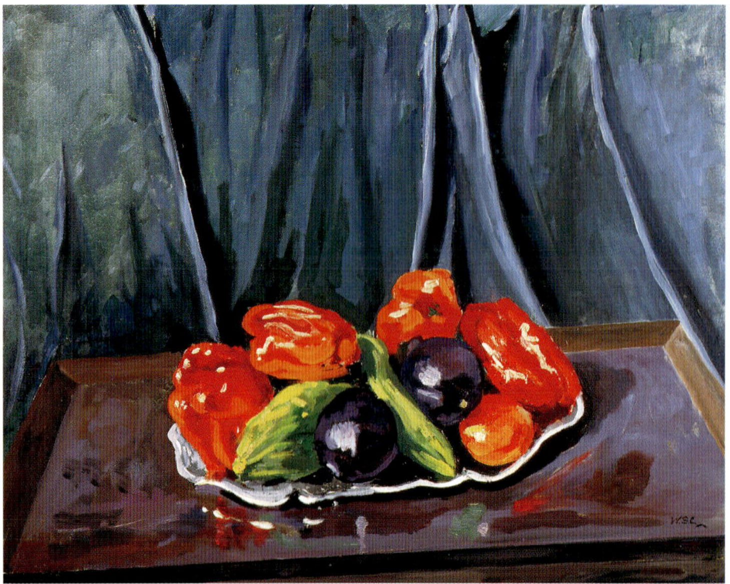

Fig 510 (C 510) above
Churchill gave this painting of Aubergines and Red Peppers on a Silver Tray to Alfred Kern in gratitude for the loan of his house at Choisy in Switzerland in 1946.

Churchill was always interested in the techniques of the masters and copied a number of paintings, as was the custom of many artists in the past schooled in this practical way of learning. But I owe a hitherto unknown example to another visitor to Chartwell, Eunice Cousins from Perth in Western Australia. She pointed out to Jan Carter, a Studio guide, that Churchill's painting, innocently entitled in 1965 'Near Marseilles' (C 333), seems in fact to be a direct copy of a Monet, 'L'Ailly Point, Low Tide, 1882', in the collection of Mr Kerry Stokes, also of Perth. Churchill's painting has always been especially intriguing because of the unusual way in which the figures in the water on the edge of the sea are painted. Mr Stokes's curator, John Stringer, kindly sent me the details of the Monet's provenance, which contains no clue whatsoever as to when or where Churchill might possibly have seen it, let alone copied it. That mystery has yet to be resolved.

Dating Churchill's paintings has always been a problem. While the dates of his visits are often known, he did not necessarily finish the picture at the time and/or might paint another version later using a photographic reference. In the case of one view of Marrakech, however (C 452), the picture can be dated to January 1959, because Mr John Whitmore, a volunteer at Chartwell, when on his honeymoon saw Churchill working on the picture, guarded by a Moroccan policeman.

In his essentially humble attitude to his painting, Churchill acknowledged three important teachers: Sir John Lavery, Walter Sickert and Sir William Nicholson. Two other artists painted with him often and were important companions of the brush: at first, Charles Montag and latterly, Paul Maze. Both were quick with encouragement and technical help, nor was Churchill ever slow to seek advice from the many professional artists he met during his lifetime.

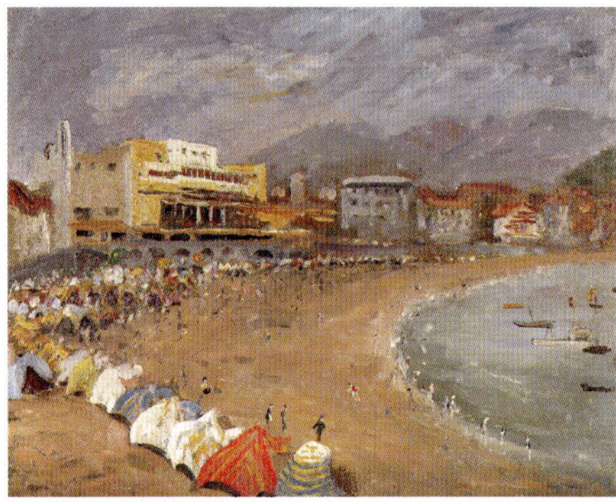

Fig 511 (C 514) above
The style of this painting of a beach on the Riviera is unusual for Churchill. He gave it to Victor Montagu on the occasion of his marriage in 1934.

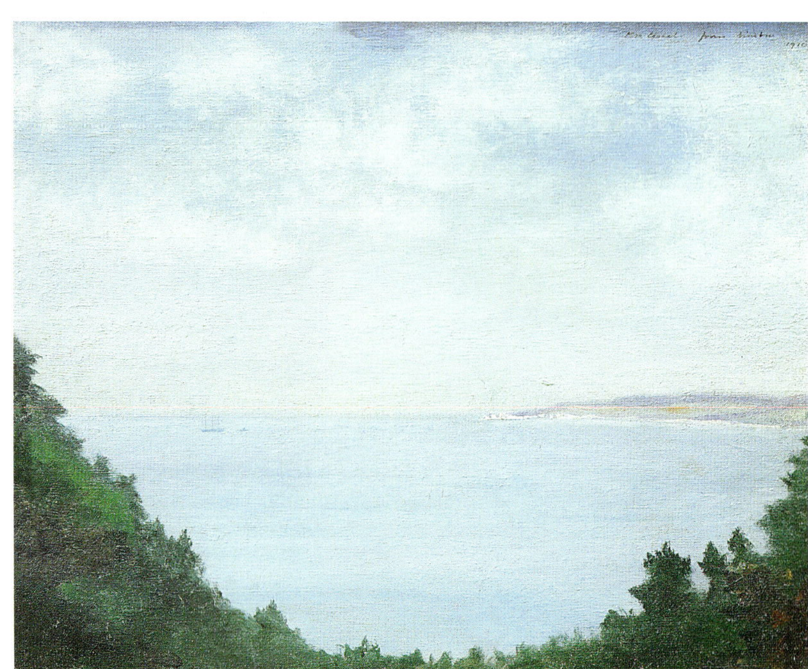

Fig 512 (C 525) right
This is a view at Branksome Dean, the home near Bournemouth on England's south coast of the financier Sir Ernest Cassel. Uniquely it is signed and inscribed: 'Mrs Cassels from Winston 1916'.

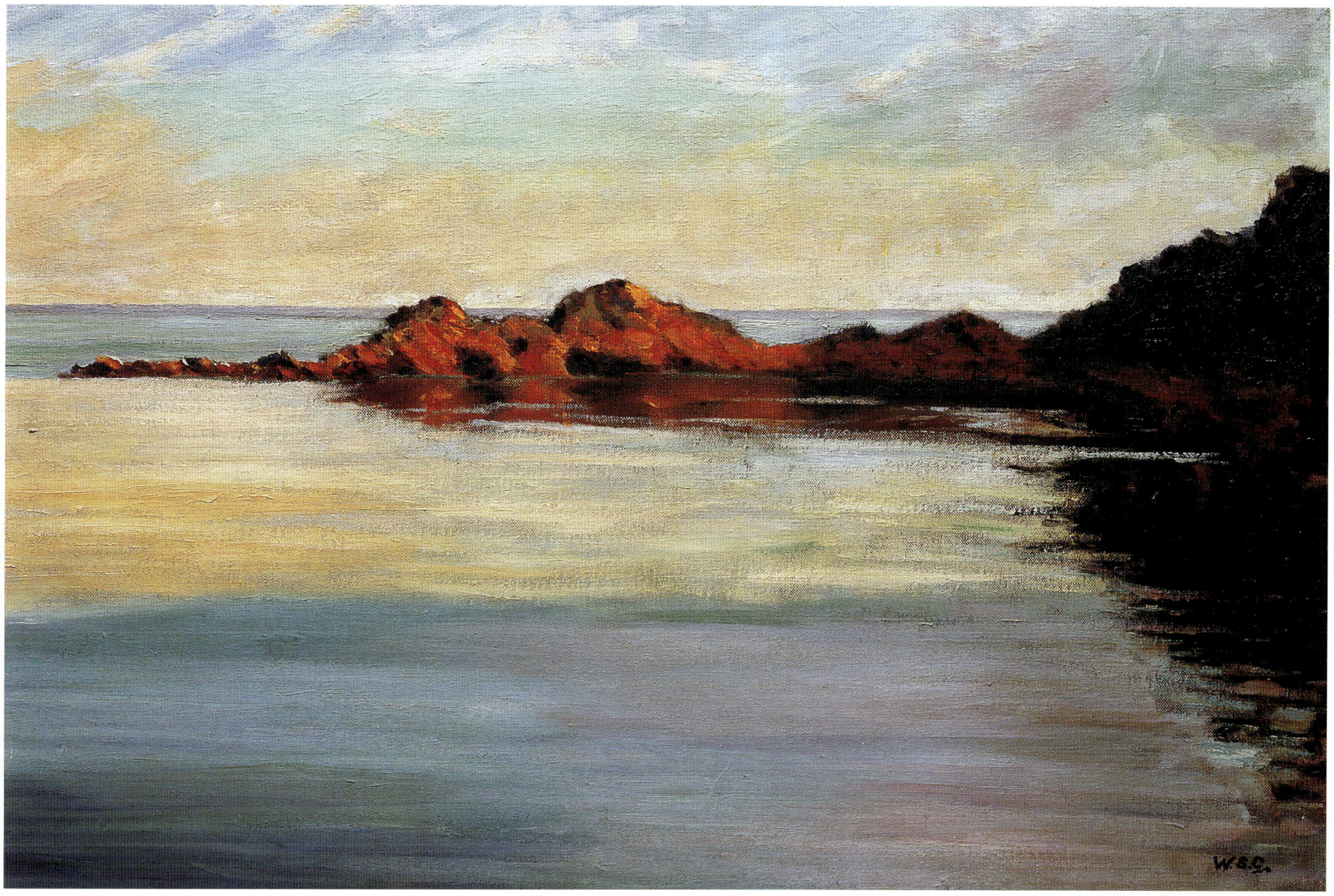

Fig 513 (C 513) above
Churchill gave this view of an inlet somewhere in the South of France in 1945 to R. J. Marnham, owner of Chartwell Farm.

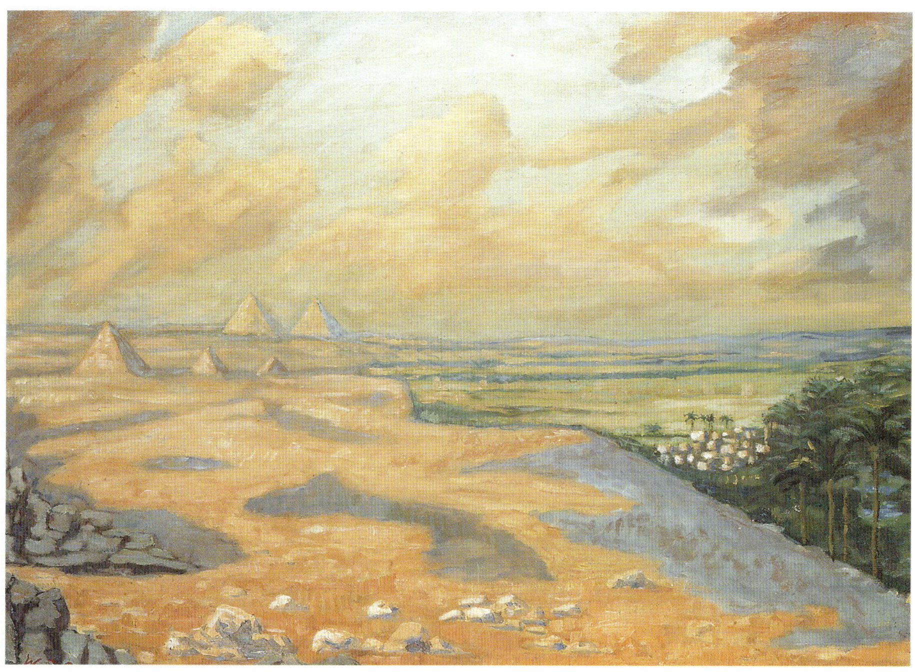

Fig 514 (C 504) left
After the Second World War, Churchill gave two paintings of the Pyramids near Cairo to Field Marshal Jan Smuts. This view of the Giza Pyramids remained with his family in South Africa; the other was stolen and has not been traced so far.

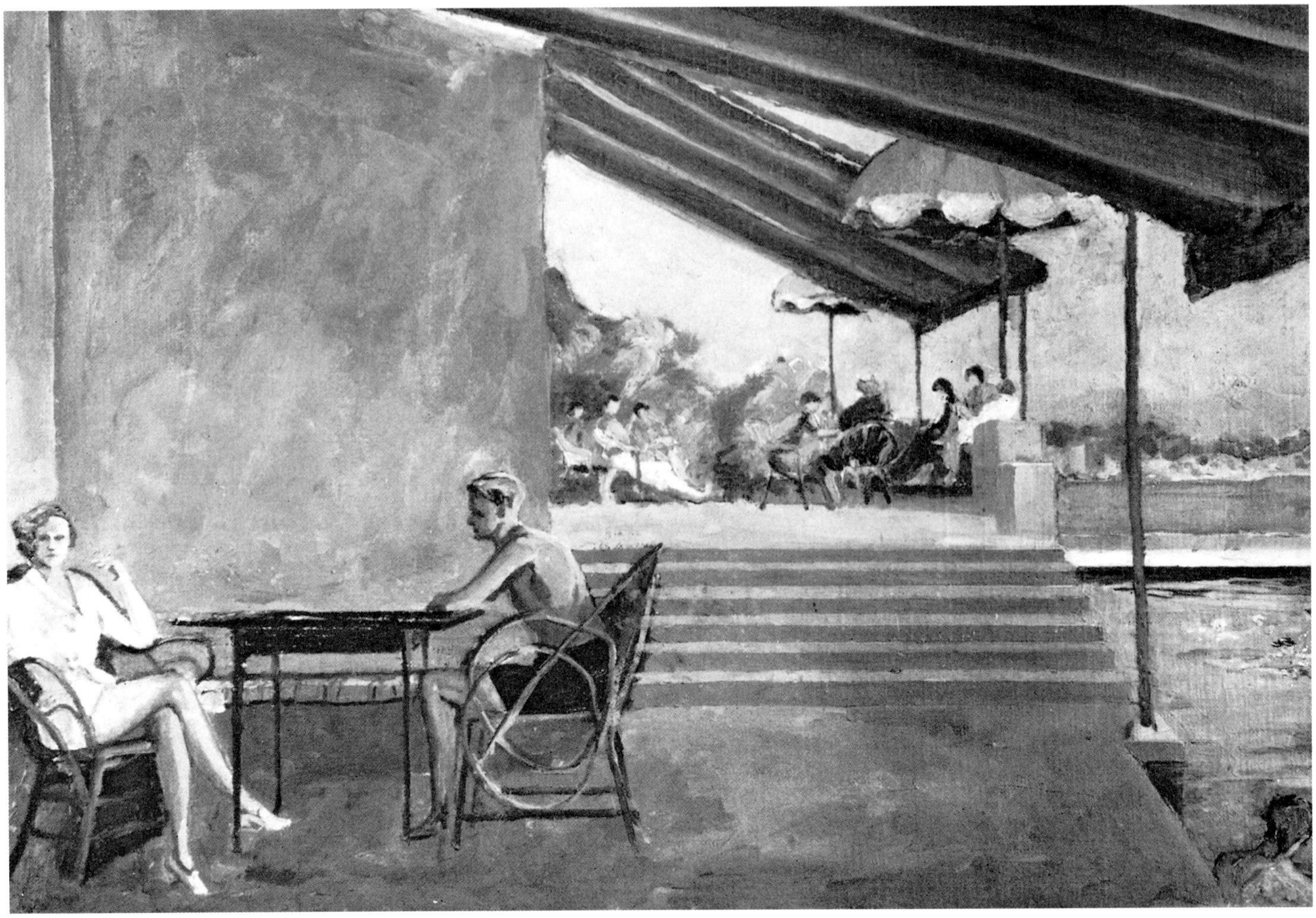

Fig 515 (C 518) above
Lady Castlerosse at Maxine Elliott's Chateau de l'Horizon with a young man thought to be her brother Dudley Delevigne. Churchill gave this little painting which is based on a photograph in the Studio archives at Chartwell, to Baron de Caters who had a house in France near Maxine's. This picture is missing. The illustration was discovered in the archives of the Witt Library at the Courtauld Institute of Art, London.

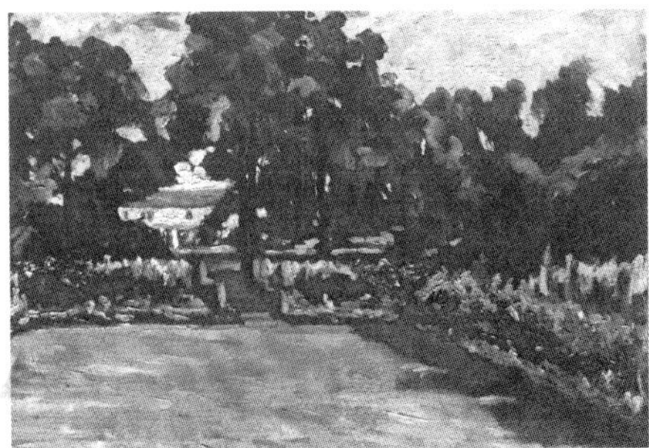

Fig 516 (C 531) above
Churchill gave this painting of the flower borders at the Chateau de l'Horizon to Maxine Elliott. This picture is missing. The illustration was discovered in the archives of the Witt Library at the Courtauld Institute of Art, London.

However, there is a small group of especially attractive early pictures by Churchill, most of them on panel, which are unusually loosely painted and which in their subjects emphasize, almost to the exclusion of everything else, sea and sky (see for example, pages 30, 31 and 35). These have always interested me not only for their bravura but because they were never repeated; this suggested that they might have been made as a consequence of Churchill's association with an artist who specialized in such subjects.

Then, out of the blue I received via Mary Soames a letter from Austin Wormleighton enquiring about the connection between Churchill and the sea painter Julius Olsson (1864-1942), whose biography he was writing. Mr Wormleighton stated that, according to family tradition, 'Olsson was one of several painters who gave lessons to your father and accompanied him to the South of France and to Cornwall on painting excursions'. Austin Wormleighton suggested that Olsson may have known Churchill from the time of the First World War, when the former worked on the camouflage of merchant ships by dazzle painting.

The existence of letters between Churchill and Olsson held by relatives of his widow Edith in Ireland was separately confirmed to me later by another relation, Jean R. Cooper, but so far these have not been found. Nor do the archives of the Royal Academy, of which Julius Olsson was a member, throw any further light on their possible relationship despite a thorough search there by Mrs Beatrice Pahlabod, although the illustrations of his paintings confirm the range of his sea pictures.

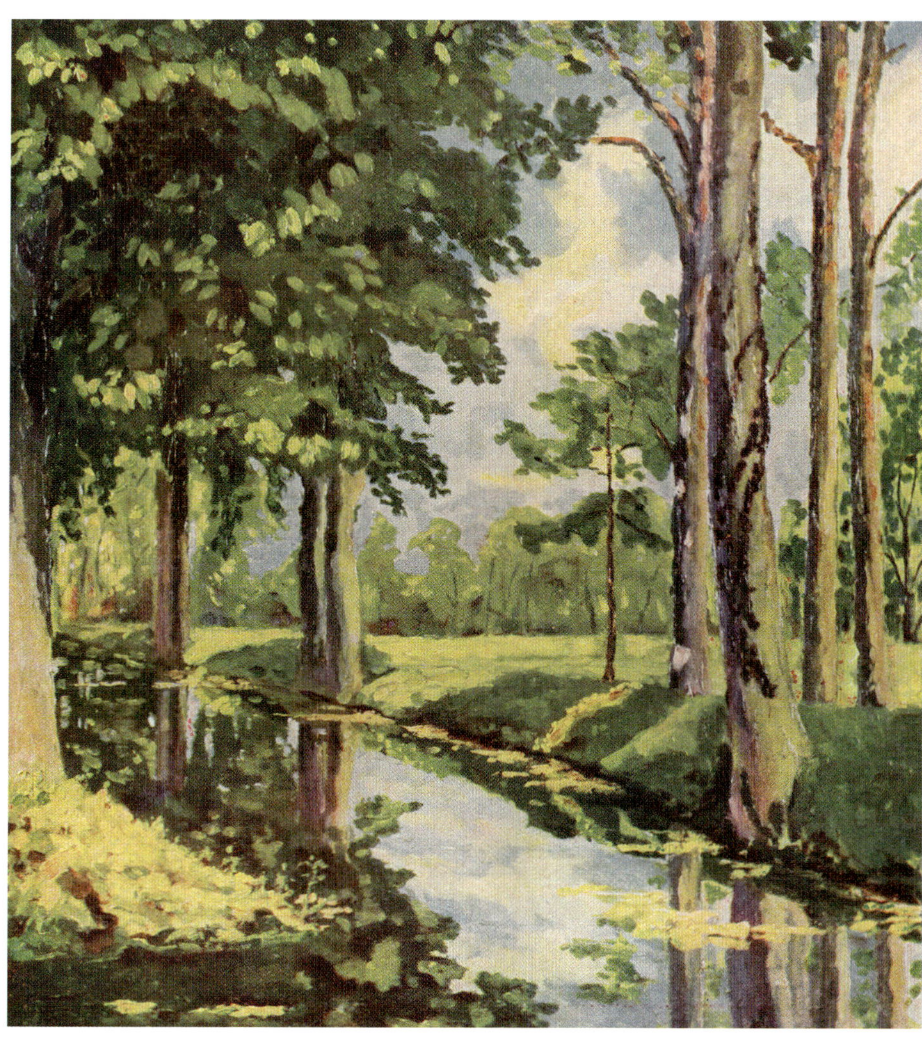

Fig 517 (C 537) left
The Moat, Breccles. This picture is missing. It was illustrated with Churchill's article 'Painting as a Pastime' in The Strand Magazine, December 1921.

Fig 518 (C 517) below
The rocks below the Chateau de l'Horizon with LadyCastlerosse and the Artist. Churchill gave this painting to Maxine Elliott. This picture is missing. The illustration was discovered in the archives of the Witt Library at the Courtauld Institute of Art, London. The releated photograph below if from the studio archives at chartwell.

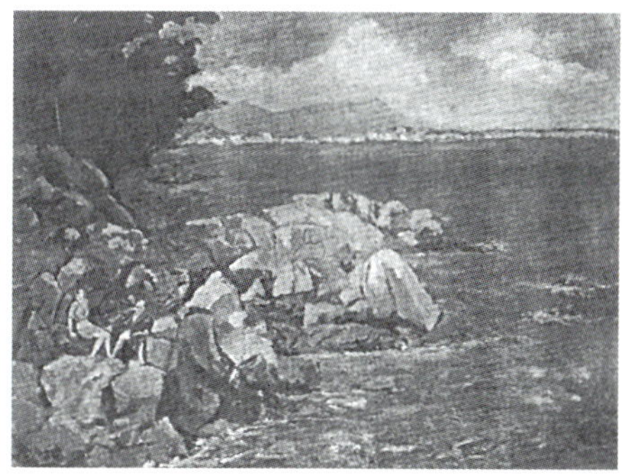

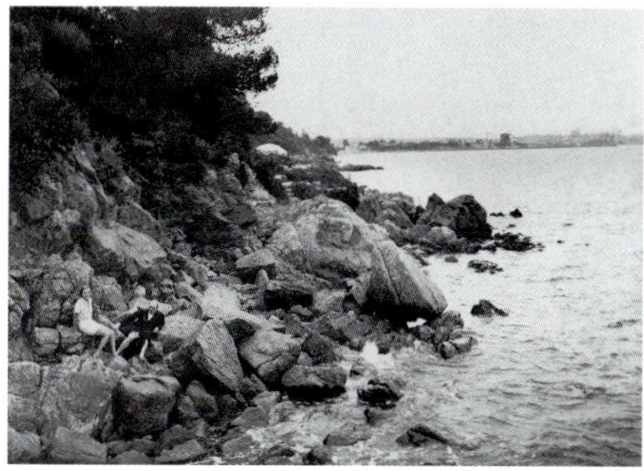

Above
Winston Churchill and Doris Castlerosse at the Chateau de l'Horizon. Photograph from the Studio Archives at Chartwell.

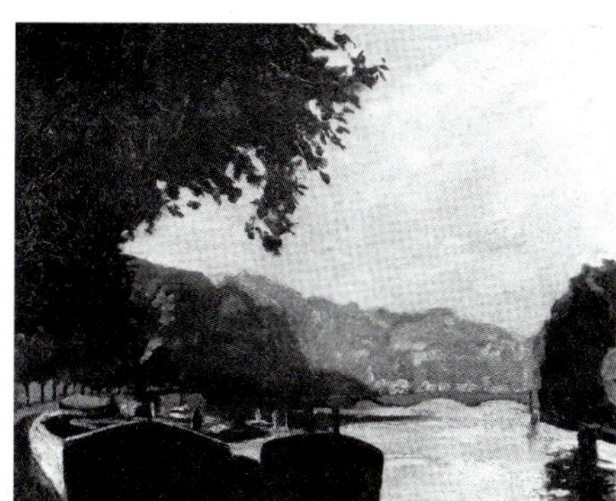

Fig 519 (C 532) above
Barges on the Seine in France. This picture is missing. The illustration was discovered in the archives of the Witt Library at the Courtauld Institute of Art, London.

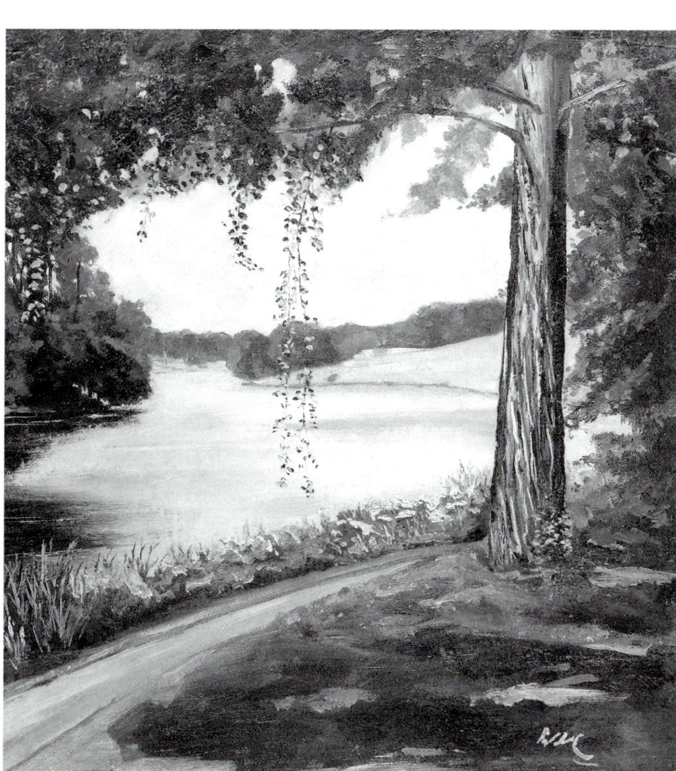

Fig 520 (C 528) left
Churchill gave this painting of the Lake at Trent Park to his butler Mr W. Greenshields. This picture is missing. The illustration was discovered in the archives of the Witt Library at the Courtauld Institute of Art.

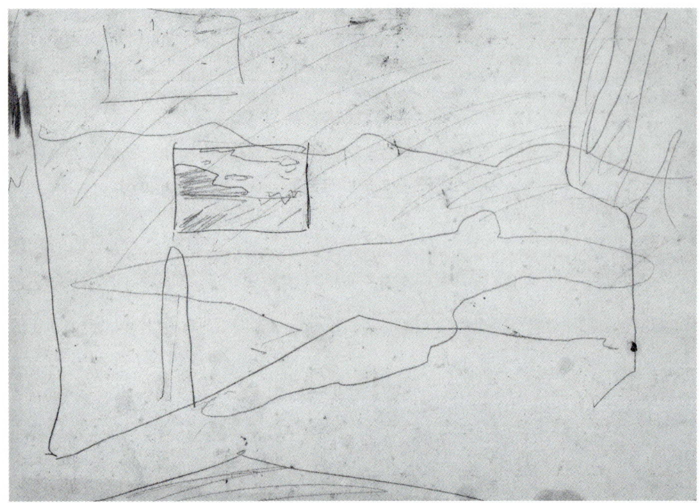

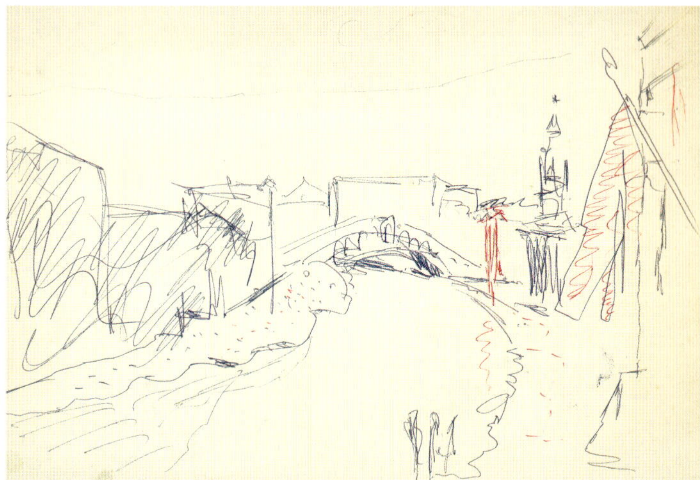

Fig 521 (C 529) above right
Sketch of the Grand Canal in Venice done by Churchill in 1951. This sketch and the squared-up photograph also illustrated right were found in the Studio archives at Chartwell. Both formed the basis of his painting on page 227, Fig 479 (C 476).

Fig 522 (C 534) above left
This series of rough sketches are on the back of a photograph (which relates to C 300) found in the Studio archives at Chartwell.

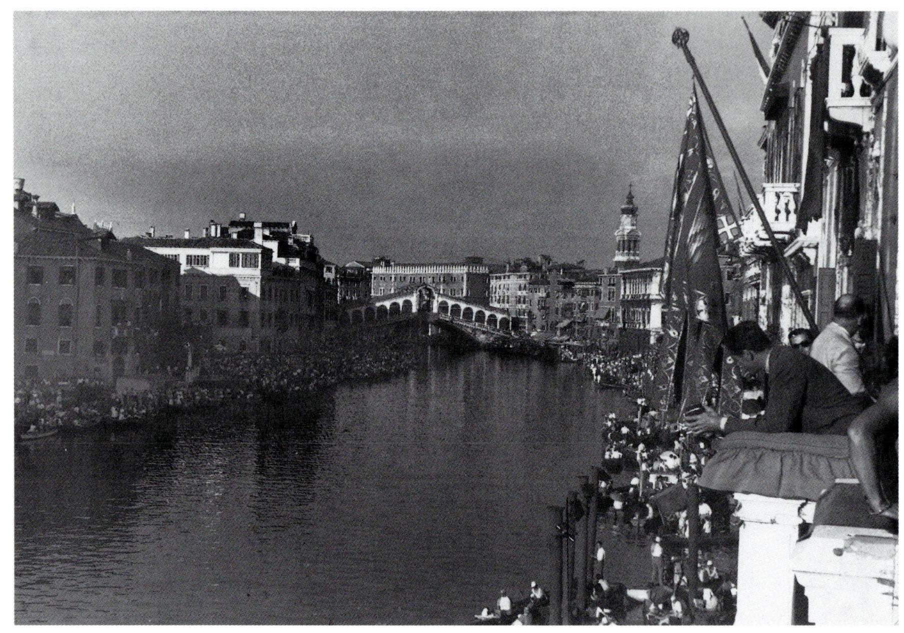

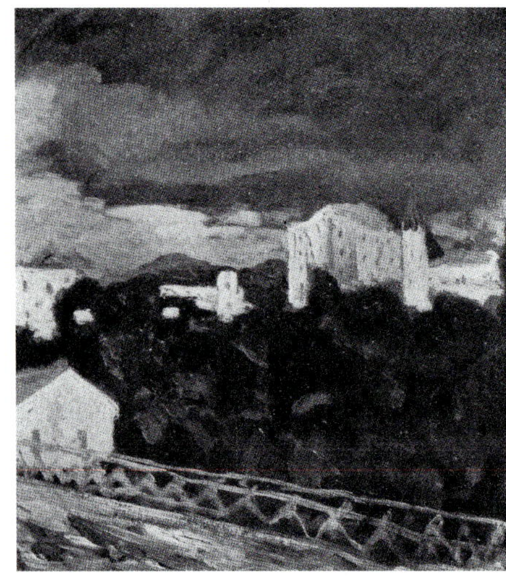

Fig 523 (C 519) above
Thunderstorm, Nice. This picture is missing. It was illustrated with Churchill's article 'Painting as a Pastime' in The Strand Magazine, January 1922.

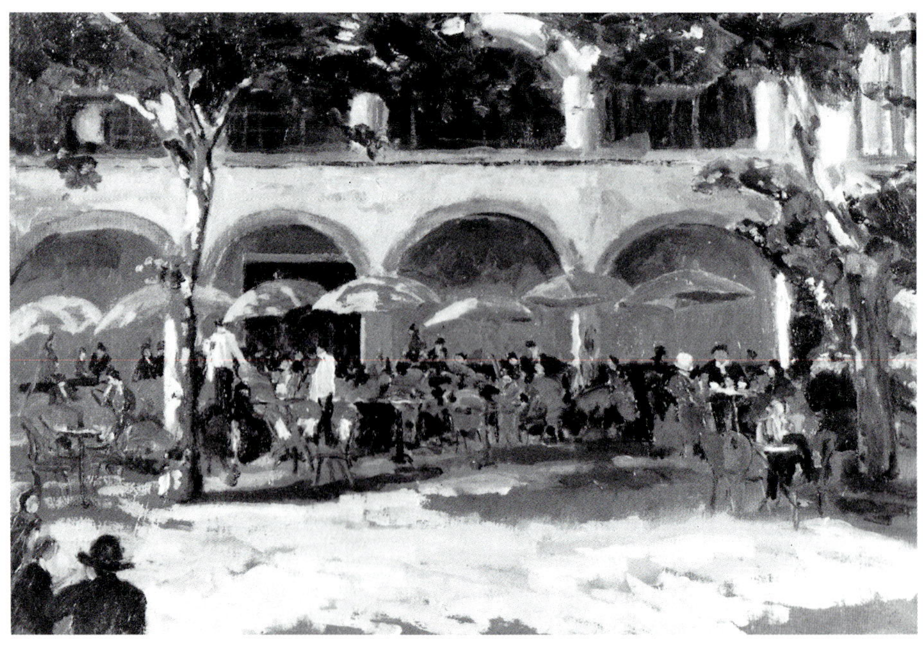

Thanks to the courtesy of the art dealer David Messum, I was able to examine a number of Olsson's paintings and there would seem to be little doubt, on the face of it, that Churchill's own pictures in a complementary style look to have been influenced by Olsson's work.

Fig 524 (C 521) below
The Valley of the Brora, Sutherlandshire. This picture is missing. It was illustrated with Churchill's article 'Painting as a Pastime' in The Strand Magazine, January 1922.

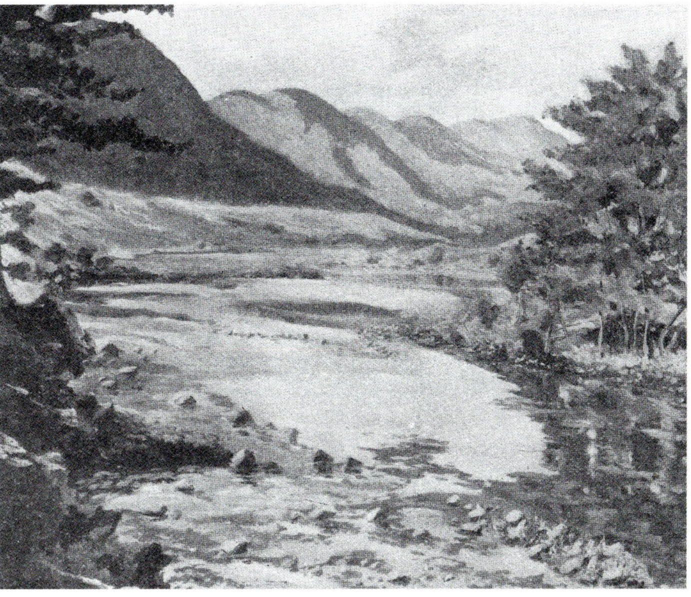

There may, however, be a clue in the original 1921/2 *Strand Magazine* version of 'Painting as a Pastime', where Churchill illustrated one of his distinctive sea pictures. The published title, 'Daybreak at Cassis, near Marseilles, September 1920', suggests a possible connection. A story related by Churchill begins: 'Chance led me one autumn to a secluded nook on the Côte d'Azur, between Marseilles and Toulon, and there I fell in with one or two painters who revelled in the methods of the modern French school. These were disciples of Cézanne.'

For the moment that is as far as it goes, for there is no evidence yet that Churchill and Olsson knew each other or, if so, when.

In his early painting days, Churchill was famously reluctant to give away his paintings. 'They are too bad to sell and too dear to me to give,' he told his aunt Leonie Leslie on one occasion. This quite reasonable attitude nonetheless created a kind of legend that it is now possible to dispel, for, as the new catalogue entries reveal, Churchill gave away more than a few in his later years, although he was never easily persuaded, unless by a fair female face, as his old friend Sir Robert Menzies related and Sir Laurence Olivier separately confirmed.

Fig 525 (C 520) below left
On the Rance, near St Malo. This picture is missing. It was illustrated with Churchill's article 'Painting as a Pastime' in The Strand Magazine, January 1922.

Fig 526 (C 522) below
Scene near the head of Lake Como. This picture is missing. It was illustrated with 'Winston Churchill's Pictures' Strand Magazine, August 1946.

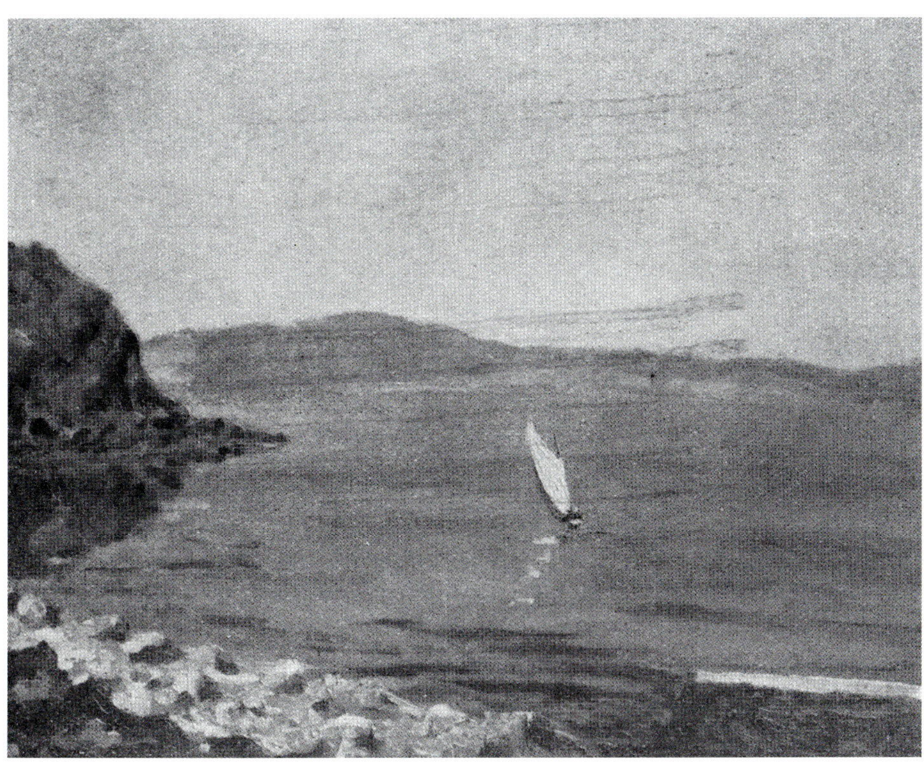

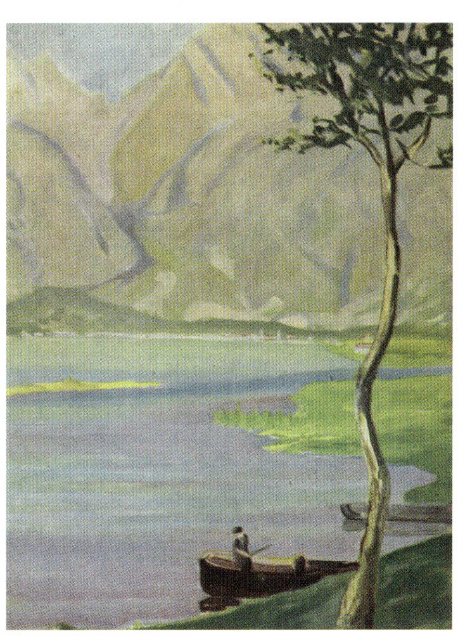

Fig 527 (C 530) opposite page bottom
Cafe at St Jean de Luz, which is on the Atlantic coast of France south of Biarritz. Churchill gave this painting to E. Merrick Tyler, his adviser at Lloyds. This picture is missing. The illustration was discovered in the archives of the Witt Library at the Courtauld Institute of Art, London.

Fig 528 (C 523) right
The Calanque, Cassis. This picture is missing. It was illustrated in 'Winston Churchill, An Eightieth Birthday Tribute' The Illustrated London News, 1954.

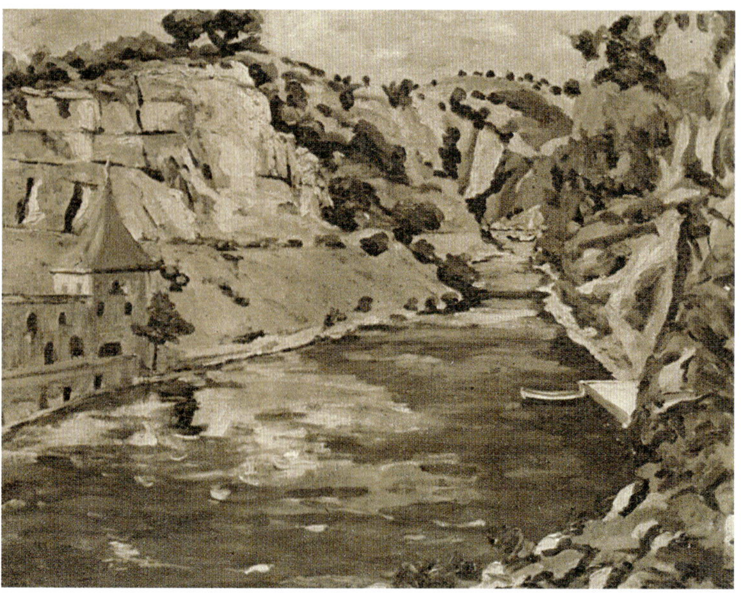

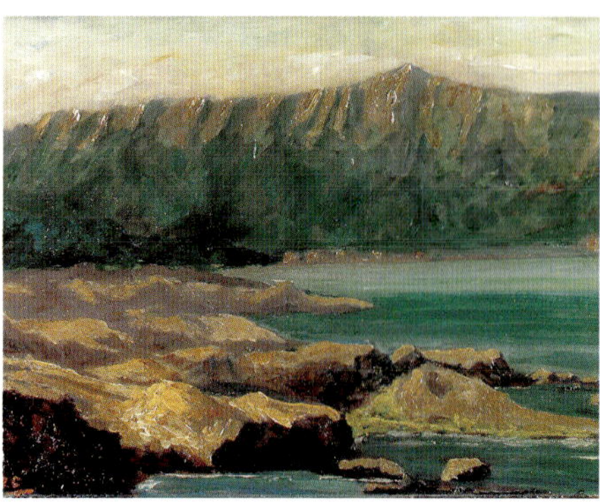

Fig 529 (C 509) above
Lake Carezza in the Dolomites. This painting cannot be authenticated yet as its early provenance is unknown.

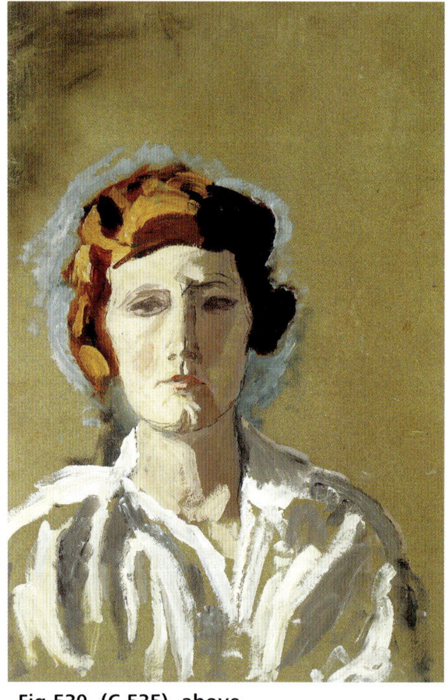

Fig 530 (C 535) above
Sketch portrait of an unknown lady. Churchill painted this on the back of C 111.

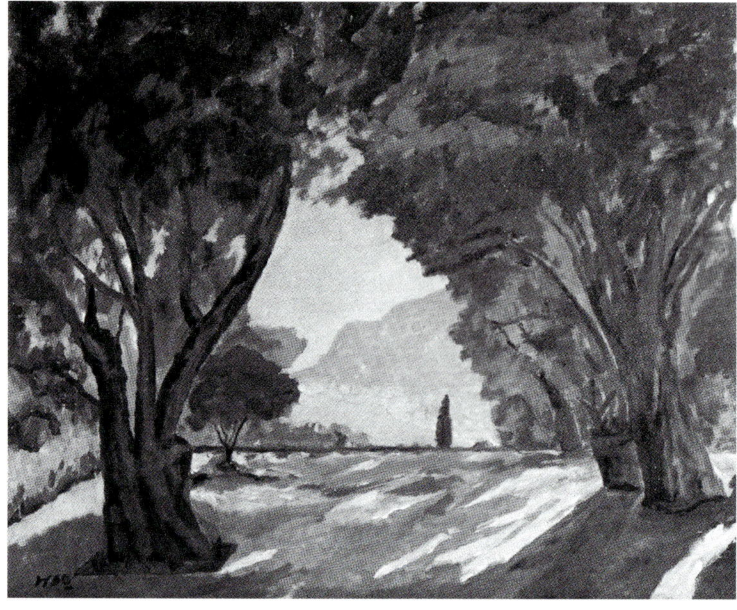

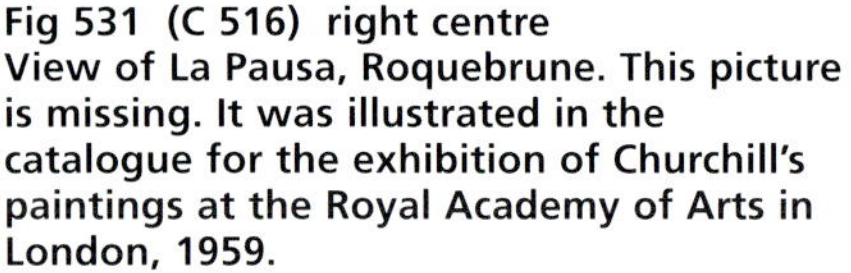

Fig 531 (C 516) right centre
View of La Pausa, Roquebrune. This picture is missing. It was illustrated in the catalogue for the exhibition of Churchill's paintings at the Royal Academy of Arts in London, 1959.

Fig 532 (C 533) right
The gardens at Port Lympne in Kent. This little painting cannot be authenticated yet as its early provenance is unknown.

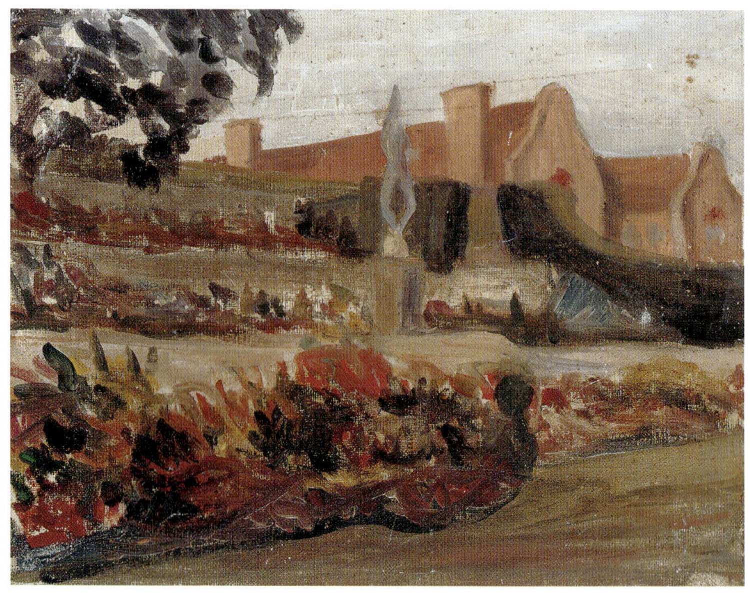

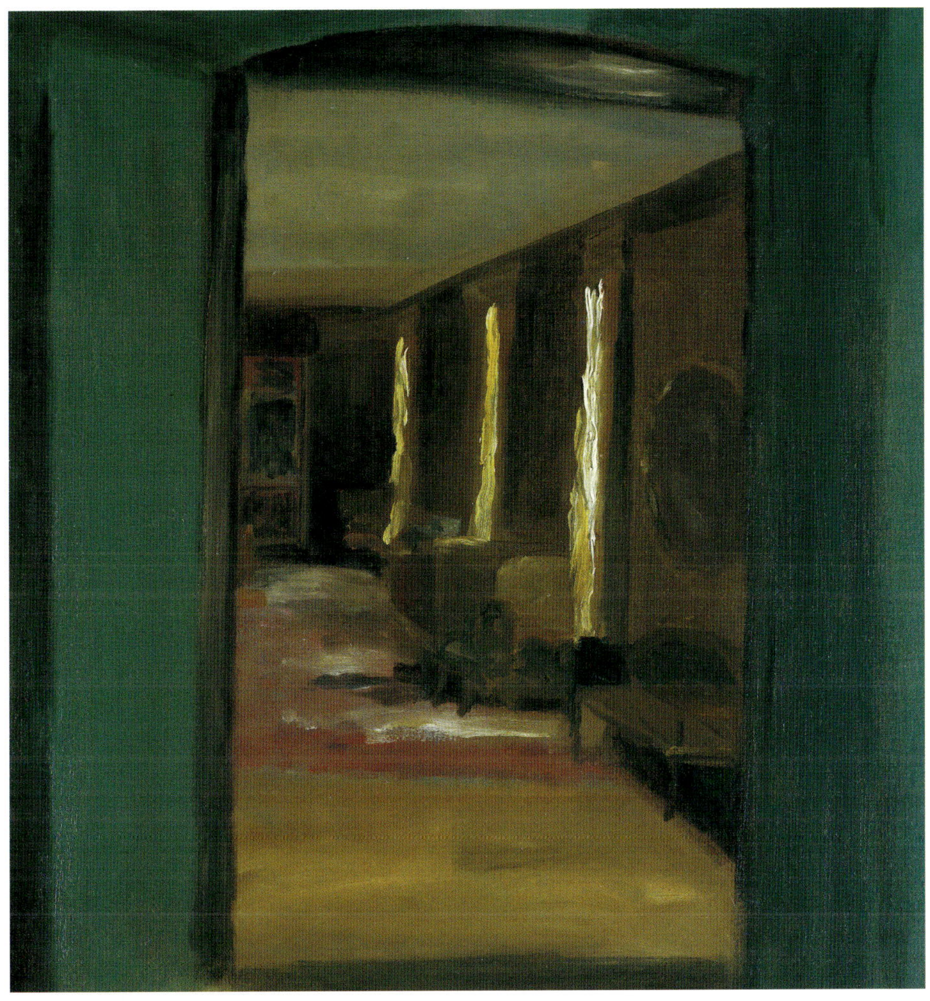

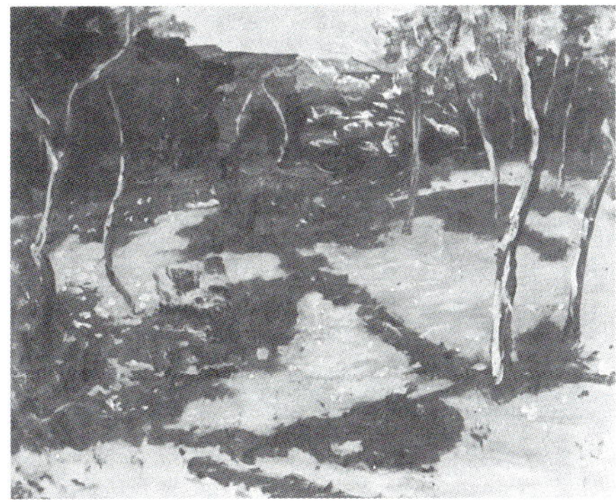

Fig 533 (C 524) above
On Cap Martin. This picture is missing. It was illustrated in the catalogue for the exhibition of Churchill's paintings at the Royal Academy of Arts in London, 1959.

Fig 534 (C 526) left
The Gallery at Esher Place. This painting is inscribed and dated '24 October 1915' on the back. It has every appearance of being by Churchill but cannot be authenticated yet until its early provenance has been established.

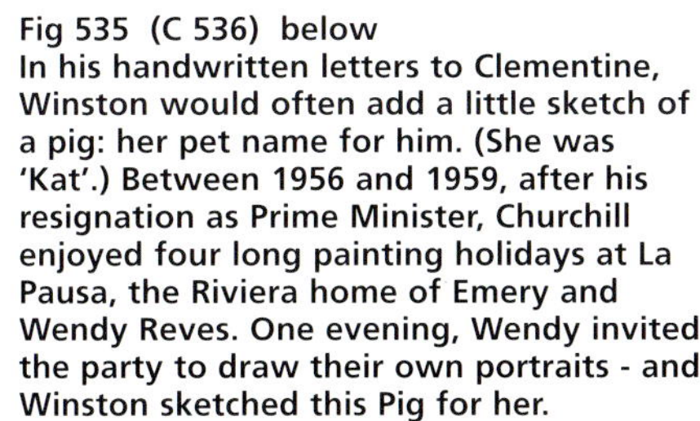

Fig 535 (C 536) below
In his handwritten letters to Clementine, Winston would often add a little sketch of a pig: her pet name for him. (She was 'Kat'.) Between 1956 and 1959, after his resignation as Prime Minister, Churchill enjoyed four long painting holidays at La Pausa, the Riviera home of Emery and Wendy Reves. One evening, Wendy invited the party to draw their own portraits - and Winston sketched this Pig for her.

Several anecdotes suggest other smaller mysteries in so far as they record Churchill painting at locations for which there is no known example extant. For example, his friend Jean Hamilton records him painting the Orangery at Panshanger in England; and his secretary Phyllis Moir recalls him painting at Bernard Baruch's ranch in South Carolina. These pictures are as likely to have been discarded or destroyed as they are to have been left behind and forgotten. Should any possible candidates be discovered, then they will have to satisfy the strict criteria, especially that of provenance, set out at the beginning of this chapter.

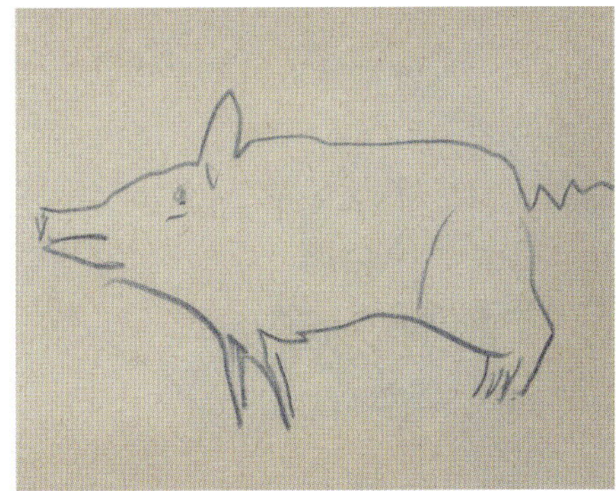

acknowledgements

MINNIE CHURCHILL would like to thank Her Majesty The Queen for her permission to reproduce the picture by Sir Winston Churchill of The Palladian Bridge at Wilton, which is in Her Majesty's collection, and HRH The Prince of Wales for his great kindness in allowing us to reproduce his picture Summer house at Trent Park.

My thanks also to The Rt Hon. Sir Edward Heath for allowing us to include his two paintings, also the Palace of Westminster and the Queens Royal Hussars. I would like to thank all the owners of the more than five hundred paintings for allowing us to include their paintings in this catalogue.

In particular, I am immensely grateful to Mary Soames for everything that she has done to help me trace so many of the owners who were either friends of her father or the children of the friends. Also to all of Sir Winston's family who own many of these paintings and allowed us to include them in this book. Many thanks to Winston S. Churchill for allowing us to reproduce photographs from Sir Winston's albums in the Broadwater Collection. I am greatly indebted to the late Peregrine Churchill for his foresight in creating Churchill Heritage.

I would particularly like to thank Carole Kenwright and the National Trust for allowing us to photograph the paintings at Chartwell. Wylma Wayne gave me enormous help and I am very grateful to her. I would like to thank the Duke of Marlborough for allowing us to include the paintings at Blenheim Palace, the Royal Academy of Arts, the Trustees of the Tate Gallery and the Winston Churchill Memorial Trust.

Thank you also to Andrew Jameson for photographing so many of the paintings both at Chartwell and in private collections, and to John Marsh, who with Tony Malone so brilliantly designed this book.

I would like to thank Allen Packwood Director of Churchill Archives Centre and his team for all their help in researching the Broadwater Collection of photographs. My thanks also go to Elizabeth Lane and Jonathan Horwich at Christie's and Hugo Swire M.P. and Susannah Pollen at Sotheby's, the Robert Harding Picture Library, the Victoria and Albert Museum Picture Library and Barbara Thompson at the Witt Library. The Eisenhower Library, The Dallas Museum of Art, The Beaverbrook Museum of Art, Westminster College, Fulton and Richard Langworth at the International Churchill Society who have all helped me greatly in my research.

It has been such fun working with David Coombs, and if we did not have his original catalogue Churchill His Paintings, designed and produced by George Rainbird and published by Hamish Hamilton in 1967, it would have been an impossible task to produce this catalogue as we would not have known about so many of these paintings.

I would particularly like to thank Hubert Schaafsma and Pegasus Publishing for commissioning this book and Anthea Morton-Saner of Curtis Brown for all her help and encouragement.

I would specially like to thank Simon Drury Bird for all his help in tracking down the paintings, nothing has been too much trouble and his resourcefulness has helped to find so many of the missing paintings.

DAVID COOMBS is very grateful first for all the information about Sir Winston Churchill's paintings either sent personally, or more often courteously forwarded by Minnie S. Churchill and Mary Soames; as well as for much other help, advice and support during the many years' making of what has proved to be a very complicated book.
In particular I must mention:

Vi Aitken; Mark Adams; Eric and Rosayn Austen Anderson; Heather Anderson; Lord Astor of Hever; Joa da Cruz Vicente de Azevedo; Sir Jack Baer; Lord Beaverbrook; Elizabeth M. Blagbrough; Sir Henry Beverley; Angela Bolger; Alan Bott; I. R. S. Bond; Paula Bongers; Robert Boutwood; Thelma Briggs; Rachel Brodie; John Brunsden; Alex Buck; Jan Carter; John Chesshyre; Nonie Chapman; Yvonne and the late Peregrine S. Churchill; Jeanne Lil Chvosta; Lord Cobbold; Faith Collins; Lady Margaret Colville; Eva Comacho; Nick and Nicole Coombs; Jean R. Cooper; Diane Courtney; Eunice Cousins; Jack Darrah; Sarah Davis; John Delavigne; Michael J. Devine; Michael Donaldson; Annabel Elliott; Nozomi Endo; Geoffrey Glassborow; Richard and Eileen Godfrey; Roger Golding; Roddy Gow; The late Grace Hamblin; Alison Hanks; Philip Harley; Deborah Hatch; David Hatter; Jane Heimlich; William J. vanden Heuvel; Dan Holt; Chloe Johnson; Breff and Jill Kelly; Carole Kenwright; Elizabeth King; Sir John Kingham; Gilly Kinloch; Alastair Laing; Richard Langworth; Victoria Law; Carolyn Leder; Celia Lee; Maxine Long; Janet McLean; Edward Maggs; Capt. Simon Maggs; Ian F. Y. Marrian; Sue Medway; Dennis Medina; Rodney Melville; David Messum; Sir Anthony Montague Browne; Misty Ellen Montier; Viscount Montgomery; Dr Jerry D. Morelock; Joan Murray; Tony and Vicky Norman; Allen Packwood; Beatrice Pahlabod; Camilla Parker-Bowles; Yvette and the late Simone Perie; Carole Perrin; Francis and Janet Quinlan; Brian Raine; Hill Carter Riddle Jr.; Melissa Rountree; John Stringer; Arthur Ochs Sulzberger; Hugo Swire; Fr. Theodore Taylor OP; Alan Taylor Smith; Viscount Thurso; Robyn Tromeur; Katherine Tunnicliffe; Susannah van Langenberg; Lucienne and the late Bart Watt; Neil Walters; Wylma Wayne; Mark Weber; A. R. Whitfield; Robin Harcourt Williams; Austin Wormleighton; David Yaxley; Karen Yiannakou; and Lara.

My thanks also for the cooperation and help of: the Churchill Archives at Churchill College; the Archives at Godalming Museum; the Tate Archives; the British Library; the Library of Congress; the National Magazine Company Library; the National Trust at Chartwell; and the London Library.

This book would never have been made without: Hubert Schaafsma; John Marsh; Tony Malone; and Ingrid Cranfield.

The photographs from the Studio archives at Chartwell are reproduced by kind permission of the National Trust.

Other photographs from the Broadwater Collection at the Churchill Archives, Churchill College, Cambridge, are reproduced by kind permission of Winston S. Churchill.

Every possible effort has been made to trace those who own paintings by, or photographs of Sir Winston Churchill. The publishers will welcome corrections or further information that can be added to any future editions.

bibliography

The outline background of my chronological chapters are based on the Encyclopaedia of Dates and Events, edited by L. C. Pascoe. Hodder and Stoughton, London 1974.

The details of Churchill's life and his painting are substantially derived from the published works of Mary Soames and Martin Gilbert. In particular: by Martin Gilbert, Churchill: A Life (Minerva, 1991) and the six volume biography of Winston Churchill by Randolph S. Churchill and Martin Gilbert (Heinemann, 1966 - 1988). And by Mary Soames, Winston Churchill: His Life as a Painter (Collins 1990) and Speaking for Themselves, The Personal Letters of Winston and Clementine Churchill (Doubleday 1998).

Many quotations are from letters and other documents in the Churchill Archives, Churchill College, Cambridge. These are copyright and reproduced by kind permission.

President Eisenhower's letters to Winston Churchill are in the Dwight D. Eisenhower Library/Museum, Abilene, Kansas USA. These are copyright and reproduced by kind permission.

Sir John Rothenstein's script for the Central Office of Information film on Churchill's Paintings is held in the archives of the Tate Gallery. It is copyright and reproduced by kind permission.

Other anecdotes and quotations are taken with respectful thanks from the following published sources:

The Alexander Memoirs, by Field-Marshal Earl Alexander of Tunis. Cassell, London. 1962.

The Glitter and the Gold, by Consuelo Vanderbilt Balsan. Harper and Brothers, [?London], 1952.

Politicians and the War 1914 - 1916, by Lord Beaverbrook. Oldbourne Book Co. London 1959.

Winston Churchill As I knew Him, by Violet Bonham Carter. Eyre & Spottiswood and Collins. London 1965.

Churchill 1874 - 1922, by the Earl of Birkenhead. Harrap, London. 1989.

The Hundred Best English Essays, edited by the Earl of Birkenhead. Cassell, London. 1929

Sir Winston Churchill Master of Courage, by Princess Bibesco. Robert Hale, London. 1957.

John Sargent by Evan Charteris. Heinemann, London. 1927.

A Thread in the Tapestry, by Sarah Churchill. Andre Deutsch, London. 1967.

Churchill, By His Contemporaries. Edited by Charles Eade. Contribution by Thomas Bodkin. Random Century, London. 1953

Maxine, by Diana Forbes-Robertson. Hamish Hamilton, London. 1964.

Art and Illusion by E. H. Gombrich. Phaidon Press, London. 1960

My dear Mr Churchill, by Walter Graebner. Michael Joseph, London. 1965.

When Your Care Enough. By Joyce C. Hall with Curtiss Anderson. Hallmark Cards, Kansas City, 1992.

The History of the Royal Academy by Sidney C. Hutchison. Chapman and Hall, London. 1968.

Lavery. The Life of a Painter by John Lavery. Cassell, London. 1940.

Jean, Lady Hamilton 1861 - 1941. A Soldier's Wife. By Celia Lee. Celia Lee, London. 2001.

My Years with Churchill, by Norman McGowan. Souvenir Press, London 1958.

A Frenchman in Khaki, by Paul Maze. William Heinemann, London. 1934.

Afternoon Light, by Sir Robert Gordon Menzies. Cassell, London. 1967.

I Was Winston Churchill's Private Secretary, by Phyllis Moir. Wilfred Funk, New York. 1941.

The Finish, by Sir Alfred Munnings. Museum Press, London, 1952.

Confessions of An Actor, by Laurence Olivier. Weidenfeld and Nicolson. London 1982.

Time's Thievish Progress. Autobiography III by John Rothenstein. Cassell, London. 1970.

Portrait and Pageant by Frank O. Salisbury. John Murray, London. 1944.

Iphigene: My Life and the New York Times. The Memoirs of Iphigene Ochs Sulzberger as written by Susan W. Dryfoos. Times Books, New York. 1981.

I Was Churchill's Shadow, by Ex-Dectective-Inspector W. H. Thompson. Christopher Johnson. London 1951.

catalogue

Every known painting by Sir Winston Churchill has a unique Coombs catalogue number indicated here by a capital letter 'C'.

All works are oil on canvas unless otherwise stated. Owners, where known, are listed in chronological order. Auctions and exhibitions are in London unless otherwise stated. Titles and dates are always subject to revision and correction.

C 1 (Fig. 7) Plug Street, Lawrence Farm, 1916, 18 x 24 in. Initialled left, Collections: Lord Thurso, Hon. Robin MacDonald Sinclair, Sold Sotheby's 9th July 1969, £1,400, Present owner unknown, Gift of the artist.

C 2 (Fig. 6) Plug Street, Battalion Headquarters, 1916, Oil on board 10 x 14 in. 25 x 35 cm, Initialled left, Exhibited: National Library of Scotland 1999 Collections: 6th Battalion, The Royal Scots Fusiliers, Trustees of the 9th Scottish Divisional Funds, The Board of Her Majesty's Commissioners for Queen Victoria School, Dunblane. Gift of the artist.

C 3 (Fig. 8) Plug Street, 1916, 20 x 24 in. Initialled right, Illustrated: Winston Churchill: His Life as a Painter by Mary Soames, 1990, Exhibited: World Tour 1958, Royal Academy 1959, New York World's Fair 1965, Marlborough Fine Art 1967, Dallas Museum of Fine Art, Minneapolis Art Institute, Sotheby's 1998, Collections: Mr Randolph S. Churchill, Mr Winston S. Churchill

C 4 (Fig. 5) Plug Street, 1916, 20 x 24 in. Initialled right, Illustrated: Winston Churchill His Life as a Painter by Mary Soames, 1990, Exhibited: World Tour 1958, Royal Academy 1959, New York World's Fair 1965, Collections: Lady Spencer-Churchill, The National Trust, Chartwell

C 5 (Fig. 249) Flowers in a Green Glass Vase, c. 1925, 36 x 24 in. Unsigned, Collections: The Studio, Chartwell, Sarah Lady Audley, Private American Collection.

C 6 (Fig. 244) Roses, c. 1928, Canvas on hardboard 20 x 14 in. 51.75 x 36 cm, Initialled right, Collections: Lady Spencer-Churchill, The National Trust, Chartwell

C 7 (Fig. 248) Mallows, c. 1928, 23 1/2 x 19 1/2 in. 61 x 50.5 cm, Initialled right, Collections: The Studio, Chartwell, The National Trust, Chartwell

C 8 (Fig. 253) Flowers, Painted in the Studio at Chartwell, c. 1928, 24 x 20 in. Initialled, Illustrated: 'The Paintings of Winston Churchill, LIFE, January 7th 1946 'Winston Churchill's Pictures', The Strand Magazine, August 1946, Painting as a Pastime by Winston S. Churchill, 1948, Exhibited: World Tour 1958 Royal Academy 1959 Collections: Lady Spencer-Churchill, Present owner unknown

C 9 (Fig. 254) Fruit and Two Jars, c. 1928, 27 x 32 in. 69 x 82 cm, Initialled right, Collections: Lady Spencer-Churchill, The National Trust, Chartwell

C 10 (Fig. 139) The Banqueting Hall, Knebworth House, 1920s, 23 x 36 in. 60 x 90 cm, Initialled left, Exhibited: Sotheby's 1998 Collections: Pamela Countess of Lytton, Knebworth House Collection Gift from the artist to Lady Lytton. The picture hangs in the room where it was painted.

C 11 (Fig. 78) Tapestries at Blenheim, c. 1930, 25 x 30 in. Initialled, Illustrated: Painting as a Pastime by Winston S. Churchill, 1948, 'An Eightieth Year Tribute to Winston Churchill', edited by Bruce Ingram, The Illustrated London News, 1954, Winston Churchill His Life as a Painter by Mary Soames, 1990, Exhibited: Royal Academy 1948 World Tour 1958, Royal Academy 1959, M. Knoedler, London 1974, Wylma Wayne Gallery, London 1982 New York and Washington, 1983, Japan Exhibition, 1998, Sotheby's 1998, Collection: The Lady Soames DBE, Gift of the artist.

C 12 (Fig. 79) State Room at Blenheim, c. 1928, 24 x 20 in. 50.8 x 61 cm, Initialled, Exhibited: New York World's Fair 1965 Tucson Art Center 1967, The Dallas Museum of Art 1986, Gerald R. Ford Museum 1991/2, Franklin D. Roosevelt Library 1992, Ronald Reagan Library 1992/3, Dwight D. Eisenhower Library 1995, Collections: Mr Joyce C. Hall from James Graham & Sons, New York, 1958, Hallmark Fine Art Collection, Kansas City

C 13 (Fig. 82) Great Hall, Blenheim, c. 1928, 30 x 25 in. 73.75 x 61.25 cm, Unsigned, Collection: Duke of Marlborough, Given by the artist to Blenheim Palace.

C 14 (Fig. 84) Tapestries at Blenheim, c. 1928, 24 1/2 x 30 in. Initialled left, Collections: Mr Randolph S. Churchill, Mr Winston S. Churchill

C 15 (Fig. 25) Pedimented doorway, c. 1922, Canvas board 20 x 14 in. Unsigned, Exhibited: Sotheby's 1998, Collections: The Studio, Chartwell, The National Trust, Chartwell

C 16 (Fig. 55) The Hallway of Wilfred Scawen Blunt's home, New Buildings, Sussex, July 1921, 24 x 20 in. Initialled, Illustrated: 'Painting as a Pastime', by Winston S. Churchill, The Strand Magazine, December 1921, Collections: The Studio, Chartwell, Mr Julian Sandys, Private English Collection

C 17 (Fig. 30) A Music Room, c. 1928, 17 x 10 1/2 in. 43 x 27 cm, Unsigned, Collections: The Studio, Chartwell, Arabella Churchill, On loan to the National Trust, Chartwell, Painting cut down and folded on to back.

C 18 (Fig. 154) The Living Room at Lympne with Lady Pamela Smith, c. 1925, 20 x 24 in. 63 x 73 cm, Unsigned, Collection: The Studio, Chartwell, The Lady Soames DBE

C 19 (Fig. 155) The Library of Sir Philip Sassoon's House at Lympne, c. 1928, 24 x 20 in. 61 x 51 cm, Initialled left, Collections: The Studio, Chartwell, Sold Sotheby's 19th May 1982, £3,200, Present owner unknown

C 20 (Fig. 148) The Blue Room, Trent Park, 1934, 19 1/2 x 13 1/2 in. 50 x 34 cm, Initialled left, Illustrated: 'Winston Churchill's Pictures', The Strand Magazine, July 1946, Painting as a Pastime by Winston S. Churchill 1948, Exhibited: Royal Academy 1948, Brazilian Embassy, Washington, DC 1965, Collection: Museu de Arte de São Paulo Assis Chateaubriand. Purchased at Christie's Charity Auction, 24th July 1949, Gift of the artist to the charity auction.

C 21 (Fig. 152) The Blue Room, Trent Park, c. 1920, Canvas board 20 x 14 in. 51 x 35.5 cm, Unsigned, Collections: The Studio, Chartwell, Miss Arabella S. Churchill, Sold at auction, £9,500, The National Trust, Chartwell

C 22 (Fig. 140) The Dining Room at Knebworth, c. 1928, 20 x 40 in. Unsigned, Collections: The Studio, Chartwell, Sarah Lady Audley, Present owner unknown

C 23 (Fig. 3) The Hall at Hoe Farm, 1915, 16 x 22 in. Initialled, Collections: The Studio, Chartwell, Sarah Lady Audley, Present owner unknown, Formerly incorrectly titled and dated 'The Inner Hall at Breccles' c. 1928; a visit to Hoe Farm by the author confirmed the revised title.

C 24 (Fig. 11) The Long Library at Blenheim with Lady Lavery and Lady Gwendeline Churchill at their Easels, 1916, 24 x 20 in. 61 x 51 cm, Initialled, Exhibited: Smithsonian Institute, Washington, DC 1983, New York State Museum 1983, Norton Gallery, West Palm Beach 1984, Franklin D. Roosevelt Library 1993, Ronald Reagan Library 1993, Winston Spencer Churchill Memorial and Library, Fulton, Collections: Lady Spencer-Churchill, Miss Edwina Sandys, sold Sotheby's 21st June 1995, Present owner unknown, Formerly entitled 'The Interior of Sir John Lavery's studio ... ' and latterly 'The Music Room at Blenheim' and dated c. 1922. The correct title and date were supplied by Mr Peregrine Churchill in a letter to Mrs Minnie Churchill: 'I can give you the date because I was there and can remember a great hush because news had just arrived on Kitchener's death, torpedoed on his way to Russia. That would I think be 1916.'

C 25 (Fig. 54) The Long Gallery at Sutton Place, c. 1921, 18 x 24 in. Initialled left, Illustrated: 'Painting as a Pastime', by Winston S. Churchill, The Strand Magazine, December 1921, Collections: The Studio, Chartwell, Sarah Lady Audley, Mr J. Paul Getty Snr, Mr and Mrs Gordon Getty, Formerly entitled 'A Long Gallery with Oak Furniture'. The correct title was supplied to the author by Mr J. Paul Getty Snr when owner of Sutton Place.

C 26 (Fig. 10) The Interior of Sir John Lavery's Studio with Two Ladies, c. 1922, Canvas board 18 x 12 in. Unsigned, Exhibited: Wylma Wayne Fine Art, London 1982, Collections: The Studio, Chartwell, Sarah Lady Audley, Sold Christie's 20th June 1996, £16,000, Mr Steve Forbes, A pencil sketch was originally noted on the back.

C 27 (Fig. 9) Studio Sketch (Sir John Lavery's), c. 1920, 20 x 24 in. Initialled, Illustrated: Winston Churchill: His Life as a Painter by Mary Soames, 1990, Exhibited: Sotheby's 1998, Collections: Lady Spencer-Churchill, The Lady Soames DBE

C 28 (Fig. 13) Interior of a Studio, Lady Kitty Somerset at an Easel, c. 1922, 27 x 20 in.Initialled,Collections: Lady Spencer-Churchill, Miss Edwina Sandys, On loan to Westminster College, The Winston Churchill Memorial and Library, Fulton.

C 29 (Fig. 12) Portrait of Lady Gwendeline Churchill, c. 1920, 30 x 25 in. 75 x 62.5 cm, Unsigned, Exhibited: Sotheby's 1998 Collections: The Studio, Chartwell, Mr Peregrine Churchill, Duke of Marlborough, Given to the Blenheim Foundation by Mr Peregrine Churchill, son of Lady Gwendeline Churchill. Inscribed on the back of the canvas: 'Painted by my husband. Clementine S. Churchill.' Relined and subsequently inscribed: 'This sketch portrait of Lady Gwendeline Churchill was painted by my Husband. Clementine S. Churchill.'

C 30 (Fig. 17) Portrait of Lady Lavery, or Lady Castlerosse, 1920s, 30 x 25 in. Unsigned, Collections: The Studio, Chartwell, Present owner unknown. Formerly said to be a portrait of Lady Lavery; Lady Spencer-Churchill subsequently decided (in 1967) that it was of Lady Castlerosse. But cf. C 152 and C 158.

C 31 (Fig. 15) Self-portrait, c. 1915, 24 x 20 in. 61.4 x 51.2, Unsigned, Illustrated: Winston Churchill: His Life as a Painter by Mary Soames, 1990, Collections: The Studio, Chartwell, The National Trust, Chartwell, Inscribed on the back: 'Self portrait, painted by my husband. Clementine S. Churchill.'

C 32 (Fig. 214) Lord Balfour and his Niece on a Log, 1920s, 20 x 24 in. Unsigned, Collections: The Studio, Chartwell The National Trust, Chartwell, Inscribed on the back: 'Painted by my husband. Clementine S. Churchill.'

C 33 (Fig. 217) Lord Balfour, 1920s, 20 x 16 in. 51 x 41 cm, Unsigned, Published: Paintings and Sculpture at Hatfield House by E. Auerbach and C. K. Adams, 1971, Illustrated: Winston Churchill: His Life as a Painter by Mary Soames, 1990, Exhibited: Sotheby's 1998, Collections: The Studio, Chartwell, Lady Spencer-Churchill. Gift to 5th Marquess of Salisbury, 1966, Marquess of Salisbury

C 34 (Fig. 215) Mme Chanel with a Dachshund, c. 1928, Board 17 1/2 x 14 in. 45 x 35.5 cm, Unsigned, Collection: The Studio, Chartwell, The National Trust, Chartwell, Based on a photograph in the archives at Chartwell. The canvas was shortened after the picture was painted.

C 35 (Fig. 216) The Guardsman, 1920s, 20 x 12 in. Initialled left, Collection: Mr Giovanni Agnelli. Donated to a charity auction at Sotheby's 9th November 1988, £14,500. Present owner unknown, 'On Sentry Go - in the snow at Buckingham Palace.' Originally, says Lady Soames, the painting was given by Churchill to Nellie Hosier, Clementine's sister, who lived in Dieppe during the war when her house was occupied by Germans.

C 36 (Fig. 213) Tea at Chartwell, c. 1928, 25 x 30 in. Unsigned, Illustrated: Winston Churchill: His Life as a Painter by Mary Soames, 1990, Collections: The Studio, Chartwell, The National Trust, Chartwell, The dining-room, 29th August 1927. [From left to right] Mrs Therese Sickert, Diana Mitford, Edward Marsh, Winston Churchill, Professor Lindemann, Randolph Churchill, Diana Churchill, Mrs Churchill, Richard Sickert. From a photograph taken by Donald Ferguson.

C 37 (Fig. 16) Sir Archibald Sinclair (Lord Thurso), 1920s, 30 x 25 in. 76 x 63.5 cm, Unsigned, Collection: The Studio, Chartwell, The National Trust, Chartwell

C 38 (Fig. 18) Group Captain Jack Scott, c. 1925, 24 x 20 in. 61 x 51 cm, Unsigned, Collections: The Studio, Chartwell, The National Trust, Chartwell

C 39 (Fig. 221) The Cockatoo, 1920s, 20 x 14 in. 50 x 61 cm, Unsigned, Collections: The Studio, Chartwell, The National Trust, Chartwell, Almost certainly based on a newspaper cutting. The title was revised by Lady Spencer-Churchill in 1967.

C 40 (Fig. 14) Lord Darling, c. 1925, 30 x 25 in. 76.2 x 63.5 cm, Unsigned, Collections: The Studio, Chartwell, The National Trust, Chartwell, Inscribed on the back by Lady Churchill 'Mr Justice Darling'.

C 41 (Fig. 222) Children Laughing, 1920s, Canvas board 14 x 20 in. 35.1 x 50.5 cm, Initialled left, Collections: The Studio, Chartwell, The National Trust, Chartwell, Based on a newspaper cutting in the archives at Chartwell entitled 'Punch and Judy: A London Street Study'.

C 42 (Fig. 93) Teatime in the Loggia at Chartwell - with Miss Marryot White, Mrs Churchill, Diana and Mary c. 1928, 16 x 24 in. Initialled right, Collections: The Studio, Chartwell, Sarah Lady Audley, Present owner unknown

C 43 (Fig. 95) Sir Winston Churchill Painting under the Loggia at Chartwell, 1927, Board 20 x 14 in. Unsigned, Collections: The Studio, Chartwell, Private English collection.

C 44 (Fig. 177) Two Ladies in a Gondola on the Lagoon at Venice, 1927, 19 3/4 x 13 3/4 in. 50 x 35 cm, Unsigned, Collections: The Studio, Chartwell, Sarah Lady Audley, Sold Sotheby's 3rd November 1982, £2,700, Sold Christie's 6th November 1992, £25,000, Wells Collection, Clementine Churchill visited Venice in September 1927 with her daughter Diana; Winston joined them there in October. This picture is probably painted from a photograph and the ladies resemble Clementine and Diana. Information supplied by Lady Soames.

C 45 (Fig. 218) Hunting Scene, c. 1928, 20 x 16 in. Unsigned, Collections: Lady Spencer-Churchill, Miss Emma Soames. Sold Christie's July 1977, £8,000, Present owner unknown, Based on a photograph in the archives at Chartwell.

C 46 (Fig. 94) Still Life: Randolph Churchill under the Pergola at Chartwell, 1920s, 24 x 20 in. 61.1 x 51 cm, Unsigned, Collections: The Studio, Chartwell, The National Trust, Chartwell

C 47 (Fig. 97) Mary's First Speech, c. 1929, 15 x 29 in. 35.7 x 50.9 cm, Unsigned, Exhibited: M. Knoedler, London 1974, Sotheby's 1998, Collection: The Lady Soames DBE, Gift of the artist. Based on a photograph in the archives at Chartwell.

C 48 (Fig. 219) Troops Going to the Front, 1917, c. 1927, 20 x 24 in. Unsigned, Exhibited: Sotheby's 1998, Collections: Lord Butler, Sir Adam Butler, Gift of the artist. Based on a newspaper cutting in the archives at Chartwell. The captions read: 'Shall We Ever Forget? War-time Memories of London ... The Gate of Good-bye: Ten years ago at Victoria Station - just before the train left for the front. The agony of farewell to men who might never come back was then part of London's everyday life. - Photograph taken in 1917 by Mr. F. J. Mortimer.'

C 49 (Fig. 220) The Fire, c. 1928, 28 x 36 in. 71 x 86.5 cm, Unsigned, Collections: The Studio, Chartwell, The National Trust, Chartwell, Based on two identical but different-sized newspaper cuttings in the archives at Chartwell. The captions read: 'Three fire brigades' combined efforts were necessary to subdue an outbreak in an omnibus garage at Bures Suffolk. A view of the fire in progress.' The canvas has been shortened.

C 50 (Fig. 19) Sunset at Roehampton, or Sunset through Fog, 1919, 24 x 20 in. Initialled right, Illustrated: Winston Churchill: His Life as a Painter by Mary Soames 1990, Exhibited: World Tour 1958, Royal Academy 1959, Sotheby's 1998, Collections: Lady Spencer-Churchill, Sarah Lady Audley, The Lady SoamesDBE, Bequeathed to Lady Soames by her sister Sarah Churchill.

C 51 (Fig. 29) Loch Choire, Scotland, August 1919, Canvas on board 17 1/2 x 13 1/2 in. Initialled, Exhibited: Royal Academy 1959, New York World's Fair 1965, Collections: Duke of Sutherland, Clare Duchess of Sutherland, Bought in at Parke-Bernet, New York 19th May 1966, $6,000, Present owner unknown

C 52 (Fig. 21) Sunset near Roehampton, c. 1919, 24 x 20 in. Initialled, Collections: Sarah Lady Audley. Sold Sotheby's 26th April 1972, £4,120, Present owner unknown

C 53 (Fig. 69) Woods at Mimizan, Landes, c. 1924, 30 x 25 in. Initialled, Illustrated: Winston Churchill: His Life as a Painter by Mary Soames, 1990, Exhibited: World Tour 1958, Royal Academy 1959, Collection: Sir Edward Heath, Gift of the artist.

C 54 (Fig. 112) Garden Scene at Breccles, c. 1925, 24 x 18 in. 61 x 46 cm, Initialled, Collections: The Studio, Chartwell, Miss Arabella Churchill. Sold Sotheby's 19th May 1982, £5,600, Sold Sotheby's 15th July 1998, £45,500, British private collection

C 55 (Fig. 113) Large Cedar in the Formal Garden at Breccles, 1920s, 24 x 20 in. Unsigned, Collections: The Studio, Chartwell, Mr Winston S. Churchill, Private collection

C 56 (Fig. 243) The Thames at Taplow, 1929s, 25 x 30 in. 63.5 x 76 cm Initialled, Collections: Lady Juliet Duff, Sold by the legatee Parke-Bernet, New York 20th October 1966, $16,000, Sold Sotheby's 4th November 1992, £21,000, Present owner unknown, Given by the artist to Lady Juliet Duff one weekend at Chartwell; it was chosen from a group of six with Viscount Montgomery's assistance.

C 57 (Fig. 111) Winter Woodland, Breccles, c. 1925, 20 x 16 in. Initialled left, Exhibited: Royal Academy 1959, Collections: Dame Pattie Menzies, Sold Christie's 10th November 1989, £20,000, Wells Collection, Gift of the artist. The painting used to hang in Sir Winston Churchill's London home at 28 Hyde Park Gate. When cleaning it for the present owner, the restorer had to remove layer upon layer of yellow residue and asked if anyone in the house might have smoked cigars!

C 58 (Fig. 233) Quiet Waters, 1920s, 20 x 24 in. 50.8 x 60.96 cm, Unsigned, Collections: Lord Beaverbrook, Lady Beaverbrook The Beaverbrook Canadian Foundation, Beaverbrook Art Gallery, Fredericton, New Brunswick, Gift of the artist on the occasion of Lord Beaverbrook's 80th birthday, May 1959.

C 59 (Fig. 81) Cannon Point, Blenheim Lake, 1920s, 26 x 31 in. 60 x 25 cm, Initialled left, Collection: Duke of Marlborough, Gift of the artist.

C 60 (Fig. 88) Wooded Water near Blenheim, 1920s, 32 x 23 in. Initialled right, Collection: Sir Anthony Montague Browne, Gift of the artist.

C 61 (Fig. 85) Boathouse, Blenheim Lake, 1920s, 28 x 25 in. 70 x 60 cm, Initialled right, Collection: Duke of Marlborough, Gift of the artist.

C 62 (Fig. 66) Mimizan, 1920s, 21 1/2 x 13 1/2 in. Initialled left, Collections: Field Marshal Viscount Montgomery, Sold Sotheby's 26th November 1969, Present owner unknown
Gift of the artist.

C 63 (Fig. 76) Evening Glow at Mimizan, 1920s, 20 x 24 in. Initialled, Exhibited: New York World's Fair 1965, Collections: Mrs Diana Sandys, Miss Edwina Sandys, Present owner unknown

C 64 (Fig. 86) The Lake at Blenheim, c. 1926-29, 20 x 24 in. Signed and initialled, Collections: Field Marshal Viscount Montgomery, Sold Parke-Bernet, New York 19th May 1966, $14,000, Present owner unknown, Gift of the artist.

C 65 (Fig. 70) Woodland Scene near Mimizan, 1920s, 24 x 20 in. 59.8 x 49.8 cm, Initialled, Exhibited: New York World's Fair 1965, Collections: Sir John Colville, Lady Margaret Colville, Gift of the artist.

C 66 (Fig. 71) Trees, Mimizan, c. 1925, 24 x 20 in. 61 x 51.1 cm, Unsigned, Exhibited: Royal Academy 1959, Collections: Lady Spencer-Churchill, The National Trust, Chartwell, Gift of the artist.

C 67 (Fig. 72) Red-roofed House at Mimizan, 1920s, 24 x 20 in. Initialled, Collections: Lady Spencer-Churchill, Mr E. Murray. Sold Sotheby's, London 14th March 1973, £3,200, Sold Sotheby's, New York 18th February 1988, $40,000, American private collector, Gift of Lady Spencer-Churchill to Mr E. Murray.

C 68 (Fig. 65) Trees by a Stream in Norfolk, c. 1923, 24 x 20 in. 61 x 51.5 cm, Unsigned, Collections: Lady Spencer-Churchill, The National Trust, Chartwell, Gift of the artist.

C 69 (Fig. 51) Mimizan, Spring 1920, 30 x 25 in. 76 x 63.5 cm, Initialled, Illustrated: 'Painting as a Pastime', by Winston S. Churchill, The Strand Magazine, December 1921, Exhibited: World Tour 1958, Royal Academy 1959, Collections: Lady Spencer-Churchill. Sold Christie's 4th March 1977, £48,000. Bought by the Tryon Gallery on behalf of Mr John Turner, Auctioned Christie's 12th November 1987. Bought in for £30,000, Auctioned Christie's 8th November 1990. Bought in for £32,000, Present owner unknown, Gift of the artist. This picture used to hang in Lady Spencer-Churchill's flat at Prince's Gate, London.

C 70 (Fig. 63) Mimizan, Landes, c. 1927, 24 1/2 x 29 1/2 in. 62.3 x 75 cm, Initialled, Collections: Mr David Lloyd George, Viscount Tenby. Sold Christie's 12th November 1965, £9,975, Anonymous owner, Sold Christie's 27th November 1997, £150,000, Lord Harris of Peckham, Gift of the artist in the late 1920s.

C 71 (Fig. 80) Mimizan, c. 1922, 24 x 20 in. Initialled, Collections: Lady Spencer-Churchill, Miss Edwina Sandys, Present owner unknown, Gift of the artist.

C 72 (Fig. 83) Mimizan Lake, c. 1922, 24 x 20 in. 61.5 x 51.5 cm, Initialled, Exhibited: World Tour 1958, Royal Academy 1959 Tokyo 1969, Wylma Wayne Fine Art, London 1982, Sotheby's 1998, British Festival, Japan 1998, Collections: Lady Spencer-Churchill, Government Art Collection, Given by Lady Churchill to the Government Whip's Office, No. 12 Downing Street, 1965, in fulfilment of a promise made by Sir Winston Churchill before his death.

C 73 (Fig. 31) View of Cherkley, 1915, 20 x 23 in. Initialled, Collections: Lord Beaverbrook, Lady Beaverbrook, The Beaverbrook Canadian Foundation, Beaverbrook Art Gallery, Fredericton, New Brunswick, Given by the artist to Lord Beaverbrook in 1974 as a 75th birthday present.

C 74 (Fig. 73) Cork Trees near Mimizan, 1924, 24 7/8 x 29 7/8 in. 63.2 x 76 cm, Signed, Exhibited: World Tour 1958, Royal Academy 1959, New York World's Fair 1965, Collections: Lady Spencer-Churchill. Sold Sotheby's, London, Charity Auction 1961, £7,400, Mrs Sigurd S. Larmon. Sold Sotheby's, New York 7th June 1984, $18,000, Mr and Mrs Christopher Nielsen, The 1961 charity auction price was then the highest ever fetched by a living English artist. The catalogue notes that the painting was 'Presented by the artist'.

C 75 (Fig. 36) The Cathedral, Hackwood Park, 1924, 32 x 25 1/2 in. 81.3 x 64.8 cm, Initialled, left and right, Collections: Lord Camrose. Sold by his executors Christie's 4th June 1999, £36,000, Present owner unknown, Gift of the artist.

C 76 (Fig. 232) Garden Scene, 1920s, 29 x 24 in. 73.6 x 61 cm, Initialled, Collections: Lady Lytton, thence by descent. Sold Christie's 20th June 1996, £22,500, Mr David Gainsborough Roberts, On permanent loan to the Jersey Museum, St Helier, Thought to be a view at Chartwell but this is unlikely as no similar scene in the garden there is known. Perhaps it is a view at the Lyttons' country house, Knebworth.

C 77 (Fig. 178) The Fountain in the Shade, c. 1925, 23 5/8 x 19 1/2 in. Initialled right, Exhibited: Franklin D. Roosevelt Library 1992, Collections: Lady Spencer-Churchill, Miss Arabella Churchill. Sold through Sotheran's July 1982, Mr Donald S. Carmichael, Gift of the artist.

C 78 (Fig. 149) Trent Park, c. 1925, Canvas board 20 x 14 in. 51 x 35.5 cm, Unsigned, Exhibited: Wylma Wayne Fine Art, London 1982, Collections: The Studio, Chartwell, Sarah Lady Audley. Sold through Wylma Wayne, 1982, Private collection, London

C 79 (Fig. 48) Cairo from the Pyramids, 1921, 25 x 30 in. Initialled, Exhibited: Royal Academy 1959, Sotheby's 1998, Collections: Lady Spencer-Churchill, Duke of Norfolk, Lady Mary Mumford, Given to the Duke of Norfolk by Lady Churchill after Sir Winston's funeral in 1965.

C 80 (Fig. 161) View over Lympne Marshes, 1925, 20 x 24 1/2 in. Unsigned, Collections: Mr Randolph S. Churchill, Mr Winston S. Churchill, Gift of the artist.

C 81 (Fig. 332) Marrakech, c. 1935, Canvas board 14 x 20 in. Unsigned, Illustrated: Winston Churchill: His Life as a Painter by Mary Soames, 1990, Collections: The Studio, Chartwell, The National Trust, Chartwell

C 82 (Fig. 49) Distant View of the Pyramids at Sunset, c. 1921, 24 3/4 x 30 in. 63 x 76 cm, Unsigned, Collections: The Studio, Chartwell, Miss Arabella Churchill. Sold Sotheby's, New York 25th May 1982, $19,000, Present owner unknown, Previously dated to c. 1926, which is unlikely as Churchill's visit to the Pyramids was in 1921.

C 83 (Fig. 342) The Entrance of the Gorge at Todhra, c. 1935, Canvas board 14 x 20 in. 35.5 x 51 cm, Unsigned, Collections: Lady Spencer-Churchill, Arabella Churchill, The National Trust, Chartwell.

C 84 (Fig. 44) Cairo from the Pyramids with the Artist Painting, c. 1946, 40 x 50 in. 102 x 127.5 cm, Unsigned, Exhibited: Sotheby's 1998, Collections: Lady Spencer-Churchill, The National Trust, Chartwell, Gift of the artist.

C 85 (Fig. 42) Distant View of the Pyramids, c. 1921, 25 x 30 in. Unsigned, Collections: The Studio, Chartwell, Sarah Lady Audley, Private collection, Lake Forest, Illinois, USA

C 86 (Fig. 50) The Pyramids. 1921, 25 x 30 in. Unsigned, Illustrated: 'Painting as a Pastime', by Winston S. Churchill, The Strand Magazine, December 1921, Winston Churchill: His Life as a Painter by Mary Soames, 1990 Collections: The Studio, Chartwell, Sarah Lady Audley, The National Trust, Chartwell

C 87 (Fig. 46) Pyramids and Sand Dunes, 1921, 25 x 30 in. Unsigned, Collections: The Studio, Chartwell, Sarah Lady Audley, Mr and Mrs Stefan Lersten

C 88 (Fig. 326) Coast Scene with a Ruined Building, c. 1920, 20 x 24 in. 51 x 61 cm, Unsigned, Collections: The Studio, Chartwell, Sarah Lady Audley, The National Trust, Chartwell

C 89 (Fig. 227) The Bow River, near Banff, Canada, c. 1929, Canvas board 14 x 20 in. 35.2 x 50.6 cm, Unsigned, Collections: The Studio, Chartwell, The National Trust, Chartwell, Formerly wrongly entitled 'In the Dolomites'. The correct title and thus the date were discovered on a visit to Canada by a volunteer guide at Chartwell.

C 90 (Fig. 228) Lake Louise, Canada, c. 1929, 24 x 32 in. 60.1 x 81 cm, Unsigned, Collection: The Studio, Chartwell, The National Trust, Chartwell

C 91 (Fig. 229) Lake Louise, Canada, c. 1929, Canvas board 14 x 20 in. Unsigned, Collection: The Studio, Chartwell, The National Trust, Chartwell

C 92 (Fig. 179) Lake Scene in the Dolomites, c. 1925, 18 x 26 in. 46 x 66 cm, Unsigned, Collections: The Studio, Chartwell, Arabella Churchill, On loan to the National Trust, Chartwell

C 93 (Fig. 270) Coast Scene in the South of France with a Cactus, c. 1925, 20 x 24 in. Unsigned, Collections: The Studio, Chartwell, Mr Jay Walton

C 94 (Fig. 290) Avignon, 1925, 19 x 29 in. Initialled, Exhibited: World Tour 1958, Royal Academy 1959, Collections: Lady Spencer-Churchill, Sold Christie's 4th March 1977, £26,000, Sultan of Brunei

C 95 (Fig. 321) The Forum in Rome, c. 1926, Canvas board 20 x 14 in. 50.5 x 35.5 cm, Unsigned, Collections: The Studio, Chartwell, Sarah Lady Audley, The National Trust, Chartwell

C 96 (Fig. 310) Coast Scene near Cannes, 1925, 20 x 28 in. Unsigned, Collections: The Studio, Chartwell, The National Trust, Chartwell

C 97 (Fig. 322) Ruined Greek Temple, c. 1934, Canvas board 20 x 14 in. Unsigned, Illustrated: Winston Churchill: His Life as a Painter by Mary Soames, 1990, Exhibited: Sotheby's 1998, Collections: The Studio, Chartwell, The Lady Soames DBE

C 98 (Fig. 134) Calm Sea near Marseilles, c. 1926, Panel 13 x 16 in. Unsigned, Collections: The Studio, Chartwell, Sarah Lady Audley, The National Trust, Chartwell

C 99 (Fig. 118) Near Lochmore, c. 1925, 25 x 30 in. Unsigned, Collections: The Studio, Chartwell, Mr Julian Sandys, Mrs Elizabeth Sandys

C 100 (Fig. 167) Copy of a Classical Landscape, c. 1925, 24 x 29 1/4 in. 61 x 74.5 cm, Initialled right, Exhibited: Wylma Wayne Fine Art, London 1982, Collections: The Studio, Chartwell, Sarah Lady Audley, An American collector. Sold Christie's, London 8th November 1990, £11,500, Mr Martin G. Lagina, The name of the artist of the painting that Churchill copied and its then owner are unknown.

C 101 (Fig. 291) The Papal Palace at Avignon, 1925, 24 x 36 in. Unsigned, Illustrated: Winston Churchill: His Life as a Painter by Mary Soames, 1990, Collections: Mr Randolph S. Churchill, Mr Winston S. Churchill, Mrs Minnie S. Churchill

C 102 (Fig. 234) East Coast Landscape, 1920s, 25 x 30 in. Unsigned, Collections: The Studio, Chartwell, Arabella Churchill

C 103 (Fig. 53) Daybreak at Cassis, near Marseilles, September 1920, 18 x 36 in. Initialled, Illustrated: 'Painting as a Pastime', by Winston S. Churchill, The Strand Magazine, December 1921, Winston Churchill: His Life as a Painter by Mary Soames, 1990, Collections: Lady Spencer-Churchill, The National Trust, Chartwell, Wrongly titled in my original catalogue as 'Seascape at Sunset'.

C 104 (Fig. 40) Sunset over the Sea - Orange and Purple, 1920s, Panel 13 x 16 in. Unsigned, Illustrated: Winston Churchill: His Life as a Painter by Mary Soames, 1990, Exhibited: Sotheby's, London 1998, Collections: The Studio, Chartwell, The Lady Soames DBE

C 105 (Fig. 41) Seascape with Rain Clouds, 1920s, Panel 13 x 16 in. 33 x 41 cm, Unsigned, Collections: The Studio, Chartwell, Miss Arabella Churchill, The National Trust, Chartwell

C 106 (Fig. 43) Sunset over the Sea - Pink and Mauve, 1920s, Panel 13 x 16 in. Unsigned, Collections: The Studio, Chartwell, Private English collection

C 107 (Fig. 38) Seascape with a Conical Buoy, 1920s, 20 x 24 in. Initialled, Collections: The Studio, Chartwell

C 108 (Fig. 39) Purple Mountains and a Blue Sea at Sunset, 1920s, Panel 13 x 16 in. Unsigned, Exhibited: Sotheby's 1998, Collections: The Studio, Chartwell, The Lady Soames DBE

C 109 (Fig. 37) Impression of a Cloud-swept Landscape in the South of France, 1920s, Panel 13 x 16 in. 32.9 x 41 cm, Unsigned, Collections: The Studio, Chartwell, Private collection

C 110 (Fig. 47) Jerusalem, 1921, 20 x 24 in. Initialled right, Illustrated: Winston Churchill: His Life as a Painter by Mary Soames, 1990, Exhibited: World Tour 1958, Royal Academy 1959, Sotheby's 1998, Collections: Lady Spencer-Churchill, Mr Winston S. Churchill

C 111 (Fig. 32) Coastal Town on the Riviera, c. 1925, Canvas board 14 x 20 in. Unsigned, Collections: The Studio, Chartwell, Private collection, Lake Forest, Illinois, USA, A sketch of a lady on the back of the canvas was noted in my orginal catalogue. Cf. C 535.

C 112 (Fig. 45) Storm over Cannes, c. 1925, 20 x 24 in. Unsigned, Collections: The Studio, Chartwell, Miss Edwina Sandys, Present owner unknown

C 113 (Fig. 320) Remains of a Greek Temple, Doorway and Pillars, c. 1934, Canvas board 20 x 14 in. 50.7 x 35.6 cm, Unsigned, Exhibited: Sotheby's 1998, Collections: The Studio, Chartwell, The Lady Soames DBE

C 114 (Fig. 319) Doorway and Pillars in Shadow, c. 1934, Canvas board 20 x 14 in. 51 x 20.5 cm, Unsigned, Collections: The Studio, Chartwell,The Lady Soame DBE

C 115 (Fig. 323) Pillars of a Ruined Temple, c. 1934, Canvas board 14 x 20 in. 36 x 51 cm, Unsigned, Collections: The Studio, Chartwell, Sarah Lady Audley, The National Trust, Chartwell, This painting has been relined and restored.

C 116 (Fig. 166) Ruins of Arras Cathedral, 1920s, 23 x 29 in. Unsigned, Collections: Mr Randolph S. Churchill, Mr Winston S. Churchill, Copy of a painting by J. S. Sargent then in the possession of Sir Philip Sassoon. The subject was incorrectly described as 'Amiens Cathedral' in my original catalogue. cf. C 440

C 117 (Fig. 201) The Palladian Bridge at Wilton, c. 1925, Canvas board 14 x 19 3/4 in. 35.5 x 50.5 cm, Unsigned, Collections: The Studio, Chartwell, The National Trust, Chartwell, This painting is unfinished.

C 118 (Fig. 202) The Palladian Bridge at Wilton, 1920s, 24 x 29 in. 60 x 73 cm, Unsigned, Collections: The Studio, Chartwell, The National Trust, Chartwell

C 119 (Fig. 176) Venice, The Bridge of Sighs, 1920s, Canvas board 19 3/4 x 13 3/4 in. 50.5 x 35 cm, Unsigned, Collections: The Studio, Chartwell, Sold Sotheby's, New York 21st May 1981, $16,000, Present owner unknown

C 120 (Fig. 206) The Palladian Bridge at Wilton, 1920s, 23 3/4 x 17 1/2 in. 60 x 44.5 cm, Initialled left, Exhibited: New York World's Fair 1965, The Dallas Museum of Art 1986, Gerald R. Ford Museum 1991/2, Franklin D. Roosevelt Library 1992, Ronald Reagan Library 1992/3, Dwight D. Eisenhower Library 1995, Collections: Captain Oswald Frewen Mrs Oswald Frewen. Sold Parke-Bernet, New York, 9th December 1965, $26,000, Hallmark Fine Art Collection, Kansas City, Missouri, A telegram is fixed to the back of the canvas. Dated 1st November 1952 and addressed to Captain Oswald Frewen, Sheep House, Brede, Sussex, it reads: 'Thank you so much for your letter Stop The subject is the Palladian Bridge at Wilton = Winston.'

C 121 (Fig. 207) The Palladian Bridge at Wilton, c. 1925, 25 x 30 in. Initialled left, Collections: Lady Spencer-Churchill, Earl of Pembroke, Gift of Lady Spencer-Churchill.

C 122 (Fig. 204) Palladian Bridge, 1925, 25 x 30 in. 76.4 x 63.7 cm. Initialled left, Illustrated: Winston Churchill: His Life as a Painter by Mary Soames, 1990, Exhibited: World Tour 1958, Royal Academy 1959, Royal Glasgow Institute 1979, New York, Albany, Washington 1983, Victoria and Albert Museum 1993, Collection: Her Majesty Queen Elizabeth II, Gift of the artist 1960.

C 123 (Fig. 99) The Water Garden at Chartwell, c. 1925, Canvas board 20 x 14 in. 50.8 x 35 cm, Initialled right, Exhibited: Wylma Wayne Fine Art, London 1982, Collections: The Studio, Chartwell, Sarah Lady Audley, Sold Christie's 20th June 1996, £16,000, Mr F. P. Spiteri Paris

C 124 (Fig. 334) Marrakech, c. 1935, 24 x 20 in. Initialled left, Illustrated: 'The Paintings of Winston Churchill', LIFE, January 7th 1946, 'Winston Churchill's Pictures', The Strand Magazine, August 1946, Collection: Hudson's Bay Company, Gift of the artist in 1956 when he was appointed the first 'Grand Seigneur [named to the Board of Directors] of the Company of Adventurers of England Trading into Hudson Bay'. This painting is based on a photograph in the archives at Chartwell.

C 125 (Fig. 141) Terrace at Hever, 1920s, Canvas board 13 3/4 x 18 1/4 in. 35.2 x 46.5 cm, Unsigned, Collections: The Studio, Chartwell, The National Trust, Chartwell

C 126 (Fig. 390) The Swimming Pool at Casa Alva, 1946, 25 x 30 in. Unsigned, Collections: The Studio, Chartwell, Sarah Lady Audley, Present owner unknown, Casa Alva was Mme Balsan's house in Palm Beach, Florida. The picture was wrongly dated in my original catalogue.

C 127 (Fig. 336) Marrakech, c. 1935, Canvas board 19 3/4 x 13 3/4 in. 50.1 x 34.9 cm. Unsigned, Exhibited: Wylma Wayne Fine Art, London 1982, Collections: The Studio, Chartwell, Sarah Lady Audley, (Other owners), Mr P. Michael Wilson. From Wilfred M. De Freitas, art dealer, Montreal. This painting is based on a photograph in the archives at Chartwell.

C 128 (Fig. 335) Marrakech, c. 1935, Canvas board 19 3/4 x 14 in. 50.5 x 36 cm, Unsigned, Collections: The Studio, Chartwell, The National Trust, Chartwell, This painting is based on a photograph in the archives at Chartwell.

C 129 (Fig. 169) Seascape, c. 1925, Panel 13 x 16 in. Unsigned, Collections: The Studio, Chartwell, Sarah Lady Audley, Present owner unknown, This picture is an unfinished copy of a painting hanging in Churchill's Study at Chartwell.

C 130 (Fig. 175) San Giorgio, Venice, 1920s, 20 x 24 in. Unsigned, Collections: The Studio, Chartwell, Present owner unknown

C 131 (Fig. 329) Harbour in the South of France, c. 1925, Canvas board 14 x 20 in. 35 x 50 cm, Unsigned, Collections: The Studio, Chartwell, The National Trust, Chartwell

C 132 (Fig. 271) The Coast near Antibes, c. 1925, 25 x 30 in. Unsigned, Collections: Mr. R. E. Golding, Mr Harry Kay, Sold Christie's 4th November 1966, £7,140, Mr R. A. Sampson, Sold Christie's 12th June 1998, £35,000, Mr Kenneth W. Rendell, Given by Churchill to his bodyguard Detective Sergeant R. E. Golding.

C 133 (Fig. 170) Seascape, 1920s, 20 x 24 in. 51 x 61.2 cm, Unsigned, Exhibited: Wylma Wayne Fine Art, London 1982, Arts Council Touring Exhibition: Kettle's Yard, Cambridge; Cornerhouse, Manchester; Camden Arts Centre, London, 1998/9, Collections: The Studio, Chartwell, Sarah Lady Audley, Government Art Collection, This is a copy of a painting hanging in Churchill's Study at Chartwell.

C 134 (Fig. 192) Flat Calm with a High-prowed Boat, c. 1925, 23 1/2 x 32 in. Unsigned, Collections: The Studio, Chartwell Miss Edwina Sandys, On loan to the Churchill Memorial at Westminster College, Fulton

C 135 (Fig. 195) The Adriatic with Venice in the Distance (or St Malo), c. 1925, 25 x 30 in. 61.9 x 74.4 cm, Initialled left, Published in 'Pictures at Harrow' by Carolyn Leder, Curator, 1998, Exhibited: M. Knoedler, London, 1977, New York International Arts Festival 1983, Japan 1998, Collections: The Studio, Chartwell, The Keepers and Governors of Harrow School Given to Harrow School by Lady Churchill in 1966 who subsequently suggested that the painting was a view of St Malo. The sailing vessels seem to have been added later by Churchill and are based on a painting in his Study at Chartwell. Cf. C 129 and C 133.

C 136 (Fig. 193) The Firth of Forth, c. 1925, 25 x 30 in. Unsigned, Collections: The Studio, Chartwell, Miss Edwina Sandys, Monsanto Company, St Louis, Missouri

C 137 (Fig. 26) The Loggia, Esher Place, Surrey, c. 1920, 19 1/2 x 23 1/2 in. Initialled right, Exhibited: New York World's Fair 1965, Collections: Lord Hailes, Sir N. F. H. Williamson Bt, Private collection, A handwritten note from Lady Churchill accompanies this painting: 'The man in the straw hat is Lord D'Abernon and Winston himself is the figure in the beige raincoat. Painted at Esher Place about 1920. C.S.C.'

C 138 (Fig. 297) Schloss Schleissheim, near Munich, c. 1932, Canvas board 14 x 20 in. 51 x 61 cm, Unsigned, Collections: The Studio, Chartwell, The Lady Soames DBE, On loan to the National Trust, Chartwell, Originally entitled 'Near Salzburg' until a visitor to the Studio at Chartwell provided the correct identification.

C 139 (Fig. 296) Schloss Schleissheim, near Munich, c. 1932, Canvas board 14 x 20 in. 35.5 x 50.5 cm, Unsigned, Collections: The Studio, Chartwell, Miss Arabella Churchill, The National Trust, Chartwell, Originally incorrectly entitled 'Near Salzburg'. Cf. C 138.

C 140 (Fig. 366) Le Moulin, St-Georges-Motel, c. 1923, 24 x 18 in. Initialled, Collections: Lady Spencer-Churchill, Private English collection

C 141 (Fig. 28) The Entrance to a Drive, c. 1920, 27 x 22 in. Initialled, Collections: The Studio, Chartwell, Present owner unknown

C 142 (Fig. 98) Winter Sunshine, Chartwell, c. 1924, Millboard 14 x 20 in. Signed left, Illustrated: Painting as a Pastime, by Winston S. Churchill, 1948, Winston Churchill: His Life as a Painter by Mary Soames, 1990, Exhibited: Sunderland House, London 1925, Royal Academy 1947, World Tour 1958, Royal Academy 1959, Collections: Lady Spencer-Churchill, Arabella Churchill, The National Trust, Chartwell

C 143 (Fig. 22) At Lullenden Manor, c. 1917, 20 x 24 in. 51 x 61 cm, Initialled left, Collections: The Studio, Chartwell, Arabella Churchill, On loan to the National Trust, Chartwell

C 144 (Fig. 62) Mells, Somersetshire, c. 1920, 24 x 20 in. 60 x 50 cm, Initialled left, Illustrated: 'Painting as a Pastime' by Winston S. Churchill, Part 2, The Strand Magazine, January 1922, Collections: The Studio, Chartwell, The Lady Soames DBE, Originally entitled 'Pergola at Chartwell'. The correct title appears in WSC's article for The Strand Magazine, 1922.

C 145 (Fig. 210) Chequers on an Autumn Evening, c. 1928, 20 x 24 in. Unsigned, Collections: The Studio, Chartwell, Mr Winston S. Churchill, Private collection

C 146 (Fig. 1) The Garden at Hoe Farm with Lady Gwendeline Churchill, 1915, 20 x 24 in. 50 x 60 cm, Unsigned, Illustrated: Winston Churchill: His Life as a Painter by Mary Soames, 1990, Exhibited: Sotheby's 1998, Collections: The Studio, Chartwell, Lady Soames, Mr Peregrine S. Churchill, Duke of Marlborough, Given by Peregrine Churchill to the Blenheim Foundation, 1998.

C 147 (Fig. 122) Trees and Shadows, c. 1928, Canvas board 20 x 14 in. 35.6 x 50.5 cm, Initialled left, Collections: The Studio, Chartwell, The National Trust, Chartwell

C 148 (Fig. 2) Entrance to the Drive at Hoe Farm, 1915, 20 x 24 in. Initialled, Collections: Mr Charles Clore (from a previous owner via Marlborough Fine Art, London), Sold Sotheby's 13th November 1985, Present owner unknown, Previously entitled 'Landscape with a Small Pool'. The correct title was confirmed on a visit to Hoe Farm by the author in 2000.

C 149 (Fig. 4) Hoe Farm, 1915, 20 x 24 in. Unsigned, Exhibited: Sotheby's 1998, Collections: The Studio, Chartwell, The Lady Soames DBEI

C 150 (Fig. 96) Snow at Chartwell, 1924, 23 1/2 x 32 in. 59.7 x 81.3 cm, Unsigned, Exhibited: World Tour 1958, Royal Academy 1959, New York World's Fair 1965, Collections: Mr Randolph S. Churchill, Mrs Natalie Barclay (formerly Mrs Bevan), Sold Christie's 23rd November 2001, £42,000. Richard Green, Private collection, Scotland, Gift of the artist. Given to Mrs Bevan by Randolph Churchill in 1966.

C 151 (Fig. 24) Lullenden Manor, 1917, 30 x 25 in. Unsigned, Exhibited: Wylma Wayne Fine Art, London, 1982, National Academy of Design, New York 1983, Smithsonian Institution, Washington, DC 1983, Gump's, San Francisco and Beverley Hills 1985, Collections: The Studio, Chartwell, Sarah Lady Audley, Russell Reynolds Associates, Incorrectly dated in my original catalogue.

C 152 (Fig. 355) Lady Castlerosse, c. 1930, 24 x 20 in. 61.3 x 51.2 cm, Unsigned, Collections: The Studio, Chartwell, The National Trust, Chartwell

C 153 (Fig. 23) Green Trees and Poppies at Lullenden, c. 1917, 29 x 24 in. Initialled, Illustrated: Winston Churchill: His Life as a Painter by Mary Soames, 1990, Exhibited: Sotheby's 1998, Collections: The Studio, Chartwell, Sir John Colville - for High Museum of Art, Atlanta, Georgia, Lady Margaret Colville, Incorrectly dated in my original catalogue.

C 154 (Fig. 252) Magnolia, c. 1930, 20 x 16 in. Initialled right, Exhibited: New York World's Fair 1965, Collections: Sarah Lady Audley, The National Trust, Chartwell

C 155 (Fig. 226) Painting Lesson from Mr Sickert, c. 1928, 20 x 14 in.Unsigned, Inscribed with the title on the back, Illustrated: Winston Churchill: His Life as a Painter by Mary Soames, 1990, Collections: The Studio, Chartwell, The National Trust, Chartwell, This painting is based on a newspaper cutting in the archives at Chartwell.

C 156 (Fig. 230) Snow under Arch, or The Messenger, c. 1935, 24 x 20 in. Initialled right, Illustrated: Winston Churchill: His Life as a Painter by Mary Soames, 1990, Exhibited: Sotheby's 1998, Collections: Lady Spencer-Churchill, Sarah Lady Audley, The Lady Soames DBE, Probably based on a photograph - as yet undiscovered.

C 157 (Fig. 100) The Dining Room at Chartwell with Miss Diana Churchill, 1933, 21 3/4 x 25 3/4 in. 55 x 65 cm, Unsigned Collections: The Studio, Chartwell, The National Trust, Chartwell, The back of the canvas is marked 'Blanchet Paris'.

C 158 (Fig. 350) Viscountess Castlerosse Relaxing on a Terrace, c. 1935, 14 x 20 in. Unsigned, Exhibited: Wylma Wayne Fine Art, London 1982, Gump's, San Francisco 1985, Sotheby's 1998, Collections: Doris Lady Castlerosse, Mr Dudley Delevingne, Marquess of Bath, Based on a photograph in the archives at Chartwell - which shows Churchill standing at the foot of the divan. Dudley Delevingne was Doris Lady Castlerosse's brother; he inherited the painting on her death in 1942 and sold it to Lord Bath in 1962.

C 159 (Fig. 223) The Line Out, c. 1928, 20 x 16 in. 51 x 40.9 cm, Unsigned, Exhibited: Sotheby's 1998, Collections: The Studio, Chartwell, The National Trust, Chartwell, Based on a newspaper cutting in the archives at Chartwell. The caption reads: 'The Waratahs jumping for the ball in their Rugby match against the South of France, at Toulouse. The Waratahs won by eleven points to three.'

C 160 (Fig. 224) The Circus, 1928, 26 x 30 in. Initialled, Exhibited: New York World's Fair 1965, Collections: Hon. Lewis Douglas, Mrs Lewis Douglas, Present owner unknown, Based on a newspaper cutting in the archives at Chartwell. Cf. C 161. The painting was incorrectly dated in my original catalogue.

C 161 (Fig. 225) Performing Elephants in the Circus Ring, 1928, 25 x 30 in. 63 x 75 cm, Unsigned, Collections: The Studio, Chartwell, Private collection, Incorrectly dated in my original catalogue. This painting is based on a newspaper cutting in the archives at Chartwell. The caption reads: 'The Circus at Olympia - The performing elephants giving one of their amusing displays in Mr Bertram W. Mills' Circus at Olympia yesterday. The Circus continues until January 24, 1928.' Cf. C 160.

C 162 (Fig. 172) After Daubigny, c. 1915, 20 x 30 in. Unsigned, Broad Street Art Galleries, St Helier, Jersey 1953, New York World's Fair 1965, Collection: Mr Charles Clore, Sold Sotheby's 13th November 1985, £5,000, Present owner unknown, Based on a painting by Daubigny. Cf. C 164 and C 165.

C 163 (Fig. 174) Copy of the Picture by John Lewis Brown Hanging in the Study at Chartwell, c. 1930, 36 x 25 in. 92 x 64 cm, Initialled right, Exhibited: Churchill Centenary Trust 1974, Collections: The Studio, Chartwell, Mr and Mrs Anthony Montague Browne, Private collection, Gift of Lady Churchill.

C 164 (Fig. 173) After Daubigny, c. 1915, 20 x 30 in. Inscribed: 'After Daubigny by W S C', Collection: Earl of Birkenhead, Private English collection,Gift of the artist. Based on a picture by the French landscape painter Charles Daubigny (1817-78) entitled 'The Ferry' acquired at Christie's for £4,515 by the Duke of Marlborough in 1910 and sold by him in 1924 at Christie's for £1,900. Information from Sir Jack Baer. Cf. C 162 and C 165.

C 165 (Fig. 171) After Daubigny, c. 1915, 14 x 22 in. Unsigned, Collections: Mr Giles Romilly, Present owner unknown, Gift of the artist. Based on a painting by Daubigny owned by the Duke of Marlborough. Cf. C 162 and C 164.

C 166 (Fig. 251) Studio Still Life, c. 1930, Canvas board 14 x 20 in. Unsigned, Exhibited: Royal Academy 1959, Collections: Lady Spencer-Churchill, The National Trust, Chartwell

C 167 (Fig. 257) Fruit and Reflections, 1930s, 16 x 22 in. 40.5 x 56 cm, Initialled left, Collections: Earl de la Warr, Sold Christie's 23rd June 1994, £17,000, Present owner unknown

C 168 (Fig. 258) A Loaf of Bread, c. 1930, 14 x 21 in. Unsigned, Illustrated: Winston Churchill: His Life as a Painter by Mary Soames, 1990, Exhibited: Sotheby's 1998, Collections: Mr Randolph S. Churchill, Mr Winston S. Churchill

C 169 (Fig. 255) Still Life, Fruit, 1930s, 25 x 30 in. estimated, initialled, Collections: Mrs Diana Sandys, Mr Julian Sandys, Private English collection, Based on a photograph in the archives at Chartwell.

C 170 (Fig. 256) Flowers in a White Bowl, c. 1930, 20 x 24 in. 51 x 61 cm, Unsigned, Collections: The Studio, Chartwell, The National Trust, Chartwell

C 171 (Fig. 260) Flowers in a Blue Vase, c. 1935, 20 x 24 in. Unsigned, Collections: The Studio, Chartwell, Sarah Lady Audley, Mr Richard M. Edelman

C 172 (Fig. 250) Nasturtiums in a Silver Presentation Bowl, c. 1935, 18 x 24 in. 46 x 62 cm, Unsigned, Collections: Lady Spencer-Churchill, The National Trust, Chartwell

C 173 (Fig. 263) Still Life, Silver, 1930s, 14 x 19 1/2 in. 35 x 50 cm, Initialled left, Illustrated: Winston Churchill: His Life as a Painter by Mary Soames, 1990, Exhibited: Sotheby's 1998, Collections: Earl of Avon, Countess of Avon, Gift of the artist to Sir Anthony Eden, the Earl of Avon.

C 174 (Fig. 262) Silver Life, 1930s, Canvas board 14 x 20 in. 50.5 x 35.5 cm, Unsigned, Collections: The Studio, Chartwell, Arabella Churchill, On loan to the National Trust, Chartwell

C 175 (Fig. 265) Silver Life, January 1937, Canvas board 14 x 20 in. Unsigned, Exhibited: Wylma Wayne Gallery, London 1982, Collections: The Studio, Chartwell, The Lady Soames DBE, This painting is mentioned in a letter from Clementine Churchill to Winston. Information from Lady Soames.

C 176 (Fig. 266) Jug and Bottles, 1930s, 20 x 14 in. Initialled, Exhibited: New York World's Fair 1965, Collections: Hon. and Mrs Averell Harriman, Mrs Pamela Harriman, Sold Sotheby's, New York, May 1997 $184,000, Present owner unknown, Gift of the artist to Mr and Mrs Harriman.

C 177 (Fig. 268) Bottlescape, 1926, 28 x 36 in. Initialled left, Exhibited: World Tour 1958, Royal Academy 1959, Collections: Lady Spencer-Churchill, The National Trust, Chartwell, Dated precisely to 1926 by Mr Peregrine Churchill, who says in a letter to Mrs Minnie Churchill: 'I was there'.

C 178 (Fig. 267) Mallows, 1930s, 24 x 20 in. Initialled left, Illustrated: Painting as a Pastime by Winston S. Churchill, 1948, Winston Churchill: His Life as a Painter by Mary Soames, 1990, Exhibited: World Tour 1958, Royal Academy 1959, Collections: Lady Spencer-Churchill, Charlotte Peel

C 179 (Fig. 168) Two Glasses on a Verandah (after Sargent), 1930s, 17 1/2 x 14 1/2 in. 45.5 x 39.5 cm, Unsigned, Illustrated: Winston Churchill: His Life as a Painter by Mary Soames, 1990, Exhibited: Sotheby's 1998, Collections: Lady Spencer-Churchill, The National Trust, Chartwell

C 180 (Fig. 259) Daffodils and Tulips, 1930s, 27 x 20 in. Unsigned, Collections: The Studio, Chartwell, Miss Arabella Churchill, Sold Sotheby's, New York 18th December 1981, $6,000, Present owner unknown

C 181 (Fig. 246) Study of Roses, 1930s, 24 1/2 x 19 in. Initialled left, Collections: Vivien Lady Olivier, Private collection, Gift of the artist to Vivien Leigh, Lady Olivier.

C 182 (Fig. 261) Magnolia, 1930s, 20 x 16 in. Initialled, Collections: Mr Randolph S. Churchill, Mr Winston S. Churchill, Mrs Minnie S. Churchill

C 183 (Fig. 264) Magnolia, 1930s, 27 x 20 in. Initialled left, Illustrated: 'An Eightieth Year Tribute to Winston Churchill', edited by Bruce Ingram, The Illustrated London News, 1954, Winston Churchill: His Life as a Painter by Mary Soames, 1990, Exhibited: Royal Academy 1951, World Tour 1958, Royal Academy 1959, M. Knoedler, London 1974, Wylma Wayne Fine Art, London 1982, New York and Washington 1983, Japan Exhibition 1998, Sotheby's 1998, Collection: The Lady Soames DBE, Gift of the artist.

C 184 (Fig. 102) A Corner of the Drawing-room at Chartwell, c. 1938, 20 x 24 in. Unsigned, Exhibited: Wylma Wayne Gallery, London 1982, Collections: The Studio, Chartwell, The Lady Soames DBE

C 185 (Fig. 203) Wilton, The Long Gallery, c. 1930, 24 x 20 in. Initialled left, Collections: The Studio, Chartwell, The National Trust, Chartwell

C 186 (Fig. 61) A Room at Breccles, Norfolk. Whitsuntide, 1920, 25 x 23 1/2 in. 63.5 x 60 cm, Initialled right, Illustrated: 'Painting as a Pastime', by Winston S. Churchill, Part 1, The Strand Magazine, December 1921, 'Winston Churchill's Pictures', The Strand Magazine, July 1946, Collections: Lady Spencer-Churchill, The Lady Soames DBE, On loan to the National Trust, Chartwell, The correct title and date are given in The Strand Magazine 1921; the painting has been folded back since it was illustrated there, with the result that the fireplace and another easy chair are now lost to view.

C 187 (Fig. 109) Interior at Breccles, 1920s, 24 x 20 in. 61.5 x 50.9 cm, Unsigned, Collections: The Studio, Chartwell, Sarah Lady Audley, The National Trust, Chartwell

C 188 (Fig. 130) The Cloisters, 1930s, 20 x 24 in. Unsigned, Collections: The Studio, Chartwell, Sarah Lady Audley, Present owner unknown

C 189 (Fig. 52) The Dining-room of Sir Philip Sassoon's House at Lympne, c. 1921, 24 x 20 in. 61 x 51 cm, Initialled left, Illustrated: 'Painting as a Pastime', by Winston S. Churchill, The Strand Magazine, December 1921, Collections: The Studio, Chartwell, The National Trust, Chartwell, There is a sketch of a woman on the back of the canvas.

C 190 (Fig. 181) Lake Maggiore, c. 1945, 22 x 28 in. 56 x 70 cm, Unsigned, Illustrated: 'The Paintings of Winston Churchill', LIFE, January 7th 1946, Collections: The Studio, Chartwell, Sarah Lady Audley, The National Trust, Chartwell, Correct title and date noted in LIFE, 1946. Painting currently without a stretcher.

C 191 (Fig. 182) In the Dolomites, c. 1935, Canvas board 14 x 20 in. 35.2 x 50.7 cm, Initialled left, Collections: The Studio, Chartwell, The National Trust, Chartwell

C 192 (Fig. 117) Loch Scene on the Duke of Sutherland's Estate, c. 1930, 22 x 28 in. Unsigned, Collections: The Studio, Chartwell, The Lady Soames DBE, Hon. Nicholas Soames MP

C 193 (Fig. 121) View at Lochmore, c. 1935, 20 x 24 in. 49 x 59.5 cm, Unsigned, Collections: The Studio, Chartwell, Anne Duchess of Westminster, Gift of Lady Spencer-Churchill in 1966.

C 194 (Fig. 120) A Loch on the Duke of Sutherland's Estate, c. 1935, 20 x 24 in. 50 x 60 cm, Unsigned, Collections: The Studio, Chartwell, The Lady Soames DBE

C 195 (Fig. 119) Mountain near Lochmore, c. 1935, 30 x 25 in. Initialled, Collections: The Studio, Chartwell, The Lady Soames DBEI

C 196 (Fig. 337) The Valley of the Ourika, c. 1935, 26 x 32 in. Unsigned, Collections: Lady Spencer-Churchill, The National Trust, Chartwell

C 197 (Fig. 347) Scene in Morocco, 1930s, 14 x 20 in. Initialled, Collections: Hon. Mrs Sylvia Henley, Wells Collection, Gift to Mrs Henley from Lady Spencer-Churchill. This is the Ourika Valley with the Atlas Mountains in the background, according to the present owner.

C 198 (Fig. 183) View in the Italian Alps, c. 1934, 25 x 30 in. 64 76 cm, Initialled left, Collections: The Studio, Chartwell, Mr Randolph S. Churchill, Mr Winston S. Churchill

C 199 (Fig. 269) Coast Scene on the Riviera, c. 1930, 20 x 24 in. Unsigned, Collections: The Studio, Chartwell, Mr Julian Sandys, Private English Collection

C 200 (Fig. 180) View in the Italian Alps, c. 1934, 20 x 24 in. Initialled, Collections: Lady Spencer-Churchill, Sarah Lady Audley, Mr Fernandez Ruiz

C 201 (Fig. 273) Coast Scene on the Riviera, 1930s, 25 x 30 in. Unsigned, Collections: The Studio, Chartwell, Private English Collection, Wedding present from Lady Spencer-Churchill. Retitled here because this painting shows a similar view to C 199 'Coast Scene on the Riviera'.

C 202 (Fig. 446) La Montagne, St Victoire, 1948, 25 x 30 in. 61 x 75 cm, Initialled right, Illustrated: 'An Eightieth Year Tribute to Winston Churchill', edited by Bruce Ingram, The Illustrated London News, 1954, Exhibited: Royal Academy 1950, Collections: The Studio, Chartwell, Celia Sandys, Asprey and Garrard, Based on two photographs in the archives at Chartwell. Re-dated to the year of Churchill's post-war visit to the area.

C 203 (Fig. 90) View of Eze, Alpes-Maritimes, c. 1930, 26 x 32 in. Unsigned, Collections: The Studio, Chartwell, Arabella Churchill, Present owner unknown

C 204 (Fig. 91) View of Eze, c. 1930, 30 x 25 in. Unsigned, Collections: The Studio, Chartwell, Private collection, Lake Forest, Illinois, USA

C 205 (Fig. 292) View of Carcassonne, 1930s, 20 x 24 in. Initialled, Collections: The Studio, Chartwell, Sarah Lady Audley, Sir Sidney and Lady Lipworth, Formerly entitled 'Loire Chateau' but Carcassonne is the likely subject.

C 206 (Fig. 293) Battlements at Carcassonne, 1930s, 10 1/2 x 8 3/4 in. Unsigned, Collection: The Lady Soames DBE, Gift of the artist to his daughter Mary. 'The first picture papa gave me, when I was a child.' – Inscribed on back.

C 207 (Fig. 123) View near Vence, Alpes-Maritimes, c. 1935, 20 x 24 in. Unsigned, Collections: The Studio, Chartwell, Sarah Lady Audley, Present owner unknown

C 208 (Fig. 294) Carcassonne, Southern France, c. 1930, 20 x 24 in.Unsigned, Exhibited: Wylma Wayne Fine Art, London 1982, Collections: The Studio, Chartwell, The Lady Soames DBE

C 209 (Fig. 92) Distant View of Eze, c. 1930, 20 x 30 in.Unsigned, Collections: The Studio, Chartwell, Mr Julian Sandys, Private English Collection

C 210 (Fig. 452) Château de Lour Mairin, Près Aix en Provence, 1948, 28 x 36 in. 71 x 92 cm, Collections: Lady Spencer-Churchill, The National Trust, Chartwell, This picture was not painted in the 1930s but in 1948; the subject has also been identified since my original catalogue.

C 211 (Fig. 341) Sunset over the Atlas Mountains, c. 1935, 20 x 24 in. Unsigned, Collections: The Studio, Chartwell, Sarah Lady Audley, Present owner unknown

C 212 (Fig. 325) Ramparts of Rhodes, 1930s, 14 x 20 in. Unsigned, Illustrated: Winston Churchill: His Life as a Painter by Mary Soames, 1990, Collection: Mr Winston S. Churchill, Gift of the artist

C 213 (Fig. 339) Scene at Marrakech, c. 1935, 23 1/4 x 36 in. 56 x 92 cm, Initialled left, Collections: Field Marshal Viscount Montgomery, Viscount Montgomery, Gift of the artist.

C 214 (Fig. 340) Marrakech, 1935-6, 25 x 30 1/8 in. 63.5 x 76.5 cm, Initialled left, Collections: Earl Lloyd George, Countess Lloyd George, The Beaverbrook Canadian Foundation, Beaverbrook Art Gallery, Fredericton, New Brunswick, Gift of the artist to David, Earl Lloyd George, 1936.

C 215 (Fig. 295) View of Carcassonne, Southern France, c. 1930
25 x 30 in. 63.6 x 76.4 cm, Initialled left, Collections: The Studio, Chartwell, The National Trust, Chartwell

C 216 (Fig. 324) The Battlements at Rhodes, 1930-38, 24 7/8 x 30 in. 63 x 76 cm, Unsigned, Collections: Mr Randolph S. Churchill, Arabella Churchill, Sold Sotheby's 21st June 1995, £30,000, The National Trust, Chartwell

C 217 (Fig. 338) Marrakech, c. 1935, Canvas board 20 x 14 in. Unsigned, Illustrated: Winston Churchill: His Life as a Painter by Mary Soames, 1990, Exhibited: Sotheby's 1998, Collections: The Studio, Chartwell,The Lady Soames DBE

C 218 (Fig. 345) Marrakech, c. 1935, 18 x 24 in. 46 x 61 cm, Unsigned, Collections: The Studio, Chartwell, Sarah Lady Audley, The National Trust, Chartwell

C 219 (Fig. 344) Marrakech, c. 1935, 16 1/2 x 18 in. 42 x 45.5 cm, Collections: The Studio, Chartwell, Arabella Churchill, The National Trust, Chartwell, Picture has been cut down and turned once.

C 220 (Fig. 346) Marrakech, c. 1935, 21 1/2 x 26 1/2 in. Initialled, Collections: Miss Elizabeth Navarro, Present owner unknown.

C 221 (Fig. 159) The Garden Entrance at Lympne, c. 1930, (size unknown), Collections: The Studio, Chartwell, Private English Collection

C 222 (Fig. 57) The Terrace at Lympne, c. 1921, 25 x 30 in. Initialled, Illustrated: 'Painting as a Pastime', by Winston S. Churchill, The Strand Magazine, January 1922, Collections: The Studio, Chartwell, The Lady Soames DBE

C 223 (Fig. 212) Porch at Cranborne, c. 1935, Canvas board 20 x 14 in. 50.5 x 35.5 cm, Initialled right, Collections: The Studio, Chartwell, The National Trust, Chartwell

C 224 (Fig. 348) The Gate at Marrakech, c. 1935, 19 1/2 x 21 1/4 in. 50.8 x 61 cm, Initialled, Exhibited: New York World's Fair 1965, The Dallas Museum of Art 1986, Gerald R. Ford Museum 1992, Franklin D. Roosevelt Library 1992, Ronald Reagan Library 1992/3, Dwight D. Eisenhower Library 1995, Collections: Sold anonymously Parke-Bernet, New York 8th September 1965, $13,000. Hallmark Fine Art Collection, Kansas City, Missouri

C 225 (Fig. 151) The House at Lympne, c. 1932, 20 x 30 in. 51 x 77 cm, Unsigned, Collections: The Studio, Chartwell, Mr Winston S. Churchill

C 226 (Fig. 208) North Porch at the Manor House, Cranborne, 1930s, 24 x 20 in. 59 x 49.5 cm, Initialled left Illustrated: Winston Churchill: His Life as a Painter by Mary Soames, 1990, Exhibited: Sotheby's 1996, Sotheby's 1998, Collections: Marquess of Salisbury, Private collection, Gift of the artist.

C 227 (Fig. 242) An English Garden in Summer with Lady Eleanor Smith, c. 1930, 24 x 20 in. Unsigned, Collections: The Studio, Chartwell, Sarah Lady Audley, Present owner unknown, Lady Eleanor Smith was the daughter of Churchill's friend F. E. Smith, later Lord Birkenhead.

C 228 (Fig. 127) Shadows on the Wall of a Village in the South of France, c. 1930, 24 x 20 in. Unsigned, Collections: The Studio, Chartwell, Sarah Lady Audley, Private collection, Lake Forest, Illinois, USA

C 229 (Fig. 374) Farm at the.Head of Lake Como, 1945, 20 x 24 in. Unsigned, Illustrated: 'The Paintings of Winston Churchill', LIFE, January 7th 1946, 'Winston Churchill's Pictures', The Strand Magazine, July 1946, Collections: The Studio, Chartwell, Sarah Lady Audley, Sold Christie's 4th March 1983, £6,500, Present owner unknown, Inscribed on the back: 'Painted by my Husband. Clementine S. Churchill.' This painting has been re-dated to 1945, the year of Churchill's post-war visit to Lake Como.

C 230 (Fig. 362) Château St-Georges-Motel, 1930s, 18 x 22 in. Unsigned, Illustrated: Winston Churchill: His Life as a Painter by Mary Soames, 1990, Collections: The Studio, Chartwell, Private Engish Collection

C 231 (Fig. 365) The Mill at La Colle, with Sarah and Randolph Churchill, 1936-39, 29 3/4 x 24 1/2 in. Initialled, Collections: Miss Maxine Elliott, Lady Forbes-Robertson, Mrs E. Rivers-Bulkeley, Sold Sotheby's 15th December 1965, £5000, Present owner unknown

C 232 (Fig. 368) Château St-Georges-Motel, c. 1935, 20 x 24 in. Initialled, Illustrated: Winston Churchill: His Life as a Painter by Mary Soames, 1990 Exhibited: M. Knoedler, London 1974, Collection: The Lady Soames DBE, Gift of the artist. Based on a photograph in the archives at Chartwell.

C 233 (Fig. 367) The Mill at St-Georges-Motel, 1930s, 20 x 24 in. 51x 61 cm, Unsigned, Collections: The Studio, Chartwell, Arabella Churchill, On loan to the National Trust, Chartwell,

C 234 (Fig. 363) The Mill at St-Georges-Motel, c. 1930, 24 x 32 in. estimated, Initialled, Illustrated: Painting as a Pastime by Winston S. Churchill, 1948, Collections: Mrs Diana Sandys, Mr Julian Sandys, Private English Collection

C 235 (Fig. 59) Ightham Mote, 1920, 19 1/2 x 23 1/4 in. Initialled, Illustrated: 'Painting as a Pastime', by Winston S. Churchill, Part 2, The Strand Magazine, January 1922, Collections: Lady Hamilton, General Sir Ian Hamilton, Mr Ian Hamilton, Sold Sotheby's April 1966, Mr Charles Henry Robinson, The National Trust, Ightham Mote, Bought from the artist by Jean Hamilton, wife of his friend Sir Ian, in 1921 for £50.

C 236 (Fig. 126) An Open Staircase in the South of France, c. 1935, 16 x 20 in. 40 x 51 cm Unsigned, Collections: The Studio, Chartwell, Arabella Churchill, On loan to the National Trust, Chartwell

C 237 (Fig. 67) The Ruins at Pompeii, c. 1921, 25 x 30 in. 63.5 x 76 cm, Unsigned, Illustrated: 'Painting as a Pastime', by Winston S. Churchill, The Strand Magazine, January 1922, Collections: The Studio, Chartwell, Sarah Lady Audley, The National Trust, Chartwell

C 238 (Fig. 309) St Jean de Vie, 1930s, 20 x 24 in. Initialled, Collections: The Studio, Chartwell, Present owner unknown, A pencil sketch on the back was noted in my original catalogue.

C 239 (Fig. 34) A Ruined Basilica, 1930s, Canvas board 20 x 14 in. Unsigned, Collections: The Studio, Chartwell, Sarah Lady Audley, The National Trust, Chartwell

C 240 (Fig. 306) A Church [probably in the South of France], c. 1935, 22 x 18 in. Unsigned, Collections: The Studio, Chartwell, Sarah Lady Audley, Private English Collection

C 241 (Fig. 314) St Jean de Vie, between Cannes and Grasse, 1930s, 20 x 24 in. Initialled right, Exhibited: Wylma Wayne Fine Art, London 1982, Dallas Museum of Art 1986, Collections: The Studio, Chartwell, Sarah Lady Audley, Russell Reynolds Associates

C 242 (Fig. 316) A Church in the South of France, 1930s, 25 1/2 x 20 1/2 in. Unsigned, Collections: Miss Marryott Whyte, Sold Sotheby's, New York 25th June 1976, $10,000, Present owner unknown, Gift of the artist.

C 243 (Fig. 317) Road in the South of France, c. 1930, Board 17 3/4 x 11 1/4 in. 45 x 29 cm, Unsigned, Illustrated: Winston Churchill: His Life as a Painter by Mary Soames, 1990, Collections: The Studio, Chartwell, Lady Soames, Mr Derek Hill, Sold Sotheby's 3rd July 2002, £18,000, Mr Herbert L. Holtz, Given by Lady Soames to the artist Derek Hill who helped her with her book Winston Churchill: His Life as a Painter.

C 244 (Fig. 311) Notre Dame de Vie above Cannes, 1930s, 20 x 24 in. Initialled, Exhibited: New York World's Fair 1965, M. Knoedler, London 1977, Collections: Mrs Diana Sandys, Mrs Piers Dixon [Celia], Mr F. Bartlett Watt, Mrs Lucienne Watt

C 245 (Fig. 318) The Porch of Notre Dame de Vie, 1930s, 30 x 20 in. 76 x 51 cm, Unsigned, Collections: The Studio, Chartwell, Miss Arabella Churchill, Sold Sotheby's 5th December 2001, £29,000, Present owner unknown

C 246 (Fig. 89) The Gardener's Cottage at Mme Balsan's House in the South of France, 1930s 21 x 25 in. 60 x 50 cm, Unsigned, Exhibited: M. Knoedler, London 1974, Wylma Wayne Fine Art, London 1982 Collections: Miss Madeleine Whyte, The Lady Soames DBE, Label on back: 'Given to me by Winston Spencer Churchill. Early study of building in Mme Balsan's garden in France.'

C 247 (Fig. 124) Pont du Gard, Nîmes, c. 1930, 30 x 25 in. Initialled, Collections: The Studio, Chartwell, Arabella Churchill, Sold Sotheby's, New York 18th December 1981, $10,000, Present owner unknown

C 248 (Fig. 448) Calanques, near Marseilles, 1948, 23 1/2 x 30 in. 60.3 x 76.8 cm, Unsigned, Collections: Lady Spencer-Churchill, Arabella Churchill, The National Trust, Chartwell

C 249 (Fig. 364), A Village Fete, St-Georges-Motel, c. 1930, 20 x 24 in. Initialled, Collections: Lady Spencer-Churchill, Sarah Lady Audley, Sold Sotheby's, New York 15th May 1985, $26,400, Present owner unknown

C 250 (Fig. 300) On the Rhine, c. 1930, Canvas board 14 x 20 in. Unsigned, Collections: The Studio, Chartwell, Arabella Churchill, Present owner unknown

C 251 (Fig. 160) Formal Garden and Pavilion at Lympne, c. 1930, Canvas board 20 x 14 in. 50.5 x 35.5 cm Unsigned, Collections: The Studio, Chartwell, Arabella Churchill, On loan to the National Trust, Chartwell

C 252 (Fig. 235) A Field of Tulips, c. 1932, Canvas board 14 x 20 in. 35.1 x 50.5 cm, Initialled right, Collections: The Studio, Chartwell, The National Trust, Chartwell

C 253 (Fig. 186) Italian Garden Scene, c. 1930, 27 x 23 in. 69 x 56 cm, Unsigned, Collections: The Studio, Chartwell, Arabella Churchill, On loan to the National Trust, Chartwell, Originally entitled 'Eastern Garden Scene' but Lady Soames suggests that it is more likely to be an Italian scene.

C 254 (Fig. 142) Colonnaded and Paved Walk at Hever, c. 1930, 24 x 20 in. 61 x 51 cm, Initialled right, Collections: The Studio, Chartwell, The Lady Soames DBE

C 255 (Fig. 27) Italian Garden at Sutton Place, 1930s, 20 x 24 in. Unsigned, Illustrated: Winston Churchill: His Life as a Painter by Mary Soames, 1990, Exhibited: M. Knoedler, London 1974, Sotheby's 1998, Collection: The Lady Soames DBE, Gift of the artist. Formerly entitled 'At Eaton Hall, Chester' the subject was correctly identified by Sir Roy Strong [?].

C 256 (Fig. 145) In the Italian Garden at Hever, c. 1930, 24 x 20 in. 62 x 51 cm, Initialled, Exhibited: Sotheby's 1998, Collections: Lady Spencer-Churchill, The National Trust, Chartwell

C 257 (Fig. 146) Summer House at Trent Park, c. 1930, 25 x 30 in. Initialled, Collections: The Studio, Chartwell, Miss Celia Sandys, Asprey and Garrard, His Royal Highness The Prince of Wales, Presented by Asprey and Garrard to the Prince of Wales on the occasion of his 50th birthday November 1998

C 258 (Fig. 143) The Colonnaded Terrace at Hever, c. 1930, 25 x 30 in. 63.6 x 76.4 cm, Unsigned, Collections: The Studio, Chartwell, The Lady Soames DBEI

C 259 (Fig. 144) View through an Arch at Hever, c. 1930, 24 x 20 in. Unsigned, Collections: The Studio, Chartwell, Arabella Churchill

C 260 (Fig. 110) Trees in the Eastern Counties, near Breccles, c. 1936, 25 x 30 in. Unsigned, Exhibited: Royal Academy 1959, Collections: Lady Spencer-Churchill, Anonymous owner, Sold Christie's 22nd November 2002, £53,000, Present owner unknown, Inscribed on the back: 'Painted by my husband. Clementine S. Churchill.'

C 261 (Fig. 20) At Lullenden, c. 1920, 30 x 20 in. Unsigned, Collections: The Studio, Chartwell, The National Trust, Chartwell, Previously entitled 'English Garden Scene'; the subject and date were identified by Mr Peregrine S. Churchill.

C 262 (Fig. 184) Fountain in a Garden near Florence, c. 1930, 20 x 26 in. 50 x 65 cm, Unsigned, Collections: The Studio, Chartwell, The Lady Soames DBE, Formerly thought to be a scene at Hever Castle, the most likely subject, identified by Mrs Annabel Elliot, is Mrs Keppel's Villa d'Ombrellino, near Florence, Italy.

C 263 (Fig. 185) Terrace at the Villa d'Ombrellino near Florence, c. 1930, 20 x 24 in. Unsigned, Collections: The Studio, Chartwell, Sarah Lady Audley, Present owner unknown, Inscribed in pencil on the back: 'Painted by my husband. Clementine S. Churchill'. Scene identified as Mrs Keppel's villa by Mrs Annabel Elliot.

C 264 (Fig. 189) Riviera Scene, 1930s, 17 1/2 x 25 1/2 in. Initialled and titled on the back, Exhibited: New York World's Fair 1965, Collections: Mr G. Huntington Hartford, Sold Sotheby's, London 20th April 1966, Sold Sotheby's, New York 3rd May 1973, $17,000, Sold Christie's, London 17th June 1977, £11,000, Present owner unknown

C 265 (Fig. 187) Garden on the Riviera, c. 1935, 25 x 30 in. 63.5 x 76 cm, Unsigned, Collections: The Studio, Chartwell, The Lady Soames DBE, Inscribed on the back: 'Painted by my husband. Clementine S. Churchill.'

C 266 (Fig. 108) Lakeland Landscape near Breccles, 1930s, 24 x 20 in. 60 x 50 cm, Initialled left, Collections: Lady Spencer-Churchill, Mr Jeremy Soames

C 267 (Fig. 358) La Dragonnière, Cap Martin, 1930s, 24 x 29 1/2 in. Signed, Collections: Lady Spencer-Churchill, Sold Sotheby's Charity Auction, London 26th April 1961, Mrs A. M. Oppenheim, Sold Sotheby's 20th April 1966, £2000, Present owner unknown

C 268 (Fig. 359) Olive Trees, Cap Martin, c. 1934, 25 x 30 in. 61 x 75 cm, Initialled left, Illustrated: Winston Churchill: His Life as a Painter by Mary Soames, 1990, Exhibited: World Tour 1958, Royal Academy 1959 Collection: The Lady Soames DBE

C 269 (Fig. 87) Blenheim Palace through the Branches of a Cedar, 1920s, 24 x 20 in. 60 x 50 cm, Initialled right, Exhibited: Arthur Ackerman, London 2000, Collections: The Studio, Chartwell,The Lady Soames DBE This view of the West Front of Blenheim Palace must have been painted in the early 1920s before the building of the water terrace.

C 270 (Fig. 272) Villa on Cap Martin, 1930s, 24 x 20 in. Initialled, Collections: Lady Spencer-Churchill, Mrs Hill, Sold Christie's 9th June 1978, £8,000, Sold Christie's 12th November 1987, £20,000, Mr John C. Turner

C 271 (Fig. 360) The Sunken Garden of La Dragonnière, Cap Martin, 1930s, 20 x 30 in.Initialled, Collections: The Studio, Chartwell, Mr Julian Sandys, Private English Collection

C 272 (Fig. 361) Olive Grove, La Dragonnière, c. 1934, 21 3/4 x 27 1/2 in. Initialled right, Illustrated: 'The Paintings of Winston Churchill', LIFE, January 7th 1946, Painting as a Pastime, by Winston S. Churchill, 1948, Collection: Mr Winston S. Churchill, Gift of the artist.

C 273 (Fig. 343) A North African Town, 1930s, 25 x 30 in. Initialled, Collections: The Studio, Chartwell, Mr Julian Sandys, Private English Collection

C 274 (Fig. 147) Avenue, Trent Park, c. 1930, 20 x 24 in. Initialled, Exhibited: World Tour 1958, Royal Academy 1959, Collections: Lady Spencer-Churchill, Mr Nicholas Soames, Sold Christie's 17th June 1977, £8,000, Sold Christie's 12th November 1987, £16,000, Mr John C. Turner

C 275 (Fig. 150) The Pergola at Trent Park, c. 1930, 25 x 30 in. 61 x 75 cm, Unsigned, Collections: The Studio, Chartwell, Mr Winston S. Churchill, Private collection

C 276 (Fig. 77) An Avenue at Frinton-on-Sea, Essex, with Miss Diana Churchill, c. 1922, 20 x 24 in. Initialled, Collections: The Studio, Chartwell, Miss Edwina Sandys, Private English Collection

C 277 (Fig. 153) Terrace at Trent Park, c. 1935, 24 x 20 in. Initialled, Collections: The Studio, Chartwell, Miss Edwina Sandys, Mr Richard J. Mahoney

C 278 (Fig. 56) A Villa at the Riviera, c. 1920, 24 x 29 in. 59.5 x 72.5 cm, Unsigned, Illustrated: 'Painting as a Pastime', by Winston Churchill, Part 1, The Strand Magazine, December 1921, Collections: The Studio, Chartwell, The Lady Soames DBE Previously wrongly titled and dated 'Pergola Overlooking a Lake' c.1930.

C 279 (Fig. 190) View of Monte Carlo and Monaco, c. 1930, 25 x 30 in. 64 x 76.5 cm, Initialled right, Collections: The Studio, Chartwell, The National Trust, Chartwell

C 280 (Fig. 188) View of Monte Carlo, c. 1935, 20 x 30 in. 51 x 61 cm, Unsigned, Collections: The Studio, Chartwell, The Lady Soames DBE

C 281 (Fig. 191) Monte Carlo and Monaco, c. 1930, 20 x 30 in. Unsigned, Collections: The Studio, Chartwell, Miss Arabella Churchill, Sold Sotheby's, New York, 21st May 1981, $20,000, Present owner unknown

C 282 (Fig. 156) View from the Stone Terrace at Lympne, c. 1932, 25 x 30 in. Unsigned, Collections: The Studio, Chartwell, The National Trust, Chartwell, This painting is shown in a photograph of Churchill sitting at his easel used in the original edition of his book Thoughts and Adventures, 1932.

C 283 (Fig. 125) Valley in the South of France, c. 1935, 25 x 30 in. 63 x 76 cm, Unsigned, Collections: The Studio, Chartwell, The National Trust, Chartwell

C 284 (Fig. 105) The Weald of Kent under Snow. Painted from Chartwell, c. 1935, 20 x 24 in. Unsigned, Illustrated: 'The Paintings of Winston Churchill', LIFE, January 7th 1946, Painting as a Pastime, by Winston S. Churchill, 1948, Exhibited: M. Knoedler, London 1974, Sotheby's 1998, Collection: The Lady Soame DBEs, Gift of the artist. The back of the canvas bears the title 'Chartwell under Snow, Kent' and an inscription in Clementine Churchill's handwriting: 'Given to Mary Churchill 1937'.

C 285 (Fig. 237) An English Valley, c. 193520 x 24 in. Unsigned, Exhibited: Wylma Wayne Fine Art, London 1982, Collections: The Studio, Chartwell, The Lady Soames DBE

C 286 (Fig. 103) View of Chartwell, c. 1938, 24 x 36 in. Unsigned, Collections: The Studio, Chartwell, The National Trust, Chartwell, Inscribed on the back: 'Painted by my husband. Clementine S. Churchill.'

C 287 (Fig. 101) Chartwell in Winter, c. 1935 25 x 30 in. Unsigned, Illustrated: Winston Churchill: His Life as a Painter by Mary Soames, 1990Exhibited: M. Knoedler, London 1974, New York and Washington, 1983, Collection: The Lady Soames DBE, Gift of the artist.

C 288 (Fig. 158) Landscape near Lympne, c. 1930, 24 x 20 in. Unsigned, Collections: The Studio, Chartwell, The National Trust, Chartwell

C 289 (Fig. 163) Coast Scene near Lympne, c. 1930, 24 x 20 in. 61 x 50.5 cm, Unsigned, Collections: The Studio, Chartwell, The Lady Soames DBE

C 290 (Fig. 162) Coast Scene near Lympne, c. 1930, 20 x 24 in. Unsigned, Illustrated: Winston Churchill: His Life as a Painter by Mary Soames, 1990, Collections: The Studio, Chartwell, Arabella S. Churchill, On loan to the National Trust, Chartwell

C 291 (Fig. 276) Coast Scene on the Riviera, c. 1935, 20 x 24 in. 51.5 x 61.5, Initialled right, Collections: The Studio, Chartwell, Mr Winston S. Churchill

C 292 (Fig. 157) Coast Scene near Lympne in Summer, c. 1930, 20 x 24 in. Initialled left, Collections: The Studio, Chartwell, The Lady Soames DBE

C 293 (Fig. 164) South-west View of the Sea from a Cliff Top at Lympne, c. 1935, 24 x 20 in. 61 x 51 cm, Unsigned, Collections: The Studio, Chartwell, The Lady Soames DBEI

C 294 (Fig. 469) Fishing Port of Madeira, c. 1950, 22 1/2 x 27 1/2 in. Unsigned, Collections: Mr Randolph S. Churchill, Mr Winston S. Churchill, Gift of the artist. Incorrectly dated in my original catalogue. Based on a photograph in the archives at Chartwell.

C 295 (Fig. 274) Riviera Coast Scene, c. 1935, 25 x 30 in. Unsigned, Collections: The Studio, Chartwell, Sarah Lady Audley, Private collection, Lake Forest, Illinois, USA

C 296 (Fig. 299) Amsterdam Harbour from Lord Beaverbrook's Yacht, c. 1938, Canvas board 13 1/2 x 19 in. 33 x 48 cm, Initialled right, Collections: Mr Walter Graebner, Sold Christie's 13th May 1966, £6,300, Sold Christie's 8th November 1990, £27,000, Wells Collection

C 297 (Fig. 470) Near Venice, 1951, 24 1/2 x 29 1/2 in. initialled right, Exhibited: Metropolitan Museum of Art, New York 1958, Collection: Mr Arthur Hays Sulzberger, American private collection, Gift of the artist. Based on a photograph in the archives at Chartwell

C 298 (Fig. 278) Study of Boats, c. 1933, 20 x 24 in. Initialled, Illustrated: Winston Churchill: His Life as a Painter by Mary Soames, 1990Exhibited: World Tour 1958, Royal Academy 1959, New York World's Fair 1965, Collections: Lady Spencer-Churchill, The National Trust, Chartwell

C 299 (Fig. 277) Harbour Scene, c. 1935, 20 x 24 in. Initialled, Collections: The Studio, Chartwell, Sir Leslie Rowan, Lady Rowan

C 300 (Fig. 301) Boats in Cannes Harbour, 1937, 24 x 30 in. Initialled, Illustrated: 'The Paintings of Winston Churchill', LIFE, January 7th 1946, 'Winston Churchill's Pictures', The Strand Magazine, August 1946, Exhibited: New York World's Fair 1965, Collections: Mrs Diana Sandys, Miss Edwina Sandys, Winston Churchill Memorial and Library at Westminster, College, Fulton, Based on a photograph in the archives at Chartwell.

C 301 (Fig. 279) Near Antibes, c. 1930, 20 x 24 in. 49 x 59.50 cm, Initialled left, Illustrated: Painting as a Pastime by Winston S. Churchill, 1948, 'An Eightieth Year Tribute to Winston Churchill', edited by Bruce Ingram, The Illustrated London News, 1954, Exhibited: Royal Academy 1953, Collections: Sir Robert Menzies, Parliament House Art Collection, Canberra, Given by the artist in 1955 to Sir Robert Menzies who bequeathed the painting to Parliament House in Canberra, seat of the Government of Australia. The Illustrated London News, 1954, captioned this painting 'Sailing-boats in Harbour at Antibes'.

C 302 (Fig. 298) Canal Scene, c. 1938, 19 7/8 x 24 1/8 in. 50.5 x 61.3 cm, Signed left 'W. Churchill' Exhibited: New York World's Fair 1965, Tucson Art Center 1967, The Dallas Museum of Art 1986, Gerald R. Ford Museum 1991/2, Franklin D. Roosevelt Library 1992, Ronald Reagan Library 1992/3, Dwight D. Eisenhower Library 1995, Collections: Mr Vic Oliver, Mrs Vic Oliver, Sold Parke-Bernet, New York 14th April 1965, $26,000, Hallmark Fine Art Collection, Kansas City, Given by the artist soon after it was painted to Mr Vic Oliver who was married to Miss Sarah Churchill. After his death it was sold by his then wife. This was the first Churchill painting to be auctioned in the USA.

C 303 (Fig. 328) Harbour in the South of France, c. 1930, 18 x 26 in. 61 x 76 cm, Unsigned, Collections: The Studio, Chartwell, Lady Margaret Colville, Gift of Lady Spencer-Churchill after Sir Winston's death.

C 304 (Fig. 304) Boats in Cannes Harbour, c. 1933, 21 x 25 in., Signed, Exhibited: World Tour 1958, Royal Academy 1959, Collections: Lord Shawcross

C 305 (Fig. 303) Sunset, Cannes, c. 1933, 20 x 30 in. 48 x 75 cm, Initialled right, Exhibited: World Tour 1958, Royal Academy 1959, Collections: Lady Spencer-Churchill, Asprey and Garrard

C 306 (Fig. 307) Harbour Scene, Cannes, 1930s, 26 x 30 in. Unsigned, Exhibited: New York World's Fair 1965 Collections: Sarah Lady Audley, Sold Sotheby's, New York 14th May 1970, $40,000, Present owner unknown

C 307 (Fig. 327) Harbour Scene in the South of France, c. 1935, 20 x 24 in. Unsigned, Collections: The Studio, Chartwell, Miss Edwina Sandys, Present owner unknown

C 308 (Fig. 308) Boat in Cannes Harbour, 1930s, 20 x 30 in. (est.), Unsigned?, Collections: Mrs Diana Sandys, Mr Julian Sandys, Private English Collection

C 309 (Fig. 58) The harbour at St. Jean Cap Ferrat, January 1921, 25 x 30 in. 64 x 76.5 cm, Unsigned, Illustrated: 'Painting as a Pastime', by Winston S. Churchill, The Strand Magazine, December 1921, Collections: The Studio, Chartwell, Mr Winston S. Churchilll

C 310 (Fig. 305) Harbour, Cannes, c. 1933, 20 x 24 in. Initialled right, Illustrated: Winston Churchill: His Life as a Painter by Mary Soames, 1990, Exhibited: World Tour 1958, Royal Academy 1959, M. Knoedler, London 1974, Japan Exhibition, 1998, Sotheby's 1998, Collections: Lady Spencer-Churchill, The Lady Soames DBE

C 311 (Fig. 302) Sunset at Cannes Harbour, 1930s, 20 x 24 1/2 in. Unsigned, Collections: Mr Randolph S. Churchill, Mr Winston S. Churchill, Gift of the artist.

C 312 (Fig. 330) St-Jean-Cap-Ferrat, 1930s, 18 x 26 in. Initialled, Exhibited: New York World's Fair 1965, Collections: Sarah Lady Audley, Present owner unknown

C 313 (Fig. 331) St-Jean-Cap-Ferrat, early 1930s, 19 1/2 x 29 1/2 in. Unsigned, Collection: Dr S. Leonard Simpson, Subject wrongly identified as 'Château de l'Horizon, Cap Ferrat' in my original catalogue.

C 314 (Fig. 333) The Club House and Jetty at St-Jean-Cap-Ferrat, c. 1930, 26 x 32 in. 64.75 x 80 cm, Unsigned, Collections: The Studio, Chartwell, The National Trust, Chartwell

C 315 (Fig. 68) The harbour at St-Jean-Cap-Ferrat, January 1921, 26 x 32 in. 65.6 x 81.2 cm, Initialled left, Illustrated: 'Painting as a Pastime', by Winston S. Churchill, The Strand Magazine, December 1921, Collections: The Studio, Chartwell, The National Trust, Chartwell

C 316 (Fig. 231) The Beach at Walmer, c. 1938, 25 x 30 in. Initialled right, Collections: General Lord Ismay, Private collection, Gift of the artist.

C 317 (Fig. 386), The Surf Club at Miami, 1946, 24 x 32 in. Unsigned, Collections: The Studio, Chartwell, The National Trust, Chartwell, Previously catalogued date incorrect, as Churchill visited Miami after the war in 1946 and painted there.

C 318 (Fig. 283) Beach Scene on the Riviera, 1930s, 20 x 24 in. 51 x 61.5 cm, Unsigned, Collections: The Studio, Chartwell, [unknown owner], Sold Sotheby's, New York 7th June 1984, $26,000, The National Trust, Chartwell, Lady Spencer-Churchill's inscription on the back and previously catalogued has been lost as the canvas has been relined. The painting is based on two complementary photographs in the archives at Chartwell.

C 319 (Fig. 197) Coast Scene, Surf Advancing on to a Sandy Shore, c. 1935, 25 x 30 in. 63.5 x 76.1 cm, Initialled right, Collections: The Studio, Chartwell, The National Trust, Chartwell

C 320 (Fig. 198) The Seashore, 1930s, 19 3/4 x 23 3/4 in. Unsigned, Collections: Mr W. Greenshields, Sold Sotheby's 20th April 1966, £650, Present owner unknown, Gift of Sir Winston to Mr W. Greenshields, his butler.

C 321 (Fig. 200) The Atlantic near Biarritz, 1930s, 24 x 30 in. 61 x 51 cm, Initialled left, Collections: Viscount Brendan Bracken, The Master and Fellows of Churchill College, Cambridge, Gift of the artist to Brendan Bracken who bequeathed the painting to Churchill College in 1959.

C 322 (Fig. 196) Distant View of Venice (or St Malo), c. 1935, 23 x 29 in. 57.5 x 72.5 cm, Unsigned, Collections: The Studio, Chartwell, Arabella S. Churchill, Sheila and Wayne Wright, San Antonio, Texas

C 323 (Fig. 194) Distant View of Venice (or St Malo), c. 1935, 20 x 24 in. 50 x 60 cm, Unsigned, Collections: The Studio, Chartwell, The Lady Soames DBE, The rocks in the right foreground led Lady Churchill and the painter Derek Hills to suggest that this painting might be a view of St Malo; on the other hand the artist is likely to have added the rocks to his original painting later. Cf. also C 135 and C 324.

C 324 (Fig. 199) Distant View of Venice, c. 1935, 25 x 30 in. 62 x 74 cm, Unsigned, Collections: The Studio, Chartwell, Mr Winston S. Churchill, Private collection, The rocks in the right foreground suggested to Derek Hills that this might be a view of St Malo; on the other hand the artist is likely to have added the rocks to his original painting later. Cf. also C 323 and C 135.

C 325 (Fig. 275) Coast Scene near Cannes, c. 1935, 26 x 32 in. 64 x 80.4 cm, Unsigned, Illustrated: Winston Churchill: His Life as a Painter by Mary Soames, 1990, Collections: The Studio, Chartwell, The Lady Soames DBE, On the back of the canvas is the maker's stamp: 'Blanchet, Rue Bonaparte, Paris'.

C 326 (Fig. 280) Coast Scene near Cannes, c. 1930, 26 x 32 in. 65 x 81.3 cm, Unsigned, Collections: The Studio, Chartwell, The National Trust, Chartwell

C 327 (Fig. 281) Coast Scene on the Riviera, c. 1930, 26 x 32 in. 65.3 x 81.2 cm, Unsigned, Collections: The Studio, Chartwell, The National Trust, Chartwell

C 328 (Fig. 282) Castle on the Riviera, c. 1935, 25 x 30 in. 63.75 x 76.5 cm, Initialled right, Collections: The Studio, Chartwell, Mr Winston S. Churchill

C 329 (Fig. 288) Coast Scene on the Riviera, c. 1930, 25 x 30 in. Initialled, Collections: The Studio, Chartwell, Mr Julian Sandys, Private English Collection

C 330 (Fig. 135) Copy of a Monet, c. 1935, 17 1/4 x 28 3/4 in. Initialled, Collections: The Studio, Chartwell, The National Trust, Chartwell, Originally entitled 'Bay near Marseilles' this picture appears to be a copy by Churchill of Monet's painting 'L'Ailly Point, Low Tide' 1882, now in the collection of Mr Kerry Stokes, Perth, Australia. The connection was recognized by Mrs Eunice Cousins, of Perth, on a visit to Chartwell.

C 331 (Fig. 136) Coast Scene near Marseilles, c. 1935, Panel 13 x 16 1/2 in. Unsigned, Collections: The Studio, Chartwell, Arabella S. Churchill, On loan to the National Trust, Chartwell

C 332 (Fig. 133) Mediterranean Coast Scene, c. 1930, 20 x 27 in. Initialled, Collections: Lady Spencer-Churchill, The Lady Soames DBE

C 333 (Fig. 138) Near Marseilles, c. 1930, 25 x 30 in. Initialled, Collections: The Studio, Chartwell, Celia Sandys, Private collection, Lake Forest, Illinois, USA

C 334 (Fig. 137) Coast Scene near Marseilles, c. 1935, 25 x 30 in. Initialled, Collections: The Studio, Chartwell, Mr Julian Sandys, Private English Collection

C 335 (Fig. 285) Coast Scene near Cap d'Ail, c. 1935, 25 x 30 in. 63.75 x 76 cm, Initialled left, Collections: The Studio, Chartwell, Mr Winston S. Churchill, Mrs Minnie S. Churchill

C 336 (Fig. 287) Antibes, 1930s, 19 3/4 x 23 3/4 in. Unsigned, Collections: Mr W. Greenshields, Sold Sotheby's 20th April 1966, Present owner unknown, Gift of Sir Winston to Mr W. Greenshields, his butler.

C 337 (Fig. 312) Coast Scene near Antibes, c. 1933, 26 x 32 in. Initialled, Collections: The Studio, Chartwell, Celia Sandys, Private collection, Lake Forest, Illinois, USA

C 338 (Fig. 313) Rocks near Cannes, c. 1935, 20 x 24 in. 51 x 61 cm, Unsigned, Collections: The Studio, Chartwell, The National Trust, Chartwell

C 339 (Fig. 315) Red Rocks near Théoule, in the South of France, c. 1933, 25 x 30 in. Unsigned, Collections: The Studio, Chartwell, Mr Julian Sandys, Private English Collection

C 340 (Fig. 483) Rocky Scene in Sicily, c. 1955, 25 x 30 in. 63.4 x 76.3 cm. Initialled, Collections: The Studio, Chartwell, Sarah Lady Audley, The National Trust, Chartwell

C 341 (Fig. 60) Racecourse, Nice, from under the Railway Bridge, January 1921, 25 x 30 in. Unsigned, Illustrated: 'Painting as a Pastime' by Winston S. Churchill, part 1, The Strand Magazine, December 1921, Collections: The Studio, Chartwell, The National Trust, Chartwell, Incorrect previous title and date: 'View through the Arch of the Bridge over the Var' c. 1930. Cf. C 342 and C 343.

C 342 (Fig. 33) Arch of Bridge over the Var, c. 1930, 25 x 30 in. Initialled, Exhibited: New York World's Fair 1965, Collections: Mrs Diana Sandys, Celia Sandys, Present owner unknown This painting is directly related to C 341 and C 343.

C 343 (Fig. 35) Arch of the Bridge over the Var, Sunset, c. 1930, 25 x 30 in. 63.5 x 76.3 cm, Unsigned, Collections: The Studio, Chartwell, The Lady Soames DBEI, This painting is directly related to C 340 and C 341.

C 344 (Fig. 107) The Goldfish Pool at Chartwell, 1932, 25 x 30 in. Unsigned, Illustrated: 'The Paintings of Winston Churchill', LIFE, January 7th 1946, 'Winston Churchill's Pictures', The Strand Magazine, August 1946, Painting as a Pastime by Winston S. Churchill, 1948, 'An Eightieth Year Tribute to Winston Churchill', edited by Bruce Ingram, The Illustrated London News, 1954, Winston Churchill: His Life as a Painter by Mary Soames, 1990 Exhibited: Royal Academy 1948, World Tour 1958, Royal Academy 1959, M. Knoedler, London 1974, New York and Washington 1983, Sotheby's 1998, Collections: Lady Spencer-Churchill, The Lady Soames DBE

C 345 (Fig. 388) View from a Bathing Hut at Miami Surf Club, 1946, 25 x 30 in. Initialled, Exhibited: Sotheby's 1998, Collections: The Studio, Chartwell,The Lady Soames DBE, The previously catalogued date, c. 1932, was incorrect. A photograph in the archives at Chartwell includes more of the interior of the bathing hut.

C 346 (Fig. 211) The Lily Pond at Coombe Place, Surrey, c. 1930, Canvas board 20 x 14 in. Initialled, Collections: The Studio, Chartwell, Lady Soames, On loan to the National Trust, Chartwell

C 347 (Fig. 284) Sketch [probably on the Riviera], c. 1930, Canvas board 14 x 20 in. Initialled, Collections: The Studio, Chartwell, Arabella S. Churchill, Present owner unknown

C 348 (Fig. 104) The Goldfish Pool at Chartwell, c. 1935, 25 x 30 in. Initialled, Illustrated: Winston Churchill: His Life as a Painter by Mary Soames, 1990, Collections: The Studio, Chartwell, The National Trust, Chartwell, Unfinished painting.

C 349 (Fig. 209) Ornamental Lily Pond at Coombe Place, Surrey, c. 1935, 14 x 20 in. 36 x 51.2 cm Initialled, Collections: The Studio, Chartwell, The National Trust, Chartwell

C 350 (Fig. 357) Les Zoraïdes, Cap Martin, c. 1935, 25 x 30 in. Initialled, Illustrated: Winston Churchill: His Life as a Painter by Mary Soames, 1990, Exhibited: Wylma Wayne Fine Art, London 1982, Dallas Museum of Art 1986, Collections: Lady Spencer-Churchill, Sarah Lady Audley, Mr Russell S. Reynolds Jr

C 351 (Fig. 356) Les Zoraïdes, Cap Martin, 1935, 20 x 24 in. Initialled, Exhibited: World Tour 1958, Royal Academy 1959, New York World's Fair 1965, Collections: Lady Birley, Sold Christie's 13th October 1980, £22,000, Present owner unknown

C 352 (Fig. 349) The Loup River, Alpes Maritimes, 1936, 20 1/8 x 24 in. 51.5 x 61 cm, Unsigned, Illustrated: Painting as a Pastime by Winston S. Churchill, 1948, Winston Churchill: His Life as a Painter by Mary Soames, 1990, Exhibited: Royal Academy 1947, Collection: The Tate Gallery, Presented by the artist to the Tate Gallery, London, in 1955 at the request of its Trustees. The painting was incorrectly dated 1930 in my original catalogue. In Painting as a Pastime, 1948, it was given the incorrect title 'The Loup River, Quebec'.

C 353 (Fig. 369) The Canal at St-Georges-Motel, 1930s, 19 1/2 x 14 in. 50 x 35 cm, Initialled right, Collections: Earl of Avon, Countess of Avon, Gift of the artist to the Earl of Avon.

C 354 (Fig. 371) Avenue and Formal Pool at St-Georges-Motel, c. 1935, 24 x 20 in. Initialled, Collections: The Studio, Chartwell, Miss Edwina Sandys, Present owner unknown

C 355 (Fig. 370) In the Park of the Château at St-Georges-Motel, 1930s, 14 x 10 in. Signed by: 'Paul Maze; A. D. de Segonzac; Winston; Simon Levy; Ivor; Balsan', Illustrated: Winston Churchill: His Life as a Painter by Mary Soames, 1990, Collections: Mr H. J. Chamberlain, Sold Sotheby's 20th April 1966, £500, Mr Roald Dahl, Sold Sotheby's 16th November 1977, £3,500, Private collection, Gift of the artist. All those who signed this, painting by Churchill contributed to its making.

C 356 (Fig. 240) English River Landscape, c. 1935, 24 x 20 in. Initialled, Collections: Lady Spencer-Churchill, The National Trust, Chartwell

C 357 (Fig. 132) On the Var, c. 1935, 30 x 25 in. Initialled, Illustrated: Winston Churchill: His Life as a Painter by Mary Soames, 1990, Collections: The Studio, Chartwell, Mr Julian Sandys, Private English Collection

C 358 (Fig. 245) The Thames from Taplow, c. 1935, 29 3/4 x 23 3/4 in. 75.5 x 63 cm, Initialled, Collections: Lady Spencer-Churchill, Arabella S. Churchill, Sold Sotheby's 7th November 1990, £18,000, American private collector

C 359 (Fig. 115) Tree-lined Stream in England, c. 1935, 20 x 20 in. Unsigned, Collections: The Studio, Chartwell, Mr Julian Sandys, Private English Collection

C 360 (Fig. 351) River Scene on the Loup, c. 1936, 25 x 30 in. 76.3 x 76.4 cm, Unsigned, Collections: The Studio, Chartwell, The Lady Soames DBE, Re-dated to the time of Churchill's first visit to the Loup.

C 361 (Fig. 354) River Scene on the Loup, c. 1936, 30 x 25 in. Unsigned, Collections: Lady Spencer-Churchill, The National Trust, Chartwell, Re-dated to the time of Churchill's first visit to the Loup

C 362 (Fig. 247) The Thames at Taplow, c. 1935, 30 x 25 in. Initialled, Illustrated: Winston Churchill: His Life as a Painter by Mary Soames, 1990, Collections: The Studio, Chartwell, The National Trust, Chartwell

C 363 (Fig. 353) Scene on the River Loup, c. 1936, 18 x 22 in. Unsigned, Illustrated: Winston Churchill: His Life as a Painter by Mary Soames, 1990, Collections: The Studio, Chartwell, Celia Sandys, Re-dated to the time of Churchill's first visit to the Loup.

C 364 (Fig. 236) A Lake in Norfolk, c. 1936, 24 x 20 in. Initialled, Exhibited: World Tour 1958, Royal Academy 1959, Collections: Lady Spencer-Churchill, [Another owner?], Sold Christie's 2nd March 1989, £28,000, Present owner unknown

C 365 (Fig. 241) A Lake in Norfolk, c. 1936, 22 1/2 x 20 in. Initialled, Collections: Lady Spencer-Churchill, Mrs S. L. Henley, Sold Sotheby's 19th May 1982, £6,600, Sold Sotheby's 20th November 1991, Present owner unknown, Gift of Lady Churchill to her cousin Mrs Henley.

C 366 (Fig. 205) The Garden at Wilton, c. 1935, 21 1/2 x 17 1/4 in. Initialled, Collections: The Studio, Chartwell, Arabella S. Churchill, Sold Sotheran's June 1982, £6,000, Present owner unknown

C 367 (Fig. 239) Lake Scene in Norfolk, c. 1935, 20 x 24 in. Unsigned, Collections: The Studio, Chartwell, Miss Edwina Sandys, Present owner unknown

C 368 (Fig. 352) A Pool on the Loup River, c. 1936, 25 x 30 in. 63.6 x 76.5 cm, Initialled left, Collections: The Studio, Chartwell, Miss Edwina Sandys, Setagaya Art Museum, Tokyo, Re-dated to the time of Churchill's first visit to the Loup.

C 369 (Fig. 238) Lake Scene in Norfolk, c. 1935, 20 x 24 in. 51 x 60 cm, Initialled left, Collections: The Studio, Chartwell, The Lady Soames DBE

C 370 (Fig. 131) View in Southern France, c. 1935, 20 x 24 in. Initialled, Collections: The Studio, Chartwell, Miss Edwina Sandys, Monsanto Company, St Louis, Missouri

C 371 (Fig. 129) Storm Scene, South of France, or The Bridge, c. 1935, 25 x 30 in. Initialled, Collections: Lady Spencer-Churchill, The National Trust, Chartwell

C 372 (Fig. 114) Lake near Breccles in Autumn, c. 1930, 21 1/2 x 29 in. Unsigned, Collections: The Studio, Chartwell, Mr Julian Sandys, Private English Collection

C 373 (Fig. 116) Near Breccles, c. 1930, 26 x 32 in. Unsigned, Collections: The Studio, Chartwell, Mr Julian Sandys, Mrs Elizabeth Sandys

C 374 (Not illustrated) The Swimming Pool at Chartwell, c. 1930, 19 1/2 x 26 in. Unsigned, Exhibited: Sotheby's 1998, Collections: Lady Spencer-Churchill, The National Trust, Chartwell, This painting is by Sir William Nicholson and was wrongly attributed to Churchill in my original catalogue. Cf. C 375.

C 375 (Fig. 106) The Swimming Pool at Chartwell, c. 1935, 25 x 30 in. Unsigned, Collections: The Studio, Chartwell, The National Trust, Chartwell, An almost identical view was painted by Sir William Nicholson and it is likely that the two works were painted in each other's company. The Nicholson also hangs at Chartwell. Cf. C 374.

C 376 (Fig. 430) Amaryllis Lily, 1948, 36 x 24 in. 90 x 60 cm, Initialled, Exhibited: M. Knoedler, London 1974 Collection:The Lady Soame DBE, The Winston Churchill Memorial Trust, Based on a photograph in the archives at Chartwell.

C 377 (Fig. 429) Buddha and Lilies, 1948, 40 x 30 in. Initialled, Exhibited: New York World's Fair 1965, Collections: Lady Spencer-Churchill, The National Trust, Chartwell, Based on a photograph in the archives at Chartwell.

C 378 (Fig. 431) Orchids, c. 1948, 25 x 30 in. 63.5 x 76.5 cm, Initialled, Illustrated: Painting as a Pastime by Winston S. Churchill, 1948, Exhibited: World Tour 1958, Royal Academy 1959, M. Knoedler, London 1977, Wylma Wayne Fine Art, London 1982, Ronald Reagan Library 1992/3, Japan 1998, Edinburgh 1999, Collection: Churchill College, Cambridge, Gift of the artist in 1964.

C 379 (Fig. 432) Black Swans at Chartwell, 1948, 28 x 22 in. Initialled, Collection: Mme Moatti, Sold Palais Galliera, Paris 1966, 50,000 Francs, Present owner unknown, Based on a photograph in the archives at Chartwell.

C 380 (Fig. 435) Miss Cecily Gemmell, c. 1949, 24 x 18 in. Initialled right 'WSC OB!', Collection: Miss Cecily Gemmell, Gift of the artist c. 1952.

C 381 (Fig. 376) Tower of the Katoubia Mosque, 1943, 20 x 24 in. Initialled right, Illustrated: Winston Churchill: His Life as a Painter by Mary Soames, 1990, Collections: President Franklin D. Roosevelt, Mr Norman Hickman, Private collection, Gift of the artist to President Roosevelt. This is the only picture painted by Churchill during the Second World War.

C 382 (Fig. 428) Buddha and Lily, 1948, 40 x 30 in. Initialled, Illustrated: Winston Churchill: His Life as a Painter by Mary Soames, 1990, Collections: Lady Spencer-Churchill, The National Trust, Chartwell ,Based on a photograph in the archives at Chartwell.

C 383 (Fig. 372), Lakeside Scene, Lake Como, 1945, 24 x 20 in. Initialled, Illustrated: 'The Paintings of Winston Churchill', LIFE, January 7th 1946, 'Winston Churchill's Pictures', The Strand Magazine, July 1946, Painting as a Pastime by Winston S. Churchill, 1948, Winston Churchill: His Life as a Painter by Mary Soames, 1990 Collections: Lady Spencer-Churchill, The National Trust, Chartwell

C 384 (Fig. 433) Black Swans at Chartwell, 1948, 22 x 27 in. 56.3 x 69 cm, Initialled, Exhibited: World Tour 1958, Royal Academy 1959, Collections: Mr Randolph S. Churchill, Arabella S. Churchill, The National Trust, Chartwell, Gift of the artist.

C 385 (Fig. 440) Water, Vaucluse, 1948, 18 x 24 in. Initialled left, Illustrated: Winston Churchill: His Life as a Painter by Mary Soames, 1990, Exhibitions: World Tour 1958, Royal Academy 1959, Collections: Lady Spencer-Churchill, Captain Nicholas Soames, The Lady Soames DBE

C 386 (Fig. 444) Fontaine de Vaucluse, 1948, 18 x 24 in. Initialled, Collections: Lady Spencer-Churchill, The National Trust, Chartwell

C 387 (Fig. 442) Fontaine de Vaucluse, 1948, 25 x 30 in. Unsigned, Collections: Lady Spencer-Churchill, The National Trust, Chartwell

C 388 (Fig. 445) Fontaine de Vaucluse, 1948, 23 1/2 x 30 in. Unsigned, Collections: Lady Spencer-Churchill, The National Trust, Chartwell

C 389 (Fig. 441) Water, Vaucluse, 1948, 20 x 17 1/4 in. Unsigned, Collections: The Studio, Chartwell, The National Trust, Chartwell

C 390 (Fig. 443) Water, Vaucluse, 1948, 24 x 18 in. Initialled, Collections: Lady Spencer-Churchill, The Lady Soames DBE I

C 391 (Fig. 463) Sketch of Lake Carezza, or The Twenty-Minute Sketch, 1949, 25 x 30 in. Initialled, Exhibitions: World Tour 1958, Royal Academy 1959, Collections: Lady Spencer-Churchill, The National Trust, Chartwell

C 392 (Fig. 449) Bridge near Aix-en-Provence, 1948, 25 x 30 in. Initialled, Collections: The Studio, Chartwell, Sarah Lady Audley, Present owner unknown

C 393 (Fig. 450) The Bridge at Aix-en-Provence, September 1948, 22 x 28 in. Initalled, Collections: Mr Willi Sax, Mrs M. Sax-Schlatter, Gift of the artist.

C 394 (Fig. 377) Lake Como, 1948, 22 x 27 in. Initialled, Collections: Lady Spencer-Churchill, The National Trust, Chartwell, Painted in about an hour.

C 395 (Fig. 379) Lake Como, 1945, 40 x 50 in. Unsigned, Exhibitions: World Tour 1958, Royal Academy 1959 Collections: Lady Spencer-Churchill, The National Trust, Chartwell

C 396 (Fig. 397) Scene on the River Meuse, with the Artist, 1946-47, 25 x 30 in. Initialled, Collections: The Studio, Chartwell, The National Trust, Chartwell, Based on a series of eleven photographs showing slightly different aspects of the view in the archives at Chartwell; seven show the artist sitting at his easel. Cf. also C 400 and C 401.

C 397 (Fig. 391) Lake Geneva, Switzerland, 1946, 25 x 30 in. 63 x 76 cm, Initialled right, Collections: The Studio, Chartwell, The Chequers Trust, Gift of Churchill's executors.

C 398 (Fig. 394) Lake Geneva and Mont Blanc, 1946, 28 x 36 in. Initialled, Exhibited: New York World's Fair 1965, Collection: Lord Moran, Private Collection, USA, Gift of the artist. Based on a photograph in the archives at Chartwell. Cf. C 399.

C 399 (Fig. 395) The Island on Lake Geneva, from Choisy, with Mont Blanc, 1946, 40 x 50 in. Unsigned, Collections: The Studio, Chartwell, The National Trust, Chartwell, Based on a photograph in the archives at Chartwell. Cf. C 398.

C 400 (Fig. 396) Scene on the River Meuse, 1946-47, 28 x 36 in. Unsigned, Exhibited: Sotheby's 1998, Collections: The Studio, Chartwell, Lady Spencer-Churchill, Mr Winston S. Churchill, This painting is based on a series of photographs in the archives at Chartwell. See also C 396 and C 401.

C 401 (Fig. 400) Scene on the Meuse, 1946-47, 28 x 36 in. Unsigned, Collections: The Studio, Chartwell, Lady Soames, On loan to the National Trust, Chartwell, Based on a series of photographs in the archives at Chartwell. See also C 396 and C 400.

C 402 (Fig. 468) Lake Garda, 1949, 25 x 30 in. 63.5 x 76.2 cm, Initialled left, Collections: Viscount Camrose, Sold Christie's 4th June 1999, £39,000, Present owner unknown, Gift of the artist.

C 403 (Fig. 456) Beaches near Antibes, c. 1945, 16 x 20 in. Initialled, Collections: Miss Horatia Seymour, Sold Christie's 12th November 1965, £8,925, The Israel Museum, Jerusalem. Gift of Handiv Foundation. London Gift of the artist. Miss Horatia Seymour was Lady Churchill's bridesmaid and a great friend; she lived at Chartwell Cottage.

C 404 (Fig. 453) Beaches near Antibes, c. 1949, 16 x 20 in. 40 x 50 cm, Unsigned, Collections: The Studio, Chartwell, Mr Peregrine S. Churchill, Duke of Marlborough for the Blenheim Foundation, Gift of Mr Peregrine S. Churchill

C 405 (Fig. 373) Menaggio, Lake Como, 1945, 19 1/2 x 29 in. Initialled, Illustrated: 'The Paintings of Winston Churchill', LIFE, January 7th 1946, 'Winston Churchill's Pictures', The Strand Magazine, July 1946, Collections: Mr. G. C. Mason, Sold Sotheby's 24th May 1965, £14,000, Present owner unknown

C 406 (Fig. 492) Monte Carlo from Cap d'Ail, August 1949, 22 x 27 in. 56 x 69 cm, Initialled left, Collections: The Studio, Chartwell, Mr Winston S. Churchill, Private collection, Based on two photographs in the archives at Chartwell.

C 407 (Fig. 447) Coast Scene near Marseilles, c. 1947, 20 x 24 in. Initialled, Collections: The Studio, Chartwell, The Lady Soames DBE

C 408 (Fig. 464) Lake Carezza in the Dolomites, 1949, 16 x 22 in. 71.5 x 92 cm, Unsigned, Collections: The Studio, Chartwell, Mr Winston S. Churchill, Based on two photographs in the archives at Chartwell. Cf. C 409, C 410, C 411, C 412.

C 409 (Fig. 462) Lake Carezza in the Dolomites, 1949, 16 x 22 in. Initialled, Collections: The Studio, Chartwell, The Lady Soames DBE, Based on two photographs in the archives at Chartwell. Cf. C 408, C 410, C 411, C 412.

C 410 (Fig. 461) Lake Carezza in the Dolomites, August 1949, 26 x 30 in. Initialled, Collections: Lord Normanbrook, Private collection, Based on two photographs in the archives at Chartwell. Cf. C 408, C 409, C 411, C 412.

C 411 (Fig. 465) Lake Carezza, Dolomites, August 1949, 22 x 27 in. Unsigned, Collections: Lady Spencer-Churchill, The National Trust, Chartwell, Based on two photographs in the archives at Chartwell. Cf. C 408, C 409, C 410, C 412.

C 412 (Fig. 467) Lake Carezza in the Dolomites, 1949, 25 x 30 in. Unsigned, Collections: Mr Anthony F. Moir, The Lady Soames DBE, Gift of the artist. Cf. C 408, C 409, C 410, C 411.

C 413 (Fig. 380) By Lake Lugano, 1945, 22 x 28 in. Initialled, Illustrated: 'The Paintings of Winston Churchill', LIFE, January 7th 1946, Painting as a Pastime by Winston S. Churchill, 1948, Collections: The Studio, Chartwell Sarah Lady Audley, Private collection, Lake Forest, Illinois, USA, Based on a photograph in the archives at Chartwell.

C 414 (Fig. 399) Canal Scene near Bruges, c. 1946, 22 x 27 in. 56 x 67 cm, Initialled left, Collections: The Studio, Chartwell, Celia Sandys, Asprey and Garrard, Based on a series of six complementary photographs in the archives at Chartwell.

C 415 (Fig. 381) St-Jean-Cap-Ferrat 1946, 20 x 24 in. Initialled, Illustrated: 'The Paintings of Winston Churchill', LIFE, January 7th 1946, Painting as a Pastime by Winston S. Churchill, 1948, Collections: Lady Spencer-Churchill, The National Trust, Chartwell, Based on three complementary photographs in the archives at Chartwell.

C 416 (Fig. 378) The Church by Lake Como, September 1945, 24 x 20 in. 60 x 50 cm, Unsigned, Illustrated: 'The Paintings of Winston Churchill', LIFE, January 7th 1946, 'Winston Churchill's Pictures', The Strand Magazine, July 1946, Painting as a Pastime by Winston S. Churchill, 1948, Collections: Lady Spencer-Churchill, Mr Jeremy Soames

C 417 (Fig. 451) Harbour Scene, probably on the Riviera, c. 1947, 24 x 18 in. Unsigned, Exhibited: Sotheby's 1948, Collections: Lady Spencer-Churchill, The National Trust, Chartwell

C 418 (Fig. 477) Torcello, August-September 1951, 20 x 24 in. Initialled left, Illustrated: Winston Churchill: His Life as a Painter by Mary Soames, 1990, Exhibited: World Tour 1958, Royal Academy 1959, New York World's Fair 1965, M. Knoedler, London 1974, Wylma Wayne Fine Art, London 1982, Sotheby's 1998 Collections: Lady Spencer-Churchill, The Lady Soames DBE

C 419 (Fig. 384) Village Scene, Lake Lugano, September 1945, 20 x 30 in. 52 x 77.5 cm, Initialled right, Illustrated: 'The Paintings of Winston Churchill', LIFE, January 7th 1946, 'Winston Churchill's Pictures', The Strand Magazine, August 1946, Painting as a Pastime by Winston S. Churchill, 1948, Collections: Mr Anthony F. Moir, United Service Club, Sold Christie's 3rd March 1978, £10,500,Anonymous owner, Sold Christie's 12th June 1988, Present owner unknown, Gift of the artist to Anthony F. Moir, his solicitor, who bequeathed the painting to the United Service Club. After the painting was illustrated in 1948, Churchill added the figure standing by the bow of the boat in the foreground. My thanks to David Hatter, a guide at Chartwell, for pointing this out.

C 420 (Fig. 382) Village near Lugano, with the Artist at his Easel, 1945, Canvas board 14 x 20 in. 35.4 x 50.7 cm, Unsigned, Collections: The Studio, Chartwell, The National Trust, Chartwell

C 421 (Fig. 385) St-Jean-Cap-Ferrat, 1946, 25 x 18 in. Initialled right, Exhibited: World Tour 1958, Royal Academy 1959, Collection: Mr Winston S. Churchill, Gift of the artist.

C 422 (Fig. 389) Scene from the Venetian Causeway, Miami Beach, Florida 1946, 25 x 30 in. Initialled right, Collection: Colonel and Mrs Frank W. Clarke, Sold Sotheby's, New York 21st May 1982, $23,000, Present owner unknown, Gift of the artist. Based on a photograph in the archives at Chartwell, which includes Churchill's empty canvas chair and this painting on the easel.

C 423 (Fig. 466), Lake Garda, San Vigilio, August 1949, 25 x 30 in. Initialled left, Exhibited: Sotheby's 1998, Collections: The Studio, Chartwell, Mr Winston S. Churchill, Based on two photographs in the archives at Chartwell.

C 424 (Fig. 481) Frankfort Beach, Jamaica, 1953, 26 x 30 in. 63.5 x 756.2 cm, Initialled right, Exhibited: New York World's Fair 1965, Collections: Mr Joyce C.Hall, Hallmark Fine Art Collection, Kansas City, Missouri, Gift of the artist, 1954

C 425 (Fig. 388) The Mediterranean near Genoa, 1945, 18 x 22 in. Initialled right, Illustrated: 'The Paintings of Winston Churchill', LIFE, January 7th 1946, 'Winston Churchill's Pictures', The Strand Magazine, August 1946, Painting as a Pastime by Winston S. Churchill, 1948, Exhibited: World Tour 1958, Royal Academy 1959, Sotheby's 1998, Collections: Lady Spencer-Churchill, Mr Winston S. Churchill, Entitled 'Rocky Seascape' in LIFE, January 7th 1946 and there said to be a view of the Mediterranean painted from the Villa Pirelli at Genoa, 'property of Albert Pirelli, Italian tire magnate ... now used as local British headquarters'.

C 426 (Fig. 484) Rocky Seascape, 1953, 22 x 27 in. Initialled, Collections: Earl Woolton, Lady Woolton, Sold Christie's 22nd November 2002, £85,000, Richard Green, London, Based on a photograph in the archives at Chartwell. The subject was identified just before the auction by the owner's agent, Robert Holden Ltd., as the Frankfort Beach at the Prospect Estate of Sir Harold and Lady Mitchell, Jamiaca, and painted there during Churchill's visit in 1953.

C 427 (Fig. 454) Rocks near Cannes, 1948, 25 x 30 in. 62 x 75 cm, Initialled right, Exhibited: World Tour 1958, Royal Academy 1959, Collections: Lady Spencer-Churchill, The University of Bristol, Gift of Lady Spencer-Churchill after Sir Winston's death; he had been Chancellor of the University since 1929.

C 428 (Fig. 404) Marrakech, c. 1949, 25 x 30 in. Initialled, Collections: The Studio, Chartwell, Sarah Lady Audley, Sold Sotheby's 3rd November 1982, Mr Malcolm Forbes Snr, Mr Steve Forbes

C 429 (Fig. 405) Marrakech, 1947, 22 x 27 in. Initialled, Collections: Lady Spencer-Churchill, Mr Julian Sandys, Private English Collection, Based on a photograph in the archives at Chartwell.

C 430 (Fig. 402) Marrakech, 1947, 22 x 27 in. Initialled left, Exhibited: World Tour 1958, Royal Academy 1959, Sotheby 1998, Collection: Mr Winston S. Churchill, Gift of the artist. Based on a photograph in the archives at Chartwell.

C 431 (Fig. 401) Valley of the Ourika and Atlas Mountains, 1948, 25 x 30 in. Initialled left, Exhibited: World Tour 1958, Royal Academy 1959, New York World's Fair 1965, Dallas Art Museum 1986, Wichita Art Museum 1986, Winston Churchill Memorial 1989, Herbert Hoover Library 1990, Franklin D. Roosevelt Library 1992, Collections: President Dwight D. Eisenhower, Dwight D. Eisenhower Library/Museum, Gift of the artist to President Eisenhower, 1958

C 432 (Fig. 406) Marrakech, 1948, 25 x 30 in. Initialled, Collections: Lady Spencer-Churchill, The National Trust, Chartwell

C 433 (Fig. 403) Valley of the Ourika near Marrakech, 1948, 25 x 30 in. Initialled right, Collections: Lady Spencer Churchill, Sarah Lady Audley, Mr Stefen Lersten

C 434 (Fig. 418) Marrakech, c.1948, 20 x 24 in. Initialled, Exhibited: New York World's Fair 1965, Collections: President Harry S. Truman, Mrs Margaret Truman Daniel, Gift of the artist. Based on a photograph in the archives at Chartwell.

C 435 (Fig. 408) Mosque at Marrakech, 1948, 28 x 36 in. Unsigned, Collections: The Studio, Chartwell, The National Trust, Chartwell, Inscribed on the back: 'Painted by my husband. Clementine S. Churchill.'

C 436 (Fig. 409) Near Marrakech, c. 1948, 25 x 30 in. 62 x 75 cm, Initialled right, Collections: Mr James Wood, The Institute of Chartered Accountants of Scotland, Gift of the artist. Mr James Wood was Churchill's accountant and bequeathed the painting to the Institute in 1972.

C 437 (Fig. 407) Village near Marrakech, 1947, 14 x 22 in. 35.8 x 56 cm, Unsigned, Collections: The Studio, Chartwell, The National Trust, Chartwell

C 438 (Fig. 412) Mosque at Marrakech, 1948, 36 x 28 in. 92 x 72 cm, Unsigned, Collections: Lady Spencer-Churchill, Mr Winston S. Churchill, Private collection, Based on a photograph in the archives at Chartwell.

C 439 (Fig. 471) Scuola di San Marco, Venice, 1951, 19 1/2 x 24 in. 51 x 61 cm, Initialled left, Collections: Mr Charles Graham-Dixon, Sold Christie 7th November 1991, £33,000 ,Joan and David Maxwell

C 440 (Fig. 165) The Ruins of Arras Cathedral (after Sargent), 1920s, 25 x 30 in. 63.5 x 76 cm, Unsigned, Illustrated: Winston Churchill: His Life as a Painter by Mary Soames, 1990, Collections: The Studio, Chartwell, Arabella S. Churchill, On loan to the National Trust, Chartwell, Wrongly catalogued previously as 'Amiens Cathedral'. The Sargent painting was owned by Churchill's friend Sir Philip Sassoon. Cf. C 116.

C 441 (Fig. 383) On Cap Martin, 1940s, 14 x 18 in. 35.5 x 46 cm, Unsigned, Collections: The Studio, Chartwell, The National Trust, Chartwell

C 442 (Fig. 439) Chartwell Landscape with Sheep, 1940s, 28 x 21 1/2 in. Initialled, Illustrated: 'Winston Churchill's Pictures', The Strand Magazine, July 1946, Collections: Mr Henry R. Luce, Mrs Clare Booth Luce, Present owner unknown, The sheep are based on a photograph in the archives at Chartwell. More were added after the painting was illustrated in The Strand Magazine, July 1946.

C 443 (Fig. 398) Le Béguinage, Bruges, 1946, 25 x 30 in. Initialled, Exhibitions: World Tour 1958, Royal Academy 1959, Collections: Miss Grace Hamblin, Sold Christie's 18th November 1968, Mr Arthur Murray, Mrs Phyllis McDowell, Gift of the artist to Miss Grace Hamblin, Lady Spencer-Churchill's secretary. This painting is based on a series of twelve complementary photographs, plus two enlarged cut-outs of figures, in the archives at Chartwell.

C 444 (Fig. 392) Inland View from Choisy, Switzerland, 1946, 22 x 20 1/2 in. Unsigned, Collections: The Studio, Chartwell, Miss Nonie Chapman, Miss Nonie Chapman was secretary to Lady Spencer-Churchill.

C 445 (Fig. 438) View from Chartwell, c. 1948, 30 x 25 in. 76.75 x 64 cm, Initialled right, Exhibited: Japan, 1998, Collections: Lady Spencer-Churchill, Mr Winston S. Churchill

C 446 (Fig. 437) Chartwell Kitchen Garden, 1948, 25 x 30 in. Unsigned, Exhibitions: World Tour 1958, Royal Academy 1959, M. Knoedler, London 1974, New York and Washington 1983, Collections: The Lady Soames DBE

C 447 (Fig. 393) Broad Landscape near Choisy, 1946, 46 x 77 in. Unsigned, Collections: The Studio, Chartwell, The National Trust, Chartwell

C 448 (Fig. 459) Distant View of a Town in the South of France, c. 1948, 22 x 27 in. Initialled, Collections: The Studio, Chartwell, Celia Sandys

C 449 (Fig. 460) Landscape in Provence - between Aix and Arles, c. 1947, 22 x 27 in. Initialled twice: lower left and lower right, Collection: Sir Edward Heath, Gift of the artist. Sir Edward Heath was Churchill's Chief Whip and a later successor as Prime Minister.

C 450 (Fig. 490) Vase of Tulips (after Cézanne) at La Pausa, 1957,28 1/2 x 16 1/2 in. Initialled left, Collections: Mr and Mrs Emery Reves, Dallas Museum of Art, The Wendy and Emery Reves Collection, Copy of a painting by Cézanne owned by Emery and Wendy Reves.

C 451 (Fig. 475) The Colleoni Memorial, Venice, c. 1951, 21 x 19 1/2 in. Unsigned, Collections: Lady Spencer-Churchill, Miss Edwina Sandys, On loan to the Winston Churchill Memorial and Library, Westminster College, Fulton

C 452 (Fig. 426) Walls at Marrakech, January 1959, 30 x 25 in. Unsigned, Collections: The Studio, Chartwell, Sarah Lady Audley, The National Trust, Chartwell, Based on a series of four complementary photographs in the archives at Chartwell. Mr John Whitmore, a volunteer at Chartwell, when on his honeymoon in Marrakech in 1959, saw Sir Winston working on this painting, guarded by a policeman.

C 453 (Fig. 425) Marrakech with a Camel, c. 1954, 22 x 27 in. Unsigned, Collections: The Studio, Chartwell, Sarah Lady Audley, Private collection, Lake Forest, Illinois, USA, Based on a series of four complementary photographs of the walls, plus one of the camel - in the archives at Chartwell.

C 454 (Fig. 472) The Bargello in Florence, c. 1951, 24 x 20 in. Initialled, Collections: Lady Spencer-Churchill Mr Julian Sandys, Private English Collection

C 455 (Fig. 493) Oranges and Lemons, 1958, 20 x 24 in. Unsigned, Illustrated: Winston Churchill: His Life as a Painter by Mary Soames, 1990, Exhibited: Royal Academy 1958, New York World's Fair 1965, Collections: Mrs Diana Sandys, Celia Sandys

C 456 (Fig. 436) Lady Churchill at the Launching of HMS Indomitable, c. August 1955, 30 x 25 in. 76 x 63 cm Unsigned, Illustrated: Winston Churchill: His Life as a Painter by Mary Soames, 1990, Collections: The Studio, Chartwell, Mr Winston S. Churchill, Mrs Minnie S. Churchill, On loan to the National Trust, Chartwell, Based on a favourite photograph on Sir Winston's desk at Chartwell, the painting is inscribed on the back: 'Painted by my husband. Clementine S. Churchill.'

C 457 (Fig. 423) Marrakech, a Man Leading a Camel, c. 1958, 25 x 30 in. 63.8 x 76.2 cm, Initialled left Collections: The Studio, Chartwell, Sarah Lady Audley, The National Trust, Chartwell, The man leading a camel is based on a photograph in the archives at Chartwell.

C 458 (Fig. 414) The Todhra Gorge, Morocco, 1951, 24 x 18 in. Initialled, Exhibited: Sotheby's 1998, Collections: The Studio, Chartwell, Sarah Lady Audley, The Lady Soames DBE, Based on two photographs, joined horizontally, in the archives at Chartwell.

C 459 (Fig. 415) The Gorge at Todhra, 1951, 24 x 18 in. Initialled, Illustrated: Winston Churchill: His Life as a Painter by Mary Soames, 1990, Collections: Lady Spencer-Churchill, The National Trust, Chartwell

C 460 (Fig. 422) Gate at Marrakech, c. 1950, 20 x 16 in. Unsigned, Collections: The Studio, Chartwell, Sarah Lady Audley, The National Trust, Chartwell

C 461 (Fig. 474) The Doge's Palace in Venicec. 1951, Initialled, Collections: Lady Spencer-Churchill, Miss Arabella S. Churchill, Bought in Christie's June 1978, £4,200, Sold Christie's 12th June 1986, £13,000, Present owner unknown

C 462 (Fig. 424) Gate at Marrakech, a Man on a Donkey, c. 1950, 25 x 30 in. 63.5 x 76.4 cm, Unsigned, Exhibited: Sotheby's 1998, Collections: The Studio, Chartwell, Sarah Lady Audley, The National Trust, Chartwell, The man on a donkey is based on a photograph in the archives at Chartwell.

C 463 (Fig. 417) Marrakech, a Group of Palms, 1950s, 28 x 21 in. Initialled, Collections: Mr and Mrs Henry Luce III, Gift of the artist. The group of palms is based on a photograph in the archives at Chartwell.

C 464 (Fig. 416) Near Marrakech, c. 1954, 27 x 22 in. Initialled, Collections: The Studio, Chartwell, Present owner unknown, The group of palms is based on a photograph in the archives at Chartwell.

C 465 (Fig. 411) Garden at Marrakech, c. 1955, 25 x 30 in. 63.5 x 76.5 cm, Initialled, Collections: The Studio, Chartwell, Miss Edwina Sandys, Sold Sotheby's 5th December 2001, £60,000, Present owner unknown

C 466 (Fig. 410) Marrakech and the Atlas Mountains, c. 1955, 25 x 30 in. Unsigned, Collections: The Studio, Chartwell, Sarah Lady Audley ,The National Trust, Chartwell

C 467 (Fig. 427) The Garden of the Mamounia Hotel, Marrakech, c. 1954, 22 x 27 in. Initialled left, Exhibited: Sotheby's 1998, Collections: The Studio, Chartwell, Mr Winston S. Churchill, Based on a photograph in the archives at Chartwell.

C 468 (Fig. 413) Marrakech, c. 1955, 18 x 30 in. Unsigned, Collections: The Studio, Chartwell, The Lady Soames DBE, Inscribed on the back: 'Painted by my husband. Clementine S. Churchill.'

C 469 (Fig. 419) The Plain of Tinerhir, 1951, 22 x 27 in. Unsigned, Exhibited: Royal Academy 1951, Collections: Lady Spencer-Churchill, Officers' Mess, The Queen's Royal Hussars (Queen's Own and Royal Irish) Inscribed on the back: 'This picture was painted by my Husband. Clementine Spencer-Churchill.' The painting was presented by Lady Spencer-Churchill 'as a token of gratitude for the part played by the Regiment during the funeral of Sir Winston Churchill. 30th Jan. 1965.'

C 470 (Fig. 421) The Valley of the Ourika, c. 1954, 22 x 27 in. 54.5 x 68.5 cm, Initialled left, Collections: The Studio, Chartwell, Miss Edwina Sandys, Setagaya Art Museum, Tokyo, Based on three related photographs, one including figures, in the archives at Chartwell.

C 471 (Fig. 494) Blue Grass - La Capponcina, 1954, 24 3/4 x 30 in. 63 x 76 cm,Initialled left, Collections: The Studio, Chartwell, Dr Roberts, Sold Sotheby's 15th July 1998, £84,000, British private collection, This painting is based on five photographs mounted together on card in the archives at Chartwell.

C 472 (Fig. 496) La Capponcina, 1950, 25 x 30 in. Initialled, Collections: Lord Beaverbrook, Present owner unknown, Gift of the artist. Subsequently sold with the villa in the early 1970s. This painting is based on three complementary photographs in the archives at Chartwell.

C 473 (Fig. 503) Cap d'Ail, 1952, 30 x 25 in. Initialled, Collections: Lady Spencer-Churchill, Present owner unknown, Based on a photograph in the archives at Chartwell; in the photograph the figure of Lady Churchill is clearly visible in the shadow of the open door on the left.

C 474 (Fig. 375) Villa on the Nivelle, 1945, 20 x 24 in. 49.5 x 60 cm, Initialled right, Illustrated: 'The Paintings of Winston Churchill', LIFE, January 7th 1946, Collections: Lady Spencer-Churchill, Arabella S. Churchill, Mr Alex Segal, The river is the Nivelle and not 'Nivello' as catalogued originally. The LIFE caption says: 'Painted at La Hendaye in southern France during a ten-day vacation that Churchill managed to sandwich in between last July's elections and the Potsdam conference.'

C 475 (Fig. 498) The Walled Garden at La Capponcina ,c. 1955, 25 x 30 in. Initialled, Collections: The Studio, Chartwell, The National Trust, Chartwell, Based on a photograph in the archives at Chartwell.

C 476 (Fig. 479) Venice, 1951, Millboard 24 x 36 in., Initialled left, Exhibited: World Tour 1958, Royal Academy 1959, Collections: Lady Spencer-Churchill, Palace of Westminster, Presented to the Palace of Westminster, seat of Britain's Houses of Parliament, by Lady Spencer-Churchill in 1965. This painting is based on a photograph in the archives at Chartwell which has been squared up with vertical and horizontal lines. Cf also the artist's sketch C 529.

C 477 (Fig. 489) La Maison Rouge, near Aix-en-Provence (after Cézanne), 1955, 20 x 24 in. Unsigned, Collections: The Studio, Chartwell, Arabella S. Churchill, Present owner unknown, Probably painted at La Pausa, home of Emery and Wendy Reves.

C 478 (Fig. 478) Venice, Canal Scene, c. 1951, 25 x 30 in. Unsigned, Collections: The Studio, Chartwell, The National Trust, Chartwell, This unfinished painting is based on two photographs in the archives at Chartwell: one has the roofline ruled up and the second is inscribed on the back by Churchill: 'lantern slide'.

C 479 (Fig. 473) River Landscape near Venice, c. 1951, 22 x 27 in. Unsigned, Collections: The Studio, Chartwell, The Lady Soames DBE, Inscribed on the back: 'Painted by my husband near Venice. Clementine S. Churchill.'

C 480 (Fig. 476) Scene near Venice, c. 1951, 25 x 30 in. Initialled right, Collections: The Studio, Chartwell, The Lady Soames DBE, Based on a photograph in the archives at Chartwell.

C 481 (Fig. 495) Monte Carlo from Cap d'Ail, c. 1955, 25 x 30 in. Unsigned, Collections: The Studio, Chartwell,The Lady Soames DBE, Based on a photograph in the archives at Chartwell.

C 482 (Fig. 434) The Lakes at Chartwell, c. 1950, 20 x 24 in. Unsigned, Collections: Lady Spencer-Churchill, The National Trust, Chartwell

C 483 (Fig. 482) Leaning Palm, Jamaica, c. 1953, 24 x 20 in. Initialled right, Collections: Lady Spencer-Churchill, Sarah Lady Audley, Present owner unknown

C 484 (Fig. 480) Jamaican Beach, c. 1953, 20 x 19 1/4 in. 51 x 48.5 cm, Unsigned, Collections: The Studio, Chartwell,The Lady Soames DBE

C 485 (Fig. 457) Red Rocks, 1951, 20 x 24 in. Unsigned, Exhibited: New York World's Fair 1965 Collections: Mrs Diana Sandys, Celia Sandys

C 486 (Fig. 458) Red Rocks in the South of France, c. 1950, 20 x 24 in. 50.7 x 61 cm, Initialled right, Collections: The Studio, Chartwell, Sarah Lady Audley, The National Trust, Chartwell

C 487 (Fig. 487) The Grotto of the Ropemakers, Syracuse, 1955, 25 x 30 in. 63.5 x 76.5 cm Initialled right, Collections: The Studio, Chartwell, The Lady Soames DBE, Based on a photograph in the archives at Chartwell - squared up with vertical and horizontal lines.

C 488 (Fig. 497) Sea from La Capponcina, 1954, 24 3/4 x 30 in. Initialled left, Exhibitions: World Tour 1958, Royal Academy 1959, Sotheby's 1998, Collections: Mr Randolph S. Churchill, Mr Winston S. Churchill

C 489 (Fig. 500) Cap d'Ail, Alpes-Maritimes, from La Capponcina, September 1952, 25 x 32 in. 63.5 x 76.2 cm, Initialled, Illustrated: Winston Churchill: His Life as a Painter by Mary Soames, 1990, Exhibited: Royal Academy 1953, Royal Academy 1960, New York World's Fair 1965, M Knoedler, London 1977, Wylma Wayne Fine Art, London 1982, National Academy of Design, New York 1983, Smithsonian Institution, Washington 1983, Milton Keynes 1987, Japan Tour 1998, Collection: The Royal Academy of Arts, Given by the artist to the Royal Academy of Arts in 1960 as his Diploma Work.

C 490 (Fig. 455) View on the Riviera, c. 1950, 24 x 18 in.Initialled, Collections: The Studio, Chartwell, Celia Sandys

C 491 (Fig. 499) The Custody of the Child, 1955, 24 3/4 x 29 3/4 in. Initialled right, Exhibited: World Tour 1958, Royal Academy 1959, Collections: Mr and Mrs Emery Reves, Dallas Museum of Art, Wendy and Emery Reves Collection, Gift of the artist.

C 492 (Fig. 502) Sea and Pine Trees, Cap d'Ail, 1955, 24 3/4 x 29 1/2 in. Unsigned, Exhibited: New York World's Fair 1965, Collections: Mrs Blanche Russell, Dallas Museum of Art, Wendy and Emery Reves Collection ?Gift of the artist.

C 493 (Fig. 491) Menton from La Pausa, 1957, 26 x 29 1/2 in. Unsigned, Collections: Lady Spencer-Churchill, The National Trust, Chartwell

C 494 (Fig. 488) View of Menton and Italy from La Pausa, 1957, 24 1/2 x 29 3/4 in. Initialled right, Exhibited: New York World's Fair 1965, Collections: Mr and Mrs Emery Reves, Dallas Museum of Art, The Wendy and Emery Reves Collection

C 495 (Fig. 485) Oscar Nemon, 1954, Bronze height 14 in. 35.5 cm, Exhibited: Japan 1988, Collections: Mr Oscar Nemon, Mr Falcon Nemon. Sold Sotheby's 12th December 2002, Mr Jack S. Churchill, Unique bronze cast from the plaster C 496.

C 496 (Fig. 486) Oscar Nemon1954, Plaster height 13 1/2 in. Illustrated: Winston Churchill: His Life as a Painter by Mary Soames, 1990, Collection: The Studio, Chartwell, The National Trust, Chartwell

C 497 (Fig. 286) Scene in the South of France, 1920s, 24 1/2 x 29 1/2 in. Unsigned, Collections: Lady Hawkey, Mrs Dinah M. Pratt, Mrs William de V. Frith, Gift of the artist to the wife of Sir James Hawkey and now owned by his grand daughter.

C 498 (Fig. 74) View at Mimizan, 1920s, 23 1/4 x 31 1/2 in. 59 x 80 cm, Initialled left, Collection: Anne Duchess of Westminster, Gift of the artist.

C 499 (Fig. 128) Scene in the South of France, possibly near Grasse, 1930s, 25 x 30 in. Initialled, Collections: Viscount Horne, Miss Emily Horne, Mr J. R. Lamberton, Present owner unknown, Gift of the artist.

C 500 (Fig. 289) Seascape near Antibes, 1930s, 19 x 23 1/2 in. Initialled left, Collections: Mr Antonio Giraudier, Sold Christie's 8th March 1990, £29,000, An American private collector, Gift of the artist. Exhibited at the Royal Academy in 1953 as 'Sailing Boat in Harbour at Antibes', as Richard Pawsey wrote to Lady Soames in 1990. This painting is based on a photograph in the archives at Chartwell.

C 501 (Fig. 420) The Atlas Mountains from Marrakech, c. 1949, 22 1/4 x 26 3/4 in. Initialled left, Collections: Mr Antonio Giraudier, Sold Christie's 1st July 1993, £28,000, Present owner unknown, Gift of the artist.

C 502 (Fig. 75) Mimizan, dated 1920, 25 x 30 in. 63.5 x 76 cm, Initialled left, Collections: Mr Bernard Baruch, Mr Harold Epstein, Sold Parke-Bernet, New York 20th October 1966, $12,000, Sold Sotheby's, London 4th November 1992, £32,000, Wells Collection, Gift of the artist.

C 503 (Fig. 501) The Sea from La Capponcina, 1955, 25 x 30 in. 63.5 x 76 cm, Initialled, Collections: Lord and Lady Beaverbrook, Dowager Lady Beaverbrook, Sold Sotheby's 22nd November 1995, £25,000, Present owner unknown, Presented by the artist on the occasion of their marriage June 1963. This painting was noted but not illustrated as C i on page 268 of my original catalogue.

C 504 (Fig. 514) The Giza Pyramids at Cairo, c. 1946, 28 x 36 in. 71.1 x 91.4 cm, Collection: Field Marshal Smuts, By family descent, Bought in at Christie's 6th November 1998, Gift of the artist. Present owner unknown. This painting was noted but not illustrated as C ii on page 268 of my original catalogue.

C 505 (Not illustrated) Close View of Cheops and Khufu at Cairo, c. 1946, 28 x 36 in. Initialled, Collection: Field Marshal Smuts, By descent, Stolen in 1972 and untraced since, Gift of the artist. This painting was noted without illustration as C iii on page 268 of my original catalogue.

C 506 (Not illustrated) Landscape [perhaps at Chartwell], Unknown, 24 1/2 x 29 1/2 in. Initialled, Collection: Mr Aristotle Onassis, Present owner unknown, Gift of the artist. This painting was noted but not illustrated as C iv on page 268 of my original catalogue. It is said that the painting was hung on the Onassis yacht, Christina.

C 507 (Fig. 509) Portrait of Sir John Lavery in His Studio, 1915, 24 x 20 in. Unsigned, Illustrated: The Life of a Painter by John Lavery, 1940, Winston Churchill: His Life as a Painter by Mary Soames, 1990, Exhibited: Royal Society of Portrait Painters, London 1919, Sotheby's 1998, Collections: Sir John Lavery, Miss Katherine Fitzgerald, Miss Geraldine Fairfax-Cholmeley, On loan to the National Trust, Chartwell, Gift of the artist. Katherine Fitzgerald was Lavery's private secretary and executor and the aunt of Miss Geraldine Fairfax-Cholmeley.

C 508 (Fig. 507) The Second Duke of Westminster (Bendor) with his Lurcher Sam, late 1920s, 16 x 13 1/2 in. Initialled right, Illustrated: Winston Churchill: His Life as a Painter by Mary Soames, 1990, Collection: Anne Duchess of Westminster, Gift of Lady Spencer-Churchill after Sir Winston's death in 1965.

C 509 (Fig. 529) Lake Carezza in the Dolomites, c. 1949, 15 x 21 1/2 in. 38.1 x 54.6 cm, Initialled left, Collections: Sold anonymously at Christie's 12th July 1973, Sold anonymously at Christie's 27th March 1997, Present owner unknown, The early provenance of this painting needs to be investigated before its authenticity can be confirmed. In 1973 it was sold at Christie's unframed and with the title 'A Bay in the South of France'.

C 510 (Fig. 510) Still Life with Aubergines and Red Peppers on a Silver Tray, 1934-35, 24 x 29 1/2 in. 61 x 75 cm, Initialled right, Collections: Mr Alfred Kern, Sold Sotheby's 14th March 1979, £3,900, Sold Christie's March 1991, £9,500, Wells Collection, Gift of the artist as a mark of gratitude for the loan of Mr Alfred Kern's house at Choisy, Switzerland, in 1946.

C 511 (Fig. 504) Landscape with Two Trees, 1922, 61 x 45.6 cm, Initialled and dated on the back, Collections: Miss Maud Elgie, Mr Michael Elgie Donaldson, Gift of the artist to Maud Elgie (later Mrs R. G. Donaldson and Mr Michael Donaldson's mother) who between 1919 and 1921 was 'employed by Mrs Churchill to help with Diana and Randolph'.

C 512 (Fig. 508) St Paul's Churchyard, c. 1927, 48.5 x 28 cm, Initialled left, Collections: Sold Balmoral Castle Charity Auction 1927, 115 guineas (£120.75), Mr Stanley Shaw Bond, Mr I. R. S. Bond,

C 513 (Fig. 513) Inlet in the South of France, 1920s, 20 x 30 in. Initialled right, Collections: Mr R. J. Marnham, Sold Christie's 1st March 1968, £1,320, (Other auctions at Christie's in 1981 and 1982), Mr F. Bartlett Watt (from Pickering and Chatto, London 1984), Mrs Lucienne Watt, Gift of the artist in 1945 to Mr R. J. Marnham, owner of Chartwell Farm.

C 514 (Fig. 511) Beach on the Riviera, c. 1930, 20 x 24 in. Unsigned, Collections: Victor Montagu, Sold Parke-Bernet, New York 21st October 1971, Sold Sotheby's, New York 7th June 1984, Sold Christie's, London 5th November 1999, £100,000, Tracey and Shanin Specter, Gift of the artist to Victor Montagu on the occasion of his marriage in 1934.

C 515 (Fig. 506) La Lieutenance, Honfleur, c. 1928, 23 x 27 1/2 in. 52.07 x 62.87 cm, Initialled left, Exhibited: Los Angeles County Museum of Art 1975, Collections: Mr P. M. Adam, Mrs Leigh Battson (from Wildenstein Gallery, New York 1967), Mr and Mrs Timothy M. Doheny, Gift of the artist to Mr P. M. Adam in 1928 in return for the latter's 'picture of my Mother's dining room which is a constant source of pleasure to me' and which still hangs over Churchill's bed in his bedroom at Chartwell.

C 516 (Fig. 531) View of La Pausa, Roquebrune, 1957, Size unknown, Initialled left, Illustrated in: Winston Churchill Honorary Academician Extraordinary, Royal Academy of Arts, London 1959, Exhibited: Royal Academy of Arts 1959, Collection: Present owner unknown, This painting is missing.

C 517 (Fig. 518) The Rocks of the Château de l'Horizon with Lady Castlerosse and the Artist, 1930s, 25 x 30 in. 53.5 x 76 cm, Initialled left, Illustrated: My Aunt Maxine by Diana Forbes-Robertson, 1964, Collection: Mrs Maxine Elliott, Lady Forbes-Robertson, J. J. Miles, Sold Sotheby's, New York 11th April 1984, $21,000, Mrs Linda Noe Lane, Gift of the artist to Maxine Elliott and thence by descent. This painting is based on a photograph in the archives at Chartwell in which the figures are clearly seen to be Churchill himself and Lady Castlerosse. The painting was sold at Sotheby's, New York, in 1984 with the title 'Seascape near Cap Ferrat, a View from Château de L'Horizon' and the figures described as Churchill and Maxine Elliott.

C 518 (Fig. 515) Lady Castlerosse at the Château de L'Horizon, c. 1935, canvas board 14 x 19 3/4 in. Initialled Collections: Baron de Caters, Mons. Guy de Caters, Sold Parke-Bernet, New York 25th September 1968, Present owner unknown, Baron de Caters had a chateau near Maxine Elliott's Château de L'Horizon in the South of France. The young man on the other side of the table from Lady Castlerosse is identified in the auction catalogue as Randolph Churchill. The related photograph in the archives at Chartwell shows this to be wrong; instead either Peter Willes or Dudley Delevingne, Doris Castlerosse's younger brother, have been suggested.

C 519 (Fig. 523) Thunderstorm: Nice, c. 1921, Size unknown, Illustrated: 'Painting as a Pastime' by Winston S. Churchill, Part 2, The Strand Magazine, January 1922, Collection: Present owner unknown, This painting is missing.

C 520 (Fig. 525) On the Rance, near St Malo, c. 1921, Size unknown, Illustrated: 'Painting as a Pastime' by Winston S. Churchill, Part 2, The Strand Magazine, January 1922, Collection: Present owner unknown This painting is missing.

C 521 (Fig. 524) The Vallery of the Brora, Sutherlandshire, c. 1921, Size unknown, Illustrated: 'Painting as a Pastime' by Winston S. Churchill, Part 2, The Strand Magazine, January 1922, Collection: Present owner unknown, This painting is missing.

C 522 (Fig. 526) Scene near the Head of Lake Como, 1945, Size unknown, Illustrated : 'Winston Churchill's Pictures', The Strand Magazine, August 1946, Collection: Present owner unknown, This painting is missing.

C 523 (Fig. 528) The Calanque, Cassis, 1920, Size unknown, Illustrated: 'Winston Churchill, An Eightieth Birthday Tribute', edited by Bruce Ingram, The Illustrated London News, 1954, Exhibited: Royal Academy 1950 Collection: Present owner unknown, This painting is missing.

C 524 (Fig. 533) On Cap Martin, 1946, Size unknown, Illustrated: Winston Churchill Honorary Academician Extraordinary, Royal Academy of Arts, London 1959, Exhibited: Royal Academy 1959, Collection: Present owner unknown, This painting is missing.

C 525 (Fig. 512) Branksome Dean, 1916, 20 x 24 in. Signed and inscribed upper right: 'Mrs Cassels from Winston/1916', Collection: Sir Harold Cassel, [With Philip Harley, Christie's, 2001]

C 526 (Fig. 534) The Gallery, Esher Place, 24th October 1915, 24 x 20 in. Unsigned, Inscribed on the back on the stretcher: 'Painted by Winston Spencer Churchill. The Gallery Esher Place. Oct. 24, 1915.' Collection: Eric A. and Rosayn Anderson (from Maggs Bros, London, 1997), Nothing is known about the early history of this picture, which is painted on a Roberson canvas, Churchill's preferred supplier. The painting could well be by Churchill but proof through provenance is so far lacking.

C 527 (Fig. 505) Sketch of Oscar Nemon, c. 1952, Pencil, size unknown, Unsigned, Illustrated: Winston Churchill: His Life as a Painter by Mary Soames, 1990, Collections: Mr F. Bartlett Watt, Toronto, Mrs Lucienne Watt, Drawn at Chequers c. 1952 while Churchill was sitting for his bust commissioned by Queen Elizabeth II from the sculptor Oscar Nemon for display at Windsor Castle.

C 528 (Fig. 520) The Lake at Trent Park, c. 1935, 28 1/4 x 24 1/4 in. Initialled right, Collections: Mr W. Greenshields, Sold Sotheby's 23rd April 1969, Present owner unknown

C 529 (Fig. 521) Sketch of Venice, 1951, Cartridge paper, approx. 290 x 450 mm. Unsigned, Collection: The National Trust, Chartwell Archives, This large sketch was done by Churchill in red and blue ballpoint pens on thick cartridge paper. It relates directly to his painting of the same subject, C 476.

C 530 (Fig. 527) Cafe at St Jean de Luz, c. 1925, Canvas board 14 x 20 in. Signed 'W. Churchill' left, Collections: Mr E. Merrick Tyler, Sold Christie's 15th March 1985, Present owner unknown, Gift of the artist. Mr Tyler was Churchill's adviser at Lloyds. The painting was accompanied by a letter from Churchill's secretary, Violet Pearman, dated 4th January 1933. 'I have despatched today by Carter Paterson to your address a picture which Mr Churchill has painted himself and which he promised to give you some time ago. He hopes the picture reaches you safely and that you like it.'

C 531 (Fig. 516) Flower Borders at Château de L'Horizon, 1930s, 20 x 30 in. Unsigned, Collections: Maxine Elliott, Mrs Fanny Vandysdadt Mons. André Vouillon, Sold Christie's 18th November 1977, Present owner unknown, Gift of the artist to Maxine Elliott before 1939. Mrs Fanny Vandysdadt was her companion/maid and Mons. André Vouillon the Mayor of Cannes.

C 532 (Fig. 519) Barges on the Seine, c. 1930, 19 1/4 x 23 1/4 in. Signed, Collections: Sarah Lady Audley, Sold Sotheby's 23rd April 1969, Present owner unknown

C 533 (Fig. 532) The Gardens at Port Lympne, Kent, 1930s, 10 x 12 in. 25.5 x 30.5 cm, Collections: 'Given by the artist to the Head Gardener of Port Lympne, and thence by descent.', Sold unframed at Phillips 17th June 1997, Present owner unknown, The early provenance of this painting needs to be investigated before its authenticity can be confirmed.

C 534 (Fig. 522) Rough Studio Sketches, Perhaps 1930s, 29.5 x 40.2 cm. Unsigned, Collection: The National Trust, Chartwell Archives, These sketches are scribbled in pencil on the back of the large photograph Churchill used for his painting 'Boats in Cannes Harbour', C 300. The subjects are not yet identified but the drawing in a rectangle, centre left, relates, when turned upside-down, to Churchill's painting 'Distant View of the Pyramids', C 85.

C 535 (Fig. 530) Portrait of an Unknown Lady, 1920s, Canvas board 14 x 20 in. Unsigned, Collections: The Studio, Chartwell, Private collection, Lake Forest, Illinois, USA, This is the painting noted in C 111 as 'Sketch of a lady on the back'.

C 536 (Fig. 535) Small Drawing of a Pig, late 1950s, 6 1/2 x 4 1/2 x 3/16 in. 16.51 x 11.43 x 0.48 cm. Unsigned, Collection: Dallas Museum of Art, The Wendy and Emery Reves Collection, Drawn by Churchill one evening while he was staying at La Pausa when Wendy Reves challenged her guests to sketch a self-portrait.

C 537 (Fig. 517) The Moat, Breccles. August, 1921, 1921, Size unknown, Illustrated: 'Painting as a Pastime', by Winston S. Churchill, Part 1, The Strand Magazine, December 1921, Collection: Present owner unknown This painting is missing.

index

This index is highly selective. It lists people of importance in Churchill's life and painting career, including members of his family, friends, critics, admirers, employees and other painters. It also lists places that particularly attracted Churchill and which he frequented for the purposes of recreation and painting, as well as the Churchill family homes. References in italics are to people pictured in the illustrations.

For additional and specific references to individual people, places and pictures, please consult the full catalogue, page 250 following

Front Endpapers
Sir Winston Churchill painting in the South of France at La Capponcina in the 1950s. A similar painting is illustrated on page 236

Back Endpapers
Sir Winston Churchill's chair and easel, Miami Beach, Florida, 1946. His painting is illustrated on page 190

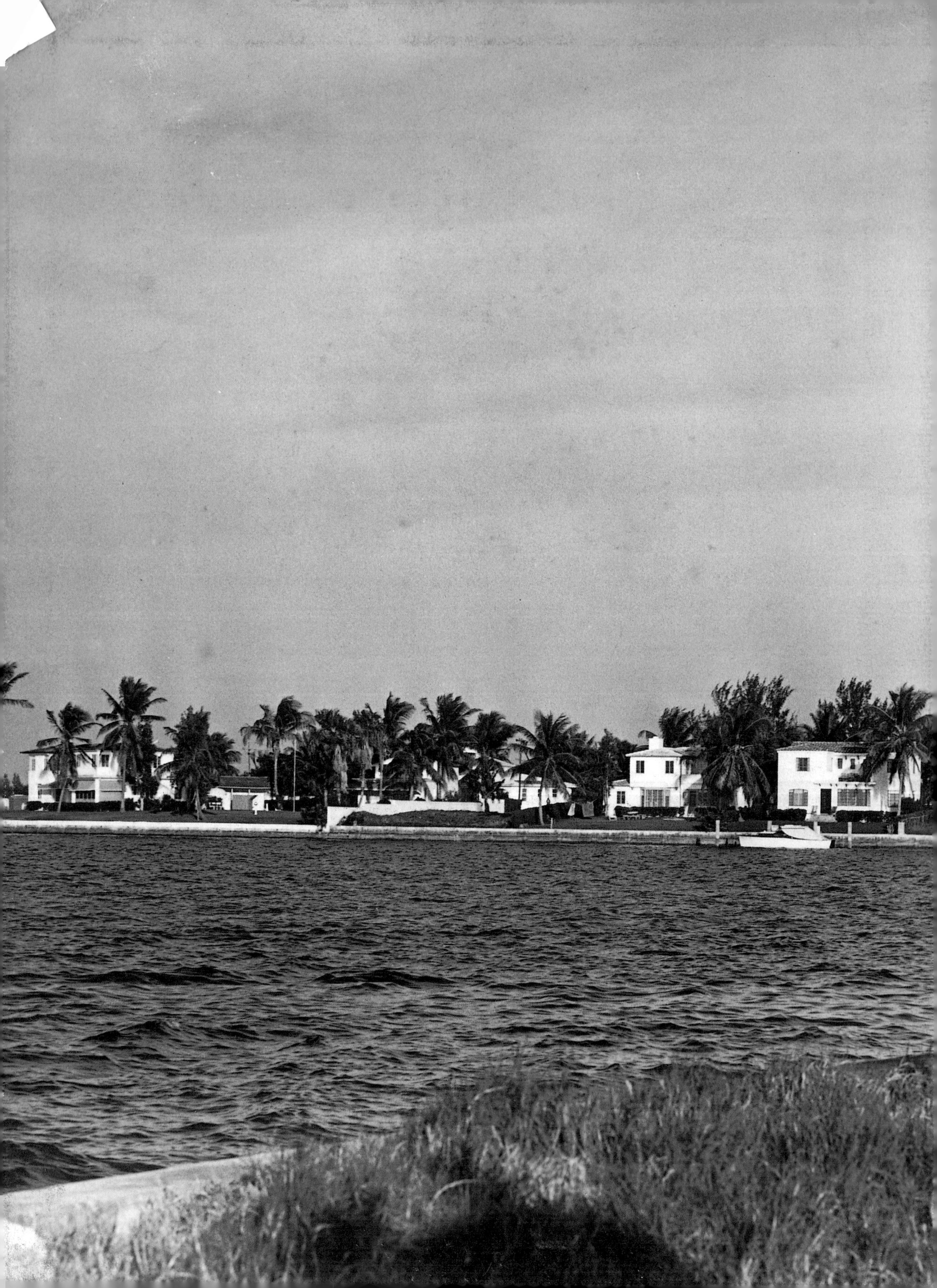